Congenial Spirits

The Selected Letters of

Virginia Woolf

Congenial Spirits

The Selected Letters of
VIRGINIA WOOLF

Edited by
Joanne Trautmann Banks

The Hogarth Press
LONDON

This edition first published in paperback 1993
1 3 5 7 9 10 8 6 4 2

Text by Virginia Woolf © Quentin Bell and Angelica Garnett
1975, 1976, 1977, 1978, 1979, 1980, 1989
Introduction and editorial notes © Joanne Trautmann Banks 1989

This edition first published in hardback in the United Kingdom in 1989 by
The Hogarth Press
Random House, 20 Vauxhall Bridge Road, London SWIV 2SA

Random House Australia (Pty) Limited
20 Alfred Street, Milsons Point, Sydney,
New South Wales 2061, Australia

Random House New Zealand Limited
18 Poland Road, Glenfield
Auckland 10, New Zealand

Random House South Africa (Pty) Limited
PO Box 337, Bergvlei, South Africa

Random House UK Limited Reg. No. 954009

A CIP catalogue record for this book
is available from the British Library

ISBN 0 7012 0982 8

Printed and bound in Great Britain by
Mackays of Chatham PLC, Chatham, Kent

Cover design and illustration by Jeff Fisher.

Jane Smith is the best lawyer in the Hamptons.

She has enemies in high places.

She's got *12 Months to Live* . . .

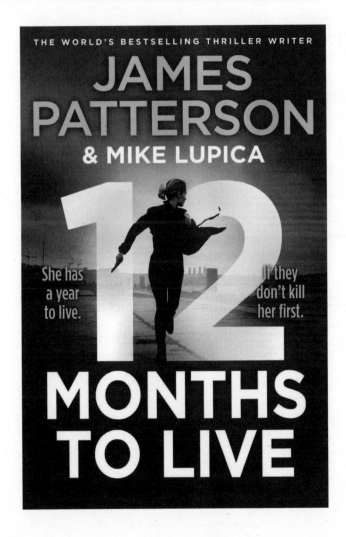

ONE

"FOR *THE* LAST TIME," my client says to me. "I. Did. Not. Kill. Those. People."

He adds, "You have to believe me. I didn't do it."

The opposing counsel will refer to him as "the defendant." It's a way of putting him in a box, since opposing counsel absolutely believe he *did* kill all those people. The victims. The Gates family. Father. Mother. And teenage daughter. All shot in the head. Sometime in the middle of the last night of their lives. Whoever did it, and the state says my client did, had to have used a suppressor.

"Rob," I say, "I might have mentioned this before: I. Don't. Give. A. Shit."

Rob is Rob Jacobson, heir to a legendary publishing house and also owner of the biggest real estate company in the Hamptons. Life was good for Rob until he ended up in jail, but that's true for pretty much everybody, rich or poor. Guilty or innocent. I've defended both.

Me? I'm Jane. Jane Smith. It's not an assumed name, even though I might be wishing it were by the end of this trial.

There was a time when I would have been trying to keep somebody like Rob Jacobson away from the needle, back when New

York was still a death penalty state. Now it's my job to help him beat a life sentence. Starting tomorrow. Suffolk County Court, Riverhead, New York. Maybe forty-five minutes from where Rob Jacobson stands accused of shooting the Gates family dead.

That's forty-five minutes with no traffic. Good luck with that.

"I've told you this before," he says. "It's important to me that you believe me."

No surprise there. He's been conditioned his entire life to people telling him what he wants to hear. It's another perk that's come with being a Jacobson.

Until now, that is.

We are in one of the attorney rooms down the hall from the courtroom. My client and me. Long window at the other end of the room where the guard can keep an eye on us. Not for my safety, I tell myself. Rob Jacobson's. Maybe the guard can tell from my body language that I occasionally feel the urge to strangle him.

He's wearing his orange jumpsuit. I'm in the same dark-gray skirt and jacket I'll be wearing tomorrow. What I think of as my sincerity suit.

"Important to *you*," I say, "not to me. I need twelve people to believe you. And I'm not one of the twelve."

"You have to know that I'm not capable of doing something like this."

"Sure. Let's go with that."

"You sound sarcastic," he says.

"No. I *am* sarcastic."

This is our last pretrial meeting, one he's asked for and that is a complete waste of time. Mine, not his. He looks for any excuse to get out of his cell at the Riverhead Correctional Facility for even an hour and has insisted on going over once more what he calls "our game plan."

Our—I run into a lot of that.

I've tried to explain to him that any lawyer who allows his or her client to run the show ought to save everybody a lot of time and effort—and a boatload of the state's money—and drive the client straight to Attica or Green Haven Correctional. But Rob Jacobson never listens. Lifelong affliction, as far as I can tell.

"Rob, you don't just want me to believe you. You want me to like you."

"Is there something so wrong with that?" he asks.

"This is a murder trial," I tell him. "Not a dating app."

Looks-wise he reminds me of George Clooney. But all good-looking guys with salt-and-pepper hair remind me of George. If I had met him several years ago and could have gotten him to stay still long enough, I might have married him.

But only if I had been between marriages at the time.

"Stop me if you've heard me say this before, but I was set up."

I sigh. It's louder than I intended. "Okay. Stop."

"I *was*," he says. "Set up. Nothing else makes sense."

"Now, you stop me if you've heard this one from me before. Set up by whom? And with your DNA and fingerprints sprinkled around that house like pixie dust?"

"That's for you to find out," he says. "One of the reasons I hired you is because I was told you're as good a detective as you are a lawyer. You and your guy."

Jimmy Cunniff. Ex-NYPD, the way I'm ex-NYPD, even if I only lasted a grand total of eight months as a street cop, before lasting barely longer than that as a licensed private investigator. It was why I'd served as my own investigator for the first few years after I'd gotten my law degree. Then I'd hired Jimmy, and finally started delegating, almost as a last resort.

"Not to put too fine a point on things," I say to him, "we're not just good. We happen to be the best. Which *is* why you hired both of us."

"And why I'm counting on you to find the real killers eventually. So people will know I'm innocent."

I lean forward and smile at him.

"Rob? Do me a favor and never talk about the real killers ever again."

"I'm not O.J.," he says.

"Well, yeah, he only killed two people."

I see his face change now. See something in his eyes that I don't much like. But then I don't much like him. Something else I run into a lot.

He slowly regains his composure. And the rich-guy certainty that this is all some kind of big mistake. "Sometimes I wonder whose side you're on."

"Yours."

"So despite how much you like giving me a hard time, you do believe I'm telling you the truth."

"Who said anything about the truth?" I ask.

TWO

GREGG McCALL, NASSAU COUNTY district attorney, is waiting for me outside the courthouse.

Rob Jacobson has been taken back to the jail and I'm finally
on my way back to my little saltbox house in Amagansett,
east of East Hampton, maybe twenty miles from Montauk and
land's end.

A tourist one night wandered into the tavern Jimmy Cunniff
owns down at the end of Main Street in Sag Harbor, where
Jimmy says it's been, in one form or another, practically since
the town was a whaling port. The visitor asked what came after
Montauk. He was talking to the bartender, but I happened to
be on the stool next to his.

"Portugal," I said.

But now the trip home is going to have to wait because
of McCall, six foot eight, former Columbia basketball player,
divorced, handsome, extremely eligible by all accounts. And an
honest-to-God public servant. I've always had kind of a thing
for him, even when he was still married, and even though my
sport at Boston College was ice hockey. Even with his decided
size advantage, I figure we could make a mixed relationship
like that work, with counseling.

McCall has made the drive out here from his home in Garden City, which even on a weekday can feel like a trip to Kansas if you're heading east on the Long Island Expressway.

"Are you here to give me free legal advice?" I ask. "Because I'll take whatever you got at this point, McCall."

He smiles. It only makes him better looking.

Down, girl.

"I want to hire you," he says.

"Oh, no." I smile back at him. "Did *you* shoot somebody?"

He sits down on the courthouse steps and motions for me to join him. Just the two of us out here. Tomorrow will be different. That's when the circus comes to town.

"I want to hire you and Jimmy, even though I can't officially say that I'm hiring you," he says. "And even though I'm aware that you're kind of busy right now."

"I'd only be too busy if I had a life," I say.

"You don't have one? You're great at what you do. And if I can make another observation without getting MeToo'ed, you happen to be great looking."

Down, girl.

"I keep trying to have one. A life. But somehow it never seems to take." I don't even pause before asking, "Are you going to now tell me what you want to hire me for even though you can't technically hire me, or should we order Uber Eats?"

"You get right to it, don't you?" McCall asks.

"Unless this is a billable hour. In which case, take as much time as you need."

He crosses amazingly long legs out in front of him. I notice he's wearing scuffed old loafers. Somehow they make me like him even more. I've never gotten the sense that he's trying too hard, even when I've watched him killing it a few times on Court TV.

"Remember the three people who got shot in Garden City?" he asks. "Six months before Jacobson is accused of wiping out the Gates family."

"I do. Brutal."

Three senseless deaths that time, too. The Carson family. Father, mother, daughter, a sophomore cheerleader at Garden City High. I don't know why I remember the cheerleader piece. But it's stayed with me. A robbery gone wrong. Gone bad and gone tragically wrong.

"Well, you probably also know that the father's mother never let it go until she finally passed," he says, "even though there was never an arrest or even a suspect worth a shit."

"I remember Grandma," I say. "There was a time when she was on TV so much I kept waiting for her to start selling steak knives."

McCall grins. "Well, it turns out Grandma was right."

"She kept saying it wasn't random, that her son's family had been targeted, even though she wouldn't come out and say why. She finally told me why but said that if I went public with it, she'd sue me all the way back to the Ivy League."

"But you're going to tell me."

"Her son gambled. Frequently and badly, as it turns out."

"And not with DraftKings, I take it."

"With Bobby Salvatore, who is still running the biggest book in this part of the world."

"Jimmy's mentioned him a few times in the past. Bad man, right?"

"Very."

"And you guys missed this?"

"Why do you think I'm here?"

"But upstanding district attorneys like yourself aren't allowed to hire people like Jimmy and me to run side investigations."

"We're not. But I promised Grandma," he says. "And there's an exception I believe would cover it."

"The case was never closed, I take it."

"But we'd gotten nothing new in all this time until a guy in another investigation dropped Salvatore's name on us."

"And here you are."

"Here I am."

"I don't mean to be coarse, McCall, but I gotta ask: who pays?"

"Don't worry about it," he says.

"I'm a worrier."

"Grandma liked to plan ahead," he says. "She was ready to go when we found out about the Salvatore connection. When I took it to her, she said, 'I told you so,' and wrote a check. She told me that she was willing to pay whatever it took to find out who took her family."

"This sounds like your crusade, not mine."

"Come on, think of the fun," Gregg McCall says. "While you're trying to get your guy off here, you can help me put somebody else away."

I know all about McCall by now. He's more than just a kick-ass prosecutor. He's also tough and honest. Didn't even go to Columbia on an athletic scholarship. Earned himself one for academics. Could have gone to a big basketball school. His parents were set on him being Ivy League. Worked his way to pay for the rest of college. The opposite of the golden boy I'm currently representing, all in all.

"I know we're supposed to be on opposing sides," McCall says. "But if I can make an exception..."

I finish his thought. "So can I."

"I'm asking you to help me do something we should have done at the time. Find the truth."

"You ought to know that my client just now asked me if

I thought he was telling the truth. I told him that I wasn't interested in the truth." I shrug. "But I lied."

"If you agree to do this, we'll kind of be strange bedfellows."

"You wish," I say.

Actually, *I* wish.

"I know asking you to take on something extra right now is crazy," he says.

"Kind of my thing."

THREE

ON MY WAY HOME, I call Jimmy Cunniff at the tavern. He used to get drunk there in summers when he'd get a couple of days off and need to get out of the city, day-trip to the beach and party at night. Now he owns the business, but not the building, though his landlord is not just an old friend but also someone, in Jimmy's words, who's not rent-gouging scum.

A Hamptons rarity, if you must know.

Jimmy's not just an ex-cop, having been booted out of the NYPD for what he will maintain until Jesus comes back was a righteous shooting, and killing, of a drug dealer named Angel Reyes. He's also a former Golden Gloves boxer and, back in the day, someone who had short stories published in long-gone literary magazines. The beer people should have put Jimmy out there as the most interesting man in the world.

He's also my best friend.

I tell him about Gregg McCall's visit, and his offer, and him telling me we can name our own price, within reason, because Grandma is paying.

"You think we can handle two at once?" Jimmy asks.

"We've done it before."

"Not like with these two," he says, and I know he's right about that.

"Two triple homicides," Jimmy Cunniff says. "But not twice the fun."

"Who knows, maybe solving one will show us how to solve the other. Maybe we'll even slog our way to the truth. Look at it that way."

"I don't know why you even had to ask if I was on board," Jimmy says. "You knew I'd be in as soon as you were. And you were in as soon as McCall asked you to be."

"Kind of."

"Stop here and we'll celebrate," he says.

I tell Jimmy I'll take a rain check. I have to go straight home; I need to train.

"Wait, you're still fixed on doing that crazy biathlon, even now?"

"I just informed Mr. McCall that crazy is kind of my thing," I say.

"Mine, too."

"There's that."

"Are you doing this thing for McCall because you want to or because the hunky DA is the one who asked you to?"

"What is this, a grand jury?"

"Gonna take that as a yes on the hunk."

"Hard no, actually," I say. "I couldn't do that to him."

"Do what?"

"Me," I say.

There was a little slowdown at the light in Wainscott, but now Route 27 is wide-open as I make my way east.

"For one thing," I tell Jimmy, "Gregg McCall seems so happy."

"Wait," Jimmy says. "Both your ex-husbands are happy."

"Now they are."

Also By James Patterson

ALEX CROSS NOVELS

Along Came a Spider • Kiss the Girls • Jack and Jill • Cat and Mouse • Pop Goes the Weasel • Roses are Red • Violets are Blue • Four Blind Mice • The Big Bad Wolf • London Bridges • Mary, Mary • Cross • Double Cross • Cross Country • Alex Cross's Trial (*with Richard DiLallo*) • I, Alex Cross • Cross Fire • Kill Alex Cross • Merry Christmas, Alex Cross • Alex Cross, Run • Cross My Heart • Hope to Die • Cross Justice • Cross the Line • The People vs. Alex Cross • Target: Alex Cross • Criss Cross • Deadly Cross • Fear No Evil • Triple Cross • Alex Cross Must Die

THE WOMEN'S MURDER CLUB SERIES

1st to Die (*with Andrew Gross*) • 2nd Chance (*with Andrew Gross*) • 3rd Degree (*with Andrew Gross*) • 4th of July (*with Maxine Paetro*) • The 5th Horseman (*with Maxine Paetro*) • The 6th Target (*with Maxine Paetro*) • 7th Heaven (*with Maxine Paetro*) • 8th Confession (*with Maxine Paetro*) • 9th Judgement (*with Maxine Paetro*) • 10th Anniversary (*with Maxine Paetro*) • 11th Hour (*with Maxine Paetro*) • 12th of Never (*with Maxine Paetro*) • Unlucky 13 (*with Maxine Paetro*) • 14th Deadly Sin (*with Maxine Paetro*) • 15th Affair (*with Maxine Paetro*) • 16th Seduction (*with Maxine Paetro*) • 17th Suspect (*with Maxine Paetro*) • 18th Abduction (*with Maxine Paetro*) • 19th Christmas (*with Maxine Paetro*) • 20th Victim (*with Maxine Paetro*) • 21st Birthday (*with Maxine Paetro*) • 22 Seconds (*with Maxine Paetro*) • 23rd Midnight (*with Maxine Paetro*) • The 24th Hour (*with Maxine Paetro*)

DETECTIVE MICHAEL BENNETT SERIES

Step on a Crack (*with Michael Ledwidge*) • Run for Your Life (*with Michael Ledwidge*) • Worst Case (*with Michael Ledwidge*) • Tick Tock (*with Michael Ledwidge*) • I, Michael Bennett (*with Michael Ledwidge*) • Gone (*with Michael Ledwidge*) • Burn (*with Michael Ledwidge*) • Alert (*with Michael Ledwidge*) • Bullseye (*with Michael Ledwidge*) • Haunted (*with James O. Born*) • Ambush (*with James O. Born*) • Blindside (*with James O. Born*) • The Russian (*with James O. Born*) • Shattered (*with James O. Born*) • Obsessed (*with James O. Born*) • Crosshairs (*with James O. Born*)

PRIVATE NOVELS

Private (*with Maxine Paetro*) • Private London (*with Mark Pearson*) • Private Games (*with Mark Sullivan*) • Private: No. 1 Suspect (*with Maxine Paetro*) • Private Berlin (*with Mark Sullivan*) • Private Down Under (*with Michael White*) • Private L.A. (*with Mark Sullivan*) • Private India (*with Ashwin Sanghi*) • Private Vegas (*with Maxine Paetro*) • Private Sydney (*with Kathryn Fox*) • Private Paris (*with Mark Sullivan*) • The Games

(*with Mark Sullivan*) • Private Delhi (*with Ashwin Sanghi*) • Private
Princess (*with Rees Jones*) • Private Moscow (*with Adam Hamdy*) • Private
Rogue (*with Adam Hamdy*) • Private Beijing (*with Adam Hamdy*) • Private
Rome (*with Adam Hamdy*)

NYPD RED SERIES

NYPD Red (*with Marshall Karp*) • NYPD Red 2 (*with Marshall Karp*) •
NYPD Red 3 (*with Marshall Karp*) • NYPD Red 4 (*with Marshall Karp*) •
NYPD Red 5 (*with Marshall Karp*) • NYPD Red 6 (*with Marshall Karp*)

DETECTIVE HARRIET BLUE SERIES

Never Never (*with Candice Fox*) • Fifty Fifty (*with Candice Fox*) • Liar
Liar (*with Candice Fox*) • Hush Hush (*with Candice Fox*)

INSTINCT SERIES

Instinct (*with Howard Roughan, previously published as* Murder Games) •
Killer Instinct (*with Howard Roughan*) • Steal (*with Howard Roughan*)

THE BLACK BOOK SERIES

The Black Book (*with David Ellis*) • The Red Book (*with David Ellis*) •
Escape (*with David Ellis*)

STAND-ALONE THRILLERS

The Thomas Berryman Number • Hide and Seek • Black Market •
The Midnight Club • Sail (*with Howard Roughan*) • Swimsuit (*with
Maxine Paetro*) • Don't Blink (*with Howard Roughan*) • Postcard Killers
(*with Liza Marklund*) • Toys (*with Neil McMahon*) • Now You See Her
(*with Michael Ledwidge*) • Kill Me If You Can (*with Marshall Karp*) • Guilty
Wives (*with David Ellis*) • Zoo (*with Michael Ledwidge*) • Second
Honeymoon (*with Howard Roughan*) • Mistress (*with David Ellis*) •
Invisible (*with David Ellis*) • Truth or Die (*with Howard Roughan*) •
Murder House (*with David Ellis*) • The Store (*with Richard DiLallo*) •
Texas Ranger (*with Andrew Bourelle*) • The President is Missing (*with Bill
Clinton*) • Revenge (*with Andrew Holmes*) • Juror No. 3 (*with Nancy Allen*)
• The First Lady (*with Brendan DuBois*) • The Chef (*with Max DiLallo*) •
Out of Sight (*with Brendan DuBois*) • Unsolved (*with David Ellis*) • The
Inn (*with Candice Fox*) • Lost (*with James O. Born*) • Texas Outlaw (*with
Andrew Bourelle*) • The Summer House (*with Brendan DuBois*) • 1st Case
(*with Chris Tebbetts*) • Cajun Justice (*with Tucker Axum*)• The Midwife
Murders (*with Richard DiLallo*) • The Coast-to-Coast Murders (*with J.D.
Barker*) • Three Women Disappear (*with Shan Serafin*) • The President's
Daughter (*with Bill Clinton*) • The Shadow (*with Brian Sitts*) • The Noise
(*with J.D. Barker*) • 2 Sisters Detective Agency (*with Candice Fox*) •
Jailhouse Lawyer (*with Nancy Allen*) • The Horsewoman (*with Mike

Lupica) • Run Rose Run (*with Dolly Parton*) • Death of the Black Widow (*with J.D. Barker*) • The Ninth Month (*with Richard DiLallo*) • The Girl in the Castle (*with Emily Raymond*) • Blowback (*with Brendan DuBois*) • The Twelve Topsy-Turvy, Very Messy Days of Christmas (*with Tad Safran*) • The Perfect Assassin (*with Brian Sitts*) • House of Wolves (*with Mike Lupica*) • Countdown (*with Brendan DuBois*) • Cross Down (*with Brendan DuBois*) • Circle of Death (*with Brian Sitts*) • Lion & Lamb (with *Duane Swierczynski*) • 12 Months to Live (*with Mike Lupica*) • Holmes, Margaret and Poe (*with Brian Sitts*)

NON-FICTION

Torn Apart (*with Hal and Cory Friedman*) • The Murder of King Tut (*with Martin Dugard*) • All-American Murder (*with Alex Abramovich and Mike Harvkey*) • The Kennedy Curse (*with Cynthia Fagen*) • The Last Days of John Lennon (*with Casey Sherman and Dave Wedge*) • Walk in My Combat Boots (*with Matt Eversmann and Chris Mooney*) • ER Nurses (*with Matt Eversmann*) • James Patterson by James Patterson: The Stories of My Life • Diana, William and Harry (*with Chris Mooney*) • American Cops (*with Matt Eversmann*) • What Really Happens in Vegas (*with Mark Seal*)

MURDER IS FOREVER TRUE CRIME

Murder, Interrupted (*with Alex Abramovich and Christopher Charles*) • Home Sweet Murder (*with Andrew Bourelle and Scott Slaven*) • Murder Beyond the Grave (*with Andrew Bourelle and Christopher Charles*) • Murder Thy Neighbour (*with Andrew Bourelle and Max DiLallo*) • Murder of Innocence (*with Max DiLallo and Andrew Bourelle*) • Till Murder Do Us Part (*with Andrew Bourelle and Max DiLallo*)

COLLECTIONS

Triple Threat (*with Max DiLallo and Andrew Bourelle*) • Kill or Be Killed (*with Maxine Paetro, Rees Jones, Shan Serafin and Emily Raymond*) • The Moores are Missing (*with Loren D. Estleman, Sam Hawken and Ed Chatterton*) • The Family Lawyer (*with Robert Rotstein, Christopher Charles and Rachel Howzell Hall*) • Murder in Paradise (*with Doug Allyn, Connor Hyde and Duane Swierczynski*) • The House Next Door (*with Susan DiLallo, Max DiLallo and Brendan DuBois*) • 13-Minute Murder (*with Shan Serafin, Christopher Farnsworth and Scott Slaven*) • The River Murders (*with James O. Born*) • The Palm Beach Murders (*with James O. Born, Duane Swierczynski and Tim Arnold*) • Paris Detective • 3 Days to Live • 23 ½ Lies (*with Maxine Paetro*)

For more information about James Patterson's novels, visit
www.penguin.co.uk.

Contents

Introduction

I N turn-of-the-century handbooks on how to write a proper letter, women were advised to be self-effacing. Ladies, they were told, do not begin a letter with 'I'. They begin instead with something that will interest their correspondents, chiefly themselves. This was the prevailing advice when Virginia Stephen first put pen to stationery. The mature Virginia Woolf sniffed at propriety, but the young woman – struggling to find any self at all and feeling the influence of her formidable father and mother – must have been powerfully tempted to be guided by conventional manners.

The proper female letter writer was simply another version of the hostess, a role Virginia had observed closely. Her exquisite mother, Julia Stephen, played it for years to rave reviews. We can applaud her skills ourselves in the famous dinner scene from *To the Lighthouse*. The successful Victorian hostess devoted herself to her guests and appeared to deny herself. She saw to it that they were entertained, drawn out, left with a flattering sense of themselves, and, not incidentally, tied to her as the source of all this pleasure.

The hostess as letter writer: here is the genesis of Virginia Woolf's great achievements in the epistolary form. What an irony for one of this century's most famous feminists. Of course, she was not satisfied with what was modelled for her. As she did with every other written form she practised, she claimed her inheritance and then changed it profoundly. She once said that she had to strangle that Victorian ideal of subservient femininity, the Angel in the House, before she could free herself to write. In the case of her letters, the Angel was not dead, only transformed. It hovered over an epistolary journey that subtly led Virginia away from self-effacement. So much for the writers of ladies' handbooks! Virginia used her letters to spin a delicate web that supported her personality almost until the end.

But she began in the feminine tradition. 'The way to get life into letters [is] to be interested in other people.' That is Virginia in an early letter (Number 501). The sentiment could have been lifted from a handbook. Virginia followed her own dictum beautifully. She may have

vii

been a shy hostess at her early Bloomsbury parties, but, wrapped in the comfort of written language, she moved with ease into the essence of the role. Over the years she seldom relinquished it. Her style alone – confident, inventive, witty – entertained lavishly. She flattered her correspondents with intelligent attention. She praised them, usually in the guise of tangential insults. She flirted with men; she flirted, even more often, with women. The middle-aged Violet Dickinson, for instance, with whom Virginia Stephen was involved in a romantic friendship, was told that her height made her 'the length of seven fine males' (224). Miss Dickinson relished the teasing and was probably mildly titillated by it. Virginia set up running jokes, peculiar to each correspondent, so that they would recognise their cues and relax into the familiar. She pretended that Vanessa Bell had no grasp of the obvious. *Antony and Cleopatra*, Virginia told her – that's a play by Shakespeare; the Sierra Nevada are mountains in Spain. For years after the event, Clive Bell received postcards with references to a supposed quarrel during their romantic entanglement. Ethel Smyth was repeatedly called an 'uncastrated cat'. It was a magnificent performance. Her friends loved it. Had she been able to tolerate the vulgarity, her mother would have approved.

Hostesses were supposed to trot out the sort of ephemeral references known as small talk. In order to avoid exercising guests unduly in a social situation, conversation was to be kept light. Never discuss religion, the handbooks ruled. Nor should a lady alarm her guests by introducing controversial politics. Virginia learned from her brothers' Cambridge friends that it was permissible to debate issues of truth, beauty and sex over tea. In her letters she often eased into these eternal verities, and a good many others, by way of charming daily details, which for her had enormous significance in themselves. Her novel about the quintessential hostess, Mrs Dalloway, set Virginia to grapple in fiction with a method she had already forged in letters. Writing to her literary friend Gerald Brenan about that novel's progress, she wailed: 'But how does one make people talk about everything in the whole of life [. . .] in a drawing room?' (1388).

Significantly, when in her letters she isolated the big issues from the charm, as in her public letters to periodicals (see, for example, 1139a), she wrote with more control and to less effect. Debate abstracted from the human element was not her strength. She did not analyse social and philosophical concepts so much as narrate them. A great deal about the servant question may be gleaned from all her letters to her sister about particular problems with Nelly or Lottie. When the nation was beset, as it was, for instance, in 1938 during the Munich Crisis, Virginia's letters (3447 and 3449) stressed what she called 'gossip about the inner history'. The public story was interlaced with personal details. Everyone knew that war was averted at the last moment when the Prime Minister, then addressing Parliament, was handed a note from Hitler. Virginia's correspondent also heard that the Prime Minister looked ten years younger as he read it. The views of Virginia's eminent friend John Maynard Keynes were aired, but so were the efforts of Mrs Ebbs, wife of the village rector. It is altogether an unusual, valuable perspective, for all its association with that form of small talk called gossip.

When gossip comes from the pen of a literary genius, it is almost certain to be lively. It may also induce shame. Ought we to be listening to such talk? 'Gentlemen,' said Henry L. Stimpson, American Secretary of State, 'do not read each other's mail.' With this pronouncement in 1929, he ended his country's code-interception programme. The Secretary was wrong. Of course gentlemen do. Most people seem to draw the line somewhere, but the popularity of Virginia Woolf's letters must be due in part to their generally amiable gossip. 'Talking of death and bullets,' she wrote cheerfully to her nephew Quentin Bell, 'have you heard that Mrs [T.S.] Eliot is on the war path, said to have a carving knife with which first to skin Tom; then Ottoline; finally me? For she says Ott and I are Tom's mistresses; now as I never had a favour from that man its rather hard to give my life on the pavement' (2767). Occasionally, Virginia went too far. 'Malicious!' cried her friends, but she was unrepentant. She could not resist the discovery of a comic character anywhere.

The delightfully wicked purveyor of gossip was normally stifled during a friend's illness. Sometimes she was irrepressible: 'Will [Arnold-Forster],' she told Vanessa Bell, 'is once more in hospital – this time with water on the knee – from what you and Duncan will doubtless draw your own conclusions' (980). But in most cases, illness brought out the caring side of Virginia Woolf and warmed up the comedy in her letters. In one of her splendid letters to Jacques Raverat, dying slowly from multiple sclerosis, she shyly dropped her mask: 'really and truly I would do a great deal to please you and can only very very dimly murmur a kind of faint sympathy and love' (1501). This caring for the sick was another aspect of her sense of responsibility as a letter writer. It may even have been the ultimate act of the hostess. True, her mother was famous for her nursing skills, and to some extent Woolf was carrying on that tradition too, but her compassion seems real enough. Her sister's terrible grief over the loss of her son was partly healed by Virginia's daily notes. Even the tiresome Barbara Bagenal received wonderful letters during her illness. The oddest example of this literary therapy occurred in 1906 after Woolf's brother Thoby had died, a young man, from typhoid. Struck by the same illness, Violet Dickinson had to be kept from the dreadful news. That much is understandable. But from the day of his death, Virginia began to invent a life for him when writing to Violet. Thoby ate this; Thoby said that. He sends a jolly message to his fellow sufferer. Is this denial? Is this the incipient fiction writer at practice? Perhaps instability of a serious order? Whatever else it is, it is certainly self-effacement carried to an extreme.

Virginia made the strongest statement of this motif in a letter to a young friend with whom she frequently discussed literary technique. She told Gerald Brenan that one of the purposes of a letter was 'to give back a reflection of the other person' (2078). The mirror is an arresting image for her epistolary method and philosophy. Unlike a realistic novel, which has been famously described by Stendhal as a mirror riding along a roadway, a letter from Virginia Woolf was not a large, flat mirror. Virginia would not have liked it half so much if it were. She would not have valued a reflection of a friend that included so complete a view of his or her surroundings as to overwhelm the real person, who was that small, luminous creature in the corner of the mirror. Nor would she have believed in the accuracy of such a reflection. That sliver of a mirror, a letter, that scrap of paper quickly covered, suited her aesthetic and philosophical purposes. Virginia's letters are like the mirrors in the finale of the pageant in *Between the Acts*. Carrying mirrors of all sizes and qualities, the actors hold the reflecting sides towards the audience while the director intones Virginia Woolf's faith: all we can ever know of ourselves are scraps, orts and fragments, held in momentary harmony and sympathy.

Over the years she refined the reflections so well that present-day aficionados of her letters can play a parlour game with them. Give the players a letter to one of Virginia's major correspondents. Cover up the name of the addressee and see if the image of the implied reader is so particular that the correspondent can be correctly guessed. The game will be easier in that Virginia tended to pick up the same general subjects each time she wrote to a certain friend. Once a connection was made on the basis of a friend's interests, she strengthened it with every letter. Eventually, she saw that she was doing so. She speculated that 'one's friendships are long conversations, perpetually broken off, but always about the same thing with the same person' (1722). With Roger Fry she spoke about art, she said; with Lytton Strachey about reading; with E. M. Forster about writing; and with Clive Bell about love. It was part of her courtesy that, even as she played to her reader's interests, she made it seem that they were her own passionate concerns as well. And so they were. Somewhere along the line, subjects and tones initiated because they were likely to be hospitable for others became just as surely reflections of Virginia's multi-faceted self.

It was at this point that her letters diverged dramatically from their origins in girlish attempts at cultural hostessing. While holding up the mirror to her friends' advantage, Virginia discovered that it was two-sided. Her own image was on the back: 'This sheet is a glass' (2162). Now the letter was an emblem of mutuality, a potential fulfilment of the offer of aesthetic love made by Bernard to Neville in *The Waves*: 'Let me create you. (You have done as much for me.)'

Virginia Woolf was never confident for long about who she was. She was frightened that the centre of her personality would not hold: 'how difficult it is to collect oneself into one Virginia' (2460). Because of the protean nature of her own form, she was lured by apparently limitless elements, such as the sky and the sea, whose vastness promised to receive her protectively. It is not too strong to say that for her psychic survival Virginia needed to keep the several strands of her identity attached to her various friends. She was the spider; the letters were the web; and the whole was spun in a hall of mirrors. Virginia needed a certain courage to return again and again to the hall. It had, after all, shifted at the times of her mental breakdowns into a funhouse of distortions. There must always have been for Virginia an underlying terror that the mirrors would reflect a void, as in her deceptively lyrical, but essentially nightmarish little story 'The Lady in the Looking-Glass'.

That possibility was diluted by Virginia's great numbers of friends, most of them very substantial people whose strengths allowed her to create herself. Writing to Katherine Mansfield, whose own credentials were unquestionable, Virginia shaped an image of herself as a writer of stature. We are alike, they told each other. With young people she created herself as the definitive aunt – never maternal (that was denied her), but wise in a way and always a welcome visitor. Seeing herself mirrored in the process of Jacques Raverat's long dying, she discovered her mysticism.

In this light, the two most satisfying correspondences of her life may have been those with Vita Sackville-West and Ethel Smyth. Vita continued the pattern of the romantic, maternal figures to whom Virginia turned for affection in her youth, but with this important difference: Vita was a ripe woman whose intimacies were physical as well as (or perhaps more than) emotional. Although not nearly in Virginia's league as a writer, Vita was fully capable of challenging her on the literary field. Virginia's creation of Vita culminated in *Orlando*, the novel Nigel Nicolson has called, in his introduction to Volume III of the complete correspondence, Virginia's 'most elaborate love-letter'. It does not obscure, however, the value of the love letters collected here. With Vita, Virginia allowed herself to be created for a time as a sexual being. That Vita also excited her imagination and her intellect gave Virginia a chance to see herself as a whole, integrated person. It didn't finally hold up, I think – this self that lived in Vita's presence – because Virginia drew back from final intimacy again and again, and so did Vita. But they were richer beings when they were together.

When she burst into Virginia's life, Ethel Smyth demanded intensity. At 70, Ethel was a rip-snorting woman who knew her own mind and thought she knew a good deal else. A younger Virginia might have backed off. But her healthiest side recognised in Ethel someone who would force her to express all her emotions, including anger, who would suck from her what she had always wanted to tell – that is, the absolute truth about her past, her writing and her values. She did not need to worry about how Ethel would take it if Virginia sounded off on Ethel's faults. The old girl could take it. Her devotion to Virginia was never in question. In her twenties, Virginia had written to a friend, 'I only ask for someone to make me vehement, and then I'll marry him' (608). Twenty years later, Ethel made her vehement, and as a consequence received, in my opinion, her best single set of letters.

With only one intimate correspondent, however, did Virginia completely abandon all attempts to play the hostess. Writing to her husband, Leonard Woolf, she reached for no flattering, entertaining phrases. She did not really attempt to address his interests. By any aesthetic criteria, the letters are bad. They are included in this volume by virtue of Leonard's central importance in her life. Virginia thought she knew why they were different: 'This is a horrid, dull scrappy scratchy letter but all letters of real affection are dull' (1927). Judging by this standard, there is no question – whatever arguments some scholars have advanced – that Leonard was, by far, the closest person to her. Virginia considered their relationship beyond words.

Words were something about which she felt ambivalent. She lived – almost literally – by her words, but she distrusted them. 'All good and evil comes from words,' she said (333). Again: 'I am always trying to get behind words' (503). Letters were especially suspicious. She told Jacques Raverat that in writing them, one 'has to put on a kind of unreal personality; which, when I write to you for example, whom I've not seen these 11 years, becomes inevitably jocular' (1501).

In the final analysis, she doubted her ability to know her friends too. Behind her back, some of them agreed that, in spite of her brilliant characterisations, she knew less than anyone. She asked Vita Sackville-West: 'Do we then know nobody? – only our own versions of them, which, as likely as not, are emanations from ourselves?' (1622). Emanations – the spider again; but the question does not really matter in this context. Whether other people are created or uncovered, it is in relation to them that Virginia Woolf existed most truly. She craved cuddling, but since, on the whole, she was not an especially physical person, relationships for her were essentially verbal. Therefore, conversations and letters were paramount. They were the prerequisite for her fragile stability. Her conversations have long since died away. But by her letters we can know her.

The same claim cannot be made for writers whose letters were carefully penned for posterity. Often the so-called great letter writers – especially the men, it must be said – filled their pages with set pieces. Virginia's letters were loved for their scintillating spontaneity. She did make self-conscious pronouncements about her technique, notably when she was young, and even on occasion wrote drafts. But she was telling the truth when she said that for her letter writing was a 'mere tossing of omelettes' (1433). Her mature letters followed her urges.

But what of that masterful, that thrilling, piece of writing, her diary? Is not the true Virginia Woolf to be found in those pages written in private to please herself? Most readers have thought that she is. Their assumption is bolstered by the diary's revelations of doubt, fear and occasional despair. Pain expressed in private must be – mustn't it? – more truthful than pleasure expressed in public. In the diary she wrote regularly about her work in progress. In the letters she did not. In private she considered the characters of her friends with greater boldness. By definition, gossip could not be admitted, for there was no ear in which to whisper it. All this argues for the sense that Virginia Woolf resides in the diary, if anywhere. Most persuasive of all is its language – direct, rich and empowered by an acutely observant person.

Granted, for many of us privacy is often more comfortable and less challenging. But even when we are scrawling in a diary, selfhood may be said to be something we *describe*. We may reveal more shameful facts about ourselves, but that is not the same thing as being real. Thinking alone, as opposed to writing, may remove us even further from our personalities in that there is less of a context. No pen and paper circumscribe us. The ultimate aloneness has been created in sensory deprivation experiments, and no one would suggest that the self is most real then. On the other hand, when we write a spontaneous personal letter, we *inhabit* our selfhood and use it to reach out to another person. It is in relationship that we form our identities as babies. It is in relationship that we continue to form them.

Thus, Virginia Woolf lives in her letters, even here in her selected letters. To be sure, condensing a life usually falsifies it. A life often comes to seem more tragic in summary than when it was lived at its normal rhythms. Loves, illnesses, achievements and disappointments pile up, and death comes in 500 pages. Sometimes, though, the process of condensing distils an essence that the whole disguised. So it is, I think, with these letters. When I had finished the selection and looked at the results, I was surprised by what I saw. The Virginia Woolf who creates herself here is different from the one who slowly emerges from the six original volumes. This Virginia is simultaneously more vulnerable and more admirable.

Furthermore, her laughter is heard even more clearly. In spite of its end, at 59, in suicide, hers does not seem a tragic life. After all, why should a life be judged by its eleventh hour? Surely that's too literary. For her and for her family, her mental illness was truly terrible, but for decades she was sane, prolific and inventively comic. In the end her supporting web dissolved almost completely. She could only throw one thin line to Vanessa and two to Leonard before giving over her fragmented self to the waters. But for most of her years she was the brilliant fulfilment of the imaginative, playful little girl whose letters begin this volume. Given her griefs, it was a courageous life.

JOANNE TRAUTMANN BANKS
Tierra Verde, Florida, 1988

Editorial Note

MOST of the letters in this book were drawn from the complete *Letters of Virginia Woolf*, edited by Nigel Nicolson and me, and published in six volumes from 1975 to 1980. Of the approximately one hundred letters discovered after 1980, the finest appeared in *Modern Fiction Studies* (*MFS*) for summer 1984. Four thousand letters had by then turned up. It seemed that the attics of her correspondents had been emptied, and not much more of interest would be found.

But there are twelve 'new' letters here. A box of files shuffled recently to Charleston – once the country home of Vanessa and Clive Bell and Duncan Grant – was found to contain four very early letters. The first two, numbered 0 and 00, are the pipings of the child Virginia, aged perhaps five. Number 1a includes one remarkable sentence that can fairly be described as the earliest Virginia Woolf narrative now in print. Number 1b is the last of the childhood cache. Of the new mature letters, the most valuable are probably the ones to Katherine Mansfield (1167a) and George Bernard Shaw (3608a). But there are other candidates: numbers 739a, 1395a, 1632a, 1957a, 2695a and 3565a. All the new letters can be identified easily because they are the only ones followed by the name of the present owner. In addition, there are four public letters to editors of periodicals (1139a, 1148b and c, 2022a). They were excluded from the complete edition on the grounds of their being another form, more polemic than correspondence. They are nonetheless cousins to her personal letters, so I have gathered them together. Three important letters to Julian Bell in China (3136a, 3146a, 3206a) and one to Duncan Grant (645a) appeared previously only in *MFS*, where not many people will have seen them. Among the new material must be counted restorations of excerpts omitted from the complete edition for fear of hurting people then alive. The passages are gossip about friends' love lives, and curious readers will have to search them out themselves.

Whether already published or new, to be chosen for this volume a letter had first to be good – one of the best, in fact – and second, if possible, able to advance the biographical narrative. The best letters were instantly recognisable. They were aesthetically pleasing, with all that such an admittedly vague phrase implies. Their rhythms flowed and romped. Their images dazzled and cohered. They were packed with insight – into Virginia Woolf, her work, her ideas, her circle and times, or, it is not too much to say, into reality itself. The best letters entertained in a broad sense: they were funny, or they were moving. I made some attempt to give an idea of the variety of Virginia's large number of personal correspondents as well as a reflection of those who received the most letters, but this was not a high priority. Occasionally I selected a letter simply because it was important to the story, not because it was a good example of Virginia's skills. Inevitably, the story told by the letters left gaps. Some of them are filled by narrative linking passages and by the footnotes. I hope that readers of the selected letters have read Quentin Bell's superb biography of his aunt, but I have not assumed it. This book is meant to be a self-contained volume that will not mystify the general reader who lacks ready access to other material on Virginia Woolf.

For the same reason, I have provided notes sufficient to explain references that would be obscure and therefore irritating to such a reader. Almost nothing, however, is repeated. In almost every case, for instance, people are fully identified only at the point of their first appearance in a letter. I am aware that some readers dislike annotations of letters, and in fact it has become fashionable to say so. They need not be bothered. Except for brief, bracketed insertions in the body of the letters, the notes are designed to be skipped if desired.

Cuts have been made within the majority of the chosen letters. This is also controversial. A good argument can be made that letters should be printed in their entirety so that a writer's rhythms and intentions, however casual, are not broken. But my reasoning ran like this. Cutting allows more letters to be printed in the space allotted. Uncut versions may be read in the complete edition, where, of course, apart from possibly libellous language, nothing was omitted within a letter. Moreover, Virginia Woolf's letters, in particular, do not suffer unduly from excerpting. For one thing, they sometimes begin slowly. They may include a series of names or events which are important to a given correspondent but bewildering to an outsider. Above all, the very spontaneity for which the Woolf letters have been admired also accounts for some careless passages in otherwise good letters. Ellipses in square brackets (to differentiate mine from Virginia Woolf's) mark all cuts from the text, with the exception of omitted postscripts. A line of trailing dots at the end of a letter distracts, unnecessarily in my opinion, from the appearance and focus of the printed page. I have also left out the names of the owners. These may be checked in the complete edition, although in some cases the letters may have changed hands since their publication. Their trails can normally be traced to one of the major public collections. I have made no cuts in the new letters.

I have followed the editing methods laid out in the Editorial Note to Volume I of the complete edition. At their core is a precise adherence to Virginia's style, even when her spelling and punctuation are erratic. But when she made an obvious slip, such as forgetting to put in a second quotation mark, I have silently corrected it. Ampersands, which she habitually used for 'and', have been spelled out. New paragraphs have been created wherever Virginia left a long space in a line and the sense clearly dictates a new thought. Dates and addresses are given as they appear in the originals. When they are incomplete, I have expanded them in square brackets. When they are missing, I have supplied them, also in brackets. In the letters from childhood, it was sometimes impossible even to guess the dates or addresses – hence the use of 'n.d.' and 'n.a.'. I have not renumbered the letters. To promote consistency in later references, each one appears with the number assigned to it in the complete edition. Some letters have been reclaimed from the 'too late' appendix at the end of Volume VI and inserted in their proper chrono-logical slot, where they take on their rightful significance. They have an 'a' or 'b' after their numbers in order to fit them into the original numbering scheme. The same system is followed for the new letters, the public letters, and the ones from *MFS*. In most cases, I have accepted the text of each letter as we transcribed it for the six volumes and *MFS*. Where there was any question, I consulted the original letter. As a result, a few changes have been made without notice. The annotations have been redone according to the demands of this volume's shape, and newly available information has been added to them.

In the complete edition, we acknowledged those scholarly books that had been the bases of our research. Since 1980, the flow of fine biographical, critical and textual studies of Virginia Woolf or her friends has continued, and I have benefited from (almost) all of them. There is space here to mention only the ones to which I have turned most frequently: Andrew McNeillie's six-volume edition of *The Essays of Virginia Woolf*, which began to appear in 1986; Paul Delaney's *The Neo-Pagans*, 1987; Frances Spalding's *Vanessa Bell*, 1983; Victoria Glen-dinning's *Vita*, 1983; Louise DeSalvo and Mitchell A. Leaska's edition of *The Letters of Vita Sackville-West to Virginia Woolf*, 1985; and Diane F. Gillespie and Elizabeth Steele's *Julia Duckworth Stephen*, 1987.

The copyright for all Virginia Woolf letters is held by her nephew, Quentin Bell, and her niece, Angelica Garnett. I want to thank them for their support of this project. Professor Bell and his wife, Olivier Bell – the meticulous editor of Virginia Woolf's *Diary* – have always been a delight to work with. In fact, Olivier Bell's assistance to scholars everywhere is the backbone of Woolf biography. She answered my questions quickly and read the typescript of this volume with great care. So did Nigel Nicolson. I treasure his wisdom, friendship, and continued presence in this work.

I am grateful to S. P. Rosenbaum and Jane Marcus – along with her editor at Indiana University Press, Joan Catapano – for providing material from forthcoming books on Edwardian Bloomsbury and Ethel Smyth, respectively. Mitchell A. Leaska answered my questions about Virginia's early diaries. I want also to express my gratitude to the following scholars and libraries for help in obtaining new Woolf letters: Sandra Bieri, Michael Boggan and C. M. Hall (British Library), Michael Bott (University of Reading), Joy Grant, Michael Hall (King's College, Cambridge), Cathy Henderson (Humanities Research Center, University of Texas), Norman Higham (University of Bristol), Sidney Huttner (University of Tulsa), Elizabeth Inglis (University of Sussex), Valerie Kettley, Lila Laakso (Victoria University in the University of Toronto), Dan H. Laurence, Alan Littel (Alfred University), Andrew McNeillie, Ruth Mortimer and Sarah Black (Smith College), Jean F. Preston and Jane Moreton (Princeton University), John D. Rateliff, Elizabeth P. Richardson, Lola Szladits (Berg Collection, New York Public Library), and Warren Keith Wright.

With the skill of master detectives, inter-library loan librarians at three institutions have searched out uncommon books and documents for me. I thank the librarians at the University of Richmond, the University of North Carolina – Asheville, and, especially, Harriet Turley at Eckerd College.

Early in this project Annette Ricker was a helpful research assistant. Her activities were funded by a grant to Dickinson College from the Dana Foundation under the Dana Student Internship Program. For research and first-rate preparation of a difficult manuscript, I am indebted to Arlene Brownstein.

My husband, Samuel Alston Banks, has been warmly supportive of this work at every stage. His ideas have so suffused my own that, in Virginia Woolf's language, we have created each other. Bless you, Sam.

JTB

1882–February 1904

Adeline Virginia Stephen, who would change the world of modern letters as Virginia Woolf, was born in 1882 into an upper-middle class household in Kensington. Her father, Leslie Stephen, nearly 50 when she was born, was a distinguished critic and philosopher, and the founding editor of the Dictionary of National Biography. Her mother, born Julia Jackson, was a member of that no longer extant species, the Great Beauty. Julia was a friend of painters and writers. She wrote several pieces herself, but spent her life mainly in caring for the needy and having children. She bore seven: three from her first marriage to Herbert Duckworth, George (b. 1868), Stella (1869) and Gerald (1870); and four Stephens, Vanessa (1879), Thoby (1880), Virginia and Adrian (1883). Virginia's other half-sister, the child of her father's first marriage to Thackeray's daughter, was called Laura (b. 1870), and by the time of Virginia's birth was known to be mentally impaired, perhaps by childhood schizophrenia.

While their brothers went away to school, Virginia and Vanessa were educated at home – not quite the deprivation Virginia later imagined in that at least she had access to her father's library and to his tutelage. Until she was 25 she moved for the most part within a circle of family and family friends, and in general extended her adolescence beyond the norm for her place and time. From childhood she wanted to write, but she did not begin to practise seriously until after the death of her father in 1904, an event towards which she was profoundly ambivalent.

The condensation of time in the first group of letters – inevitable because few fine letters were written and fewer kept – makes Virginia's early life go by in a rush. The important events, the illnesses and deaths, appear to happen off-stage. Of course they were central. By the time she was 22, Virginia had lost her mother, her sister Stella, and her father. On two occasions – in 1895 and 1897 – she had also lost her mental stability. Fortunately, she had the comfort of her sister Vanessa and the intimate friendship of Violet Dickinson, the first of Virginia's major correspondents.

o: To Leslie Stephen   [n.a.]
[n.d.]¹

MY DEAR FATHER
WE HAVEENT BATHED YET WE ARE GOING TO TO MORROW WE SANG
IN THT TRAIN YOUR LOVING VIRGINIA.

Quentin Bell

oo: To George Duckworth   *22 Hyde Park Gate, S.W.*
[n.d.]

MY DEAR GEORGE
I AM A LITTLE BOY AND ADRIAN IS A GIRL I HAVE SENT YOU SOME
CHOCOLATES GOOD BYE VIRGINIA

Quentin Bell

1: To James Russell Lowell   [*22 Hyde Park Gate, S.W.*]
20.8.88

MY DEAR GODPAPA² HAVE YOU BEEN TO THE ADIRONDACKS AND
HAVE YOU SEEN LOTS OF WILD BEASTS AND A LOT OF BIRDS IN THEIR
NESTS YOU ARE A NAUGHTY MAN NOT TO COME HERE GOOD BYE
                                        YOUR AFFECT^e
                                        VIRGINIA

1. The only one of Virginia's five childhood letters that can be dated is Number 1, which was enclosed with a dated letter from Leslie Stephen to James Russell Lowell. She was then aged 6½. Two of the others (o and oo) appear, from their printing and content, to be earlier. By the time she wrote the letter numbered 1a, she was using script. In 1b she has learned some further spelling, punctuation, and syntax.
2. A fiercely articulate agnostic, Leslie Stephen did not have his children baptised, but he did choose for them 'sponsors', of whom Lowell, the poet, critic, and American Minister in London, 1880–85, was Virginia's. Lowell and Stephen had been friends since the latter's trip to the United States during the Civil War.

1a: To Julia Stephen   [*22 Hyde Park Gate, S.W.*]

[n.d.]

My dear Mother

We went out for a walk with Stella this morning up to the pond and there were a lot of big boats. We cleaned the little room out this morning and we cleaned up the silver things cos they were awfully dirty. It was awfully jolly at the stuffed beasts.[1] Edwin[2] came with us to them. Mrs Prinsep[3] says that she will only go in a slow train cos she says all the fast trains have accidents and she told us about an old man of 70 who got his legs caute in the weels of the train and the train began to go on and the old gentleman was draged along till the train caute fire and he called out for somebody to cut off his legs but nobody came he was burnt up. Good bye

your Loving Virginia

Quentin Bell

1b: To Julia Stephen   *Limnerslease, Guildford*
 [*Surrey*]

[n.d.]

My dear Mother

We have just come back from a [3-mile] walk to Guildford. I caught a frittilary [fritillary butterfly] this morning. Mrs Crane[4] stayed quite late yesterday. We have breakfast and tea in our play room but dinner with Mr and Mrs Watts.[5] Has father done anything shocking yet, and has he found any flowers. The beds are so soft that you sink down ever such a way when you get in. Mr and Mrs Watts go to bed at about

1. The children's name for the Natural History Museum.
2. Virginia's cousin, Edwin Fisher, born the year after she was.
3. Virginia was related to the Prinseps through the marriage of her mother's aunt, Sara Pattle, to Thoby Prinsep.
4. Mary, wife of the artist Walter Crane, whom Watts painted in 1891. The Cranes lived near the Stephens in Kensington.
5. The painter G. F. Watts (1817–1904) and his wife, Mary Fraser Tytler Watts, also an artist. They had completed Limnerslease in 1891. Therefore, the most likely date for this letter is 1892 or 1893. We know that Virginia stayed at Limnerslease in February 1894, but the letter's spring references and its level of sophistication make the later date unlikely. Watts had known Virginia's mother since her girlhood when he lived with the Prinseps.

half-past eight, and they get up about 5. Mrs Watts went to church this morning at half past seven. We gave Emma[1] some wild roses, the place is simply swarming with them. Nessas eye is all right to day only rather shut up, so she has left off her bandage. It is very fine here but as I have said that I suppose it will begin to rain. Adrian has picked up an old whip with which he means to beat Shag [a dog]. The Cuckoo has been singing just in front of us, but we have not heard a nightingale, have you? I expect that the others are writing the same things as I. Good bye.

Your loving Ginia

Quentin Bell

2: To Thoby Stephen   [*22 Hyde Park Gate, S.W.*]

Friday March 6th [1896]

My dear Thoby,[2]

How does the [family entomological] Museum get on? Father says that they have discovered an ape which is nearer to a man than anything else which has been yet found.[3] Of course they mean the genus 'Sambo', which doubtless you remember capturing twenty years ago with me. Mr Gibbses[4] Butlers wife, keeps a venerable dachshund. This animal resolutely refuses to wear a muzzle,[5] she says it screams at the sight of one, and so they are going to buy a cage to take it out in!

It is so windy to day, that Miss Jan[6] is quite afraid of venturing out. The other day her skirt was blown over her head, and she trotted along in a pair of red flannel drawers to the amusement of the Curate

1. Presumably Virginia's cousin, Emma Vaughan, who was several years older but became a good friend later. See p. 5, n. 2.
2. Thoby, a student at Clifton College, was 15 years old. Virginia was 14, and, like her sister Vanessa, being educated at home. This letter was typewritten under the supervision of her father.
3. *Pithecanthropus erectus*, whose fossilised remains were discovered in Java by Eugene Dubois in 1891. His published report appeared in 1894.
4. Frederick Waymouth Gibbs (1821–98), a barrister and friend of Leslie Stephen.
5. As required by the anti-rabies Metropolitan Streets Act (1867) for any dog not on a lead. The Act was repealed in 1903.
6. Virginia herself. Fuelled by Virginia's imagination, the Stephen children led fanciful lives, which included the elaborate use of nicknames for each other and for their family friends. Thoby, for instance, was 'Your Highness', 'Your Mightiness' or 'Grim'. An intimate cousin (see the next three letters) was 'Toad'. Virginia, whose haplessness – as in the incident described here – was part of the family lore, was also known as 'Goat'.

who happened to be coming out of Church. She swears that she blushed the colour of the said drawers, but that must be taken for granted. I have nothing to tell you, Your Highness; and my candle insists upon tumbling over every five minutes; and Nessa is snarling at the noise; and my Virgil must be looked out; and I expect that you must go into school; so Good Bye, your Mightiness; write to me when feel so inclined; your loving Goatus Esq. . . .

Are you interested in the Italians, and what is it all about, and which side am I?[1]

26: To Emma Vaughan[2]   *Warboys Rectory, Warboys, Huntingdonshire*[3]

12 August 1899   (this is all the address necessary)

Dearly beloved Toad,

[. . .] You see, my dear toad, that the terrible depression of this climate has not yet affected my spirits. I suspect you and Marny of ulterior motives in thus blackening our minds, or perhaps you are too unimaginative and soulless to feel the beauty of the place. Take my word for it Todkins, I have never been in a house, garden, or county that I liked half so well, leaving St Ives out of account. Yesterday we bicycled to Huntingdon – and paid a visit to our relatives.[4] Coming back we forgot all our cares – (and they were many – Nessa and I each had a large string bag full of melons which bumped against our knees at every movement) in gazing – absorbing – sinking into the Sky. You dont see the sky until you live here. We have ceased to be dwellers on the earth. We are really made of clouds. We are mystical and dreamy and perform

1. On 1 March 1896 an Italian invasion force was crushed by the Abyssinians at Adowa. The battle led to a treaty which acknowledged the independence of Ethiopia.
2. Virginia's first cousin (1874–1960), who later studied music in Dresden and then, unmarried, spent a great deal of time in charitable work. Her sister Margaret ('Marny', 1862–1929) devoted her life to assisting the poor. Another sister, Augusta (1860–1953), also mentioned in this letter, was married to Robert Croft; and their brother, William Wyamar Vaughan (1865–1938), was married to the travel writer and memoirist Margaret ('Madge') Symonds (1869–1925), a daughter of the critic John Addington Symonds. Her *Days Spent on a Doge's Farm* was published in 1893.
3. The house taken by the Stephens for their annual summer holiday. After the death of Julia Stephen four years earlier, the family had given up their beloved Talland House in St Ives, Cornwall, so closely associated with her memory.
4. The family of Lady Stephen, widow of Leslie's brother.

Fugues on the Harmonium. Have you ever read your sister in laws Doges Farm? Well that describes much the same sort of country that this is; and you see how she, a person of true artistic soul, revels in the land. I shall think it a test of friends for the future whether they can appreciate the Fen country. I want to read books about it, and to write sonnets about it all day long. It is the only place for rest of mind and body, and for contentment and creamy potatoes and all the joys of life. I am growing like a meditative Alderney cow. And there are people who think it dull and uninteresting!!!!

This all flowed from my lips without my desire or knowledge. I meant only to be short and businesslike. Poor Toad – when you come I shall say to you – Have you read my letter – And you will confess that you did try a bit on the road and you really do mean to have another shot on the way back. And you are only waiting for a rainy day to finish it altogether. Augusta thinks it bad for your eyesight and Marny has telegraphed 'Forbid you to read Virginias letters'. I am a little cracky this afternoon, its the hottest day I have yet lived thro'. I have read a whole long novel through; beginning at breakfast this morning and ending at 4 p.m.[1] [. . .]

Yr always,

Goatus

35: TO EMMA VAUGHAN   *22 Hyde Park Gate, S.W.*

23rd April [1901]

My dearest Toad,

[. . .] The only thing in this world is music – music and books and one or two pictures. I am going to found a colony where there shall be no marrying – unless you happen to fall in love with a symphony of Beethoven – no human element at all, except what comes through Art – nothing but ideal peace and endless meditation.[2] This world of human beings grows too complicated, my only wonder is that we don't fill more madhouses: the insane view of life has much to be said for it – perhaps its

---

1. The exaggeration is part of Virginia's performance. In her journal for this period (to be published in 1989), she says on 6 August that she is reading Mrs Gaskell's *Cranford* (1853), and on 10–11 August, Trollope's *Barchester Towers* (1857).
2. Virginia had recently seen Will and Madge Vaughan, whose conjugal inseparability irritated her, largely because she was infatuated with the artistic Madge.

the sane one after all: and *we*, the sad sober respectable citizens really rave every moment of our lives and deserve to be shut up perpetually.[1] My spring melancholy is developing in these hot days into summer madness. [. . .]

Goodbye dearest Toad, dear lovely charming gifted Toad!!

37: TO EMMA VAUGHAN   *Fritham House [Lyndhurst, Hampshire]*

Aug 8th [1901]

Dearest Todger,

[. . .] Our London season about which you ask, was of the dullest description. I only went to three dances – and I think nothing else. But the truth of it is, as we frequently tell each other, we are failures.[2] Really, we can't shine in Society. I don't know how it's done. We aint popular – we sit in corners and look like mutes who are longing for a funeral. However, there are more important things in this life – from all I hear I shan't be asked to dance in the next, and that is one of the reasons why I hope to go there. [. . .]

Your loving,
Goat

39: TO THOBY STEPHEN   *[22 Hyde Park Gate, S.W.]*

Nov 5th [1901]

My dear Grim,

[. . .] My real object in writing is to make a confession – which is to take back a whole cartload of *goatisms* which I used at Fritham[3] and

1. Emma and Virginia's first cousin, Hervey Fisher (1869–1921), was now in the Lambeth mental hospital, St Mary of Bethlehem. Virginia herself had a serious breakdown at 13, following her mother's death. Two years later, in 1897, during her half-sister Stella's fatal illness, Virginia's mental health was once again precarious.

2. The motherless Vanessa, whose social debut had been arranged by her ambitious half-brother, George Duckworth, detested society's frivolity and her brother's plans for her. She was more interested in painting. Hugely disappointed, George now turned to Virginia, who compounded her sister's condescension and awkwardness with fear.

3. Fritham House, Lyndhurst, Hampshire, which the Stephens had taken in August and September of this year.

elsewhere in speaking of a certain great English writer – the greatest: I have been reading Marlow [*sic*], and I was so much more impressed by him than I thought I should be, that I read Cymbeline just to see if there mightnt be more in the great William than I supposed. And I was quite upset! Really and truly I am now let in to [the] company of worshippers – though I still feel a little oppressed by his – greatness I suppose. I shall want a lecture when I see you; to clear up some points about the Plays. I mean about the characters. Why aren't they more human? Imogen and Posthumous and Cymbeline – I find them beyond me – Is this my feminine weakness in the upper region? But really they might have been cut out with a pair of scissors – as far as mere humanity goes – Of course they talk divinely. I have spotted the best lines in the play – almost in any play I should think –

Imogen says – Think that you are upon a rock, and now throw me again! and Posthumous answers – Hang there like fruit, my Soul, till the tree die [*Cymbeline:* V. v. 262–5]! Now if that doesn't send a shiver down your spine, even if you are in the middle of cold grouse and coffee – you are no true Shakespearian! Oh dear oh dear – just as I feel in the mood to talk about these things, you go and plant yourself in Cambridge.

Tomorrow I go on to Ben Jonson, but I shant like him as much as Marlow. I read Dr Faustus, and Edward II – I thought them very near the great man – with more humanity I should say – not all on such a grand tragic scale. Of course Shakespeares smaller characters are human; what I say is that superhuman ones *are* superhuman. Just explain this to me – and also why his plots are just cracky things – Marlows are flimsier; the whole thing is flimsier, but there are some very 'booming' (Stracheys word[1]) lines and speeches and whole scenes – when Edward dies for instance – and then when Kent is taken away to be executed, and the little King wont have it done, and his mother tries to make him forget and asks him to ride with her in the Park, and he says 'And will Uncle Edmund ride with us?' That is a human touch! What a dotard you will think me! but I thought I must just write and tell you – [. . .]

Yr. Goat

1. The future biographer and critic, Lytton Strachey (1880–1932), was a close friend of Thoby at Trinity College, Cambridge, and later became one of Virginia's intimates.

57: To Violet Dickinson[1]   *22 Hyde Park Gate, S.W.*

[October/November 1902]

My Woman,

[. . .] Nessa has got Sargent at the Academy now, and the Denty's daughter sitting to her tomorrow.[2] Sargent is worth all the other teaching she's ever had. As far as I can make out, he likes her things but artists are so inarticulate. Anyhow she likes him – his voice – even his green eyes. He stands staring straight at the canvas for 10 minutes, and then says 'Youve got the right idea.' All the other scrubby creatures turn green with jealousy. What women are! I go and rummage in the London Library now. I got into the vaults where they keep the Times yesterday, and had to be fished out by a man. But too many books have been written already – its no use making more. Eleanor[3] is said to be a worse Prig acted than written – all talk. I'm going to write a great play which shall be all talk too – but so exciting you'll squirm in your seat. That is a plan of mine and Jacks[4] – we are going to write it together – it could be done Im sure. Im going to have a man and a woman – show them growing up – never meeting – not knowing each other – but all the time you'll feel them come nearer and nearer. This will be the real exciting part (as you see) – but when they almost meet – only a door between – you see how they just miss – and go off at a tangent, and never come

---

1. Violet Dickinson (1865–1948), almost twenty years older than Virginia, was her first intimate from outside the family. She was a friend of the Duckworths, chiefly Stella, but Virginia only came to know her well when she stayed with them at Fritham a few weeks before this letter was written. Many of Violet's other friends were wealthy and titled, and Virginia's letters to Violet (over 400 of them survive) are sprinkled with references to that set. To Virginia, Violet was valuable because of her outgoing and sympathetic maternal nature and because she was convinced that Virginia would one day be a great writer. On Virginia's side, at least, the friendship was also flirtatious, romantic, and, to a limited extent, passionate. When writing to Violet, Virginia called herself 'Sparroy', a fantastical small animal – half-bird, half-monkey, perhaps – capable of snuggling.
2. The great portraitist John Singer Sargent (1856–1925) was teaching at the Royal Academy Schools, where Vanessa had been accepted in 1901.
3. A play by Mrs Humphry Ward (1851–1920), based on her novel (published in 1900) of the same name. Mrs Ward was a friend of Leslie and Julia Stephen, and occasionally called at Hyde Park Gate.
4. John Waller Hills (1867–1938), solicitor and later MP, was Stella Duckworth's widower.

anywhere near again. There'll be oceans of talk and emotions without end.[1] [...]

71: TO VIOLET DICKINSON   [*22 Hyde Park Gate, S.W.*]

[February? 1903]

Woman,

Come any day you can – everyday – if you come here you will see father who rampages for you – but whistle and Sparroy will come to you. Father is a fraud, only an invalid for the sake of his ladies.[2] I wish I could be an invalid and have ladies. I am so susceptible to female charms, in fact I offered my blistered heart to one in Paris, if not to two.[3] But first by a long way is that divine Venus who is Katie[4] and you and Nessa and all good and beautiful (which are you I wonder?) women – whom I adore. I weep tears of tenderness to think of that great heart of pity for Sparroy locked up in stone – never to throw her arms round me – as she would, if only she could – I know it and feel it. Honestly there was a look of Katie in her stupid beautiful head, and Katie in a bath towel would have what you call a bust just like hers, only Katie wont ever open her arms (which aren't of stone – the Venus hasn't got any by the way) for this poor Sparroy to enter. Then there was another, but the woman waits for the letters. Gerald [Duckworth] insults me – says I drink whiskey – utterance so thick – *I* say mixture of Venus and Violet.

Yr. S[parroy].

1. A structure that is very like Virginia's novel of 1925, *Mrs Dalloway*.
2. Not quite true. Sir Leslie Stephen (he was awarded a KCB in 1902) had in fact undergone surgery for abdominal cancer in December. He seemed to make a good recovery, but by late April it would be clear that the cancer had spread. It was true, however, that his illness called forth visits from numerous female friends and relatives, whose dutiful sobriety annoyed Virginia.
3. There is no evidence that Virginia had yet been to Paris. The one to whom she offered her heart, however, was the Venus de Milo, of which she would have seen many reproductions.
4. Lady Cromer, *née* Lady Katherine Thynne (1865–1933), daughter of the 4th Marquess of Bath and wife of the 1st Earl of Cromer.

76: To Violet Dickinson   *22 Hyde Park Gate, S.W.*

[10 April 1903]

My woman,
    [. . .] Do you see that there are 40 illegits: to every 1000 legal births? Doesn't it make you feel nervous. The risk of going wrong seems to be enormously increased, in fact inevitable practically, since I read that. [. . .]

                                                    Yr. Sparroy

80: To Violet Dickinson   [*22 Hyde Park Gate, S.W.*]

[4 May? 1903]

My Beloved Woman,
    Your letters come like balm on the heart. I really think I must do what I never have done – try to keep them. I've never kept a single letter all my life – but this romantic friendship ought to be preserved. Very few people have any feelings to express – at least of affection or sympathy – and if those that do feel dont express – the worlds so much more like a burnt out moon – cold living for the Sparroys and Violets. This is because you think, or say, you oughtn't to write nice hot letters. Kitty[1] never pierces my tough hide, or tries to. She came to see father the other day, the first time since his illness, and asked him why he hadn't been to call on her, all this time, which was rather *too* fashionable, I thought. And didnt volunteer more than a fishy white glove to *me* – perhaps naturally – only this explains why in crises of emotion, Violet is the Sympathetic Sink, not Kitty.
    All Stephen's are self centred by nature; taking more than giving – but if you once understand that, and it cant be helped you can get on all right with them. Indeed some of them are really rather loveable people. [. . .]

                                                    Yr. Sparroy

1. Katherine Maxse, *née* Lushington (1867–1922). Her family and Virginia's had long been friends, and Vanessa, especially, felt close to her. She was one of the models for the socially adept Mrs Dalloway.

107: TO VIOLET DICKINSON   *22 Hyde Park Gate, S.W.*

[11? October 1903]

My Violet,

[. . .] Kitty is in the very heart of the politix – at Birmingham with Joe and Milner.[1] Her head will spin right off with theories. George has moved to the treasury[2] – has a rise of salary and is head secretary. When we came to breakfast this morning there was a giant man in the hall. The treasury messenger with important letters from Cabinet ministers, which mustn't wait even the Sabbath. George touches his high water mark of worldly happiness at moments like these. But Sparroy has come to one mournful egoistical conclusion – she's a fool. I cant understand all these facts and figures for the life of me – and all the rest talk glibly. Do you understand? The British brain feeds on facts – flourishes on nothing else – but I cant reason. Do you mind – do you think it'll make me a foolish writer? [. . .]

No talking to Georgie or Gerald; they are a marvelous pair. A dinner with them is something to laugh over ten days later. Character is what amuses me. Lord – they are comic – Gerald a little jealous and Georgie the good boy whose virtue has been rewarded. If ever I write a novel, those two shall go in large as life.[3] 'People always tell me George ought to have been a diplomat' says Gerald – 'now I think I should have made a good diplomat' – and waits for our answer. Georgie explains very earnestly how one should always get up to open the door for a lady in a diplomatic household! Pixton is the diplomatic household for him.[4] [. . .]

My Violet goodbye, and Bless you.

Yr. AVS

1. The Secretary of State for Colonies, 1895–1903, Joseph Chamberlain (1836–1914), and Alfred Milner (1854–1925), High Commissioner for South Africa, 1897–1905, and later a member of Lloyd George's War Cabinet. Viscount Milner was the brother-in-law of Kitty's husband, Leopold Maxse, editor of the *National Review*.

2. George Duckworth was secretary to Austen Chamberlain (1863–1937), who had just been appointed Chancellor of the Exchequer.

3. She apparently carried out this threat about this time. A character based on George appears in the two chapters of an untitled novel which constitute Virginia's earliest surviving attempts at long fiction. The manuscript is held by the University of Sussex in its Monk's House Papers among the items collected as A.26, 'Early Writings ca. 1904'.

4. Pixton Park, Dulverton, Somerset, the house of Elisabeth, the Dowager Countess Carnarvon – a fashionable rather than a political household. Virginia liked to imagine that her half-brother was considering whether it was expedient to propose marriage to the widow. In fact, he married her stepdaughter, Lady Margaret Herbert (1870–1958) on 10 September 1904.

145: To Violet Dickinson   *22 Hyde Park Gate, S.W.*

Thursday night [31 December 1903]

My Violet,

[Dr] Wilson thought Father weaker this morning – his pulse not so good.[1] His temp. has been 100 all day; at 2 AM. it goes up to 102. Wilson thinks the temp. may go down as it did before – but I dont know whether father will be able to live through the weakness which must come afterwards. He has been asleep most of today, very quietly. He sleeps more and more, but is perfectly conscious when he wakes. I think he gets weaker every day – and he takes nothing but a little milk and meatjuice, and that with difficulty. But in a way I feel happier about him – he is less able to think and to worry – and that is the worst thing. But however you look at it, it is a miserable time. If he had died at first it would have been easier, but now one has to give up more – I mean all these days he has been there, and able to talk a little, and one has had time to think – however, I know I shall be glad for him.

We have been tramping Bloomsbury this afternoon with Beatrice, and staring up at dingy houses.[2] There are lots to be had – but Lord how dreary! It seems so far away, and so cold and gloomy – but that was due to the dark and the cold I expect. Really we shall never get a house we like so well as this, but it is better to go.

We are the sanest family in London and talk and laugh as though nothing were happening; Adrian and Thoby are going to sing the new year in! We should never get on without this kind of thing.

I write letters all about ourselves. Dont really hurry back because of us. It will make your husband angry,[3] and there's no real reason except that we want you, which isnt sufficient.

The nurses are rather bothersome, but have now settled to dignity

1. Sir Leslie had been in a slow decline since April. Though he rallied from time to time, it was clear to everyone that he was dying. Virginia sent frequent bulletins to Violet, especially as the end neared.
2. The four Stephen children were already planning to move from Kensington after their father's death and to set up a household of their own in unfashionable but liberating Bloomsbury. Their companion was Katie Cromer's sister, Lady Beatrice Thynne (1867–1941).
3. Violet Dickinson never married. 'Your husband' was a running joke begun by Virginia, who often used such devices for cementing friendships. She may have had a particular man in mind, such as Violet's neighbour, a Mr Crum, or even her brother Ozzie, with whom she lived.

and silence, which is peaceful at anyrate. [Nurse] Traill is depressed, I think a little tired of it all.

Yr. AVS

158: To Violet Dickinson   *22 Hyde Park Gate, S.W.*

[February 1904]

My Violet,

Wilson says he is practically the same. He has no doubt that the growth or a clot of blood is preventing the poison from reaching the bladder as quick as it was doing, but he says this may break down at any moment.

Oh dear – it is very hard. He may live a week or so I suppose, or the end may come at any time! They cant tell, and we just have to sit here. But he has no pain, and the fever just now is less. I begin to wish for anything to end this. The waiting is intolerable – but Lord, these things have to be and we have to grin and bear them! The worst of it is he is so tired and worn out, and wants to die I think, and is just kept alive. I shall do my best to ruin my constitution before I get to his age, so as to die quicker!

Yr. AVS

March 1904–December 1906

Virginia's father died on 22 February 1904. The Stephen children, sometimes accompanied by George or Gerald Duckworth or by Violet Dickinson, immediately went away, first to Manorbier on the Welsh coast in Pembrokeshire, then to northern Italy and Paris. In May 1904, haunted by prolonged grief and guilt, Virginia suffered her second major mental collapse. It was serious: she required the care of three nurses; she was plagued by hallucinations, paranoia and fear of eating; she even attempted to commit suicide by throwing herself from a window at Violet Dickinson's house in Welwyn, where she stayed for three months. Shaky, but sane at last, she joined her brothers and sister, who were spending their summer holidays in Nottinghamshire before their move to Bloomsbury. There she slowly began to resume her writing.

In a very short time she was prolific and published. Beginning with a review and an essay at the end of 1904, she published over fifty short pieces of these types in the next two years. She was no longer living in isolated fantasy about her writing. She had not only Violet's encouragement, but, more important, that of the author Margaret Symonds Vaughan. She further expanded her life by teaching at an adult education school, by participating in the Thursday evening discussions that are generally regarded as the origins of the 'Bloomsbury Group' and by travelling abroad. On an expedition to Greece, Vanessa became ill. Two of Virginia's other supports, Violet and Thoby, also fell ill, in their cases, gravely. The situation prompted several of the strangest letters Virginia ever wrote.

182: To Violet Dickinson
Manor House, Teversal [Nottinghamshire]

26 Sept. [1904]

My Violet,

[. . .] Oh my Violet, if there were a God I should bless him for having delivered me safe and sound from the miseries of the last six months! You cant think what an exquisite joy every minute of my life is to me now, and my only prayer is that I may live to be 70. I do think I may emerge less selfish and cocksure than I went in and with greater understanding of the troubles of others.

Sorrow, such as I feel now for Father, is soothing and natural, and makes life more worth having, if sadder. I can never tell you what you have been to me all this time – for one thing you wouldn't believe it – but if affection is worth anything you have, and always will have, mine.

It is queer now that I am better that I feel physically so much more. I am rather bothered with neuralgia, but that goes away with food and fresh air, and I hardly attempt to do more than bask and eat.

It will be nice to see you again. Nessa so happy.

Yr. loving,
AVS

I am longing to begin work.

186: To Violet Dickinson   *The Porch, Cambridge*[1]

30th Oct: [1904]

My Violet,

I was very glad of your letter. Nessa's visit was delightful, and we talked the whole time, not on altogether soothing subjects though. I cant make her, or you, or anybody, see that it is a great hardship to me to have to spend two more long months wandering about in other peoples comfortless houses, when I have my own house waiting for me and rent paid regular on Quarter day. It is such a natural thing from an outsiders point of view, that I get only congratulations, and people say how lucky I am, and how glad I ought to be to be out of London. They dont realise that London means my own home, and books, and pictures, and music, from all of which I have been parted since February now, – and I have never spent such a wretched 8 months in my life. And yet that tyrannical, and as I think, shortsighted Savage[2] insists upon another two. I told him

1. Virginia was staying in Cambridge with her father's sister, Caroline Emilia Stephen (1834–1909). 'Nun' or 'the Quaker', as the family called her, was a Quaker convert who wrote on mysticism. It had been decided – by her doctor, who convinced her family – that Virginia should not move to the Stephens' new house in Gordon Square, Bloomsbury, just yet, but should continue to rest in the country, first with her aunt, then with her cousin, Will Vaughan, and his wife Madge in Yorkshire.
2. Dr George Henry Savage (1842–1921), distinguished clinician and scholar. Though he had long been one of the Stephens' family doctors, his reputation was based largely on his knowledge of neurological and mental illnesses.

when I saw him that the only place I can be quiet and free is in my home, with Nessa: she understands my moods, and lets me alone in them, whereas with strangers like Nun I have to explain every random word – and it *is* so exhausting. I long for a large room to myself, with books and nothing else, where I can shut myself up, and see no one, and read myself into peace. This would be possible at Gordon Sq: and nowhere else. I wonder why Savage doesn't see this. As a matter of fact my sleep hasn't improved a scrap since I have been here, and his sleeping draught gives me a headache, and nothing else. However I shall have a few days in London next week, which will be some relief, and meanwhile I can let off my irritation upon you! Nessa contrived to say that it didn't much matter to anyone, her included, I suppose, whether I was here or in London, which made me angry, but then she has a genius for stating unpleasant truths in her matter of fact voice!

I have written to ask Madge to have me about the 16th, as Savage approves – really a doctor is worse than a husband! Oh how thankful I shall be to be my own mistress and throw their silly medicines down the slop pail! I never shall believe, or have believed, in anything any doctor says – I learnt their utter helplessness when Father was ill. They can guess at what's the matter, but they cant put it right.

This is a long and egoistical grumble, but I do get so sick of it all at times; this eternal resting and fussing, and being told not to do this and that. I wish I could cut off my leg at once and have done with it rather than go through the endless bothers and delays of a nervous breakdown. [. . .]

Yr. AVS

190: To Violet Dickinson   *46 Gordon Square, Bloomsbury*

Thursday [10 November 1904]

My Violet,

I came upon this kind of essay which I wrote at Manorbier.[1] It aint up to much, as I was writing then to prove to myself that there was nothing wrong with me – which I was already beginning to fear there was. Also I wrote very quick and hasty – without thought, as they say, of publication. But the Quakers words bear fruit; and I think I may as well

1. In March 1904. This work has not survived.

send this to Mrs Lyttelton to show her the kind of thing I do.[1] Of course I dont for a moment expect her to take *this* which is probably too long or too short, or in some way utterly unsuitable. I only want to get some idea as to whether possibly she would like me to write something in the future – at Giggleswick[2] for instance. Could you address this to her office address, which I dont know. I dont want her to think that she has got to show me the *least* favour, because of you! [. . .]

Yr. AVS

193: To Violet Dickinson   *Giggleswick School, Settle, Yorkshire*

21st Nov. [1904]

My Violet,

Here I am, sitting at my window under the moors, which are all white with snow and frost, and the temperature is below freezing. I keep warm with a fire, and a fur rug; and I might be in the heart of the Alps. The snow stays sometimes on the Hills till June or July, they say. The School is in a little hollow by itself, with great craggy moors on all four sides. I am longing to get a good walk out among them, but so far Madge has had bothersome little School duties to do, and I have not had a chance to get beyond the garden hardly. The country with its moors breaking into gray stone and gray stone walls instead of hedges and stone houses reminds me of Cornwall, and I always expect to find the Atlantic.

I have done my round of School duties – Lectures, Concerts, Chapel, Hall – and my word it is deadly. We have not had a meal alone so far – always either boys or masters. So I dont get much talk with Madge, and whenever we are alone for a minute in blunders Will, like George, and begs me not to let Madge talk morbidly. He is rather afraid that my influence upon her is not a good one, she says – and is always reminding her of her duties as the Headmasters wife. He *is* curiously like George: only with more solid brains; but he is conventional to the back bone, and loves all the small dignities and duties of his position. Madge only longs for amusing unconventional people – artists and writers – and as she

1. Mary Kathleen Lyttelton (d. 1907), the widow of Bishop Arthur Lyttelton, and the mother of Violet's friend, Margaret, was the editor of the Women's Supplement of the *Guardian*, a weekly journal for the clergy.
2. Giggleswick School, Settle, Yorkshire, where Will Vaughan was Headmaster.

says – only Madge says many things without meaning them – Will is a Philistine and thinks there's something wrong in cleverness. I cant help wondering whether she wouldn't have been happier unmarried – at least to Will. She does seem thrown away here. She loves the country of course, but the life is deadly, and she has no friends – there aren't any people for her to be friends with – except among the masters and one or two old Maids in the village. She is very charming, and artistic, and works away like a hero, and tries to take an interest in football and school contests but I cant conceive a drearier life for anyone – let alone Madge. She is probably planted here for life. Will is an excellent old Blunderbuss, very sterling and honest, but thickheaded and conventional till, as I say, he rivals his cousin George. He has none of George's tact, so that daily life is not made smooth by him.[1] The children are delightful; very healthy independent little animals, not in the least shy of me; indeed I have just had to drive them all off my knee, and to refuse to tell them another long story about a Dog. I have already invented a great many wonderful facts about Wolves and Horses which they absorb very literally, and ask me all kinds of impossible questions. I was amused yesterday when in answer to Janets[2] demands I described the appearance and habits of the dragon – whose picture I wear in my watch chain. I had to make him as horrid as possible; and suddenly I found that Wills paternal eye was on me disapprovingly; he didn't like his children to be told fables, especially on Sunday. They have their Sunday books – but I must say, they dont seem to suffer in spirit. Madge is always trying to make them go their own way, and have their own ideas – and Will wants to 'discipline' them in true pedagogic manner. However he is a most devoted Father, and husband for the matter of that – though somewhat a blind one, I think. [. . .]

Here a maid comes in to say that the gardener is taken very ill, and may she go for a doctor. Madge of course has to go off in the snow to the

1. Nevertheless, Vaughan went on to become Master of Wellington College (1910–21) and Headmaster of Rugby (1921–31). And Virginia changed her mind. In Letter 194, written five days later to Violet, Virginia says: 'Madge is delightful, and we discuss literature and other things for hours on end. She is like a clever and loveable child, but not in the least mature. She and Will as I see more every day, are perfectly happy. [. . .] He is really the saving of her, and keeps her going in all kinds of ways. I cant imagine what she would do without him to decide things for her. They are a charming pair.'
2. The oldest of the Vaughan children, born in 1899. She grew up to be a scholarly physician, the Principal of Somerville College, Oxford, and a Dame of the British Empire. There were three children at this time; a fourth was born in 1906.

gardeners cottage – Will wont let her take brandy unless the doctor orders it. So here she comes back again; the doctor *does* order Brandy, as the man's heart is bad in the sudden cold; so she makes another journey, and then the maid tells her that she must have a Char in to help – and so it goes on – and the unfortunate novel which Madge is longing to write at, having the mood on her, wont get much done to it this morning I foresee.[1] Will takes it all as part of the days work, and novel writing and everything else of an artistic kind must give way before it. I must say Madge takes it like an angel. It makes me rather angry though. [. . .]

Yr. AVS

198: TO MADGE VAUGHAN   *46 Gordon Square, Bloomsbury*

1st Dec. [1904]

My dearest Madge,

I wish you would send your long rigmaroles – but in default I like your coherent letters very much too – too much. I do enjoy flattery! I never seriously meant to deny myself the pleasure of writing, however bad it be for the public morals! – As a matter of fact I am vain enough to think it had better read me than more popular authors. 'Genius' is not a word to be used rashly; it gives me enormous pleasure, and something more than pleasure, that you should find anything of that kind in me. I am no judge; and honestly dont know from hour to hour whether my gifts are first – second or tenth rate. I go from one extreme to another; but when I am in my lowest depths I shall haul myself out of the water by reading your words of encouragement because, however extravagant, I know you mean them honestly. I cant help writing – so there's an end of it. I am very glad too, that in spite of my imperfections I did not seem to you finally intolerant and hard – which are two things I very much dislike. Your researches into my hand went to show that my heart was just as strong as my head, remember; and if I'm not sure of my brains power I am quite sure of my hearts power; and that I do care for certain people – you for example and those heavenly – (and earthly) Babies. Quite permanently. So let us strike a friendship! [. . .]

Yr. AVS

1. Margaret Symonds did not publish her novel, *A Child of the Alps*, until 1920.

202: TO MADGE VAUGHAN   *46 Gordon Square, Bloomsbury*

[Mid-December 1904]

Dearest Foster Madge,[1]

[. . .] My real delight in reviewing is to say nasty things; and hitherto I have had to [be] respectful. The worst of it is, I find, that very few people have the brains to write a really *bad* novel; whereas anyone can turn out a respectable dull one. [. . .]

Yr. loving AVS   *Write.*

224: TO VIOLET DICKINSON   *46 Gordon Square, Bloomsbury*

Bank Holiday [24 April 1905]

My Violet,

Thanks to our boat we only reached Liverpool last night late,[2] and came up by the first train this morning, when I found your letter, which I now answer, after writing I dont know how many letters, so my hand is cramped, my brain barren, and Heaven knows what kind of letter you expect, as you live in a country cottage where the postman calls once a week, and not then if it rains, and which is a house, a prison rather, of unpleasant memories for one poor unfortunate at anyrate!![3] *That* is a sentence worthy of the Guardian at its best – might be printed just as it stands, without a single editorial comma – and would make the Church of England shiver in its vitals. The sea leaves my head in a state of swimmy swammy swampiness, so that I have sat the whole afternoon on Nessa's lap, in a maudlin condition. Didnt I say in one of my inspired writings, which you threw into the fire, that coming home was the best part of being away? It really is. Especially when you travel in Spain, where the trains stop to breathe every 5 minutes and then the idiotic boat is late at Lisbon. But to take up my pen again when we got to Granada – There we were very comfortable in the Washington Irving – I asked if anyone remembered an English Lady the length of seven fine males,[4]

---

1. Virginia also addressed Madge Vaughan as 'Mama', calling herself 'your infant' (Letter 197).
2. On 29 March Virginia and her brother Adrian had sailed to Portugal and Spain. They visited Lisbon, Seville and Granada.
3. A reference to Virginia's stay during her illness in 1904.
4. Violet was well over 6 feet tall.

travelling with a beautiful but haughty aristocrat, with their own bath in a waterproof jacket – but your fame has left Granada at anyrate.

It is far and away the best place we saw – almost have seen I think – I basked like a lizard in the gardens, and it was as hot as an English August, which conveys nothing to your mind but think of orange trees, with oranges, and every other kind of tree with large green leaves, and all the blossoms you can think of. The cottage garden is nothing to it. There my descriptive faculty is blasted.

Then we had to travel 24, or 48 hours to Lisbon, and slept one night at a little country wayside inn – where the fire burnt in the middle of the room, and the company of Spanish peasants sat round and drank and stared at us, and we expected to have knives in our throats every moment. Then we were given one room -- the only sleeping room – with one bed – and a canvas door between us and the family who undressed outside, and we locked our door as best we could – and lay down delicately side by side in our clothes, and heard the old woman counting her money, and swearing and spitting, and by degrees we went to sleep, and at 9 they brought us goats milk, and told us to get up and be gone. This all happened on the edge of an arid desert, lit by stars, smelling of meadow sweet beneath the shadow of a Moorish Castle!

Next day we went on to Badajoz – and came on Tuesday to Lisbon, where we had baths, and that is the most delightful thing we did there. We had to wait 2 days for the ship, and sailed on Thursday. The ship was very small, very sea-smelly, and the moment we got out to sea it began to roll like an inebriate, and I sat down to dinner, and suddenly got up, and without words left the room. It was beastly cold and dreary – however next day was better and after all we had a fair voyage, and last night at eleven we got into the dock, and slept still in our berths.

So now our travels are over. [. . .]

Yr. AVS

237: TO VIOLET DICKINSON   [*46 Gordon Square, Bloomsbury*]

[July 1905]

My Violet,

[. . .] I have been trying to analyse Mrs Carlyle all the morning; and find I write such marvellous dry nonsense. I sometimes doubt the value of words, which is a terrible confession for a journalist to make. Proofs come of the Andalusian Inn, and a short review, which is a shade more scornful than I meant.[1] But I dont suppose the most sensitive of authors cares what the Guardian says of him – preaching the charities of the parish in the next breath. Perhaps Mrs Lyttelton will have some sea sanity blown into her brains.[2] [. . .]

We take chairs and sit on our balcony after dinner, and watch the servant girls giggling with waiters in the shade of the trees. Really Gordon Square with the lamps lit and the light on the green is a romantic place – even hangouts may be will o'the wisps. I say in my Carlyle article 'Coruscations are more in letters'!![3] Such and so profound is my wisdom. Do you like my fluent rounded style, or my curt and mordant style the best? – or the better – as the Sichels[4] of this world have it.

I am dining with Savage tomorrow night,[5] and I think I shall ask him what bee gets into my bonnet when I write to you. Sympathetic insanity, I expect it is. You know you must really be insane to leave England and think to widen your mind by knocking round the world. You will bring back photographs to show us! Here I state my firm refusal to look at one of them. I am treated with sympathy now, as one about to lose her solitary friend. Indeed I cant conceive a more pathetic case, and I shed secret and bitter tears over it. No one to ask me if my back aches, or if I have written anything lately – or to promise well for my future. Letters must come hot from the Equator with praise, or I shall give up literature and take to marriage. We saw Georges baby take his bottle the other day, looking more like a Christian now he can eat. His eyes are still shut, and squint; and he is supposed to be like his cousin, Lord Porchester![6]

1. All Woolf's essays can now be read in the six-volume *Essays of Virginia Woolf,* edited by Andrew McNeillie. These three articles, all published in the *Guardian,* are 'The Letters of Jane Welsh Carlyle', 'An Andalusian Inn' and a review of *Rose of Lone Farm,* by Eleanor G. Hayden. (*Essays,* I, 54, 49, 49).
2. Mrs Lyttelton and Violet Dickinson were leaving soon for a long sea voyage.
3. Virginia wrote that Charles Lamb's coruscations were unspontaneous and that Thomas Carlyle's letters were written with his biographer in mind, but that Jane Carlyle had epistolary sincerity.
4. Edith Sichel (1862–1914), whose *Catherine de Medici The Times Literary Supplement* asked Virginia to review in April of this year as her second commission. The editor, Bruce Richmond (1871–1964), rejected it, saying, Virginia told Violet, that 'the Times is an academic paper, and treats books in the academic spirit – whereas I do not' (Letter 225).
5. George Savage was not only Virginia's doctor, he had also been a friend of her family and now attempted to draw her into his social circle.
6. One of the Carnarvon family, into which George Duckworth had married.

But all this is profoundly uninteresting; and I begin to think that one sentence of my article at any rate is true. I am going to dine with the Buxtons[1] to discuss my good – would be good at any rate – works – Letters are not literature! It is so odd to plunge into philanthropic society, living on the other side of the river of a sudden.

Now I must write 2 other letters.

Yr. AVS

250: To VIOLET DICKINSON   *Trevose View, Carbis Bay, Cornwall*

1st Oct: [1905]

My Violet,

[...] We have had visitors for the last 4 weeks; Kitty and Leo [Maxse] in lodgings; Gerald, Imogen Booth,[2] Sylvia Milman,[3] Jack [Hills], and now two Cambridge youths.[4] These last are a great trial. They sit silent, absolutely silent, all the time; occasionally they escape to a corner and chuckle over a Latin joke. Perhaps they are falling in love with Nessa; who knows? It would be a silent and very learned process. However I dont think they are robust enough to feel very much. Oh women are my line and not these inanimate creatures. [...]

I have written quite a lot, always with your stern eye searching me out across the world. I wish I had you here to encourage. No one really takes very much interest, why should they, in my scribblings. Do you think I shall ever write a really good book? Anyhow I can manage rather better than I did though there are still awful bare and unprolific patches.

1. Earlier in the year Virginia had been persuaded to teach at Morley College, an evening institute for working people. Now she was invited by Violet's friend Ella Crum to meet Mr Buxton, the Principal of Morley. Virginia taught there for three years.
2. A daughter of Charles Booth, author of *Life and Labour of the People in London*, to whom George Duckworth had been temporarily a secretary. The Booths were friends of Virginia's parents.
3. The Milmans had been friends of the Stephen family for three generations. Sylvia was the daughter of Arthur Milman, a barrister, and studied at the Royal Academy Schools with Vanessa.
4. Two of Thoby Stephen's closest and most brilliant friends, Lytton Strachey and Saxon Sydney-Turner (1880–1962). Sydney-Turner, who afterwards became a great friend of Virginia, was, like Strachey, a member of the famous Cambridge intellectual society, the Apostles. His career was subsequently in the Treasury.

Also I have read a good deal, mostly 18th century; that was my weak point. Writing is a divine art, and the more I write and read the more I love it. [. . .]

Yr. loving AVS

266: TO VIOLET DICKINSON   *At Mrs Turners, Giggleswick,*
Settle, Yorkshire[1]

Monday [16 April 1906]

My Violet,
[. . .] I lead the life of a Solitary: read and write[2] and eat my meal, and walk out upon the moor, and have tea with Madge, and talk to her, and then dine alone and read my book, which I might be doing now if I weren't writing to you.

There is a discreet elderly person called Mrs James who waits on me, and provides meals whenever I want them; I had sausages for dinner last night. But she is taciturn, and has a family somewhere downstairs. When I want my bath I stand in the hall and shout for it; and a man answers. Mrs Turner is *gone below* Miss. In the morning she brings a thing like a childs coffin to my room, which she calls 'it.' Coffins are neither sex, but strictly impersonal.

There is a Greek austerity about my life which is beautiful and might go straight into a bas relief. You can imagine that I never wash, or do my hair; but stride with gigantic strides over the wild moorside, shouting odes of Pindar, as I leap from crag to crag, and exulting in the air which buffets me, and caresses me, like a stern but affectionate parent! That is Stephen Brontëised; almost as good as the real thing. [. . .]

Yr. AVS

272: TO MADGE VAUGHAN   *46 Gordon Square, Bloomsbury*

[July 1906]

My dearest Madge,
I feel rather guilty to have made you write so much and read so much

---

1. Virginia returned to Giggleswick 12–25 April, staying this time in a boarding house which was ten minutes' walk from the Vaughans.
2. She was reading Walter Savage Landor's *Pericles and Aspasia* (1836), and writing, as was her habit during this time, a description of her surroundings (unpublished).

in the midst of everything else.[1] But I am *most grateful*, and that I hope you will believe.

I do agree with every word you say, and I think I understand your meaning.

My only defence is that I write of things as I see them; and I am quite conscious all the time that it is a very narrow, and rather bloodless point of view. I think – if I were Mr Gosse writing to Mrs Green![2] I could explain a little why this is so from *external* reasons; such as education, way of life etc. And so perhaps I may get something better as I grow older. George Eliot was near 40 I think, when she wrote her first novel – the Scenes [*of Clerical Life*].

But my present feeling is that this vague and dream like world, without love, or heart, or passion, or sex, is the world I really care about, and find interesting. For, though they are dreams to you, and I cant express them at all adequately, these things are perfectly real to me.

But please dont think for a moment that I am satisfied, or think that my view takes in any whole. Only it seems to me better to write of the things I do feel, than to dabble in things I frankly dont understand in the least. That is the kind of blunder – in literature – which seems to me ghastly and unpardonable: people, I mean, who wallow in emotions without understanding them. Then they are merely animal and hideous. But, of course, any great writer treats them so that they are beautiful, and turns statues into men and women. I wonder if you understand my priggish and immature mind at all? The things I sent you were mere experiments; and I shall never try to put them forward as my finished work. They shall sit in a desk till they are burnt! But I am very glad that you were so frank; because I have had so very little criticism upon my work that I really dont know what kind of impression I make. But do

1. In her role as literary mentor, Madge had been reading some of Virginia's short narratives, all apparently lost, unless one was 'Phyllis and Rosamond', dated June 1906 (published for the first time in *The Complete Shorter Fiction of Virginia Woolf*, ed. Susan Dick, 1985). This was about two sisters, raised for marriage, who spend an evening with a group of free-spirited young men and women in Bloomsbury. In any case, writing to Violet, Virginia says: 'Madge tells me I have no heart – at least in my writing: really I begin to get alarmed. If marriage is necessary to one's style, I shall have to think about it. [. . .] "The air is full of it" says Madge: but I breathe something else.' (Letter 273).
2. The critic Edmund Gosse (1849–1928) and Charlotte Green, *née* Symonds, Madge's aunt and the widow of T. H. Green, the philosopher. Virginia had recently been in correspondence with Mrs Green.

please remember, that if I am heartless when I write, I am very sentimental really, only I dont know how to express it, and devoted to you and the babies; and I only want to be treated like a nice child. [. . .]

Yr. loving AVS

295: TO VIOLET DICKINSON   [*46 Gordon Square, Bloomsbury*]

Wednesday [14 November 1906]

My Violet,

I'm as hot – I can only think of one comparison, and I believe that aint proper. It isn't hell fire, so dont guess that. We are really merry grigs in this family, and any allusion to Greece is received with hysterial applause.[1]

Visitors come and use their handkerchiefs a great deal; I begin now by saying my brother has typhoid my sister appendicitis – dont laugh. Thoby has had an excellent day and the doctor says we can be quite happy, his temp. is going down, and everything is satisfactory.

[Nurse] McKechnie came today, and the rest cure has begun – but it is a very jovial business, and [Dr] Thompson says she has made excellent progress, and will be completely right in a very short time. He is surprised at the way she has picked up. So here I sit and think of many things: such as drains and boilers and carbolic and bedpans – why they always will come in I dont know. I think my heroic conduct in Greece has stayed in my mind. I discuss enemas at afternoon tea with Peter[2] – whether you call them ènēma or enĕma – or enigma – what the

1. On 8 September 1906 Virginia, Vanessa and Violet Dickinson had set out for Greece, where they joined Thoby and Adrian at Olympia. Together they visited Corinth, Athens, Nauplia and Mycenae, but Vanessa fell ill (apparently with appendicitis) on the return journey to Athens and remained there with Violet, while Virginia and her brothers visited family friends in Euboea. Vanessa recovered sufficiently to continue to Constantinople, where she fell ill again. The Stephens brought her back to London by train, arriving on 1 November, only to find that Thoby (who had returned home ahead) was also ill. He had typhoid. So did Violet. Almost daily Virginia sent her cheerful bulletins, sparing her the truth. Vanessa was getting better, but Thoby was not.

2. The future art critic Clive Bell (1881–1964). Virginia may have called him Peter as a teasing reference to the Wordsworth poem 'Peter Bell', about an itinerant potter who has a dozen 'wives'. Clive was present in the Stephen household for two reasons – his deep friendship with Thoby, whom he had known at Cambridge, and his love for Vanessa, to whom he had proposed unsuccessfully.

difference between turpentine and glycerine may properly be thought to be. This is humanising him. Is this hot enough? old furry fleasome one? Beatrice [Thynne] comes as punctually as a piano tuner, and from the same excellent motives. But when she goes we kiss each other, and sometimes there is a tender passage on the chest in the hall, while she prods her umbrella on my toe. [. . .]

Yr. loving,
AVS

301: TO VIOLET DICKINSON   [*46 Gordon Square, Bloomsbury*]

Tuesday [20 November 1906][1]

My Violet,

How you can trust any nurse to write down your vocabulary I dont know. My patient [Vanessa] is only allowed to write a very occasional letter to Miss Snowden[2] – thats the drs. orders. He thinks you agitate – any woman that size must be eccentric – whereas he saw Snow for himself, and diagnosed her case.

We are going on well through our stages. It's a long business, but there's no need to be anxious. I must get out my pen again, and make that do its business. I reviewed 2 silly novels; no 3 – and a 4th remains.[3] My aim now is to pour out 500 chaste words in order, symmetry and taste – no matter what they mean.

Why dont you read the Creevey Papers through?[4] I cant stop imbibing disreputable gossip; I begin to see what it is to have a taste for memoirs – like Lady Hilton, and Margaret [Lyttelton]. Is this conceited? but take the leavings of my brains when they have spent themselves on appendicitis and they stick like a leech to Creevey. I think I shall write an article for the Academy. But this dont interest you. What you like is

---

1. Thoby Stephen died this morning. During the next month – for fear that she might impede Violet's recovery, but also for deeply personal reasons – Virginia continued to pretend in frequent letters that Thoby was coming along well.
2. Margery Snowden (1878–1966?) had studied with Vanessa at the Royal Academy Schools.
3. These reviews have not been traced. They may have been part of Virginia's campaign to convince Violet that life was going along normally.
4. Thomas Creevey (1768–1838) was a politician whose journals and the letters he received comprise the *Creevey Papers* (1903).

oaths and scandal. So mark then, my weazened pimpernel, I shall have a niece in February.[1]

Susie Grosvenor is engaged to John Buchan;[2] and the wise – that is Jack [Hills] – predict tragedy. How is she to live with a clever man all the days of her life? She is pretty and flaxen and brainless (this is Jacks voice) must have a man to hold her handkerchief – but her heart is excellent – He has a brain, edits the Spectator and thinks of politics. Now make a story out of this as you lie in bed, and think of me.

Weighing day tomorrow I think, if the machine aint broke by Gerald.

Goodnight and God – have I a right to a God? send you sleep.

Wall[3] nuzzles in and wants love.

Yr. AVS

306: To Violet Dickinson   *46 Gordon Square, Bloomsbury*

25th [November 1906]

My Violet,

[. . .] Nessa also increases steadily. Really I think we are through our troubles – but it has been the devil of a time. I have tried to write – but perpetual sense has consolidated my brains. Thoby has been reading reviews of the Life,[4] and wants to know if you are up to that? The dr. says his brain is the strongest he knows; and his heart is fit to do the work of two men. Still, it is a long job, as you have to be so careful with food – and then as his lungs were bad there is the danger of cold – and he is like a child. We hope he will get away in 3 weeks, with Bell; and Nessa will be more than ready to go before that. She is to get up and come down if she likes this week – but I have made her promise to stay more or less in her room till she goes away – at least to make that her headquarters. She really is a wonderful woman. She sat down solidly to

1. This was no scandal; only the pregnancy of George Duckworth's wife, Lady Margaret. In February she gave birth to her second son.
2. Susan Grosvenor (1882–1977), a longtime friend of Virginia, married in July 1907 the author and future Governor-General of Canada, John Buchan (1875–1940), later Lord Tweedsmuir.
3. For 'Wallaby', another of Virginia's animal names for herself when writing to Violet.
4. *The Life and Letters of Leslie Stephen* (1906), by his friend, the historian Frederic William Maitland (1850–1906). Virginia had contributed a short memoir of her father (*Essays*, I, 127).

get well, confronted all the doctors, and has proved that she was right all the time. She saw Kitty [Maxse] one day, but as a rule she only sees us. They let her do as she thinks fit now; I feel happier about her than I have done for months. She does seem to me rested all through – brain and body – and ready to begin again as fresh as paint.

And now that Thoby is out of danger things will go swimmingly: only my dear old furry one must heal up – and come to a festal dinner. This is perhaps the dullest letter that *my* pen ever wrote; of course if Snow [Margery Snowden] had written it, or Ella [Crum], or Herbert Paul[1] – one would have thought differently of them. I went to the zoo this morning with Adrian; and a Kingajou hung on to my hand: O Kingajou, I said – if I were you! You will understand that that is exclamatory, and it is a poem too. And I saw the kangaroo, with its baby in its pouch, and it licked its nose, and wiped its eyes. That is Violet I cried.

Yr. AVS

318: To Violet Dickinson   *46 Gordon Square, Bloomsbury*

Monday [10 December 1906]

My Violet,

[. . .] Thoby is going on well; he has chicken broth of a kind, and will be up by Christmas. The dr. approves of his trip with Peter [Clive Bell], but wont say yet when that will be. I suppose early in January. He has a great many flowers and attentions, and is very good and delights his nurses. The dr. says he has a remarkable mind. [. . .]

We will turn to more interesting subjects – as, Walter Headlam and my manuscripts. Now Violet raises herself in bed, and calls to the nurse to draw the blind a little higher, and bids them tell Mrs Crum not to come in yet awhile.

I am to send him all my unpublished works; and he will write me a sober criticism. Doesn't that do you good, and make you believe that life holds possibilities? Further, he wishes to dedicate his translation of the Agamennon to me, instead of to Swinburne; in gratitude for 3 pages of the finest criticism known to him which I wrote and despatched 4 years

---

1. The politician and author (*Life of Froude*, 1905), whom Violet knew.

ago! How many of my letters will thus rise up and bear fruit? I may be incubating heaven knows what glories.[1] [. . .]

Are you in what state of body or mind? My plan is to treat you as detached spirit; maybe your body has typhoid; that is immaterial (you will be glad to hear) I address the immortal part, and shoot words of fire into the upper aer which spirits inhabit. They pierce you like lightning, and quicken your soul; whereas, if I said How have you slept, and what food are you taking, you would sink into your nerves and arteries and your gross pads of flesh, and perhaps your flame might snuff and die there. Who knows?

Yr. AVS

326: To Violet Dickinson   *46 Gordon Square, Bloomsbury*

[18 December 1906]

Beloved Violet,

Do you hate me for telling so many lies?[2] You know we had to do it. You must think that Nessa is *radiantly happy*[3] and Thoby was splendid to the end.

These great things are not terrible, and I know we can still make a good job of it – and we want you more and more. I never knew till this happened how I should turn to you and want you with me when no one else could help.

This is quite true, my beloved Violet, and I must write it down for once. I think of you as one of the people – Adrian is the other – who make it worth while to live and be happy. You are part of all that is best, and happiest in our lives. Thoby was always asking me about you. I know you loved him, and he loved you.

1. The Greek scholar Walter Headlam (1866–1908) was a Fellow of King's College, Cambridge. Twenty years older than Virginia, he had been a visitor to the family's house in Cornwall during her childhood. They now began an erudite flirtation. But neither was very serious, and the relationship had run its course some time before Headlam's sudden death in June 1908. His *Agamemnon of Aeschylus* was not published until 1910, when it appeared with a letter of acceptance from Swinburne, to whom Headlam had offered in 1900 to dedicate the book.
2. Violet had learned that Thoby was dead. She read it in the December issue of the *National Review*, which published a review of Maitland's biography of Leslie Stephen. The reviewer wrote: 'This book appeared almost on the very day of the untimely death of Sir Leslie Stephen's eldest son, Mr Thoby Stephen, at the age of 25.'
3. Two days after Thoby's death, Vanessa had agreed to marry Clive Bell.

The only thing I feel I could not bear would be to think that this news should make you worse. It would not be right. I can feel happy about him; he was so brave and strong, and his life was perfect.

Now we must be more to each other than ever; and there will be all Nessa's life to look forward to. She is wonderfully well.

'I think on the whole I get happier every day – though it's difficult to think that I can ever be much happier than I have often been at moments during the last few weeks.' That is what she writes today.

Beloved, get well and come back to your Wall who loves you.

Yr. AVS

December 1906–1909

*Vanessa's engagement and marriage brought the first important male correspon-
dent into Virginia's life. Clive Bell was well read and worldly. Virginia responded
to both qualities. With Clive she discussed her first novel, which would take many
years to complete, and with him she carried on her first serious flirtation. Her
dangerous actions were motivated by her jealousy of Clive and, later, the Bells'
new baby, both of whom had displaced her intimacy with Vanessa.*

*The marriage meant that she and Adrian had to find a new home. They
moved to another Bloomsbury address, and there continued to entertain Thoby's,
and now Adrian's, Cambridge friends. Maynard Keynes came. So did Duncan
Grant, Desmond MacCarthy and Lady Ottoline Morrell. The location was not
'good'; young men and women discussed what they pleased – Virginia's women
friends were scandalised. So was Henry James, the old friend of her father. But the
contacts were creatively stimulating for Virginia, who gradually added lively new
correspondents, such as Lytton Strachey – to whom she was, very briefly, engaged
– and dropped old ones.*

*Intellectual friends induced a new style in Virginia's letters. With Clive and
Lytton, Virginia was less breathless than in her early letters and more deliberately
clever. But to Vanessa, whom Virginia still needed above all others, she wrote with
warm, witty spontaneity.*

328: To Clive Bell   *46 Gordon Square, Bloomsbury*

Thursday [20 December 1906]

My dear Clive,
    [. . .] I wish you would write a description of yourself – your features
your gifts your prospects your parents – that I might know exactly who
you are and what you are and above all whether you are worthy of
Vanessa. The general opinion seems to be that no one can be worthy of
her; but as you are unknown this is no reflection upon you. Only it will
show you the kind of reputation she has; perhaps you know it already. I
begin to wish she were a little more various – but I do homage all day

long prostrate and acquiescent, before her shrine. And I suppose incense rises in the fields of Wiltshire also;[1] the last worshipper was Pippa Strachey[2] who lunched with me today. She has an imm*ense* admiration – you can put the accents on — for Vanessa – and thinks *no* man good enough. This letter can be divided into equal parts if necessary; but I have an instinct that one word does for the two of you. [...]

Your aff.
AVS

331: To Violet Dickinson   *[Lane End]* Bank
                                  Lyndhurst [*Hampshire*][3]

[25 December 1906]

My Violet,

[...] I am reading now a book by Renan called his Memories of Childhood [*Cahiers de Jeunesse*, 1906]: O my word it is beautiful – like the chime of silver bells; and when his old peasant mother writes it is the same thing, so that I think it a virtue in the French language that it submits to prose, whereas English curls and knots and breaks off in short spasms of rage. Also I am reading my dear Christina Rossetti with her kind voice and her prominent eyes, and her acquiescent piety: but all the same she sings like a robin and sometimes like a nightingale – the first of our English poetesses. She doesn't think, I imagine; but just throws up her head and sends forth her song, and never listens, but makes another. O you Christians have much to answer for! She died surrounded by all the horrors of the Church, poor woman. Then I am reading your Keats,[4] with the pleasure of one handling great luminous stones. I rise and shout in ecstasy, and my eyes brim with such pleasure that I must drop the book and gaze from the window. It is a beautiful edition.

Yr. AVS

1. Vanessa and Clive were spending the Christmas holidays with his parents, William and Hannah Bell, at Cleeve House, Seend, Wiltshire.
2. Philippa Strachey (1872–1968), the third of Lytton's five sisters, was a steadfast worker in the causes of women's suffrage and education. Like all the other members of her family, her speech was marked by extravagant stresses.
3. Virginia and Adrian were staying in Hampshire for Christmas. On New Year's Eve they went to Cleeve House to join Vanessa and Clive.
4. Violet's Christmas gift.

332: To Violet Dickinson　　　　　[*Lane End, Bank,*
　　　　　　　　　　　　　　　　Lyndhurst, Hampshire]

[28? December 1906]

My Violet,

[. . .] I think housekeeping is what I do best, and I mean to run our house on very remarkable lines.[1] Does housekeeping interest you at all? I think it really ought to be just as good as writing, and I never see – as I argued the other day with Nessa – where the separation between the two comes in. At least if you must put books on one side and life on t' other, each is a poor and bloodless thing. But my theory is that they mix indistinguishably. [. . .]

I met an old man on the village green yesterday, lame and frost bitten and ruddy and white haired who told me he had had goose for dinner and 'really thought he was the happiest old man in the world'. He looked so convinced of it and so stealthy as though happiness was not altogether respectable that I told him he was a credit to the race and upon wh. he shambled off to the public house, and I nearly followed.

Get well; read, and flourish. [. . .]

Yr. AVS

333: To Violet Dickinson　　　　　[*Lane End, Bank,*
　　　　　　　　　　　　　　　　Lyndhurst, Hampshire]

[30? December 1906]

My Violet,

[. . .] I shall want all my sweetness to gild Nessa's happiness. It does seem strange and intolerable sometimes. When I think of father and Thoby and then see that funny little creature [Clive] twitching his pink skin and jerking out his little spasm of laughter I wonder what odd freak there is in Nessa's eyesight. But I dont say this, and I wont say it, except to you. Tell me if it bores you; I dont want to make things worse for you, and I know my letters aren't soothing. [. . .]

I have been reading Keats most of the day. I think he is about the greatest of all – and no d——d humanity. I like cool Greek Gods, and

1. Vanessa and Clive were to keep the Gordon Square house. Adrian and Virginia, who had hitherto relied on Vanessa to manage the domestic side of their lives, planned to move to another house after the marriage.

amber skies, and shadow like running water, and all his great palpable words – symbols for immaterial things. O isn't this nonsense? Adrian plays patience at my side. I have done my 5 reviews also, and my mind feels as though a torrent of weak tea had been poured over it. I do think all good and evil comes from words. I have to tune myself into a good temper with something musical, and I run to a book as a child to its mother. Dont you think the flesh is a cumbersome illustration, and the text is all written or spoken in half a dozen words? [. . .]

AVS

334: TO VIOLET DICKINSON   *Lane End* [*Bank,*
                                             Lyndhurst, Hampshire]

[31 December 1906]

My Violet,

[. . .] The world is full of kindness and stupidity, I wish everyone didn't tell me to marry. Is it crude human nature breaking out? I call it disgusting. [. . .]

Yr. AVS

336: TO VIOLET DICKINSON   *46 Gordon Square, Bloomsbury*

Thursday [3 January 1907]

My Violet,

[. . .] We spent the day at Bath – a Meredithian expedition – so far as Nessa and Clive were concerned. They swung along the streets arm in arm; she had a gauze streamer, red as blood flying over her shoulder, a purple scarf, a shooting cap, tweed skirt and great brown boots. Then her hair swept across her forehead, and she was tawny and jubilant and lusty as a young God. I never saw her look better. Indeed our two days [at Cleeve House] were more of a treat than I expected; I am not unselfish, as you know; but selfishly I do enjoy life and beauty and audacity, and all that freedom and generosity which seem to bathe her like her own proper atmosphere. And Clive as I think I said, is perfectly fit to receive all this; I think he has a very sweet and sincere nature, and capable brains and great artistic sensibility of every kind. What you miss is inspiration of any kind, but then old Nessa is no genius, though she has all the human gifts; and genius is an accident. They are the most honest couple I ever saw; a little more imagination and they would be less scrupulous – but on the whole, I doubt that man and woman are made much better in the world. I did not see Nessa alone, but I realise that this is all over, and I shall never see her alone any more; and Clive is a new part of her, which I must learn to accept. [. . .]

Yr. AVS

338: To Lady Robert Cecil[1]   *46 Gordon Square, Bloomsbury*

Monday [January 1907]

My dear Nelly,

[. . .] Why is there nothing written about food – only so much thought? I think a new school might arise, with new adjectives and new epithets, and a strange beautiful sensation, all new to print. How generous I am! I might have kept this all to myself. But the fur is another matter. It is a very subtle and serious matter, wrapped round the most secret fibres of our consciousness; you dont know what a lot might be said and felt and thought – what reams, therefore might be written – about such a gift;[2] and here am I going to squeeze all this in to the usual Thank you. I think I ought to be hurt, and then angry, and then apologetic, and then generous, and then sentimental and then philosophical, and then merely friendly. Whereas I am none of these things; only I think I am grateful – because, if I have none of the finer feelings, I am yet fitted with a marvellous simplicity of nature so that to buy a fur is impossible to me, but to accept a fur is quite easy and pleasant. O well – this is the way we writers write – when we wish not to say something. As you are a novelist yourself you need no further explanation.

I think you ought to write novels: you can write letters which is far harder. [. . .]

Yr.

AVS

1. Nelly Cecil (*née* Lady Eleanor Lambton, 1868–1956), daughter of the 2nd Earl of Durham, and wife of Lord Robert Cecil, a son of the 3rd Marquess of Salisbury. She was another of the aristocratic friends of Violet Dickinson. Lady Robert had a special attraction in that she was bookish and a would-be writer. She and Virginia exchanged manuscripts at this stage, as well as frequent letters. Later this year, the editor of the *Cornhill Magazine* asked the two women to share a monthly column of book reviews. This they did for several months.
2. Received by Virginia either for Christmas or for her 25th birthday on 25 January. Lady Robert had earlier sent pheasants, which occasioned Virginia's thoughts about food as a critical subject.

339a: To Vanessa Stephen   [*46 Gordon Square, Bloomsbury*]
[6 February 1907]

Address of Congratulation
to our
Mistress
on her
Approaching Marriage[1]

Dear Mistress,

We the undersigned three Apes and a Wombat[2] wish to make known to you our great grief and joy at the news that you intend to marry. We hear that you have found a new Red Ape of a kind not known before who is better than all other apes because he can both talk and marry you: from which we are debarred.

We have examined his fur and find it of fine quality, red and golden at the tips, with an undergrowth of soft down, excellent for winter. We find him clean, merry, and sagacious, a wasteful eater and fond of fossils. His teeth are sharp, and we advise that you keep him on Bones. His disposition is Affectionate.

We therefore commend your marriage, and testify that you will make an excellent Mistress for any Ape or Wombat whatsoever. You are very understanding of Apes, loving and wholesome, vigilant after fleas, and scourging of all Misdoing.

We have been your humble Beasts since we first left our Isles, which is before we can remember, and during that time we have wooed you and sung many songs of winter and summer and autumn in the hope that thus enchanted you would condescend one day to marry us. But as we no longer expect this honour we entreat that you keep us still for your lovers, should you have need of such, and in that capacity we promise to abide well content always adoring you now as before.

With Humble Obeisance to our Mistress
We sign ourselves,
Her devoted Beasts
Billy

1. Vanessa and Clive were married at St Pancras Registry Office the next day, 7 February.
2. This letter was composed and signed by Virginia only. She sometimes referred to herself collectively as 'the apes'. 'Wombat' was one of the familiars created by the Stephen children and about whom they told each other tales.

Bartholomew
Mungo
and
WOMBAT

The Sixth of February,
nineteen hundred and seven.
Year of our Lord.

345: To Clive Bell   *46 Gordon Square, Bloomsbury*

[February 1907]

My dear Clive,

[...] A true letter, so my theory runs, should be as a film of wax pressed close to the graving in the mind; but if I followed my own prescription this sheet would be scored with some very tortuous and angular incisions. Let me explain that I began some minutes since to review a novel and made its faults, by a process common among minds of a certain order or disorder, the text for a soliloquy upon many matters of importance; the sky and the breeze were part of my theme. A telegram however, with its necessary knock and its flagrant yellow, and its curt phrase of vicious English – I know not which sense was most offended – hit me in the wing and I fell a heaped corpse upon the earth. The sense, if that can be said to have sense which had so little sound, was to discredit the respectability of a house in Fitzroy Square.[1] And there you see me in the mud. Shall I argue that a mind that knows not Gibbon knows not morality?[2] or shall I affirm that bad English and respectability are twin sisters, dear to the telegram and odious to the artist? I state the question and leave it; for it will ramify if I mistake not through all the limbs of my soul and clasp the very Judgment seat of God. So then let us turn – and where? First, I think, to Vanessa; and I am almost inclined to let her name stand alone upon the page.[3] It contains all the beauty of the sky,

1. Virginia had found a house at 29 Fitzroy Square, but some of her friends, particularly Violet Dickinson and Beatrice Thynne, thought the neighbourhood disreputable and begged her not to move there. That George Bernard Shaw and his mother had recently lived there alleviated some worries, and Virginia and Adrian moved to their new house in March.
2. Letter 345 begins with a reference to Gibbon, presumably one of the literary topics through which Clive and Virginia were endeavouring to know each other better.
3. Cf. the dedication to *Night and Day* (1919): 'To Vanessa Bell but, looking for a phrase, I found none to stand beside your name.'

and the melancholy of the sea, and the laughter of the Dolphins in its circumference, first in the mystic Van, spread like a mirror of grey glass to Heaven. Next in the swishing tail of its successive esses, and finally in the grave pause and suspension of the ultimate A breathing peace like the respiration of Earth itself.

If I write of books you will understand that I continue the theme though in another key; for are not all Arts her tributaries, all sciences her continents and the globe itself but a painted ball in the enclosure of her arms? But you dwell in the Temple, and I am a worshipper without. It behoves me then to speak of common things, that are and cease to be; of people and of houses, of Empires and of governments.

I read then, and feel beauty swell like ripe fruit within my palm: I hear music woven from the azure skeins of air; and gazing into deep pools skimmed with the Italian veil I see youth and melancholy walking hand in hand. Yet why separate and distinguish when all are pressed to your ardent lips in one clear draught?

Let us then have make [*sic*] an ending: for in truth I must copy out this sheet.[1]

Yours ever,
AVS

355: To Clive Bell   *46 Gordon Square, Bloomsbury*

Friday [22 March 1907]

My dear Clive,

[...] Well then, how am I to write a letter? But perhaps you have observed that this is a favourite device with letter writers, they are always in haste, or in discomfort, or in a temper, so that you only get the dregs of their genius, and you can speculate what a letter it would have been – seeing there are six careful sheets already – had he had time or temper, or so on. And I put 'he' because a woman, dear Creature, is always naked of artifice; and that is why she generally lives so well, and writes so badly. [...]

Yr.
AVS

1. This may have been a rather nasty joke; in Letter 408 Virginia maliciously tells Lytton that Clive always rewrites his letters. Or she may not be joking at all. As she began to write to men, to the educated men who were Thoby's friends, she was a little anxious about her literary style and her own lack of formal education.

371: To Violet Dickinson   *29 F[itzroy] Sq[uare]*

Saturday [20 July 1907]

My Violet,

Here is a nice pleasant tawny old book, which I daresay you have got already, or wont read anyhow. If so, do send it me back. I got it from an old Jew, who always spends an hour or so in discourse with me; and we stroke all the venerable books, and discuss title pages, which he can read, whatever the language, and print, and the degeneracy of people who buy new books, and all sorts of interesting subjects, even Tristram Shandy 'no one would wish for a complete set – I myself have never read it through, though I take it up often' – So it dont matter that the book is without a title page, and 3 sheets of introduction: it is white as driven snow within, and outside like a ripe fiddle. 'Have you a friend with a garden, he said; who likes sullets – sullads you understand' That is the amount of his learning. So my good woman, – this is a specimen of my narrative style, which is far from good, seeing that I am forever knotting it and twisting it in conformity with the coils in my own brain, and a narrative should be as straight and flexible as the line you stretch between pear trees, with your linen on drying – I felt in my pocket and counted out minute silver pieces, and gross coppers, which fell short, as I piled them in a row on the table. So he forgave me the rest, magnanimously, as between scholars. Now after some conversation between us, I have never read the book, but I like snatches, it is going down to Welwyn [Violet's country house, Hertfordshire], where it shall live among trees. [. . .]

Last night I dined out in Chelsea, and mauled the dead and rotten carcases of several works written by my friends; how I hate intellect! There were several brilliant young men, whose lights had been kindled at Cambridge, and burnt all of them precisely in the same way; and some said they were artificial, supplied by the county loan at so much the cube. You turn them off, when company isnt there, to prevent waste; and you know what you have spent, to a penny. An elderly man who had somehow got my name right, said to me 'In the course of your life Miss Stephen, you must have known many distinguished people. Stevenson, I suppose?' Yes and George Eliot, and Tennyson before he grew a beard I said. But the astonishing thing is that these great people always talked much as you and I talk; Tennyson, for instance, would say to me, 'Pass the salt' or Thank you for the butter. 'Ah indeed; you should write your memoirs; one gets paid for that kind of thing' he said; being a dealer in pictures.

At this moment I should be cobbling a terrific passage in my article on Lady Fanshawe;[1] which begins reptile and turns quadruped in the middle. If only my flights were longer, and less variable I should make solid blocks of sentences, carven and wrought from pure marble; or the Greek marble which absorbs colours. [. . .]

Yr. AVS

378: To Clive Bell
The Steps, Playden, Sussex[2]

[18 August 1907]

My dear Clive,

[. . .] I am reading Henry James on America;[3] and feel myself as one embalmed in a block of smooth amber: it is not unpleasant, very tranquil, as a twilight shore – but such is not the stuff of genius: no, it should be a swift stream. [. . .]

Yr.
AVS

380: To Violet Dickinson
[*The Steps, Playden, Sussex*]

Sunday [25 August 1907]

My Violet,

[. . .] we went and had tea with Henry James[4] today, and Mr and Mrs Prothero,[5] at the golf club; and Henry James fixed me with his staring

1. In her review for the *TLS* of *The Memoirs of Ann, Lady Fanshawe*, Virginia found the story of this conventional Restoration lady pleasantly bland (*Essays*, I, 143).
2. Where Virginia and Adrian had rented a house. The Bells stayed nearby at Rye. They shared visitors, including Lytton Strachey and Saxon Sydney-Turner.
3. *The American Scene* (1906), reflections on his native country, which he had visited after an absence of twenty years in England.
4. Henry James lived at Lamb House, Rye, from 1898 until his death in 1916. He had been a friend of Leslie and Julia Stephen.
5. George Walter Prothero (1848–1922), the historian and Fellow of King's College, Cambridge.

blank eye – it is like a childs marble – and said 'My dear Virginia, they tell me – they tell me – they tell me – that you – as indeed being your fathers daughter nay your grandfathers grandchild – the descendant I may say of a century – of a century – of quill pens and ink – ink – ink pots, yes, yes, yes, they tell me – ahm m m – that you, that you, that you *write* in short.' This went on in the public street, while we all waited, as farmers wait for the hen to lay an egg – do they? – nervous, polite, and now on this foot now on that. I felt like a condemned person, who sees the knife drop and stick and drop again. Never did any woman hate 'writing' as much as I do. But when I am old and famous I shall discourse like Henry James. We had to stop periodically to let him shake himself free of the thing; he made phrases over the bread and butter 'rude and rapid' it was, and told us all the scandal of Rye. 'Mr Jones has eloped, I regret to say, to Tasmania; leaving 12 little Jones, and a possible 13th to Mrs Jones; most regrettable, most unfortunate, and yet not wholly an action to which one has no private key of ones own so to speak.' [. . .]

From our garden we look over a dead marsh; flat as the sea, and the simile has the more truth in that the sea was once where the marsh is now. But at night a whole flower bed of fitful lighthouses blooms – O what a sentence! – but irritants are good I am told – along the edge; indeed you can follow the sea all round the cliff on which we stand, till you perceive Rye floating out to meet it, getting stranded halfway on the shingle, like – nothing so much as a red brick town. But then 'red brick towns dont float; and these semi metaphors of yours are a proof that you dip hastily into a pocket full of words, and fling out the first come; and that is why your writing is so . . .' Anyhow, we have a real country cottage – white walls, and bright pictures, and cheerful manly books, Stevenson and Thoreau, and a garden, and an orchard; I dont really enjoy any of these things; it bores me dreadfully to cut the flowers, and I am determined that Mrs Dew Smith is a vague weak shallow kind of person; who has realised all her dreams in this house, and will be told forever, how charming it is, and how clever she is.

Gerald [Duckworth] has been here today; my spirits spring like fire now that he is gone; Adrian and I had the heaviest work; for we ran out of our talk on the way up from the station, and then we each took turns with a question, till when it came to mine I could only say 'What do you usually have for lunch on Sunday Gerald?' Which however was best of all, for he remembered the lunches of 20 years ago. 'O those puffs! not short pastry, but puff pastry – There was one dish, my dear, just black at the bottom, all flaky, done with more butter than she[1] uses now – which I shall remember till my dying day.' Then we talked about beef; and at last he fell asleep; as a prize pig, well entertained might sleep. This is brutal, because he took a great deal of trouble to come; and I should be affectionate. [. . .]

Yr. AVS

397: TO VIOLET DICKINSON   *29 Fitzroy Square, W.*

[December 1907]

My Violet,
    [. . .] I have been staying at Oxford, and stretching my brains with trained Arabs, with not an ounce of flesh on them. The atmosphere of Oxford is quite the chilliest and least human known to me; you see brains floating like so many sea anemonies, nor have they shape or colour. They are bloodless, with great veins on them. (This reads like a school childs exercise – so precise and true is it.) Of course Herbert Fisher[2] has his merits; but what can you do with a brain so competent that nothing resists it – because after all, it attempts only solid things – histories, and triumphant little text books. Now my brain I will confess, for I dont like to talk of it, floats in blue air; where there are circling clouds, soft sunbeams of elastic gold, and fairy gossamers – things that cant be cut – that must be tenderly enclosed, and expressed in a globe of exquisitely coloured words. At the mere prick of steel they vanish. [. . .]

Yr. AVS

406: TO CLIVE BELL   [*29 Fitzroy Square, W.*]

Wednesday [15 April 1908]

My dear Clive,
    [. . .] I gather that you are going to a dance; and I believe you go because you think your wife the most beautiful woman in England, and

---

1. Sophia ('Sophie') Farrell (c. 1861–1942), who came as cook to the Stephens in the 1880s, and was now working for Virginia and Adrian.
2. Virginia's distinguished cousin, H. A. L. Fisher (1865–1940), the historian and Fellow of New College, Oxford. His scholarly work included *Studies in Napoleonic States-manship* (1903) and *A History of England, 1485–1547* (1906). He was later President of the Board of Education and Warden of New College.

she goes because she thinks so too. Kiss her, most passionately, in all my private places – neck –, and arm, and eyeball, and tell her – what new thing is there to tell her? how fond I am of her husband?[1]

Your AVS

410: To Clive Bell   [*29 Fitzroy Square, W.*]

Wednesday [6 May 1908][2]

My dear Clive,

[...] Why do you torment me with half uttered and ambiguous sentences? my presence is 'vivid and strange and bewildering'. I read your letter again and again, and wonder whether you have found me out, or, more likely, determined that there is nothing but an incomprehensible and quite negligible femininity to find out. I was certainly of opinion, though we did not kiss – (I was willing and offered once – but let that be) – I think we 'achieved the heights' as you put it. But did you realise how profoundly I was moved, and at the same time, restricted, by the sight of your daily life. Ah – such beauty – grandeur – and freedom – as of panthers treading in their wilds – I never saw in any other pair. When Nessa is bumbling about the world, and making each thorn blossom, what room is there for me? Seriously nature has done so much more for her than for me. I shrank to my narrowest limits, and you found me more than usually complex, and contained. Chivalrous as you are, however, you took infinite pains with me, and I am very grateful. [...]

Yr. aff.

AVS

412: To Violet Dickinson   *29 Fitzroy Sq.*

May 13th [1908]

My Violet,

[...] I had a fortnight at St Ives; Adrian and Nessa and Clive came for

1. This was beginning to be true in a new and disruptive way. See the next letter.
2. Virginia had just returned from a holiday in Cornwall, where she had been joined by Adrian and the Bells with their new baby (Julian, born in February). During that time Clive and Virginia, both feeling ousted from Vanessa's affections, turned to each other. Their flirtation continued for several months. It did not end in bed, and somehow the family relationships were preserved, if damaged.

the last week. I doubt that I shall ever have a baby. Its voice is too terrible, a senseless scream, like an ill omened cat. Nobody could wish to comfort it, or pretend that it was a human being. Now, thank God, it sleeps with its nurse. Now and then it smiled at Nessa, and it has a very nice back; but the amount of business that has to be got through before you can enjoy it, is dismaying. Clive and I went for some long walks; but I felt that we were deserters, but then I was quite useless, as a nurse, and Clive will not even hold it. [. . .]

AVS

435: To Saxon Sydney-Turner   *5 Cathedral Green, Wells, Somerset*[1]

[14 August 1908]

My dear Saxon,

[. . .] I have been horribly disabused by visiting Glastonbury and Cheddar; Cheddar is exactly like the scenic railway at the Exhibition, and I was not in the least anxious to be reminded of that; besides there was no switch back, and the populace was disgusting as usual. In my absence, – this was yesterday – (you must put up with small beer) Hans and Gurth were taken for a walk by the slavy; they both escaped, raced round the town, and were taken in charge by a policeman, who put them into prison. Mr Oram, a verger, and my landlord, had released them, but I found the household almost hysterical, and I had a solemn interview with Mr Oram, who begged me not to be agitated, and assured me that I was not, strictly speaking, a criminal. Gurth had no name on his collar, and the law etc., etc., Mr Oram has an impediment in his speech, which makes him repeat everything twice over. He also insists upon calling Hans 'Miss Hans' and was very arch about 'His Lordship' (Gurth) running after 'this young lady'. 'You know how it is with gentlemen, Miss Stephens – pardon me the liberty' I had to pretend that I was deeply moved. Do you think all the lower classes are naturally idiotic? I can't conceive how this man who is the father of two children, gets through his life, or for the matter of that, buttons his waistcoat in the morning.

1. With her dogs Hans and Gurth for companions, Virginia stayed for two weeks in Wells, but went twice to meet Vanessa and Clive in Bath. She spent another two weeks in Manorbier, Pembrokeshire.

His youngest, or as Clive would have it, younger, daughter, has just declared her wish that I should be her stepmother. [. . .]

Your affate VS

438: To Clive Bell

Sea View, Manorbier
[*Pembrokeshire*]

Aug. 19th [1908]

My dear Clive,

There is no doubt but that I was well advised in telling you to come here for your honeymoon. I am surprised to find how beautiful it all is – more than I remembered – how lovely, and how primitive. I have not been on the cliffs yet, my business yesterday keeping me on the trot, but directly this letter is done, I am off to Proud Giltar.

Ah, it is the sea that does it! perpetual movement, and a border of mystery, solving the limits of fields, and silencing their prose. [. . .]

I think a great deal of my future, and settle what book I am to write –[1] how I shall re-form the novel and capture multitudes of things at present fugitive, enclose the whole, and shape infinite strange shapes. I take a good look at woods in the sunset, and fix men who are breaking stones with an intense gaze, meant to sever them from the past and the future – all these excitements last out my walk, but tomorrow I know, I shall be sitting down to the inanimate old phrases. [. . .]

I split my head over Moore every night,[2] feeling ideas travelling to the remotest part of my brain, and setting up a feeble disturbance, hardly to be called thought. It is almost a physical feeling, as though some little coil of brain unvisited by any blood so far, and pale as wax, had got a little life into it at last; but had not strength to keep it. I have a very clear notion which parts of my brain think. [. . .]

Yr. AVS

Kiss my old Tawny [Vanessa], on all her private places – kiss her eyes, and her neck socket.

---

1. By this time Virginia had completed 100 pages of her first novel *Melymbrosia*, which was to become *The Voyage Out* (1915).
2. *Principia Ethica* (1903) by the philosopher, Apostle, and Fellow of Trinity College, Cambridge, G. E. Moore (1875–1958). Clive, who had taken over the post of literary confidant from Violet and Madge, was in many ways also a mentor. Probably it was he who recommended the book, but it could just as easily have been Lytton or Saxon in that the book was something of a bible for the current Apostles and their friends.

444: TO VANESSA BELL   *Manorbier [Pembrokeshire]*

Saturday [29 August 1908]

Beloved,

[. . .] Do you call this well written? careful, and rhythmical? if so, my good beast, your ear is stuffed with feathery down. I am also sunk into such a simple inarticulate mood, that I doubt whether you will understand my bleatings. The only words I have spoken for four weeks, except when I saw you, have been very loud and hearty. 'Fine day! No, he wont bite. I should like a fowl tonight.' One has to be so cheerful with the lower classes, or they think one diseased. [. . .]

Yr. B.[1]

469: TO LYTTON STRACHEY   *29 Fitzroy Square, W.*

Thursday [28 January 1909]

[. . .] Why do you tantalise me with stories of your novel?[2] I wish you would confine your genius to one department, it's too bad to have you dancing like some (oh well – I'll drop the metaphor) over all departments of literature – poetry, criticism (both scientific & humane) art – belles lettres – and now fiction. A painstaking woman who wishes to treat of life as she finds it, and to give voice to some of the perplexities of her sex, in plain English, has no chance at all. [. . .]

Yrs.
VS

1. For 'Billy', one of the Apes (see Letter 339a). Virginia normally signed herself 'B' when writing to Vanessa.
2. *Lord Pettigrew*, a political novel of which Lytton completed only the first four chapters before abandoning the project.

470: To Lytton Strachey   *29 Fitzroy Square, W.*

Feb. 1st [1909]

Dear Mr Hatherly,[1]

I shall be happy to give you tea tomorrow. If there's one thing a Yorkshire woman can cook, it's a muffin.

I missed you by 10 minutes at the Philips' the other day.

So you've noticed it then? How clever you are, and how unkind! For don't you think that these 'extraordinary conclusions' you like so much may be rather uncomfortable for me and perhaps (though I really won't admit it) a little uncomfortable for Clarissa? We were not happy – no – and yet I know its dangerous to imagine people in love with one, and so I told myself all the time. But James is really – sometimes a woman feels so much older than a man.[2] There! that's worthy of Lady Eastnor.[3] I am thinking of his face, as he helped me on with my cloak, and said good night. I don't admit for a moment that you have any real ground for your 'extraordinary conclusions', and I suppose I should do better to say no more about them. You always tempt me to run on, and justify myself and explain myself, with your hints and subtleties and suggestive catlike ways. Could you come early tomorrow – by the bye? Mr Ilchester[4] has sent me a ticket for the Wagner opera – what d'you call it – and I don't want to miss the overture.

Your very sincerely,
Eleanor Hadyng

1. Lytton, as Vane Hatherly, and Virginia, as Eleanor Hadyng, were participants in a game in which they and several of their friends adopted fictional roles in order to create an epistolary novel. Clive and Vanessa were known as James and Clarissa Philips.

2. Lytton suspected a love affair between Virginia and Clive. Using the cover of Mr Hatherly, he was able to voice his suspicions. He had more than a passing interest. On 19 February he proposed to Virginia, who accepted him. Lytton, however, immediately panicked. Virginia knew of his homosexuality and, although probably somewhat disappointed, kindly consented to a mutual breaking off.

3. Lady Ottoline Morrell (1873–1938), half-sister of the 6th Duke of Portland, and wife of the barrister and Liberal MP, Philip Morrell (1870–1943). She was a fascinating hostess and patron of the arts, whom Virginia had met in 1908.

4. Saxon Sydney-Turner, who, like Virginia and Adrian, was deeply devoted to Wagnerian opera at this time.

471: To Clive Bell   *29 Fitzroy Square, W.*

Sunday [7? February 1909]

My dear Clive,

You are really angelic to take so much pains to give reasons and advice.[1] They seem to me excellent; for you have laid your finger on spots already suspected by me. I will only offer some explanation of the wretched first volume. Those bare passages of biography were not meant to remain in the text. They are notes to solidify my own conception of the peoples characters. I thought it a good plan to write them down; but having served their purpose, they shall go. Helen's letter also was an experiment. When I read the thing over (one very grey evening) I thought it so flat and monotonous that I did not even feel 'the atmosphere': certainly there was no character in it.[2] Next morning I proceeded to slash and rewrite, in the hope of animating it; and (as I suspect for I have not re-read it) destroyed the one virtue it had – a kind of continuity; for I wrote it originally in a dream like state, which was at any rate, unbroken. My intention now is to write straight on, and finish the book; and then, if that day ever comes, to catch if possible the first imagination and go over the beginning again with broad touches, keeping much of the original draft, and trying to deepen the atmosphere – Giving the feel of running water, and not much else. I have kept all the pages I cut out; so the thing can be reconstructed precisely as it was. Your objection, that my prejudice against men makes me didactic 'not to say priggish', has not quite the same force with me;[3] I dont remember what I said that suggests the remark; I daresay it came out without my knowledge, but I will bear it in mind. I never meant to preach, and agree that like God, one shouldn't. Possibly, for psychological reasons which seem to me very interesting, a man, in the present state of the world, is not a very good judge of his sex; and a 'creation' may seem to him 'didactic'. I admit the justice of your hint that sometimes I have had an

1. Clive had again written her his criticisms of *Melymbrosia*. She had first asked for his help in October 1908.
2. Clive had written: 'For the first volume, I suggest, less definition, and a reversion to the original plan of giving an atmosphere' (his letter is published in Quentin Bell's *Virginia Woolf: A Biography* (1972), Vol. I, Appendix D).
3. '[. . .] to draw such sharp and marked contrasts between the subtle, sensitive, tactful, gracious, delicately perceptive, and perspicacious women, and the obtuse, vulgar, blind, florid, rude, tactless, emphatic, indelicate, vain, tyrannical, stupid men, is not only rather absurd, but rather bad art, I think.'

inkling of the way the book might be written by other people. It is very difficult to fight against it; as difficult as to ignore the opinion of one's probable readers – I think I gather courage as I go on. The only possible reason for writing down all this, is that it represents roughly a view of one's own. My boldness terrifies me. I feel I have so few of the gifts that make novels amusing.

I expect your praise is immensely exaggerated:[1] you (I guess) have so much more of the dramatic instinct than I have that you see it into my scenes. But I take praise very gratefully; long for some assurance that all my words aren't vapour. They accumulate behind one in such masses – dreadful, if they are nothing but muddy water. I think myself that the last part is really the best; at least I have written it with far greater relish, and with the sense of having the thing before me. What vanity these sheets will seem, one of these days, when Melymbrosia is a dusty book on your shelves, which Julian [Bell] tries to read, but cant! However, there are numbers of things that I should be interested to say about the book; and we need not always be thinking of posterity. I too write in haste, just before dressing to go out. I will only add here I have blind faith in my power of making sentences presentable, so that I leave bald patches gaily, to furbish up next winter.

I was a little afraid that you would accuse me of compromise; but I was also quite sure that, made as I am, that sequel was the only one possible. I want to bring out a stir of live men and women, against a background. I think I am quite right to attempt it, but it is immensely difficult to do. Ah, how you encourage me! It makes all the difference. Are you really interested? I suppose so, since you say it; but you have no notion how pale and transparent it reads to me sometimes – though I write with heat enough. [...]

Yr. aff^ate,

VS

---

1. Clive thought the novel 'wonderful', that her prose came near the best poetry, and that the picnic scene was even better than the Box Hill scene in Jane Austen's *Emma*.

500: TO VANESSA BELL   *Bayreuth*[1]

Sunday [8 August 1909]

Beloved,

No letter has yet come from you. I hope this heat has not turned you apoplectic: it is roasting like Hell here. We heard Parsifal yesterday – a very mysterious emotional work, unlike any of the others I thought. There is no love in it; it is more religious than anything. People dress in half mourning, and you are hissed if you try to clap. As the emotions are all abstract – I mean not between men and women – the effect is very much diffused; and peaceful on the whole. However, Saxon and Adrian say that it was not a good performance, and that I shant know anything about it until I have heard it 4 times. Between the acts, one goes and sits in a field, and watches a man hoeing turnips. The audience is very dowdy, and the look of the house is drab; one has hardly any room for ones knees, and it is very intense. I think earnest people only go – Germans for the most part, in sacks, with symbolical braid. Everything is new art – the restaurants have single lines drawn up the walls, with triangles suddenly bursting out – the kind of thing one sees in the Studio [the art magazine]. The grossness of the race is astonishing – but they seem very clean and kind. They suit Saxon very well. He thinks them so sensible.

So far, we have got on without more than a temporary tartness. Saxon cant decide anything – even what he wants to eat – but Adrian is very prompt and business like. I am haunted by the thought that I can never know what anyone is feeling, but I suppose at my age it cant be helped. It is like trying to jump my shadow. [. . .]

How does Sophie [Farrell, the cook] do?

Give her my love.

                                                            Yr. B.

501: TO VANESSA BELL   [*Bayreuth*]

Tuesday [10 August 1909]

Beloved,

I believe Saxon sent you a long and erudite letter this morning. He

1. On 5 August Virginia, with Saxon Sydney-Turner and Adrian, left for a month's holiday in Germany. They went first to Bayreuth for the Wagner Festival and afterwards to Dresden.

has been composing it at meal times, and humming it all day. Some of it 'rather pleased' him.

We have got into our stride, I think, and it is really rather an amusing life. I spend the morning writing,[1] and the others go for a walk; we meet for lunch, and this afternoon, as it is an off day, we walked out to the Hermitage. This is a place built in imitation of Versailles; and it is all overgrown and deserted, with little French Temples, and ruins, and courtyards. Wherever one goes, one finds a garden set with tables, where monster men and women drink great jugs of beer and eat meat – although it is a blazing hot day. The weather tends to break up. The colours are very beautiful – yellow and leaden. We walked home through the fields. I dont much admire the country, because it is very florid and without shadow; and one feels wedged into the earth, with no sea anywhere. However the town is charming; most of it built in the 18th century; there are very wide streets, with solid grey houses, like Cambridge houses, only somehow rather rustic. Last night we walked about after dinner, and all the people were singing over their beer. As there was very little light, and a few people peeping out of windows, and virgins tripping by in cloaks, and a great yellow coach standing in the middle of the road, one might have been in the year 1750. Saxon is dormant all day, and rather peevish if you interrupt him. He hops along, before or behind, swinging his ugly stick, and humming, like a stridulous grasshopper. He reminds me a little of father. He clenches his fists, and scowls in the same way; and stops at once if you look at him. Adrian and I wink at each other, and get caught sometimes. About 11 o'clock at night, when we begin to yawn, he brightens up, and comes out with some very acute and rather acid question. We argued till 1.30 this morning. It was about something Adrian had said two or possibly three Thursdays ago, which Saxon had not understood. He hoards things, like a dormouse. His mind is marvellously accurate, but I am rather surprised by his intellect. He sometimes seems quite fresh and about 26, and manly. I think he suspects that we think him obsolete, and wants to assert himself. I dont know what Adrian has told you, but I am surprised at our good temper, so far. We are rather austere, like monks and nuns, speak little, and – oh I long for you! There are bullocks here, with eyes like yours, and beautiful trembling nostrils.

Adrian has just brought me your letter, for which I thank God; I was

1. Virginia sent an article on the Festival to *The Times*, which published it on 21 August (*Essays*, I, 288).

fretting the drought. You are a tawny devil to talk of your letters being dull! My conclusion was that the way to get life into letters was to be interested in other people. You have an atmosphere. Ah! there's no doubt I love you better than anyone in the world! I dont think I am selfish about you. I wish you were out of London; and I am seriously alarmed to think that you contemplate another Bunting.[1] Do wait another year, if you fill her veins with salt, she may take after her aunt; but a watered child would very likely be a true woman. I dont in the least mind your showing Clive my letters; because I dont make much difference between you; only they are dull. He mustn't criticise. As for 'genius', even I have done with that. [. . .]

B.

503: TO VANESSA BELL   *Bayreuth*

Monday [16 August 1909]

Beloved,

[. . .] writing seems to me a queer thing. It does make a difference. I should never talk to you like this. For one thing, I dont know what mood you are in, and then – but the subtleties are infinite. The truth is, I am always trying to get behind words; and they flop down upon me suddenly. When I write to Ottoline [Morrell] or Lytton, I honour all the conventions, and love them. And then, you are much simpler than I am. I thought about that at the opera last night. How do you manage to see only one thing at a time? Without any of those reflections that distract me so much, and make people call me bad names. I suppose you are, as Lytton once said, the most complete human being of us all; and your simplicity is really that you take in much more than I do, who intensify atoms. [. . .]

Yr. B.

The Apes kiss you. [. . .]

1. Vanessa and Clive's second son, Quentin, was born in August 1910.

512: To Vanessa Bell   *Lelant Hotel, Lelant R.S.O.,*
                                        Cornwall

Christmas Day [1909]

Beloved,

I went for a walk in Regents Park yesterday morning, and it suddenly struck me how absurd it was to stay in London, with Cornwall going on all the time. I bought an A.B.C. and found there was a train at 1. It was then 12.30. However, I caught it, and arrived at 10.30 last night.

Adrian simultaneously made up his mind to go to Brockenhurst [New Forest]. At breakfast we had both decided to stay in London. Sophie was hysterical, and I have no pocket handkerchief, watch key, notepaper, spectacles, cheque book, looking glass, or coat. However, it is a hot spring day. I have been walking along the sands, and sitting in the sun, and when I have done this, I am going to Trick Robbin.[1] Lytton came to tea on Thursday, and we were very intimate and easy[2] and I have no doubts of his charm. But Duncan Grant[3] also arrived, which was a little difficult. He went in ten minutes.

At seven o'clock Desmond MacCarthy appeared, wanting tea. I suppose the scandal will be spread now. He told me how much he disliked going to South Africa, and how his novel was becoming ridiculous.[4] He seemed whimsical, but slightly tragic. He gave me a small humming bird – dead – which he had bought near the British Museum. Then Castle[5] came to dinner, and I was very much bored. He has a dull fluent mind, tinged with romanticism – but I daresay Irene[6] would never find it out. I doubt though that he would master her sufficiently for her respect.

Then there came Lytton and James and Frankie Birrell, Duncan

---

1. Virginia's childhood rendering of 'Trecrobben', the older name for Trencrom, a flat-topped hill behind Lelant.
2. After their February 'disengagement'.
3. Lytton's cousin, the painter Duncan Grant (1895–1978), who was to become one of the most important members of her circle.
4. Another major figure in Bloomsbury, Desmond MacCarthy (1877–1952), the journalist and critic, and a Cambridge Apostle. He never published a novel.
5. One of Adrian's friends, Tudor Castle, who worked in the Admiralty and died young.
6. Irene Noel (d. 1956), daughter of Frank Noel of Euboea, Greece, with whom the Stephens had stayed in 1906. She later married Philip Baker (subsequently Noel-Baker).

Grant, Keynes, Norton, and Cole.[1] They sat round mostly silent, and I wished for any woman – and you would have been a miracle. I talked to Frankie and Keynes most of the time. But it was desperate work. However Frankie (if that is his name) told me how he had an idiot brother, and we discussed sex and illegal rites. Cole, of course, was disastrous. He began to tell stories about shooting policemen and challenging Hugh Lane[2] which I had to answer, across the room, and everyone sat silent. Then he stayed till 2 talking about Mildred and the Pasolinis.[3]

Everyone left – even Norton couldn't sit him out. I told Norton that you were asking him to dinner on Thursday; if you aren't he is going to dine with us. I saw him blush at your name – but all the intimacies were impossible.

It was like climbing a wall perpetually. I am so drugged with fresh air that I cant write, and now my ink fails. As for the beauty of this place, it surpasses every other season. I have the hotel to myself – and get a very nice sitting room for nothing. It is very comfortable and humble, and infinitely better than the Lizard or St Ives. The subtleties of the landscape – they must wait. How I wish you were coming out with me now – it is very warm, bright blue sky and sea, and no wind and smells heavenly. What a mercy about H.P.G.[4]

Yr. B.

1. James Strachey (1887–1967) was Lytton's younger brother and also an Apostle. He later made his name as a psychoanalyst and, with Ernest Jones, translated and edited the Standard Edition of Freud. Francis Birrell (1889–1935) was the older son of the author and Liberal statesman, Augustine Birrell, whose younger son, Anthony, was retarded but lived at home. 'Frankie', who had been at King's, became a journalist and later co-owner of a popular Bloomsbury bookshop. 'Keynes' was, of course, the future economist John Maynard Keynes (1882–1946). At this time he had a Fellowship at King's, but had also taken rooms with Duncan Grant at 21 Fitzroy Square and was getting to know Virginia well. H. T. J. ('Harry') Norton (1886–1937) was a Cambridge mathematician and Apostle, who had an unrequited love for Vanessa. Horace de Vere Cole (1881–1936), another of Adrian's Cambridge friends, was best known as a practical joker.
2. The art collector and critic (1875–1915).
3. The Pasolinis were a noble Florentine family known to the Stephen children through their mother. Three members of their own generation – Guido Pasolini with his cousins Lucrezia (Rezia) and Nerino Rasponi – had stayed with them in 1898. Mildred's identity is not definitely known, but she may have been the socially active Mildred Squash (?), whom Virginia called on, according to her journal, in March 1905.
4. The Stephen family home in Kensington, 22 Hyde Park Gate, which they had been trying to sell or lease.

513: To Clive Bell   *Lelant Hotel, Lelant*
                                             [*Cornwall*]

26th Dec [1909]

My dear Clive,

    [. . .] The life I lead is very nearly perfect. A horrid tone of egoistic joy pervades this sheet I know. What with the silence, and the possibility of walking out, at any moment, over long wonderfully coloured roads to cliffs with the sea beneath, and coming back past lighted windows to one's tea and fire and book – and then one has thoughts and a conception of the world and moments like a dragon fly in air – with all this I am kept very lively in my head. For conversation there are the maid and the landlady, who tell me about the moon and the chickens and the wreck. A ferryman this morning told me about trawling and angling and drowned sailors. I pick up a certain amount of gossip by stretching my head out of the window and listening to the leaning men beneath. Now, suddenly at half past nine, the carols have stopped, and there is only one man walking quickly, and whistling. A strange affair is life! However, one might run on and on, covering sheets, with mysticism, ridiculous in the daylight. My Lady Hester[1] got into the habit of talking so that she could never read, and must dictate letters, and took herself for the Messiah. Suppose I stayed here, and thought myself an early virgin, and danced on May nights, in the British camp! – a scandalous Aunt for Julian, and yet rather pleasant, when he was older, like Norton, and wished for eccentric relations. Can't you imagine how airily he would produce her, on Thursday nights. 'I have an Aunt who copulates in a tree, and thinks herself with child by a grasshopper – charming isn't it? She dresses in green, and my mother sends her nuts from the Stores'. But Norton will become a politician, and cease to woo the arts with hairy arms. Spite toils in me, you see, even by the side of the green ocean. [. . .]

                                                          Yr. VS

1. Virginia was reading the *Memoirs* of Lady Hester Stanhope, the early nineteenth-century traveller who went to the Middle East in men's clothing, in order to review a biography of her (*Essays*, I, 325).

1910–1912

1910 was, in many ways, a lost year for Virginia. She published only four articles and wrote very few letters. True, she began her work for women's suffrage and participated in the infamous Dreadnought Hoax, but by March she was mentally unstable again. Eventually, she entered a nursing home for such therapy as was available at the time.

In the meantime, Vanessa and Clive had met the great art critic Roger Fry, who mounted his notorious Post-Impressionist Exhibition in November 1910. Vanessa found in him a lover, and Virginia, a wonderful friend. By 1911, Virginia was spending time with younger friends from Cambridge and Oxford, especially the crowd she called the 'Neo-Pagans' – Ka Cox, Rupert Brooke, and others. She revived her relationship with her old Greek tutor, Janet Case, to whom she confided the story of her half-brother's sexual molestations of her.

As she neared 30, the pressure to marry increased. When Leonard Woolf, who had been at Cambridge with Thoby, returned on leave from the Ceylon Colonial Service, everyone seemed to recognise that a potential husband was at hand. Virginia invited him to stay at her new cottage in Sussex, and then, as a friend, to share the communal house she and Adrian set up in Brunswick Square. Soon after, Leonard proposed. Virginia wavered. She retreated into illness again. But at last she agreed, and in June 1912 they were able to share the happy news with their friends.

518: To Violet Dickinson   *29 Fitzroy Square, W.*

Sunday [27 February 1910]

My Violet,
  [...] I spend hours writing names like Cowgill on envelopes.[1]

1. Virginia's first active involvement in politics was addressing envelopes for the Women's Suffrage Movement. This campaign, led by Mrs Pankhurst, had been gaining popular support for years, but the Prime Minister, Asquith, was a strong opponent of the cause, and his refusal to grant the vote to women led to increasing protest and violence between 1910 and the outbreak of war. Virginia's inspiration in this work was Janet Case (1862–1937), who had been at Girton College, Cambridge, and in 1902–3 had tutored Virginia in Greek.

People say that Adult Suffrage is a bad thing; but they will never get it owing to my efforts. The office, with its ardent but educated young women, and brotherly clerks, is just like a Wells novel. [. . .]

Yr. VS

519: To Violet Dickinson   *Lelant Hotel, Cornwall*

[8? March 1910]

My Violet,

I dashed off here, and forgot to write. The whole affair is at an end; and without a scratch. Adrian and Mr [Duncan] Grant saw McKenna.[1] He merely laughed at them, and supposed they had come to save themselves. When they said that they wished to apologise in order to get the officers out of the scrape, he was amazed. He said that it was ridiculous to suppose that anyone on board could be blamed for an instant. In fact, he seemed to think the suggestion impertinent, and said that an apology was not to be thought of. He advised us not to do it again; but it is certain that it has had no bad results for anyone. The story about the Admiral must be pure fiction.[2]

We came here suddenly – Nessa and I and Clive. We have had one beautiful day, and now it pours. I will try to come to tea on Wednesday, but I mayn't be able to.[3]

Yr. VS

1. Reginald McKenna (1863–1943), First Lord of the Admiralty. Adrian and Duncan had called on him about the 'Dreadnought Hoax', orchestrated by Horace Cole. On 10 February Virginia and five friends visited H.M.S. *Dreadnought* at Weymouth in the disguise of the Emperor of Abyssinia and his suite. They were received with dignity, and later Cole leaked the story to the press.
2. The *Dreadnought* was the flagship of the Commander-in-Chief Home Fleet, Admiral Sir William May, and his Flag-Commander was William Fisher, Virginia's first cousin. Both officers had received the party. It was alleged in Parliament that the 'Emperor' had conferred the Royal Abyssinian Order on Admiral May, who applied to the King for permission to wear it, but McKenna denied the story.
3. After returning from Cornwall, Virginia was ill in bed with the physical symptoms (headache, insomnia, anorexia) that had in the past accompanied her mental breakdowns. Dr George Savage recommended that she rest, so with the Bells she went for three weeks to Studland in Dorset. Her health remained precarious throughout the spring and summer. At the end of June, Vanessa, who was pregnant and felt the strain of being responsible for Virginia, turned again to Dr Savage. He recommended that Virginia take the rest cure then popular, particularly for women, at Jean Thomas' private nursing home, Burley Park, Twickenham. Virginia was a patient there for about six weeks.

531: To Vanessa Bell   *Burley, Cambridge Park,*
                                        Twickenham
July 28th [1910]

Beloved, or rather, Dark Devil,

I meant to write several days ago, although you do say you dont care a damn. But in that too I was hoodwinked by Miss Thomas. I gather that some great conspiracy is going on behind my back. What a mercy we cant have at each other! or we should quarrel till midnight, and Clarissas [the coming 'niece'] deformities, inherited from generations of hard drinking Bells, would be laid at my door. She – (Miss T.) wont read me or quote your letters. But I gather that you want me to stay on here.

She is in a highly wrought state, as the lunatic upstairs has somehow brought her case into court; and I cant make her speak calmly. Do write and explain. Having read your last letter at least 10 times – so that Miss Bradbury [nurse] is sure it is a love letter and looks very arch – I cant find a word about my future. I had agreed to come up on *Monday*; which would leave time for walking.[1] Savage wanted me to stay in bed more or less this week. As I must see him again, I suppose I must wait over Monday. But I really dont think I can stand much more of this.

Miss T. is charming, and Miss Bradbury is a good woman, but you cant conceive how I want intelligent conversation – even yours. Religion seems to me to have ruined them all. Miss T. is always culminating in silent prayer. Miss Somerville [patient], the absent minded one with the deaf dog, wears two crucifixes. Miss B. says Church Bells are the sweetest sound on earth. She also says that the old Queen the Queen Mother and the present Queen represent the highest womanhood. They reverence my gifts, although God has left me in the dark. They are always wondering what God is up to. The religious mind is quite amazing.

However, what I mean is that I shall soon have to jump out of a window. The ugliness of the house is almost inexplicable – having white, and mottled green and red. Then there is all the eating and drinking and being shut up in the dark.[2]

1. During the second half of August, Virginia, accompanies by Jean Thomas, went for a walking tour in Cornwall.
2. What Virginia describes is the essence of the famous rest cure developed by the nineteenth-century American physician (and novelist), S. Weir Mitchell. It had been brought to England about 1880 and was widely thought to be especially helpful in treating nervous women. Milk was the ingredient around which the Weir Mitchell diet was built.

My God! What a mercy to be done with it!

Now, my sweet Honey Bee, you know how you would feel if you had stayed in bed alone here for 4 weeks. But I wont argue, as I dont know what you have said. Anyhow, I will abide by Savage.

Miss T. and I have long conversations. She has a charming nature; rather whimsical, and even sensual. But there again, religion comes in; and she leads a spotless life. Apparently she is well off, and takes patients more or less as a spiritual work. She has harboured innumerable young women in love difficulties. They are always turning up to lunch, and I creep out of bed and look at them. At present there is one upstairs, and a barren wife across the passage. The utmost tact is shown with regard to our complaints; and I make Miss T. blush by asking if they're mad.

Miss Somerville has periods of excitement, when she pulls up all the roses, and goes to church. Then she is silent for weeks. She is now being silent; and is made very nervous by the sight of me. As I went out into the garden yesterday in a blanket with bare legs, she has some reason. Miss Bradbury is the woman you saw out of the window and said was homicidial [*sic*]. I was very kind with her at dinner, but she then put me to bed, and is a trained nurse.

Miss T. talks about you with awe. How you smile, and say such quaint things – how your eyes fill with tears – how beautiful your soul is – and your hands. She also thinks you write such beautiful English! Your language is so apt and so expressive. Julian is the most remarkable child she ever saw. The worst of her is that she is a little too emotional.

I have been out in the garden for 2 hours; and feel quite normal. I feel my brains, like a pear, to see if its ripe; it will be exquisite by September.

Will you tell Duncan that I was told he had called, and that I am furious that they didn't let me see him. Miss T. thought him an extremely nice young man.

Do write, today. I long to see you. Its damned dull being here alone. Write sheets. Give Clive my love. His visits are my brightest spots. He must come again.

I will be very reasonable.

Yr. B.

551: TO CLIVE BELL   *Bagley Wood, Oxford*[1]

[23 January 1911]

Dearest Clive,

Tuesday would be best and, I need hardly say, delightful. On Friday I dont really get back till 5.30. Here I am in the heart (or perhaps that isnt the typical feature) of young womanhood.[2] I like clever young women, in spite of my brother in law (That was said to tease).

Gumbo[3] is seated at the piano, dressed in a tight green jersey, which makes her resemble the lean cat in the advertisement, singing O Dolche Amor, to her own accompaniment. The accompaniment ends: she flings her hands up, and gives vent to a passionate shriek; crashes her hands down again and goes on. A dry yellow skin has formed round her lips, owing to her having a fried egg for breakfast. Save that her songs are passionate, we have not mentioned the subject. But Roger[4] is discussed perpetually, and she has a letter from him, about her Friday Club[5] paper, which he takes to be a direct attack upon himself. Beginning my dear Marjorie: it ends Yrs. very sincerely. I have not seen her alone, as I went first to Court Place,[6] and was there made to play Scramble patience for some hours. We had an icy motor drive over to Bagley. The motor broke down on the slope of a steep muddy hill; and Gumbo was seized with hysterics, imagining that a dog would run between her legs. I said that she need fear nothing of the kind, but did not give my reasons: and the baying of a hound in a far away farm made her fling herself upon

1. The home of Mr and Mrs Bertrand Russell (1872–1970). The philosopher had already published his *Principia Mathematica* (1910) with Alfred North Whitehead. His wife at this time was Alys, *née* Pearsall Smith.
2. From Newnham College.
3. Marjorie Strachey (1882–1964), the youngest of Lytton's five sisters. Her career was in teaching.
4. Here enters another major Bloomsbury figure, the painter and critic Roger Fry (1866–1934). He had recently begun a close friendship with Clive and Vanessa, who supported his efforts to bring the work of Cézanne and other artists to England for the First Post-Impressionist Exhibition of November 1910. It caused a scandal, and Fry's significant but conventional reputation changed overnight. In April of this year, during a trip to Turkey with the Bells, Roger and Vanessa fell in love. It was a serious affair, which turned the Bells' marriage into an amicable friendship.
5. Founded by Vanessa, Clive, and others in October 1905 for the discussion of the fine arts. The club met regularly until 1912 or 1913.
6. Court Place, Iffley, Oxford, the home of the transplanted American writer, Logan Pearsall Smith (1865–1946), Bertrand Russell's brother-in-law.

Ray.[1] Last night Gumbo gave us a long disquisition upon her character, talents, passions, and so forth; and told us that she would give all the praise she has for brilliance, if one person (preferably a man) would say she was lovely. No one rose. She has improved; and we get on better. No one makes me laugh more. She is a real figure.

Thus far I got; and then Ray's Miss Cox arrived. Miss Cox is one of the younger Newnhamites, and it is said that she will marry either a Keynes or a Brook.[2] She has a superficial resemblance to a far younger and prettier Sheepshanks.[3] She is a bright, intelligent, nice creature; who has, she says, very few emotions, but thinks so highly of Gwen[4] that she even copies her way of speech. I am writing this in the waiting room at Oxford, having caught an unexpected omnibus on the high road, and thus arrived ½ an hour early. We played patience to an early hour this morning; and became very frank and indecent. Gumbo told us how her period affected her entrails, and finally destroyed her voice, upon which we all asked (she had been singing Brahms) whether she was now indisposed. It appeared that she was suffering from diarrhoea – all this pleased me very much, and I repeat that I like clever young women. Also I had a compliment on my beauty. This was a little dashed by hearing that Gumbo had felt a distinct emotion of love upon last seeing Nessa.

Yrs.

V.S.

1. Rachel (Ray) Costelloe (1887–1940), daughter of Logan's sister Mary Pearsall Smith (married first to Frank Costelloe and second to Bernard Berenson). Ray, who later married Oliver Strachey, an older brother of Lytton, became a writer and worker for women's causes. Her sister Karin (1889–1953) was to marry Virginia's brother Adrian.
2. Katharine Cox, known as 'Ka' (1887–1930), became an immediate friend of Virginia. She married neither a Keynes (Maynard and his brother Geoffrey) nor a Brooke (the poet Rupert Brooke and his friend Justin), all of whom were associated with a young intellectual group, chiefly at Cambridge, whom Virginia called the Neo-Pagans, based on their avowed love for the romantic rural life. Depressed by Rupert Brooke's death, Ka did not marry until 1918. Her husband was a painter, Will Arnold-Forster.
3. Mary Sheepshanks (c. 1870–1958), a daughter of the Bishop of Norwich, devoted her considerable energies to social causes, particularly the rights of women. It was she who in 1905 persuaded Virginia to teach at Morley College, of which Miss Sheepshanks was effective Principal.
4. Gwendolen Darwin (1885–1957), a granddaughter of the biologist. A member of the Friday Club, she was a painter and a writer. Later this year she married another painter, Jacques Raverat. Both were Neo-Pagans.

570: To Vanessa Bell   *29 Fitzroy Square, W.*

Thursday [8? June 1911]

Beloved,

A dreadful Whitsunday blankness has descended upon us. We hoped that the storm would lighten the air – far from it. The storm was terrific. As nearly as possible Synge [Virginia] was taken from you. A great flash almost came in at the window. A church was set on fire.

Did you feel horribly depressed? I did. I could not write, and all the devils came out – hairy black ones. To be 29 and unmarried – to be a failure – childless – insane too, no writer. [. . .]

Mauds [her maid] brother has had four fingers cut off by a machine for making pear drops. The sweets stuck – he put his hand in to free them, and it was drawn into the mill. The misery of the lower classes impresses me very much. Think of losing a hand making pear drops! [. . .]

This haste explains the dulness of this letter: nevertheless every word glows like a horseshoe on the anvil with passion. These June nights! – how amorous they make one. Tell me how you are and any adventures.

Yr. B.

571: To Leonard Woolf[1]   *29 Fitzroy Square, W.*

8 July [1911]

Dear Mr Wolf [*sic*],

Would you come down to Firle[2] for a week end? It is a cottage in the Sussex downs. Either the 22nd or the 29th would suit.

I hope you will.[3]

Yours sincerely,
Virginia Stephen

1. Thoby Stephen's Cambridge friend and an Apostle, Leonard Woolf (1880–1969) had arrived in London in June on leave from seven years' Colonial Service work in Ceylon. He at once began to see his old friends. On 3 July he had dinner with Vanessa and Clive; Virginia came in afterwards.
2. Little Talland House, in the village of Firle, Sussex, which Virginia had taken earlier this year.
3. Leonard was unable to accept this first invitation, but he stayed at Little Talland House in September of this year. Back in London, Virginia and Leonard continued to see a good deal of each other, both at Gordon Square and Fitzroy Square.

576: To Vanessa Bell   *29 Fitzroy Square, W.*

[25? July 1911]

Beloved,

[...] I have just come back from Firle, where I had an interesting time with [Janet] Case. She is a woman of great magnanimity, and even said some things in praise of you. (you can see me curling up to your side). She said how great your beauty was, and your dignity of character.

We talked incessantly.

I gathered that she has had several proposals, but, cherishing the image of a deceased father, who kept a school, she refused them all.[1]

Doesn't it seem to you odd that she has never told either Emphie or Margaret Davies[2] about any of them – 'but we have sometimes discussed marriage in an abstract way.' She had brought down a handsome reticule, into which she drops bits of torn lace from time to time; and this she takes away on visits. So she sat stitching with an expression such as Marny [Vaughan] has when she goes watercolour sketching, and listened to a magnificent tirade which I delivered upon life in general.

She has a calm interest in copulation (having got over her dislike of naming it by the need of discussing Emphies symptoms with a male doctor) and this led us to the revelation of all Georges malefactions.[3] To my surprise, she has always had an intense dislike of him; and used to say 'Whew – you nasty creature', when he came in and began fondling me over my Greek. When I got to the bedroom scenes, she dropped her lace, and gasped like a benevolent gudgeon. By bedtime she said she

1. No doubt Virginia confided the story of *her* proposals. In order, they were from Lytton Strachey (February 1909); old family friend and barrister Hilton Young (1879–1960) (May 1909); and a few days before this letter, on 20 July, Clive and Thoby's contemporary at Trinity, Walter Lamb (1882–1968), later Secretary to the Royal Academy of Arts. Of these men, Lytton was the dearest to her, but she was in love with none of them, nor with ex-Trinity student and diplomat, Sydney Waterlow (1878–1944), who, although married, would propose to her in November of this year.
2. Emphie Case lived with her sister Janet; Margaret Llewelyn Davies (1861–1944) had been at Girton College, Cambridge, with Janet Case. From 1889–1921 Llewelyn Davies was General Secretary of the Women's Co-operative Guild. She was influential in the political development of both Virginia and Leonard.
3. Under the guise of consoling them after their mother's death, both Vanessa and Virginia had been sexually caressed by their half-brother, George Duckworth.

was feeling quite sick, and did go to the W.C., which, needless to say, had no water in it. [. . .]

I have also had 3 letters from W. [Walter Lamb]. What to say to him, I dont know. He wants to come here. I have written to say that I can only repeat what I said before, and that it seems not worth while to come up and hear that. However, as I said he could choose for himself, I must let him – this time.

With all my gross and inordinate vanity, my vampire like suction and (I know my faults by this time) I dont see that I can go on letting him praise me, unless I shall fall in love – and that seems as though one said unless I grow a beak. I've no doubt there is vanity in this too. [. . .]

Janet C. said suddenly in the train 'What are you thinking of, Virginia?' Imprudently I answered 'Supposing next time we meet a baby leaps within me?' She said that was not the way to talk.

I suppose Duncan [Grant] has seduced A[drian]. I imagine a great orgy on the river tonight.

Yr. B.

581: To Vanessa Bell   *Little Talland House, Firle,*
                                         Lewes, Sussex

Tuesday [22? August 1911]

Beloved,

I am very sorry about Quentin.[1] It does seem abominable that you should have all these bothers, and I'm afraid that you're not feeling very well – poor honey-buzzard. I wonder if your affairs [menses] have stopped. [. . .]

I am cursing domesticity too, but only in a very mild way. The servants [Sophie and Maud] have arrived, and made everything pompous and heavy-footed. Why we have them, I cant think. There is always a certain amount of grumbling to be lived down, because of the heat of the kitchen etc.

But of course this is a gnats bite to your miseries.[2] I suppose though there is a kind of unity in marriage (barring children) which one doesn't get from liaisons. I'm thinking a good deal, at intervals, about marriage. My quarrel with it is that the pace is so slow, when you are two people.

1. Now one year old.
2. Vanessa was lately recovered from a miscarriage suffered at Broussa in Turkey. She had been staying at a house near Guildford to be close to her lover, Roger Fry.

As a painter, I believe you are much less conscious of the drone of daily life than I am, as a writer. You *are* a painter. I think a good deal about you, for purposes of my own, and this seems to me clear. This explains your simplicity. What have you to do with all this turmoil? What you want is a studio where you can see things. [. . .]

Yr. B.

595: To Leonard Woolf   *38 Brunswick Square, W.C.*

Dec 2nd [1911]

Dear Leonard,

Here is the scheme of the house.[1] I think I told you about most of the things before. The servants are quite amenable. All they beg is that we shall be punctual. I'm expecting you to come in for tea on Monday. Your rooms are now papered white and look much nicer. There aren't any curtains; but there are blinds and I think we can rig something up. I hope it wont be very uncomfortable at first.

As to the rent of the room, Adrian and I think that probably 35/- a week would be about fair. This is to include light, coals, hot baths, and service.

We dont want to do anything but share the expenses of the house – Possibly this is too high a rent. I'm going to wait and examine the expenses after the first week, and then tell you, if you dont mind, what the cost of living and washing is.

I feel quite sanguine, because having gone into it all with the servants, they seem prepared and rather amused than otherwise. I want to ask you about other small things: whether you like fish – but that can wait.

Yrs.
VS

There is a book case in your room.

1. This was for its day a most unusual household. To the horror of old friends like Violet Dickinson, when the lease ran out on their Fitzroy Square house, Virginia and Adrian had moved to 38 Brunswick Square, Bloomsbury, which they proposed to run communally with Duncan Grant, Maynard Keynes and Leonard Woolf.

[*Enclosure*]
    Meals are:

Breakfast	9 a.m.
Lunch	1.
Tea	4.30 p.m.
Dinner	8 p.m.

Trays will be placed in the hall punctually at these hours. Inmates are requested to carry up their own trays; and to put the dirty plates on them and carry them down again *as soon as the meal is finished.*

Inmates are requested to put their initials upon the kitchen instruction tablet hung in the hall against all meals required that day before 9.30 am.

If notice of absence is given before 6 p.m. the dinner can be cancelled; if given before 12 a.m. the lunch can be cancelled.

The meals will consist of tea, egg and bacon, toast or roll for breakfast: meat, vegetables, and sweet for lunch: tea, buns, for tea: fish, meat, sweet, for dinner. It is not possible as a general rule to cater for guests as well as inmates. If notice is given, exceptions can sometimes be made. Particular desires will be considered. A box will be placed in the hall in which it is requested that inmates shall place their requests or complaints.

It is hoped that inmates will make a special effort to be punctual, for thus the work of service will be much lightened.

The proprietors reserve the right of ceasing to supply service at any time: there will probably be holidays at Christmas, Easter, and in the summer. But at these times, a caretaker will be in the house, capable of supplying breakfast, and doing rooms.

600: To Leonard Woolf   *38 Brunswick Square, W.C.*

Saturday [13 January 1912]

My dear Leonard,

    I am rushing for a train so I can only send a line in answer.[1] There

1. On 11 January Leonard had rushed to London from Somerset, where he was staying with a friend, and asked Virginia to marry him. He returned at once and wrote to her breathlessly that night, telling her how he loved her, but saying he would do whatever she wished. Again the next day he wrote, listing his faults: 'selfish, jealous, cruel, lustful, a liar and probably worse still', and her virtues: 'magnificence intelligence wit beauty directness' (see Quentin Bell, I, 181).

isn't anything really for me to say, except that I should like to go on as before; and that you should leave me free, and that I should be honest. As to faults, I expect mine are just as bad – less noble perhaps. But of course they are not really the question. I have decided to keep this completely secret, except for Vanessa; and I have made her promise not to tell Clive. I told Adrian that you had come up about a job which was promised you. So keep this up if he asks.

I am very sorry to be the cause of so much rush and worry. I am just off to Firle.

Yrs.
VS[1]

608: TO MOLLY MACCARTHY   *38 Brunswick Square, W.C.*

[March 1912]

My dear Molly,[2]

[. . .] I didn't mean to make you think that I was against marriage. Of course I'm not, though the extreme safeness and sobriety of young couples does apall me, but then so do the random melancholy old maids. I began life with a tremendous, absurd, ideal of marriage, then my bird's eye view of many marriages disgusted me, and I thought I must be asking what was not to be had. But that has passed too. Now I only ask for someone to make me vehement, and then I'll marry him! The fault of our society always seems to me to be timidity and self consciousness; and I feel oddly vehement, and very exacting, and so difficult to live with and so very intemperate and changeable, now thinking one thing and now another. But in my heart I always expect to be floated over all crises, when the moment comes, and landed heaven knows where! I

1. For the next several months, Virginia hesitated over this, the only proposal she had really taken seriously. Perceiving Leonard as strong enough to be equal to Virginia, Vanessa was enthusiastic for the match, and said so to both of them. One of the reasons for Virginia's reluctance became clear at the end of the month when she had some of the old symptoms of approaching mental illness – headaches and insomnia. In February she felt so ill that she had to re-enter Jean Thomas' nursing home at Twickenham for a rest cure. She left at the end of the month.
2. Molly MacCarthy (1882–1953), was born Mary Warre-Cornish, a daughter of the Vice-Provost of Eton. It's interesting that Virginia was sharing her views about marriage with her in that Molly had suffered a mental breakdown in 1904, six weeks after her engagement to Desmond MacCarthy.

don't really worry about W[oolf]: though I think I made out that I did. He is going to stay longer anyhow,[1] and perhaps he will stay in England anyhow, so the responsibility is lifted off me.

No, I shan't float into a bloodless alliance with Lytton – though he is in some ways perfect as a friend, only he's a female friend. [. . .]

Yrs. aff.
VS

615: TO LEONARD WOOLF   *Asheham [Rodmell, Sussex]*[2]

May 1st [1912]

Dearest Leonard,

To deal with the facts first (my fingers are so cold I can hardly write) I shall be back about 7 tomorrow, so there will be time to discuss – but what does it mean? You can't take the leave, I suppose if you are going to resign certainly at the end of it. Anyhow, it shows what a career you're ruining!

Well then, as to all the rest. It seems to me that I am giving you a great deal of pain – some in the most casual way – and therefore I ought to be as plain with you as I can, because half the time I suspect, you're in a fog which I don't see at all. Of course I can't explain what I feel – these are some of the things that strike me. The obvious advantages of marriage stand in my way. I say to myself, Anyhow, you'll be quite happy with him; and he will give you companionship, children, and a busy life – then I say By God, I will not look upon marriage as a profession. The only people who know of it, all think it suitable; and that makes me scrutinise my own motives all the more. Then, of course, I feel angry sometimes at the strength of your desire. Possibly, your

1. Determined to resign from the Ceylon Civil Service if Virginia would agree to marry him, and perhaps even if she would not, Leonard had asked the Colonial Office on 14 February to extend his leave by four months.
2. Disliking her 'suburban villa', as she called Little Talland House, Virginia was delighted to discover a few miles west of Firle a larger, remarkably graceful, and isolated house. She and Vanessa leased it from the beginning of this year.

being a Jew comes in also at this point. You seem so foreign.[1] And then I am fearfully unstable. I pass from hot to cold in an instant, without any reason; except that I believe sheer physical effort and exhaustion influence me. All I can say is that in spite of these feelings which go chasing each other all day long when I am with you, there is some feeling which is permanent, and growing. You want to know of course whether it will ever make me marry you. How can I say? I think it will, because there seems no reason why it shouldn't – But I don't know what the future will bring. I'm half afraid of myself. I sometimes feel that no one ever has or ever can share something – Its the thing that makes you call me like a hill, or a rock. Again, I want everything – love, children, adventure, intimacy, work. (Can you make any sense out of this ramble? I am putting down one thing after another). So I go from being half in love with you, and wanting you to be with me always, and know everything about me, to the extreme of wildness and aloofness. I sometimes think that if I married you, I could have everything – and then – is it the sexual side of it that comes between us? As I told you brutally the other day, I feel no physical attraction in you. There are moments – when you kissed me the other day was one – when I feel no more than a rock. And yet your caring for me as you do almost overwhelms me. It is so real, and so strange. Why should you? What am I really except a pleasant attractive creature? But its just because you care so much that I feel I've got to care before I marry you. I feel I must give you everything; and that if I can't, well, marriage would only be second-best for you as well as for me. If you can still go on, as before, letting me find my own way, as that is what would please me best; and then we must both take the risks. But you have made me very happy too. We both of us want a marriage that is a tremendous living thing, always alive, always hot, not dead and easy in parts as most marriages are. We ask a great deal of life, don't we? Perhaps we shall get it; then, how splendid![2] [. . .]

Yrs.
VS

1. Virginia had been casually anti-Semitic, and thought nothing of dropping the derogatory phrase 'Portuguese Jew' into her earlier letters. Now her attitude toward Jews became for a while self-conscious. During World War II when it became clear that should England be invaded, Leonard as a Jew would be especially at risk, Virginia made plans with him for a double suicide.
2. This letter persuaded Leonard to offer his resignation, which was accepted on 7 May. On 29 May Virginia told him that she would marry him.

620: To Violet Dickinson   *38 Brunswick Square, W.C.*

[4 June 1912]

My Violet,

I've got a confession to make. I'm going to marry Leonard Wolf [*sic*]. He's a penniless Jew. I'm more happy than anyone ever said was possible – but I *insist* upon your liking him too. May we both come on Tuesday? Would you rather I come alone? He was a great friend of Thobys, went out to India – came back last summer when I saw him and he's been living here since the winter.

You have always been such a splendid and delightful creature, whom I've loved ever since I was a mere chit, that I couldn't bear it if you disapproved of my husband. We've been talking a great deal about you. I tell him you [are] 6 ft 8: and that you love me.

My novels just upon finished.[1] L. thinks my writing the best part of me. We're going to work very hard. Is this too incoherent? The one thing that must be made plain is my intense feeling of affection for you. How I've bothered you – and what a lot you've always given me.

Yr. Sp.

623: To Lytton Strachey   *38 Brunswick Square, W.C.*

6th June [1912]

Ha! Ha!

Virginia Stephen
Leonard Woolf

628: To Madge Vaughan   *38 Brunswick Square, W.C.*

[June 1912]

Dearest Madge,

[. . .] how am I to begin about Leonard? First he is a Jew: second he is 31; third, he spent 7 years in Ceylon, governing natives, inventing ploughs, shooting tigers, and did so well that they offered him a very

---

1. The manuscript of Virginia's novel, now called *The Voyage Out*, was delivered to her publisher – her half-brother, Gerald – in March 1913 and was finally published two years later.

high place the other day, which he refused, wishing to marry me, and gave up his entire career there on the chance that I would agree. He has no money of his own. He has been living at Brunswick Sq. since December – we know each other as I imagine few people do before marriage. I've only known him 6 months, but from the first I have found him the one person to talk to. He interests me immensely, besides all the rest. We mean to marry in August, and he wants to find out about labour and factories and to keep outside Government and do things on his own account.[1] He has also written a novel,[2] and means to write as well as be practical. We shall, I think, take a small house and try to live cheaply,[3] so as not to have to make money. [. . .]

At first I felt stunned, but now every day the happiness becomes more complete – even though it does seem a fearful chance – my having found any man who gives me what Leonard does. [. . .]

Yr. loving,
VS

1. Leonard realised his ambitions fully. He was a prolific writer on economics, politics, and literature, and from time to time a practical influence on the Government. For the next few years his growing friendship with Margaret Llewelyn Davis focused a large part of his attention on the Co-operative Movement, begun in 1844, and based on consumer control of manufacturing, sales and financing. Already on the political Left, Leonard began now to call himself a Socialist.
2. *The Village in the Jungle*, published in 1913.
3. For the first several months of their marriage, the Woolfs' London base was 13 Clifford's Inn.

1912–1915

Virginia and Leonard were married on 10 August. The honeymoon was a great success in most ways: the Woolfs found that they loved each other's constant company. It was, however, a disappointment sexually. Virginia was not roused by the conjugal act. Moreover, her vulnerable psyche could not long stand up to the other forms of intimacy enforced by marriage. Still, she poured forth cheerful letters while travelling – always a great inspiration to her epistolary genius – and for months after her return to London. By 1913 she was apparently so unstable that Leonard consulted doctors about the wisdom of Virginia's having children, much though she wanted them. In September of that year, she attempted suicide. Afterwards she alternately raged and despaired. She appeared to recover in 1914, but in retrospect that period was only a long respite, during which she wrote a few letters that show her trying to reclaim her style. The illness returned, more vehemently than ever, but by the end of 1915 Virginia was at last well. She would remain so, more or less, until just before her death.

During this period the war also raged, but Virginia was scarcely aware of it. She was in the midst of madness during two important personal events as well, the publication of her first novel, The Voyage Out, *and the move to Hogarth House, Richmond, to which she was taken as a violent patient.*

644: To Lytton Strachey   *Tarragona [Spain]*[1]

Sept. 1st 1912

Dear Lytton,

I wonder if you got a card written at the beginning of our tour, from the home of Coleridge and Southey.[2] That is now remembered by us chiefly for its leg of mutton. We've travelled far, and beef has become mutton, chicken partridge – I should hardly know now if you gave me

1. Virginia and Leonard had married on 10 August at St Pancras Registry Office. They had a honeymoon of nearly two months, first at the Plough Inn, Holford, Somerset, and then on the Continent, where they stayed in Provence, Spain, and Italy.
2. Alfoxton House, Holford, where William and Dorothy Wordsworth stayed in 1797 and 1798, while Coleridge was living nearby at Nether Stowey.

pork to eat. This is a sad state of things only balanced by the beauties of nature and the antiquities of man, upon which I would discourse if you would listen, but to tell the truth it is the food one thinks of more than anything abroad. When I tell you that the W.C. opposite our room has not been emptied for 3 days, and you can there distinguish the droppings of Christian, Jew, Latin and Saxon – you can imagine the rest. This is Tarragona; we go on to Madrid, and from Madrid to Venice. Our habits are simple; 2 days in a place, one day in a train; we walk in the morning, read in the afternoon, make our tea, which is the point we have just passed, then walk on the sea-shore; and after dinner sit by a café, and, as its Sunday tonight, listen to the military band. Several times the proper business of bed has been interrupted by mosquitoes. They bloody the wall by morning – they always choose my left eye, Leonard's right ear. Whatever position they chance to find us in. This does not sound to you a happy life, I know; but you see, that in between the crevices we stuff an enormous amount of exciting conversation – also literature. My God! You can't think with what a fury we fall on printed matter, so long denied us by our own writing! I read 3 new novels in two days: Leonard waltzed through the Old Wives Tale[1] like a kitten after its tail: after this giddy career I have now run full tilt into Crime et Châtiment, fifty pages before tea, and I see there are only 800; so I shall be through in no time. It is directly obvious that he [Dostoevsky] is the greatest writer ever born: and if he chooses to become horrible what will happen to us? Honeymoon completely dashed. If he says it – human hope – had better end, what will be left but suicide in the Grand Canal. Have you been writing about him?

As you can imagine, we mean to be very various and active in the winter. Just about this moment, you're settling down over the fire, having returned from a brisk walk among the Scotch firs in a Scotch mist, and saying (something I can't spell – it's French) to the effect that life holds nothing but copulation, after which you groan from the profundities of the stomach, which reminds you that there is venison? – partridge? mutton? – for dinner, whereupon you take down Pope, your pocket copy, and proceed for the 150th time to read . . . , when the bell rings and the sandy haired girl, whom you wish was a boy, says 'Dinner on the table' . . . whereas I'm just off to walk by the shores of the Mediterranean, by the beams of the dying sun, which is still hot enough

1. Arnold Bennett (1908).

to make a cotton dress and a parasol necessary, while the military band plays the Barcarolle from Hoffman's Tales, and the naked boys run like snipe along the beach, balancing their buttocks in the pellucid air. [. . .]

Leonard sends love.

Yrs.

V.W.

645: To Katharine Cox   *Zaraʒoga – Saragossa*
                                          [Spain]

Sept 4th [1912]

My dear Bruin,

[. . .] Why do you think people make such a fuss about marriage and copulation? Why do some of our friends change upon losing chastity? Possibly my great age [30] makes it less of a catastrophe; but certainly I find the climax immensely exaggerated.[1] Except for a sustained good humour (Leonard shan't see this) due to the fact that every twinge of anger is at once visited upon my husband, I might be still Miss S. [. . .]

Yr V.W.

645a: To Duncan Grant   *Toledo [Spain]*

Sept 8th [1912]

My dear Duncan,

[. . .] We came here yesterday from Madrid. Madrid is without exception the beastliest place I have ever seen. We saw the pictures . . . [*sic*];[2] unfortunately Leonard had an attack of his fever [malaria], which made it more dismal than it is by nature, and we came on here in blazing sun, with his temperature 101. Apparently it is produced by the sudden determination of microbes to copulate, incited to love by an East wind. Happily he's all right again today.

We have had a most splendid time however in every way, and happily there's still a good deal to come. Spain is far the most

1. On returning from their honeymoon, Virginia and Leonard consulted Vanessa about her sister's inability to experience orgasm, a fact Vanessa passed on in a letter to Clive.
2. It was a running joke between Virginia and Duncan that he could not bear to read descriptions of nature or works of art, in this case those at the Prado.

magnificent country I have ever seen. It's on a much larger scale than Italy, and the colour... you begin with sand colour, go on with – however, when I come to describe I can't even name the colours right. Then there are vast rivers; every evening we go for a walk somewhere, in fact we are very lazy about sights. The Cathedral here is the best thing we've seen; I expect this town is too, but at present it is ringing with barrel organs, and the vociferations of voluptuous women. The middle class women grow to an immense size, which is shot forward to such a degree that's its wonderful how they keep their feet at all. The poor women are sometimes most lovely; they have such good shaped heads, and beautiful clothes. We come in for immense interest, and amusement, especially our shoes. Almost the best thing we did was to go to the top of Mont Serrat, only I was never so frightened in my life. We went up in a motor bus which dashes round and round a ledge, just big enough for it, on one side a precipice sheer into the valley, with no wall, on the other a steep rock. The bus whizzed round the corners, and if the breaks [*sic*] had not acted we should have been over in an instant. This went for an hour until we were right on the top. I insisted upon walking down. [. . .]

Leonard wants me to send his love. [. . .]

Yrs
V.W.

660: To Katharine Cox   *Grand Hotel, Leicester*[1]

[18 March 1913]

My Dear Ka,

Having lost my spectacles I can hardly see to write, but the female gynaecologist at the table and Leonard over the fire scribble scribble scribble so I suppose I must too. You would like to have my impressions of the condition of the working classes (the reason why I think she is a female g. is that when I came in she was pointing very low down in the body of a large diagram of the female body and saying to a sad elderly woman, 'That's what we must have out' – ovaries, I presume).

We have been to Manchester, Liverpool, Leeds, Glasgow, and now end with the boot factory here. Many valuable things come into my head

---

1. Virginia had accompanied Leonard on a trip to study the Co-operative Movement in Midland and northern cities.

at once; it is as if the thaw were beginning – seeing machines freezes the top of one's head. It's the oddest feeling, providential, I suppose, so as to keep the poor quiet. The melancholy thing is that they seem perfectly respectable and content, rather like old gentlemen in Clubs, supposing they were worn down and out at elbows. I cant help thinking that fiery reformers fly completely over their heads. But my dear Ka, I see at a glance that nothing – except perhaps novel writing – can compare with the excitement of controlling the masses. The letters you'd get! The jobs you'd be sent on – and then people would always be telling you things, and if you could move them you would feel like a God. I see now where Margaret [Llewelyn Davies] and even Mary MacArthur[1] get their Imperial tread. The mistake I've made is in mixing up what they do with philanthropy. Why don't you force yourself into some post when you get back[2] – in 6 months time you'd be driving about 6,000 helpless women in front of you. L. and I seriously consider branching out in some such line. I mean, he should branch: reviewing French poetry which is what he is now doing is only fit for crazy creatures, who have been in asylums.

We go back tomorrow. What are you doing? I'm glad you liked L's novel – (you can't see how insincerely I say that, and its no use grinning at me in Berlin). He gets a terrible lot of praise, and it seems to make no difference. My novel – but having said that, I'm now trained to stop short: isn't it wonderful? Its all Leonard's doing.†

Things in London were much the same as usual 10 days ago. A good deal of love, spite, art gossip, and opera. We dine at the Cock, and see the usual run. However, we shall probably retire after Easter and live sensibly. By the way, we want to buy a horse.[3] How does one do it?

Yes, I'm *very* fond of you, and often think how I'd like to have my Bruin opposite. When shall I? Don't marry till you're 30 – if then.*

Yr. V.W.

[*in Leonard's handwriting*]
  *No reflection on me. Vide†.

---

1. Mary MacArthur (1880–1921) was organiser of the Women's Trade Union League and a champion of reform for women's working conditions.
2. Ka Cox was in Berlin helping a friend after childbirth. She afterwards travelled alone in Poland and Russia, returning to England in July of this year.
3. This plan was never realised.

665: To Violet Dickinson   *Asheham House, Rodmell,*
                                             Lewes [Sussex]

Friday, April 11th [1913]

My Violet,

[. . .] We aren't going to have a baby, but we want to have one, and 6 months in the country or so is said to be necessary first.[1] [. . .]

All the morning we write in two separate rooms. Leonard is in the middle of a new novel[2] but as the clock strikes twelve, he begins an article upon Labour for some pale sheet, or a review of French literature for the Times, or a history of Co-operation.[3]

We sew [*sic*] articles over the world – I'm writing a lot for the Times too, reviews and articles and biographies of dead women – so we hope to make enough to keep our horses. I've sent my book to Gerald, but have heard nothing so far, and expect to have it rejected – which may not be in all ways a bad thing.[4]

We are only waiting for £2,000 to start the best magazine the world had ever seen.[5] Everyone agrees that it is the best idea in the world, but also hints that they cant support the bankrupt. Still, we go on looking up to Heaven.

We spent a fortnight moving from factory to factory in the North, getting as far as Glasgow and seeing every kind of horror and miracle. As you can imagine, I dont follow these economic questions very easily, but Leonard seems to be able to read and write and talk to enthusiasts without turning a hair. His book seems to be a great success – the reviews all compare him with Kipling – but I cant see that he has the vanity of the true author – which is a serious reason against his being one. *I've* never met a writer who didn't nurse an enormous vanity, which at last made him unapproachable like Meredith whose letters I am

---

1. In fact, worried about Virginia's mental health, which had been bad at the beginning of the year, Leonard had sought medical advice about whether or not she should have children. The doctors were divided in their opinions, but Leonard agreed with their general impression that it would be unwise at this time. This letter may indicate that Virginia had not yet agreed.
2. *The Wise Virgins* (1914).
3. *Co-operation and the Future of Industry* (1919).
4. The next day she heard from her half-brother Gerald Duckworth, the publisher, that *The Voyage Out* had been recommended for publication by his reader Edward Garnett.
5. The plan came to nothing.

reading – who seems to me as hard as an old crab at the bottom of the sea. [. . .]¹

Yr

V.W.

679: TO LEONARD WOOLF   *Burley, Cambridge Park,*
                                         *Twickenham*²

Monday [4 August 1913]

Darling Mongoose,³

I did like your two letters this morning. They make all the difference.

But I wish you weren't working. I'm enormously fat, and well – very sleepy.

Have you ridden?

Nothing you have ever done since I knew you has been in any way beastly – how could it?⁴ You've been absolutely perfect to me. Its all my fault. But when we're together – and I go on thinking – it must be all right. And we shall be on Thursday – How are you? you dont say – I think about you and think of the things we've had together. Anyhow, you've given me the best things in my life.

Do try and get out, and rest, my honey mongoose. You did look so bad. When you say sleepy you mean tired, poor beast.

I have been trying to read American magazines which are lent to me by Miss Funk a tall American.

I do believe in you absolutely, and never for a second do I think you've told me a lie –

Goodbye, darling mongoose – I do want you and I believe in spite of my vile imaginations the other day that I love you and that you love me.

Yr *M*[andrill]⁵

1. George Meredith had been a friend of Leslie Stephen.
2. At the end of July, Virginia was back in the nursing home, from which she sent plaintive daily letters to Leonard.
3. Virginia was still calling herself and her intimates by animal names. Her favourite name for Leonard was 'Mongoose', and for herself when writing to him 'Mandrill'.
4. During her illness Virginia sometimes railed against her husband.
5. Virginia left the nursing home on 11 August, and on 23 August went with Leonard to Holford, where, in their honeymoon inn, her illness intensified. She became so disturbed that Leonard telegraphed to Ka Cox for help, and the two of them took Virginia back to London. On 9 September she attempted to kill herself with an overdose of her sleeping medicine, veronal, and very nearly succeeded. On 20

682: To Leonard Woolf   *Asheham House, Rodmell,*
                                         Lewes, Sussex

Sunday [7? December 1913][1]

Immundus Mongoosius Felicissimus, I could write this letter in beautiful silver Latin, but then the scurvy little heap of dusty fur could not read it. Would it make you very conceited if I told you that I love you more than I have ever done since I took you into service, and find you beautiful, and indispensable? I am afraid that is the truth.

Goodbye Mongoose, and be a devoted animal, and never leave the great variegated creature. She wishes me to inform you delicately that her flanks and rump are now in finest plumage, and invites you to an exhibition. Kisses on your dear little pate. Darling Mongoose.

                                                        Mandril

699: To Leonard Woolf   *Asheham House, Rodmell,*
                                         Lewes [Sussex]

Saturday [14 March 1914]

Dearest,
    [. . .] Do come back a brisk well mongoose, with a feather in your cap.[2]
    My pet, you would never doubt my caring for you if you saw me wanting to kiss you, and nuzzle you in my arms. After all, we shall have a happy life together now, wont we?

                                                        Yr. M.

1. Occasionally, Leonard was able to get away for a short stay in London. This letter may have been written during the time he was there to end the lease on their London rooms.
2. Leonard, who was feeling the strain of looking after Virginia during her long illness, had gone to stay with Lytton Strachey for a few days. In his absence, Virginia was cared for in turn by Ka Cox, Janet Case, and Vanessa. He returned in much better health.

September she was taken to Dalingridge Place, Sussex, lent by George Duckworth. Nurses were engaged to help Leonard with her care. Her symptoms included terrors about eating, deep guilt and despair, insomnia, delusions, and manic excitement. In mid-November the Woolfs moved to Asheham House. Between 5 August and 4 December, she was apparently unable to write any letters. None, at least, survive. From December, and throughout 1914 and the early months of 1915, Virginia was slowly recovering. Her letters during this period are few, and when they exist, they are for the most part uncharacteristically lacklustre.

709: TO KATHARINE COX   *The Cottage Hotel, Wooler,*
                               Northumberland[1]

Aug. 12th [1914]

My dear Ka,

We've been having an argument as to whether you really went to
Ireland or not – so I write to find out, though it seems as unlikely as
possible that you will ever get this letter. It is thought that you are
probably doing service somewhere, either as a nurse, or part of the
military.[2] I never felt anything like the general insecurity. We left
Asheham a week ago, and it was practically under martial law. There
were soldiers marching up and down the line, and men digging trenches
and it was said that Asheham barn was to be used as a hospital. All the
people expected an invasion – Then we went through London – and oh
Lord! what a lot of talk there was! Roger [Fry], of course, had private
information from the Admiralty, and had been seeing the German
Ambassadress [Princess Lichnowsky], and Clive was having tea with
Ottoline, and they talked and talked, and said it was the end of
civilisation, and the rest of our lives was worthless. I do wish you would
write and tell us what you hear – They say there must be a great battle,
and here, where we are 15 miles from the North Sea, they expect to be in
the midst of it, but then so they did at Seaford.

Your future is practically blasted, because you will be on 20 different
committees. The very earnest and competent are already coming to
town, with their practical habits – but I never could see the use of
committees.

We have struck about the most beautiful country I've ever seen here.
Except that it has no sea, I think it is better than Cornwall – great moors,
and flat meadows with very quick rivers. We are in an Inn full of north
country people, who are very grim to look at, but so up to date that one
blushes with shame. They discuss Thomson's[3] poetry, and post im-
pressionism, and have read everything, and at the same time control all
the trade in Hides, and can sing comic songs and do music hall turns – in
fact the Bloomsbury group was stunted in the chrysalis compared with

1. The Woolfs had gone to Northumberland for a five-week holiday.
2. War had been declared on 4 August. For the first eighteen months Virginia made
   almost no written comments on it, apart from this letter.
3. The poet James Thomson (1700–48), author of *The Seasons*.

them – But why did you never prepare me for the Scotch dialect, and the melodious voice which makes me laugh whenever I hear it? [...]

Yrs
V.W.

716: To Molly MacCarthy   *17 The Green, Richmond*[1]

15th December [1914]

Dearest Molly,

[...] I've just been taking a course of cookery lessons, at an institution in Victoria St.

I do hope you're going to have Rachel[2] taught plain cooking and needle-work, as well as Icelandic and Portuguese. It is dreadful how we were neglected, and yet its not hard to be practical, up to a point, and such an advantage, I hope.

Yes, that damnable book[3] is coming out. To my great relief, I find that though long and dull, still one sentence more or less follows another, and I had become convinced that it was pure gibberish. [...]

Yr. loving,
V.W.

719: To Thomas Hardy   *17 The Green, Richmond*

17th Jan. 1915

Dear Mr Hardy,[4]

I have long wished to tell you how profoundly grateful I am to you for your poems and novels, but naturally it seemed an impertinence to do so. When however, your poem to my father, Leslie Stephen,

---

1. The Woolfs lived at this address for only a few months while they looked for larger quarters. They had decided to settle just outside London so that Virginia could avoid some of its stresses.
2. Desmond and Molly MacCarthy's daughter Rachel (1909–82), who in 1932 married Lord David Cecil.
3. The publication of *The Voyage Out* had been delayed during Virginia's long illness. It appeared at last on 26 March 1915.
3. Thomas Hardy was then nearly 75.

appeared in *Satires of Circumstance* this autumn,[1] I felt that I might perhaps be allowed to thank you for that at least. That poem, and the reminiscences you contributed to Professor [F. W.] Maitland's Life of him [1906], remain in my mind as incomparably the truest and most imaginative portrait of him in existence, for which alone his children should be always grateful to you.

But besides this one would like to thank you for the magnificent work which you have already done, and are still to do. The younger generation, who care for poetry and literature, owe you an immeasurable debt, and in particular for your last volume of poems which, to me at any rate, is the most remarkable book to appear in my lifetime.

I write only to satisfy a very old desire, and not to trouble you to reply.

>Believe me
>Yours sincerely
>Virginia Woolf

723: To Lytton Strachey   *17 The Green [Richmond]*

Friday [26 February 1915]

Dearest Lytton,

This is just to say that I am now well again and it is very wonderful, but I dont want to talk about it. I should like to see you. I wonder where you are. I want oceans of gossip. Ottoline's teeth for instance – has she got new ones?

Also a bright idea strikes me. Let us all subscribe to buy a Parrot for Clive. It must be a bold primitive bird, trained of course to talk nothing but filth, and to indulge in obscene caresses – the brighter coloured the better. I believe we can get them cheap and gaudy at the Docks.

The thing is for us all to persuade him that the love of birds is the last word in Civilisation – You might draw attention, to begin with, to the Pheasants of Saxby, which heard the guns on the North Sea before the

1. The poem called 'The Schreckhorn' was composed in June 1897. Hardy felt that the mountain, 'In its quaint glooms, keen lights, and rugged trim', expressed the personality of his Alpinist friend Leslie Stephen.

Parson did[1] – We must interest him in birdlife of all forms; he has already a pair of Zests [Zeiss] glasses. The advantages of the plan are in the first place that Vanessa, in his absence, could put the Parrot in the basement, or cover the cage with a towel – and secondly, he would very likely after a year or two, write another book on Birds[2] – The fowl could be called Molly or Polly. I commend this to you: get subscriptions. I heard the list with 6d.

I have to keep lying down, but I am getting better.

Our happiness is wonderful.

Your loving
V.W.[3]

1. On 28 January 1915 the vicar of Saxby, Lincolnshire, the Rev. W. L. Evans, wrote to *The Times* to say that the pheasants at Saxby Hall had begun clucking at an early hour when they heard the guns of the Battle of the Dogger Bank on 24 January. The bombardment had been inaudible to humans.
2. Clive Bell's *Art* had been published in February 1914. It propounded his concept of 'significant form', but Virginia, reading it in the midst of her illness, did not much appreciate it.
3. Virginia was wrong; she was not well again, and this nasty little letter may be one of the symptoms of her recurring illness. Within days she was once again raving. Leonard went on duty. Nurses were recalled. A break of six months occurs in her letters, after which she truly was well.

1915–1918

Once Virginia had recovered, she was soon writing letters with her old verve and maybe even something more. From the suburban safety of Richmond, the Woolfs made careful forays into the social and intellectual life of London and elsewhere. Leonard was taken up by the Fabian Socialists, which meant that Virginia met the Webbs and Shaw. She took some tentative political steps of her own by joining the Women's Co-operative Guild and providing a meeting place and speakers for these working women. Younger friends came into their lives. Dora Carrington had fallen in love with Lytton. Barbara Hiles, Saxon's lifelong love, married someone else, but stayed in the Bloomsbury circle. Of all her new friends, Katherine Mansfield was the most influential.

Within the family, the cast of characters regrouped. Vanessa fell in love with the basically homosexual Duncan Grant, with whom she would live for the rest of her life, and by 1918 they were expecting a child. Clive, still devoted to Vanessa, frequently stayed with her and their children, but his passions were directed towards Mary Hutchinson.

Early in 1917 the Woolfs bought a printing press. This was the beginning of The Hogarth Press, which hereafter published their own work, as well as pieces by Eliot, Mansfield and other distinguished writers. For practical reasons, the Woolfs declined to publish Ulysses. *Virginia also had aesthetic reservations. Never a good judge of contemporaries' work, particularly when they were her rivals, Virginia was appalled by Joyce's vulgarity, as she thought it. 1917 was also the year in which she began in earnest the diary she would write for the rest of her life.*

In November 1918 the war ended. For Virginia it had meant little beyond the threat of conscription for her family and friends, most of whom were conscientious objectors. In the same month she finished her second novel, Night and Day, *having said almost nothing in her letters about its composition.*

732: TO LYTTON STRACHEY   *Asheham, Rodmell,*
                                            Lewes [Sussex]

22nd Oct. [1915]

Dear Lytton,

I think it is about time we took up our correspondence again. Surely you must have amassed a million adventures since we met. I can't feel altogether sure that you still persist in the flesh – my friends – ah, but Sydney Waterlow tells me I have none. By God! What a bore that man is! I don't know why exactly, but no one I've ever met seems to me more palpably second rate and now the poor creature resigns himself to it and proposes to live next door to us at Richmond and there copulate day and night and produce 6 little Waterlows. This house for a long time stank to me of dried semen.[1] And its only a kind of mutton fat in his case. You see what straits we are reduced to.

I am really all right again, and weigh 12 stone! – three more than I've ever had, and the consequence is I can hardly toil uphill, but it's evidently good for the health. I am as happy as the day is long, and look forward to being rid of the nurse soon (she is at present dusting the room, and arranging the books). We come up on the 5th; as the summer seems to have broken up.

I should think I had read 600 books since we met. Please tell me what merit you find in Henry James. I have disabused Leonard of him; but we have his works here, and I read, and can't find anything but faintly tinged rose water, urbane and sleek, but vulgar, and as pale as Walter Lamb. Is there really any sense in it? I admit I can't be bothered to snuff out his meaning when it's very obscure. I am beginning the Insulted and Injured [Dostoevsky, 1862]; which sweeps me away. Have you read it. But this will not lead you (O God, how this woman annoys me with her remarks 'The Dardanelles, Mrs Woolf, would they be in France?') to think that I am spending long hours with my favourites, as Ott. used to say she delighted to do, in the long country days. Have you seen her? Have you seen anyone? What are you writing? Please lend us your last Edinburgh [*Review*] article. Leonard is writing so many different books – one for the morning, another for the afternoon. His life, so he said yesterday, is to be spent on a History of Diplomacy, but as the

---

1. Waterlow had married Margery Eckhard as his second wife in 1913. During the winter of 1914/15 they had rented Asheham House.

Webbs have their claws fixed in his entrails, I see no hope for him.[1]

Nurse now thinks I must stop writing. I tell her I'm only scribbling to a relative, an elderly spinster, who suffers from gout, and lives on scraps of family news. 'Poor thing!' says nurse. 'Arthritis it is', I remark. But it won't do!

Yrs.

V.W.

739a: To Margery Olivier   *Hogarth House, Paradise Rd., Richmond*[2]

13th Jan. [1916]

My dear Margery,[3]

Can't you come and dine and sleep this Sunday – arriving, with a very small bag containing one night gown, soon after, or for tea, and departing by any train you choose on Monday.

From what we observed at Asheham we fully expected you to fail in chemistry. If you'd never looked at that book you'd have come out top. Still, I feel sure that you will make an excellent doctor, and please remember that I entrust the care of my body to you and Noel. Even without hearts, you have appearances, and one can get within speaking distance of you, which is quite impossible with the ordinary male

1. The social historians and political lobbyists, Sidney (1859–1947) and Beatrice (1858–1943) Webb, always looking out for bright young people for the Socialist Fabian Society, had spotted an article by Leonard on the Women's Guild. They now asked him to write a report on international relations, which was first published in a special supplement of the *New Statesman* (10 July 1915) under the title 'An International Authority and the Prevention of War'. Later Leonard wrote a second essay, and they were published together by the Fabian Society in 1916 as *International Government: Two Reports*. The book had a strong influence on Government thinking about a future League of Nations.
2. In March 1915, while Virginia was very ill, Leonard moved their belongings into the house in Richmond where they were to live for nine years. Hogarth House was the name given to half of a handsome eighteenth-century townhouse (Suffield House was the name of the other) when it was divided in the nineteenth century.
3. One of the four lovely daughters of Sir (later Lord) Sydney Olivier, the Colonial administrator and Fabian Socialist. They were members of the Neo-Pagan set surrounding Rupert Brooke. Margery (1886–1974) was the oldest, Noel (1892–1969) the youngest. Although Noel, later Richards, did become a doctor, Margery did not. Later this year she began to have schizophrenic breaks, and she spent the rest of her long life in institutions.

doctor. But have you no heart? I mean, used you to have one, and did it wither and turn to dust, or did you never have one?

But we will discuss this on Sunday. We shall be alone. Please ask us to come and see you sometime – I am beginning to creep about.

Yours
Virginia Woolf

Excuse this paper – the only bit I can find. Dinner 7.30.

Smith College Library Rare Books Room

740: To Margaret Llewelyn Davies
Hogarth House [Richmond]

Sunday [23 January 1916]

Dearest Margaret,

[. . .] The big mouthed red haired woman was, alas, my sister in law Karin [Stephen, *née* Costelloe]. There can be no doubt of it. She sat 2 seats from L. at the [Bertrand Russell] lecture, and fills him with such physical repulsion that he can hardly endure to look at her. He says the lecture[1] was interesting, though hard to follow. I hope to go next Tuesday, more to see the audience than to listen, I'm afraid. Then there'll be Mrs Sidney Webb, who attacks at great length. I don't see that there's much good in Lectures – clever people go home and gossip about them, and thats about all. But then, my dear Miss Davies, what does do good? You say sitting on Town Councils and upholding one's ideals. I incline to think that that merely improves one's own soul – still, I daresay the Women's Guild has done something; isn't it touching how I return to that achievement of yours always for comfort?

I've been reading Carlyle's Past and Present [1843], and wondering whether all his rant has made a scrap of difference practically. But Bertie [Russell], according to Bob Trevelyan[2] who lunched here, takes his lectures very seriously, and thinks he's going to found new civilisations. I become steadily more feminist, owing to the Times, which I read at breakfast and wonder how this preposterous masculine fiction [the war] keeps going a day longer – without some vigorous young woman

1. One of several published later this year as *The Principles of Social Reconstruction*.
2. R. C. Trevelyan (1872–1951), a poet and translator from the classical languages, had shared a house with Roger Fry in the 1890s.

pulling us together and marching through it – Do you see any sense in it? I feel as if I were reading about some curious tribe in Central Africa – And now they'll give us votes; and you say – what do you say Miss Ll.D? I wish I could borrow your mind about 3 days a week. [. . .]

Yr. V.W.

745: To Lytton Strachey   *Hogarth [House], Richmond*

28th Feb. [1916]

Dearest Lytton,

[. . .] Your praise [of *The Voyage Out*] is far the nicest of any I've had[1] – having as you know, an ancient reverence for your understanding of these things, so that I can hardly believe that you *do* like that book. You almost give me courage to read it, which I've not done since it was printed, and I wonder how it would strike me now. I suspect your criticism about the failure of conception is quite right. I think I had a conception, but I don't think it made itself felt. What I wanted to do was to give the feeling of a vast tumult of life, as various and disorderly as possible, which should be cut short for a moment by the death, and go on again – and the whole was to have a sort of pattern, and be somehow controlled. The difficulty was to keep any sort of coherence, – also to give enough detail to make the characters interesting – which Forster says I didn't do.[2] I really wanted three volumes. Do you think it is impossible to get this sort of effect in a novel; – is the result bound to be too scattered to be intelligible? I expect one may learn to get more control in time. One gets too much involved in details – [. . .]

Yr.

V.W.

---

1. Lytton had written to her on 25 February, praising her novel in the highest possible terms, but adding that 'it perhaps lacked the cohesion of a dominating idea – I don't mean in the spirit – but in the action' (Virginia Woolf and Lytton Strachey, *Letters*, ed. Leonard Woolf and James Strachey, 1956, p.73).
2. E. M. ('Morgan') Forster (1879–1970), a Cambridge Apostle and a close friend of Leonard, had already published four successful novels and was working on *A Passage to India*. He made the point about Virginia's weak characterisations in a generally favourable review in the *Daily News and Leader* for 8 April 1915.

771: TO VANESSA BELL   *Hogarth House [Richmond]*

28th June [1916]

Dearest,

[...] I always keep a sort of pouch of gossip for you in my mind – I imagine you have a very soft trembling silken nose – but let me think now about our weekend with the Webbs. The Bernard Shaws[1] were there. We talked quite incessantly – we were taken for brisk walks, still talking hard, through kind of Dalingridge[2] countyr. Mrs Webb pounces on one, rather like a moulting eagle, with a bald neck and a bloodstained beak. However, I got on with her better than I expected. She seems very open minded, for an elderly person, and with no illusions or passions, or mysteries, so I daresay one would find her rather dull in the long run; she reminded me of one of the undergraduates of our youth. Shaw went fast asleep apparently, in the midst of all the talk and then woke up and rambled on into interminable stories about himself, and his backbone which is crooked, and his uncle who tried to commit suicide by shutting his head in a carpet bag, and his father who played on the ophicleide and died insane as they all do, and so on and so on. Poor Mrs Shaw was completely out of it, and she took me for a motor drive, and confided to me that Beatrice and Sidney, though wonderful people, had no idea of religion; and then she told me all about her conversion to Indian mysticism, and lent me little books, which unluckily, Mrs Webb got hold of, and she jeered at poor old Mrs Shaw, who sat in her corner, like a fat white Persian cat, making straw mats. I think I should be driven to mysticising if I saw much of the Webbs. [...]

Yr B.

778: TO VANESSA BELL   *Asheham [Rodmell, Sussex]*

16th August [1916]

Dearest,

[...] We are once more in domestic difficulties. After saying she was quite content, Nelly told me two days ago that she finds Asheham too

1. George Bernard Shaw (1856–1950) had, in 1898, married Charlotte Payne-Townshend, a fellow member of the Fabian Society.
2. The Sussex house of their half-brother George Duckworth.

depressing to stay, and, though Lottie would stay with her, she wont without her. They like Richmond, and its only a question of Asheham, but it seems to me too difficult to arrange to get different people every time we come here; so I must find a new couple by Oct. 1st. Do you think there is any chance that Blanche and Jessie would come, if Maynard doesn't take Gordon Square? Or, if he does, what sort of person is Miss Chapman? Would she come as cook?

I should be very grateful if you would answer as soon as possible about Blanche and Jessie, as I foresee we shall have difficulties in getting anyone.

I have been considering the question of having Sophy back. She wrote me another melancholy letter the other day, but I daresay she would prefer to stay with Aunt Minna in H. P. G. to coming out to Richmond, and being rather humble. Also, I dont know whether she would be very expensive – in weekly books I mean, for the expense of a slopper isn't much – and very tyrannical.

I wish you would give me your sage advice on the subject. Lottie cheerfully says we shall find no one who likes Richmond and Asheham; and of course Asheham, without the train, and no shops sending out, is very lonely, if one doesn't care for the country. [. . .]¹

Yr B.

818: To Margaret Llewelyn Davies

Hogarth House, Paradise Road,
Richmond

Jan. 24th [1917]

Dearest Margaret,
        [. . .] We had a very remarkable Guild meeting² last night, which I

1. This letter is representative of two dozen others written during these years to Vanessa about domestic difficulties. Virginia was regularly and intricately involved in problems with her servants. Nelly Boxall (a cook) and her friend Lottie Hope (maid) were to be with her for many years. Blanche Bam and Jessie were Vanessa's servants, Miss Chapman was Maynard Keynes' housekeeper in Gower Street, and the faithful Sophie Farrell was with Julia Stephen's sister-in-law, Sarah Emily (Aunt Minna) Duckworth.

2. The Women's Co-operative Guild, led by Margaret Llewelyn Davies, was the women's organisation of the Co-operative Societies. Its main purpose was to create educational and economic opportunities for its 30,000, mostly working-class,

must tell you about. A speaker [Mrs Bessie Ward] from the Civil Liberty Council, lectured us upon Venereal Diseases, and moral risks for our sons. I felt that the audience was queer, and as no one spoke, I got up and thanked her, whereupon two women left the room, and I saw that another gigantic fat one was in tears. However, they all went, except Mrs Langston who told the lecturer it was a most cruel speech, and only a childless woman could have made it 'for we mothers try to forget what our sons have to go through'. Then she began to cry. Did you ever hear such – nonsense it seems to me. The poor speaker said she was used to it. I do think its odd – the servants tell me that great indignation was expressed by most of the women at the mention in public of such subjects – [. . .]

Yr. V.W.

837: TO VANESSA BELL   *Hogarth [House, Richmond]*

May 22nd [1917]

Dearest,

[. . .] We've been so absorbed in printing[1] that I am about as much of a farmyard sheep dog as you are. I can hardly tear myself away to go to London, or see anyone. We have just started printing Leonards story; I haven't produced mine yet, but there's nothing in writing compared with printing. I want your advice about covers.

We've got about 60 orders already, which shows a trusting spirit, especially as most of them come from old ladies and poets in the North, recommended by Bob Trevelyan, whom we've never heard of. Not one of our intimates has yet bought a copy (this arrow is not aimed at you.)

However, I did rouse myself to go and see Ott[oline Morrell]. I was so much overcome by her beauty that I really felt as if I'd suddenly got into the sea, and heard the mermaids fluting on their rocks. How it was done I cant think; but she had red-gold hair in masses, cheeks as soft as

members. In the autumn of 1916 Virginia joined the Richmond Branch of the WCG and thereafter for four years provided speakers for the monthly meetings, which were held at Hogarth House.

1. The Woolfs, who had long planned to buy a hand-press, acquired one in March of this year. They constituted themselves The Hogarth Press and, working from their dining-room table, soon issued an appeal for subscribers. The Press's first publication was *Two Stories* (July 1916), one, 'Three Jews', by Leonard, the other, 'The Mark on the Wall', by Virginia. 134 copies were sold.

cushions with a lovely deep crimson on the crest of them, and a body shaped more after my notion of a mermaids than I've ever seen; not a wrinkle or blemish – swelling, but smooth.

Our conversation was rather on those lines, so I'm not surprised that I made a good impression. She didn't seem so much of a fool as I'd been led to think; she was quite shrewd, though vapid in the intervals. I begged her to revive Bedford Sqre and the salon, which she said she would, if anyone missed her. Then came protestations, invitations – in fact I dont see how we can get out of going there,[1] though Leonard says he wont, and I know it will be a disillusionment. However, my tack is to tell her she is nothing but an illusion, which is true, and then perhaps she'll live up to it. She was full of your praises. 'That exquisite head, on the lovely body – a Demeter – promising loaves and legs of mutton for us, and such *sympathy*, more *feeling* for others now. I *did* so enjoy my time at Wissett.'[2]

Emma Vaughan came; and I was plunged fathoms deep in St Albans Road [the Vaughan house], and Sunday tea. She is rather more set, and has a blankness in the eye which is precisely that of a toad glutted with large moths. Do you remember the look – how desperate it makes one feel – and then some perfectly banal remark or laugh in the manner of Aunt Virginia.[3] She woke up however about the war, and was very pro-German within limits. She visits wounded Germans in camps, and works from 10 to 7 every day, and has a great many sensible things to say, so I daresay she is going to become a respectable middle aged person. Then we had a visit from Violet [Dickinson], who assured us from private sources that the war will be over in August – but really the ramshackleness of the aristocratic mind is a marvel. They seem to be incapable of thinking and skate along from one extraordinary rumour to another. She said the King would certainly buy copies of our pamphlet – and I got her to tell me a series of death bed scenes of the Lyttelton family – the poor old Bishop Arthur L.[4] was pestered to death by them. 'Now you're practically dead, Arthur, you *must* collect yourself and tell us what you see. Dont you feel anything like immortality coming on?'

1. Garsington Manor, near Oxford, where for fourteen years the Morrells entertained and encouraged many of the distinguished writers and painters of the time.
2. In August 1916 Ottoline had visited Vanessa at Wissett Lodge, Suffolk.
3. Countess Somers (1827–1910), great-aunt of both Virginia and Emma.
4. Arthur Lyttelton (d. 1903) was the Bishop of Southampton.

and so on, till he was forced to say that [he] was merely bored and nothing else. [. . .]

Yr

B.

905: To Vanessa Bell   *Hogarth [House, Richmond]*

Tuesday [29 January 1918]

Dearest,

I now begin another letter, partly that should I die tonight you may know that my last thoughts were of you. Not that you care – but think of all the gossip you'd miss – yes, that touches the one sensitive spot. My chief item – Barbara[1] – is stale by this time. I daresay you've written her an expressive letter in your best style. She burst in this morning saying she was going to be married on Friday. With consummate presence of mind I exclaimed 'Then you've chosen the right man!' I hadn't the least notion which. She said 'Yes, its Nick.' So I said 'Of course Nick's the right man', and she said, 'Yes, he's the right man to marry, but Saxon is very wonderful as a friend. And its not going to make the least difference to any of us. We've all discussed it, and we're all agreed, and we're going to Tidmarsh for the honeymoon, and Carrington and Lytton'll be there – which makes it all the nicer.' I cant say I altogether understand the young; I'm not sure, I mean, that I dont see a reversion to the devoted submission of our grandmothers. Do you think she's in love? Isn't she merely doing what will make him happy? However the sober sense of it all is sublime; in many ways this method of abolishing private property in love has its exaltation. Perhaps it doesn't imply the highest mental gifts; one might hint at physical deficiencies; or do you think that absolute sublimity in emotion is reserved for eunuchs? Think of the three of them discussing the question over the stove in her studio, and Nick saying 'No, Saxon: you must marry her;' and Saxon refusing to be happy save in their happiness, and Barbara suggesting copulation with

1. Barbara Hiles (1891–1984) had been an art student before the war. Her closest friend at the Slade was Dora Carrington (1893–1932), who was in love with Lytton and lived with him at the Mill House in Tidmarsh, Berkshire. Barbara had two suitors, one of them the unlikely Saxon Sydney-Turner, and the other, Nicholas Bagenal (1891–1974), who was currently serving in the Irish Guards. Nick won Barbara, but Saxon remained devoted to her all his life. She was at this time regularly helping with The Hogarth Press.

each on alternate nights, but at once realising her own selfishness and saying she'd marry either – only it must be the one she didn't most want to – Or how did they settle it? I'm told Saxon has written a full account to you.

Thursday. Well, you almost lost me. Nine bombs on Kew; 7 people killed in one house, a hotel crushed – but not a hair of Wattie's [Walter Lamb] head was touched. I know raids dont interest you when no one you know is killed, so I won't describe our night in the kitchen. Barbara was with us and we all slept on the floor – We have mattresses laid there every night. Talking to the servants from 8 to 1.15 (as we did the first time) is so boring – 'but not so boring as a description' as you justly remark – so I pass rapidly to Ottoline. [. . .]

Well, old Desmond [MacCarthy] turned up the other day, and I have scented a minute romance for you – I'm afraid only a figment, but still better than nothing. Did you ever meet a woman called Enid Bagnold[1] – would be clever, and also smart? who went to Ottoline's parties, and now lives at Woolwich and nurses soldiers? 'That disagreeable chit?' Yes, that is my opinion too. But she has evidently enmeshed poor old Desmond. She has written a book, called, as you can imagine, 'A diary without dates', all to prove that she's the most attractive, and popular and exquisite of creatures – all her patients fall in love with her – her feet are the smallest in Middlesex – one night she missed her Bus and a soldier was rude to her in the dark – that sort of thing. Desmond insists that I shall review it in the Times. First he writes a letter; then he comes and dines; then he gives me the book; then he invites me to lunch with a Prince Bibesco,[2] who is apparently one of Bagnolds lovers; then he writes again – and every visit and letter ends with the same command – For God's sake review this book!

So far I have resisted; but I don't know that Desmond's charms won't overcome me in time. The Roumanian Prince too has the most exquisite voice. To charm me further, Desmond rang him up, and I listened – but the appalling thing is that Desmond is now, whether from

1. The novelist and playwright (1889–1981). *A Diary Without Dates* was her first book. She and Desmond MacCarthy had a close friendship, but no serious romance. Virginia refused to review her book.
2. Prince Antoine Bibesco (1879–1951), the grandson of the reigning Prince of Roumania. His career was in diplomacy, but he was also a playwright and edited the letters of Marcel Proust. One of his many love affairs was with Enid Bagnold.

drink, Bagnold or bankruptcy in such a state of dissolution that one has to be very careful what one says. In the middle of a silence, he suddenly starts up and cries out, 'O dear! O dear! O dear!' something father used to do. I guess that Molly's novel has been refused.[1] I suspect that he has finally lost or burnt his proof sheets; and then, as he says, he feels it incumbent on him to eat and drink as much as he can when he dines out, so that his digestion is ruined.

Bagnold has said to him 'Now I won't kiss you' (or whatever it is they do) 'until you've got my book reviewed in the Times.' Bagnold has him in her toils.

The question is, am I a match for Bagnold? You would be, of course, but then I'm so susceptible. Bagnold paints too. [. . .]

Yr
B.

910: To Saxon Sydney-Turner   *Asheham [Rodmell, Sussex]*

Feb. 25th [1918]

Dearest Saxon,

[. . .] I'm thinking of reading Measure for Measure this afternoon, and I wish you could be here, and then we'd ramble on about all sorts of things. I daresay you share my feeling that Asheham is the best place in the world for reading Shakespeare. Asheham is very lovely at this moment. I started upon Sophocles the day after we came – the Electra, which has made me plan to read all Greek straight through. Why doesn't one? why shouldn't we combine? I suppose life's too short or too merciless for such felicity – what with the trains going so early, and human nature being so imperfect: (this refers to myself, I need hardly say.) Still, the classics *are* very pleasant, and even, I must confess, the mortals. I found great consolation during the influenza in the works of Leonard Merrick,[2] a poor unappreciated second rate pot-boiling writer of stories about the stage, whom I deduce to be a negro, mulatto or quadroon; at any rate he has a grudge against the world, and might have

1. Molly MacCarthy's *A Pier and A Band* was published in this year.
2. Author (1864–1939) of *While Paris Laughed* and *Conrad in Quest of His Youth*, which Virginia reviewed in the *TLS*, 4 July 1918 (*Essays*, II, 265).

done much better if he hadn't at the age of 20 married a chorus girl, had by her 15 coffee coloured brats and lived for the rest of the time in a villa in Brixton, where he ekes out his living by giving lessons in elocution to the natives – Now if this were about a Greek writer, it would be what is called constructive criticism, wouldn't it? I'm not at all pleased with Jebb[1] by the way, he never risks anything in his guesses: his sense of language seems to me stiff, safe, prosaic and utterly impossible for any Greek to understand. Now surely they launched out into flowering phrases not strictly related, much as Shakespeare did. Jebb splits them up into separate and uncongenial accuracies. But I'm too lazy to look up the particular one I mean: something about an old man's hair. I can remember Jebb coming to dinner with us, and sitting at the far end of the room with Nessa and Thoby. I there and then saw and perhaps said that he had the souls and innumerable legs of a black beetle. I am appalled at the number of things I can remember. Meredith, Henry James; a great many others too, if I could think of their names; Lowell, Mrs Humphry Ward; Herbert Spencer, once; John Addington Symonds, and any number of Watts', Burne Jones' and Leightons.

Its so nice writing to you that I just run on, and it strikes me that this may seem to you not only foolish, which I don't mind, but lacking in understanding, which I should mind – I've been sitting in the garden all the afternoon, reading Measure for Measure, looking at the trees, and thinking as much of you as of anything. I suppose it would be merely silly to try to say *what* one thinks of you – moreover I hope that by this time you know.

Nessa is coming over[2] on Thursday for the night. The new tutor [Henry Moss] arrives tomorrow. I gather that he is recovering from a nervous breakdown, which is supposed to give him a chance of suiting the general atmosphere. [. . .]

Yrs.
V.W.

1. R. C. Jebb (1841–1905), whose edition of Sophocles appeared in seven volumes (1883–1896). Like the other well-known writers and painters mentioned at the end of this paragraph, he was a friend of Leslie and Julia Stephen.
2. From Charleston, a farmhouse four miles away, near Firle. Vanessa and her family had taken the house in the autumn of 1916. That 'family' now included Duncan Grant, with whom Vanessa would share the rest of her life.

924: To Lytton Strachey   *Hogarth* [*House, Richmond*]

23rd April [1918]

[. . .] We've been asked to print Mr Joyce's new novel,[1] every printer in London and most in the provinces having refused. First there's a dog that p's – then there's a man that forths, and one can be monotonous even on that subject – moreover, I don't believe that his method, which is highly developed, means much more than cutting out the explanations and putting in the thoughts between dashes. So I don't think we shall do it. [. . .]

                                                                        Yr.
                                                                        V.W.

978: To Lytton Strachey   *Hogarth House, Paradise Road,*
                                Richmond

Oct. 12th [1918]

Dearest Lytton,

I'm extremely sorry to hear distressing accounts of your diseases. Goldie[2] has been having the shingles too, and goes to a marvellous doctor, a quack, I suppose, who is curing him quickly and completely. He lays his fingers upon the tips of the nerves, and you can see the poison withdrawing as you watch. Would it be worth while to find out something more strictly accurate?

However, you must consider that boils, blisters, rashes, green and blue vomits are all appointed by God himself to those whose books go into 4 editions within 6 months.[3] Shingles, I can assure you, is only a

---

1. Harriet Weaver, owner and editor of the *Egoist Press*, had come at the suggestion of T. S. Eliot to offer *Ulysses* to The Hogarth Press. Because it was too long for the Woolfs to set, Leonard attempted to find a commercial publisher, but no one would touch it due to its 'obscenity' and its publisher's almost certain prosecution.
2. Goldsworthy ('Goldie') Lowes Dickinson (1862–1932), Fellow of King's College, Cambridge, was a philosopher, political scientist, and an older Apostle, whom Leonard and Lytton knew well.
3. Since *Eminent Victorians* had been published in May 1918, it had required five further impressions of 1000 each. Its success continued and established Lytton's reputation as a debunking biographer.

first instalment; don't complain if the mange visits you, and the scurvy, and your feet swell and the dropsy distends and the scab itches – I mean you won't get any sympathy from *me*. Did I tell you that Violet Dickinson encountered Mrs H. Ward who was raging publicly against the defamation of her grandfather,[1] and thereby giving the liveliest joy to Lady Horner,[2] who feels that you have worked off several old scores beyond her reach, and therefore blesses you every night as a benefactor? I'm now going to discover the Cromer attitude to Gordon in private.[3]

Here we are back in Richmond again, and even plunged into a mild form of society, mild to you that is – to me the climax of dissipation. What with the approach of peace and the Russian dancers,[4] the gallant Sitwells, and the poetical Edith,[5] Ottoline utterly abandoned and nefarious, Duncan covered with paint from head to foot, Nessa abounding in babies,[6] Saxon wrung with rheumatics, Robbie Ross[7] found dead in his shirtsleeves, Roger [Fry] going to lay him out, Oscar Wilde's widow bursting in dead drunk – and so forth – all the things that invariably happen in London in October – it's a pleasant change. [. . .]

Then there was the Sitwells' party, at which it was proposed to read aloud a sentence of banishment upon Ottoline (whose conduct seems to have surpassed itself – and yet even in vice what a magnificence she has!) – but this of course meant no more than that we withdrew to somebody's bedroom in great numbers and left Ottoline, got up to look precisely like the Spanish Armada in full sail, in possession of the drawing room. Perhaps more happened after I left. But how fearfully old one's getting! There I left her, with equanimity, to have her feathers

---

1. The popular novelist Mrs Humphry Ward was a granddaughter of Dr Thomas Arnold, the Headmaster of Rugby, one of Lytton's 'Victorians'.
2. Whose house, Mells, Somerset, was a centre of cultural and political society in late Victorian and Edwardian times.
3. Virginia's friend Katie Cromer was the second wife of the 1st Earl of Cromer, the virtual ruler of Egypt when General Gordon, another of Lytton's subjects, was murdered at Khartoum in 1885.
4. The Russian troupe of Sergei Pavlovich Diaghilev.
5. Edith Sitwell (1887–1964), whose book of poems, *Clowns' Houses*, Virginia had reviewed in the *TLS* of 10 October 1918 (*Essays*, II, 306). Sitwell's brothers were Osbert (1892–1969) and Sacheverell (1897–1988). Virginia had attended a party at their house in Carlyle Square, Chelsea, on 10 October.
6. Vanessa's sons were now 10 and 8, and she and Duncan were expecting a baby.
7. Robert Ross, the writer an art, literature, and theatre, who had died on 5 October. He had been the friend and editor of Oscar Wilde.

pulled out by the vicious old Roger,[1] who has a febrile senility coming on, as I told him in the cab, quite unlike our elderly benignity – It's an attempt at youth perhaps – Do you feel this tolerance creeping into your veins too? Literature remains of course – however there's no room to begin upon that. I read the Greeks, but I am extremely doubtful whether I understand anything they say; also I have read the whole of Milton, without throwing any light upon my own soul, but that I rather like. Don't you think it very queer though that he entirely neglects the human heart? Is that the result of writing one's masterpiece at the age of 50? What about your masterpiece? And when are you coming to London? Please tell Carrington that we are waiting for her wood-cuts.[2] Leonard sends his love.

Yr.
V.W.

980: To Vanessa Bell   *Hogarth [House, Richmond]*

Saturday [19 October 1918]

Dearest,

[. . .] I expect the tide is already setting back to service again, and few things give me a greater sense of being like other mature women, which as you know is the ambition of my life, than going to registry offices, and talking about 'my sister has a governess and two small boys.' I feel at once on the road to reality or whatever one may call it. As for my domestics, they are now unfortunately, grovelling at our feet; Lottie and Leonard twit each other about their bad tempers, and of course its all very expensive and not really to my taste so nice as being with Mrs Geall at Asheham, except for the comfort.[3] [. . .]

Then we had old Ka to dinner. Will's once more in hospital – this time with water on the knee – from what you and Duncan will doubtless

1. Roger Fry's quarrel with his former friend and supporter went back to 1911, when, in love with Vanessa, he had accused Ottoline of saying that he was in love with *her*.
2. Four of Carrington's woodcuts had been published with *Two Stories*. She did not illustrate another Hogarth Press book until 1921.
3. For many months the sisters had exchanged letters about Vanessa's need for domestic help. Virginia had gone to agencies on Vanessa's behalf and had once lent her Nelly Boxall. Soon Virginia was embroiled in the servants' intrigues, which both vexed and interested her. In the latest row about their duties, Lottie Hope and Nelly had threatened to resign, hoping secretly to work at Charleston. Now the crisis had passed.

draw your own conclusions.[1] Clive and Mary[2] whom I floundered in upon at Gordon Sqre are of opinion that some enlargement of his parts is necessary, though I dont believe they'd consent to undertake that at a naval hospital, and anyhow Ka doesn't mean to have a family until they're settled in the country. They are going to live on the top of one of the Wiltshire downs, so that Will can see nothing but the sky, which is the only thing he likes to paint though a certain amount of green is admitted very low down on the edge of the canvas. She said that his pictures – which are the passion of his life – are very old fashioned, but very remarkable.

It sounds to me about as bad as it can be, which is of course very satisfactory, and she also has to make out that he is very wild and mad – He is heir to an estate and a large income; but he has given it all up to his younger brother – so you can judge exactly the sort of pictures he must paint and in fact all about him. We're going to dine with them, so I'll let you know more, if the subject interests you. Unfortunately I've got my affairs and can't go to a large family tea party which Ka's sister is giving in Harley St today – though it would give me infinite pleasure.

Then we had Saxon. Everybody, of course, has entirely failed to see what I saw at the first glance; he is happier than he has ever been in his life. After a short conversation I saw that Mrs Stagg[3] is far more to him than Barbara [Bagenal]; and then he has got a complete or almost complete set of gold teeth. This is one of the great interests of his life. He takes them out and hands them round, and explains exactly which of the teeth are useful, which ornamental, and at what points others will probably – not certainly – have to be added next year. He has got through love, and has got down to the solid foundations – Stagg and false teeth. He is already talking of Bayreuth, and whether we shall have an opera next year – if so, will [Arthur] Nikish or [Richard] Strauss conduct – then the singers – and so on – Barbara was merely an interlude owing to there being no opera.

I have begun my artistic education again. I went to see the Rodins at the Albert Museum [posthumous exhibition]. I didn't think at all highly of them, except from the literary point of view, and even so they're not

1. Ka Cox and Will Arnold-Forster had married on 9 September.
2. Mary Hutchinson, *née* Barnes (1889–1977), a cousin of Lytton Strachey and the wife of the barrister St John Hutchinson, had begun an open affair with Clive Bell early in the war. It continued for many years.
3. Saxon Sydney-Turner's landlady in Great Ormond Street.

as good as [Jacob] Epsteins. But I see I shall have to write a novel entirely about carpets, old silver, cut glass and furniture. The desire to describe becomes almost a torment; and also the covetousness to possess. I dont think this has much to do with their artistic value though. Please tell me what picture shows there are.

How are you, and the remarkable [as yet unborn] baby upon whom all my future hopes for the world may be said to rest?

Yr

B

986: To Vanessa Bell *Hogarth [House, Richmond]*

11.30, Nov. 11th [Armistice Day, 1918]

Dearest,

The guns have been going off for half an hour, and the sirens whistling; so I suppose we are at peace, and I cant help being glad that your precious imp will be born into a moderately reasonable world. I see we're not going to be allowed any quiet all day, as people seem to be whistling and giving catcalls and stirring up the dogs to bark, though its all done in such an intermittent kind of way that its not in the least impressive – only unsettling. Besides its very grey and smoky, – oh dear, now drunken soldiers are beginning to cheer.

How am I to write my last chapter[1] with all this shindy, and Nelly and Lottie bursting in to ask – here is Nelly with 4 different flags which she is putting in all the front rooms. Lottie says we ought to do something, and I see she is going to burst into tears. She insists upon polishing the door knocker, and shouting out across the road to the old fireman who lives opposite. O God! What a noise they make – and I, on the whole though rather emotional (would you be, I wonder?) feel also immensely melancholy; yes, you're well out of it [at Charleston], because every taxi is now hooting, and the school children I know will form up round the flag in a moment. There is certainly an atmosphere of the death bed too. At this moment a harmonium is playing a hymn, and a large Union Jack has been hoisted onto a pole. But this must be fearfully dull to read about.

1. This is one of only two references in her letters to her second novel, *Night and Day* (1919), which she had begun to write early in 1917. She finished it on 21 November.

As to gossip, we went to tea with Nelly [Cecil] yesterday, and afterwards to a concert given at Shelley House;[1] but first imagine poor Nelly more shrivelled and sunken than ever, wearing the most piteous expression, like an imprisoned monkey; I've never seen anyone who seemed to ask one more to put her out of her misery. They've moved to a horrid little house on the Embankment, which she has done up in the old Kitty [Maxse], chinz curtains, white walls, green boards style. I rather liked her though. She agreed that Leo and Lord Northcliffe[2] ought to be banished as well as the Kaiser, and said she thought the English in many ways worse than the Germans. And then we went on to this appalling [Shelley] house, where I'd been asked by Bruce Richmond, and there I saw our entire past, alive, incredibly the same as ever – Mrs Rathbone, Mrs Muir MacKenzie, Enid M. M., precisely as she was at Hyde Park Gate, Hervey Vaughan Williams,[3] any number of people who weren't exactly George [Duckworth] but might have been; all dressed up so irreproachably so nice, kind, respectable – so insufferable – . You remember the kind of politeness, and the little jokes, and all the deference, and opening doors for one, and looking as if the mention of the w.c. even would convey nothing whatever to them. I enjoyed it immensely; but I couldn't help seeing us in white satin Mrs Young's[4] being taken down to supper. The house itself is incredible – an enormous, cultivated, sham 18th century house, with vast portraits of young girls holding bunches of roses, and looking into the future, while a small white path meanders away under apple trees in the distance. And then, painted on the panels, were those sort of geographical pictures which are meant to be not quite serious but very charming; maps of Chelsea hospital, with decorative clouds, all very flat, and brightly coloured. And pale green Morris curtains; and china pots standing on

1. The Chelsea house belonging to St John Hornby, where he had installed his Ashendene Press in 1902 and gave frequent concerts.
2. Leopold Maxse, as editor of the *National Review*, had consistently argued against a League of Nations and in favour of maintaining Britain's imperial position. Lord Northcliffe, founder of the *Daily Mail* and chief proprietor of *The Times*, was urging Lloyd George to 'Hang the Kaiser' and make Germany pay for the war.
3. Mrs William Rathbone was the mother of Mrs Bruce (Elena) Richmond. Mrs Muir MacKenzie, a daughter of Lord Aberdare, had married Montague Muir MacKenzie in 1888, and Enid was their only child; they had been neighbours of the Stephens in Hyde Park Gate. Hervey Vaughan Williams was the elder brother of the composer, Ralph, who had married one of Virginia and Vanessa's first cousins.
4. Sally Young had made the Stephen girls' evening gowns.

little wooden stools; Italy represented too, by casts of the Virgin and child; scrolls of Japanese figures; but all infinitely pale, watery, and ugly, far worse than any plush lodging house.

This, by the way, applies also to the decorations of Wills and Ka's flat, which impressed me very disagreeably; acid lemon colours against black curtains, and one white rose against a wall the colour of skim milk. There's no doubt that you have done a great work in rolling up the shams;[1] at least I dislike a great many things now with an intensity which owing to my punishment in the case of Mary I daresay I should be wise to hide.[2]

What one instinctively says about Will is 'What a Whippersnapper!' but I implore you, don't give this out as my considered opinion. Its the effect of his little mongrel cur's body; his face which appears powdered and painted like a very refined old suburban harlots; and his ridiculous little voice. I saw Ka get nervous when my eyes rested too long upon him. She was much relieved when he began to use slang and talk manly; and I daresay he has his parts, (I dont mean only in the physical sense) but I'm as convinced as I am that the church bells have now begun to ring that he'll never be a painter. I saw one worried and fretful work of his – the downs by moonlight; but he said it was a sketch, and hinted very modestly that he didn't belong to the Omega school. He expressed great admiration for you and Duncan, as painters; and you'd be amused to hear what an impression you as a human being made on him. You had only to come into the Friday Club he said to change the feeling completely; I gathered you made things real, and large, and infinitely composed and profound.

'Yes, I'll always maintain, said old Ka, who sat on the hearthrug stitching at one of her usual cushions, that Vanessa is one of the few great people I've ever known.'

'Ah but my dear Ka, try and explain how she does it!' I cried.

Then we set to and analysed the famous remark of mine about your reality, which they both said that they felt strongly, and thought most remarkable, so I'm not alone.

You will have heard of Barbara's brat.[3] Saxon seems fairly

1. Through her work with the Omega Workshops, founded in 1913 by Roger Fry for the creation of painted furniture, fabrics, rugs and other decorative arts. The Omega closed in 1919.
2. Vanessa, Clive and Mary Hutchinson were angry that Virginia had gossiped about Vanessa's being bored with Mary, who was Clive's lover. Virginia was unrepentant.
3. Barbara and Nicholas Bagenal's first child, Judith, born 8 November 1918.

composed, and means to call it Judith. According to Oliver[1] he assumes that he is the spiritual begetter at any rate, and Nick scarcely counts even for that act; Oliver agrees with me that Saxon is happier than usual.

Then we had [H. T. J.] Norton to dinner, and I felt a kind of reverence for him, as the representative of old Cambridge, as we knew it, in the days of 'personal emotions'; I must say I think it probably the highest type in the world, and it solves all my religious feelings. We've now had marriage bells, one hymn, God save the King twice over, about a dozen separate cheers, and the old gentleman opposite has climbed to the top of a tree with an immense Union Jack.

Yr
VW

987: To Vanessa Bell   Hogarth [House, Richmond]

Wednesday [13 November 1918]

Dearest,

Modesty requires me to say that you will be sick of the sight of my handwriting – So now thats said. The truth is that its still very difficult to settle to anything. Peace seems to make much more difference than one could have thought possible, though I think the rejoicing, so far as I've seen it, has been very sordid and depressing. I expect it was much better in the country, and I wish we'd been at Asheham, and come over and had a civilised debauch with you and the brats.

I had to go to the dentist in Wigmore St on Monday, at 3, and by 4 the streets were in such a state that if I hadn't met L[eonard]: and buffeted through the crowd with him I dont think I should have got home. As it was a small boy was almost crushed in the tube at my feet; we were so packed we could hardly pick him out; everyone seemed half drunk – beer bottles were passed round – every wounded soldier was kissed, by women; nobody had any notion where to go or what to do; it poured steadily; crowds drifted up and down the pavements waving flags and jumping into omnibuses, but in such a disorganised, half hearted, sordid state that I felt more and more melancholy and hopeless of the human race. The London poor, half drunk and very sentimental or completely stolid with their hideous voices and clothes and bad teeth, make one doubt whether any decent life will ever be possible, or

1. Lytton's older brother, Oliver Strachey (1874–1960), a cryptographer in the Foreign Office.

whether it matters if we're at war or at peace. But I suppose the poor wretches haven't much notion how to express their feelings. At present it seems to be a mixture of Bank Holiday and Sunday. The clocks strike incessantly, in a very disordered way. So far the only change I've noticed is that we get no newspapers because the boys won't deliver them, and the buses are lit up, but our lamps are as dark as ever, and the telephones have practically broken down. [. . .]

Poor Katherine Mansfield seems very bad, though I dont like to ask her how bad, and she says she's going to Switzerland with Murry and will be cured.[1] I can't help finding her very interesting, in spite of her story ['Bliss'] in the English Review; at least she cares about writing, which as I'm coming to think, is about the rarest and most desirable of gifts. I had a fearfully depressing talk with old Janet Case the other day; at the end of which I came to the conclusion that when nice educated people who've spent their lives in teaching Greek and ought to know something about it, have less feeling for modern fiction, including my own which she advised me to give up and take to biography instead since that was 'useful', than a stranded jelly fish on which the flies have already settled, its high time for us writers to retire to the South Seas.

There's practically no one in London now whom I can talk to either about my own writing or Shakespeares. I'm beginning to think that I'd better stop writing novels, since no one cares a damn whether one writes them or not. Do you ever feel that your entire life is useless – passed in a dream, into which now and then these brutal buffaloes come butting? or are you always certain that you matter, and matter more than other people? I believe having children must make a lot of difference; and yet perhaps its no good making them responsible for one's own inefficiency – but I mean rather transparency – nonentity – unreality.

Here I am now at the 17 Club.[2] London seems quieted down – only

1. Of tuberculosis. The date of Virginia's first meeting with Katherine Mansfield (1888–1923) is not known for certain, although it may have been as early as November 1916. In July 1918 the Woolfs brought out as their third publication Mansfield's long story 'Prelude'. In many ways the friendship between the two women was close. Unfortunately, only two letters to Mansfield survive (1156 and 1167a, the latter published here for the first time). Virginia disliked Mansfield's husband, the critic John Middleton Murry (1889–1957).

2. A club which had been founded in October 1917, and named for its own origins as well as the February 1917 revolution in Russia. Its membership was a mixture of left-wing politicians, from Ramsay MacDonald downwards, and intellectuals such as Leonard, Virginia and Lytton. Its premises were in Gerrard Street, Soho.

one drunken soldier abusing an officer – only one old lady making a speech in the train about 'what we owe you boys'. [. . .]

B.

992: To Vanessa Bell   *Hogarth [House, Richmond]*

Monday [9 December 1918]

Dearest,

[. . .] we had Sydney Waterlow to dinner, who told us a most dismal story of Saxon's condition. 'I am bored when I am with other people, and lonely when I'm by myself' he said. He agreed that the only remedy was to find some one to marry, but he said that he had now no opportunities of meeting young women, and was inclined to think that he had better emigrate. He was not actively unhappy, according to Sydney, but completely hopeless. Of course I can't help thinking that this is a judgment upon Cambridge generally; its what happens if you go on telling the truth. You lose all generosity and all power of imagination. Moreover, you inevitably become a complete egoist. Please impress this upon Julian and Quentin, to say nothing of the nameless one, whom I dreamt of last night, and of course it was a boy.[1]

Roger has now told me the story about our birth. His latest discovery is Mrs McColl,[2] as you probably know. He told her to read The Voyage Out. She asked Mr Cox,[3] the elderly gentleman at the London Library, for it. 'Thats by Virginia Woolf isnt it?' he said. 'She's a sister of Mrs Clive Bell. Strange whats come to those two girls. Such a nice home they had. Sir Leslie our President. But of course they weren't baptised!' So you see, how even in the London Library they follow us up; its thought you're slightly worse than I am; but Mrs McColl said there wasn't much to choose between us. Your life's pretty bad, but my writing is considered coarse. [. . .]

Your

B.

1. Nevertheless, on Christmas Day Vanessa gave birth to a daughter. Her name, Angelica, was not chosen until March.
2. Andrée MacColl, *née* Zabe (d. 1945), the French wife of the painter and art critic D. S. MacColl, at this time Keeper of the Wallace Collection.
3. Frederick Cox (1865–1955), who from the age of 16 until the year of his death worked at various jobs for the London Library. For decades he was a familiar sight in his post near the entrance, where he impressed readers with his encyclopaedic knowledge of the Library's books.

1919–1921

Virginia's life during these years was routine but productive. She and Leonard moved back and forth between Hogarth House and Sussex, where in 1919 they acquired the cottage, Monk's House, that would henceforth be their country home. They did not venture abroad, but travelled to stay with friends or to conduct Leonard's business. With Ralph Partridge as an assistant, The Hogarth Press slowly built its list, transforming itself from a hobby to a professional venture, and Virginia was involved in all its editorial and technical aspects. For financial and intellectual reasons, she steadfastly continued her journalism. She corresponded with the readers of Night and Day, *but her fiction was already changing. The experimental vision that began with her short stories found its full expression in* Jacob's Room, *completed at the end of 1921. Another new form for Virginia was the confrontational public letter. Her correspondence with the* Woman's Leader *and the* New Statesman *was a token of her rising feminist anger.*

1016: To Katharine Arnold-Forster
Hogarth House, Richmond

5th Feb. [1919]

Dearest Ka,

[...] You can't conceive what existence is like without trains or tubes,[1] a heavy snow falling, no coal in the cellar, a leak in the roof which has already filled every possible receptacle, and probably no electric light tomorrow. We in Richmond can still get to Waterloo; but Hampstead is entirely cut off. Leonard's staff[2] of course live upon the northern heights, and hardly get to the office at all, so the poor man has to go up himself, and here I sit waiting, and God knows, what with the snow and

---

1. The inflation which followed the Armistice led to a series of strikes, particularly in the mining and transport industries.
2. Leonard was editor of a new journal, the *International Review*, backed by Arnold Rowntree. It did not achieve sound financial standing and ceased publication after one year.

the fog, when he'll be back. Then the experts say that the working classes have behaved with such incredible stupidity that the Government will beat them; and this strike is only the beginning of others far worse to follow. They say we are in for such a year as has never been known. [. . .]

Have you heard of the catastrophes at Charleston? I cant go into them in any detail, since they would fill volumes. But imagine a country doctor ordering some medicine for the baby which made it ill by day and by night – Nessa commands him to stop – he refuses – he wont say what it is – the gamp has to obey him – child loses more and more pounds – Duncan goes over to Brighton and interviews Saxon's father[1] about the quality of Nessa's milk – without result – Noel[4] telegraphed for – lady doctor[3] arrives secretly – finds the doctor is ordering some form of poison – Mrs Brereton[4] thinks it her duty to inform the Dr of his rival's presence – scenes, explosions, dismissal – triumph of Nessa and the lady doctor and partial recovery of the Baby. Just as this was over, the servants took to drink or worse, and had to be got rid of; frantic efforts of course to get others; none to be had; telegrams sent, interviews arranged, cook discovered, fails at the last moment – whole thing begins over again; more cooks discovered; just about to start when their father falls dead in the street, upon which both Nessa and I rush about in a fury, with the result that we each engage cooks without telling the other, and one has to be dismissed at enormous expense and terrific cost of energy. You cant think what a lot of time this has all taken up, or how sick I am of beginning my letters, 'Jane Beale, I am writing for my sister – ' For one thing I detest that style of sentence, and then the bold abrupt handwriting is what I can't compass. [. . .]

Yrs
V.W.

1020: To Vanessa Bell   *Hogarth* [*House, Richmond*]

Wednesday [12 February 1919]

Dearest,
    [. . .] O dear, when shall I ever see you, and my adorable Niece?

1. Dr Alfred Sydney-Turner, the proprietor of a private home for mental patients.
2. Noel Olivier had qualified as a doctor in the autumn of 1917.
3. Her friend, Dr Marie Moralt.
4. Julian and Quentin's governess, who had come to Charleston in January 1918.

Paula is a name of character, and so is Susanna; and I see one must consider Bell as part of the colour scheme,[1] though, if she marries a man called Tristram or McCawney it will be sad to have sacrificed Sidonia, Esther, Vashti and the others. I like a name that has the look of a clear green wave; there's distinct emerald in Sidonia, just as there's the splash of the sea in Vanessa; and a chandelier or lustre in Miriam, with all its eyes. By the way, Leonard wants you to call her Fuchsia; that is his favourite name, and he long ago decided to call his daughter that. [. . .]

Yr
B.

1023: To Vanessa Bell   *Hogarth [House, Richmond]*

Monday [24 February 1919]

Dearest,

[. . .] Chiefly for your benefit I went to a concert and a tea party yesterday, and sat between Sir Valentine Chirrol,[2] Katie [Cromer], and Sir Henry Newbolt.[3] I walked with Sir Henry to the concert, and with Katie back again.

Then there's the house[4] to describe to you. But the pen falters. It faces the Stuffed Beasts. Inside they have a complete collection of autotypes of the Dutch school – old women in white bonnets – Rembrandt heads – all chocolate brown in gilt frames. This is on the staircase. The drawing room has gilt mirrors, triangular shaped, several important oil sea scapes, and heads of horses, to the shoulder, in water colour on little easels. There are photographs of soldiers and babies on every prominence. Sir Henry smelt me very suspiciously at first. He has the appearance of a grey weasel, tapering to a point at both ends.

'I never listen to music, but I think my own thoughts', he said. 'I see

---

1. Although she was Duncan Grant's child, the new baby was being presented to the world as the daughter of Clive Bell, to whom Vanessa was still married. The baby was first registered as Helen Vanessa Bell. In March her mother added Angelica, by which name she was known.
2. A traveller and journalist, Chirol (1852–1929) had been the head of the foreign department of *The Times* and a friend of Leslie Stephen.
3. The poet and barrister (1862–1938), whose wife was a Duckworth and therefore also known to the Stephens at Hyde Park Gate.
4. In the Cromwell Road facing the Natural History Museum, and belonging to Mrs Samuel Bruce.

things. I find it very difficult to write poetry without hearing music – yes, Mrs Woolf, probably something will come of this – something almost always does come of a concert –'

'Surely you ought to keep a quartet', I said – which I thought a very pretty compliment; and I see I could shine in South Kensington, which I don't believe either you or Duncan could do. They have a simplicity which is very engaging – they dont hunch up in corners, like [John Middleton] Murry, and say nothing. Bruce and Elena [Richmond] are infinitely polite. And yet, I wonder how far one could go – I feel like a rabbit, who's really a hare, on a lawn with other rabbits, who are really rabbits. Or is this my conceit? Anyhow, Sir Valentine and Katie are full of doubts about the future.

'For myself, I'm a fatalist', said Katie. 'We may be shot at any moment – any how we shall all be shot together.' 'But why?' I asked. 'Who's going to shoot you?' 'O the Jews – the Russian Jews,' she replied. 'Yes, said Sir Val; Nobody can accuse me of being a pacifist, but after 4 years of war the people are not the same people they were. We shall never see 1914 again: They're strung up – they're unreasonable – they want higher wages – and, as Lady Cromer says, there are the Jews, the Russian Jews. There are Jews in every town – colonies of them. They will supply the motive power, and – once the shooting begins – well, I'm a fatalist too, like Lady Cromer.' I almost proclaimed myself a Russian Jew, but I'm keeping this for the next concert. [. . .]

Yr
B.

1069: To Janet Case   *Hogarth House, Richmond*

Wednesday [23 July 1919]

My dear Janet,

[. . .] Have you read the poems of a man, who is dead, called Gerard Hopkins?[1] I liked them better than any poetry for ever so long; partly because they're so difficult, but also because instead of writing mere rhythms and sense as most poets do, he makes a very strange jumble; so that what is apparently pure nonsense is at the same time very beautiful, and not nonsense at all. Now this carries out a theory of mine; but the

1. Gerard Manley Hopkins (1844–89) never published his poems during his lifetime. The first edition, prepared by his friend Robert Bridges, appeared in 1918.

poor man became a Jesuit, and they discouraged him, and he became melancholy and died. I couldn't explain this without quoting however, and now I must go and wash. [. . .]

Your affate
V.W.

1073: To Katharine Arnold-Forster *Asheham, Rodmell, Lewes [Sussex]*

Aug. 12th [1919]

Dearest Ka,

[. . .] Of course, literature is the only spiritual and humane career. Even painting tends to dumbness, and music turns people erotic, whereas the more you write the nicer you become. Do write the Life of somebody – a vast fat book, running over into the margins with reflections and cogitations of all kinds. Do my dear Bruin – I assure you your style is perfectly fitted to some rich thick compound, infinitely humane and judicious, not of course to be run off in a hurry. But in the long winter evenings you might fill page upon page.

Katherine [Mansfield] Murry is, poor woman, very ill; she has been all the winter, and gets no better. Probably she will go to San Remo; but I feel rather dismal about her. You thought her too painted and posed for your more spartan taste I think. But she is all kinds of interesting things underneath, and has a passion for writing, so that we hold religious meetings together praising Shakespeare. I dont much care for Murry's poems though. As for Sydney[1] his good opinion is much in his favour; but alas – his literary judgement has always reminded me of an elephant in a tea cup – His blunders are monstrous there as I suppose they are in office. [. . .]

Yr
V.W.

1. Sydney Waterlow and Katherine Mansfield were second cousins.

1084: To Katharine Arnold-Forster
Hogarth [House, Richmond]

Thursday [9 October 1919]

My dear Bruin,

It was charming to hear from you. After many wanderings, your letter dropped into the box as we got home. We did our best to keep the [railway] strike going in our neighbourhood, and doled out potatoes to the signalman at dusk, but it was all very heroic of us. One's household doesn't like a strike; the servants' point of view is that the lower classes should be kept down.

But this is all moonshine compared with your news. Haven't I always said that I could practically see the shapes of little Bruins[1] attached to your neck? It will be a superb nursery – the old mother bear occasionally rolling over to give her cubs a lick, and everything smelling so nice of milk and straw. But I can't pretend that I'm not envious. Well, well – I think all good mothers ought to consider me half their child, which is what I really like best.

London is, so they say, in an intellectual ferment. Maynard [Keynes] was speaking last night, but instead of going to hear him, we snuggled over a fire and read our books. I've got to write articles without end. I'm very highly thought of – as a reviewer. Did you ever read George Eliot?[2] Whatever one may say about the Victorians, there's no doubt they had twice our – not exactly brains – perhaps hearts. I don't know quite what it is; but I'm a good deal impressed.

Turning, however, to the immediate present, I see that *Night and Day* will be out shortly. Gerald Duckworth[3] lost the last chapter, so I daresay it will be November instead of October. I don't feel nervous; nobody cares a hang what one writes, and novels are such clumsy and half extinct monsters at the best; but, oh dear, what a bore it will be! All one's friends thinking they've got to say something; old Bob Trevelyan hustling up, and saying, of course, the wrong thing; and when people praise me, I never know how to answer, and if they don't praise me,

1. Mark Arnold-Forster was born in April 1920.
2. Virginia was writing about Eliot for the *TLS*.
3. Her half-brother, who had published her first novel, brought out her second on 20 October.

that's not exhilarating either. Leonard is completely callous. His book[1] may be out any day too. [. . .]

Yrs.
V.W.

1087: To Lytton Strachey   *Hogarth [House], Richmond*

Oct. 28th [1919]

Ah, how delightful to be praised by you [for *Night and Day*]! I tell myself that of course you're always too generous about me, and one ought to discount it, but I can't bring myself to. I enjoy every word. I don't suppose there's anything in the way of praise that means more to me than yours. There are myriads of things I want to ask you; about the male characters for instance. Do they convince? Then was Rodney's change of heart sufficiently prepared for to be credible? It came into my head on the spur of the moment that he was in love with Cassandra, and afterwards it seemed a little violent. I take your point about the tupping[2] and had meant to introduce a little in that line, but somehow it seemed out of the picture – still, I regret it. Never mind; I've an idea for a story where all the characters do nothing else – but they're all quadrupeds! However, as I'm afflicted with rheumatism, this had better wait, I only wanted to say how happy your letter had made me, – dialogue was what I was after in this book – so I'm very glad you hit on that; I mean it was one of the things – there are so many million others! – but I can't help thinking it's the problem, if one is to write novels at all, which is a moot point. [. . .]

Your
Virginia

1095: To Janet Case   *Hogarth [House, Richmond]*

[19 November 1919]

My dear Janet,
    [. . .] I shall like very much to discuss my [*Night and Day*] people with you – save that I'm beginning to feel that they're not mine at all. I'm told

---

1. *Empire and Commerce in Africa* was published by George Allen & Unwin and The Labour Research Department in 1920.
2. 'An old black ram/Is tupping your white ewe' (*Othello*, I, i, 96–7).

so many different things about them. But try thinking of Katharine [Hilbery] as Vanessa, not me; and suppose her concealing a passion for painting and forced to go into society by George [Duckworth] – that was the beginning of her; *but* as one goes on, all sorts of things happen. Its the conflict that turns the half of her so chilly; but I daresay this was overdone; and then there's the whole question, which interested me, again too much for the books sake, I daresay, of the things one doesn't say; what effect does that have? and how far do our feelings take their colour from the dive underground? I mean, what is the reality of any feeling? – and all this is further complicated by the form, which must sit tight, and perhaps in Night and Day, sits too tight; as it was too loose in The Voyage Out. And then there's the question of things happening, normally, all the time. But Leonard is typewriting at this table; and someone's coming into dinner, and my niece Angelica who is staying with us has pulled my hair down; so I must stop. [. . .]

Yr.
V.W.

1100: To Lytton Strachey   *Hogarth* [*House, Richmond*]

Sunday [30 November 1919]

[. . .] I'm in the 2nd vol. of Ethel Smyth.[1] I think she shows up triumphantly, through sheer force of honesty. It's a pity she can't write; for I don't suppose one could read it again. But it fascinates me all the same. I saw her at a concert two days ago – striding up the gangway in coat and skirt and spats and talking at the top of her voice. Near at hand one sees that she's all wrinkled and fallen in, and eyes running blue on to the cheeks; but she keeps up the figure of the nineties to perfection. Of course the book is the soul of the nineties. Did you ever know Sue Lushington?[2] Much the same type. Then Ethel's passion for the W. C. (it occurs in every chapter) is of the highest merit. [. . .]

Yr.
V.W.

1. The composer, writer, and feminist (1858–1944), who was to become a close friend of Virginia in the 1930s. Her two-book autobiography was called *Impressions that Remained* (1919). She later wrote five additional volumes of autobiography.
2. Sister of Kitty Maxse and, like her, a frequent visitor with their parents, Judge Vernon Lushington (1832–1912) and his wife, to the Stephens at Hyde Park Gate.

1120: TO DUNCAN GRANT   *Hogarth [House, Richmond]*

Wednesday [11 February 1920]

My dear Duncan,

[...] Ottoline yesterday was in fine feather about your show.[1] The poor old thing undulated and eulogised till really it was like talking to some poor fowl in delirium – her neck became longer and longer and you know how she always hangs to 'wonderful' as if it were a rope dangling in her vacuum – but as Nessa says, this is nonsense –. Poor Tony Birrell was there, said to be underdeveloped, but to me most sympathetic and in fact I wish we'd married. He sat on a low stool eating sugar cakes and laughing – God knows about what – but I saw nothing lamentable in his state. However, we shall meet. This is an endeavour to thank you without allowing myself to describe your pictures.

V.W.

1126: TO VANESSA BELL   *Monk's House [Rodmell,*
                                Sussex][2]

Good Friday [2 April 1920]

Dearest,

I was very glad to get your post card [from Italy], though some passages were obliterated, I suppose by the channel spray.

Here we are with the bells ringing for church – daffodils out – apple trees in blossom – cows mooing – cocks crowing – thrushes chirping – this is to move your compassion. I suppose you're sitting in a Roman street sucking iced soda through a straw while Duncan, having made friends with the waiter – and there are goats, and large spotted dogs – and nice brown and yellow pots – donkeys – mules – beautiful girls for me – and etc – I wont describe it all, as I daresay you can see it for yourself. Still I do shoot forth a pang of odious envy. England is a little soft and sappy after all. I haven't much news, as we've been here for a week, and our only prospect is a visit from the Sturgeon

---

1. His first one-man exhibition, at the Carfax Gallery.
2. In July 1919 the Woolfs purchased this small house in the village of Rodmell. It was to remain their country house for the rest of their lives, and now belongs to the National Trust.

family[1] tomorrow and the possible advent of Saxon, Nick, and Barbara [Bagenal].

I went in and saw the yellow bird [Clive] in bed with some complaint (nothing much) before I came away, and as I deposited my humble oranges in plain paper, who should trip from her taxi but the blue one [Mary Hutchinson], with plovers' eggs and orchids of course, all dressed in yellow with purple spots and as daring and devilish as I was muffled and discreet. Still I faced her out and from my moral heights crushed her, – I hope – I doubt it though. Still its better to be dowdy on one's own ground than a failure on hers – and as a matter of fact I was half a street away and may have invented the whole thing. Still, you can imagine – Oh and the yellow bird so prosperous and perky upstairs – strewn with compliments. [. . .]

Isn't it exciting to start a new epoch as you're doing? – not A. D. I wouldn't say that, oh no – but an entirely new Pagan Era, with dear old Dolphin[2] in her many coloured multiplicity presiding and ladling out scents and spices from the steaming obscenity – what a sentence! but I've been reading Henry James' letters[3] till my brain rings and swings – do pictures affect you like that? He stayed in your hotel, by the way, and no doubt wore out some rich leather seat with his rotundity. This, however, you skip; and want to know about Mrs Clifford[4] – who was, indeed, all that you've ever imagined her to be – wattled all down her neck like some oriental Turkey, and with a mouth opening like an old leather bag, or the private parts of a large cow. Her stories were magnificent – about Ruddy Kiplings wedding – and how [the publisher, William] Heinemann came too late with a bouquet – and picture Sundays[5] – and how Professor Sylvester[6] suddenly sank on his knees on the black hearth rug and recited his sonnets to her, with Ethel [her

1. Leonard's younger sister Flora (1886–1975), her husband George Sturgeon, and their daughter Molly.
2. Virginia's favourite animal nickname for her sister.
3. Edited by Percy Lubbock and reviewed by Virginia in the *TLS* for 8 April (*Essays*, III, 198).
4. As the widow of Leslie Stephen's friend, the mathematician W. K. Clifford, Lucy Clifford (*née* Lane, c. 1855–1929) supported herself and her two children by writing novels and plays.
5. On the Sunday before sending-in day at the Royal Academy, artists were in the habit of inviting their friends to their studios to view their work.
6. Professor James Sylvester (1814–97), a brilliant mathematician, who also wrote verse and *The Laws of Verse* (1870).

daughter] at her breast – and then 'yes, a great many young men have come to me in their troubles, for a lone woman who has once been married and considers herself married still, is a great help to young men – and they all know that Lucy Clifford never gives away a secret and never thinks harm of a friend' – upon which we all fell silent and almost sobbed – This was to explain why she wouldn't write her memoirs. Moreover, she moves about all in black, lurching like a beetle thats lost a front leg, so I suppose I shall have to review her novel after all – her courage and fertility move my heart to tears. [. . .]

Yr
B.

1128: To Vanessa Bell   *Hogarth House [Richmond]*

April 15th [1920]

Dearest,

[. . .] There is a good deal doing in the art world. A show of Negro carvings at the book club – the X group – pictures in Shaftesbury Avenue, and the entire works of Bach played; Beethoven next week. I went to see the carvings and I found them dismal and impressive, but Heaven knows what real feeling I have about anything after hearing Roger [Fry] discourse. I dimly see that something in their style might be written, and also that if I had one on the mantelpiece I should be a different sort of character – less adorable, as far as I can make out, but somebody you wouldn't forget in a hurry. But then an unknown young man wrung me by the hand – Hannay[1] he said he was – and Desmond [MacCarthy] came in with a highly respectable male aristocrat, of whom I could see he was slightly ashamed. – as I should be ashamed if you passed me by when I was walking with Elena Richmond. How much simpler life is for painters! How can I possibly afford not to know South Kensington? You cant think how much this problem puzzles me – the humanity of South Kensington, I mean. You see, to go to the grave with that problem unsolved would be a bitter failure in my eyes. If you see me kick and stir in my death bed, that'll be it.

Adrian and Karin have sent out cards for a large evening party on the 28th, I think; so you wont be back; and I daresay its a kind of assertion of independence on their part. I shall try to go, but not in the same spirit

1. Alexander Hannay (1889–1955), the art critic of the *London Mercury*.

that I bound up your flight, – still always expecting a romance at the top; whereas, in the case of the Stephen's, I feel that I'm the romance. Its really very dismal now that you're away. I didn't think I should miss you so much. There's no conversation to [be] had in my style, and I have to have my tea at the 17 Club, and altogether there's something about Dolphin [Vanessa] and her ménage that can't be matched. For sheer ridiculous comedy partly, of course, for you're not altogether in the high classic style – and poor old Duncan, well – there's a good deal to be said about him. The Athenaeum has ceased to talk about Wyndham Lewis.[1] On the other hand, they've adopted Katherine [Mansfield] as their writer of genius,[2] which means, I'm afraid, that poor Mrs Woolf – but we writers are never jealous. Thank Heaven, I say to myself that genius has arisen, though not in my particular headpiece. Whereas, what you painters say is, – but I'd much rather hear about Susan Lushington. Do tell me, not on a postcard, the whole history of your liaison, and what your future relations are to be; and whether she had to swallow scruples to have tea with you; I'm sure she got over them in fine style; what I remember chiefly about her is that she had to move on after 5 minutes because her head piece gave out; then she took to giving high shrieks. Is this still true? [. . .]

Yr
B.

1139a: To The Editor, The *Woman's Leader*
[*Monk's House, Rodmell,*
Lewes, Sussex]

[6 August 1920][3]

Madam,

There is little use, I am afraid, in writing articles; still less in answering those who disagree with them. To Mr. Massingham my meaning is ambiguous, and my ways untruthful; to me, his meaning is plain enough but almost, if not entirely, off the point. Let me clear up

1. Percy Wyndham Lewis (1882–1957), the writer and artist.
2. The editor of the *Athenaeum* was John Middleton Murry, the husband of its 'writer of genius'.
3. The date given is for the publication, not the composition, of the letter, and this will be true for all the 'public' letters that appear in this volume.

some at least of my ambiguities. Not for an instant did I accuse Mr Massingham[1] of bias or partiality. I am wholly against the plumage trade. At the age of ten or thereabouts I signed a pledge never to wear one of the condemned feathers, and have kept the vow so implicitly that I cannot distinguish osprey from egret. Cocks, hens, parrots, and ostriches are the only birds whose feathers I recognise or wear. The huge majority of women are as ignorant and as innocent as I am. With this in my mind, I picked up the *Nation* and read the half sentimental and wholly contemptuous phrases about 'What do women care?' and 'Look at Regent Street this morning!' which I quoted in my article. I have no reason to suppose that Mr Massingham either wrote the sentences of which I complain, or approved the tone of them. But it was against them that my article, with sufficient plainness as I thought, was directed. Had I wished to attack the plumage trade I should not have lumbered my space with the statement, in that case irrelevant, that men are more to be blamed for it than women.[2] I should have stuck simply to the fact that the trade is abominable and the cruelty repulsive. But to make such a denunciation in your columns seemed to me superfluous. To denounce as forcibly as I could the injustice of Wayfarer's remark seemed, on the contrary, an odious but obvious necessity. It was with that end in view that I endeavoured to prove that in this instance men, rather than women, are to be charged with cruelty and indifference. I did not confound a statement of fact with its moral implications. To torture birds is one thing, and to be unjust to women is another, and it was, I hope, plain to some of my readers that I was attacking the second of these crimes and not the first. Thus, when Mrs Bradley[3] asks 'Does it matter in the least to the birds so foully slain whether the blame rests most with men or women?' I reply that I am not writing as a bird, or even a champion of birds; but as a woman. At the risk of losing such little reputation for humanity as I may still possess I hereby confess that it seems to me more necessary to resent such an insult to women as Wayfarer casually lets fall than to protect egrets from extinction. That is my way of 'raising the moral currency of civilised nations.' But that does

1. H. W. Massingham (1860–1924), editor of the *Nation* since 1907, and writer of the 'Wayfarer' column, had replied to an article (23 July) on the Plumage Bill that Ray Strachey, editor of the *Woman's Leader*, had asked Virginia to write.
2. I.e., because men torture and kill birds for economic gain.
3. Meta Bradley and E. Florence Yates also participated in the exchange of views in the *Woman's Leader* on the Plumage Bill.

not mean that I have not the highest respect for Mr Massingham's way also.

Had you placed six columns of your paper at my disposal, instead of a thousand words, I might have given some of my reasons for attaching so great, some will say excessive, an importance to a phrase in a newspaper. On some future occasion you will, perhaps, allow me to explain why it is that such phrases, common as they are, serve not merely to produce an outburst of sex antagonism, but seem to me for the more serious harm they do to deserve trouncing and denial until either they are forced down their writers' throats or justified up to the hilt. But what the effect of them is, and why the damage is so disastrous not merely to women's relations with men but to her art and her conduct are questions far too broad and too complex to broach at the tail end of a letter.

In conclusion, as I have lost my temper, caused Mr Massingham to waste his time, and in his opinion (though I think he overrates the power of my pen) done more harm to the cause than 'a round score of Miss Yateses,' I should like to make whatever reparation I can. Plainly with this example of my own ambiguity as a writer before me, it would never do to write another article solely from the birds' point of view. But I will give myself the pleasure of spending whatever sum I receive for my article, not upon an egret plume, but upon a subscription to the Plumage Bill Group.

> With prayers to you therefore to make it
> as handsome as possible,
> Virginia Woolf

1148b: To The Editor, The *New Statesman*
[Hogarth House, Richmond]

[9 October 1920]

Sir,

Like most women, I am unable to face the depression and the loss of self respect which Mr Arnold Bennett's blame and Mr Orlo Williams' praise – if it is not the other way about – would certainly cause me if I read their books in the bulk.[1] I taste them, therefore, in sips at the hands

---

1. The novelist Arnold Bennett had just published a collection of essays called *Our Women*, in which his thesis was that men were cognitively and creatively superior to

of reviewers. But I cannot swallow the teaspoonful administered in your columns last week by Affable Hawk. The fact that women are inferior to men in intellectual power, he says, 'stares him in the face'. He goes on to agree with Mr Bennett's conclusion that 'no amount of education and liberty of action will sensibly alter it'. How, then, does Affable Hawk account for the fact which stares me, and I should have thought any other impartial observer, in the face, that the seventeenth century produced more remarkable women than the sixteenth, the eighteenth than the seventeenth, and nineteenth than all three put together? When I compare the Duchess of Newcastle with Jane Austen, the matchless Orinda with Emily Brontë, Mrs Heywood with George Eliot, Aphra Behn with Charlotte Brontë, Jane Grey with Jane Harrison,[1] the advance in intellectual power seems to me not only sensible but immense; the comparison with men not in the least one that inclines me to suicide; and the effects of education and liberty scarcely to be overrated. In short, though pessimism about the other sex is always delightful and invigorating, it seems a little sanguine of Mr Bennett and Affable Hawk to indulge in it with such certainty on the evidence before them. Thus, though women have every reason to hope that the intellect of the male sex is steadily diminishing, it would be unwise, until they have more evidence than the great war and the great peace supply, to announce it as a fact. In conclusion, if Affable Hawk sincerely wishes to discover a great poetess, why does he let himself be fobbed off with a possible authoress of the Odyssey? Naturally, I cannot claim to know Greek as Mr Bennett and Affable Hawk know it, but I have often been told that Sappho was a woman, and that Plato and Aristotle placed her with Homer and Archilocus among the greatest of their poets. That Mr

1. The women listed – other than those of the first rank of fame – are Margaret Cavendish, Duchess of Newcastle (1624?–74), who led her husband in their joint writing of twelve volumes of plays, poems, and philosophical essays; the poet Katherine Phillips (1631–64), sometimes called 'Orinda', the first female commoner to be celebrated as a writer; Eliza Haywood (1693–1756), an actress, popular novelist and political satirist, who appears in Pope's 'The Dunciad'; Aphra Behn (1640?–89), novelist, playwright, and perhaps the first woman to make her living as a writer; Lady Jane Grey (1537–54), the learned but hapless political tool of those who would have her Queen after Edward VI; and Jane Harrison (1850–1928), the distinguished classical scholar and lecturer at Newnham College, Cambridge, whom Virginia knew.

women. It was favourably reviewed, together with Orlo Williams' *The Good English-woman*, by the *New Statesman* columnist 'Affable Hawk', who was none other than Virginia's friend Desmond MacCarthy.

Bennett can name fifty of the male sex who are indisputably her superiors is therefore a welcome surprise, and if he will publish their names I will promise, as an act of that submission which is so dear to my sex, not only to buy their works but, so far as my faculties allow, to learn them by heart.

Yours, etc.,
Virginia Woolf

1148c: To The Editor, The *New Statesman*
[*Hogarth House, Richmond*]

[16 October 1920][1]

Sir,

To begin with Sappho. We do not, as in the hypothetical case of Burns suggested by 'Affable Hawk', judge her merely by her fragments.[2] We supplement our judgement by the opinions of those to whom her works were known in their entirety. It is true that she was born 2,500 years ago. According to 'Affable Hawk' the fact that no poetess of her genius has appeared from 600 B.C. to the eighteenth century proves that during that time there were no poetesses of potential genius. It follows that the absence of poetesses of moderate merit during that period proves that there were no women writers of potential mediocrity. There was no Sappho; but also, until the seventeenth or eighteenth century, there was no Marie Corelli and no Mrs Barclay.[3]

To account for the complete lack not only of good women writers but also of bad women writers I can conceive no reason unless it be that there was some external restraint upon their powers. For 'Affable Hawk' admits that there have always been women of second or third rate ability. Why, unless they were forcibly prohibited, did they not express these gifts in writing, music, or painting? The case of Sappho, though so remote, throws, I think, a little light upon the problem. I quote J. A. Symonds:

1. 'Affable Hawk' (Desmond MacCarthy) had not been convinced by Virginia's arguments and had written a rebuttal, to which Virginia replied the following week.
2. MacCarthy had suggested that Robert Burns too might be considered a great poet if, like Sappho, his work had survived only in fragments.
3. The popular novelists Marie Corelli (Mary Mackay, 1855–1924) and Florence Barclay (1862–1921).

'Several circumstances contributed to aid the development of lyric poetry in Lesbos. The customs of the Aeolians permitted more social and domestic freedom than was common in Greece. Aeolian women were not confined to the harem like Ionians, or subjected to the rigorous discipline of the Spartans. While mixing freely with male society, they were highly educated and accustomed to express their sentiments to an extent unknown elsewhere in history – until, indeed, the present time.'[1]

And now to skip from Sappho to Ethel Smyth.

'There was nothing else [but intellectual inferiority] to prevent down the ages, so far as I can see, women who always played, sang and studied music, producing as many musicians from among their number as men have done,' says 'Affable Hawk'. Was there nothing to prevent Ethel Smyth from going to Munich [Leipzig, actually]? Was there no opposition from her father? Did she find that the playing, singing and study of music which well-to-do families provided for their daughters were such as to fit them to become musicians? Yet Ethel Smyth was born in the nineteenth century. There are no great women painters, says 'Affable Hawk', though painting is now within their reach. It is within their reach – if that is to say there is sufficient money after the sons have been educated to permit of paints and studios for the daughters and no family reason requiring their presence at home. Otherwise they must make a dash for it and disregard a species of torture more exquisitely painful, I believe, than any that man can imagine. And this is in the twentieth century. But, 'Affable Hawk' argues, a great creative mind would triumph over obstacles such as these. Can he point to a single one of the great geniuses of history who has sprung from a people stinted of education and held in subjection, as for example the Irish or the Jews? It seems to me indisputable that the conditions which make it possible for a Shakespeare to exist are that he shall have had predecessors in his art, shall make one of a group where art is freely discussed and practised, and shall himself have the utmost of freedom of action and experience. Perhaps in Lesbos, but never since, have these conditions been the lot of women. 'Affable Hawk' then names several men who have triumphed over poverty and ignorance. His first example is Isaac Newton. Newton was the son of a farmer; he was sent to a grammar school; he objected to working on the farm; an uncle, a clergyman, advised that he should be exempted and prepared for college; and at the age of nineteen he was

---

1. From John Addington Symonds' *Studies of the Greek Poets* (1873).

sent to Trinity College, Cambridge. (See D.N.B.)[1] Newton, that is to say, had to encounter about the same amount of opposition that the daughter of a country solicitor encounters who wishes to go to Newnham in the year 1920. But his discouragement is not increased by the works of Mr Bennett, Mr Orlo Williams and 'Affable Hawk'.

Putting that aside, my point is that you will not get a big Newton until you have produced a considerable number of lesser Newtons. 'Affable Hawk' will, I hope, not accuse me of cowardice if I do not take up your space with an enquiry into the careers of Laplace, Faraday, and Herschell, no compare the lives and achievements of Aquinas and St Theresa, nor decide whether it was Mill or his friends who was mistaken about Mrs Taylor.[2] The fact, as I think we shall agree, is that women from the earliest times to the present day have brought forth the entire population of the universe. This occupation has taken much time and strength. It has also brought them into subjection to men, and incidentally – if that were to the point – bred in them some of the most lovable and admirable qualities of the race. My difference with 'Affable Hawk' is not that he denies the present intellectual equality of men and women. It is that he, with Mr Bennett, asserts that the mind of woman is not sensibly affected by education and liberty; that it is incapable of the highest achievements; and that it must remain for ever in the condition in which it now is. I must repeat that the fact that women have improved (which 'Affable Hawk' now seems to admit), shows that they may still improve; for I cannot see why a limit should be set to their improvement in the nineteenth century rather than in the one hundred and nineteenth. But it is not education only that is needed. It is that women should have liberty of experience; that they should differ from men without fear and express their difference openly (for I do not agree with 'Affable Hawk' that men and women are alike); that all activity of the mind should be so encouraged that there will always be in existence a nucleus of women who think, invent, imagine, and create as freely as men do, and with as little fear of ridicule and condescension. These conditions, in my view of great importance, are impeded by such statements as those of 'Affable Hawk' and Mr Bennett, for a man has still much greater facilities that a woman for making his views known and respected. Certainly I cannot

1. The *Dictionary of National Biography*, whose first editor, 1882–91, was Leslie Stephen.
2. Mrs Taylor, whom MacCarthy used to support his argument along with the others named in this sentence, married John Stuart Mill in 1851. The philosopher thought her his superior in every way, but his friends disagreed with him.

doubt that if such opinions prevail in the future we shall remain in a condition of half-civilised barbarism. At least that is how I define an eternity of dominion on the one hand and of servility on the other. For the degradation of being a slave is only equalled by the degradation of being a master.

Yours, etc.,
Virginia Woolf

1167a: To Katherine Mansfield

*Hogarth House, Paradise Road,
Richmond, Surrey*

Feb. 13th [1921]

My dear Katherine,

I was so delighted to get your letter.[1] It came as I was having my tea alone, – a half-spring evening, rather pale, and a bunch of mimosa smelling very sweet. I read it twice, and then I read the envelope [*missing*].

I saw Murry two nights ago when I dined at Gordon Square; but Clive bawls so that one can scarcely say anything – still, we talked a little about you, which I liked. I'm always thinking of things to say to you. They have to be put in my diary. I'm wondering what you think about your book,[2] and what people have said about it. The reviews are enthusiastic, but then the reviews are stupid. Shall I write you a criticism of it one of these days? I sometimes think that though we're so different we have some of the same difficulties. I'm in the middle of my novel now,[3] but have to break off, of course, to make a little money. I shall write an article on Dorothy Wordsworth,[4] and so pay for our new sheets, and then get back again. I don't know that its readable though. What I admire in you so much is your transparent quality. My stuff gets

---

1. From Mentone, France, where Mansfield had gone in another attempt to treat her tuberculosis. John Middleton Murry had asked Virginia to write to his wife, who was feeling isolated and miserable.
2. *Bliss and Other Stories*, published in December 1920. Murry had indicated that Katherine was not pleased with it.
3. Since the spring of 1920 Virginia had been writing *Jacob's Room* (1922), the first of her experimental novels.
4. This article, if completed, has not yet been found.

muddy; and then in a novel one must have continuity, but in this one I'm always chopping and changing from one level to another. I think what I'm at is to change the consciousness, and so to break up the awful stodge. Does this convey anything to you? And you seem to me to go so straightly and directly, – all clear as glass – refined, spiritual.[1] But I must read them over again properly. I feel as if I didn't want just all realism any more – only thoughts and feelings – no cups and tables. When will your next book come out?[2]

Like an idiot I lost my temper with Arnold Bennett for abusing women, and wasted my time writing a foolish violent, I suppose unnecessary satire.[3] Somehow it seems to me worse than lazy impertinence on his part. Suppose some poor wretch who wanted to write was put off by that little grocer? And so I lashed out. It seems to me very important that women should learn to write. Does it to you?

God knows I don't much like them when they do it – or men either for the matter of that. Mr Beresford[4] gave a lecture upon fiction the other day at the 1917 Club – a deplorable exhibition. At the end, up jumped an unshaven Jew and said he had no use for Dorothy Richardson,[5] Katherine Mansfield, or Virginia Woolf. And then Morgan Forster said that [Mansfield's] Prelude and The Voyage Out were the best novels of their time, and I said Damn Katherine! Why can't I be the only woman who knows how to write?

Still I never go anywhere where I see writers, and I hope not to talk about editions and reviews and how Squire has written a poem, and

---

1. Cf. Letter 1228 to Janet Case, in which Virginia claims to despise *Bliss*. Sometimes her intense jealousy of a contemporary's work, particularly that with which her own was likely to be compared, prevented her from seeing it clearly.
2. The next volume was *The Garden Party and Other Stories* (February 1922).
3. She does not mean the letters to the *New Statesman*, but a biting feminist story called 'A Society'. She published it in her collection, *Monday or Tuesday* (April 1921), but had decided – so Leonard Woolf says in his introduction to her posthumous volume of short stories *A Haunted House* (1943) – not to reprint it. It is included in *The Complete Shorter Fiction of Virginia Woolf* (1985).
4. John Davys Beresford (1873–1947), whose novels were widely read and regarded in his day. Virginia had just reviewed one of them, *Revolution*, in the *TLS* for 27 January 1921 (*Essays*, III, 279).
5. The novels of Dorothy Richardson (1873–1957) were often compared to Virginia Woolf's because both employed the 'stream of consciousness' technique, but in this case, the linking seems to have been made mostly on the basis of gender.

Blunden an article.[1] Can one keep out of it? And why does one hate it so? We had Rose Macaulay[2] here the other night – rather a harum-scarum woman, very modest, and incredibly benighted. If you take Miss Royde Smith seriously, and believe that Clemence Dane and Mr Beresford need be read, what hope for you is there? But their modesty – thats what impresses me. Isn't Potterism one of the successes of the age? She almost apologized for having written it. I've been seeing Lytton and Eliot,[3] a little, and old Sydney [Waterlow], and we have our memoir club,[4] which gets more and more brilliant and more and more unreal. I like Eliot, and pity him, as if he suffered a great deal from having acquired a shell which he can't lift off. Meanwhile all sorts of things grow underneath, very painfully. But this is guesswork. We only make signs to each other. Lytton is as mellow as a pear. Queen Victoria is done, and he is set up for life on the proceeds.[5] But I must say of my friends that with all their faults they get nicer with success.

My dear Katherine, what a ghastly long letter! My church bells are ringing as yours were. But Sunday evening in Richmond needn't be

1. J. C. Squire (1884–1958), poet, critic, and at this time editor of the *London Mercury*; and the poet and critic Edmund Blunden (1896–1974), who was currently writing for the *Athenaeum*.
2. The novelist (1881–1958), whose reputation was then largely based on her satire, *Potterism* (1920). The novelists whom she recommended to Virginia were, in addition to Beresford, Naomi Royde Smith (d. 1964), Macaulay's close friend, and Clemence Dane (d. 1965), all of whom Virginia considered conventional and whose popularity promised no good for her own.
3. Virginia had invited T. S. Eliot to dinner in November 1918, after writing to ask him for something for The Hogarth Press. They knew of each other before that meeting, and, in fact, Leonard believed that they may have met earlier. It was Eliot who was responsible for sending the *Ulysses* manuscript to the Woolfs, via Harriet Weaver, whose assistant editor he was at the *Egoist*. In May 1919 the Press brought out a small book of Eliot's poetry, called simply *Poems*. Virginia and Eliot continued to see each through the years, and they became good friends, but her letters to him were never relaxed.
4. This fascinating, long-lived group, organised by Molly MacCarthy, consisted of a small circle of friends who vowed to gather from time to time to read frank autobiographical essays to one another. It met from March 1920 until 1956. Death made it necessary to add members to the original thirteen: Virginia and Leonard Woolf, Vanessa and Clive Bell, Molly and Desmond MacCarthy, Lytton Strachey, Maynard Keynes, Duncan Grant, Roger Fry, Morgan Forster, Saxon Sydney-Turner and Sydney Waterlow. Vanessa and Duncan's housemate, the novelist David ('Bunny') Garnett (1892–1981), was invited to join soon after the Club began.
5. Lytton's biography of Queen Victoria, which was dedicated to Virginia, was published in April of this year and was immensely successful.

described. L. and I are now going to cook eggs and bacon on the gas stove; then I shall learn some Russian words for Koteliansky,[1] who insists upon teaching us; then I shall read Dorothy Wordsworth – but probably I shall think a good deal about writing and about Katherine; and get half dazed over the fire. Please Katherine, let us try to write to each other.

Your affate
V.W.

Smith College Library Rare Book Room

1169: To Vanessa Bell   *The Queen's Hotel, Manchester*[2]
Thursday, March 17th, 1921

Dearest,

I am reminded of you at every turn in this hotel – How you would love it! in fact, why you and Duncan don't do a series of hotel scenes I cant conceive. A vast green plush room – pillars – candelabra – silver trays – urns – coffee pots – large British family groups reading newspapers – drinking – the clergy – mothers and daughters – all grey tidy skimpy incredibly respectable – save for one or two hippotamus females basking in corners all stuck about with diamonds – and old gentlemen bursting through their waistcoats – indeed they never stop eating fried fish, tea, and meringues. But I can give you no idea; and then just outside the window are trams, Queen Victoria, the Duke of Wellington, and the man [James Hargreaves] who invented the Spinning Jenny [in 1764] – now who was he? – all black as soot, noble, – pointing at the opposite houses – I say I can't finish this sentence, and

1. S. S. Koteliansky (1882–1953) had come to England from the Ukraine. A friend of the Murrys, 'Kot' was collaborating with both Virginia and Leonard on some translations from the Russian published by The Hogarth Press, including Gorky's *Reminiscences of Tolstoi* (1920) and *The Note-Books of Anton Tchekhov Together with Reminiscences of Tchekhov* (1921), I. A. Bunin's *The Gentleman from San Francisco and other stories* (1922), and Dostoevsky's *Stavrogin's Confession and The Plan of the Life of a Great Sinner* (1922).
2. The Woolfs had gone to Manchester where Leonard was adopted as Labour candidate for the Combined Universities. Out of a field of six candidates – one of whom was Virginia's cousin, the historian and member of Lloyd George's Government, H. A. L. Fisher – Leonard came in fourth in the General Election of November 1922.

then there's Mrs Snowden[1] clearly writing to Lily (was that her name?) about airing the curtains.

Last night Leonard made a speech in a chemistry theatre, and I talked to Mrs Unwin [the wife of a professor] about the beauties of Derbyshire, which are indeed surprising, but too melodramatic for your taste. This was at the University, where Watties [Walter Lamb] father is professor, and they're all somehow like Wattie, provincial, smug, destitute of any character, hopelessly suburban, yet trying to live up to the metropolitan intellect (me, I mean) which they can't do. Somehow, we have got off the rails for real middleclass intellectual political life. Does that ever strike you? Tonight we're dining at what they call the Refectory with Professor Weiss and Professor – I forget; and I've prepared 2 things to say. The first is 'I am Herbert Fisher's cousin' the 2nd is 'I am Leslie Stephen's daughter.' But supposing nothing whatever happens? And why did you bring me into the world to go through these ordeals?

I spent the morning at the Art gallery. There's Work by Ford Madox Brown, the Hireling Shepherd by Holman Hunt, Love and death by Watts; and I assure you the number of incidents one can pick out is amazing. If Leonard hadn't got impatient I could have found grasshoppers copulating in the very background of Holman Hunt. The shepherds hair is done one by one. Then there's a lamb with 8 separate whiskers. Theres Aunt Susie by Dodd[2] – and Mr Beccles by Aunt Susie, and Nymphs by Waterfield and – God knows what all – Your art is far more of a joke than mine. But dont think that I am unaware how dull this letter is – We spent the afternoon at the Zoo. Imagine (oh God, says poor old Dolphin, how much longer is this going on? Why should I imagine the Manchester Zoo) well, but you must admit it was exciting to find a dromedary and an Indian buffaloe, with ingrowing toe nails, poor beast, in a grotto of pale grey stone, totally forgotten, there being only 2 charwomen about the place, which is the size of Regents Park, and almost entirely given over to the scaffolding of a panorama, and a lake. But how I love these places! The whole expedition is one long rapture of

1. The mother of Margery Snowden (1878–1966?), who had studied painting with Vanessa at the Royal Academy Schools and remained a close friend. Lily was Margery's sister.
2. Aunt Susie was Isabel Dacre (1844–1933), a member of the Manchester Academy of Fine Arts, and an associate of Francis Dodd (1874–1949), who had done several drawings of Virginia in 1907–8.

romance – and if I could live in hotel lounges I think I should be – Yes, here are more people come in. Mrs Snowden has settled down beside me after a very tiring day, she says – When you know a waiter by name, in fact shake him by the hand, what does it mean? Its the clergy who do it. However, I will say no more. When I'm old, when Julian and Quentin and Angelica are out in the world, do let us become travelling matrons, and go round the provinces together, in handsome style, having buried our husbands, for I think its best to be a widow (I mean in a hotel –)

Did you hear that Lytton has thrown us over on what must be a pretext about Lady S.?[1]

So Leonard and I are going alone; but there's more in it than meets the eye. Ralph has a fixed and gloomy look which reminds me of his father the suicidal Colonel.[2] I imagine (but for Gods sake dont shout this about Gordon Square,[3] that there's been a crisis. Anyhow I hope so. I hope they're all at daggers drawn. I think Carrington is losing Lytton and spurning poor Ralph – but here is Leonard – I must wash and rehearse my 2 speeches. I am Leslie Stephen's Cousin – thats what it will be. [. . .]

Yr
B.

1. Lytton had cancelled his plans to go to Cornwall with the Woolfs, saying that his mother was ill, but Virginia believed that a crisis in his domestic arrangements was behind his decision. In 1918 Ralph Partridge (1894–1960), who had risen during the war to the rank of Major, returned to Oxford to complete his studies. From there he often visited Carrington and Lytton at Tidmarsh. He soon fell in love with Carrington, who was, of course, devoted to Lytton. The situation was complicated when Lytton fell in love with Ralph. The way to keep them all together, Carrington reasoned, was to give in to Ralph's insistence on marriage, which she did in May 1921. Virginia followed these convolutions partly through Ralph, who in October 1920 had begun to work at The Hogarth Press.

2. Whom Ralph had once brought to dinner with the Woolfs in order to take his mind off a problem with which he had become obsessed. Many years after neglecting to declare to the Inland Revenue some dividends earned in India, the senior Mr Partridge fell into a deep guilt, reported his negligence to the authorities, and then – when they took no action after three letters – decided that his honour required that he shoot himself if he did not hear from them within ten days. A desperate letter from Ralph to the Revenue brought their prompt assessment, and his father survived to die of natural causes.

3. Where many of Virginia's circle, including Vanessa, Duncan, Maynard Keynes, the Stracheys and the Tidmarsh group, had houses or rooms, and where Virginia's love of gossip had made trouble before.

1173: To Lytton Strachey   *Ponion, Zennor,*
                                   St Ives [Cornwall]

Wednesday [30] March [1921]

The enclosed card gives you no idea of the place, which is indescribable – far better than the Lizard or the Land's End, or St Ives, or indeed anywhere. (I have just had to move my chair out of the blazing sun). One walks out of the window on to the cliff. There are 2 seals bathing in the bay. Two adders curling round my ankles. Gorse, cowries, Cliffs, Choughs, Ravens, Cream, solitude, sublimity and all the rest of it. It's true that Ka is perched on the hill a mile and a half away, with the oddest collection of good little grey men who spend their time scrambling up chimneys and funnels and are hardly articulate in consequence.[1] But there is Henry Lamb[2] for you – not for me. I've not seen him. We take our books out and lie in the sun; occasionally I say, why aren't you here? – but even so, a general benignity pervades us. I like Will better, and have looked through [his] portfolios of grey-blue rock-scapes – not of Cornwall; of Italy as it was before the war. I met a man yesterday by appointment to discuss literature – 'which is my whole life, Mrs Woolf.' But I can give you no idea – He lives with a half perished dumb wife on a headland in a cottage with Everyman's Library entire. 'I read no moderns. Life is not long enough for anything save the best. Hardy has taught me to look into my heart. I have enjoyed this conversation, Mrs Woolf. It has confirmed me in my own opinions.' This stunted animal was a clerk in the post office, became infected with books, and is now like the oldest kernel of a monkey's nut in the Gray's Inn Road. However – why is it that human beings are so terribly pathetic? God knows. Or am I becoming rotten with middle age? I did refrain from asking him to correspond; but left with tears in my eyes – almost. I can't help thinking that we are hopelessly muddled. Then there was the theosophist, Mr Watt in the cottage which I once hired; and he lives on nuts from Selfridges, and a few vegetables, and has visions, and wears boots with soles like slabs of beef and an orange tie; and then his wife crept out of her hole, all blue, with orange hair, and cryptic ornaments,

1. Ka Arnold-Forster and her husband Will now lived at Eagle's Nest overlooking Zennor, Cornwall. The 'little grey men' were simply visitors who had come there to climb.
2. The painter Henry Lamb (1883–1960), younger brother of Walter Lamb, and formerly the object of Lytton's affections.

serpents, you know, swallowing their tails in token of eternity, round her neck. The rain, they said, often comes through the walls on a wet day, so I'm glad I didn't settle there. But can you explain the human race at all – I mean these queer fragments of it which are so terribly like ourselves, and so like Chimpanzees at the same time, and so lofty and high minded, with their little shelves of classics and clean china and nice check curtains and purity that I can't see why its all wrong. We tried to imagine you there, snipping their heads off with something very witty.

Well, I shall read Queen Victoria and try to see how its done. I see the New Republic is publishing it, and it's an incredible gem, and a masterpiece of prose. I quite believe it, though my jealousy is twinged – and I thought I had no vices left in me after this week. I thought I was going to read the whole of Shakespeare and I haven't; but I come back longing to get my teeth into your book – Is it quite magnificent? And why weren't you here? And now I must take a last look at the country: which will dissolve me in tears.

Give my love to your mother.

Yr.
V.W.

1181: To Molly MacCarthy   *Monk's House, Rodmell,*
                                    Lewes [Sussex]

[20 June 1921]

My dear Molly,

[...] I am reading the Bride of Lammermoor – by that great man Scott: and Women in Love by D. H. Lawrence, lured on by the portrait of Ottoline which appears from time to time.[1] She has just smashed Lawrence's head open with a ball of lapis lazuli – but then balls are smashed on every other page – cats – cattle – even the fish and the water lilies are at it all day long. There is no suspense or mystery: water is all semen: I get a little bored, and make out the riddles too easily. Only this puzzles me: what does it mean when a woman [Gudrun] does eurythmics in front of a herd of Highland cattle? [...]

Your
V.W.

1. Lawrence drew an unpleasant portrait of Ottoline Morrell, his friend and patroness, in the character of Hermione Roddice.

1196: TO ROGER FRY   *Hogarth House, Richmond*

Oct. 17th 1921

My dear Roger,

Your letter arrived precisely one hour ago, and here I am sitting down to answer it. Whether the answer will be sent is, of course, another matter. Your last – slightly tipsy, very brilliant, sympathetic, inspiring and the best you ever wrote, – sent me flying to the inkpot, but when I read my production and compared it with yours my vanity as an author refused to be pacified.[1] I can't endure that you should write so well. If you want answers let your letters be like bread poultices: anyhow I tore up what was, I now think, the best letter I ever wrote. Would you like it if I dashed off a little sketch of the eclipse of the moon last night, which entirely surpassed your great oil painting of the Rape of Euridyce – or whatever it is?

You will say that you don't have eclipses of the moon on the shores of the Mediterranean:[2] Well, its true we have been having the devil of a time – the influenza. Leonard refusing to go to bed; Nelly [Boxall] like a hen run over, but unhurt, by a motor car; Lottie [Hope] something after the pattern of an intoxicated Jay: the house ringing with laughter and tears. Do other people go on like this, I sometimes wonder, or have we somehow (this includes you, by the way) slipped the coil of civilisation? I mean, we've jumped the lines. There you are bathing naked with 50 prostitutes; yesterday we had Goldie [G. Lowes Dickinson] to tea. I do my best to make him jump the rails. He has written a dialogue upon homosexuality which he won't publish, for fear of the effect upon parents who might send their sons to Kings: and he is writing his autobiography which he won't publish for the same reason.[3] So you see what dominates English literature is the parents of the young men who might be sent to Kings. But Goldie won't see this – having a mystic sense, in which I am deficient. He was as merry as a grig, though; and had forgotten whatever it was – the ruin of civilisation I suppose – that used to distress him.

1. Roger replied: 'You needn't be afraid – your letter reduced me to a state of abject admiration at the Virginian style. I know quite well that this queer business of writing is quite as odd and peculiar as ours of putting paint on. It only looks like ordinary writing because we both use words but we use them quite differently and certainly I'm not taken in by the similarity' (*Letters of Roger Fry*, II, 515, ed. Denys Sutton, 1972).
2. Roger was in St Tropez with Vanessa, Duncan, and the children.
3. Dickinson's *Autobiography* was published in 1973, 40 years after his death.

Tonight we go to Weybridge to dine with Mrs Forster[1] and read an address upon article 22 of the Covenant. Wells[2] has asked us to a party. George Booth[3] has asked us to another. Life, as you see, whizzes by with incredible rapidity, and its all I can do to cling to my arm chair in Richmond, and add page upon page to a story [*Jacob's Room*] which you wont like but will have to say you do. That reminds me of the Nation; of Murry;[4] of Sydney; of a thousand things which I long to say but can't see how to get in on this sheet of paper. Murry has bred in me a vein of Grub Street spite which I never thought to feel in the flesh. He has brought out a little book of those clay-cold castrated costive comatose poems[5] which he has the impertinence to dedicate to Hardy in terms which suggest that Hardy has adopted him as his spiritual son. Thank God, he is soundly drubbed in the newspapers. But his article on you has drawn his fangs for ever; he has no sting: all one hopes is that he may bite each one of us in turn before he is finally discredited and shuffled off to some 10th rate Parisian Café, where you'll find him, 20 years hence, laying down the law to the illegitimate children of Alaister Crawley,[6] Wyndham Lewis, and James Joyce. Eliot says that Joyce's novel [*Ulysses*] is the greatest work of the age – Lytton says he doesn't mean to read it. Clive says – well, Clive says that Mary Hutchinson has a dressmaker who would make me look like other people. Clive has cut his hair, drinks wine only once a day, says eggs and sausages is his favourite dish, and comes to Richmond to confess his sins – after which, I suppose, he sins them worse than ever. But he is trying to reform.

Love to Nessa – I don't write to her on principle. Nor do I read over what I have written to you: but now, send me another.

V.W.

1. Morgan's mother, Alice Forster; he was at this time in India.
2. The Woolfs knew H. G. Wells (1866–1946) chiefly because of his and Leonard's overlapping political interests.
3. The shipowner, George Booth (1877–1971), son of Charles Booth, and known to Virginia in her youth.
4. John Middleton Murry had published an unflattering article on Fry's *Some Architectural Heresies of a Painter* in the *Nation and Athenaeum* for 27 August 1921.
5. *Poems: 1916–20.*
6. Aleister Crowley (1875–1947), an undistinguished poet and a Satanist who proclaimed himself the Beast from the Book of Revelations.

1200: To Dorothea Stephen[1]   [*Hogarth House, Richmond*]

[28? October 1921]

My dear Dorothea;

[...] Your view that one cannot ask a friend who has put aside the recognised conventions about marriage to one's house because of outsiders and servants seems to me incomprehensible. You, for example, accept a religion which I and my servants, who are both agnostics, think wrong and indeed pernicious. Am I therefore to forbid you to come here for my servants sake? Yet I am sure you agree with me that religious beliefs are of far greater importance than social conventions. I am quite willing to suppose that all you said to Vanessa was dictated by kindness and good will, though I do not think it struck her quite in the same way. Anyhow my point is different – it is simply that I could not let you come here without saying first that I entirely sympathise with Vanessa's views and conduct – since, for your own reasons, you have drawn attention to them. If after this you like to come with Katharine, by all means do; and I will risk not only my own morals but my cook's.

Yours affly. V.W.

1204: To Vanessa Bell   *Hogarth House [Richmond]*

Sunday, Nov. 13th 1921

Dearest,

[...] But you want to hear about Dorothea [Stephen]. I enclose a copy of the letters. I don't see that I was indiscreet; and I am sure I triumphed; but only with the mind. She came to tea, of course, with Kate; devoured huge quantities of muffin and cake; and so oppressed me with her moral depravity – her sheer repulsiveness and obtuseness and stodge – that I was practically fainting. Really, she makes one dizzy with dislike. It all came over me at the first sight of her – She said how d'y do in her condescending way, and began to eat like a poor woman at a charity tea, fast, stealthily, every crumb, thanking me with insincere sweetness; but happily Leonard had her. He loathed her. They talked about Ceylon. Meanwhile poor dear old Kate half blind, all blurred and

1. Virginia's cousin (1871–1965) was a missionary in India. Her sister Katherine (1856–1924) had been the Principal of Newnham College, Cambridge.

worn and misty, kept eating butter by mistake for bread and putting her cup down on the tea pot, crunched up in her chair, with her hat over her eyes, and those good leather gloves that she always wears, and shoes like some old statues. She told me about Laura;[1] who is the same as ever, and never stops talking, and occasionally says, 'I told him to go away' or 'Put it down, then', quite sensibly; but the rest is unintelligible. Then I was accosted by Dorothea. 'Virginia, do you like having that book about the Queen [Lytton's *Queen Victoria*] dedicated to you? I should. It seems to me a very intimate kind of book. But I do not know that I should like the Brahmans to read it, or the Americans. You see, we can laugh in the right places, because we understand; they would laugh in the wrong, because they do not understand. I should not like that.' Does that bring her back to you? – her odious selfcomplacency; her extreme brutality – I felt as if she had a thick stick as well as a thick leg; and if I did anything unseemly she would kick and beat. She lives in a village; can't talk a word of the language, which is Candarese; learns sanskrit with a pundit, and intends to expound the fallacies of Buddha. I pretended that I had not heard of her book.[2] Being excessively vain, she was furious. 'Then you do not read your Literary Supplement. There was a very long review of me there – by an exceedingly ignorant man. I also had one in the Indian Observer. That was slightly more intelligent.' As she stumped out of the house she drew herself up, pressed her hands to her forehead and muttered some gibberish which she said was the Eastern form of farewell upon leaving a dear friend for some time. 'How long will it be?' I asked. 'Five years' she replied. – Thank God! [. . .]

Yr
B.

1. Laura Stephen (1870–1945) was the only child of Leslie Stephen's first marriage, to Harriet Thackeray, a daughter of the novelist. The contemporary descriptions do not make clear what was wrong with Laura, but it seems more likely that she was psychotic than mentally retarded, as the Stephens seemed to think. At any rate, some of Virginia's earliest memories were of Laura's bizarre behaviour. She had for years been living in an institution, where Virginia seems never to have visited her.
2. *Indian Thought* (1918).

1922–1923

In 1922 Virginia was 40. The year began with illness. Physical symptoms, such as headache and 'flu, merged into mental ones. As in the past, Virginia's recovery was slow, and in fact she was ill several times during the year. It may have been her own illness that made her particularly compassionate to sick friends, to whom she wrote some of her best letters. One such correspondence stands out: the letters to the French painter Jacques Raverat, who suffered from multiple sclerosis.

Another significant friendship that was sustained largely by letters was with Gerald Brenan, who lived in Spain, but came to England to pursue his love of Carrington. The Woolfs visited him in a remote part of Andalusia. Virginia took a leading role in trying to help her friend T. S. Eliot break away from financial dependence on his bank job in order to write full time. At the end of 1922 Virginia met Vita Sackville-West, but the event contained nothing that signalled their later intimacy.

Convinced that with Jacob's Room *she had found her own voice, Virginia continued to develop her kind of novel in* Mrs Dalloway. *She was aware, as she told her friends, of the accompanying voices of Proust and Joyce. Leonard's appointment as literary editor of the* Nation *enlarged the cultural influence of both Woolfs.*

1210: To E. M. Forster   *Hogarth House, Richmond*

21st Jan: 1922

My dear Morgan,

It was a great pleasure to get your letter [from India]. I meet Goldie [Dickinson] at dinner and I say 'I've just had a letter from Morgan' 'Ah, what wonderful letters he writes!' says Goldie. Clive and Maynard, who are the other guests at table, feel jealous, as I intended they should.

Does this present Bloomsbury with sufficient force? Two days later I was stricken with the influenza, and here I am, a fortnight later, still in bed, though privileged to take a stroll in the sun, for half an hour – after lunch.

But its not going to be sunny today.

Writing is still like heaving bricks over a wall; so you must interpret with your usual sympathy. I should like to growl to you about all this damned lying in bed and doing nothing, and getting up and writing half a page and going to bed again. I've wasted 5 whole years (I count) doing it; so you must call me 35 – not 40 – and expect rather less from me. Not that I haven't picked up something from my insanities and all the rest. Indeed, I suspect they've done instead of religion. But this is a difficult point. [. . .]

Every one is reading Proust. I sit silent and hear their reports. It seems to be a tremendous experience, but I'm shivering on the brink, and waiting to be submerged with a horrid sort of notion that I shall go down and down and down and perhaps never come up again.[1] [. . .]

So good bye, and write to me again. I am feeling ever so much better since beginning this letter.[2]

Yours ever
Virginia

1218: To Vanessa Bell   *Hogarth House [Richmond]*

Monday, Feb. 20th, 1922

Dearest Dolphin,

[. . .] Yes, I was rather depressed when you saw me – What it comes to is this: you say 'I do think you lead a dull respectable absurd life – lots of money, no children, everything so settled: and conventional. Look at me now – only sixpence a year – lovers – Paris – life – love – art – excitement – God! I must be off'. This leaves me in tears. [. . .]

1228: To Janet Case   *Hogarth House, Richmond*

March 20th 1922

My dear Janet,

[. . .] Literature still survives. I've not read K. Mansfield [*The Garden Party*], and don't mean to. I read Bliss; and it was so brilliant, – so hard,

---

1. See Letter 1244.
2. In fact, Virginia was quite seriously ill during January, February and March, first with 'flu, then with a chronic, low-grade temperature and an irregularity of her heartbeat.

and so shallow, and so sentimental that I had to rush to the bookcase for something to drink. Shakespeare, Conrad, even Virginia Woolf. But she takes in all the reviewers, and I daresay I'm wrong (don't be taken in by *that* display of modesty.) Middleton M[urry]. is a posturing Byronic little man; pale; penetrating: with bad teeth; histrionic; an egoist; not, I think, very honest; but a good journalist, and works like a horse, and writes the poetry a very old hack might write – but this is spiteful. [. . .]

Yr V.W.

1239: TO CLIVE BELL   *Monks House, Rodmell,*
                                       Lewes [Sussex]

Good Friday [14 April 1922]

Dearest Clive,

This is the sixth letter I have written this evening, my principle being, as you observe, to keep the treat for the last; only by the time one's ordered the coffee and politely bandied compliments with the aristocracies of birth and intellect – [Nelly] Cecil's and [H.G.] Wells – (see how proud I am!) and addressed a perhaps too familiar gossip to Tom Eliot, and also dashed off a kind of one syllable, one idea, one page epistle to the Homeopathic Hospital in Great Ormond Street[1] one has small control of pen, ink, grammar, or manner. Do you like very long sentences that cant be read in a breath? I do. It's part of my anti-naturalistic bias.

Now Mr Joyce . . . yes, I have fallen; to the extent of four pounds too. I have him on the table. His pages are cut. Leonard is already 30 pages deep. I look, and sip, and shudder. But why do I not simply attend to business, which is to thank you for the chocolates – How I relish these old world observances! You shall have a skyblue valentine next 14th of February. Indeed, indeed, you are too good. It sends me back to the old days of Peter Studd[2] and sugar tongs: yes, in the old days there were sugar plums, and little tongses, and now there is Wyndham Lewises and Tonks.[3] Did you read the Herald? What is the psychology of the underworld? What scurvy of the soul are they afflicted with that they

---

1. Where her maid, Lottie Hope, was recuperating from surgery.
2. Arthur Studd (1863–1919), the artist and collector, who was a friend of Virginia's family at Hyde Park Gate.
3. Henry Tonks (1862–1937), the painter.

must scratch in public? These questions are mere rhetoric, addressed to miles of sodden downs and pouring rain, for I shan't get an answer; and did I ever wring a word from you about your play?[1] True, I was stirred by the white bosoms of your actresses: Diana, Pamela, Olga, and the rest. I like to stitch a bright page to my sober one of Good Friday bells, and a child's funeral, now being despatched in the rain. Mr Deadman[2] dug the grave – and oh God! – you said a bitch was on heat for 3 days: its a fortnight. We let ours loose; she was lined in the churchyard by the Vicar's pomeranian, Jimmy, who had lived chaste for 10 years as the Vicar's wife told Nelly; 'and now he's lost' she said – 'running wild in the Brooks' and indeed they didn't catch him till eleven that night. The village rings with the scandal, in passion week too.

Yrs
V.W.

1244: To Roger Fry   *Hogarth House, Paradise Road,*
                                      Richmond, Surrey

Saturday [6 May 1922]

My dear Roger,

[...] Here I am sweating out streams of rheumish matter from eyes, mouth, ears, solely in order to attend your lecture. I have the most violent cold in the whole parish. Proust's fat volume comes in very handy. Last night I started on vol 2 [*A l'Ombre des jeunes filles en fleurs*] of him (the novel) and propose to sink myself in it all day. Scott Moncrieff[3] wants me to say a few words in an album of admiration – will you collaborate? If so, I will: not otherwise.

But Proust so titillates my own desire for expression that I can hardly set out the sentence. Oh if I could write like that! I cry. And at the moment such is the astonishing vibration and saturation and intensification that he procures – theres something sexual in it – that I feel I *can* write like that, and seize my pen and then I *can't* write like that. Scarcely

---

1. On 9 April Virginia had written to Clive about his farcical comedy in three acts, *Love and Liberty*. It was not performed or published.
2. William Dedman, the Rodmell village sexton, who worked in the garden at Monk's House, and whose wife sometimes cooked and cleaned for the Woolfs when they were in Sussex.
3. C. K. Scott-Moncrieff (1889–1930), who was translating *A la Recherche du Temps Perdu* into English. His tribute to Proust has not been found.

anyone so stimulates the nerves of language in me: it becomes an obsession. But I must return to Swann. [...]

> Ever your
> V.W.

1250: To Janet Case   *Hogarth [House, Richmond]*

Sunday [21 May 1922]

My dear Janet,

[...] We've been sitting in the Park and listening to the Band and having a terrific argument about Shaw. Leonard says we owe a great deal to Shaw. I say that he only influenced the outer fringe of morality. Leonard says that the shop girls wouldn't be listening to the Band with their young men if it weren't for Shaw. I say the human heart is touched only by the poets. Leonard says rot, I say damn. Then we go home. Leonard says I'm narrow. I say he's stunted. But don't you agree with me that the Edwardians, from 1895 to 1914, made a pretty poor show. By the Edwardians, I mean Shaw, Wells, Galsworthy, the Webbs, Arnold Bennett. We Georgians have our work cut out for us, you see. There's not a single living writer (English) I respect: so you see, I have to read the Russians: but here I must stop. I just throw this out for you to think about, under the trees. How does one come by one's morality? Surely by reading the poets. And we've got no poets. Does that throw light upon anything? Consider the Webbs – That woman has the impertinence to say that I'm a-moral: the truth being that if Mrs Webb had been a good woman, Mrs Woolf would have been a better. Orphans is what I say we are – we Georgians – but I must stop.

1275: To Lady Ottoline Morrell   *Monk's House, Rodmell,*
Lewes [Sussex]

Aug. 18th [1922]

My dear Ottoline,

[...] Poor Rebecca Wests novel[1] bursts like an over stuffed sausage.

1. The novelist, journalist, critic, and feminist, who was born Cicily Fairfield (1892–1983), and took her pseudonym from the Ibsen character she played during her youthful foray into acting. Her first book was a study of Henry James (1916), and Virginia was now reading her second novel, *The Judge* (1922). West's personal life interested people too. As a young woman she had fallen in love with the already married H. G. Wells, and was raising their child, Anthony West.

She pours it all in; and one is covered with flying particles; indeed I had hastily to tie the judge tight and send it back to Mudies [Library] half finished. But this irreticence does not make me think any the worse of her human qualities. I imagine she talks a great deal. Mary Hutchinson met her in a furniture shop and says she looked like a large wet dog, in a waterproof, very shaggy. I cannot write with this debauched pen, but I must stumble along and tell you that I do admire poor old Henry [James], and actually read through the Wings of a Dove [1902] last summer, and thought it such an amazing acrobatic feat, partly of his, partly of mine, that I now look upon myself and Henry James as partners in merit. I made it all out. But I felt very ill for some time afterwards. I am now reading Joyce, and my impression, after 200 out of 700 pages, is that the poor young man has only got the dregs of a mind compared even with George Meredith. I mean if you could weigh the meaning on Joyces page it would be about 10 times as light as on Henry James'.

They say it gets a little heavier. It is true that I prepared myself, owing to Tom [Eliot], for a gigantic effort; and behold the bucket is almost empty.

I tremble as I write. I shall be struck down by the wrath of God. Next I go on to Proust; and then – I think something old. [. . .]

V.W.

1280: To Jacques Raverat[1]   *Monks House, Rodmell,*
                                       Lewes [Sussex]

Aug. 25th [1922]

Dear Jacques,

Anyhow you haven't forgotten one feature in your old friend's character – vanity. I enjoyed your praises[2] immensely, and Gwen's, and

1. The French painter Jacques Raverat (1885–1925) had been at Cambridge with the Neo-Pagans and, after pursuing Ka Cox, had married another of their number, Virginia's old friend, the painter Gwen Darwin. They lived near Vence in the Alpes Maritimes, where Jacques was nearing the end of his long struggle with multiple sclerosis. The disease left him unable to paint or, finally, to write except by dictation to his wife. Always extremely sympathetic to sick people, Virginia wrote to him regularly and intimately during this time, even though she had not seen him for years and never knew him particularly well.
2. Of *Monday or Tuesday*, a collection of Virginia's stories which the Woolfs published in March 1921 as The Hogarth Press's seventeenth publication.

felt quite set up for many days. I rather expect abuse for that book. Now you must give me your opinion of my novel [*Jacob's Room*] which comes out soon – foreigner you may be, but you're a highly interesting character still.

Shall we really come out sometime next January? Could you find us rooms in your village? We talk perpetually of going abroad, but I want to settle in where one can read and write, and if you were there it would be great fun. Then perhaps we could talk off some of our arrears. I feel a little shy, do you? Not fundamentally, superficially. My impression is that we used to argue a great deal about the way we live. Now we have solved all that. You have a house in France, and we in Richmond. It's rather nice, shabby, ancient, very solid and incredibly untidy (I'm talking of Hogarth House) but then we print all over the place. One of Ka's gallant youths – I mean the sort of person Ka used to have about – is our partner [Ralph Partridge]. We meet at lunch and tea. We gossip. The poor young man tries to tell us what Lytton Strachey thinks about Proust (he lives with Lytton and has married Carrington). Then I go up to London: walk the streets, on the excuse of buying something – nothing so amazing; drop in to tea at the 1917 Club, where one generally falls into gloom at the extreme insignificance, dowdiness, of the intellectual race – darkies, actresses, cranks, Alix, James[1] – that's the sort of creature one meets there. Well, I don't boast. I'm only one of them myself, but inwardly one still feels young and arrogant and frightfully sharp set. I can't resist boasting still – can you? and trying to talk people down. Still, we have grown a little mellow. Everyone in Gordon Square is now famous.

Clive has taken to high society. I assure you, he's a raging success, and his bon mots are quoted by lovely but incredibly silly ladies. Really they give parties to meet Clive Bell. Maynard of course scarcely belongs to private life any more, save that he has fallen in love with Lydia Lopokhova,[2] which is, to me, endearing. Nessa and Duncan potter along in extreme obscurity. That is all I can think of at the moment, and I am afraid that it may sound vague and dismal in your ears. The truth is

1. In 1920 Alix Sargant-Florence (1892–1973) married Lytton's younger brother James Strachey, who was on the fringe of the Neo-Pagans, and they both went to Vienna to train as psychoanalysts under Freud.
2. Lydia Lopokova (1891–1981) had captured London, and most especially Maynard Keynes, as one of the stars of Diaghilev's ballet company. Keynes, who was at this time leading a busy life as an academic, an editor, and a respected author on international politics and economics, married Lopokova in 1925.

you must write me a proper letter and expose yourself as I hereby expose myself.

I feel that in the great age of the world, before this present puling generation had come along, you and I and that remarkable figure Gwen Darwin were all congenial spirits. By the way you'll have to give up calling Woolf Woolf: Leonard, that is his name. I assure you, I couldn't have married anyone else – But when Ka praises Will the sound is unpleasant in my ears. So I refrain. I have nothing whatever to say against Ka and Will. At first sight he is a mere sandhopper; but later I think he has some sort of spine – indeed, he's a muscular little man, considering his size. Ka, of course, keeps a medicine chest and doses the village, and gets into a blue dress trimmed with fur for tea, when county motor cars arrive, and she is much in her element. Is this malicious? Slightly, perhaps, but you will understand.

I wish I could discuss the art of writing with you at the present moment. I am ashamed, or perhaps proud, to say how much of my time is spent in thinking, thinking, thinking about literature. It is a dangerous seed to plant in your children. Still, I doubt whether anything else in life is much worth having – so there is the philosophy of an old woman of 40. Do you maintain that one can think about painting? Is Gwen Raverat still so extreme? And what about Lady Darwin [Jacques' mother-in-law] and dear poor pin-cushion Eily?[1]

But I am drivelling. Tell me when you write if there are any good French books, and say if you would like me to send you anything from England.

Love to Gwen,
Yours ever,
Virginia Woolf

1303: TO ROGER FRY   *Hogarth House, Paradise Road,*
                            Richmond, Surrey

Sunday Oct. 22nd 1922

My dear Roger,

I am racking my brains to think of some gossip to send you but as I

---

1. Elinor Monsell (d. 1954), one of Virginia's friends in her youth, was married to Gwen's cousin, Bernard Darwin, the writer on golf.

suppose this to mean something spicy – Dora Sanger[1] for example, raping Goldie [Dickinson] in Piccadilly, or Ottoline redeeming her soul by some act of unparalleled magnanimity – I wait and wait – sitting over the fire, Lottie [Hope] chattering about the best way to toast muffins and how the woman next door has had half her toe cut off because of an ingrowing nail; rain, I suppose, falling; and the autumnal church bells beginning as usual, it being now 20 minutes to six, to summon the Christians – an outrage upon my peace which always makes my gorge rise with indignation.

I have been involved in an appalling shindy about poor Tom Eliot's annuity.[2] Were you asked to subscribe £10 a year towards it? The story is long, and reflects credit upon no one save myself: but the upshot of it is that Tom remains in the Bank, and I am in correspondence with Ezra Pound. A complete muddle, as you may imagine. But Tom's psychology fascinates and astounds. There he has let us all go on writing and appealing for the past 6 months, and at last steps out and says he will take nothing less than £500 a year – very sensible, but why not say so at first; and why twist and anguish and almost suffocate with humiliation at the mere mention of money? Its on a par with not pump shipping[3] before your wife. Very American, I expect; and the more I see of that race the more I thank God for my British blood, which does at any rate preserve one from wearing 3 waistcoats; enamel buttons on one's overcoat, and keeping one's eyes perpetually shut – like Ezra Pound.

Morgan and Herbert Read[4] were dining here last night, and Read, who has been in the Wyndham Lewis pigsty without wallowing in it, had some amazing stories of the brutes. Lewis now paints in a shed

1. Dora Sanger (*née* Pease, 1865–1955) had been a student at Newnham College and a teacher before marrying the barrister Charles Sanger. She concerned herself with social causes throughout the world and was considered by Virginia to be rather too morally upright and condescending.

2. In July Ottoline Morrell had enlisted Virginia's help in establishing the Eliot Fellowship Fund, a complement to the Bel Esprit project begun for his friend by the American poet Ezra Pound (1885–1972). The Eliot Fund committee sought to raise enough money to enable T. S. Eliot to leave his job at Lloyd's Bank and devote himself to writing. Virginia worked hard towards this goal, but Eliot was vacillating and evasive. In any event, the plan did not succeed, and five years after it was begun, the money was returned to the subscribers.

3. 'Pumping ship', a now obsolescent term for urinating.

4. The art historian and critic (1893–1968), who was then Assistant Keeper in the Victoria and Albert Museum.

behind a curtain – rites are gone through before you enter; but this is all
very dull and out of date, and I'm sure Oscar Wilde did it all much better.
Morgan was very charming, and we went a walk in Richmond Park
together and talked entirely about very very minute domestic details:
the cat; the maid; the cousin; and Miss Partridge of Ashstead. He is
finishing his novel,[1] and utterly refuses to stay with the Asquiths[2] or
dine with Lady Colefax.[3]

Margery[4] was here the other night – your sister I mean, not Marjorie
Strachey who ramps in Gordon Square – a menagerie without cages.
The animals prowl in and out, and Nessa was laying the law down the
other night with some force. If only she could never see any of her
friends, she says, life might be tolerable: but there's Karin [Stephen],
there's Mary Hutch[inson]: there's the telephone, there's Kitty Maxse
falling over the bannisters and killing herself – ought one to write to
Susan Lushington [her sister]? No, one would say the wrong thing. Still
it seems a pity that Kitty did kill herself: but of course she was an awful
snob. No, one couldn't go on with people like that. One had to make a
break somewhere. Then, of course, in comes Angelica [Bell]; all the
beads are upset on the floor; et cetera, et cetera.

I'm sending you my novel tomorrow – a little reluctantly. It has *some*
merit, but its too much of an experiment. I am buoyed up, as usual, by
the thought that I'm now, at last, going to bring it off – next time. I
suppose one goes on thinking this for ever; and so burrowing deeper
and deeper into whatever it is that perpetually fascinates. Why don't
you come back and explain it? – you are the only person who ever does;
so for God's sake, get perfectly cured, and moderate your activity. It will
accumulate in the cistern, and you can draw it off at leisure. I mean,
you'll paint your masterpiece if you have a rest. But then nothing except
painting and writing is really interesting: and as one's time is limited,
how can one sit and smile?

I wish you would consider, seriously, bringing out a series of

---

1. *A Passage to India* (1924).
2. The Liberal Prime Minister (1908–16), Herbert Asquith (1852–1928), and his wife
   Margot (*née* Tennant, 1864–1945).
3. Sibyl Colefax (d. 1950), wife of Sir Arthur Colefax, KC, was a lively London hostess,
   who had made her house, Argyll House, Chelsea, a centre for political and cultural
   society.
4. Margery Fry (1874–1958), who shared a home with her brother Roger until she
   became Principal of Somerville College, Oxford, in 1926.

modern paintings, with introductions, through the Hogarth Press.[1] The Press takes up all my time, and I ought to be translating Kots Russian,[2] instead of running on like the kitchen tap. I think it is now firm on its legs, and might branch out: I think a shop and gallery combined must come next, but this waits for you.

Yrs V.W.

1310: To Dora Sanger   [*Hogarth House, Richmond*]

[30 October 1922]

My dear Dora,

[. . .] Why do you accuse Leonard of indifference to public affairs? Here he is slaving all day to make the world safe for democracy or some trash like that. Its on the cards he will be Woolf M.P. before long, and I may dedicate my life to tea parties on the terrace. What have you and Charlie done compared with this? I have been telling Charlie on the other page that you must come and see us. I suppose you'll say you haven't time for frivolity, and make off with my matches again, having first said all the disagreeable things you can think of, because you are upset about the Chinese rice pickers and their famines and earthquakes. [. . .]

Yours ever
(with apologies for not writing more
seriously)
Virginia Woolf

1317: To Ralph Partridge   *Hogarth [House, Richmond*]

Friday [10 November 1922]

My dear Ralph,

I think I had better explain why you made me so angry this evening by asking me to see that Leonard did not sell the press during the

---

1. In 1923 The Hogarth Press published a book of Duncan Grant's paintings, with an introduction by Roger Fry, but the planned series went no further.
2. The collaborative translations begun in 1920 by S. S. Koteliansky with both Virginia and Leonard Woolf continued in 1923 with the publication by The Hogarth Press of *Tolstoi's Love Letters* and *Talks with Tolstoi*, by A. B. Goldenveizer.

weekend to Constables, and why I was further indignant with you for
going on to suggest that we were ready, as you said, to 'sell the press to
the highest bidder.' I suspect that you didn't mean either of these
remarks seriously.

But I think I may have left you with the impression that I am myself
in favour of amalgamation with some big firm in order to increase the
publicity of my own books and profits. If you do think this, you are quite
wrong; but the fault (being angry) may be mine.

What did make my blood boil was your assumption that Leonard
and I are quite ready to be bamboozled with a bargain which would
destroy the character of the press for the sake of money or pride or
convenience; and that you must protect its rights. After all we have
given the press whatever character it may have, and if you're going to
tell me that you care more about it than I do, or know better what's good
for it, I must reply that you're a donkey. You will retaliate by telling me
that I'm another to take your chance remarks seriously. No doubt I am;
but I was left with a feeling that you would base some weekend
discussions upon the assumption that the Woolves are out to make a
good bargain, and that Virginia, consumed with vanity, and blown with
ambition, is going to persuade Leonard etc and etc – In short, that the
days of an independent Hogarth are doomed.

This was not at all my meaning, I assure you.[1]

Yours ever
Virginia Woolf

Tell Carrington, if she is not sick altogether of these fiery quadrupeds
[the Woolfs], that she never did give me the receipt for the toffee; which
might sweeten my temper.

---

1. Behind this letter lies what Leonard saw as the ambiguous position of The Hogarth
   Press as neither the hobby the Woolfs had originally envisaged, nor yet the
   commercial, professional publisher towards which it was headed. Some of the books
   were still being printed at home by Leonard, Virginia and Ralph, but the work was
   increasingly jobbed out to commercial printers. At this time, there had been several
   approaches, including ones from Constable and Heinemann, offering amalgamation
   with The Hogarth Press. The Woolfs ultimately refused all the offers in order to
   preserve their independence in choosing whom to publish, but, realising that the
   Press needed to become a full-time venture, brought in some additional help in
   January. The decision to keep the Press independent was also based on its ability to
   give Virginia freedom as a writer, for the Press had, with *Jacob's Room*, begun to
   publish her novels.

1330: TO JACQUES RAVERAT   *Hogarth House, Paradise Road,*
                            Richmond, Surrey

Dec. 10 1922

My dear Jacques,

It was very nice to get your letter – to which Gwen's handwriting adds an unmistakable smack of that lost but unforgotten woman. I'm glad you liked Jacob better than the other novels; one always wishes the last to be best. I'm not blind, though, to its imperfections – indeed it is more an experiment than an achievement. Is your art as chaotic as ours? I feel that for us writers the only chance now is to go out into the desert and *peer* about, like devoted scapegoats, for some sign of a path. I expect you got through your discoveries sometime earlier. [. . .]

I heard praises of your pictures from Roger Fry the other night. He thinks you are now doing the interesting things – but I don't know if his praises, or any one's praises, mean much to you. We are so lonely and separated in our adventures as writers and painters. I never dare praise pictures, though I have my own opinions. Raspail was spelt wrong [in *Jacob's Room*] owing to Duncan and Vanessa, whom I consulted. A letter more or less means nothing to them. Toads are (essentially) insects, I maintain. Women may be worse, or may be better, than men, but surely the opinions of the writer of Jacobs Room on that point, or any other, are not *my* opinions. This is a very old quarrel though.

I'm glad you are fat; for then you are warm and mellow and generous and creative. I find that unless I weigh 9½ stones I hear voices and see visions and can neither write nor sleep. It is a necessity, I suppose, to part with youth and beauty, but I think there are compensations. [. . .]

Yours ever,
Virginia Woolf

1337: TO GERALD BRENAN[1]   *Monk's House, Rodmell,*
                             Near Lewes, Sussex

Christmas Day 1922

Dear Gerald,

[. . .] I have been thinking a great deal about what you say of writing

1. Gerald Brenan (1894–1987) had become a close friend of Ralph Partridge during the war. Through him, Brenan met Carrington, with whom he was in love for years. In

novels. One must renounce, you say. I can do better than write novels, you say. I don't altogether understand. I don't see how to write a book without people in it. Perhaps you mean that one ought not to attempt a 'view of life'? – one ought to limit oneself to one's own sensations – at a quartet for instance; one ought to be lyrical, descriptive: but not set people in motion, and attempt to enter them, and give them impact and volume? Ah, but I'm doomed! As a matter of fact, I think that we all are. It is not possible now, and never will be, to say I renounce. Nor would it be a good thing for literature were it possible. This generation must break its neck in order that the next may have smooth going. For I agree with you that nothing is going to be achieved by us. Fragments – paragraphs – a page perhaps: but no more. Joyce to me seems strewn with disaster. I can't even see, as you see, his triumphs. A gallant approach, that is all that is obvious to me: then the usual smash and splinters (I have only read him, partly, once). The human soul, it seems to me, orientates itself afresh every now and then. It is doing so now. No one can see it whole, therefore. The best of us catch a glimpse of a nose, a shoulder, something turning away, always in movement. Still, it seems better to me to catch this glimpse, than to sit down with Hugh Walpole,[1] Wells, etc. etc. and make large oil paintings of fabulous fleshy monsters complete from top to toe. Of course, being under 30, this does not apply to you. To you, something more complete may be vouchsafed. If so, it will be partly because I, and some others, have made our attempts first. I have wandered from the point. Never mind. I am only scribbling, more to amuse myself than you, who may never read, or understand: for I am doubtful whether people, the best disposed towards each other, are capable of more than an intermittent signal as they forge past – a sentimental metaphor, leading obviously to ships, and night and storm and reefs and rocks, and the obscured, uncompassionate moon. I wish I had your letter for I could then go ahead; without so many jerks.

You said you were very wretched, didn't you? You described your liver rotting, and how you read all night, about the early fathers; and then walked, and saw the dawn. But were wretched, and tore up all you

1. The best-selling novelist Hugh Walpole (1884–1941), who was to become one of Virginia's friends.

1920 he had gone to live in the remote mountains of Granada in Spain, in order to pursue a life of writing. During one of his visits to England, in May 1922, the Woolfs had met him at Tidmarsh, and Virginia had been impressed by the young man's intense devotion to literature.

wrote, and felt you could never, never write – and compared this state of yours with mine, which you imagine to be secure, rooted, benevolent, industrious – you did not say dull – but somehow unattainable, and I daresay, unreal. But you must reflect that I am 40: further, every 10 years, at 20, again at 30, such agony of different sorts possessed me that not content with rambling and reading I did most emphatically attempt to end it all; and should have been often thankful, if by stepping on one flagstone rather than another I could have been annihilated where I stood. I say this partly in vanity that you may not think me insipid; partly as a token (one of those flying signals out of the night and so on) that so we live, all of us who feel and reflect, with recurring cataclysms of horror: starting up in the night in agony: Every ten years brings, I suppose, one of those private orientations which match the vast one which is, to my mind, general now in the race. I mean, life has to be sloughed: has to be faced: to be rejected; then accepted on new terms with rapture. And so on, and so on; till you are 40, when the only problem is how to grasp it tighter and tighter to you, so quick it seems to slip, and so infinitely desirable is it.

As for writing, at 30 I was still writing, reading; tearing up industriously. I had not published a word (save reviews). I despaired. Perhaps at that age one is really most a writer. Then one cannot write, not for lack of skill, but because the object is too near, too vast. I think perhaps it must recede before one can take a pen to it. At any rate, at 20, 30, 40, and I've no doubt 50, 60, and 70, that to me is the task; not particularly noble or heroic, as I see it in my own case, for all my inclinations are to write; but the object of adoration to me, when there comes along someone capable of achieving – if only the page or paragraph; for there are no teachers, saints, prophets, good people, but the artists – as you said – But the last sentence is hopelessly unintelligible. Indeed, I am getting to the end of my letter writing capacity. I have many more things to say; but they cower under their coverlets, and nothing remains but to stare at the fire, and finger some book till the ideas freshen within me, or they once more become impartible.

I think, too, there is a great deal of excitement and fun and pure pleasure and brilliance in one's fellow creatures. I'm not sure that you shouldn't desert your mountain, take your chance, and adventure with your human faculties – friendships, conversations, relations, the mere daily intercourse. Why do young men hold books up before their eyes so long? French literature falls like a blue tint over the landscape.

But I am not saying what I mean, and had better stop. Only you must write to me again – anything that occurs to you – And what about something for the Hogarth Press?[1]

Leonard adds his wishes to mine for the future.

Yours
Virginia Woolf

P.S.

I add a postscript, which is intended to explain why I say that one must not renounce. I think I mean that beauty, which you say I sometimes achieve, is only got by the failure to get it; by grinding all the flints together; by facing what must be humiliation – the things one can't do – To aim at beauty deliberately, without this apparently insensate struggle, would result, I think, in little daisies and forget-me-nots – simpering sweetnesses – true love knots – But I agree that one must (we, in our generation must) renounce finally the achievement of the greater beauty: the beauty which comes from completeness, in such books as War and Peace, and Stendhal I suppose, and some of Jane Austen; and Sterne; and I rather suspect in Proust, of whom I have only read one volume. Only now that I have written this, I doubt its truth. Are we not always hoping? and though we fail every time, surely we do not fail so completely as we should have failed if we were not in the beginning, prepared to attack the whole. One must renounce, when the book is finished; but not before it is begun. Excuse me for boring on: you may have said nothing of the kind. I was wondering to myself why it is that though I try sometimes to limit myself to the thing I do well, I am always drawn on and on, by human beings, I think, out of the little circle of safety, on and on, to the whirlpools; when I go under.

---

1. Gerald Brenan published nothing with The Hogarth Press, but he continued to write and, beginning in the forties, published works on Spain, novels and memoirs which earned him great respect, particularly in his adopted country.

1341: To V. Sackville-West[1] *Hogarth House, Paradise Road, Richmond, Surrey*

3rd Jan. [1923]

Dear Mrs Nicolson,

I should never have dared to dun you if I had known the magnificence of the book. Really, I am ashamed, and would like to say that copies of all my books are at your service if you raise a finger – but they look stout and sloppy and shabby. There is nothing I enjoy more than family histories, so I am falling upon Knole the first moment I get.

I am shameless enough to hope that the poems[2] won't go to the wrong address. I was prepared to sniff at Eddie's Georgians,[3] and so I did; but not at yours.

I wonder if you would come and dine with us? Say Monday 8th, 7.45.

We don't dine so much as picnic, as the press has got into the larder and into the dining room, and we never dress.

I would look up a train, and give you directions if you can come, as I hope.

Yours very sincerely
Virginia Woolf

1348: To Molly MacCarthy *Hogarth House, Paradise Road, Richmond, Surrey*

Friday [19 January 1923]

Dearest Molly,

I was just taking up my pen when struck down by the usual old temperature, which sinks my head fathoms deep in the mud. Ought one not to find one's father's eyes when one sinks fathoms deep [*The Tempest*, I, ii]? But no such luck.

1. The poet, novelist and gardener Victoria ('Vita') Sackville-West (1892–1962) was the daughter of the 3rd Baron Sackville and the wife of the diplomat and author Harold Nicolson (1886–1968). She was destined to become, next to Vanessa, Virginia's greatest female friend. They first met on 14 December, dining with Clive Bell. Vita had just published the history of her family, *Knole and the Sackvilles*, which she sent Virginia.
2. Vita's *Orchard and Vineyard* (1921).
3. The fifth and last volume of *Georgian Poetry* (1922), an annual anthology of contemporary verse edited by Edward Marsh (1872–1953).

This is, primarily, in answer to your letter to the Hog. Press. Of course we will bully the old wretch.[1] Perpetual letters? Telegrams? Telephone? What do you advise? He must be coerced. I hate to think that all his words vanish into the cesspool (a horrid figure of speech – but then, I sometimes think we ladies, of the old guard, you and I, that is, the solitary survivors, ought to invigorate our language a little) – I've been talking to the younger generation all the afternoon. They are like crude hard green apples: no halo, mildew or blight. Seduced at 15, life has no holes and corners for them. I admire, but deplore. Such an old maid, they make me feel. 'And how do you manage not- not - not - to have children?' I ask. 'Oh, we read Mary Stopes of course.'[2] Figure to yourself my dear Molly – before taking their virginity, the young men of our time produce marked copies of Stopes! Astonishing! Think of Aunt Gussie![3]

This is all incoherent drivvle: but then I'm above normal. You want news of that old bubble, now flown over St Paul's and far away, Nessa's party. Well, we were all awfully nice: I kept thinking of Shakespeare. We were so mellowly and good fellowly: not any intensity or bitterness, but all serene and melodious. Miss Sands; Sickert;[4] Roger [Fry]; then dancing, acting; it's a great thing to have done with copulation and to be merely a bag of pot pourri. Do you recognise any of your friends in that? Bunny Garnett went away and had a son the very next morning.[5] Everyone was so clever too. They sang. Marjorie Strachey acted, and her obscenity was really sublime. I want very much to come down. I figure us two, old friends, ladies, straying hand in hand down the glades

1. Desmond MacCarthy, whose friends regularly urged him to organise his writings into book form. Virginia never persuaded him to publish a book with The Hogarth Press.
2. Dr Marie Stopes, author of *Married Love* and *Wise Parenthood*, both published in 1918. The latter dealt with contraception and was a huge popular success.
3. Mrs Douglas (Augusta) Freshfield (d. 1911), a sister of Sir Richmond Ritchie, who married Anne Thackeray. She was related by marriage to the Stephens, and was Molly MacCarthy's aunt.
4. Ethel Sands (1873–1962) was an American-born painter of independent means, who entertained elegantly at her houses in Normandy and Chelsea. She was a friend of fellow painter Walter Sickert (1860–1942), who was active in some of the London artists' associations, and well known to Roger Fry and the other Bloomsbury painters.
5. David Garnett married Rachel ('Ray') Marshall in 1921. Their son was Richard Duncan Garnett.

of Savernake[1] – talking. Harry Norton was at the party: very very old, no teeth: no flesh, no lusts.[2] I felt that he was nothing but a pouch, a sort of puff ball, gone dry – but so amiable it made one weep. How is Mona Wilson?[3] Please write to me, a diary letter: beginning 'I was woken by a sunbeam at 8 a.m.' going on through every detail until the schoolmaster calls in the evening.

But I must stop.

Ever Yr.
V.W.

1355: To Maynard Keynes   *Hogarth House, Paradise Road, Richmond*

12th Feb. 1922 [*error for* 1923]

Dear Maynard,

May I lay the following facts about [T.S.] Eliot before you? of course in the strictest confidence.

He has now decided to give up the Bank. It is obvious that it is impossible to collect enough money to provide him with anything like a sufficient income. He is anxious therefore to get some permanent job which would bring him in £3 or £400 a year. If possible he would like work in some way connected with literature. Is there any chance that the Nation could give him employment as literary editor,[4] or in any capacity which would bring him in an assured income? I suggested the very vague possibility of such work, and he said it was of all others what he should prefer.

If this is out of the question could you give us any advice or suggestions? He has a degree at Harvard, where he studied philosophy; then went to Paris and Oxford but left without taking a degree. He would prefer not to teach, but would do secretarial or librarian's work. He is clearly getting into a bad state of health, and the efforts of the Eliot

1. The MacCarthys lived at Oare, Wiltshire, near the Savernake Forest.
2. H. T. J. Norton was at this time only 36.
3. The MacCarthys' neighbours in Oare included the writer Mona Wilson.
4. Maynard Keynes, together with a few other Liberals, had just acquired controlling interest of the *Nation & Athenaeum*, and Keynes was to become Chairman of the Board. Because of his financial obligations and his wife's objections, Eliot was reluctant to take the literary editorship. The post went instead to Leonard Woolf.

fund are so slow that it is useless to wait, on the chance that that will eventually support him. At present, the fund would pay him £300 a year, perhaps, for three years or so. If he could rely on a small certain income from regular work he would risk giving up the Bank. If it were not for his wifes constant illness[1] he would have left the Bank before now.

His address is,

9 Clarence Gate Gardens, N.W.1.

I told him I was writing to you.

If there is anything you would like to ask me, I am on the telephone, or would come up.

Please excuse this pestering on my part, which is to relieve my own conscience, for I feel we have made a muddle [of the Eliot Fund] and ought to try and do something sensible if possible.

Yours Ever
Virginia Woolf

He is, of course, extremely anxious that none of this should be talked about.

1365: To Dorothy Brett[2]   *Hogarth House, Paradise Road,*
Richmond, Surrey

March 2nd [1923]

My dear Brett,

No you didn't tire me in the least – of course not. It was selfish of me, I felt, to make you talk about Katherine. I have wanted to so much since she died. But it must be very difficult for you. I've been looking in my diary and see that I must have written to her sometime in March 1921.[3] From what you say, perhaps she never did get my letter. It makes me

1. Vivien Eliot, *née* Haigh-Wood (1888–1947), had married the poet in 1915. Almost immediately she began to suffer from recurrent physical ills of several varieties, most of which seem to have been compounded – or even caused – by a severe mental instability that finally led Eliot to leave her in 1933.
2. The Hon. Dorothy Brett (1883–1977), daughter of the 2nd Viscount Esher, was a painter and a friend of Carrington from their Slade days. She was even closer to Katherine Mansfield, whose death on 9 January of this year had deeply distressed Virginia (see *Diary*, II, 225–8).
3. It was February. See Letter 1167a.

sorrier than ever that I did not simply persist – and yet I like to think that she had not, as I thought, taken some dislike to me, or got tired of hearing from me. I had been meeting [John Middleton] Murry, who was just going to join her, and he said she was lonely, and asked me to write. So I wrote at once, a very long letter, saying that she need only send one line, and I would go on regularly writing. It hurt me that she never answered, and then, as I was telling you, those gossips assured me that this was her game, and so on, and so on; until though I wanted to write, I felt that I no longer knew where we stood together; and so waited to see her – as I thought I certainly should.

I have been typing out her letters this morning,[1] and it is terrible to me to think that I sacrificed anything to this odious gossip. She gave me something no one else can. But here I am being selfish again. No one of my friends knew her, except you; and that is why I cant help going on to you. [. . .]

Ever yours
V.W.

1376: To Vanessa Bell   *Carmen de los Fosos, Generalife, Granada, Spain*[2]

1st April [1923]

Dearest,

We arrived here last night, and are staying with the Temples;[3] she being a Miss McLeod, lord of the Scottish Isles, who says she once met you. Anyhow they're very anxious that you and Roger [Fry] should come here, which I said I would pass on to you at once, and hereby do. It's an awful long journey – and we still have 2 days on mules and in diligences before we reach Gerald's house, up in the Sierra Nevada –

1. For Murry, who published twelve of the thirty in his two-volume edition of Mansfield's letters, 1927–8.
2. The Woolfs were on their way to Gerald Brenan's house in Yegen. It was their first trip abroad since their honeymoon in 1912.
3. Charles Lindsay Temple (1871–1929), formerly Governor of Northern Nigeria. His wife was Olive, daughter of Sir Reginald Macleod, 27th Chief and Baron of Dunvegan, Skye.

mountains, I may tell you,[1] always with snow on them. Nevertheless I am determined never to live long in England again. The rapture of getting into warmth and colour and good sense and general congeniality of temper is so great. I was overcome by the beauty of Dieppe – don't you think we might share a Chateau, so large that we never met? Not to run up against suburbs and old respectable creatures at every step is such a joy. I shall learn French at once.

We had no adventures to speak of. Travelling is very easy. I managed to avoid the Aldous Huxleys[2] who crossed with us. I can't think it right to look precisely like an illustration to Vogue; and I daresay they thought the same t'other way round about us. Spain is quite different from France, but I leave all that for you. There was a great religious festival at Madrid, and stuffed images of great beauty (emotional, not aesthetic) were parading; and Christ was showered under with confetti. Why not bring the children up Roman Catholics? I think it induces to warmth of heart. Gerald is staying here, and we have been walking in wind and rain through the Generalife gardens, which I visited in 1904 [1905] with Adrian [Stephen]. Much has happened since. The Temples are an elderly couple [52 and 37], he racked with malaria, always wrapped in a great coat, and was at Cambridge and knew the Ll[ewelyn] Davies',[3] and used to be taken to Roger's studio in Battersea. He jumped at the mention of him. He said he understood he had become very advanced; but himself stuck to Corot. She is a Scottish gentlewoman, clean, discreet, shabby, with blue eyes like poor Marny's [Margaret Vaughan], but is a woman of character, since her betrothed died exploring Lake Chad, when she was a girl in the Isle of Skye, and was buried (naturally enough) on the spot without a tomb. She at once went to Edinburgh, bought a marble slab, had it engraved, and started for Lake Chad, against the wishes of all her family; deposited it on the very spot and married the governor. Mrs [Margot] Asquith is coming on Tuesday, but we shall be gone.

Leonard and Gerald are at a bull-fight. I am afraid I am not going to be offered any tea. It is a wonderful modern house, with electric

1. Vanessa's lack of basic knowledge was a running joke between the sisters.
2. Virginia had met the novelist Aldous Huxley (1894–1963) at Ottoline Morrell's in 1917. In 1919 he married Maria Nys, a Belgian refugee whom Ottoline had sheltered. His fame began with the publication in 1921 of *Crome Yellow*.
3. Brothers of Margaret Llewelyn Davies, who were educated at Cambridge and known to the Stephens in their youth.

saucepans in every room. Mr Temple is an engineer. I regret to say that I had difficulty with the W.C. this morning. Remember, if you come, to screw the handle round and round – otherwise nothing happens.

I ought to be writing an article for the Nation;[1] but the worst of travelling for writers is that it freezes all their functions. To write to a dolphin is all very well – perhaps though Leonard's terms are rejected. I hope not. I think it might be great fun. Does it strike you that we are all now elderly? – elderly, accomplished, successful, looked up to? It doesn't reach to Granada however. Murry wrote me a wormish letter, by the way, about the differences between us, and our memories and so on. I tried to imitate you, and replied that our differences are too great to admit of any further communication; so that we had better rely on the past. Poor Tom [Eliot] said he was only capable of creeping into the country.[2] His problem still remains – God knows what we can do about it. Please, however, be as discreet as marble. Mary, I gather, is the [person] they most dread[3] – she wrote me a most affectionate letter about looking at the cliffs of Dover and thinking of her, which is more than I get out of some people I could touch with a short stick.

Did you think Rodmell very inferior to Charleston?[4] I suppose so: but then what a pleasure that was! How the Wolves can live here: how stuffy; how ridiculous their decorations are etc etc. That was what Dolphin said to Duncan when they settled in at night.

Yr

B.

1380a: To Mary Hutchinson   *Alicante* [*Spain*]

perhaps Wednesday 18th April [1923]

Dear Mary,

I was much touched to get your letter, and if there had been white cliffs should have looked at them tenderly – but there was only Aldous

---

1. Virginia's article, 'To Spain', was published in the *Nation and Athenaeum* on 5 May 1923 (*Essays*, III, 361), the first issue after its reorganisation under Keynes, with Leonard as literary editor.
2. The Eliots, both in poor health, had taken a cottage in Fishbourne, Sussex. Mainly as a result of his wife's bills, Eliot's financial situation was still precarious.
3. Mary Hutchinson was a friend of the Eliots.
4. During the Woolfs' absence, Vanessa, Duncan and the children stayed at Monk's House.

Huxley's head. It is all a very very long time ago. We have climbed so high, and talked such a lot. I have become a confirmed continentalist, and can't think why we submit to a mitigated version of life at Hammersmith and Richmond. Here it is always fine, always indolent; one drinks coffee, listens to the Band, ships come in, old men spit; last night I did not sleep till 4, because of bugs. At 4 Leonard extricated a camel shaped lump of purple tissue from the hairs of my blanket. It burst with an odious smell into thick blood. So do not expect much continuity, cogency, or clarity from me. I am sitting in a Spanish gentleman's Club, to which travellers are admitted. There is only one old gentleman and his spittoon in the midst of a vast yellow chamber, set tight round the walls with wicker chairs, and in the midst breadths of white marble and vistas of billiard tables and courtyards and arum lilies beyond.

We are waiting for a ship to take us to Barcelona, but owing to the feast of the conception of the Virgin the ship remains at Carthagena, and so we grill here, watching the ships, listening to the band as I say. But we have been among the eternal snows [at Yegen], on mule back, and crouched over olive wood fires with deformed Catalans at midnight. Also at Granada with the Temples – highly aristocratic elderly people, expecting Mrs Asquith the day after. In short, I cannot even begin to chatter. I should overpower the whole of River House [Hutchinsons' house, Hammersmith]. My voice would begin with the boiled egg and continue with the heavenly mushrooms and grilled chops at lunch. The 8ts would row past and row back and still I should be talking.

Gerald is a very sympathetic, but slightly blurred character, who owing to solitude and multitudes of books has some phantasmagoric resemblance to Shelley. Otherwise he is intelligent, and as we share certain views upon English prose, our tongues wag – mine like a vipers, his like a trusty farmyard dogs. He has a slight impediment in his speech. I like young men who have not had the dew frozen hard at Cambridge. In short, he admires a sentence or two in one of my books. Hush! Hush! Mary is looking for the ruler – ebony black – with which she snubs my perspiring snout.

I hope for a week in Paris. Leonard, of course, has to rush back in order to issue Maynards paper – to which Mary Hutchinson is going to contribute some serious and well informed articles upon *Dress*. This, which I mean simply and affectionately, you take like a nervous mare with your ears laid back and one long white tooth showing. Ah, how hard it is to establish communication with any human being! I must stop. But, observe, I have said nothing about olives, oranges, lemons, palms;

or the Eliots. I am reading Proust, I am reading Rimbaud. I am longing to write.

yrs V.W.

1382: To Leonard Woolf   *Hotel de Londres [Paris]*

Tuesday [25 April 1923]

Dearest Mong[oose],

Here I am already in bed at 10.30, and I shall be asleep within the half hour. I've had quite a successful though a lonely day. I wrote – found nothing to do to my Nation article, so began Gissing;[1] lunched at a new place; good; 3 courses; bought china and went to the Louvre; took bus to Notre Dame; was there pursued by the Headmaster of Eton and wife and family whom I knew,[2] and had to escape; had tea; again pursued – hid behind a pillar; bought more china; again pursued, hid behind a pot; so home by bus; rung up by Hope,[3] who wants to treat me to ices at Rumpelmayers tomorrow, and asks me to dine on Thursday; says I shall easily get tickets for the Misanthrope. Now I've dined at our usual place – omelette, ham and pots, and spinach; suisse, coffee and cream, then chocolate, very good, at the orchestra café, but the music was such that even I could dream no dreams, so came away, got straight into bed, and finished reading my Gissing book; which brings me to the present moment. You, I suppose, have arrived, and are surrounded by innumerable letters. I'll now put out the light and fall fast asleep – it being 25 to 11. Goodnight, sweetest tiny mouse.

Wednesday

Here I am on Wednesday morning, having had a very good night, no aspirin – slept till 7.45.

---

1. Her review of *George Gissing: An Impression* by May Yates appeared in the *New Statesman* of 30 June (*Essays*, III, 373).
2. Cyril Alington (1872–1955), Head Master of Eton, 1917–1933. His wife was Hester Lyttelton, whom Virginia had known through Violet Dickinson.
3. Hope Mirrlees (1887–1978) was a contemporary of Virginia's sister-in-law, Karin Stephen, at Newnham, and a friend of the former Newnham scholar Jane Harrison, with whom she lived in Paris. In May 1920 The Hogarth Press had published Mirrlees' *Paris: a Poem.*

I have written at Gissing, and now I am going to dress and go about my business. It is fine, almost hot. I must go first and get money changed: then to the [Galeries] Lafayette, and then home to meet Hope and have tea. I'm already rather lonely, and home sick. No letter from Nessa, so I shall come certainly on Friday. So far I've found my way without difficulty. Just before I came to the Boul. St Germain a drunk taxi driver drove straight onto the pavement into a tree and knocked five people down and bent the tree right over. But I was too late to see it.

I long to hear from you. It was bitterly cold here yesterday; how is your cold? and I wonder how Margery[1] has done, and what news there is, – if I've many letters – but it's no use asking questions.

I must now get ready; and kiss my Mong a thousand times.

I am honestly being very good, shall go to bed again tonight and read till 10.30, then sleep: and of course the way to make me want Mong is to be away from him: It is all rather pointless and secondrate away from him.

MANDRILL

1388: To Gerald Brenan *Hogarth House, Paradise Road,*
Richmond, Surrey

Sunday, it may be 12th [13th] of May [1923]

My dear Gerald,

If I don't seize this moment, inauspicious as it is, I shan't write. Every cranny of my day is filled with the most degrading occupations. I think of you as a Saint on a hill top – someone who has withdrawn, and looks down upon us, not condescendingly but with pity. Indeed, all my memories of you are of an extraordinary pleasantness. What do the old ladies at Granada say about you? So sweet a nature, such tact, combined, my dear, with all an Englishman's dignity, and never in the way, and so considerate, with charming manners too. I can well believe that he will write something very very wonderful one of these days. With all these sentiments I entirely agree.

---

1. In March Ralph Partridge had left The Hogarth Press, but the Woolfs had already taken on a full-time employee, Marjorie Thomson (c. 1900–31), known as Marjorie Joad, formerly a student at the London School of Economics.

Please let me know exactly what your allowance comes to.[1] Is it enough for travel? Shall you alter your way of life? Here we are with our noses to the grindstone.[2] The grindstone is made of innumerable books which have to be transubstantiated into precisely the right number of articles, containing the right sentiments, views and facts, in the right number of words at the right moment. This not once, but weekly, every week, every month, every year – till all our precious time is over, and life, which surely has other uses, has poured in cataracts of printers ink, down the main gutter to the Thames. Perhaps the horror will mitigate. I have had only 4 days writing at my novel[3] since I got back. Tomorrow, I say to myself, I shall plunge into the thick of it. But how does one make people talk about everything in the whole of life, so that one's hair stands on end, in a drawing room? How can one weight and sharpen dialogue till each sentence tears its way like a harpoon and grapples with the shingles at the bottom of the reader's soul? Did we discuss dialogue at Yegen? I lose myself in metaphors when I begin to write, being dissipated, interrupted, – here is Leonard with the title page of the Feather Bed, a poem in the manner of Browning by Robert Graves.[4] We are printing all day long, Mrs Joad and I, while Leonard goes to his office. No news, except a postcard from Palermo from Carrington.[5] I am sending Valéry's poem which I got for you in Paris. The Nation with a poor article by Lytton ['Sarah Bernhardt'] and a poor article by me ['To Spain']. This is to fulfil my promise – not to make you think well of me as a writer. Then, I shall send the Proust book, which one day I should like back again.

Did I not say this was an inauspicious moment? The church bells are ringing, through a watery evening atmosphere: I sit by a solid coal fire, and hear vaguely the motor buses accumulating power to return to London stuffed with wet clerks and girls in bright woollen dresses. To

1. Gerald Brenan was receiving £50 a year from his great-aunt Adeline, Baroness von Roeder, and a further allowance from his father.
2. Leonard's literary editorship of the *Nation & Athenaeum*.
3. *Mrs Dalloway* (1925), then called *The Hours*.
4. Robert Graves (1895–1987), the poet and novelist, had not yet achieved the recognition that would come to him with the publication of his early autobiography, *Goodbye to All That* (1929). The Hogarth Press published his long poem as its thirty-third publication in July of this year.
5. Carrington, with Lytton Strachey and Ralph Partridge, was on her way back through Sicily after visiting North Africa.

your eye, these girls might have something attractive. I wonder whether your manly passions are a help to your writing? I wonder what your father and mother do and say? I shall recoup myself for the extreme coldness, colourlessness, and insipidity of the external world by going to the Italian marionettes[1] tomorrow: by having Tom Eliot to dinner; by dining at the Cock with some brave spirit like – can't think of anyone at the moment: and with luck, some small adventure will turn up. This I say to lure you here. Beevor Bevan[2] makes his appearance in about 2 weeks time. Let me have your Aunt's address and a copy shall go to her.

Your
Virginia Woolf

1390: To ROGER FRY   *Hogarth [House, Richmond]*

Saturday 18th May [1923]

My dear Roger,

[...] I try to pity you; indeed, I am much concerned about the damnable intestines;[3] only conceive England at this moment – leaden grey at half past five, so cold one wraps in wool to cross the hall, fires blazing, tents at the dog show blown over, the first class of Pekinese irretrievably mingled with the second to the despair of a thousand hearts: and to cap it all, Murry abroad again – I should say in Fleet Street again – blowing the enclosed nonsense through a megaphone.[4] That bloodless flea to talk about life! that shifty ruffian who can't keep his hands out of other people's pockets to prate of honesty! But there is a charm in complete rottenness. Leonard met him in the street, and Murry at once lied so splendidly about his duty to Massingham,[5] and 'sticking

1. The Marionette Players of Teatro dei Piccoli, who were performing Charles Perrault's *Puss in Boots*.
2. A satirical article by Gerald Brenan, which Leonard had accepted for the *Nation & Athenaeum*.
3. 'I am marooned in Nancy, tied by my intestines, which have rebelled again' (*Letters of Roger Fry*, II, 535).
4. Murry was distributing a prospectus for a new journal, the *Adelphi*, which he successfully edited until 1930. He had formerly (1919–21) been editor of the *Athenaeum*.
5. H. W. Massingham, the long-standing editor of the *Nation*, could not entirely agree with the brand of Liberal politics espoused by Keynes and the other new backers of his journal. A new editor was appointed, and Massingham transferred his column to the *New Statesman*, which was sympathetic to the Labour Party.

to the old Nation' (he offered to edit the new) that Leonard couldn't help loving him.

What gossip is there? That strange figure Eliot dined here last night. I feel that he has taken the veil, or whatever monks do. He is quite calm again, Mrs Eliot has almost died at times in the past month. Tom, though infinitely considerate, is also perfectly detached. His cell, is I'm sure, a very lofty one, but a little chilly. We have the oddest conversations: I can't help loosing some figure of speech, which Tom pounces upon and utterly destroys. Never mind: I loose another. So we go on. But at my time of life, I begin to resent inhibitions to intercourse; and these poor damned Americans so respect them. But I can't really hit it off with Lady [Sibyl] Colefax. Can you advise me how to acquire the social manner – neither cold nor hot? When I go to these tea parties, they all seem like people enchanted, and chained to a particular patch of the carpet, which they can't cross for fear of death – But you know it all of old. What irritates me is to see – anybody, Mrs W. K. [Lucy] Clifford it may be – possessed of a sense which I have not. And I believe – but here you mightn't agree – that it is one essential for a writer. I think Proust had it. [. . .]

Yours Ever
V.W.

1395a: TO CLIVE BELL   *Hogarth House, Paradise Road,*
Richmond, Surrey

May 29th [1923]

Dearest Clive,

I wrote you the most brilliant charming, and flattering letter that I have ever written, or you received, at Rodmell last weekend, when Shanks[1] coming in, I stuffed it between the pages of the Rose Growers Annual, where it remained. So now I can only plod in my own footsteps. There was a great deal of praise in it. First I praised your article in the Nation;[2] which, too, I made the theme of some very perspicacious

1. The poet and critic Edward Shanks (1892–1953), first winner of the Hawthornden Prize in 1919, was a Rodmell neighbour of the Woolfs. His romantic arrangements provoked avid village gossip because his wife had recently left him for another man, and he was consorting with Boen Hawkesford, mentioned later in this letter, the daughter of the local rector.
2. 'Elegance Down the Ages' (19 May 1923).

remarks to Tom Eliot and my husband. For, I said, there's all these young men, Mortimer, Lucas[1] and so on, being clever and cocking the snook, but all afraid to have an idea. Which I said, Clive has, and owns to; and thus, besides perking it with the best of them; something solid remains. Tom Eliot, who was dining with us – and it was a lovely night for a wonder, and for a wonder we were all very gay and outspoken, and he was in the best of spirits – Tom said 'I only wish Clive would write for the Criterion',[2] whereupon a slight gloom overtook us, as if the corpse were in the room, and Tom being surgeon, proposed to infuse a little cordial, as a last effort to avert rigor of the dead – that stiffening which has already, I fancy, set in. 'No, Clive is to write for me' said my husband. Well, as you see, it was all very flattering.

Then I went on a great deal of stuff about you and Mary – and how you were like Byron and Lady Car;[3] but the cap don't fit Mary's head very well. She's not been in the madhouse, anyhow. But all this gaiety, these parties, these conquests, this debauchery – its all a little Byronic, you must admit. Doesn't your head swim, or turn? Dont you sometimes think of [G.E.] George Moore, speaking the truth; or of the match box which you hid, because it was not 18th century? I am only trying to annoy.

I assure you life here is full, in its quieter way, of wonders. Lytton is back, and has had his Benson medal[4] slung about his neck by Sir Henry Newbolt. He is disillusioned, with Africa and with Tidmarsh. We are to meet him at Garsington on Saturday. And we are to meet Puffin and Lord David;[5] and so on and so on; and I'm nibbling, just nibbling, at Siegfried Sassoon[6] who says – but no: I mustn't repeat compliments; not

---

1. Raymond Mortimer (1895–1980), the critic, journalist and assistant literary editor at the *New Statesman*; and F. L. Lucas (1894–1967), the critic, novelist, poet and Fellow of King's College, Cambridge.
2. Which Eliot edited from its first appearance in October 1922.
3. The novelist Lady Caroline Lamb (1785–1828). She was obsessively in love with Byron, whose death unsettled her mind.
4. Endowed by the biographer and essayist A. C. Benson (1862–1925) and presented by the Royal Society of Literature for Lytton's achievements as a biographer and critic.
5. Ottoline Morrell's guests on this occasion included Anthony ('Puffin') Asquith (1902–68), the son of the former Prime Minister. Young Asquith, who would become a film director, was then an Oxford undergraduate, as was the future biographer and critic, Lord David Cecil (1902–86), the son of the 4th Marquess of Salisbury.
6. The poet Siegfried Sassoon (1886–1967) had become known through his vehement protestations against the war, in which he served as an officer. He was now literary editor of the Socialist *Daily Herald*.

if Mary's there; and oh dear I've had such a lot for an article ['To Spain']
you and she didn't like; and Desmond has been in a stew about his
young reviewers going to the Nation and Bob [Trevelyan] has made
matters infinitely worse; and they're now all composed, save that Sharp
says he is going to come the strongman over Woolf;[1] and Woolf
thereupon bristles like Beatrice Thynnes chow, and I have to pull all my
weight on his harness – thats what chows wear isn't it? So we go on.

Mary wants to know about Shanks. Well, he's a nice, quiet,
snubnosed little creature, with one of those faces which seem always to
be coveting pennybuns in bakers shops – Whether he's engaged to
Bowen [*sic*] or no did not, as they say, transpire. Only he had prevented
her from reading Ulysses. Tom, tell her, has once more fallen ill, and
gone back to Chichester [Fishbourne]; and Vivien is rather better – and
Murry, meeting Leonard in the street, looks like a grocer who's had a
vision of God, and says sanctimoniously, how he had to stand in with
the rest – and won't write for the Nation, though, as we all know, the
poor worm offered to edit it himself,[2] if they'd have him, which they
wouldn't. And Brett tells me that she has *not* been left a fortune and is *not*
financing the Adelphi; and Katherine no longer visits her; and the ghosts
use such long words she can't follow them. Fancy [the deaf] Brett with
her trumpet up interrogating the air! And the Sitwells[3] – but I told you
all this in the letter Shanks interrupted – So no more: only write again,
all your boasts.[4]

Yr
V.W.

Herrick Memorial Library, Alfred University

1. The *New Statesman*, edited from its founding in 1913 by Clifford Sharp (1883–1935),
   gave its literary editor, Desmond MacCarthy, a good deal less money for reviewers
   than the *Nation* allowed Leonard, who was recruiting writers from among his and
   Desmond's mutual acquaintances.
2. When Virginia later realised that she had been spreading this apparently false rumour
   about Murry, she took pains to set the record straight with her correspondents. See
   Letters 1400 and 1402 in the complete edition.
3. See Letter 1414, p. 176, n. 1.
4. 'Clive's just written me a prodigious letter all about his compliments, and his parties,
   and his ladies, and gentlemen, and [the painter, André] Derain, young Oxford men
   who admire Mrs Woolf so much – for, of course, I am sprinkled with compliments
   too, and I suppose its all part of the game, but at our time of life it seems a little noisy
   and splashy don't you think. (vain as I am)' (Letter 1395, to Vanessa Bell).

1405: TO BARBARA BAGENAL   *Hogarth House, Paradise Road,*
                                  Richmond, Surrey

24th June 1923

My dear Barbara,

I should have written to you before, but I have had so many disasters lately from writing letters,[1] that nothing short of death or bankruptcy will in future draw one from me. I hope scarlet fever isn't about as bad as going bankrupt. I have often thought of you in your hospital, as I take my way about the streets in comparative freedom. Yet I would have changed places with you last Sunday fortnight, when Ottoline completely drew the veils of illusion from me, and left me on Monday morning to face a world from which all heart, charity, kindness and worth had vanished. How she does this, in 10 minutes, between 12 and 1, in the best spare bedroom, with the scent of dried rose leaves about, and a little powder falling on the floor, Heaven knows. Perhaps after 37 undergraduates, mostly the sons of Marquises, one's physical life is reduced, and one receives impressions merely from her drawl and crawl and smell which might be harmless in the stir of normal sunlight. Only is the sunlight ever normal at Garsington? No, I think even the sky is done up in pale yellow silk, and certainly the cabbages are scented. But this is all great rubbish. We've had a desperate afternoon printing, and I'm more in need of the love of my friends than you are. All the 14pt quads have been dissed into the 12 pt boxes! Proof taking has been made impossible; and Eliots poem[2] delayed a whole week. I'm sure you'll see that this is much more worth crying over than the pox and fever and the measles all in one. Do you have horrid old gamps who come and cheer you up? by which I meant tell you stories about their past grandeur, and how they have come down in the world or they wouldn't be nursing the likes of you – by which they mean that you haven't got silk chemises. I could write you a whole page of their talk, but refrain.

Here is a quotation from a letter I've just had from Roger, in Salamanca. 'I was really rather surprised to see Saxon Turner approach

---

1. Virginia was in trouble again for her spontaneous gossip. In Letter 1416 she tells a correspondent: 'I'm breaking myself of the habit of profuse and indiscriminate letter writing. [. . .] Letter writing as a game is not safe'. But she didn't mean it.
2. *The Waste Land*, typeset entirely by Virginia herself, appeared in September 1923. 460 copies were printed, and by February 1925 it was sold out. This was not the poem's first publication. It had burst upon a small but astonished world in the first issue (October 1922) of the *Criterion*.

the table at Segovia where I was seated with one Trend, a Cambridge musician; he approached the table in perfect style with just a little guttural noise, a sort of burble which expressed everything the moment demanded and sat down and we went about very happily for some days. He became quite talkative. And really what a nice creature he is.' So our poor Saxon is moving among the living. He disappeared in such gloom, owing to your loss,[1] that I've since thought of him as a kind of sea gull wailing forlornly round the coast on windy nights. You won't be lacking though in letters from him. And they will tell you every detail. London is spasmodically gay, that is to say I dine out in humble places and went to the opera one night, and one night to the Italian puppets, and one night to see Nessa, and another to dine with Maynard, and Leonard is frightfully busy. We meet on the stairs oftener than anywhere, and I'm not sure that the glories of the Nation are quite worth so much energy.

Mrs Joad is doing very well – much better, to be honest, than dear Ralph [Partridge], but then she is a daily worker, enthusiastic, sanguine, and much impressed by small mercies. If only she didn't scent herself, rather cheaply, I should have nothing to say against her. She is a character so entirely unlike my own that I can't help gaping in astonishment, as we sit at lunch. Fancy playing tennis in Battersea Park! Fancy having a mother who lives at Harpenden! Fancy eating up all the fat, because it's good manners! Carrington insisted upon meeting her – I don't think they received good impressions of each other. How is that couple doing at Tidmarsh? I hear that Ralph is to become a bookbinder: also that he is to write articles, say on the hibernation of toads, on the maternal instinct of weasels, for which he is to be paid £50 guineas an article, if Lytton will co-operate. Of course Lytton won't, and so we shall soon read 'Saturday, with the Buff Orpingtons' by Lytton Strachey: or 'Hints on Wireworm,' by the same author. Oh how glad I am I'm not married to Ralph (he's in love with Mrs Dobrée!).[2]

Duncan was very severely treated by Simon Bussy in the Nation.[3] Nevertheless he has sold almost every picture, I hear: and they say this

1. Saxon Sydney-Turner had courted Barbara Hiles, as she then was, in 1918 while she was an assistant at The Hogarth Press. She was to have accompanied him to Spain.
2. Valentine Dobrée, *née* Brooke-Pechell (1894–1974), was married to the literary scholar Bonamy Dobrée. She was a painter, a friend of Ralph's wife Carrington, and – Virginia was right – Ralph's lover.
3. On 9 June Bussy had written of Duncan Grant's exhibition at the Independent Gallery that he had 'a manner of using paint which makes the canvas look more like stuff that has been dipped in a dye than like a painted picture'.

will revive poor Roger's miseries about his own failure; but Roger, of course, is far the nicest human being of any of us, and will as usual be incomparably more generous than one could suspect Christ to be, should Christ return, and take to painting in the style of Cézanne at the age of 56. Clive, who has nothing Christlike about him, has had to give up eating tea, because, when Lady Lewis[1] gave a party the other night and Rosenthal[2] played Chopin, a waistcoat button burst and flew across the room with such impetuosity that the slow movement was entirely spoilt. The humiliation, which would have killed you or me – the room was crowded with the élite of London – only brushed him slightly – he won't eat bread and butter any more: but his spirits are superb, and he says that life grows steadily more and more enchanting, the fatter one gets. Mr Bernard Shaw almost agreed to review his book[3] for the Nation; and said so on a postcard, but Clive is very touchy about postcards from Bernard Shaw, and has never forgiven Carrington,[4] nor ever will. Lydia has got a new bed: Very tactlessly I asked her if it was a double one.[5] No it isn't yet, she said; I saw that one must not make jokes about beds, however many Russian Generals and Polish princes or Soho waiters she's lain with. Her respectability is something your gamps would revere. But I find that talk about the Ballet has its limitations. Not indeed that she dances anymore: unfortunately she sometimes writes.

I hope you realise that though I am chattering like a pink and yellow cockatoo (do you remember Mrs Brereton's poem, Pink and yellow, pink and yellow?) I'm a chastened raven underneath: I mean I am very much concerned at your miseries, which besides being in themselves odious, show a mean malignity on the part of Providence which makes me, for one, a Christian and a believer. If there were not a God, of course you would have gone to Spain with Saxon: as it is, there you are in bed at

---

1. Elizabeth, *née* Eberstadt (1845–1931), whose house in Portland Place had been a cultural gathering place since the turn of the century.
2. Moriz Rosenthal, who was born in Austria in 1862 and was Court Pianist to the Emperor of Austria and the Queen of Roumania.
3. *On British Freedom* (1923).
4. Early in the previous year, Clive Bell had written an unflattering review of Bernard Shaw's *Back to Methuselah*. Carrington forged a caustic letter from Shaw complaining of the insult and sent it to Clive, who was completely taken in. He replied to Shaw, who, of course, denied that he had written such a letter.
5. Lydia Lopokova, now living in Gordon Square near Maynard Keynes, was not yet divorced. She married Keynes in August 1925.

Maidstone. Our only alleviation of HIS afflictions is to send you our latest, Talks with Tolstoi – a very amazing book, even when it has passed through the [hospital] furnace, which I suppose it must do, before reaching you.

Leonard is still trying to take proofs in the basement. I have cheered myself up by writing to you, so please don't say that I've plunged you into despair, as another invalid [Vivien Eliot] did the other day, when I cheered myself up by writing to her.

Please get well, and come and see me. Barbara Chickybidiensis[1] is one of those singular blooms which one never sees elsewhere, a rare and remarkable specimen. I wish I could write an article for Outdoor Life about you, and get £50. £25 should then be yours.

Love to Nick [Nicholas Bagenal].

Let me know how you are.

Yr V.W.

1414: To Jacques Raverat   *Hogarth House, Richmond*

July 30th 1923

My dear Jacques,

I only got your letter two hours ago, on my English breakfast tray, with its bacon and egg: and I will answer at once. No, no, no. Nothing you said offended me: all delighted me; and I should have written ages ago if I had not always said 'I'll write Jacques a nice long letter' – and so waited for the proper moment, and wrote meanwhile myriads of dreary drudgery. I find I never write to people I like. Jacques and Gwen require a good state of mind: whereas, – now you shall fill in the names of our old friends who can be put off with miserable relics.

We are all packed to go to Sussex tomorrow. This conveys nothing to you who have never seen the Hogarth Press. We travel with a selection of our books packed in hampers. Add to this a dog and a tortoise, bought for 2/- yesterday in the High Street. My husband presides with considerable mastery – poor devil, I make him pay for his unfortunate mistake in being born a Jew by discharging the whole business of life. This induces in me a sense of the transitoriness of

---

1. A nickname coined by Virginia during one of Barbara Bagenal's visits to Monk's House when she had impressively identified some yellow flowers as *Tropaeolum Canaryensis*.

existence, and the unreality of matter, which is highly congenial and comfortable. Now what do *you* think real? Gwen used to have views about that. Gwen was a highly dogmatic woman. Her breed is, alas, quite extinct. I assure you I can knock over the freeest thinker and boldest liver with the brush of a feather – nincompoop though I am, as far as logic goes.

This brings me, rather helter skelter, (but forgive thimble headed-ness in your old friend) – to the question of the religious revival: which concerns you both a good deal more nearly than you suspect. On my way back from Spain I stayed a week in Paris and there met Hope Mirrlees and Jane Harrison. This gallant old lady, very white, hoary, and sublime in a lace mantilla, took my fancy greatly; partly for her superb high thinking agnostic ways, partly for her appearance. 'Alas,' she said, 'you and your sister and perhaps Lytton Strachey are the only ones of the younger generation I can respect. You alone carry on the traditions of our day.' This referred to the miserable defection of Fredegond[1] (mass; confession; absolution, and the rest of it.) 'There are thousands of Darwins' I said, to cheer her up. 'Thousands of Darwins!' she shrieked, clasping her mittened hands, and raising her eyes to Heaven. 'The Darwins are the blackest traitors of them all! With that name!' she cried, 'that inheritance! That magnificent record in the past!' 'Surely', I cried, 'our Gwen is secure?' 'Our Gwen,' she replied, 'goes to Church, (if not mass, still Church) every Sunday of her life. Her marriage, of course, may have weakened her brain. Jacques is, unfortunately, French. A wave of Catholicism has invaded the young Frenchmen. Their children are baptised; their –' Here I stopped her. 'Good God', I said, 'I will never speak to them again! Whats more, I've just written a flippant, frivolous, atheistic letter to that very household, which will arrive precisely as the Host is elevated; they'll spit me from their lips, spurn me from their hearts – and, in short, religion has accomplished one more of her miracles, and destroyed a friendship which I'm sure began in our mother's wombs!' All this eloquence left me dejected as a shovelful of cinders. Next week arrived your letter, which was the greatest relief in the world. Gwen is a militant atheist: the world renews itself: there is

---

1. Fredegond Shove, *née* Maitland (1889–1949), was the daughter of Virginia's cousin Florence Fisher and F. W. Maitland, the historian. As a widow, Mrs Maitland married Gwen Darwin's uncle. After her mother's death in 1920, Fredegond grew very pious, and was received into the Catholic Church in 1927.

solid ground beneath my feet. I at once sent word to dear old Jane, who replied, a little inconsistently, 'Thank God'.

But speaking seriously, (and I need not say that the hand of art has slightly embellished the preceding) this religious revival is a glum business. Poor Middleton Murry has had a conversion, which has had an odious Bantam – the Adelphi – which I wish you'd take in and comment upon monthly. I'm too much prejudiced to be fair to him. As literature, it seems to me worthless – (only strong words are out of place): it seems to me mediocre then. The spirit that inspires it, with its unction and hyprocrisy, and God is love, which still leaves room for flea bites, pin pricks, and advertising astuteness, would enrage, were it not that there's something so mild and wobbly about that too that I can't waste good wrath. Most of my friends find it deplorable. Ka [Arnold-Forster], the usual exception, rather likes it. But the story of the Murrys, is long and elaborate, and I'm getting so harassed by household affairs that perhaps I'd better stop.

Leonard: Here's a man from the typewriter shop. Shall we be rash and buy a new one?

Cook: I think I'd better make the pie tomorrow. Monday meat is never trustworthy.

Virginia: I shall have to take my pink dress, if we're going to stay with Maynard.

Leonard: Well you can't take your pink dress, because the luggage has gone.

Virginia: Gone? Good God! Gone?

Leonard: I told you twenty times it was going at eleven.

etc. etc. etc.

I knew both the Murrys. Please read Katherine's works, and tell me your opinion. My theory is that while she possessed the most amazing *senses* of her generation so that she could actually reproduce this room for instance, with its fly, clock, dog, tortoise if need be, to the life, she was as weak as water, as insipid, and a great deal more commonplace, when she had to use her mind. That is, she can't put thoughts, or feelings, or subtleties of any kind into her characters, without at once becoming, where she's serious, hard, and where she's sympathetic, sentimental. Her first story which we printed, Prelude [1918], was pure observation and therefore exquisite. I could not read her latest [*The Garden Party*]. But prejudice may be at work here too. As for the Sitwells, though I paid 3/6 to hear Edith vociferate her poems accompanied by a small and nimble orchestra, through a megaphone, I understood so little that I could not judge.[1] I know Osbert slightly. They take themselves very seriously. They descend from George the IVth. They look like Regency bucks. They have a mother who was in prison.[2] They probably need careful reading, which I have never given them, and thus incline to think them vigorous, but unimportant, acrobats. Literature is in a queer way, however: as I shall explain next letter. By the way, do send me your version of Mrs Litchfield's remarks on my article.[3] Gerald Brenan's aunt [Baroness von Roeder] sent him the same unfortunate work, picked out with red lines in ink. She was outraged. (She is 85). She said it was done for notoriety and was only printed because 'Mrs Woolf has the dibbs, and would cut Mr Woolf short if he didn't'. But Mrs L., being Gwens Aunt, is much too refined to say that.

What a letter! What a letter! It is like the interminable monologue of an old village woman standing at her door. Each time you say good day and try to move off, she bethinks her of something fresh and it all begins again. And my hand shakes, so I cant write legibly. I have a queer illness, which consists of a permanent slight fever, which the Drs. diagnosed consumption, but have almost cured now by injecting pneumonia germs in multitudes. This must be my excuse for febrile verbosity. Please write to Monks House, Rodmell, Lewes.

Ever Yrs.

V.W.

1417: To Gerald Brenan   *Monks House, Rodmell,*
                                          Lewes [Sussex]

10th Aug. 1923

My dear Gerald,

[. . .] We came down here last week, and here we remain till October,

1. This avant-garde performance of Edith Sitwell's *Façade*, in which her voice was intended to be an instrument, was given at the Aeolian Hall on 12 June 1923. The poems were recited through a Sengerphone and appeared to emanate from a grotesque head in the centre of a curtain.
2. Lady Ida Sitwell (1869–1937), daughter of the 1st Earl of Londesborough, had before the war naively fallen prey to a fraudulent moneylender, and in 1915 spent three months in prison.
3. 'To Spain', which Leonard published in the *Nation*. Mrs Litchfield was Gwen Raverat's aunt, Henrietta Darwin (1843–1929), who married R. B. Litchfield.

a very happy life, on the whole, though I become rather restless with my desire to write, my desire to read, my desire to talk, and to be alone, and to explore Sussex and find a perfect house, and arrive at some conception of the meaning of all things. Why nature dangles this ancient carrot before me, I do not know. Every book is to me a glass through which I may possibly behold – I don't know what; and so with people; and so with my solitary walks on the downs, when suddenly I find I am breaking through myriads of white convolvulus, twined about the grass, and then I think there are more flowers here than in Spain. . . . I will write to Gerald when I get home.

Eliot will come and stay with us. At first I shall find him very pompous and American. Later, rather young and simple. I will send you The Waste Land when it is out – in a week or two. All marked styles are to be avoided, I think, because they limit one. He begins to repeat himself. He creaks: he angles, (if there is such a verb from angular) but I insist, against his many detractors that these are only the impediments of a very good brain. [. . .]

Tonight I shall read the plays of Marlowe; tomorrow I shall walk across the meadows to Lewes and buy a chicken. Does this sketch in great blobs produce any likeness of a character? or what do you get out of these careless, random diluted letters? I can no longer write careful letters. Moreover I am too sleepy with the heat (it is as hot to-day as it was in Alicante) to visualise you, your room, Maria [servant at Yegen], the brassero, the mountains, the little begging children, the pigeons, the mules, the figure of Don Giraldo, in corduroys, with a knotted tie, sitting by a plate of grapes, from which he picks a handful now and then, while he reads – Then he jumps up. Then he goes to the other room. Then he writes. Then he tears up. Then he runs out up the mountain alone making phrases? stories? deciding profound matters of art? or scarcely thinking at all? – God knows. I do not pretend to know much about that young man, whom, at this moment – the church has just struck 6 – I see with extreme plainness. Yes, but what is he thinking? How does it feel to be inside him? I am tormented by my own ignorance of his mind. And there is something absurd, and perhaps even insincere, in keeping up this semblance of communication in purple lines upon great white sheets. [. . .]

Please write.

V.W.

1432: TO JACQUES RAVERAT   *Hogarth House, Paradise Road, Richmond*

Nov. 4th 1923

My dear Jacques,

You were saying that you would like a little gossip about Maynard and Lydia. On Sept. 7th we went to stay with them at Studland – a ducal home,[1] in which they fared, rather uneasily I thought, because the dukes servants were in the pantry; and Lydia's habits, of course, are not ducal. I do not know how far I transgress the bounds of good taste, if I allude (oh it must be in a whisper, only in the presence of Gwen) to – well things called Sanitary Towels – you see blue bundles discreetly hidden beneath lace in the windows of small drapers. When used they should be burnt. Lydia, whose father was porter in a Petersburg hotel, and whose entire life has been spent hopping from foot to foot with the daughters of publicans, did not know this perhaps the most binding of all laws of female life (Ask any Darwin, excepting Mrs Litchfield – they'll tell you). She put her weeks supply on the grate. The grate was filled with white shavings. Imagine the consequences. There she left them. The cook's husband, and Duke's valet, did the room. Soon the Cook herself requested to speak with the lady. There was such a scene, it is said, as shook the rafters, – rage, tears, despair, outrage, horror, retribution, reconciliation: and – if you knew Lydia you'll see how naturally it follows – lifelong friendship upon a basis of – well, bloody rags. Really, there is a curious feeling about that menage, as well may be with such a foundation. Lydia has the soul of a squirrel: anything nicer you cant conceive: she sits by the hour polishing the sides of her nose with her front paws. But, poor little wretch, trapped in Bloomsbury, what can she do but learn Shakespeare by heart? I assure you its tragic to see her sitting down to King Lear. Nobody can take her seriously: every nice young man kisses her. Then she flies into a rage and says she is like Vanessa, like Virginia, like Alix Sargent Florence [Strachey], or Ka Cox [Arnold-Forster] – a seerious wooman.

Ka Cox dined with us two nights ago. Is malice allowed? Is it deducted from the good marks I have acquired or hope to acquire with the Raverat family? But then you've always known the worst of me – my incorrigible mendacity; my leering, sneering, undependable disposition.

---

1. The Knoll, the seaside retreat of the Duke of Hamilton. It became a hotel in 1931.

You take me as I am, and make allowances for the sake of old days. Well, then, Ka is *intolerably dull.* I am quoting my husband. I am not quite of that opinion myself: but why, I ask, condescend to the Woolfs? Why be so damned matronly? Why always talk about Will [Arnold-Forster] – that parched and pinched little hob goblin, whom I like very much but think an incorrigibly bad painter, as if he were Shelley, Mr Gladstone, Byron and Helen of Troy in one? I dont carry on about Leonard like that, nor yet Gwen about Jacques. What I suspect is that dear old Ka feels the waves of life withdraw, and there, perched high on her rock,[1] makes these frantic efforts to pretend, to make the Woolfs believe that she is still visited by the waters of the great sea.

Indeed, once upon a time, when we all swooned upon her in our love affairs and collapsed in our nervous breakdowns,[2] she was. She was wetted punctually, and shone in her passive way, like some faintly coloured sea anemone, who never budges, never stings, never – but I am getting wrapped up in words.

Anyhow, both Leonard and I lost our tempers. We said nothing. We went to bed in the devil of a gloom. Are we like that? we said. Are we middle aged and content? Do we look like old cabbages? Is life entirely a matter of retrospect and county families and trying to impress people with ringing up men at the foreign office about French conscription of Natives in Africa? No, no, no. Let us change the subject.

Duncan [Grant] has just been in to tea. I may tell you it is rather a fine November day, but dark by half-past four. Duncan was going on to Twickenham to see his mother to choose some silks for a chair cover – bright sunlight being essential. Its no good. One goes to the window and shows him the church all lit up. Off he wanders murmuring something about getting there by daybreak – Half his buttons seemed to be off; his braces are too long. He has always to be hitching himself together; and odd bits of shirt stick out. [. . .]

What other news is there? Very little I think of interest, so far as facts go. And to convey feelings is too difficult. I try, but I invariably make enemies. I go to parties, very occasionally, and there get rather random headed, and *say too much.* I assure you its fatal – but I never can resist the

---

1. Her house, Eagle's Nest, in Zennor, Cornwall.
2. Before his marriage Jacques had been in love with Ka Cox and Gwen Darwin at the same time, and Ka had seemed like a great sensual earth mother. It was also Ka who was called upon by Leonard when Virginia needed nursing during the breakdown following their marriage.

desire for intimacy, or reconcile myself to the fact that all human relations are bound to be unsatisfactory. Are they? I rather expect Jacques, in his thick black beard, surveying the country from his motor car, knows all about it. I still play my game of making up Jacques and Gwen as I walk about London. No doubt I shall be picked off by a motor omnibus in the thick of it. After half an hours acute discomfort, should we settle down to the old relationship, whatever it was? Jacques I think was rather dictatorial; he called us silly women; he said the Oliviers[1] were *real*: but not most people. Gwen sat on the floor and said something very positive – being, poor woman, a Darwin to the backbone, and Virginia of course, shied and shilly-shallied, and – no, you must write Virginia's part, because she is oddly enough, the last woman I have any idea of. About coming, to Vence – this must be done somehow, and I aim at Easter, or later, or earlier. But we are tied by the navel string to the Nation; and – what awful, indecent things I keep thinking of this evening!

Please write someday soon; and explain what you think about, as you survey the world. And please think kindly of me. How I depend upon my friends! You wouldn't believe it, either of you.

Ever yrs

V.W.

1433: To Gerald Brenan   *Monks House, Rodmell,*
                                          Lewes [Sussex]

Dec. 1st 1923

My dear Gerald,

I am ashamed to say that I left a long unfinished letter to you behind at Richmond, and now have my doubts that I can accomplish, as I wish and have wished for long, a finished one. I am coming to the age when I sit staring at the fire and saying 'I'm so busy: I'm so fearfully hard at work: I've not got a word to throw at a dog:' and so I do nothing. Oh, yes, I ought to be reading *4* manuscripts for the Hogarth Press, one by a young Frenchman, another by a paralysed girl, and a third by an astute

---

1. The four Olivier sisters, two of whom (Noel and Margery) have appeared in this narrative before (the others were Bryn and Daphne) as Neo-Pagans, like the Raverats.

and bold American, who was Henry James' secretary,[1] and a fourth by a Spaniard.

In the unfinished letter in the drawer of my Roman cabinet I went at some length into several points of disagreement between us. I disagreed entirely and with some heat in your estimate of Conrad: I repeated, with qualifications, my remark that he is a great, though limited, novelist and then I observed that Vanity Fair is inferior as a work of art to Wuthering Heights: and then I joked at you for taking me seriously when I was writing humorously (but humour never crosses the Channel) for your Aunt. Do you indeed accuse me of writing for money? Do you have the temerity to bid me forsake journalism? And in God's name, what do you mean by 'working working working at my novel'?[2] How does one 'work' at one's novel? Well, scribbling journalism is one way, and lunching with Lady Colefax to meet Hugh Walpole, is another. But do not let us quarrel over these misfits of meaning. Come to England and let us adjust them in hours of endless talk.

I saw Carrington two days ago, and we had a long long consultation, such as you can imagine, about Ralph, among other things. Since your advice, I have tried to be cordial; as to quarrel was none of our wish; indeed I always like him, but Carrington says, he suspects us – you're evidently right – he suspects all brain workers, who don't rampage about the purlieus of Soho chasing pretty powdered girls. I quite like seeing him do it: I don't bear the shadow of a grudge against him; but life is life. Surely that is a Spanish proverb? Interpreted it means, women of 41 can't be intimate with rowing blues of 28. Carrington was very sincere. She interests me more than he does. And don't think that your ruse was altogether successful. I suspected – but as you'll be seeing them, I shall drop this subject, as I don't want to be quoted, mentioned, or twisted like a figure of wax in front of your 6 eyes.[3]

Now we have a card to say you're in Morocco, and a picture of camels ploughing sandhills; so that my letter begins to evaporate. There

1. Theodora Bosanquet, who was not in fact American, worked with Henry James from 1907 until his death in 1916. The Press published her *Henry James at Work* in November 1924.
2. Brenan was working on *A Holiday by the Sea*, which he put aside, finishing it only in 1960. It was published the next year.
3. Brenan had confessed to Ralph Partridge that he and Ralph's wife, Carrington, were in love. The news led to a temporary breach between the two men. Carrington and Partridge stayed with Brenan on his return from Morocco in January 1924, and the friendship of the three was restored.

it will be on the table over the braziers in your room among all the littered foolscap, and you'll never find it. Perhaps as you say, you'll marry a lady in a veil, and live among the palm trees like a sultan for ever.

That is not the life to make a good writer of you, however. I have a feeling that a street would put a backbone into your sentences, which, if you will excuse the frankness, I think they begin to want. For your story of Mr Unwin,[1] you should live in Birmingham, and have to eat in A.B.C. shops. Or, more boldly, live in Bloomsbury, and hear Clive Bell chattering. You asked me about him and Murry. Clive is a great source of pleasure to me, for one thing because he says outright what I spend my life in concealing. Never was there anyone so petty, conceited, open and good at bottom of heart. I always think of him as a mixture of Pepys and Boswell. Sometimes I imagine him the only one to survive of us all – for 50 years or so after his death. I should be more sure of this if he had not been slightly corrupted by Lytton. When I first knew him, he was perfection: a hunting squire who thought himself a Shelley. But he is always a delight to watch: and no one more annoys and outrages me: and also I am on perfectly friendly terms with him; and he pays my cabs, and stands me 'Cold Snacks' at the Café Royal, where the waiter brings him the cold red beef to look at before he cuts it – but I can't trouble to go on with this account, or get it very like.

Please believe that I could write better if I took a little more time. But letter writing is now a mere tossing of omelettes to me: if they break and squash, can't be helped. Then, of course, you should know Roger, whose mind, far subtler and more richly stocked than Clives, never ceases for a second to glow, contract, expand, like some wonderful red-tinted sea anemone, which lives in the deepest water and sucks into itself every scrap of living matter within miles. He is close on sixty, and gets, so it seems to me, richer and suppler, richer and suppler – but they say his painting is very bad. As for Murry, I can no longer follow him even with amusement, much less with dislike. Eliot says he has unbuttoned his waistcoat and found his level. One might as well listen to a half starved clerk spouting religious revival on a tub at Hyde Park Corner. But you are right about him. His friend (he has one disciple left, Sydney Waterlow – a kind of spaniel who follows anybody who will beat him) his friend says that in the Adelphi he is purging his sins: and the process is holy to watch, and salutary to us, the unconverted, too. He

1. A story about lower middle-class life which Brenan began but never completed.

is one of those Dostoevsky relics. He sees himself pulled asunder by the angels of darkness and light. As a matter of fact – but no: I can't go on with Murry either.

What about your defence of Joyce? Our press has its mouth wide gaping for *prose*. Did we tell you that Rylands,[1] a young man at Cambridge, is coming in June to be our partner? So we shall be more capable of undertaking masterpieces. I rather agree that Joyce is underrated: but never did any book [*Ulysses*] so bore me. But then, as you think criticism is not my line (*meant humorously*) I will not go on to analyse. I will not send you my next book, which consists of criticism pure and simple.[2] I will work work work – I wish I could laugh in person instead of trying to make my pen laugh. My ink pot is stood upon the hob; and the faint sizzling sound of boiling purple ink is now to be heard. We have been weeding onions in the light of a towering rose pink cloud, which, tugging a little at its anchor, moved very slowly across the sky, and over Mount Caburn, and so away. Indeed, I could spend my whole life describing clouds.

I am now going to read Greek.

Ever yr.
V.W.

For Gods sake, send me your sonnets, and my Proust.

1. George ('Dadie') Rylands (b. 1902) was a Cambridge Apostle, whom the Woolfs met through Maynard Keynes. He stayed at The Hogarth Press for only a short time, afterwards returning to Cambridge as a Fellow of King's, where his particular interests were literature and drama. His friendship with the Woolfs was lasting.
2. Virginia was preparing her first collection of critical essays, *The Common Reader* (1925). She was also writing some new pieces, including 'On not Knowing Greek', to which she refers at the end of this letter (*Essays*, IV).

1924–1925

During these years Virginia alternated between two entirely different kinds of books. Part of the time she wrote her novel, Mrs Dalloway, *and part of the time, her analytical volume,* The Common Reader. *The experience was satisfying, but very hard work – which she never revealed to her friends in letters.*

Early in 1924 the Woolfs moved back to Bloomsbury. The Hogarth Press was set up in the basement of 52 Tavistock Square as a proper business, and one of its new recruits was the best-selling author Vita Sackville-West. The relationship between the two women now began to warm up. Virginia spoke of Vita almost recklessly in letters to Jacques Raverat. Not that he was likely to tell anyone, for he was near death, which came in March 1925.

1440: To Clive Bell   *Hogarth [House, Richmond]*

Wednesday [23 January 1924]

Dearest Clive,

[...] As for gossip, what? Lord Berners,[1] Vita, Siegfried [Sassoon]: thats my style these last days: and oh dear for a carving knife to scrape the numbskulls a little sharper! Dear Vita has the body and brain of a Greek God; Berners is by all means admirable, and Siegfried the most delightful, and sensitive etc etc etc: but when it comes to sitting tight, 2 feet apart, over the fire from 8 to 11.30 – more brain, O God, more brain! So Meredith cries, in a sonnet which in our youth we quoted:[2] and here, to solace myself, I've been reading a Maynard-Lytton 1906 correspondence, all about Hobby and Duncan[3] – oh so far away, and vivid, and

1. Lord Berners was Gerald Tyrwhitt-Wilson (1883–1950), 14th Baron Berners. He was an amateur musician and artist of great talent, and later wrote several novels and books of autobiography. He was a friend of Vita Sackville-West, whose presence with Berners at the Woolfs' dinner party prompted Virginia to write in her diary: 'we have got into the peerage. [...] Still, rank, nowadays, at my age, is slightly vulgar, like a fringe to the mantelpiece' (II, 287).
2. 'More brain, O Lord, more brain!' (George Meredith, *Modern Love*, XLVIII).
3. Arthur Hobhouse ('Hobby', 1886–1965) came to Cambridge just after Maynard Keynes and Lytton Strachey, who were both infatuated with him and saw to his

bringing back, as charwomen say of hardboiled eggs, which 'repeat'. Again vulgarity, its Penkala's fault – (It's a red pen, with a *real* nib; gilt, but virile, none of that smooth mush the fountain pens have. I'll give you one. Remind me.)

And what else? Logan [Pearsall Smith] came to tea, a little censorious, mildly buggeristical, a young Spaniard having come to Chelsea all the way from his Estaňcia on the Steppe of Paraguay to translate Trivia. Its the American salt I dont relish, something coarse and briny in the blood.[1] Vita was well laughed at about P.E.N.,[2] but the poor girl has lost her way and dont know which light to turn on next. Would I introduce her to the Robert Lynds?[3] 'Well, if you'll introduce me to Lord Lascelles.'[4] 'Why dont you contribute to the Queen's dolls House,[5] Virginia?' 'Is there a W.C. in it, Vita?' 'You're a bit hoity toity, Virginia.' Well, I was educated in the old Cambridge School. 'Ever heard of Moore?' 'George Moore the novelist?'[6] 'My dear Vita, we start at different ends'. The poor girl looks divinely lovely, a little tousled, in a velvet jacket. But let us meet, for no more letter writing at my age; only a St Vitus' dance. [. . .]

V.W.

1. Born in New Jersey, Logan Pearsall Smith came to England with his family when he was a young man and became a British subject in 1913. He was known for his collections of aphorisms, especially the first one, *Trivia* (1902).
2. Vita was a member of the Committee of P.E.N., the international authors' society, and in the spring of 1923 had proposed Virginia for membership. She described the scene in her first letter to Virginia, dated 26 March 1923: 'There was a little shout of excitement from the Committee about you, and Galsworthy (so to speak) got up and made a curtsey' (*The Letters of Vita Sackville-West to Virginia Woolf*, ed. Louise DeSalvo and Mitchell A. Leaska, 1985, p. 47). But Virginia declined to join, as she had on a previous occasion.
3. The essayist (1879–1949), who for many years contributed to the *New Statesman* under the pseudonym Y.Y. He was literary editor of the *Daily News*, which after 1930 became the *News Chronicle*. His wife was Sylvia, *née* Dryhurst (1888–1952), also a writer.
4. Henry Lascelles (1882–1947), son of the 5th Earl of Harewood, whom he succeeded in 1929. He had been much in love with Vita in 1911–13, and in 1922 married Princess Mary, only daughter of George V.
5. The doll's house, now at Windsor Castle, which Sir Edwin Lutyens designed for Queen Mary in 1922. Virginia had refused an invitation to contribute a miniature manuscript to its library, but Vita had accepted.
6. The two Moores were the Cambridge philosopher, G. E. Moore (1873–1958), and George Moore (1852–1933), the Irish novelist.

election as an Apostle. More seriously, they were also rivals for the affections of Duncan Grant, who had an affair with Maynard.

1450: To Jacques Raverat   *52 Tavistock Square, W.C.1*[1]

March 8th 1924

My dear Jacques,

This you see [her new address] is the reason why I havent written and cant write now and won't be able, so far as I can see to cross the channel this year – a new house, to which we move in a few days, which has had to be cleaned, scoured, painted and lighted, all in a hurry, leaving me a mere drudge, without a thought in my head, or, what is much worse, a penny in my purse. I dont therefore see how we can possibly take precedence of your better off friend. Let us creep into a cranny, if we can come. Otherwise assume we can't.

But thats no reason why our letters should languish. You don't want to hear about my new house, I know by experience. It has a basement for the Press and a large studio: 2 floors full of solicitors [Messrs Dolman & Pritchard], L. and I on top looking at all the glories of London, which are romantically, sentimentally, incredibly dear to me. The Imperial Hotel, all pink and blue, in Russell Square: St Pancras Church spire, carved from white plaster – do you know it? These are the things I love, better than olive trees and mountains, but not so much as Jacques and Gwen, after all.

You said very tactfully in your last letter, why did Adrian and Karin separate, or rather how did he stand that d—d American[2] all these years? I must say your language is a trifle strong. She is a good, honest woman: and in her place I'd have done the same, and in his too. Incompatible, is what they say: and this they've realised for 8 years, and ground their teeth over, while appearing in public the most love-locked of couples. We Stephen's are difficult, especially as the race tapers out, towards its finish – such cold fingers, so fastidious, so critical, such taste. My madness has saved me; but Adrian is sane – that's all the light I can throw. [...]

Ever V.W.

1. Eager to get back into the excitement of London life, and concerned too that Leonard was wasting time commuting from Richmond to the *Nation & Athenaeum* offices, Virginia had been looking for a London house for months. By the middle of March the Woolfs were back in Bloomsbury.
2. Karin's mother, Mary Berenson (*née* Pearsall Smith) had been born an American. The Stephens continued to see each other during their separation, and after about a year they gradually rebuilt their marriage.

1497: To V. Sackville-West   *Monk's House, Rodmell,*
                                     Lewes [Sussex]

Monday [15 September 1924]

My dear Vita,

I like the story very very much – in fact, I began reading it after you left,[1] was interrupted by Clive, went out for a walk, thinking of it all the time, and came back and finished it, being full of a particular kind of interest which I daresay has something to do with its being the sort of thing I should like to write myself. I don't know whether this fact should make you discount my praises, but I'm certain that you have done something much more interesting (to me at least) than you've yet done. It is not, of course, altogether thrust through; I think it could be tightened up, and aimed straighter, but there is nothing to spoil it in this. I like its texture – the sense of all the fine things you have dropped in to it, so that it is full of beauty in itself when nothing is happening – nevertheless such interesting things do happen, so suddenly – barely too; and I like its obscurity so that we can play about with it – interpret it different ways, and the beauty and fantasticallity of the details – the butterflies and the negress, for instance. This is all quite sincere, though not well expressed.

I am very glad we are going to publish it, and extremely proud and indeed touched, with my childlike dazzled affection for you, that you should dedicate it to me. [. . .]

                                     Yrs Ever
                                     V.W.

1500: To Molly MacCarthy   *Monk's House, Rodmell*
                                   [Sussex]

Oct. 2nd [1924]

Dearest Molly,

   [. . .] we are publishing all Dr Freud,[2] and I glance at the proof and

1. Vita spent the night of 13 September with Virginia and Leonard, her first visit to Monk's House. She brought with her the manuscript of her long story, *Seducers in Ecuador*, which The Hogarth Press published in November.
2. Sigmund Freud's *Collected Papers* in four volumes. This was the beginning of The Hogarth Press's connection with the International Psycho-Analytic Library. In essence, the Press now had the rights to Freud's work in English translation, as well as to books by other important analysts. The relationship continues to this day.

read how Mr A. B. threw a bottle of red ink on to the sheets of his marriage bed to excuse his impotence to the housemaid, but threw it in the wrong place, which unhinged his wife's mind, – and to this day she pours claret on the dinner table. We could all go on like that for hours; and yet these Germans think it proves something – besides their own gull-like imbecility. [. . .]

V.W.

1501: To Jacques Raverat   *Monks House, Rodmell*
                                            [Sussex]

Oct. 3rd 1924

My dear Jacques,

Certainly the painters have a great gift of expression. A highly intelligent account you seem to me to give of the processes of your own mind when I throw Neo Paganism in. In fact I rather think you've broached some of the problems of the writer's too, who are trying to catch and consolidate and consummate (whatever the word is for making literature) those splashes of yours; for the falsity of the past (by which I mean Bennett, Galsworthy and so on) is precisely I think that they adhere to a formal railway line of sentence, for its convenience, never reflecting that people don't and never did feel or think or dream for a second in that way; but all over the place, in your way.[1]

I'm writing now, partly because I was so much intrigued by your letter, and felt more in touch, partly because this is my last evening of peace. I go back to London tomorrow. Then there'll be people upon people; and I shall dash in and out, and go to concerts, and make engagements, and regret making engagements. The difficulty of writing letters is, for one thing, that one has to simplify so much, and hasn't the courage to dwell on the small catastrophes which are of such huge interest to oneself; and thus has to put on a kind of unreal personality; which, when I write to you for example, whom I've not seen these 11

1. Jacques had written to Virginia about the problems of writing and painting, suggesting that a word like Neo-Pagan aroused many associations, like throwing a pebble into a pond: 'There are splashes in the outer air in every direction, and under the surface waves that follow one another into dark and forgotten corners' (see Quentin Bell, II, 196).

years, becomes inevitably jocular. I suppose joviality is a convenient
mask; and then, being a writer, masks irk me; I want, in my old age, to
have done with all superfluities, and form words precisely on top of the
waves of my mind – a formidable undertaking.

About your letter, however; I didn't mean that private relations bore
me: which is indeed an intolerable perversion of my real meaning, who
find relations of all kinds more and more engrossing, and (in spite of
being made a fool of so often by one's impulse to surrender everything –
dignity and propriety – to intimacy) final, in some way; enduring:
gigantic; and beautiful. Indeed, I find all this in my relations with people,
and what I can guess of theirs. What I meant was that *sexual* relations
bore me more than they used: am I a prude? Am I feminine? Anyhow for
two years past, I have been a spectator of I daresay a dozen affairs of the
heart – violent and crucial; and come to the conclusion that love is a
disease; a frenzy; an epidemic; oh but how dull, how monotonous, and
reducing its young men and women to what abysses of mediocrity! Its
true that all my lovers were of the simplest type; and could only flush
and fade crudely like sea anemones bathed now blue, now red. That's
what I meant, I think.

Our loves, yours and mine and that granite monolithic Gwens –
(until she writes to me, I shall say what I like in abuse of her to her
husband) were of a very different kind. But then we were creatures of
temperament. No: your admiration of me was not apparent; but then I
was alarmed of your big nose, your bright eyes, your talking French,
and your having such a quick easy way with you, as if you had solved
the problems of life, – gone straight into the middle of the honeycomb
without one miss. Yes – thats how I figure you: thats still (vaguely now)
the image I have of my dear and adorable Jacques – but I should never
have dared call him so to his face. And then, (this is a secret) for some
reason, your and Gwen's engagement, being in love, took on for me a
symbolical character; which I even tried to put down in writing. All very
absurd I suppose: still you were very much in love, and it had an ecstatic
quality. Indeed, you will laugh, but I used to think of you, in a purely
literary way, as the two people who represented that passion in my
mind: and still, when I think of you, I take out my brush, and
paint both of your faces a divine sunset red. How oddly composed
are one's feelings! You would never have guessed, I daresay,
that Jacques and Gwen always appear to Virginia in a sunset
glow? [. . .]

I'm awfully shy of saying how really and truly I would do a great deal to please you and can only very very dimly murmur a kind of faint sympathy and love.

Yrs
V.W.

1520: To Jacques Raverat   *Monk's House, Rodmell*
[Sussex]

Dec. 26th 1924

My dear Jacques,

[...] Who is there next? Well, only a high aristocrat called Vita Sackville-West, daughter of Lord Sackville, daughter of Knole, wife of Harold Nicolson, and novelist, but her real claim to consideration, is, if I may be so coarse, her legs. Oh they are exquisite – running like slender pillars up into her trunk, which is that of a breastless cuirassier (yet she has 2 children) but all about her is virginal, savage, patrician; and why she writes, which she does with complete competency, and a pen of brass, is a puzzle to me. If I were she, I should merely stride, with 11 Elk hounds, behind me, through my ancestral woods. She descends from Dorset, Buckingham, Sir Philip Sidney, and the whole of English history, which she keeps, stretched in coffins, one after another, from 1300 to the present day, under her dining room floor. But you, poor Frog, care nothing for all this. [...]

Yours aff.
V.W.

1524: To Jacques Raverat   *52 Tavistock Sqre., London*

Jan 24th 1925

My dear Jacques,

[...] Have you any views on loving one's own sex? All the young men are so inclined, and I can't help finding it mildly foolish; though I have no particular reason. For one thing, all the young men tend to the pretty and ladylike, for some reason, at the moment. They paint and powder, which wasn't the style in our day at Cambridge. I think it does imply some clingingness – a tiny lap dog, called Sackville West,[1] came

---

1. Edward Sackville West (1901–65), the son and heir of the 4th Baron Sackville, was Vita's first cousin. He had just come down from Oxford and was to become a writer and music critic.

to see me the other day (a cousin of my aristocrat and will inherit Knole) and my cook said, Who was the lady in the drawing room? He has a voice like a girls, and a face like a persian cats, all white and serious, with large violet eyes and fluffy cheeks. Well, you can't respect the amours of a creature like *that*. Then the ladies, either in self protection, or imitation or genuinely, are given to their sex too. My aristocrat (oh, but I have now 2 or 3, whom I'll tell you about – they interest me) is violently Sapphic, and contracted such a passion for a woman cousin, that they fled to the Tyrol, or some mountainous retreat together, to be followed in an aeroplane by a brace of husbands.[1] The mothers of girls are said to take it to heart. I can't take either of these aberrations seriously. To tell you a secret, I want to incite my lady to elope with me next. Then I'll drop down on you and tell you all about it. [. . .]

Yrs. aff.
V.W.

1534: To Jacques Raverat   *52 Tavistock Square* [*W.C.1*]

Feb: 5th 1925

My dear Jacques,

[. . .] Clive is now shaped like a spade and thick as an oak tree. He wears bright blue socks, which he is forever hitching up, and his trousers, for some reason which a man may know, are always above his knees. But how good hearted he is – bunches of grapes arrive for me; and yet I never do anything but bite his nose off when I see him, and laugh at him behind his back. I have an idea you and Gwen hated him. Let me assure you, you were wrong. Not that I claim for him any of the heroic virtues. Being bred a Puritan, (in the main – but I had a French great grandmother to muddle me) I warm my hands at these red-hot-coal men. I often wish I had married a foxhunter. It is partly the desire to share in life somehow, which is denied to us writers. Is it to you painters? Ever since I was a child I have envied people who did things – but even influenza shall not mislead me into egoistical autobiographical

---

1. Virginia gives a slightly distorted version of Vita's elopement with Violet Trefusis, who was not a cousin but a friend since childhood. In February 1920 they ran away, intending to spend the rest of their lives together, but only got as far as Amiens in France, where their husbands, Harold Nicolson and Denys Trefusis, caught up with them and persuaded them to separate and return.

revelations – Of course, I long to talk to you about myself, my character, my writings, but am withheld – by what?

Karin's party came off last night, and I lay in bed and imagined it all very brilliant. Leonard put on his deceased brother-in-law's (who died in a Bath at Eastbourne) dress clothes, and went off to brew the punch. Hope Mirrlees arrived half an hour early (do you admire her novels? – I can't get an ounce of joy from them, but we like seeing her and Jane [Harrison] billing and cooing together). Then came 40 young Oxford men, and three very pretty girls; Vanessa, Mary Hutch, Clive and Lytton – Lytton gravitated to the 40 young men, and was heard booming and humming from flower to flower. Vanessa, who had not dressed, sat commandingly on a sofa, talking to a sculptor called Tomlin,[1] and to no one else, for she is beyond the pale now, makes no attempt to conciliate society, and often shocks me by her complete indifference to all my floating loves and jealousies, but with such a life, packed like a cabinet of drawers, Duncan, children, painting, Roger – how can she budge an inch or find a cranny of room for anyone? Clive came in late, having been dining with Mary at her new house in Regent's Park. She has a ship's steward to serve at table, and whether for this reason or another provides the most spicy liquors, foods, cocktails and so on – for example an enormous earthenware dish, last time I was there, garnished with every vegetable, in January – peas, greens, mushrooms, potatoes; and in the middle the tenderest cutlets, all brewed in a sweet stinging aphro-disiac sauce. I tell you, I could hardly waddle home, or compose my sentiments. So Clive gets a little warm, and very red about the gills towards midnight.

Then Karin, who felt the approach of disillusionment about eleven, ran down to the kitchen and borrowed the housemaid's gramophone. The 40 young men began waltzing, and the three lovely girls sat together flirting in corners. Isn't it an odd thing that Bloomsbury parties are always thus composed – 40 young men; all from Oxford too, and three girls, who are admitted on condition that they either dress exquisitely, or are some man's mistress, or love each other. Much preferring my own sex, as I do, or at any rate, finding the monotony of young mens' conversation considerable, and resenting the eternal pressure which they put, if you're a woman, on one string, find the disproportion excessive, and intend to cultivate women's society en-

1. Stephen Tomlin (1901–37). He later modelled the bust of Virginia now in the National Portrait Gallery.

tirely in future. Men are all in the light always: with women you swim at once into the silent dusk. But to return. They danced. Leonard got horribly bored. He was set upon by little Eddie Sackville West, who is as appealing as a kitten, a stray, a mangy, unloved kitten; and this poor boy, after pouring forth his woes (all men confide in Leonard – especially such as love their own sex) sat by mistake down on the best tea cups. Being an aristocrat out of his element, he was considerably discomposed. Sweets and jams stuck to his behind, and Leonard had to dust him, and pat him, and finally leave him; trying I believe, to smoke a pipe in full evening dress, and white waistcoat. They work very hard, the aristocracy. Karin was heard to say, between the waltzes, Isn't this jolly? – On being assured it was, she plucked up heart, and means to give another party, with another hostess,[1] next month.

Really, you have done me good. This is the first time I have cantered out on paper this fortnight. I find a great pleasure in waking all the doves in their dovecots – in stirring my words again. But this I can never explain to a painter, I suppose; how words live in companies, never used, except when one writes. [. . .]

Yours,
V.W.

1541: To Gwen Raverat   *52 Tavistock Square, W.C.1*

11th March [1925]

Dearest Gwen,

Your and Jacques' letter came yesterday, and I go about thinking of you both in starts, and almost constantly underneath everything, and I don't know what to say.[2] The thing that comes over and over is the strange wish I have to go on telling Jacques things. This is for Jacques, I say to myself; I want to write to him about happiness, about Rupert [Brooke], and love. It had become to me a sort of private life, and I believe I told him more than anyone, except Leonard; I become mystical as I grow older and feel an alliance with you and Jacques which is

---

1. Virginia was to have been Karin Stephen's co-hostess for this party, but missed it due to influenza.
2. Jacques Raverat's last letter to Virginia was about *Mrs Dalloway*, which she had sent him in proof. To it Gwen appended a note telling Virginia about his death, from multiple sclerosis, on 7 March. For a narrative of the Raverats' lives and Gwen's widowhood, see Letter 2498.

eternal, not interrupted, or hurt by never meeting. Then of course, I have now for you – how can I put it? – I mean the feeling that one must reverence? – is that the word – feel shy of, so tremendous an experience; for I cannot conceive what you have suffered. It seems to me that if we met, one would have to chatter about every sort of little trifle, because there is nothing to be said.

And then, being, as you know, so fundamentally an optimist, I want to make you enjoy life. Forgive me, for writing what comes into my head. I think I feel that I would give a great deal to share with you the daily happiness. But you know that if there is anything I could ever give you, I would give it, but perhaps the only thing to give is to be oneself with people. One could say anything to Jacques. And that will always be the same with you and me. But oh, dearest Gwen, to think of you is making me cry – why should you and Jacques have had to go through this? As I told him, it is your love that has forever been love to me – all those years ago, when you used to come to Fitzroy Square, I was so angry and you were so furious, and Jacques wrote me a sensible manly letter, which I answered, sitting at my table in the window. Perhaps I was frightfully jealous of you both, being at war with the whole world at the moment. Still, the vision has become to me a source of wonder – the vision of your face; which if I were painting I should cover with flames, and put you on a hill top. Then, I don't think you would believe how it moves me that you and Jacques should have been reading Mrs Dalloway, and liking it. I'm awfully vain I know; and I was on pins and needles about sending it to Jacques; and now I feel exquisitely relieved; not flattered: but one does want that side of one to be acceptable – I was going to have written to Jacques about his children, and about my having none – I mean, these efforts of mine to communicate with people are partly childlessness, and the horror that sometimes overcomes me.

There is very little use in writing this. One feels so ignorant, so trivial, and like a child, just teasing you. But it is only that one keeps thinking of you, with a sort of reverence, and of that adorable man, whom I loved.

Yours,
V.W.

1560: To Gerald Brenan   *52 Tavistock Square, W.C.1*

[14 June 1925]

My dear Gerald,

It was very good of you to write. But I shan't answer your criticisms (and I daresay you don't want me to) because at the moment I can only pit them against other peoples' criticisms, and cannot make them refer to Mrs Dalloway itself. This is partly, I suppose, that I have just had a long talk with Roger [Fry], and he gave me an entirely different view of Mrs D from yours – in fact I think you and he contradict each other on practically every point of importance (the two I now remember being Septimus: to him the most essential part of Mrs D: And this I certainly did mean – that Septimus and Mrs Dalloway should be entirely dependent upon each other – if as you say he 'has no function in the book' then of course it is a failure. And fate – no book to him more full of fate). Meanwhile, as I finished it 8 months ago, and am now at work on something different [*To the Lighthouse*], I feel very far away, and as if I saw you and Roger turning a little wax model this way and that – something that I have, at the moment, very little connection with.

Perhaps it is this lack of criticism, or rather the fact that I affect different people so differently, that makes it so difficult for me to write a good book. I always feel that nobody, except perhaps Morgan Forster, lays hold of the thing I have done: they meet in conflict up in the air; and so I have to create the whole thing afresh for myself each time. Probably all writers now are in the same boat. It is the penalty we pay for breaking with tradition, and the solitude makes the writing more exciting though the being read less so. One ought to sink to the bottom of the sea, probably, and live alone with ones words. But this is not quite sincere, for it is a great stimulus to be discussed and praised and blamed; I shall keep your letter and read it very carefully in a few months time. At the moment, I am letting the different opinions (here are two letters, from highly intelligent people – one [from Lytton Strachey] to say that Mrs D herself is a failure, the whole interest centering in Septimus and Rezia – another [from Charles Sanger] imploring me to write more like Tchekhov, and lamenting the fact that I 'contemplate the lives of the idle rich') – I say, I am letting these opinions accumulate, and then, when all is quiet, I shall creep out of my hole, and piece them together. [. . .]

Yours

V.W.

1572: To V. Sackville-West   *Monks House, Rodmell*
                                     [Sussex]

Monday [24 August 1925]

My dear Vita,

[. . .] I have a perfectly romantic and no doubt untrue vision of you in my mind – stamping out the hops in a great vat in Kent – stark naked, brown as a satyr, and very beautiful. Don't tell me this is all illusion. We came away from London so parched and cynical that all we wanted was to sit in the damp and observe insects. Naturally, this being so, telegrams pursued us, and the Morrells would have been on us, Ottoline and Philip, demanding beds, and weaving the whole smoke cloud over us again, had it not been for some valiant lying on my part. One can't tell the Truth to Ottoline. She found it out, – as indeed a babe in arms could; but showed it. Now dont you, as a born aristocrat (which is said to annoy) call this damned bad manners? I do. So we are under a ban. If I say that I have to meet my mother in law in Bexhill, you ought to believe it. Still – no doubt this bores you. [. . .]

But please tell me about your poem. Are you writing it? Is it very beautiful? I rather think I shall like it: but I am very old fashioned in my poetry, and like reading Crabbe.[1] What I wish is that you would deal seriously with facts. I dont want anymore accurate descriptions of buttercups, and how they're polished on one side and not on the other. What I want is the habits of earthworms; the diet given in the workhouse: anything exact about a matter of fact – milk, for instance – the hours of cooling, milking etc. From that, proceed to sunsets and transparent leaves and all the rest, which, with my mind rooted upon facts, I shall then embrace with tremendous joy. Do you think there is any truth in this? Now, as you were once a farmer, surely it is all in your head ready. Tennyson, you see, was never a farmer: Crabbe was a parson, which does as well. [. . .]

                                                              Yr VW.

---

1. George Crabbe (1754–1832), author of *The Village* and *The Borough*, whose distinction lay partly in his ability to write realistically about nature. Vita was writing her long traditional poem, *The Land*, which was published in 1926 and was awarded the Hawthornden Prize.

1575: To Janet Case   *Monks House [Rodmell,*
                                        Sussex]

Tuesday [1 September 1925]

My dear Janet,
    [...] dont, I beg of you, father on me that doctrine of yours about the
way things are written mattering and not the things: how can you accuse
me of believing that? I don't believe you can possibly separate expression from thought in an imaginative work. The better a thing is
expressed, the more completely it is thought. To me, [Robert Louis]
Stevenson is a poor writer, because his thought is poor, and therefore,
fidget though he may, his style is obnoxious. And I don't see how you
can enjoy technique apart from the matter – [...]

                                             Your aff
                                             V.W.

1583: To Roger Fry   *Monk's House, Rodmell,*
                                       Sussex

Sept. 16th 1925

    [...] We are lying crushed under an immense manuscript of
Gertrude Stein's.[1] I cannot brisk myself up to deal with it – whether her
contortions are genuine and fruitful, or only such spasms as we might all
go through in sheer impatience at having to deal with English prose.
Edith Sitwell says she's gigantic, (meaning not the flesh but the spirit).
For my own part I wish we could skip a generation – skip Edith and
Gertrude and Tom and Joyce and Virginia and come out in the open
again, when everything has been restarted, and runs full tilt, instead of
trickling and teasing in this irritating way. I think its bad for the
character too, to live in a bye stream, and have to consort with
eccentricities – witness our poor Tom, who is behaving (I can't go
into details – I don't suppose you need them) more like an infuriated

1. In November 1926 The Hogarth Press published *Composition as Explanation*, by the
   American experimental writer Gertrude Stein (1874–1946).

hen, or an old maid who has been kissed by the butler than ever.[1] [...]

Yrs ever
V.W.

1588: To V. Sackville-West   *Monks House* [*Rodmell, Sussex*]

Wednesday [23 September 1925]

My dear Vita,

[...] I'm going to live the life of a badger, nocturnal, secretive, no dinings out, or gallivantings, but alone in my burrow at the back. And you will come and see me there – please say you will: if you're in London, let me know. A little quiet talk in the basement – what fun! And then I'm going this winter to have one great gala night a month: The studio will be candle lit, rows of pink, green, and blue candles, and a long table laid with jugs of chocolate and buns. Everybody will be discharged into this room, unmixed, undressed, unpowdered. You will emerge like a lighthouse, fitful, sudden, remote (Now that is rather like you) This way of seeing people might be gigantically successful, and then your cousin [Eddy Sackville West] has lent me his piano, and I intend to break up the horror of human intercourse with music. It struck me on my snails walk to the river this afternoon (I have now had tea and lit the fire, unsuccessfully) that the fear and shock and torture of meeting one's kind come from the conditions – being clasped to each other unmitigatedly, on a sofa – pure, neat, entire (I cant think of the word I want). Now if we could be dispersed a little – could we visit St Pauls, or the Tower or Ken Wood, where the scenery or the noble buildings would intervene between us, then we should sail gradually and calmly into latitudes of intimacy which in drawing rooms are never reached. Do you agree? Every Wednesday I shall take a trip in an omnibus with someone to mitigate the shock of human intercourse. [...]

Your V.W.

1. In reply to a letter from her saying that The Hogarth Press wished to reprint *The Waste Land*, Virginia had received from T. S. Eliot a fawning, flattering letter in which he put off their Press discussions. Immediately afterwards she saw in the *TLS* an announcement of Eliot's *Collected Poems* from his new employer, Faber, an event he had chosen not to mention.

1599: To V. Sackville-West   *52 Tavistock Square, W.C.1*

Monday [16 November 1925]

My dear Vita,

Its perfectly enchanting and has lasted me two whole days – your picture: the chauffeur, the secretary your mother the night.[1] There are at least 3 novels in it. Send me some more: If only all novels were that – balls of string for one to pull out endlessly at leisure.

I want you to invent a name by the way which I can use instead of 'novel'. Thinking it over, I see I cannot, never could, never shall, write a novel. What, then, to call it?

I've flashed to the top of Hampstead Heath in a motor car, sat on a bench and seen three fir trees in the fog; flashed back and seen Nancy Cunard,[2] whose father has left her, to be kept perpetually, an entire fox of solid silver. And why dont I see you?

Owing to standing or sitting 3 minutes too long in the Press I am put back into bed[3] – all the blame now falling on the Hogarth Press. But this is nothing very bad – I feel as if a vulture sat on a bough above my head, threatening to descend and peck at my spine, but by blandishments I turn him into a kind red cock.

I am very sorry for you – really – how I should hate Leonard to be in Persia![4] But then, in all London, you and I alone like being married.

And where's your poem [*The Land*]?

Yr VW.

1. Vita had just spent four days with her mother, Lady Sackville, in her house at Brighton and had described the visit in a letter to Virginia.
2. Nancy Cunard (1896–1965), the fast-living but cultivated daughter of the wealthy Sir Bache Cunard and his socialite wife. The Hogarth Press had published Nancy's poem, *Parallax*, in April.
3. Virginia had been ill off and on since August, when she collapsed at Charleston after months of strenuous social activity in London. Great care was taken by Leonard and Virginia to prevent any return of her mental instability.
4. On 4 November Vita's husband, Harold Nicolson, had left for the legation in Teheran to assume his duties as Counsellor. After the first of the year, Vita planned to join him for a few months.

1926–1927

Disappointed that Vita had not yet invited her to stay, Virginia reflected in her diary for 7 December that 'if I do not see her now, I shall not – ever: for the moment for intimacy will be gone, next summer'. The invitation came, and on 17 December Virginia went to stay with Vita for three nights. It was the beginning of their love affair. They slept together only a few times, but their emotional tie was strong, even when Vita took other lovers, as she soon did. Virginia's jealousy was doubtless one of the motives behind the composition of Orlando: *she would woo Vita as others could not.*

Several events evoked particularly interesting letters from Virginia. There was the 1926 General Strike, which both Woolfs, but particularly Leonard, tried to move towards a just end. Then Vita travelled twice to Persia, which demanded correspondence, and Virginia herself went to Italy, from which she sent Vanessa letters in return for a promised painting. In May 1927 her important novel To the Lighthouse *was published, and, as usual, she was more willing to discuss her work after its appearance.*

1613: To V. Sackville-West   *52 Tavistock Sqre [W.C.1]*

Tuesday, January 26th, 1926

Your letter from Trieste came this morning – But why do you think I don't feel, or that I make phrases? 'Lovely phrases' you say which rob things of reality.[1] Just the opposite. Always, always, always I try to say what I feel. Will you then believe that after you went last Tuesday – exactly a week ago – out I went into the slums of Bloomsbury, to find a barrel organ. But it did not make me cheerful. Also I bought the Daily

---

1. 'I just miss you, in a quite simple desperate human way. You, with all your undumb letters, would never write so elementary a phrase as that; perhaps you wouldn't even feel it. And yet I believe you'll be sensible of a little gap. But you'd clothe it in so exquisite a phrase that it would lose a little of its reality' (Vita to Virginia, 21 January 1926).

Mail – but the picture is not very helpful. And ever since, nothing important has happened – Somehow its dull and damp. I have been dull; I have missed you. I do miss you. I shall miss you. And if you don't believe it, your a longeared owl and ass. Lovely phrases? [. . .]

To tell you the truth, I have been very excited, writing. I have never written so fast [*To the Lighthouse*]. Give me no illness for a year, 2 years, and I would write 3 novels straight off. It may be illusion, but (here I am rung up: Grizzle barks: settles in again – it is a soft blue evening and the lights are being lit in Southampton Row: I may tell you that when I saw crocuses in the Sqre yesterday, I thought May: Vita.[1]) What was I saying? Oh only that I think I can write now, never before – an illusion which attends me always for 50 pages. But its true I write quick – all in a splash; then feel, thank God, thats over. But one thing – I will not let you make me such an egoist. After all, why don't we talk about *your* writing? Why always mine, mine, mine? For this reason, I expect – that after all you're abundant in so many ways, and I a mere pea tied to a stick. [. . .]

As for the people I've seen, I've fallen in love with none – but thats not exactly my line. Did you guess that? I'm not cold; not a humbug; not weakly; not sentimental. What I am; I want you to tell me. Write, dearest Vita, the letters you make up in the train. I will answer everything. [. . .]

But of course (to return to your letter) I always knew about your standoffishness. Only I said to myself, I insist upon kindness. With this aim in view, I came to Long Barn. Open the top button of your jersey and you will see, nestling inside, a lively squirrel, with the most inquisitive habits, but a dear creature all the same –

Your Virginia

Are you perfectly well? Tell me.

1621: To V. Sackville-West   *52 Tavistock Sqre.* [*W.C.1*]

Feb. 17th 1926

[. . .] Then there was Rodmell. Now that was a joy – I cant tell you how lovely, – the water meadows soaking wet, but now and then the sun coming out and stroking the downs. D'you remember how they turn from green to blue, like opals? I don't think you ever walk. You are always charging at the head of an army – but I walk, nosing along,

1. When Vita would be back in England.

making up phrases, and I'm ashamed to say how wrapped up I get in my novel. Really, I am a little alarmed at being so absorbed – Why should one engross oneself thus for so many months? and it may well be a mirage – I read it over, and think it is a mirage: but I can scarcely do any thing else. I got up on to the Downs though, where you went plunging in the motor, and then came down to tea, and sat over a wood fire, and read some poetry, and a manuscript, (thinking still of my own novel) then cooked an omelette, some good coffee; and wanted a little drop of wine, with you. (Have you been tipsy often? Do you know it was 4 weeks yesterday that you went?) Yes, I often think of you, instead of my novel; I want to take you over the water meadows in the summer on foot, I have thought of many million things to tell you. Devil that you are, to vanish to Persia and leave me here! – dabbling in wet type, which makes my fingers frozen; and setting up the poems of Mrs Manning Sanders,[1] which the more I set them, the less I like. And, dearest Vita, we are having *two* waterclosets made, one paid for by Mrs Dalloway, the other by The Common Reader: both dedicated to you.

Then I lunched with Lytton at Kettners. First I was so dazzled by the gilt and the warmth that in my humility I felt ready to abase myself at the feet of all the women and all the waiters; and really humbled at the incredible splendour of life. Halfway through lunch, reason triumphed; I said this is dross; I had a great argument with Lytton – about our methods of writing, about Edmund Gosse, about our friendship; and age and time and death and all the rest of it. I was forgetting Queen Elizabeth – He is writing about her [*Elizabeth and Essex*, (1928)]. He says that she wrote to an ambassador 'Had I been crested and not cloven you would not have dared to write to me thus.' 'Thats style!' I cried. 'It refers to the male and female parts' he said. Gosse told him this, adding that of course, it could not be quoted. 'You need some excuse for lunching with Gosse,' I said. But Lytton thinks me narrow minded about Gosse. I say I know a mean skunk when I see one, or rather smell one, for its his writing I abominate. And, Vita, answer me this: why are all professors of English literature ashamed of English literature? Walter Raleigh[2] calls Shakespeare 'Billy Shaxs' – Blake, 'Bill' – a good poem 'a bit of all right.' This shocks me. I've been reading his letters. But dear old Lytton – he was infinitely charming, and we fitted like gloves, and I was very happy,

1. Ruth Manning-Sanders' *Martha Wish-You-Ill* was published by the Press in July.
2. Sir Walter Raleigh (1861–1922), Professor of English Literature at Oxford. His letters, edited by his widow, were published in two volumes in 1926.

we nosed about the book shops together, and remarked upon the marvellous extent of our own reading. 'What haven't we read?' said Lytton. 'Its a question of life, my dear Lytton' I said, sinking into an arm chair: And so it all began over again. [...]

Yr VW.

1622: To V. Sackville-West   *52 Tavistock Sqre* [*W.C.*[1]]

March 1st, 1926

[...] The people who took us were Leonards brother and his wife.[1] I promptly fell in love, not with him or her, but with being stock brokers, with never having read a book (except Robert Hitchens)[2] with not having heard of Roger, or Clive, or Duncan, or Lytton. Oh this is life, I kept saying to myself; and what is Bloomsbury, or Long Barn either, but a contortion, a temporary knot; and why do I pity and deride the human race, when its lot is profoundly peaceful and happy? They have nothing to wish for. They are entirely simple and sane. She has her big dog. They turn on the Loud Speaker. When they take a holiday they go to the Spring of the Thames where it is as big as a man's arm, not big enough for a boat; and they carry their boat till they can put it in, and then they skull all the way down to Marlow. Sometimes, she said the river is level with the banks; and it is perfectly deserted. Then she said to me suddenly, as we were looking down at the wood from her window 'Thats where the poet Shelley wrote Islam. He tied his boat to the tree there. My grandfather had a walking stick cut from that tree.' You always run up against poetry in England; and I like this dumb poetry; and I wish I could be like that. She will live to be a hundred; she knows exactly what she enjoys; her life seems to me incredibly happy. She is very plain; but entirely unvexed, unambitious; and I believe, entirely right. Yes; that what I've fallen in love with – being a stockbroker. [...]

Tuesday [2 March]

[...] But to write a novel in the heart of London is next to an impossibility. I feel as if I were nailing a flag to the top of a mast in a

1. Leonard's brother Herbert Woolf (1879–1949) and his wife Freda, *née* Major, who lived at Cookham, Berkshire.
2. Robert Hichens (1864–1950), the popular novelist, whose best-known book was *Garden of Allah* (1904).

raging gale. What is so perplexing is the change of perspective: here I'm sitting thinking how to manage the passage of ten years, up in the Hebrides.[1] then the telephone rings; then a charming bony pink cheeked Don called [F.L.] Lucas comes to tea well, am I here, asking him about the Life of Webster, which he's editing, or in a bedroom up in the Hebrides? I know which I like best – the Hebrides. I should like to be with you in the Hebrides at this moment. [. . .]

Another break. Now its the next day. I'm so orderly am I? I wish you could live in my brain for a week. It is washed with the most violent waves of emotion. What about? I dont know. It begins on waking; and I never know which – shall I be happy? Shall I be miserable. I grant, I keep up some mechanical activity with my hands, setting type; ordering dinner. Without this, I should brood ceaselessly. And you think it all fixed and settled. Do we then know nobody? – only our own versions of them, which, as likely as not, are emanations from ourselves. [. . .]

Yr V.W.

1624: To V. Sackville-West

52 Tavistock Square, London, W.C.1

16th March 1926

[. . .] I like your letters I was saying, when overcome by the usual Hogarth Press spasm. And I would write a draft if I could, of my letters; and so tidy them and compact them; and ten years ago I did write drafts, when I was in my letter writing days, but now, never. Indeed, these are the first letters I have written since I was married. As for the *mot juste*, you are quite wrong. Style is a very simple matter; it is all rhythm. Once you get that, you can't use the wrong words. But on the other hand here am I sitting after half the morning, crammed with ideas, and visions, and so on, and can't dislodge them, for lack of the right rhythm. Now this is very profound, what rhythm is, and goes far deeper than words. A sight, an emotion, creates this wave in the mind, long before it makes words to fit it; and in writing (such is my present belief) one has to recapture this, and set this working (which has nothing apparently to do with words) and then, as it breaks and tumbles in the mind, it makes words to fit it: But no doubt I shall think differently next year. Then there's my

---

1. 'Time Passes', the second section of *To the Lighthouse*.

character (you see how egotistic I am, for I answer only questions that are about myself) I agree about the lack of jolly vulgarity. But then think how I was brought up! No school; mooning about alone among my father's books; never any chance to pick up all that goes on in schools – throwing balls; ragging: slang; vulgarity; scenes; jealousies – only rages with my half brothers, and being walked off my legs round the Serpentine by my father. This is an excuse: I am often conscious of the lack of jolly vulgarity but did Proust pass that way? Did you? Can you chaff a table of officers? [. . .]

Yr VW

1626: To V. Sackville-West
The Hogarth Press, 52 Tavistock Square, London, W.C.1

29th March 1926

[. . .] a ghastly party at Rose Macaulays,[1] where in the whirl of meaningless words I thought Mr O'donovan[2] said Holy Ghost, whereas he said 'The Whole Coast' and I asking 'Where is the Holy Ghost?' got the reply 'Where ever the sea is' 'Am I mad, I thought, or is this wit?' 'The Holy Ghost?' I repeated. 'The Whole Coast' he shouted, and so we went on, in an atmosphere so repellent that it became, like the smell of bad cheese, repulsively fascinating: Robert Lynds, Gerald Goulds,[3] Rose Macaulays, all taking shop; and saying Masefield[4] is as good as Chaucer, and the best novel of the year is Shining Domes by Mildred Peake; until Leonard shook all over, picked up what he took to be Mrs Gould's napkin, discovered it to be her sanitary towel and the foundations of this tenth rate literary respectability (all gentlemen in white waistcoats, ladies shingled, unsuccessfully) shook to its foundations. I kept saying 'Vita would love this' Now would you? [. . .]

1. Rose Macaulay's essay *Catchwords and Claptrap* was published by The Hogarth Press in 1926.
2. Jeremiah (Gerald) O'Donovan (1872–1942) was a former priest, who later married and became a novelist. He was Rose Macaulay's lover.
3. Gerald Gould (1885–1936), journalist, and his wife, Barbara Ayrton Gould (d. 1950), who went from journalism to politics, and was elected as a Labour candidate in 1945.
4. John Masefield (1878–1967) would become Poet Laureate in 1930.

1632a: To Raymond Mortimer *52 Tavistock Square, London,*
W.C.1

April 27th 1926

Dear Raymond

It was very nice to get your letter, and I will try to answer it, but it is almost impossible to write to people in Paris.[1] Here's Vita telling me how you let pearls filter through your fingers, crush emeralds under your boots. Then how can I tell you about Clive and Mary [Hutchinson] and Leonard and Virginia and the Nation and the country and Sybil [Colefax] and all the rest of it after that? I am also in a state of absolute disgust with all letters. That beast Walter Raleigh fills my soul with loathing. He was always being what they call 'so like Walter Raleigh.' I dont want to be so like Virginia – But then, all my inclinations are setting (I must warn you) in the direction of comfortable middle class stupidity. None of us are clever enough to count – thats my opinion. So why not be nice? Then it seems to me that all young women are infinitely nicer than all young men – not that its their fault, if they're sent to Cambridge and stuffed with chopped hay, and sent out to parade Bloomsbury like dummies; I mean they seem to me only half alive, and rigid with conceit, and self assertive, and positive, and opinionated, and ugly, and snob-bish, and brainy, and unaesthetic – and, in short, all the things I most dislike. (One good point about writing to Persia is that one can fire off one's little pistols, and no harm done.) Now a girl may not be clever, but her modesty has kept her fresh, and her training – which is the most exacting form of spiritual gymnastics continued all day long – has given her a suppleness and variety of reactions which I find infinitely interest-ing, and envy, for I have it not myself, being man-trained; and shall never be able to do my hair, as you know.

All your friends are saying nice things about you. I often pass your windows and look up and I agree that you have some reason to plume yourself, when you wake in Teheran (Vita spells it Tehran) and think how you might be lunching with Chrissie to meet Lesley Jowitt[2] to meet

1. Mortimer had gone to Persia to see Vita and, more especially, Harold Nicolson, with whom he was in love.
2. Christabel McLaren (1890–1974), the wife of Henry McLaren, later 2nd Lord Aberconway, a patron of the arts, and the hostess of a distinguished salon in Mayfair; Lesley Jowitt, wife of the political leader William Jowitt (1885–1957), moved in the same circles, as did Clive Bell and his lover, Mary Hutchinson.

Mary to meet – here I run out of names. Most people are away. We stole off and were divinely happy for 5 days at Iwerne Minster, in a country, at a moment, which really made one almost ashamed of England being so English; and carpeting the woods, and putting cuckoos on trees, and doing exactly what Shakespeare says.[1] Yes, I like poetry better than prose, in my mid-age; and had a good argument with Lytton the other day on that subject, and many others. We old creatures now dribble away for 3 hours untouched; I never think what I'm going to say next, and the talk goes on, through the open door, with Lytton making torrents of water in the w.c. He has been dropped on in the Times for his metaphors, his clichés; and Joyce and myself patted on the back.[2] The truth is, of course, only scraping one's mind on imaginary things ever makes metaphors; for truth is the devil; it waters down everything. Still, bad metaphors, rightly used, are good; you cant go dotting and starring your page when its about [Lord] Cromer and Victoria. He is getting on with his book; and I wish everyone would pinch and scratch him; if he had his back to the wall, he would write much better.

What are you writing? But then you're so modest, so nice natured (fundamentally) that you never say. Have you disinterred some astonishing fossils, walking the Persian mountains? Shall you come back bearded and fierce and disdainful? Do, do.

As for news we are all in the air about giving up the Nation, or not; as Maynard has a new idea every week.[3] Either way, I think we shall end by being freer, which is what we want. Nessa and Duncan are off to Italy, and Angus[4] goes with them. I think I am going to the Ring. I think I am going to see Hardy[5] – also to motor about France a little, also to

1. 'When daisies pied and violets blue, / And lady-smocks all silver-white, / And cuckoo-buds of yellow hue / Do paint the meadows with delight, / The cuckoo then, on every tree, / Mocks married men; for thus sings he, cuckoo; / Cuckoo, cuckoo: o word of fear, / Unpleasing to a married ear' (*Love's Labours Lost*, V, ii, l. 902 ff).

2. On 4 March 1926 in the *TLS* Herbert Read wondered why *Mrs Dalloway* and *Ulysses* had not been selected for Sir Arthur Quiller-Couch's *Book of English Prose* (1925) when Lytton Strachey, whose death scene from *Queen Victoria* Read deplored, was included in the anthology.

3. Leonard at first resigned his position as literary editor of the *Nation*, but, pressured by Keynes to reconsider, stipulated that he would come to the office only two days a week. Keynes agreed, and Leonard stayed in his post until 1930.

4. Angus Davidson (1898–1980) succeeded George Rylands at The Hogarth Press in December 1924 and remained until 1927.

5. The Woolfs visited Thomas and Florence Hardy in Dorchester on 23 July. For a description of the visit, see *Diary*, III, 96–101.

spend a week at Rodmell, and then settle in and see no one, do nothing, but wrap myself about in my book, and live there till its done. But why do you think one imposes these extraordinary tasks on oneself?

It will be very nice to see you again.

Leonard sends his love.

Yr aff

Virginia Woolf

Please remember me to Harold

Princeton University

1635: To Vanessa Bell   *52 Tavistock Square, W.C.1*

Wednesday 12th May 1926

Dearest,

We have just been told as a dead secret that the [General] strike will be settled this afternoon. This comes from Laski,[1] but as nobody tells the truth, it may well be another maresnest. However, everybody agrees that something is happening – either there will be peace today or strike going on for several weeks. It beggars description. Recall the worst days of the war. Nobody can settle to anything – endless conversations go on – rumours fly – petitions to the Prime Minister are got up. The past 3 days Leonard and I have been getting signatures from writers and editors to the Archbishop of Canterburys proposals.[2] That is to say Miss Bulley[3] arrives at 9.30: Gerald Brenan with his bicycle at 11: Ralph Partridge, just out of a railway accident on the Cambridge line, at 11.15. Clive is in and out all day. The telephone rings 8 times in 20 minutes. I have to argue with [J.C.] Jack Squire at Aldershot. Desmond [MacCarthy] is expected. Francis Birrell begs us to come and see his father [Augustine] – or better still go to the Oval and talk to Hobbs.[4] Desmond arrives fresh from Asquith [Lord Oxford]; has a whisky and soda.

1. Harold Laski, Professor of Political Science at the London School of Economics from 1926 until his death in 1950.
2. For a compromise solution between employers, Government, and workers, which would not leave the latter embittered after the failure of the strike. Leonard was invited to support the Archbishop (Randall Davidson) by collecting signatures from prominent writers and artists.
3. The art historian Margaret Bulley, later Mrs G. W. Armitage, a Bloomsbury neighbour.
4. Jack Hobbs, the most famous cricketer of this period.

Maynard rings up from Cambridge – where he has been driven with Lydia in search of coal – to command us to print the Nation on the Hogarth Press. Leonard refuses twice, though several undergraduates have volunteered to motor up and act as compositors. Leonard is now employed by the Labour party to write articles; I have to take despatches to the House of Commons.

Meanwhile, there are no tubes and no buses and no taxis – except those run by special constables often with fatal results. They charge 3d a ride anywhere; but after going to Westminster by bus, with a policeman on the box, and boards up to protect us from stone throwers (the streets in the West End are perfectly peaceful, as a matter of fact) walking seems preferable. Suddenly Roger and Helen[1] arrive – it is now tea time, carrying a market basket containing chocolate and melons, which nourish and provide drink, in case of bloodshed at Camden town, which is the most riotous part of London. Roger is wilder than ever, but agrees with me in thinking it all unutterably boring and quite unimportant and yet very upsetting – Between telephone calls from Arnold Bennett and Mr Garvin[2] and despairing interviews with Miss Bulley who has been insulted by Edmund Gosse – Roger explains that the Gower Street house is off, as the Bedford agent exacts complete respectability and no subletting except to members, by blood, of one's own family – which says Roger he can't guarantee: so he's now after a house in Bernard Street. He has tried, but failed, to get your show put off;[3] and then to have it broadcast. Well, with 3 weeks, I think its not so bad. (The press by the way carries on dismally – Mrs C.[4] arrives on Faith Henderson's bicycle, red with rust; she, too, red with exercise and fury at strikers. She and Leonard argue. But she is a monument of virtue and motherliness and at intervals I sob on her shoulder – for instance when Bob [Trevelyan] arrives having bicycled from Leith Hill, wanting cold meat at 3.30. and brings two poetic dramas for us to read – But now it is tea time, and Desmond suddenly assumes the rôle of Mussolini – marches

1. After Vanessa Bell shifted her affections from Roger Fry, he turned to Helen Anrep, *née* Maitland (1885–1965). She had trained as an opera singer and married the mosaicist Boris Anrep in 1917. She lived happily with Fry until his death.
2. J. L. Garvin, editor of the *Observer*, and one of two people approached by the Woolfs and their circle (John Galsworthy was the other) who refused to sign the petition.
3. The London Artists' Association exhibition, which opened on 12 May.
4. Mrs Cartwright, who worked at The Hogarth Press from 1925 until 1930; she lived in Hampstead near Faith Henderson, *née* Bagenal, wife of the editor of the *Nation & Athenaeum*, Hubert Henderson.

off to see Lord Beaverbrook[1] and the Editor of the Morning Post – which he does with great success, while Clive complains bitterly that if only we had got Mary's car, which we cant have, because Jack [Hutchinson, her husband] has tonsilitis, and refuses to let Mary or the car out of his sight, we might have tackled Winston Churchill himself.[2] Miss Bulley arrives for the 6th time – will not sit down – but would like 20 copies of the [Archbishop's] letter, which I proceed to type. It is now 7 o'clock, and Roger and Helen put on their boots and decide that it is time to start off for Dalmeny, with their melons, by a back road, to avoid rioters. Walking has almost cured Roger's disease. At last they go, as Desmond returns. We then argue a little about psycho-analysis and Swinburne, which is some relief –

Soon however, Hubert Henderson rings up to say that this is the gravest moment of the strike, and there is imminent danger of civil war in South Wales. Winston has tear gas bombs in readiness: armoured cars are convoying meat through Piccadilly; all the T.U. leaders in Birmingham have been arrested. The Roneo printers refuse to print L's article on the Constitution. Will L. come to the office at once? Now it is 7.30 and we have to dine with Eileen Power and Romer Wilson:[3] Desmond has to dine with the Asquiths: Clive is going to stand by in case he can get through to Manchester on the telephone – So we dine with Eileen Power who has heard that there is no hope of a settlement for 3 weeks; and says at intervals 'This is the death blow of Trades Unionism in England' –

So we go home at 11, to find Nelly [Boxall] hanging over the stairs to say that a man called Cook and a woman called Brown want us urgently and have been calling at intervals since 8 o'clock. As we talk, the bell rings, and Janet Vaughan appears, who says that Lord Haldane[4] and a friend of hers are bringing out an emergency paper and will we give

1. William Aitken, 1st Baron Beaverbrook (1879–1964), the Tory publisher of the *Evening Standard* and *Daily Express*.
2. During the General Strike, Churchill edited the official Government newspaper, the *British Gazette*. He was then Chancellor of the Exchequer, and the most resolute opponent of the strikers.
3. Eileen Power (1889–1940), a medieval historian, was now a Reader in Economic History at the London School of Economics. The novelist Romer Wilson (1891–1930) had won the Hawthornden Prize in 1921 for *The Death of Society*.
4. Richard Haldane, Viscount Haldane (1856–1928) held office in pre-war Liberal Governments and became Lord Chancellor in the 1924 Labour administration. He wrote on philosophical and political subjects.

them our letter and list of names to be printed at once. She has a bicycle outside, and though she has just bicycled from Wandsworth where she has been acting to strikers,[1] she will bicycle with it to Fleet Street (all papers are about the size of foolscap, and mostly typewritten.) While this is being prepared, Brown or Haldane rings up to say it is now too late. At last we go to bed. At 9.30 this morning, as I began by saying, Laski rings up – and so we go on.

Strike settled 1 P.M. This has just been broadcast – as you'll probably have heard by now. Everyone is in the greatest spirits. Books at once begin to sell – I've spent the afternoon in wild discussions with Viola,[2] who is beside herself to get her book floated – We are probably having 24 sandwichmen on Monday. I hope your show is now safe – Work begins tonight. Miners still have to settle terms finally wh. they do on Friday. The Nation is coming out – Maynard is up – In short everybody is jubilant and almost hysterical. You probably think this all nonsense – but the relief after all these days of misery with lights half out, nobody doing anything, and the only news coming at intervals in Nelly's bedroom from the wireless is terrific. We're going to have a strike dinner and drink champagne with Clive, the Frys, and other spirits.

Please write.

We shall now be rushed off our feet I hope with orders.

Yr B.

1644: To Vanessa Bell   *52 Tavistock Square, W.C.1*

2nd June. 1926

Dearest,

[. . .] We were at a party at Edith Sitwell's last night, where a good deal of misery was endured. Jews swarmed. It was in honour of Miss Gertrude Stein who was throned on a broken settee (all Ediths furniture is derelict, to make up for which she is stuck about with jewels like a drowned mermaiden.) This resolute old lady inflicted great damage on

1. Madge Vaughan's daughter Janet, now aged 27 and a pathologist, was organising concerts for the strikers.
2. Viola Tree (1884–1939), the performer and daughter of the famous actor-manager Sir Herbert Beerbohm Tree, placed her memoirs, *Castles in the Air*, with The Hogarth Press, who had published it the previous month. Its distribution had been halted by the General Strike.

all the youth. According to Dadie [Rylands], she contradicts all you say; insists that she is not only the most intelligible, but also the most popular of living writers; and in particular despises all of English birth. Leonard, being a Jew himself, got on very well with her. [. . .]

Then I went to your show. [. . .] What I think is this: there is a divinely lovely landscape of yours of Charleston: one of flashing brilliance, of sunlight crystallised, of diamond durability. This I consider your masterpiece. I do not think the big picture of Angelica etc. in the garden quite succeeds. I expect the problem of empty spaces, and how to model them, has rather baffled you. There are flat passages, so that the design is not completely comprehended. Of the smaller works, I think the blue boat by the bridge is my favourite. Indeed, I am amazed, a little alarmed (for as you have the children, the fame by rights belongs to me) by your combination of pure artistic vision and brilliance of imagination. A mistress of the brush – you are now undoubtedly that; but still I think the problems of design on a large scale slightly baffle you. For example the Aunt Julia photograph.[1] It seems to me that when you muffle the singing quality of your tone, and reduce the variety and innumerability of colour (The pigeon breast radiance in which you are so supreme that, before hot pokers, or the asters (?) my mind shivers with joy) to bone, where the frame of the design is prominent, then, now and again, you falter, or somehow flatten. But I was hugely impressed, and kept on saying that your genius as a painter, though rather greater than I like, does still shed a ray on mine. I mean, people will say, What a gifted couple! Well: it would have been nicer had they said: Virginia had all the gifts; dear old Nessa was a domestic character – Alas, alas, they'll never say that now. [. . .]

Yr B

1655: To V. Sackville-West   *52 Tavistock Square, W.C.1*

[15 July 1926]

Dear Mrs Nicolson,

   [. . .] Oh what an evening! I expected a ravishing and diaphanous dragonfly, a woman who had spirited away 4 husbands, and wooed from buggery the most obstinate of his adherents: a siren; a green and

1. The distinguished photographer, Julia Margaret Cameron, *née* Pattle (1815–79), Virginia and Vanessa's great aunt on their mother's side.

sweetvoiced nymph – that was what I expected, and came a tiptoe in to the room to find – a solid hunk: a hatchet minded, cadaverous, acid voiced, bareboned, spavined, patriotic nasal, thick legged American.[1] All the evening she declaimed unimpeachable truths; and discussed our sales: hers are 3 times better than mine, naturally; till thank God, she began heaving on her chair and made a move as if to go, gracefully yielded to, but not, I beg you to believe, solicited, on our parts. Figure my woe, on the stairs, when she murmured, 'Its the *other* thing I want. Comes of trying to have children. May I go in there?' So she retired to the W.C., emerged refreshed; sent away her cab, and stayed another hour, hacking us to pieces. But I must read her book [*The Venetian Glass Nephew* (1925)]. [. . .]

> Your devoted
> Virginia Woolf.

1677: To Gerald Brenan   [*Monk's House, Rodmell, Sussex*]

Oct 3rd [1926]

My dear Gerald,
    [. . .] Ralph said he had read enough of your novel [*A Holiday by the Sea*] to perceive a masterpiece. Why aren't I allowed to read it then? Am I inferior to Ralph? Certainly, in some ways. I dont think I shall ever possess his sexual powers, for one thing, which must be a cause of endless pleasure to him: though a little mystifying, I daresay, to Frances Marshall.[2] Do the sexes differ greatly here? I wish you would explain what this vein in the thigh does to the vision of the world – slip a purple shade over it, or what? [. . .]

> Yrs V.W.

1687: To V. Sackville-West   *52 Tavistock Sqre* [*W.C.1*]

[19 November 1926]

    [. . .] But you dont see, donkey West, that you'll be tired of me one of

---

1. Virginia was speaking of Elinor Wylie (1885–1928), the American poet and novelist. She was married three times, not four.
2. Frances Marshall (b. 1900) was a young Newnham graduate, with whom Ralph Partridge had fallen in love in the summer of 1923. She was soon part of the unusual social mix at Ham Spray, where Lytton Strachey and Carrington also lived. After Carrington's death in 1932, Ralph and Frances married.

these days (I'm so much older) and so I have to take my little precautions. Thats why I put the emphasis on 'recording' rather than feeling. But donkey West knows she has broken down more ramparts than anyone. And isnt there something obscure in you? There's something that doesn't vibrate in you: It may be purposely – you dont let it: but I see it with other people, as well as with me: something reserved, muted – God knows what. Still, still, compare this 19th Nov – with last, and you'll admit there's a difference. It's in your writing too, by the bye. The thing I call central transparency – sometimes fails you there too. I will lecture you on this at Long Barn. Oh why does [Robert] Bridges say my essays are poor, and Mr [Goldsworthy Lowes] Dickinson say I'm the finest critic in English literature? I cannot believe that anybody has ever been so mis-rated as I am: and it makes it much harder to go full tilt at fiction or essays: Let them damn my novels, and I'd do essays: damn essays and I'd do novels. This is one of those glib lies one's pen slips out: of course I shall go on doing precisely what I want. Only with me two inches in the top are so tremendously susceptible. Darling donkey West – will you come at 2.30 – to the Press, I think: and then how nice I shall lie on the sofa and be spoilt. But my [headache] pain is going already. Was Irene[1] nicer than I am? Do you know this interesting fact. I found myself thinking with intense curiosity about death? Yet if I'm persuaded of anything, it is of mortality – Then why this sense that death is going to be a great excitement? – something positive; active?

Yr
VW.

P.S.
The flowers have come, and are adorable, dusky, tortured, passionate like you – And I've had lunch and feel ever so much better, and have read my letter, and am ashamed of its egotism, and feel tempted to tear it up, but have no time to write another. And don't I lecture you nicely? Thats what comes of attacking your poor Virginia and dog Grizzle. They bite instantly.

But at the same time they adore: and if you hadn't the eyes of a newt and the blood of a toad, you'd see it, and not need telling –

---

1. Irene Cooper Willis, a barrister, writer and feminist.

1711: To V. Sackville-West   *52 Tavistock Sqre* [*W.C.1*]

Wednesday, Feb. 2nd. [1927]

[. . .] Yes, I like you to write good poetry. My parting lecture was not very coherent. I was trying to get at something about the thing itself before its made into anything: the emotion, the idea. The danger for you with your sense of tradition and all those words – a gift of the Gods though – is that you help this too easily into existence. I dont mean that one ought to strain, to write showily, expressively, or so on: only that one ought to stand outside with one's hands folded, until the thing has made itself visible: we born writers tend to be ready with our silver spoons too early: I mean I think there are odder, deeper, more angular thoughts in your mind than you have yet let come out. Still, you'll get the Hawthornden [Prize], Oh yes, and I shall be vaguely jealous, proud, and disgusted. [. . .]

                                                            Yr V.

1716: To Ethel Sands   *52 Tavistock Square* [*W.C.1*]

Wednesday [9 February 1927]

Dearest Ethel,
    [. . .] was I very absurd about children last night? I was rather shocked that you should think I didn't care for Nessa's. They are such an immense source of pleasure to me. But I see what it is: I'm always angry with myself for not having forced Leonard to take the risk in spite of doctors; he was afraid for me and wouldn't; but if I'd had rather more self-control no doubt it would have been all right. That's I suppose, why I don't talk of Nessa's children – it's true I never do – whom I adore. This is only a small contribution to feminine psychology, and don't I beg dream of answering. I daresay your charming character is to blame for confidences. [. . .]

                                                            Yr aff
                                                            V.W.

1717: To V. Sackville-West   *52 Tavistock Sqre* [*W.C.1*]

Wednesday, Feb. 16th [1927]

[. . .] There's nothing I wouldn't do for you, dearest Honey. Its true, the other night, I did take a glass too much. Its your fault though – that

Spanish wine. I got a little tipsy. And then Bobo Mayor[1] is a great seducer in her way. She has gipsy blood in her: she's rather violent and highly coloured, sinuous too, with a boneless body, and thin hands; all the things I like. So, being a little tipsy about twelve o'clock at night, I let her do it.

She cut my hair off. I'm shingled. That being so – and it'll look all right in a month or two, the hairdresser says – bound to be a little patchy at first – lets get on to other things. Its off; its in the kitchen bucket: my hairpins have been offered up like crutches in St Andrews, Holborn, at the high altar. Darling Honey, if anything could make me say Vita's a villain it is that you didn't tell me, you'll be happier, wiser, serener, cleverer a thousand times shingled than haired. As for beauty, I looked in the glass a week ago; and I assure you, its an illusion: a mirage: I'm a plain woman; shall be plainer; so a bingling and shingling more or less dont matter: but let us get on to something interesting.

Nothing occurs to me at the moment. [. . .]

I must post this, but like lingering over it, though my hand is so cold I cant write, in order to be with you. You shall ruffle my hair in May,[2] Honey: its as short as a partridges rump. [. . .]

> Your
> Virginia

1722: To V. Sackville-West   *Monks House, Rodmell*
                                      [Sussex]

Sunday, Feb 28th 1927

[. . .] does it strike you that one's friendships are long conversations, perpetually broken off, but always about the same thing with the same person? With Lytton I talk about reading; with Clive about love; with Nessa about people; with Roger about art; with Morgan about writing; with Vita – well, what do I talk about with Vita? Sometimes we snore – [. . .]

> Yr
> Virginia

---

1. Beatrice Mayor, *née* Meinertzhagen (1885–1971), the author of several plays.
2. On Vita's return from her second long trip to Persia.

1735: To V. Sackville-West   *52 Tavistock Sqre [W.C.1]*

March 23rd 1927

Dearest Honey,

[...] Why do I think of you so incessantly, see you so clearly the moment I'm in the least discomfort? An odd element in our friendship. Like a child, I think if you were here, I should be happy. Talking to Lytton the other night he suddenly asked me to advise him in love – whether to go on, over the precipice, or stop short at the top. Stop, stop! I cried, thinking instantly of you. Now what would happen if I let myself go over? Answer me that. Over what? you'll say. A precipice marked V.

I had a visit from Edith Sitwell whom I like. I like her appearance – in red cotton, many flounced, though it was blowing a gale. She has hands that shut up in one's own hands like fans – far more beautiful than mine. She is like a clean hare's bone that one finds on a moor with emeralds stuck about it. She is infinitely tapering, and distinguished and old maidish and hysterical and sensitive. She told me awful Brontë stories about being cursed by her mother as a child and made to kill blue bottles in a hot room. I like talking to her about her poetry – she flutters about like a sea bird, crying so dismally. But honey, can one make a new friend? Can one begin new intimate relations? Dont mistake me. No precipice in this case – Only I was discussing friendship with Morgan Forster. One cannot follow up human relations any more he said. Theres Dante to read. Solitude – ones soul. He is half a monk. An elderly bugger is always something of a priest. [...]

Yr
Virginia

1741: To V. Sackville-West   *Villa Corsica, Cassis*
[France][1]

Tuesday, 5th April (1927]

[...] I am writing, with difficulty, on a balcony in the shade. Everything is divided into brilliant yellow and ink black. Clive is seated at a rickety table writing on huge sheets of foolscap, which he picks out

1. On their way to Italy, the Woolfs had stopped in Cassis to stay with Vanessa and Duncan, who for the next few years spent several months a year there. Clive Bell, recovering from his broken relationship with Mary Hutchinson, was in Cassis too.

from time to time in red ink. This is The history of Civilisation [1928]. He has by him Chamber's Dictionary of the English Language. We all sit in complete silence. Underneath, on the next balcony, Vanessa and Duncan are painting the loveliest pictures of rolls of bread, oranges, wine bottles. In the garden, which is sprinkled with saucers of daisies, red and white, and pansies, the gardener is hoeing the completely dry earth. There is also the Mediterranean – and some bare bald grey mountains, which I look at, roasting in the sun, and think Vita is climbing over hills like that at this moment. I hope your rubber shoes are doing well. Talk of solitude – I think your analysis highly subtle (oh yes and you're a clever donkey West: an original donkey: for all your golden voice, which has the world by the ears) It is the last resort of the civilised: our souls are so creased and soured in meaning we can only unfold them when we are alone. So Leonard thinks; and is determined to buy a farm house here and live alone, with me, half the year. It may be our form of religion. But then what becomes of friendship, love, intimacy? Nessa says, suddenly, she has been wondering why one is supposed to attend to people. Other relations seem to her far more important. I say, thats what Vita says in her letter this morning. Heard from Vita? says Clive, pricking up his ears, like a war horse, out at grass – (for he has renounced the world, and puts water in his wine, and looks incredibly pink and fresh) Yes, I say. And off we go, discussing you and Harold and Dottie,[1] whom we gather, (Clive and I that is) is not altogether cut out for the life of a diplomatists friend in Teheran. This may be over subtle, and malicious, on our part. But you know what Clive is, and Virginia too, when they get together. [. . .]

Are you well?

Virginia

1742: To Vanessa Bell   *Hotel de France, Palermo*
                                         [Sicily]

9th April 1927

Dearest,

Will there be a special allowance for letters written under circumstances of great difficulty? If so, this one must be paid at a rate of 17

1. Dorothy Wellesley (1891–1956) was married to Lord Gerald Wellesley (later Duke of Wellington). She was a poet and, most important in this context, one of Vita's loves and a lifelong friend. She had stayed with the Nicolsons in Persia.

inches by 8¾: oil: canvas: still life.[1] We are sitting in our bedroom after dinner. The light is suspended in thick glass some feet above my head. Leonard is dusting the table with his bandanna. I have made an awful mess with various odds and ends accumulated during my travels: several packets of cigarettes for instance have been ground to powder. There are explosions going on in the street and a general buzz and hum which rather entice me to step out into the Square and go to the movies; but we are off to Segesta[2] early tomorrow so we are having a quiet night. However, they are at this moment marching through the Square, playing a band, with lanterns, and some sacred object under a panoply – It is Easter, I suppose – I like the Roman Catholic religion. I say it is an attempt at art; Leonard is outraged – We burst into a service of little girls in white veils this morning which touched me greatly. It seems to me simply the desire to create gone slightly crooked, and no God in it at all. Then there are little boys brandishing palms tied in red ribbon and sugar lambs everywhere – surely rather sympathetic, and to me more attuned than those olive trees which the old gentlemen are for ever painting at street corners in Cassis.

Looking out of the carriage window at Civita Vecchia, whom should we see, sitting side by side on a bench, but D. H. Lawrence and Norman Douglas[3] – unmistakable: Lawrence pierced and penetrated; Douglas hoglike and brindled – They were swept off by train one way and we went on to Rome. I am sure Rome is the city where I shall come to die – a few months before death however, for obviously the country round it is far the loveliest in the world. I dont myself care so much for the melodramatic mountains here, which go the colour of picture postcards at sunset; but outside Rome it is perfection – smooth, suave, flowing, classical, with the sea on one side, hills on the other, a flock of sheep here, and an olive grove. There I shall come to die; and I suggest, as an idea you may consider, the foundation of a colony of the aged – Roger, you, Lytton, I: all sunken cheeked, tottering and urbane, supporting each others steps along Roman roads; I dont mind if one does die at the street corner: you with a beautiful handkerchief over your head (how ashamed you made me feel of my poor partridges rump!) and the rest of

1. Vanessa had promised Virginia a painting in return for her letters.
2. The Doric temple, late 5th century B C, a few miles from Palermo.
3. Woolf and Lawrence never met, but she saw him twice, the first time in Cornwall, and in 1919 she briefly rented his cottages there. Lawrence was now 42 and had only three more years to live. Douglas (1868–1952), the author of *South Wind* (1917), lived in Italy.

us with large sticks in our hands. A death colony will certainly become desirable. However we only had time to see the Coliseum and to eat a vast dish of maccaroni. Then we crossed over to Palermo by night and I shared a cabin with an unknown but by no means romantic Swedish lady who complained that there was no lock on the door, whereupon I poked my head out from the curtains and said in my best French 'Madame, we have neither of us any cause for fear' which happily she took in good part. Its odd how much the Scandinavians scrape, scent, gurgle and clean at night considering the results next morning: as hard as a board, and as gray as a scullery pail. She suggested nothing but paring potatoes. Much though I love my own sex, my gorge heaves at the travelling female. We had two with us from Toulon to Mentone, arch and elderly, with handbags packed with face powder and complexions that not all the thyme and mint in England could sweeten – elderly virgins from Cheltenham, playing golf in France; but one feels sure they cant hit the ball – they cant do anything – they spend enough to keep you and me a year on their clothes – they have no reason to exist in this world or the next. [. . .]

Otherwise I find the clergy and the old ladies very fascinating; I find the architecture divine. Pillars of pale green and pink marble like avenues of birch trees disappearing one behind another: immense distances; vast spaces; people like ants; everything very light, gay and spacious – Why, I ask you, cant we build like that? You cant think how beautiful the human figure looks properly displayed on these staircases. I have seen the mosaics [at Monreale]: there is one of hunting which I liked; but the gilt tends to be tinselly. My taste is naturally so bad that I dont in the least mind exposing it. [. . .]

Yr B

1743: To Vanessa Bell   *Hotel de Rome, Syracuse*
                                          [Sicily]

14th April [1927]

Dearest,

This is again written in great difficulties sitting beside the fountain of Arethusa (she was pursued by Alpheus as you know and they now spout together eternally) in a glare of sun and dust with Italians asleep, one singing, a man playing a mandoline; a beggar. But the worse I write, the better you must paint: were it not for a picture, I should not bring myself to write at all. We got here last night, and who should we meet driving from the station, but Osbert Sitwell, who stopped the cab and was very friendly, but he is lodged in a grand hotel outside the town, whereas we lodge in a cheap Italian inn, where no one speaks English, and we get delicious food, and there are only Italian officers and widows, and thank God, no Germans – so I dont suppose we shall see Osbert. There is a courtyard, with two cats in a basket, a waiter varnishing a table and an old woman picking over mattresses: I am rapidly falling in love with Italy. I think it is much more congenial than France – All the men must be womanisers. The old innkeeper cooks an omelette specially for me. I dreamt all night of Duncan and Carrington. She asked him to get her with child, which he did. This was so vivid I woke and asked Leonard if he would think it a compliment should Bea[1] ask the same of him. But alas – my dream is gone like smoke; Carrington bears none of Duncan's children within her, I'm sure. Aint it odd how all the flowers of female youth will die with their buds unopened – Carrington, Alix [Strachey], Frances,[2] – This is the sort of thing Leonard and I maunder on about as we sit in the ruins.

Last night we explored Syracuse by moonlight. But how am I to describe without boring you, particularly as you won't have drunk a bottle of wine, and be half tipsy as I was – the bay, the schooners, the blue sky, with the white pillars, like paper, and clouds crossing, and people sauntering, and a man on stilts – no it cant be done. One's mind is such a hotch potch of different things, always on the bubble – I daresay painters are more concentrated, but less amiable and lovable in their marmoreal chastity than we are – you and Duncan always seem to me, though some appearances are against it, marmoreally chaste – You have cast out so many of the devils that afflict poor creatures like me – Ever since I left Cassis I have thought of you as a bowl of golden water which brims but never overflows. A back hander? Eh? Well, I am being brushed off my seat by an old man who is sweeping the ground. [. . .]

I dont bear my friends ill will, but I think of them all as dead, or far removed behind a painted curtain, which I have no wish to draw aside – I should like to go on travelling from town to town all my life. rambling about ruins and watching schooners come in, and falling in love with Italian girls, who all look like Millais drawings in the Cornhill. I should

1. Beatrice Howe, later Lubbock, a friend of Clive Bell, and author of the novel *A Fairy Leapt Upon My Knee*.
2. Frances Marshall and Ralph Partridge had a son in 1935.

rather like to write; which one cant do; but perhaps it is nicer to imagine books, which I do all day long, until I have to tell them to poor old Leonard – We spend a lot of time on the balcony looking at people in the street. All the horses wear ostrich feathers. Tell Angelica I woke up in the night travelling to Rome and found her matchbox. It came in very handy – I have several secrets to tell her, in great private – I have seen three new witcherinas. They sent her their love. I said she had a beautiful tribe of Elves, and also a crested newt but this is *very private*.

Did Tommie and Julia[1] confide in you? How anyone can think him attractive, physically, passes me – But I am not a judge of the manly form, I suppose – He reminds me of Georges [Duckworth] opera hat – the thing he carried under his arm to make him look diplomatic – and God knows why, here is a letter from George about some book of his, which he wants Leonard to praise. I dont think I shall ever come home. But please, good Dolphin, write to Rome. You have kept your hair. You are beautiful, beloved, chaste: and I am none of these things.

V.W.

1745: To Vanessa Bell   *Hotel Hassler-New York*
                                         Piazza Trinita dei Monti, Rome

21st April 1927

Dearest.

[. . .] I'm sure, to return to your letter, that I should make a vile mother. For one thing (though this I try to hide from you) I slightly distrust or suspect the maternal passion. It is obviously immeasurable and unscrupulous. You would fry us all to cinders to give Angelica a days pleasure, without knowing it. You are a mere tool in the hands of passion. Other mothers are much worse, and I've no doubt I should be worst of all – Helen Anrep and Faith [Henderson] appal me when they talk of their children: In fact what you feel about marriage I feel about motherhood, except that of the two relations motherhood seems to me the more destructive and limiting. But no doubt I'm merely trying to make out a case for myself: there's some truth in [it] though; I dont like profound instincts – not in human relationships. [. . .]

B.

1. Stephen Tomlin and Lytton's niece, the writer Julia Strachey (1901–79), visitors at Cassis, married in July of this year, but the marriage was unhappy.

1750: To Vanessa Bell   *52 Tavistock Square* [*W.C.1*]

Sunday 8th May 1927

Dearest,

[...] Quentin [now aged 16] came to lunch. That boy is really a marvel. He drank two full tumblers of strong Spanish wine, where I can only take a wine-glass; and it was a hot day; and then he went off to shop, and seemed quite as steady as usual, and came back to tea, and had a long argument with me about poetry and painting. Probably I am almost as spotted with the maternal taint as you are. My pride rises at the sight of him, and I find myself boasting to the char about his height and his age as if I were Aunt Mary. I only wish they didn't both (Quentin and Julian, I mean) think Bernard Shaw greater than Shakespeare. Quentin sees nothing in poetry. For God's sake dont tell me you put in by mistake a drop too much of the old Bell in them – I always thought you were playing with gunpowder in that marriage, and you scarcely deserved to come off as well as you did. [...]

By the way, your story of the Moth so fascinates me that I am going to write a story about it. I could think of nothing else but you and the moths for hour's after reading your letter.[1]

Isn't it odd? – perhaps you stimulate the literary sense in me as you say I do your painting sense.

God! How you'll laugh at the painting bits in the Lighthouse!

Yr B.

1754: To V. Sackville-West   *52 Tavistock Square* [*W.C.1*]

Friday [13 May 1927]

Darling Vita,

What a generous woman you are! Your letter [in praise of *To the Lighthouse*] has just come, and I must answer it, though in a chaos. (Nelly returning: her doctor; her friends; her diet etc) I was honest though in thinking you wouldn't care for The Lighthouse: too psychological; too many personal relationships, I think. (This is said not of the dummy

1. From Cassis Vanessa had described the great numbers of moths that regularly circled her lamp, particularly one enormous one that, captured for her children, refused to be killed by the usual chloroform. The narrative, or rather the image, was one of the inspirations for Virginia's *The Moths*, which became her most experimental novel, *The Waves* (1931).

copy)[1] The dinner party the best thing I ever wrote: the one thing that I think justifies my faults as a writer: This damned 'method'. Because I don't think one could have reached those particular emotions in any other way. I was doubtful about Time Passes. It was written in the gloom of the Strike: then I re-wrote it: then I thought it impossible as prose – I thought you could have written it as poetry. I don't know if I'm like Mrs Ramsay: as my mother died when I was 13 probably it is a child's view of her: but I have some sentimental delight in thinking that you like her. She has haunted me: but then so did that old wretch my father: Do you think it sentimental? Do you think it irreverent about him? I should like to know. I was more like him than her, I think; and therefore more critical: but he was an adorable man, and somehow, tremendous. [...]

VW.
(oh I forgot –
Virginia Woolf)

1756: To Vanessa Bell   *52 Tavistock Sqre, WC1*

Sunday 15th May 1927

Dearest,

No letter from you – But I see how it is –

Scene: after dinner: Nessa sewing: Duncan doing absolutely nothing.

Nessa: (throwing down her work) Christ! There's the Lighthouse! I've only got to page 86 and I see there are 320. Now I cant write to Virginia because she'll expect me to tell her what I think of it.

Duncan   Well, I should just tell her that you think it a masterpiece.

Nessa   But she's sure to find out – They always do. She'll want to know why I think its a masterpiece

Duncan   Well Nessa, I'm afraid I cant help you, because I've only read 5 pages so far, and really I dont see much prospect of doing much reading this month, or next month, or indeed before Christmas.

---

1. In addition to the real thing, Virginia had sent Vita a copy of *To the Lighthouse* inscribed 'In my opinion the best novel I have ever written.' Inside Vita found all the pages blank.

Nessa   Oh its all very well for you. But I shall have to say something: And I dont know who in the name of Jupiter all these people are (turns over some pages desperately) I think I shall make a timetable: its the only way: ten pages a day for 20 days is –

Duncan   But you'll never be able to keep up ten pages a day.

Nessa   (rather dashed) No – I suppose I shant. Well then, one may as well be hung for a sheep as for a goat – though whats the sense of saying that I never could see: a sheep is almost identical with a goat in some countries; except that one can milk a goat of course. Lord! I shall never forget Violet Dickinson at Athens and the goats milk! But what was I saying when you interrupted me? Oh yes: I shall take the bull by the horns. I shall write to Virginia and say 'I think its a masterpiece –' (she takes the inkpot and prepares to write, but finds it full of dead and dying insects). 'Oh Duncan, what have you done with the inkpot? used it to catch flies in? But thats a beetle! Yes it is. Beetles have 12 legs: flies only 8. D'you mean to say you didn't know that? Well, I suppose you're one of those people who think a spider's an insect: Now if you'd been brought up in Cornwall you'd know that a spiders not an insect; its – no I dont think its a reptile: its something queer. I know. Anyhow, I cant write to Virginia, because the ink is nothing but a mass of beetles or spiders legs – I really dont know what they are: but one man's meat is another man's poison; and if you will use the ink pot to catch flies in, then I dont see how even Virginia herself could possibly expect, or even wish me to write to her – (they settle down again to discuss spiders etc etc etc)

Now isn't this word for word the truth? [. . .]

I'm engulfed in writing a paper on poetry to read to some Oxford undergraduates on Wednesday – Vita comes with me – We stay at an hotel. Let us hope for nightingales, moons, and love – [. . .]

Adrian and Karin [Stephen] have patched, she tells me, a working marriage; which means she will visit American asylums 6 months of the year; and the other 6 live here. But her sterling qualities are now uppermost, and I was deeply touched – I dont quite know by what – It came over me sitting with her, dumb, and deaf, and resolute, in front of the open window, watching Alix and Waley[1] march round and round

1. Arthur Waley (1889–1966), the translator from Asian languages.

the square together. These things do come over me – Its what makes me so undependable as a friend – Tomorrow I am lunching at Simpsons with Saxon [Sydney-Turner] to meet some Swedes – 'not exciting people exactly' he said; so I expect an uproarious time. We are, by the way, taking a first class carriage to see the Eclipse in June.[1] Will you share? It stops in Yorkshire as the sun disappears, for 5 seconds; we all get out and look up; hot coffee is then served and we return to London – Saxon is coming; also the Swedes. [. . .]

Yr B.

1760: TO VANESSA BELL   *Monks House, Rodmell,*
                                         [Sussex]

Sunday – 22nd May 1927

Dearest,

I was so pleased and excited by your letter[2] that I trotted about all day like a puppy with a bone. In fact you entirely destroyed my powers of work: I was always taking it out and reading it again, until I thought perhaps I exaggerated, and ran off to Leonard with it to ask him if he thought you really meant it. Taking into account your well known character, he decided, finally, that you probably did. So then I settled down to complete satisfaction, which no one else's letters have given me – (here's one that may recall the character of Dora Sanger to you – I dont want it back)

But what do you think I did know about mother? It can't have been much – What would Quentin have known of you if you had died when he was 13? I suppose one broods over some germ; but I specially refrained either from reading her letters, or father's life. He was easier to do, but I was very much afraid you would think me sentimental. I seem to make people think that the Stephen family was one of insane gloom. I thought it was a cheerful enough book. I don't defend my accuracy, though I think Watts used to buy lapis lazuli, break it up with a small hammer, and keep it under damp cloths. I think, too, the pre-raphaelites thought it more like nature to use garden clay, whenever possible; to

1. On 28 June Virginia, Leonard, Vita, Harold, Eddy Sackville West, Quentin and Saxon left London by train for Richmond, Yorkshire, where early next morning they watched the total eclipse of the sun from Bardon Fell.
2. Vanessa had been deeply moved by the portraits of their parents in the Ramsays.

serve for colours. Lord Olivier writes that my horticulture and natural history is in every instance wrong: there are no rooks, elms, or dahlias in the Hebrides; my sparrows are wrong; so are my carnations: and it is impossible for women to die of childbirth in the 3rd month – He infers that Prue had had a slip (which is common in the Hebrides) and was 9 months gone. This is the sort of thing that painters know nothing of. [. . .]

Ottoline impends; but she never fades – She's still at Garsington; Philip sits in the Nation chucking Mrs Jones[1] on the chin, and Leonard comes in to find 'P.M' [Philip Morrell] marked on all the best books. 'Uncle Philip would like these, please, Mr Woolf' says Mrs Jones archly. Leonard says nothing. He says, going out, casually, 'Mr Morrell may do a briefer notice of the Aztecs if he likes: but if he writes more than 50 words, I shall cut it.' With the Morrells in London, this snuggling and chucking, to put it euphemistically, may increase; and not wanting a whole clutch of bastards, Ottoline may stay away.

Then I went to Oxford to speak to the youth of both sexes on poetry and fiction. They are young; they are callow; they know nothing about either – They sit on the floor and ask innocent questions about Joyce – They are years behind the Cambridge young, it seemed to me; Quentin and Julian could knock them into mud pies. But they have their charm – There was a man called Martin (I think) an adorer and disciple of Roger's, who was the most intelligent. We went on to somebodies rooms, and there they sat on the floor, and said what a master they thought Roger Fry; and were Bell and Grant able to make a living by decorations; and was Tom Eliot happy with his wife. They're oddly under our thumb, at the moment – at least this particular group. Roger, the old wizard, has them all entranced – I pretended to a degree of intimacy which, alas, is not mine, to colour my cheeks for them. Clive, they said, was very good fun; but we always feel Roger Fry's the real mind. Then there was Vita, very striking; like a willow tree; so dashing, on her long white legs with a crimson bow; but rather awkward, forced indeed to take her stockings down and rub her legs with ointment at dinner, owing to midges – I like this in the aristocracy. I like the legs; I like the bites; I like the complete arrogance and unreality of their minds – for instance buying silk dressing gowns casually for £5 and then

1. Alice Jones (1878–1970), whose 'Mrs' was a courtesy title, was the secretary to the editor of the *Nation & Athenaeum*. Her affair with Philip Morrell, who had been her employer during the war, produced a son in 1917.

lunching off curd cream (a yellow mess) which she picked out of tartlet with a fork, dropping the pastry back into the dish; and then tipping porters a shilling for doing nothing; and then – the whole thing (I cant go into details) is very splendid and voluptuous and absurd. Also she has a heart of gold, and a mind which, if slow, works doggedly; and has its moments of lucidity – But enough – You will never succumb to the charms of any of your sex – What an arid garden the world must be for you! What avenues of stone pavements and iron railings! Greatly though I respect the male mind, and adore Duncan (but, thank God, he's hermaphrodite, androgynous, like all great artists) I cannot see that they have a glowworm's worth of charm about them – The scenery of the world takes no lustre from their presence. They add of course immensely to its dignity and safety: but when it comes to a little excitement – ! (I see that you will attribute all this to your own charms in which I daresay you're not far wrong). [. . .]

I creep up and peer into the Stephen's dining room where any afternoon, in full daylight, is to be seen a woman in the last agony of despair, lying on a sofa, burying her face in the pillow, while Adrian broods over her like a vulture, analysing her soul.[1] It is exactly like a picture by John Collier. [. . .]

Yr B.

1764: To Roger Fry   *52 Tavistock Sqre [W.C.1]*

May 27th 1927

My dear Roger,

[. . .] I meant *nothing* by The Lighthouse. One has to have a central line down the middle of the book to hold the design together. I saw that all sorts of feelings would accrue to this, but I refused to think them out, and trusted that people would make it the deposit for their own emotions – which they have done, one thinking it means one thing another another. I can't manage Symbolism except in this vague, generalised way. Whether its right or wrong I don't know, but directly I'm told what a thing means, it becomes hateful to me. [. . .]

Yr
V.W.

1. Adrian Stephen was in his last year of training as a psychoanalyst.

1780: To V. Sackville-West   [52 Tavistock Square, W.C.1]

Monday [4 July 1927]

Yes you are an agile animal – no doubt about it, but as to your gambols being diverting, always, at Ebury Street for example, at 4 o'clock in the morning, I'm not so sure. Bad, wicked beast! To think of sporting with oysters – lethargic glucous lipped oysters, lewd lascivious oysters, stationary cold oysters, – to think of it, I say.[1] Your oyster has been in tears on the telephone imploring Clive to come back to her – thats all the faith there is in oysters. But what did I come back to? A message from Dadie [Rylands], and he's coming in next minute, and I'm alone, and Leonards motoring, and we shall have 2 or 3 hours tête à tête – I and Dadie. Hah Hah! Bad Wicked Beast.

At the same time, there were the mushrooms: the crab: the bed; the log fire: All shall be credited to you. I'm a fair minded woman. You only be a careful dolphin in your gambolling, or you'll find Virginia's soft crevices lined with hooks. You'll admit I'm mysterious – you don't fathom me yet – Who knows what – but here's Dadie: [. . .]

Yr Virginia

1783: To V. Sackville-West   52 Tavistock Sqre, W.C.1

18th July 1927

My dear Mrs Nicolson,

I cant tell you how I enjoyed myself on Sunday. It was so good of you and your husband to let me come. And what a lovely garden! I cant think how you can ever bear to leave it. But then *everything* was so delightful. London seemed more commonplace than ever after your delightful Long Barn. And I still have some of your lovely flowers to remind me of the happy time I had with you, and your husband, to whom please give my best thanks and remembrances, and with much love to you both, I am. There, you ramshackle old Corkscrew, is that the kind of thing you like? I suppose so.

What I think will be so nice next time is the porpoise in my bath – steel blue, ice cold, and loving hearted. Some prefer dolphins – I dont.

---

1. Vita had spent an unchaste night with Mary Hutchinson, and had told Virginia about it during her recent stay at Vita's house, Long Barn.

I've known one dolphin, the Mediterranean kind, ravage a whole bedfull of oysters. A lewd sort of brute that. [...]

Honey dearest, don't go to Egypt please. Stay in England. Love Virginia. Take her in your arms. [...]

Yr Virginia

1800: TO SAXON SYDNEY-TURNER   *Monk's House, Rodmell*
[Sussex]

Sunday Aug 21st (1927]

My dear Saxon,

[...] I am reading a new classic every night. But what is happening to you? and to Barbara [Bagenal] and to Barbara's child and to Mrs Stagg [his landlady] and to your uncle the ichthyologist? This is the group, you see, in which I compose you. Then there's your great grandfather's life.[1] Do you agree that one never thinks of Saxon or Barbara singly, but always as the centre of a nest of other objects? This fact has never been observed by the novelists – but my word, what a set of dunderheads and duffers they are! Even Scott has passages of an incredible imbecility. Trollope has gone up in my estimation however. But then, as its all a question of mood, and of what one's just read, or whom one's just seen, whats the good of criticism? And, anyhow, vile as they are, the novelists outdo the critics. You probably have no notion what the criticism of fiction amounts to – you, who have passed your entire life on the highest peaks of Parnassus where only a few asphodels grow in the snow. Grow and Snow ought not to be there; but there they are. [...]

Yrs
V.W.

1820: TO V. SACKVILLE-WEST   *52 Tavistock Sqre. [W.C.1]*

9th Oct. [1927]

[...] Yesterday morning I was in despair: You know that bloody book which Dadie and Leonard extort, drop by drop, from my breast? Fiction, or some title to that effect [*Phases of Fiction*]. I couldn't screw a

---

1. Saxon had suggested that the diary of his great-grandfather, Sharon Turner, might be made into a book for The Hogarth Press, but the idea died.

word from me; and at last dropped my head in my hands: dipped my pen in the ink, and wrote these words, as if automatically, on a clean sheet: Orlando: A Biography. No sooner had I done this than my body was flooded with rapture and my brain with ideas. I wrote rapidly till 12. Then I did an hour to Romance. So every morning I am going to write fiction (my own fiction) till 12; and Romance till 1. But listen; suppose Orlando turns out to be Vita; and its all about you and the lusts of your flesh and the lure of your mind (heart you have none, who go gallivanting down the lanes with Campbell)¹ – suppose there's the kind of shimmer of reality which sometimes attaches to my people, as the lustre on an oyster shell (and that recalls another Mary [Hutchinson]) suppose, I say, that Sibyl [Colefax] next October says 'Theres Virginia gone and written a book about Vita' and Ozzie [Dickinson] chaws with his great chaps and Byard [of Heinemann] guffaws, Shall you mind? Say yes, or No:² Your excellence as a subject arises largely from your noble birth. (But whats 400 years of nobility, all the same?) and the opportunity thus given for florid descriptive passages in great abundance. Also, I admit, I should like to untwine and twist again some very odd, incongruous strands in you: going at length into the question of Campbell; and also, as I told you, it sprung upon me how I could revolutionise biography in a night: and so if agreeable to you I would like to toss this up in the air and see what happens. [. . .]

I am reading Knole and The Sackvilles. Dear me; you know a lot: you have a rich dusky attic of a mind. O yes, I want very much to see you.

Yr V.W. (thats because of Campbell)

1835: E. M. FORSTER   *52 Tavistock Square, W.C.1*

21st Nov. [1927]

Dear Morgan,

I'm so glad I was not annoying – only wrong. (I dont think I'm as wrong as Arnold Bennett in the Standard, all the same.) But where we

1. Vita's affair with the 28-year-old Mary Campbell, wife of the South African poet Roy Campbell, both of whom were living in the children's cottage at Long Barn, was to have nearly disastrous effects when Roy threatened violence. Virginia's disgust was masked for the most part by her jealousy.
2. Vita was thrilled with the prospect of the new book and immediately began calling herself 'Orlando' with Mary Campbell.

differ is I think plain from your letter. Both bunches have been lost, you say, 'and yet we persist in reading fiction.'[1] But I don't. Nothing induces me to read a novel except when I have to make money by writing about it. I detest them. They seem to me wrong from start to finish – my own included. And I suppose I wanted you to say something to explain to me why I feel this. Naturally you didn't, because you dont feel it. Youve lost your bunch; but still you go on. And I dont want to go on, either writing them or reading them. This only proves I think that I am not a novelist and should not criticise them either. As for your book – its perfect I think, better than anything I could ever write; (I mean this) only it doesnt light up my own particular boggle. Never mind. It is delightful and brilliant beyond words. [. . .]

Yr
Virginia

1. This letter is part of an exchange begun when Virginia reviewed Forster's *Aspects of the Novel* in the *Nation* for 12 November. Their argument was about the importance of 'life' in fiction (Forster) and 'art' (Woolf). Forster had written to her that both led to exquisite caskets, the keys to which had been lost.

1928–1929

Virginia's life continued lively and ambitious. Orlando *appeared and made its subject, as well as its reviewers, very happy. Virginia lectured on women and fiction at Cambridge, then published the work as* A Room of One's Own. *Her struggle with* Phases of Fiction *was understandable in that she was attempting to define methods that would account for most English novels and a good deal of Continental fiction as well. She also began her most daring novel,* The Waves, *imagining it barely visible on the horizon but infinitely beautiful if only she could net it.*

Her relationship with Vita grew during a trip with her to Burgundy in September 1928, but both Woolfs were miserable over their separation from each other. Leonard went with Virginia to see the Nicolsons at Harold's post in Berlin in January 1929. The popular novelist Hugh Walpole was a new correspondent. Her nephews, Julian and Quentin, were, at 20 and 18, old enough to become intriguing correspondents themselves, and Virginia was refreshed by writing to the young. Letters to Mary Hutchinson, with whom Vita had dallied, took on a flirtatious tone.

1858: To Vanessa Bell   *52 Tavistock Sqre* [*W.C.1*]

Saturday, 11th Feb. [1928]

Dearest

[. . .] I have had a most shameful and distressing interview with poor dear Tom Eliot, who may be called dead to us all from this day forward. He has become an Anglo-Catholic, believes in God and immortality, and goes to church. I was really shocked. A corpse would seem to me more credible than he is. I mean, there's something obscene in a living person sitting by the fire and believing in God. [. . .]

Yr B.

1891: To Quentin Bell   *52 Tavistock Sqre, WC1*

May 6th [1928]

My dear Quentin,

Your letter has been rather a surprise to me; because, if you can write as well as all that, with such abandonment to devilry and ribaldry, – for I dont believe a word of what you say – how in Gods name can you be content to remain a painter? Surely you must see the infinite superiority of the language to the paint? Think how many things are impossible in paint; giving pain to the Keynes', making fun of one's aunts, telling libidinous stories, making mischief – these are only a few of the advantages; against which a painter has nothing to show: for all his merits are also a writers. Throw up your career, for God's sake. [. . .]

I was fascinated and appalled by the story of your adventures – That a nephew of mine! I cried, between tears and laughter – Should one be proud of you or the very opposite – climbing the Monument naked, and sleeping with a professor of divinity, who is, unfortunately, but its the way in Germany, of the female sex – such is your way of life, and I tell it at many a merry party, half crying, half laughing.

I wish though you would come home. I want to visit the Museums with you and to consult you on many points. I dreamt of you all last night, but I shant tell you what we were doing, for fear it should shock you.

Julian is a very odd sort of phenomenon – about the size of a moderate Indian rhinoceros; said to be good tempered – I doubt it. He's a clever reptile, and is writing – there, that's what you should do.

I have had no news from your blessed mother for a fortnight, except about letting her rooms to an American. Of course Duncan went and let them to another American; of course Mrs Uppington [Vanessa's daily help] went off with the keys; of course I was blamed for everything – of course – of course.

I am scribbling away to finish my nonsense book. Have I your permission to mention you in the Preface?[1] Because I've done it.

Now sit down and write to me, dearest Quentin, a long long letter. I

---

1. In the Preface to *Orlando* Virginia acknowledges 'my nephew Mr Quentin Bell (an old and valued collaborator in fiction)', a reference to their joint comic writings within, and usually about, the family circle.

assure you, without flattery, and we know each other too well for that, you write the best letters of anyone I know.

And do come back because of our Libel.

Yr loving V.W.

1895: To Vanessa Bell   *Monk's House, Rodmell*
                                                   [Sussex]

Saturday May 25th [1928]

Dearest,

[. . .] I am feeling extremely barren and dry without you – Angelica will be a small shower of rain; but not enough – What happens when you leave me too long is that I go gadding wherever I'm asked and finally end in a rage of misery against my kind – I saw nothing but celebrities last week; Rebecca West at Todds;[1] Maurois[2] and Arnold Bennett at Colefaxes, and had Rose Macaulay to dine alone. Rebecca was much the most interesting, though as hard as nails, very distrustful, and no beauty. She is a cross between a charwoman and a gipsy, but as tenacious as a terrier, with flashing eyes, very shabby, rather dirty nails, immense vitality, bad taste, suspicion of intellectuals, and great intelligence. She gave me the true history of Isadora Duncan's life[3] – (I sent you the life, by the way, which is rather valuable, as the libraries are banning it). Rebecca has knocked about with all the mongrels of Europe. She talks openly of her son,[4] who has got consumption: They say she is a hardened liar, but I rather liked her – The Todd ménage is incredibly louche: Todd in sponge bag trousers; Garland in pearls and silk; both rather raddled and on their beam ends. Maurois was disappointing, but then Sibyl makes everyone stony, and breaks up talk with a hammer – good, deserving, industrious, kindhearted woman as she is. Rose Macaulay was a great disappointment – Some houses have gone too far to be repaired – she is one. If we had rescued her before she was 30 – but she is now 45 – has lived with the riff raff of South

1. Dorothy Todd, the editor of *Vogue* from 1922–6, had enlarged its reputation by publishing articles by sophisticated writers, including Virginia herself. Todd shared her flat with Madge Garland, the magazine's fashion editor.
2. The French biographer André Maurois (1885–1967).
3. The American dancer and free spirit, whose autobiography had just been published. She was killed in a car accident on Nice on 14 September 1927.
4. Anthony West, son of H. G. Wells.

Kensington culture for 15 years; become a successful lady novelist, and is rather jealous, spiteful, and uneasy about Bloomsbury; can talk of nothing but reviews, yet being the daughter of a Cambridge Don, knows she shouldn't; and has her tail between her legs. She made me determined not to allow Angelica, whatever happens, to become a novelist. All this fame that writers get is obviously the devil; I am not so nice as I was, but I am nicer than Rose Macaulay – also she is a spindle shanked withered virgin: I never felt anyone so utterly devoid of the sexual parts. [. . .]

B.

1918: TO V. SACKVILLE-WEST   *Monks House, Rodmell*
                                                          [Sussex]

30th Aug 1928

How do you live the life you do? Sixty people to dinner.[1] One for three days entirely dissipates my soul, and sends it floating, like duckweed, down a dirty river. I am very hot. I have been mowing the lawn. It looks now like a calm sea through which several large ships have passed leaving wakes behind them. Then I ate two plums which make my hands sticky. For many days I have been so disjected by society that writing has been only a dream – something another woman did once. What has caused this irruption I scarcely know – largely your friend Radclyffe Hall (she is now docked of her Miss owing to her proclivities) they banned her book;[2] and so Leonard and Morgan Forster began to get up a protest, and soon we were telephoning and interviewing and collecting signatures – not yours, for *your* proclivities are too well known. In the midst of this, Morgan goes to see Radclyffe in her tower in Kensington, with her love [Lady Troubridge] and Radclyffe scolds him like a fishwife, and says that she wont have any letter written about her book unless it mentions the fact that it is a work of artistic merit – even genius. And no one has read her book; or can read it: and now we have to explain this to all the great signed names – Arnold Bennett and so on. So our ardour in the cause of freedom of speech gradually cools, and instead of offering to reprint the masterpiece, we are already beginning to wish it unwritten.

1. In Berlin, where Vita was visiting her husband at his new diplomatic post.
2. *The Well of Loneliness* (1928), the famous novel about lesbianism by Radclyffe Hall (1886–1943).

I am observing with interest the fluctuations of my own feelings about France.[1] Leonard says he can't come. Like an angel he says but of course go with Vita. Then he somehow conveys without a word the fact of his intolerable loneliness without me – upon which I give it all up; and then suddenly think, what an unwholesome sentimental state this is! I will go. And then visualise myself saying goodbye to him and cant face it; and then visualise a rock in a valley with Vita in an Inn: and *must* go. So it goes on. Meanwhile Ethel Sands advises us to go to Auxerre, Vézelay, Autun, Semur, Saulieu (Hotel de la Poste has wonderful food) and we are to stay at least two nights with her and Nan.[2] I think I must manage to come. But it will be the greatest proof of devotion. And Leonard may make it impossible – Can you put up with these vacillations:? Anyhow I shall see you before anything need be done.

I am very happy and not very happy. Do you like these states of mind to take precedence of all else in letters? I am happy because it is the loveliest August; downs so brown and grey, and the meadows so – I forget what. On the other hand, I have to work all day – it seems – grinding out a few notes like those a blunt knife makes on a whetstone, at novels and novels. I read Proust, Henry James, Dostoevsky; my happiness is wedged like (but I am using too many metaphors) in between these granite blocks (and now that they are granite blocks I can compare my happiness to samphire, a small pink plant I picked as a child in Cornwall).

Why need you be so timid and pride-blown, both at once, over writing your novel? What does donkey West mean about her ambition and failure?[3] Why should you fail at this prosy art, when you can please Jack Squire with poetry? (Thats a nasty one) I am entirely of your opinion that Heaven has made us and not we ourselves. I accept no responsibility for anything I write or do. I like your fecundity. And; surely, for the last ten years almost, you have cut back and pruned and root dug – What is it one should do to fig trees? – with the result that you write sometimes too much like a racehorse who has been trained till his tail is like a mouses tail and his ribs are like a raised map of the Alps. Please write your novel, and then you will enter into the unreal world,

1. Vita had suggested that the Woolfs travel with her to Burgundy in September. In the event, Virginia went, but Leonard stayed behind, unhappy.
2. Nan Hudson (1869–1957), the American painter with whom Ethel Sands shared her life. One of their two houses was near Dieppe.
3. Vita was thinking about her next novel, *The Edwardians* (1930), and had written to Virginia that it was better to 'fail gloriously than dingily succeed' (21 August 1928).

where Virginia lives – and poor woman, can't now live anywhere else. [. . .]

Yr[1]

1922: TO V. SACKVILLE-WEST   *Monks House, Rodmell, Sussex*

Saturday, Sept 8th 1928

[. . .] I have a thousand things to say, and as usual am in a flying rush, Pinka[2] having had four puppies yesterday so that I have to go and buy Lactol or something in Lewes. They are 2 male 2 female; and she is a model of all the maternal vices – absorbed, devoted, zealous, cowish. But I was going to say that I like your Tolstoy [article] very much. I think it is your best criticism, so far as I've seen. And as I always take credit for your good writing, I'm pleased with myself. I think you have got nearer the old Sphinx than any of the other anniversarists – who abound; but blither. The question you should have pushed home – had there been room – is precisely the one you raise, what made his realism which might have been photographic, not at all; but on the contrary, moving and exciting and all the rest of it. Some dodge there must have been; some very queer arrangement – I dont know what – of perspective. But I like you when you write such interesting things – and I have a great deal to say – if only the puppies could be fed without my going to Lewes – about your novel. I thought out, indeed, a long and it seemed then very profound essay upon writing novels, and how one can know if they are only foam and gush or not, on the downs the other evening: I cant remember it now. I believe that the main thing in beginning a novel is to feel, not that you can write it, but that it exists on the far side of a gulf, which words can't cross: that its to be pulled through only in a breathless anguish. Now when I sit down to an article, I have a net of words which will come down on the idea certainly in an hour or so. But a novel, as I say, to be good should seem, before one writes it, something unwriteable: but only visible; so that for nine months one lives in despair, and only when one has forgotten what one meant, does the

1. Here, instead of her usual signature, Virginia drew a squiggly design, meant to stand for one of her intimate names with Vita, 'Bosman's Potto', a lemur.
2. Or Pinker, a spaniel, whom Vita had given the Woolfs from the litter of one of her own dogs. Pinka was the model for the main character in Virginia's book about Elizabeth Barrett Browning's dog, *Flush*.

book seem tolerable. I assure you, all my novels were first rate before they were written. [. . .]

                                                                    Yr

1924: To V. Sackville-West   *52 Tavistock Square, W.C.1*
                                 [Monk's House, Rodmell,
                                 Sussex]

Sunday [16 September 1928]

Dear Mrs N.

[. . .] I am melancholy and excited in turn. You see, I would not have married Leonard had I not preferred living with him to saying good bye to him. But at the same time, the Roman ruins in Auxerre excited my interest. Also the stained glass.

(This is what I call my fun). [. . .]

1927: To Leonard Woolf   *Saulieu [France]*

Tuesday [25 September 1928]

Dearest Mongoose, darling Mongoose,

I am writing in a field overlooking Burgundy; 4.30: very hot and fine. It rained in Paris last night; but as usual completely cleared about 8 this morning. We got up at six and arrived at one, and then we had the vastest most delicious meal I have ever eaten. It is the usual small French inn, with farmers lunching; but as I say we began with paté of duck, went on to trout, gnocchi, stuffed chicken and spinach made with cream and then sour cream and a delicious cake and then pears ad lib; as the marmots say. Then it is the annual fair in Saulieu, and we walked about looking at roundabouts and paying twopence for a chance to win a live pigeon in a lottery. I am now getting melancholy for you, and thinking that perhaps the downs are more beautiful than Burgundy. What is odd is that there is no sign of vintage. We passed through vineyards this morning, and I saw some few black bunches hanging, but here there is nothing. It seems purely French, only two naval Englishmen at lunch, and some French motorists. Then – here it got so cold that we had to come back to the hotel. I am going to sit and read I think till dinner and then there are fireworks at the fair. You will be dining at Charleston, and I hope I may get some report of Lytton. I think we must come to France with the car, doing about 30 miles a day and seeing the small towns – it certainly has great advantages, not being in a hurry and walking about looking at the country. [. . .]

Lord! I do hope you'll be careful motoring tonight! – and that you eat and sleep and dont give away all your affection to the poos [the puppies]. Poor Mandril does adore your every hair of your little body and hereby puts in a claim for an hour of antelope kissing the moment she gets back.

I forgot the timetable and my writing paper – nothing much else. This is a horrid, dull scrappy scratchy letter but all letters of real affection are dull. Do you think we are extremely intimate? I do; because, why should I, a born dandy as I am, write so carelessly – [. . .]

                    Mandrill. DUSKY DARKY Marmot esquire.

Love to Nelly [Boxall].

1932: TO LEONARD WOOLF   *Hotel de la Poste, Vézelay,*
                                       Yonne [France]

Friday 28th Sept [1928]

Dearest Mon,

I am afraid I must have seemed to you more than usually foolish to telegraph, but there were no letters at Avallon, and as we were coming here, without sleeping, I couldn't hear till Saturday at Auxerre. I wonder what happened? Vita heard from Harold, who wrote on Tuesday, by the first post; and we waited for the second and none came from you. I hope you didn't have to go into Lewes. But I admit I was ready to bother you any amount to be put out of my misery. Your answer came at 8.30 this morning. Mercifully it did, for its a pouring wet day: here we are cooped up in our bedrooms in a clean but primitive, cheap, but well cooking little inn, with Vézelay as black as London in November. [. . .]

I wonder if Quentin finished [painting] the gramophone and what you think of it. I left my address here and may get your letter this evening, more likely tomorrow morning. Vézelay is 12 miles from Avallon, 8, I think from Sermizelles: and thus we are dependent upon motor buses which come twice a day for letters.

I wonder if Lytton was heckled [at Charleston]; whether you have 'gathered' as you would say, being such a little prig – no daddies *not* a prig – we adore dadanko do-do – we want to talk with him; and kiss the

poos. Have they really begun to play the violin, daddie? Are you fonder
of them than of the marmoteski? – Now stop mots; go under the table. I
cant hear myself speak for their chatter. How they sobbed when there
was no letter from Dinkay at Avallon! Shall you be glad to see us all
again? Remember I am coming by the *Monday* boat, not Tuesday: but if
you have to go to London I suppose I could get a bus. Lord! How I adore
you! and you only think of me as a bagfull of itching monkeys, and ship
me to the Indies with indifference!

I think we shall have a very happy and exciting autumn, in spite of
the complete failure of Orlando. It is clearing slightly – we may visit the
museum.

Yrs Mandrill
D.D.

1937a: To V. Sackville-West   [*52 Tavistock Square, W.C.1*]
[12 October 1928]

Your biographer is infinitely relieved and happy.[1]

1957a: To Rebecca West   *52 Tavistock Square, W.C.1*
November 10th 1928

Dear Rebecca West,

I keep saying to myself that I will write and thank you for your
article on Orlando,[2] and then I hesitate because it seems impossible to
take all that praise to oneself. However, then my critical lobe points out
that after all the intelligence and the insight and the brilliance can be
thanked for apart from the fact that you have spent all this richness upon
me.

I can't tell you how it exhilarates me to feel your mind rushing along
where mine tried to go (what a lot more you have guessed of my

1. Virginia's telegram was a reply to Vita's letter, calling *Orlando* 'the loveliest, wisest,
richest book that I have ever read' (11 October 1928).
2. In the *New York Herald Tribune* for 21 October, West had labelled *Orlando* 'a poetic
masterpiece of the first rank', describing Virginia as a highly self-conscious writer
'whose left lobe (which is critical) is obviously without cease letting her right lobe
(which is creative) know what it doeth'. This was one of only two letters that Rebecca
West framed.

meaning than anybody else!) and expanding and understanding and making everything ten times more important than it seemed before.

So I must thank you for being the critic you are, even if I cant take all the praise you give me.

This of course needs no answer. But I hope that someday you may be in England and that we may meet.

Meanwhile I am with many thanks,

Your Virginia Woolf

University of Tulsa

1976: To V. Sackville-West   *Monk's House, Rodmell, Lewes [Sussex]*

[3 January 1929]

[...] I am light headed at the moment; why, heaven knows. I have been walking alone down a valley to Rat Farm, if that means anything to you: and the quiet and the cold and the loveliness – one hare, the weald washed away to vapour – the downs blue green; the stacks, like cakes cut in half – I say all this so excited me; and my own life suddenly became so impressive to me, not as usual shooting meteor like through the sky, but solitary and still that, as I say – well how is the sentence to end?: figure to yourself that sentence, like the shooting star, extinct in an abyss, a dome, of blue; the colour of night: which, if dearest Vita you can follow, is now my condition: as I sit waiting for dinner, over the logs. [...]

Do you really love me? Much? passionately not reasonably?

V.

1980: To V. Sackville-West   *52 Tavistock Sqre, WC1.*

Tuesday 8th January 1928 [1929]

[...] I have written myself out of breath – 30,000 words [of *Phases of Fiction*] in 8 weeks, and now want to dive and steep myself in other peoples books. I want to wash off all my own ideas. So I have been reading and reading, and making up a new little book for the Hogarth Press (if it survives) on six novels.[1] A good idea, d'you think? Picking six

1. She did not carry out this plan.

novels from the mass, and saying everything there is to be said about the whole of literature in perhaps 150 pages. I've been reading Balzac, and Tolstoy. Practically every scene in Anna Karenina is branded on me, though I've not read it for 15 years. *That* is the origin of all our discontent. After that of course we had to break away. It wasn't Wells, or Galsworthy or any of our mediocre wishy washy realists: it was Tolstoy. How could we go on with sex and realism after that? How could they go on with poetic plays after Shakespeare? It is one brain, after all, literature; and it wants change and relief. The text book writers cut it up all wrong (the telephone: Leonards mother: is sending us a cake –) and where was I? Literature is all one brain. [. . .]

1995: To V. Sackville-West   [*52 Tavistock Square, W.C.1*]
Thursday, Feb. 7th [1929]

[. . .] He [Leonard] is a perfect angel – only more to the point than most angels – He sits on the edge of the bed and considers my symptoms[1] like a judge. He brings home huge pineapples: he moves the gramophone into my room and plays until he thinks I'm excited. In short, I should have shot myself long ago in one of these illnesses if it hadn't been for him. As it is, I hope to go into the Square next week: but as I say this sort of thing takes time; it must be let to wander about one's body like a policeman trying bolts; and theres no doubt I get many more times of complete comfort now. [. . .]

Virginia

2005: To V. Sackville-West   [*52 Tavistock Square, W.C.1*]
Tuesday, Feb. 19th [1929]

[. . .] You think reading Sterne is real life. I am sometimes pleased to think that I read English literature when I was young; I like to think of myself tapping at my father's study door, saying very loud and clear 'Can I have another volume, father? I've finished this one'. Then he would be very pleased and say 'Gracious child, how you gobble!'

---

1. On returning with Leonard from a visit to Berlin to see Vita and Harold, Virginia began a 'flu-like illness that lasted for a month. Vita blamed it on 'SUPPRESSED RANDINESS' (6 February 1929), but it was generally attributed to exhaustion and an unwise overdose of a drug for seasickness, Somnifène.

(There's Miss Matheson[1] ringing up to say they want to broadcast the frost and thaw in Orl—do tomorrow – Do I mind? No. thats all right –) and get up and take down, it may have been the 6th or 7th volume of Gibbons complete works, or Speddings Bacon,[2] or Cowper's Letters.' 'But my dear, if its worth reading, its worth reading twice' he would say. I have a great devotion for him – what a disinterested man, how high minded, how tender to me, and fierce and intolerable – But I am maundering. [. . .]

Virginia

2020: TO VANESSA BELL

Monks House, Rodmell
[Sussex]

April 24th 1929

Dearest Dolphin,

[. . .] Julian came in, very late, – we had expected him to dine – but Fred[3] caught him and they got talking. He has got thinner, I thought; there was a lot to be said about cars, also about Apostles.[4] He is growing like a crab – I mean he is only half covered with shell: he is very queer; one finds him noticing, and feeling, and taking up what last year was imperceptible to him. We argued about poetry as usual, and he said he has written a long essay on poetry, which he is sending us. The Bell sociability is so odd, mixed with the Stephen integrity. I daresay he'll give you a lot of trouble before he's done – he is too charming and violent and gifted altogether: and in love with you, into the bargain. It is very exciting – the extreme potency of your Brats; they might have been nincompoops – instead of bubbling and boiling and frizzling like so many pans of sausages on the fire. (I am just about to cook an omelette) I am so lost without any young life that I meditate plunging into Ann[5] – only what would happen? [. . .]

B.

1. Hilda Matheson (1888–1940), first Director of Talks for the BBC, and – though Virginia did not know it – now passionately involved in an affair with Vita.
2. James Spedding edited *The Life and Letters* of Sir Francis Bacon in seven volumes (1861–74).
3. Fred Pape, husband of Angelica's nurse Louie, and chauffeur for Lady Bowen of Cadogan Square. He had given Virginia driving instructions in 1927 when the Woolfs bought their first car.
4. Julian Bell, now at Cambridge, had been elected to the Apostles, which he thought the most important event of his undergratuate career.
5. Ann Stephen, 13, daughter of their brother Adrian.

2022a: To The Editor,
  The New Republic
                            [*52 Tavistock Square, W.C.1*]

[24 April 1929]

Sir:

I hasten to submit to your correspondent's correction and to retract my opinion that because Henry James was born in Boston [in New York, actually] he therefore did not write English like a native.[1] I will do my best to believe that the language of Tennyson and the language of Whitman are one and the same. But may I explain that the responsibility for my error rests with Walt Whitman himself, with Mr Ring Lardner, Mr Sherwood Anderson, and Mr Sinclair Lewis?[2] I had been reading these writers and thinking how magnificent a language American is, how materially it differs from English, and how much I envy it the power to create new words and new phrases of the utmost vividness. I had even gone so far as to shape a theory that the American genius is an original genius and that it has borne and is bearing fruit unlike any that grows over here. But in deference to your correspondent I hasten to cancel these views and will note for future use that there is no difference between England and America; climate and custom have produced no change of any sort; America is merely a larger England across the Atlantic; and the language is so precisely similar that when I come upon words like boob, graft, stine, busher, doose, hobo, shoe-pack, hiking, cinch and many others, the fact that I do not know what they mean must

1. A reader called Harriot T. Cooke had written to the *New Republic* in reply to Virginia's article 'On Not Knowing French' (13 February 1929, *Essays*, V), complaining of her condescension towards Americans' use of English. On the same page as Virginia's rebuttal, the magazine printed a letter by the great American man of letters, Edmund Wilson, who called Mr Cooke 'touchy' and Mrs Woolf's view rather 'perverse'. What Virginia actually wrote was: 'Thus a foreigner with what is called a perfect command of English may write grammatical English and musical English – he will, indeed, like Henry James, often write a more elaborate English than the native – but never such unconscious English that we feel the past of the word in it, its associations and attachments.'
2. These three writers are the contemporaries who most interest Virginia in 'American Fiction', which she published in the *Saturday Review of Literature* for 1 August 1925 (*Essays*, IV). She begins by saying that Whitman (1819–92) is 'the one American writer whom the English wholeheartedly admire'. She goes on to discuss Lardner's (1885–1933) *You Know Me, Al* (1916), Anderson's (1876–1941) *The Triumph of the Egg* (1921) and *A Story Teller's Story* (1924), and Lewis's (1885–1951) *Babbitt* (1922).

be attributed to the negligence of those who did not teach me what is apparently my native tongue.

Having thus admitted my error, may I 'just as a matter of curiosity' [used by Cooke in his letter] ask to be enlightened on another point? Why, I wonder, when I say that Henry James did not write English like a native is it assumed that I intend an insult? Why does your correspondent at once infer that I accuse the Bostonians of talking Choctaw? Why does he allude to 'condescension' and refer to 'us poor benighted Americans' and suppose that I look upon them as 'newcomers to the English language' when I said nothing of the sort? What have I done to make him angry? [James Russell] Lowell's essay 'On a Certain Condescension in Foreigners' (for such he apparently thought the English) should, I think, have for pendant 'On a Certain Touchiness in' – dare I say it? – 'Americans.' But may I implore you, Sir, if I use that word, not to infer that I thereby imply that you wear a pigtail and paint your forehead red? If I speak of 'Americans' it is merely because our common ancestors some centuries ago agreed, for reasons best known to themselves, to differ.

Virginia Woolf

2026a: To Mary Hutchinson

Monks House, Rodmell
[Sussex]

Monday [6 May 1929]

Well, Weazel,[1] I was very sorry not to see you at the lecture but the truth was I had to take my niece [Judith Stephen] to the Coliseum, and by the time we had seen the last juggler and lady in yellow satin my head spun. Weazels would have seemed snakes.

But when shall I see you? Life seems nothing but a cascade. Shall you come to tea with me one day? But I suppose you are flitting in the dusk from one arc lamp to another. My vision of you is almost entirely unreal. You come out at night; you drop orchids in the mud, and have them washed in warm water with cotton wool.

I am running on because Leonard is in the W.C. and I am left in charge of Pinka, who is on heat and therefore all agog for life. We are

1. Since Vita's night with Mary Hutchinson, Virginia had adopted one of her animal names for Mary, with whom she had not always been on easy terms during the long years of Mary's relationship with Clive Bell. The name in this case seems to have been used ambivalently; it's erotic, but vaguely hostile.

down here to see about making a new room[1] – this we have been seeing about for 3 months now, and not a stone is laid. But when the stones are laid you will have to brave the eternal sea mist and south west gale and come here. I should provide you with the works of Ronald Firbank[2] which I am reading with some unstinted pleasure and we would walk on the terrace and see the lights of Lewes twinkle like the necklace which you are just letting curl in a circlet on your dressing table.

Clive is in Cassis, to me rather dreary and like coffee cups after a party; but he won't go to Saigon apparently. He means to live in Paris for a year. Dear, dear, how depressing is all this, this yellowing and falling of one's friends. He seems to me still redeemable, but how?

Here is Leonard. I must go to my lodge and write a page of the dullest book in creation [*Phases of Fiction*]. And then we drive up to London: and then – and then – what will happen then?

I like Weasels to kiss: but as they kiss to bite: and then to kiss. I like alternations and variety.

V

And Tom – Have you heard the latest?[3]

2028: TO QUENTIN BELL   *52 Tavistock Square, W.C.1*

May 11th 1929

Dearest Quentin – oh, but youre Claudian. Well then Claudian

How you have seduced me by the charm of your language! I have thrown on to the floor the last page of my most hated book – it is dry as a captains biscuit – there is no food even for the weevil in it – and turned to this succulent sheet. For now thank God I need not say what I think of fiction and Proust and the future and the new orientation of the human soul, as Leonard and Dadie [Rylands] insist – never were such task-masters; now I can throw myself onto the back of life and grasping hard

---

1. The Woolfs were planning two rooms, a sitting room opening onto the garden, and a bedroom for Virginia above it. But in the next year, they changed the rooms around to get a view of the downs from the sitting room.
2. The novelist (1886–1926), whose highly stylised works included *Valmouth* (1919) and *Sorrow in Sunlight* (1925).
3. During a telephone conversation in April, Eliot had complained that Vivien Eliot's legs were so swollen she was bedridden, the Eliots were having humiliating servant problems, they had to move constantly, and no one came to see them any more. 'This is our man of genius' (*Diary*, III, 223).

to the mane fly away and away. Where? How could I write when you were at Cassis and every page was left in the drawing room to be read by Clive Vanessa Angelica Duncan Sabine Miss Campbell and Colonel Teed?[1] You have a very elementary notion of the principles which should guide epistolary correspondence; though letter-writing on a typewriter is a mongrel, a mule; a sterile thing, compared with the handwritten letter. I say only what the typewriter likes to say. But I might have said things even so that I should not wish the whole population of Cassis to read. You admit your trousers have holes in them. Why at Lewes station you had to be covered with a potato sack in order to save the blushes of the young women who sell violets. But what was I going to say that is indiscreet? Only that I wish Clive would progress beyond love where he has been stationed these many years to the next point in the human pilgrimage. One cant kick ones heels there too long. One becomes an impediment. At your age a little talk and hubble-bubble of the kind does very well. One would not wish to cut you off from the society of your sex and mine. But take warning; dont outstay your welcome there. – I mean don't let people say Oh he thinks of nothing but love; oh he's off on that old subject again. Why do I say this? Something Christabel MacClaren said about Clive and Miss – I dont know the name of the enchantress any more. I saw Julian twice last week. He is a most marked and peculiar figure; so bulky, but so agile. We had an odd conglomeration – Roger and Helen and Mauron and Mr Plomer and Mr Blunden, the nature poet, and Miss Jenkins,[2] who teaches; and they all talked of every sort of thing; Julian vociferating at the top of his voice – Whats pure poetry? Whats assocation? Whats abstract? Whats concrete – half in French too; while little Miss Jenkins who is the size and shape of a mouse, piped up in the best Strachey voice – Lord how that persists! – its echoes will be heard when Pauls Cathedral is tumbling stone from stone; she piped up (forgive this

1. Sabine was the young French woman who looked after Angelica at Cassis. Lt. Col. A. S. H. Teed (rtd), who lived with Jean Campbell, rented La Bergère to Vanessa and Duncan.
2. The Woolfs' guests, in addition to Julian Bell, Roger Fry, and Helen Anrep, were: Charles Mauron (1899–1960), the scientist-turned-litératteur, who had been lecturing on French literature in Bloomsbury recently; two young poets, William Plomer (1903–73) and Edmund Blunden (1896–1974), both of whom had been teaching in Japan; and the novelist Elizabeth Jenkins (b. 1905), whose first novel, *Virginia Water*, was published in this year and who taught English at King Alfred's School, Hampstead.

typewritten incoherency) 'But what am I to do if a young man asks me to go to France with*out* saying if he inc*lu*des copu*la*tion?' She said, what seemed odd, that it is now the convention that no young woman can demand a statement of intentions beforehand. She said that Bloomsbury has muddied the pure pool of convention and the young know not one hand from another, nor which is land nor which water.

Last night we had a terrific revivication; the resurrection day was nothing to it. Old Sydney Waterlow who dandled you as a babe, turned up from Abyssinia, which has nothing to do with dulcimers, he says; there he had a breakdown and is back again, ruminating, questing, like some gigantic hog which smells truffles miles and miles away. It is now Spengler.[1] But then, my dear, you were too young to know him; so what does it convey to you, this reference of mine to a tortured soul? He was impotent for years; and Clive heard his miracle, how he found a woman in Piccadilly and brought it off there and then – and [G.E.] Moore converted him and Bertie [Russell] fathered him and I refused him and Leonard dished him; and still he quests like a hog for the Truth. So we all did once; save for myself; who was always distracted by some other flippancy. [. . .]

Write; at once

yr loving

Virginia

2036a: To Mary Hutchinson   *Fontcreuse, Cassis*
                                         [France]

8th June 1929

Dearest Weasel,

[. . .] Does London exist? Here all is heat and vineyards; people swim about naked in the air. One prays that a ladies legs may be shapely. The human figure has regained the place which, as you may know, it had in Greece. Shapely or not – and alas, often it is a mere barrel of flesh, in which bones are lost like needles and perhaps dont exist, – everyone is shameless – the effect of the wine and the heat. I like the

---

1. Oswald Spengler (1880–1936), the German philosopher and author of *Decline of the West* (1918–22), by which Waterlow, lately British Ambassador in Addis Ababa, was deeply influenced.

atmosphere so much that I think of buying a house in a wood this afternoon.[1]

Nessa and Duncan live a kind of bubbling seraphic life, with Angelica and Judith [Bagenal, 11] sporting like dolphins, naked too. They are infinitely happy, busy, full of small errands and businesses; giving lifts to old ladies, entertaining the Colonel, (whose mistress has gone off to induce a miscarriage, her 6th, in Geneva); and today there is a grand swimming race, and a picnic, and presents, bought in Cassis, for everybody. It is certain that Mrs Curry will lose; for among other curiosities, we have all sorts of cups without saucers, broken teapots, by which I mean – but dont ask me in this heat to be exact – that there is not a single whole couple in Cassis. They are all odds and ends. Some breed cocker spaniels, all paint.

But this will be boring you horribly. You will be dining at Boulestin's [restaurant] tonight, with a lady. And you will be wearing a tight black dress with many flounces and a white camellia. We, on the contrary, dine out on the terrace; and I'm not allowed to say 'theres a shooting star' because by the time they look, its shot. Suddenly it becomes very cold and we go and sit in the studio. Then Leonard and I stumble to bed, through the vines, to the croak of frogs. A pleasant life – yes: but I should like a little gossip with Weasel; and shall be back in 10 days. Leonard sends his love –

Virginia

2056: To V. Sackville-West   *Monks House [Rodmell, Sussex]*

Aug 15th [1929]

Dearest Creature

I am quite well again, and spent the morning writing. It wasn't you; as you were only the tailend – I had been badgered by people in London, and then this writing of four articles,[2] all pressed as tight as hay in a stack (an image that comes you see from [Vita's] The Land) – that was what did it – not that it was bad. These headaches leave one like sand which a

1. This was a serious plan, but the Woolfs soon realised that having three houses was impractical.
2. All were printed originally in the *Nation* and reprinted in the *New York Herald Tribune*. Their subjects were Cowper, Beau Brummell, Mary Wollstonecraft, and Dorothy Wordsworth (*Essays*, V).

wave has uncovered – I believe they have a mystic purpose. Indeed, I'm not sure that there isnt some religious cause at the back of them – I see my own worthlessness and failure so clearly; and lie gazing into the depths of the misery of human life; and then one gets up and everything begins again and its all covered over. [. . .]

Yr
V.

2057: To V. Sackville-West   *Monks House* [*Rodmell, Sussex*]

Sunday 18th Aug. [1929]

[. . .] I am recovered, and have, more or less, finished my articles. The last was Dorothy Wordsworth, and if the written word could cure rheumatism, I think her's might – like a dock leaf laid to a sting; yet rather astringent too. Have you ever read her diaries, the early ones, with the nightingale singing at Alfoxden [Somerset], and Coleridge coming in swollen eyed – to eat a mutton chop? Wordsworth made his head ache, thinking of an epithet for cuckoo. I like them very much; but I cant say I enjoy writing about them, nine pages close pressed. How can one get it all in? [William] Plomer is a nice young man, rather prim and tight outwardly, concealing a good deal I think; though I'm completely bored by speculating as to poets' merits. Nobody is better than anybody else – I like people – I dont bother my head about their works. All this measuring is a futile affair, and it doesn't matter who writes what. But this is my grey and grizzled wisdom – at his age I wanted to be myself. And then, – here is a great storm of rain. I am obsessed at nights with the idea of my own worthlessness, and if it were only to turn a light on to save my life I think I would not do it. These are the last footprints of a headache I suppose. Do you ever feel that? – like an old weed in a stream. What do you feel, lying in bed? I daresay you are visited by sublime thoughts – [. . .]

Virginia

2063: TO HUGH WALPOLE   *Monks House, Rodmell,*
25th Aug. 29   *Lewes, Sussex*

My dear Hugh,[1]

[...] When I was young I liked writing letters. Now I cannot remember how one does it. It is a fine hot day, and I am sitting in my garden room which has a fine view of the downs and marshes and an oblique view of Leonard's fish pond, in which it is our passion to observe the gold fish. There should be four, and one carp; but it is the rarest event to see them all together – and yet I can assure you that so to see them matters more to us both than all that is said at the Hague.[2] We are going off tomorrow to a pond at Slindon [Sussex] where goldfish are so thick in the water that the village children ladle them out in their caps for passers by.

Why then am I reading La Fontaine with obdurate passion? I mean, why is human life made up of such incongruous things, and why are all one's events so perfectly irrational that a good biographer would be forced to ignore them entirely?

Here the church bells begin ringing and I am plunged as usual into anger and confusion – I hate to be disturbed; I hate the arrogance and monopoly of Christianity (and I'm writing to the son of a Bishop too!) but then I love the old women doddering along in their black bonnets, and the thought of all the years, and all the processions; and how buried there are their ancestors for centuries – I must explain that our garden abuts on the churchyard, and when we are looking at our beehives, they are often burying someone on the other side of the wall. Where shall you be buried, and shall you have a tombstone over you or none, and what do you feel about posterity, and have you any desire to be thought of in your grave – which questions bring me by a path which you will discern beneath the brambles – to your works: to your play; to the novel which I'm to be allowed to read. But you dont say when its coming out. Is it this one that you are rushing up to Cumberland to write?[3] Please

1. The popular novelist (1884–1941) had presented Virginia with the *Femina Vie Heureuse* prize in 1928 for *To the Lighthouse.*
2. In August 1929 a conference at The Hague endorsed the Young Plan, which removed Allied control from Germany.
3. In the late summer Walpole went home to Cumberland to begin *Judith Paris* (1931). The novel which Virginia was 'to be allowed to read' was *Hans Frost* (September 1929), about which Walpole wrote in his diary: 'I like this book. It's in a new vein for me, the vein of humour I ought to have tried long ago. Virginia Woolf has perhaps liberated me' (Rupert Hart-Davis, *Hugh Walpole*, 1952. p. 279).

send me, what I'm sure there must be – a picture postcard of Hugh Walpoles house; or anyhow a view of the valley where he lives. I have a childish wish to consolidate my friends and embed them in their own tables and chairs, and imagine what kind of objects they see when they are alone. Of course, it is quite true that I know nothing about human character, and to be frank, care less; but I have a cosmogony, nevertheless, – indeed all the more; and it is of the highest importance that I should be able to make you exist there, somehow, tangibly, visibly; recognisable to me, though not perhaps to yourself. Now *your* gift as a novelist – I was going to write an essay upon you, but I shan't, because you wont let me read your works.

Aren't you singularly vain, for a man of your reputation? I should have thought, selling ten million copies in a month, you would have long ago disregarded Virginia – perhaps you have – Perhaps it is only your sublime urbanity, and the quality which I most adore and that is man-of-the-worldliness, that lets her think that you care what she says.

Ought I to read Mr Priestley's book?[1] by the way – From the reviews, chiefly by Jack Squire, I am sure that I should hate it – but I suspect that I may be wrong, and if you say so I will send a card to the Times bookclub at once. What I am suspicious of is this manufactured breeze – what they call humanity – But you know my foibles in that respect – what I hate is having it done by electric fans and other machinery for making one sunburnt and rosy and jolly and cheery – but I may wrong him – he may be the real thing, not manufactured. [. . .]

Your affte
Virginia

2068: To V. Sackville-West   [*Monks House, Rodmell, Sussex*]

Tuesday [17 September 1929]

[. . .] What can I say about Hugh? – and I've got to write to him [about *Hans Frost*]. The truth is its a day dream, unreal, all spangles, like a Christmas tree, and to me rather exhilarating for that reason – all shivers to violet powder. I expect all his books are gloried dreams of Hugh; Hugh a great man, Hugh a sinner, Hugh a lover, Hugh prodigiously wicked and so on – never a glimpse of any reality; and thats

1. The best-selling novel, *The Good Companions* (1929), by J. B. Priestley (1894–1984).

the trick – thats the glamour and the illusion and the spangle: thats why he sells, and why nothing is left but a little dent. I've only read 30 pages of Rebecca,[1] but I think really she is another pair of shoes. I agree that the convention is tight and affected and occasionally foppish beyond endurance, but then it is a convention and she does it deliberately, and it helps her to manufacture some pretty little China ornaments for the mantelpiece. One could read some of it again, but Hugh never, never. [. . .]

Potto and Virginia

2078: TO GERALD BRENAN   *Monks House, Rodmell*
                                          [Sussex]

Oct 4th 1929

My dear Gerald,

I have just taken out your letter and re-read it. Probably you have forgotten that you wrote to me on the 11th July; and it is now the 4th of October. And I am not in a good mood for writing, being dirty – you know how physical states affect one – and lazy – so that I cant get up and wash; and lonely, Leonard is in London. But it is for this last reason that I write, because it is the last night for some months, perhaps, that I shall be lonely. Tomorrow I shall go back to London, and there already awaits me a string of inevitable experiences – what is called 'seeing people'. You don't know what that means – it means one can't get out of it. It means that Miss Winter has asked us to ask Mr Robinson Jeffers[2] to tea because he is only in London for a week and will then return to a cave in California and write immortal poetry for ever. Mr Jeffers is a genius so one must see him. Then Hugh Walpole is passing through London; Hugh is not a genius, and its precisely because of that sad deficiency, which so many of us share by the way, that he must be 'seen'. It torments him, his lack of genius, when, if only (so he says) the Bishop his father had had an ounce more spunk in him he, Hugh might have been something Titanic. Feel my biceps, he is always saying; and there's something so curious in his state, that again one must say I shall be in on Thursday at 4.

And then there's that automaton [Sibyl] Colefax your friend. Do you

1. Rebecca West's *Harriet Hume* (1929).
2. The American poet Robinson Jeffers (1887–1962) lived austerely near Carmel, California. The Hogarth Press published his work in 1928, in 1929, and again in 1930. His friend Ella Winter married the American journalist Lincoln Steffens.

remember a curious autumnal tea party, with Logan [Pearsall Smith] and Clive and God knows who else, and how she forgot your name, and kept saying 'Mr—I can't remember who you are!' Happily time makes all these past scenes unspeakably beautiful – if one remembered the truth, life would no doubt be unbearable. And theres the Sidney Webbs – they have to be seen. I wont go on. I only want you to realise how little control I have over my London; yours you say (July 11th) is all that it should be. To counteract it I have bought a hut at Cassis, in a vineyard. There I shall imagine that I see Africa and hear nightingales and so attain to something of a prophetic strain, now lacking.

For, Lord, Lord, how much one lacks – how fumbling and inexpert one is – never yet to have learnt the hang of life – to have peeled that particular orange. As I said I am out of the mood for writing, and write because I shall never do it once I am 'seeing': this being so, I shake these brief notes onto the page, like – what can I think of – only lice – instead of distilling the few simple and sweet and deep and limpid remarks which one would like to send to Spain in a letter. Suppose one could really communicate, how exciting it would be! Here I have covered one entire blue page and said nothing. One can at most hope to suggest something. Suppose you are in the mood, when this letter comes, and read it in precisely the right light, by your Brazier in your big room, then by some accident there may be roused in you some understanding of what I, sitting over my log fire in Monks House, am, or feel, or think. It all seems infinitely chancy and infinitely humbugging – so many asseverations which are empty, and tricks of speech; and yet this is the art to which we devote our lives. Perhaps that is only true of writers – then one tries to imagine oneself in contact, in sympathy; one tries vainly to put off this interminable – what is the word I want? – something between maze and catacomb – of the flesh. And all one achieves is a grimace. And so one is driven to write books – you see I'm shaking down unripe olives (if you like that better than lice.)

You say you can't finish your book because you have no method, but see points, here and there, with no connecting line.[1] And that is precisely my state at the moment, beginning another book [*The Waves*]; What do all the books I have written avail me? Nothing. Is it the curse of

1. Virginia is interjecting her own concepts, partly to help the younger writer, partly because his intelligence and respect spurred her to think through literary matters in his 'presence'. Brenan had actually written (11 July 1929, University of Sussex): 'there remain some difficult passages which I owe to my incapacity for thinking out a suitable plot'.

our age or what? The will o' the wisp moves on, and I see the lights (when I lie in bed at night, or sit over the fire) as bright as stars, and cant reach them. I daresay its the continuity of daily life, something unlustrous and habitual that we lack. I give it up. Not writing books I mean; only understanding my own psychology as a writer. I thought I had anyhow learnt to write quickly: now its a hundred words in a morning, and scratchy and in [hand-]writing, like a child of ten. And one never knows after all these years how to end, how to go on: one never sees more than a page ahead; why then does one make any pretensions to be a writer? Why not pin together one's scattered sheets – I daresay one would be wise to. [. . .]

And if it should occur to you one night to attempt this curious effort at communicating what Gerald Brenan thinks on his mountain top, then I will first read it through very quickly, at breakfast, and come upon it a little later, and read it again and try to amplify your hieroglyphs – It is an interesting question – what one tries to do, in writing a letter – partly of course to give back a reflection of the other person. Writing to Lytton or Leonard I am quite different from writing to you. And now my log, shaped like an elephants foot, has fallen over, and I must pick up the tongs – goodnight.

V.W.

2094: To G. L. Dickinson   *52 Tavistock Square, W.C.1*

Nov. 6th [1929]

Dear Goldie,

It was very good of you to write. I cant tell you how pleased I am that you like my little book[1] – seeing that I nourish a deep if inarticulate respect and affection for you. I'm so glad you thought it good tempered – my blood is apt to boil on this one subject as yours does about natives, or war; and I didnt want it to. I wanted to encourage the young women – they seem to get fearfully depressed – and also to induce discussion. There are numbers of things that might be said, and that arent said. The double soul[2] is one of them; and also education – I dont believe, though

---

1. *A Room of One's Own* (1929), based upon Virginia's gently feminist lectures on women and literature at the women's colleges of Cambridge in 1928.
2. One of the *Room*'s most famous themes was that there are male and female parts of the mind in everyone and that they must unite before an artist can become fully creative.

I'm a complete outsider,[1] that its right for either sex as it is. But I'm certainly outstaying my welcome here. I was among your [BBC] listeners the other night and would have liked (this hardly ever happens to me – I mean with lectures in general) that you had gone on. And I laughed aloud.

Yours sincerely
Virginia Woolf

2097: To V. Sackville-West   [*52 Tavistock Square, W.C.1*]

Wednesday [13 November 1929]

Dearest Creature,

[. . .] Yesterday I was in mischief – in the arms of Osbert [Sitwell], and very fat they are too; on the carpet of Mrs Courtauld,[2] and that is as thick and resilient as Osberts arms. Lord! what a party? I flirted and I flirted – with Christabel [McLaren], with Mary [Hutchinson], with Ottoline [Morrell]; but this last was a long and cadaverous embrace which almost drew me under. Figure us, entwined beneath Cezannes which she had the audacity to praise all the time we were indulging in those labyrinthine antics which is called being intimate with Ottoline; I succumb: I lie; I flatter; I accept flattery; I stretch and sleek, and all the time she is watchful and vengeful and mendacious and unhappy and ready to break every rib in my body if it were worth her while. In truth, she's a nice woman, eaten with amorosity and vanity, an old volcanoe, all grey cinders and scarcely a green plant, let alone a shank left. And this is human intercourse, this is human friendship so I kept saying to myself while I flattered and fawned. [. . .]

I hope, oh I hope, you are now comfortable and quiet and warm and loving your

Potto and V.

---

1. The intellectually sophisticated woman as 'outsider' was a theme that Virginia would pick up more aggressively in *Three Guineas* (1938).
2. Elizabeth (d. 1931), wife of the wealthy industrialist and art collector, Samuel Courtauld. Her house at 20 Portman Square was a centre of cultural life in London.

2099: To V. Sackville-West

52 T[avistock] S.[quare, W.C.1]

Tuesday [19 November 1929]

[. . .] Everyone seems to be ill. Going to the garage yesterday the man said to me, 'I've been ill for a fortnight; my wife has been ill for a fortnight; our little boy died of double pneumonia last night; and *the dog has distemper.*' This he repeated three times, always winding up solemnly and *the dog has distemper* as if it were the most important of the lot. But there was the child dead in the cottage. [. . .]

V.

1930–1931

At the beginning of 1930, the composer Ethel Smyth marched into Virginia's life. In her 70s and tremendously energetic, she would be the last of Virginia's major correspondents. Ethel provoked sharp, honest qualities in Virginia's letters. In answer to her probing questions, Virginia wrote what amounted to an epistolary autobiography. In love with the woman, Ethel was equally interested in the work. She brought her own work and causes into the middle of Virginia's life. It was an exciting, exasperating friendship.

In 1931 the Woolfs met John Lehmann, who kept them in touch with the young generation of poets and became deeply involved with The Hogarth Press. The Waves was published. Leonard, and many others, considered it as masterpiece. At the end of the year, Lytton Strachey was dangerously ill.

2127: TO CLIVE BELL   *52 Tavistock Sqre. [W.C.1]*

Sunday Jan 18th [19]30

[. . .] But now, having prepared our dress,[1] which consisted – and the point is not made vainly as you will perceive if you read on – in my case of a pair of hare's ears, and a pair of hare's paws (you remember the March hare) we went round to Fitzroy Street. Roger [as the White Knight] had taken the place by storm. The children crowded round him like the piper. He was a masterpiece, having called out all the resource and ingenuity of Woolworths stores. Candles, mousetraps, tweezers, frying pans, scales – I know not what all – dangled from him by brass chains, infinite in number; his legs were bound in cricket pads; he wore chain armour on his breast; his cheeks flowered in green whiskers, and the surface of the body where visible was covered in white yeager [Jaeger] tights. Encouraged by the extravaganza I turned lightly on my heels (a hare, you remember and mad at that) and tapped Dotty [Wellesley] on the nose. Whether she was tipsy already or merely sour by nature, God knows; anyhow she flared up like a costermonger; damned my eyes; and this not in play; and swore I had wiped all the

1. That is, their costumes for Angelica Bell's 11th birthday party, to which the guests were invited to come as characters from *Alice in Wonderland*.

powder from her face. The worst of it was, that having recovered her temper she went by natural precipitation, into the opposite extreme of facetious and persistent amorosity, with the result that I spent the evening with her at my side – petulant, peevish, disconnected, incapable of a sensible, sober, let alone intelligent remark – all was high flown, rhapsodical and pert.

Enough, enough, I have vented my spleen where I dare hope it will be understood. In every other way the party was a complete success – hams disappearing – Angus [Davidson] assiduous and more than gentlemanly; Barbara [Bagenal] owing to her disguise negligible; and Angelica ravishing, flirtatious, commanding and seductive. Vanessa presided unperturbed – and going home Leonard, wearing a green baize apron and a pair of chisels as the Carpenter came in conflict with the police on behalf of a drunken prostitute, who, being insulted by three tipsy men, answered them back in their own coin. 'Why dont you go for the men who began it? My name's Woolf, and I can take my oath the woman's not to blame. She called them bugger; but they called her whore' – and so on – holding his apron and chisel in one hand; upon which Lydia [Keynes] suddenly appeared out of the crowd; and by hook or by crook the affair subsided and we went home to bed. [. . .]

yr Virginia

2129: To Ethel Smyth   52 *Tavistock Square, W.C.1*

30 Jan. 1930

Dear Miss Smyth,[1]

If you only knew how often I have wanted to write to you – and only didn't for fear of boring you – to thank you for your books and articles and to ask you about my great grandfather Pattle who shot up out of a barrel, as you say, in the Indian ocean[2] – then you wouldn't apologise.

1. Dame Ethel Smyth (see Letter 1100 and n. 1) wrote her first letter to praise *A Room of One's Own* and to seek advice for a planned BBC broadcast on women and war. Later Virginia learned that Ethel had already fallen in love with her, based solely upon the mind that had created that lyrically feminist pamphlet.
2. James Pattle (1775–1845) was the grandfather of Julia Jackson, Virginia's mother. Quentin Bell, summarising the legends about him, writes that he was 'the greatest liar in India; he drank himself to death; he was packed off home in a cask of spirits, which cask, exploding, ejected his unbottled corpse before his widow's eyes, drove her out of her wits, set the ship on fire and left it stranded in the Hooghly' (Quentin Bell, I, 14). Ethel had heard this story from her father, Major General J. H. Smyth, and retold it in her autobiography, *Impressions that Remained* (1919), where Virginia read it.

There is nothing I should like better than to see you – and you might like me. Who knows?[1] Thursdays my husband, whom you would like, is here – but as you only come sometimes, please say which day suits you and we will keep it.

I am very glad you liked my little book. It was rather a wild venture, but if you think there is something in it, I am satisfied.

Yours sincerely and with as much admiration as you will accept,

Virginia Woolf

2145: TO QUENTIN BELL   *52 Tavistock Sq. [W.C.1]*

17th Feb. 1930

My dear Quentin,

I have been having influenza, and being in bed, could not write to you, because I could not type, and so the most amazing letter in the world (which it would have been) remains unwritten. My brain was packed with close folded ideas like the backs of flamingoes when they fly south at sunset. They are now all gone – a few grey draggled geese remain, their wing feathers trailed and mud stained, and their poor old voices scrannel sharp and grating – that's the effect of typing; every sentence has its back broke, and its beak awry. Nevertheless, as I want nothing so much as another letter from you, I must eke it out.

I am sitting over the fire with masses of virgin – what d'you think I'm going to say? – typescript by my side; novels six foot thick to be read instantly [for The Hogarth Press] or I shall be knived by cadaverous men at Bournemouth whose life depends on my verdict; and amorous typists. They write because they cant have their nights to their liking. This is hard on me. They write to revenge themselves upon the young man at the fish shop, or the young woman in red at the flower shop. So what news have I? Helen's [Anrep] been here; Roger's been here; and Nessa; and Vita; and just before I fell ill, your Miss Watson.[2] She is a nice girl – yes, I liked her. She stood fire from Roger very well. He was at this most sweeping and searching, raking her with terrific questions and denunciations. There was Julian's Mr Empson[3] too – a black and red sort

1. A slight reworking of a sentence from Ethel's letter: 'You might (who knows??) quite like me' (Berg Collection, New York Public Library).

2. Elizabeth Watson, later Sproule (1906–55), an art student, a Communist, and a friend of Quentin Bell.

3. William Empson (1906–84), the poet and critic, who in 1930 at the age of 24 published his famous *Seven Types of Ambiguity*.

of rook, very truculent, and refreshing. None of your etiolated, sophisticated, damp, spotted, you know what I mean – Tonight theres a grand meeting, which I cant attend, of the new paper promoters,[1] at Rogers. How young and ardent we all are at our age, flinging guineas on the waves and believing in the rule of reason and the might of art and the downfall of our enemies! But Raymond [Mortimer] says the paper must be shiny; Roger says shine means shoddy; shine means Mayfair. Well, you can fancy how the argument goes and the tempers fly and the old friends are excoriated. [. . .]

Your poor dear old dotty Aunt V.

2148: To Ethel Smyth   *52 T.[avistock] S.[quare, W.C.1]*

27th Feb. [1930]

Well if I did what I want, I should ring up whatever your number is and ask you to come tomorrow. But – oh damn these medical details! – this influenza has a special poison for what is called the nervous system; and mine being a second hand one, used by my father and his father to dictate dispatches and write books with – how I wish they had hunted and fished instead! – I have to treat it like a pampered pug dog, and lie still directly my head aches. That is what I am doing; and on Saturday we shall go to Rodmell where I shall lie still out of doors, and then creep along the water meadows, and then perhaps read a novel, and not write a word, except this kind of word, and not see a soul except Leonard and Mrs Thompsett, who cooks the chicken, for a week perhaps: when suddenly I shall be cured and dash about the house inventing pleasures – of which the first will be to ring up Ethel Smyth and ask her to come instantly to tea. Will she come? I dont think the cure this time will take more than a week. I'm taking prodigious care. You're at the bottom of all the spoonfulls of codliver oil and malt that I gulp down. But you see, I dont dare ask you tomorrow. Lord! what a bore! To think that my father's philosophy and the Dictionary of National Biography[2] cost me this! I never see those 68 black books without cursing them for all the jaunts they've lost me.

1. The indefatigable Roger Fry had launched yet another project. His magazine, to be called the *Antidote*, never appeared.
2. Of which Leslie Stephen was the founding editor, beginning in the year of Virginia's birth.

I too feel that the book – not that book – *our* book – is open, and at once snatched away. I want to talk and talk and talk – About music; about love; about Countess Russell.[1] Dont you think you might indulge me this once and tell me what she said thats so interesting [about Virginia]? Yes. I think you are a kind woman, besides being such a . . . etc etc. Those two happy dodges of yours come in useful on occasion, dot dot, dot – et cetera. I will write your character in that style one of these days. Years ago, 3 or 4 at least, when I first met Maurice Baring[2] he made my heart jump by saying 'You must come and meet Ethel Smyth.' but nothing came of it and I was, as you say, too 'delicate' to press. What a fool one is. Here is Leonard, come back from his committee – yes, yes, you showed your discrimination by what you say of him. But I cant write the history of my marriage on what remains of this paper, so good bye, and my address is

Monks House
Rodmell
Lewes. Sussex

Should you give me the great pleasure of a letter

Our love
Yr Virginia

2149: To Saxon Sydney-Turner

52 Tavistock Sqre. [*W.C.1*]

27th Feb. [1930]

My dear Saxon,

[. . .] What is your opinion of Ethel Smyth? – her music, I mean? She has descended upon me like a wolf on the fold in purple and gold, terrifically strident and enthusiastic – I like her – she is as shabby as a washerwoman and shouts and sings – but the question of her music crops up – I don't mean that she cares what I think, being apparently indomitable in her own view, but one day you must tell me the truth

1. Countess Russell, *née* Mary Beauchamp and previously Countess von Arnim (1866–1941), who wrote several popular novels under the name of 'Elizabeth', after her most famous, *Elizabeth and Her German Garden* (1898). She was a cousin of Katherine Mansfield and a friend of Ethel Smyth, who had stayed with her at Cannes during the previous summer.
2. Another of Ethel's friends, the former diplomat, novelist and man of letters (1874–1945), whose biography she wrote in 1938.

about it. Anyhow, as a writer she is astonishingly efficient – takes every fence. [...]

Love
Virginia

2157: To Ethel Smyth   *52 Tavistock Square, W.C.1*

15th March
Sunday March 17th [16, 1930]

[...] Where can I begin all the things that might be said. My mother? Your Niece?[1] The hermaphrodite?[2] Being vain, I will broach the subject of beauty – just for a moment – and burst out in ecstasy at your defence of me as a very ugly writer – which is what I am – but an honest one, driven like a gasping whale to the surface in a snort – such is the effort and anguish to me of finding a phrase (that is saying what I mean) – and then they say I write beautifully! How could I write beautifully when I am always trying to say something that has not been said, and should be said for the first time, exactly. So I relinquish beauty, and leave it as a legacy to the next generation. My part has been to increase their stock in trade, perhaps. But to leave this fascinating subject – Yes I would like to know all about your niece. Why briefly? Haven't you got a ream of paper which you might just as well fill, sitting over your fire (what sort of fire?) in your room (what sort of room?) alone? For what other purpose than to write letters to me brim full of amusement and excitement were you gifted with a pen like a streak of hounds in full scent? And the more odds and ends you stuff in the better I like it, for I have a habit of making you up in bed at night. Lets imagine Ethel Smyth, I say to myself. We will begin with the servant bringing in the breakfast etc etc. Marriage – yes? – What about marriage? I married Leonard Woolf in 1912, I think, and almost immediately was ill for 3 years. Nevertheless we have nothing to complain of. Youth – I will give you scenes from my youth one day. But I cant take another blue slip now, so must trust that you will continue shooting letters into pillar boxes

1. Elizabeth Williamson (1901–80), Ethel's great-niece, taught mathematics and astronomy at University College, London.
2. During her 1914 journey through the Nubian desert, described by Ethel in *Beecham and Pharaoh* (1935), she had met and photographed a hermaphrodite, the cast-off 'wife' of a sheik.

with a fling of your wrist – better still, that you may come and see me – [. . .]

Yr
Virginia

2162: To Ethel Smyth   *52 T[avistock] S[quare, W.C.1]*

Sunday [6 April 1930]

Good God, Ethel, I daresay you're perfectly right. I daresay I'm a d——d intellectual. I know nothing about myself. And you coming in with your rapidity and insight probably see whats what in a flash. The party wasn't my choice – I warned you.

But I think I see what you mean. – The [F. L.] Lucases. I've struggled and rebelled against them all my life, but their integrity always makes me their slave. Much though I hate Cambridge, and bitterly though I've suffered from it, I still respect it. I suppose that even without education, as I am, I am naturally of that narrow, ascetic, puritanical breed – oh what a bore; and its too late now. It cant be helped.

You'd be amused to see how I fret and worry when I am suddenly made aware of my own character. For months I forget all about it, and then someone says But you're the most appalling liar I've ever met, and I rush to the glass (this sheet is a glass) as if I'd been told my dress was upside down, or my nose bleeding. As I told you, I am not a good psychologist.

The sort of thing I like is when you twist up a note out of a cover in the train – Thats life, I say. And I am only a spectator. I happened the other day to read an old article of my own, and I said 'Good God, what a prig that woman must be!' I think I must go to some more parties – perhaps they would help. Only I hate dressing and coming into rooms. [. . .]

Virginia

2178: To Dorothy Brett   *Monk's House, Rodmell,*
Lewes [Sussex]

May 10th 1930

My dear Brett,

[. . .] It is monstrous that Lawrence should have died.[1] I never spoke

1. D. H. Lawrence, Dorothy Brett's good friend, died on 2 March, aged 44, three and a half years younger than Virginia.

to him, and only saw him twice – once, swinging a spirit lamp in a shop at St Ives, and once, two or three years ago when our train stopped outside Rome in the early morning and there was Lawrence talking to Norman Douglas on the other platform.

The papers have been hypocritical beyond belief: I almost blazed into print in a rage; first abusing her [Frieda Lawrence] and then slobbering over him. I dont suppose it matters – And I couldn't write because I have never read any of his books, or more than half of two of them.[1] I hate preaching – and I can't read contemporaries; and I dont want to read novels, whoever writes them. [...]

yr
Virginia Woolf

2183: To Ethel Smyth   *52 Tavistock Sqre. WC1*

Monday [26 May 1930]

[...] If only I weren't a writer, perhaps I could thank you and praise you and admire you perfectly simply and expressively and say in one word what I felt about the Concert yesterday. As it is, an image forms in my mind; a quickset briar hedge, innumerable intricate and spiky and thorned; in the centre burns a rose. Miraculously, the rose is you; flushed pink, wearing pearls. The thorn hedge is the music; and I have to break my way through violins, flutes, cymbals, voices to this red burning centre. Now I admit that this has nothing to do with musical criticism. It is only what I feel as I sat on my silver winged (was it winged?) chair on the slippery floor yesterday. I am enthralled that you, the dominant and superb, should have this tremor and vibration of fire round you – violins flickering, flutes purring; (the image is of a winter hedge) – that you should be able to create this world from your centre. Perhaps I was not thinking of the music but of all the loves and ages you have been through. Lord – what a complexity the soul is! But I wont scratch all the skin off my fingers trying to expound. But my dear Ethel it was frightfully good of you to let me come – dear me yes – what a generous woman you are – and how I adore your generosity and the vehemence with which you scatter the floor with hairpins and fumble in your placket for a spectacle case and embrace the Governor of Cyprus and enfold us all in the spontaneity and ruthlessness of your career.

1. She had read at least the following Lawrence novels: *Trespassers*, *The Lost Girl* (which she reviewed, *Essays*, III, 271), and *Women in Love*. In 1931 she wrote 'Notes on D. H. Lawrence', after having read *Sons and Lovers* (see Letter 2354 and *Essays*, V).

Thats what I call living; thats the quality I would give my eyes to possess. Of course, in my furtive and sidelong way (being like a flat fish with eyes not in the usual place) I had read a good deal of this years ago in your books, and now I begin to read it and other oddities and revelations too in your music. It will take a long time not merely because I am musically so feeble, but because all my faculties are so industriously bringing in news of so many Ethels at the same moment. There I sit a mere target for impressions and try to catch each one as it flies and find its gold or its white or its blue ring for it. I only offer this explanation of my dumbness and fatuity yesterday. I couldn't say 'I like that best' or 'that' because I was sorting out, in a rapid elementary way, a myriad arrows: But perhaps you saw, with your hawk's glance, to the bottom of my silence.[1] [...]

Virginia

2194: To Ethel Smyth   [*52 Tavistock Square, W.C.1*]

Sunday, 22nd June [1930]

[...] I did not mean, though I must have said, that Leonard [like Jacob] served 7 years for his wife. He saw me it is true; and thought me an odd fish; and went off next day to Ceylon, with a vague romance about us both [Virginia and Vanessa]! And I heard stories of him; how his hand trembled[2] and he had bit his thumb through in a rage; and Lytton said he was like Swift and would murder his wife; and someone else said Woolf had married a black woman. That was my romance – Woolf in a jungle. And then I set up house alone with a brother [Adrian], and Nessa married, and I was rather adventurous, for those days; that is we were sexually very free – Elizabeth [Williamson] owes her emancipation and mathematics partly to us – but I was always sexually cowardly, and never walked over Mountains with Counts as you did, nor plucked all the flowers of life in a bunch as you did. My terror of real life has always kept me in a nunnery. And much of this talking and adventuring in London alone, and sitting up to all hours with young men, and saying whatever came first, was rather petty, as you were not

1. A splendid letter, but Virginia was ambivalent. She was also writing to her nephew Quentin Bell: 'An old woman of seventy one has fallen in love with me. It is at once hideous and horrid and melancholy-sad. It is like being caught by a giant crab' (Letter 2181).
2. A lifelong physical condition. Leonard Woolf was exempted from military service partly on the grounds of his 'inherited nervous tremor'.

petty: at least narrow; circumscribed; and leading to endless ramifi-
cations of intrigue. We had violent rows – oh yes, I used to rush through
London in such rages, and stormed Hampstead heights at night in white
or purple fury. And then I married, and then my brains went up in a
shower of fireworks. As an experience, madness is terrific I can assure
you, and not to be sniffed at; and in its lava I still find most of the things I
write about. It shoots out of one everything shaped, final, not in mere
driblets, as sanity does. And the six months – not three – that I lay in bed
taught me a good deal about what is called oneself. Indeed I was almost
crippled when I came back to the world, unable to move a foot in terror,
after that discipline. Think – not one moment's freedom from doctor
discipline – perfectly strange – conventional men; 'you shant read this'
and 'you shant write a word' and 'you shall lie still and drink milk' – for
six months.

But enough. [. . .]

Virginia

2218: To Ethel Smyth

*Monks House [Rodmell,
Sussex]*

15th Aug. 1930

As it is a pouring wet afternoon, I will write a few disjected
observations, like offerings to a magpie. (These birds make their nests
of straw, haircombings, and other things that have been thrown away.)
Ethels great grandmother on the paternal side was a Magpie. [. . .]

(2) As a psychologist I am myopic rather than obtuse.[1] I see the
circumference and the outline not the detail. You and Nessa say I
am so frightfully stupid because I dont see that fly on the floor: but I
see the walls, the pictures and the Venus against the pear tree [in
The Monk's House garden], so that the position and surroundings
of the fly are accurately known to me. Say that you are a fly: what
you actually do and say I may misinterpret; but your standing in the
world being known to me, I never get you out of perspective as a
whole. Therefore act and speak as frantically as you like; having
(while I lay on the sofa that first afternoon) sketched your ambit –
your wall, statue and pear tree, no minor agitation in the foreground
will upset me. You see I like your circumference.

1. Ethel had written: 'You are supposed to be inexpert as a psychologist, not very
"human" and so on. And it is so. And yet I have a feeling of security with you in the
matter of being understood' (11 August 1930, Berg Collection).

(3) Hence if I were ill I should be quite as ready to come to you as to Vita, though for entirely different reasons. When I was ill, 4 years ago, and had to spend 3 months in bed, she took me to Long Barn: there I lay in Swansdown and recovered. The sense of peace dwells thus, about her – those are some of my associations. But loving lights, pillows, and all luxury as I do, aesthetically largely, and often merely spectacularly, for I never acquire possessions myself, you, if I were ill, would be as soothing; no, not that; perhaps supporting would be the better word. Sanity is what I want. A robust sense of fact. Well, wouldn't you give me that? Haven't you – anyhow to my sense, warred with the world sufficiently to have made intervals of peace?

The object of this remark is I think to prove that I am diverse enough to want Vita and Ethel and Leonard and Vanessa and oh some other people too. But jealousy is not a very bad fault is it? I am often jealous of other people's gifts. Only to think I want the swansdown only is not an accurate picture of my mind.

(4) Then Perversion.

Yes, I am afraid I do agree with you in thinking it silly. But I suspect we are wrong. I suspect the ramrod and gunpowder of our East Indian grandfathers here influences us. I think we are being provincial and petty. When I go to what we call a *Buggery Poke party, I feel as if I had strayed into the male urinal; a wet, smelly, trivial kind of place. I fought with Eddy Sackville over this; I often fight with my friends. How silly, how pretty you sodomites are I said; whereat he flared up and accused me of having a red-nosed grandfather. For myself, why did I tell you that I had only once felt physical feeling for a man when he felt nothing for me? I suppose in some opium trance of inaccuracy. No – had I felt physical feeling for him, then, no doubt, we should have married, or had a shot at something. But my feelings were all of the spiritual, intellectual, emotional kind. And when 2 or 3 times in all, I felt physically for a man, then he was so obtuse, gallant, foxhunting and dull that I – diverse as I am – could only wheel round and gallop the other way. Perhaps this shows why Clive, who had his reasons, always called me a fish. Vita also calls me fish. And I reply (I think often while holding their hands, and getting exquisite pleasure from contact with either male or female body) 'But what I want of you is illusion – to make the

* There is a Farm here called Muggery Poke.

world dance.' More than that, I cannot get my sense of unity and coherency and all that makes me wish to write the Lighthouse etc. unless I am perpetually stimulated. Its no good sitting in a garden with a book; or collecting facts. There must be this fanning and drumming – of course I get it tremendously from Leonard – but differently – Lord Lord how many things I want – how many different flowers I visit – and often I plunge into London, between tea and dinner, and walk and walk, reviving my fires, in the city, in some wretched slum, where I peep in at the doors of public houses. Where people mistake, as I think, is in perpetually narrowing and naming these immensely composite and wide flung passions – driving stakes through them, herding them between screens. But how do you define 'Perversity.'? What is the line between friendship and perversion?

Well, enough – especially as I read in your last letter that you dont want remarks about character. And I've no doubt these are all wrong; but I'm treating you as a woman whose paternal Grand-mother was a magpie.

V.

2222: To Ethel Smyth   *Monks House [Rodmell, Sussex]*

Tuesday [19 August 1930]

(1) 'I dont suppose I am really very fond of anyone'
I woke up in the night and said 'But I am the most passionate of women. Take away my affections and I should be like sea weed out of water; like the shell of a crab, like a husk. All my entrails, light, marrow, juice, pulp would be gone. I should be blown into the first puddle and drown. Take away my love for my friends and my burning and pressing sense of the importance and lovability and curiosity of human life and I should be nothing but a membrane, a fibre, uncoloured, lifeless to be thrown away like any other excreta. Then what did I mean when I said to Ethel "I dont suppose I am really very fond of anyone"?'
(2) It is true that I only want to show off to women. Women alone stir my imagination – there I agree with you:

(3) [. . .] So – I now come to the point – might I one day read some of your letters? Your diary? Remember what a lot has to be packed in. And remember – not I confess that you seem in any danger of forgetting this elemental fact – what a crazy piece of work I am – like a cracked looking glass in a fair. Only, as I write this, it strikes me that as usual I am romancing, led on irresistibly by the lure of some phrase; and, that in fact Virginia is so simple, so simple, so simple: just give her things to play with, like a child. [. . .]

Yr V

2239: To Ethel Smyth   *Monks House* [*Rodmell, Sussex*]

Monday 21st [22] Sept. [1930]

[. . .] We are throwing our hats up – no great exaggeration – about your essay. Morgan Forster (E. M. Forster the novelist, whose books once influenced mine, and are very good, I think, though impeded, shrivelled and immature) said 'Lord! I should think you would like an essay by Ethel Smyth! She should write pamphlets – my word (he said) how good her thing in the train was[1] – how I laughed – what a born writer' and then, by a natural transition, passed to Lady Russell, and said (he's the quietest, but most inflexible of men) 'No; I dont like her. I think she is unkind and selfish. But she has a wonderful way of making one wish to be nice to her' – and nothing I could say would change his inflexible opinion 'I dont like her' – but then he was very young when he knew her,[2] and she was rude to the old mother whose sister, son, daughter and husband he is. They share a Surrey house; and live like mice in a nest. [. . .]

And its raining, Ethel, sweeping in filaments of mist across my marshes; but Ethel, all the same I walked to the top of the down this afternoon, and surveyed Sussex, and then tore my skirt my knickers and some tender parts not mentioned even between ladies on a barbed wire fence. Do you know, if I could sit still all the morning I could write straight ahead now – if I were you, and could drive one hour into another, I could finish the Waves in one blast – as it is I wake filled with a

1. 'An Adventure in a Train' from *Streaks of Life* (1921). But Ethel wrote no essay at this time for The Hogarth Press.
2. As tutor to her children in 1905, when she was Countess von Arnim and living in Germany.

tremulous yet steady rapture, carry my pitcher full of lucid and deep water across the garden, and am forced to spill it all by – some one coming – Never mind. And write to me.

V.

2244: To Ethel Smyth · *Monks House, Rodmell*
[Sussex]

Sept. 28th [1930]

[. . .] Ah, but now they are gone, and I wrote this morning; and then took one of Leonards large white pocket handkerchiefs and climbed Asheham hill and lost a green glove and found 10 mushrooms, which I shall eat in bed tomorrow, with bacon, toast and hot coffee. I shall get a letter from Ethel. I shall moon slowly dressing; shall loiter talking, shall hear about the funeral of our [Rodmell] epileptic, Tom Fears, who dropped dead after dinner on Thursday; shall smell a red rose; shall gently surge across the lawn (I move as if I carried a basket of eggs on my head) light a cigarette, take my writing board on my knee; and let myself down, like a diver, very cautiously into the last sentence I wrote yesterday. Then perhaps after 20 minutes, or it may be more, I shall see a light in the depths of the sea, and stealthily approach – for one's sentences are only an approximation, a net one flings over some sea pearl which may vanish; and if one brings it up it wont be anything like what it was when I saw it, under the sea. Now these are the great excitements of life. Once I would have written all this twice over; but now I can't; it has to go, with its blood on its head. I have 3 whole days of solitude still – Monday, Thursday and Friday. The others are packed with this damnable disease of seeing people. Please tell me what psychological necessity makes people wish to 'go and see' so-and so? I never do. Do they resent obscurely, the effort that L. and I make to be alone? that I make to write? [. . .]

V.

2252: To Margaret Llewelyn Davies
52 Tavistock Sq. [W.C.1]

Oct. 10th 1930

Dearest Margaret,
[. . .] I am very pleased that Mrs Barton on the whole approves – at

the same time I'm amused at the importance attached to the size of the Guilders.[1] Vanity seems to be the same in all classes. But I swear that Mrs Barton shall say exactly what she thinks of the appearance of me and my friends and I wont think *her* unsympathetic. Indeed I wish she would – what fun to hand her a packet of our letters and let her introduce it! What rather appals me (I'm writing in a hurry, and cant spell, and dont please take my words altogether literally) is the terrific conventionality of the workers. Thats why – if you want explanations – I dont think they will be poets or novelists for another hundred years or so. If they cant face the fact that Lilian[2] smokes a pipe and reads detective novels, and cant be told that they weigh on an average 12 stone – which is largely because they scrub so hard and have so many children – and are shocked by the word 'impure' how can you say that they face 'reality'?, (I never know what 'reality' means: but Lilian smoking a pipe to me is real, and Lilian merely coffee coloured and discreet is not nearly so real). What depresses me is that the workers seem to have taken on all the middle class respectabilities which we – at any rate if we are any good at writing or painting – have faced and thrown out. Or am I quite wrong? And how do you explain away these eccentricities on the part of your swans? It interests me very much. For you see, it is that to my thinking that now makes the chief barrier between us. One has to be 'sympathetic' and polite and therefore one is uneasy and insincere. And why, with such a chance to get rid of conventionalities, do they cling to them? However, I must stop. And we must meet and go into the question by word of mouth – if you want me to make them sylphs I will.

Yours Virginia

2254: To Ethel Smyth   *52 Tavistock Square [W.C.1]*

Thursday, 16th Oct [1930]

[. . .] *Monday* or (or is it 'and'? – see, how seldom I look at my own

1. At the invitation of Margaret Llewelyn Davies, formerly Secretary of the Women's Co-operative Guild, Virginia had written the introduction to a book of autobiographical essays and letters by Guild members. From the first, Llewelyn Davies and others – among them Eleanor Barton, the current General Secretary – had requested changes in the manuscript, which greatly annoyed Virginia. But the book was published later this year by The Hogarth Press under the title *Life as we have known it.*
2. Lilian Harris (c. 1866–1949), formerly Assistant Secretary to the Guild, lived with Llewelyn Davies.

works) *Tuesday*.[1] If one put comparatives for all your superlatives, you're a very good critic – that is, have singled out the phrase I liked (the pigeon)[2] and the stories I liked; and lighted with your aeroplane eye upon the generally acclaimed successes – that is Mark on the Wall and Kew. You are perfectly right about Green and blue and the heron one ['Monday or Tuesday']: thats mainly why I won't reprint. They are mere tangles of words; balls of string that the kitten or Pan [Ethel's dog] has played with. One of these days I will write out some phases of my writer's life; and expound what I now merely say in short – After being ill and suffering every form and variety of nightmare and extravagant intensity of perception – for I used to make up poems, stories, profound and to me inspired phrases all day long as I lay in bed, and thus sketched, I think, all that I now, by the light of reason, try to put into prose (I thought of the Lighthouse then, and Kew and others, not in substance, but in idea) – after all this, when I came to, I was so tremblingly afraid of my own insanity that I wrote Night and Day [1919] mainly to prove to my own satisfaction that I could keep entirely off that dangerous ground. I wrote it, lying in bed, allowed to write only for one half hour a day. And I made myself copy from plaster casts, partly to tranquillise, partly to learn anatomy. Bad as the book is, it composed my mind, and I think taught me certain elements of composition which I should not have had the patience to learn had I been in full flush of health always. These little pieces in Monday or (and) Tuesday were written by way of diversion; they were the treats I allowed myself when I had done my exercise in the conventional style. I shall never forget the day I wrote The Mark on the Wall – all in a flash, as if flying, after being kept stone breaking for months. The Unwritten Novel was the great discovery, however. That – again in one second – showed me how I could embody all my deposit of experience in a shape that fitted it – not that I have ever reached that end; but anyhow I saw, branching out of the tunnel I made, when I discovered that method of approach, Jacobs Room [1922], Mrs Dalloway [1925] etc – How I trembled with excitement; and then Leonard came in, and I drank my milk, and concealed my excitement,

1. Virginia's collection of short stories, *Monday or Tuesday* (1921), included 'A Haunted House', 'A Society', 'Monday or Tuesday', 'An Unwritten Novel', 'The String Quartet', 'Blue and Green', 'Kew Gardens', and 'The Mark on the Wall'. All these stories, with the exception of 'A Society' and 'Blue and Green' were among those reprinted by Leonard after Virginia's death in *A Haunted House* (1943).
2. 'The shadow of a thrush crossed the carpet; from the deepest wells of silence the wood pigeon drew its bubble of sound' ('A Haunted House').

and wrote I suppose another page of that interminable Night and Day (which some say is my best book). All this I will tell you one day – here I suppress my natural inclination to say, if dear Ethel you have the least wish to hear anymore on a subject that cant be of the least interest to you. And, I add, Green and Blue and the heron were the wild outbursts of freedom, inarticulate, ridiculous, unprintable mere outcries. [. . .]

Yr V.

2263: To Quentin Bell   *52 Tavistock Sq. [W.C.1]*

28th Oct. [1930]

Dearest Quentin,

You see how obediently I answer your letter at once. For all your illiteracy and difficulty with the pen – your letter might be written by a large wild cat that had fallen with all its paws into a well – you yet contrive to make me see you and your miraculous companions. Now if Wyndham Lewis instead of writing a Bloomsbury Black Book in which every sinner of either school is to be pilloried were to write what is the truth – that we are merely wild, odd, innocent, artless, eccentric and industrious beyond words, there would be some sting to it. But to represent us as he does one seething mass of correlated villainy is so beside the point (I cant remember any of the right words – but I have been writing for two hours and they have flown) that it glances from the back.[1] No, not from Eddy [Sackville West] and Harold [Nicolson], and Raymond [Mortimer]. They are all providing escapes for themselves, it is said; they propose to live abroad. That is what we are talking of at the moment. Today I am going to a party at the Austrian Embassy to hear a Viennese string quartet with Ethel Smyth. She will be in an old rabbit fur coat and thick boots; I feebler but dowdier. There will be princes and dukes. Tea and cakes. Women and violins. Ethel will almost certainly commit some rape. That is why I go, to tell the truth, for God knows I cant listen to quratets at Austiran embassies. (There you see how this typewriter seplls.)

It has been the finest October on record. The gravel pits at

1. In 1924 the author and painter Wyndham Lewis had satirised Lytton Strachey and others in an article entitled 'Apes of God'. In 1930 he expanded it into a novel. He described Bloomsbury as substituting 'money for talent as a qualification for membership. [. . .] The tone of "society" (of a spurious donnish social elegance) prevails among them.'

Warlingham [Surrey] where we went on Sunday are precisely like Cézanne pictures – why go to the South of France where the wind blows and the mosquitoes bite, then? What I most envy is Rome. Oh to be Quentin and going to Rome! But my dear child, do you know that in half a century there will be methods of circumventing these divisions of Aunt and Nephew? By attaching a small valve something like a leech to the back of your neck I shall tap all your sensations; the present system is a mere anachronism; that I should be here and you there and nothing between us but a blue sheet (of paper I mean). [. . .]

Love to all the oddities.

Virginia

2265: To Ethel Smyth   *52 Tavistock Square. [W.C.1]*

30th Oct 1930

[. . .] By the way, what are the arguments against suicide? You know what a flibberti-gibbet I am: well there suddenly comes in a thunder clap a sense of the complete uselessness of my life. Its like suddenly running one's head against a wall at the end of a blind alley. Now what are the arguments against that sense – 'Oh it would be better to end it'? I need not say that I have no sort of intention of taking any steps: I simply want to know – as you are so masterly and triumphant – catching your train and not running too fast – what are the arguments against it?

V.

2274: To Vanessa Bell   *52 Tavistock Square [W.C.1]*

Nov. 8th [1930]

Dearest Dolphin,

[. . .] I've got no news. Yet I've seen so many people I could fill 8 pages: but its only chatter. My most horrid experience was a visit from Tom Eliot. This had been arranged for weeks. At the last moment he rang up to say that Vivien [Eliot] wanted to come too, and would we pretend that we had asked her. This sounded ominous, but was nothing to the reality. She is insane. She suspects every word one says. 'Do you keep bees?' I asked, handing her the honey. 'Hornets' she replied. 'Where?' I asked. 'Under the bed.' Thats the style, and one has to go on talking, and Tom tries, I suppose, to cover it up with longwinded and facetious stories. And she smells; and she throws cheap powder over the bread; and she opens his letters, suspects me of being his mistress, so far as we could gather; and finally said that I had made a signal which meant that they were to go. So they did go, in about half an hour, and now he writes that he wants to come and see me alone, to explain I suppose; but I expect Vivien will appear too. I went to Ottolines [Morrell] yesterday, and must unsay my abuse, as there I found Yeats, whom I think (naturally, wrongly) our only living poet – perhaps a great poet: anyhow a good poet; and there was also de la Mare,[1] who is very odd, very charming, rather daft, but at the same time surprisingly on the spot. Being now almost incapable of discretion I said all the wrong things about poetry and we had a long discourse – very amusing to me: as I can't think why they dont write poetry about interesting things any longer. Yeats admitted it – but then, as he believes in the unconscious soul, in fairies, in magic, and has a complete system of philosophy and psychology – it was not easy altogether to understand: at the same time, I agreed with many of his views; and he also is surprisingly sensible. He has grown tremendously thick, and is rather magnificent looking; in fact seeing how seldom one meets interesting people (with Dolphin [Vanessa] away) this was a great success. It is old Ottolines function, undoubtedly. She has the atmosphere for that, though she now has a black trumpet hung to her side for she is rapidly growing deaf. [. . .]

Also we had a terrific visitation from Hugh Walpole. If you want a book from the Times, get Cakes and Ale by Somerset Maugham. All London is ringing with it. For there poor Hugh is most cruelly and maliciously at the same time unmistakably and amusingly caricatured [as Alroy Kear]. He was sitting on his bed with only one sock on when he opened it. There he sat with only one sock on till 11 next morning reading it. Also, we gathered in tears. He almost wept in front of Hilda Matheson, Vita and Clive, in telling us. And he couldn't stop. Whenever we changed the conversation he went back. 'There are things in it that nobody knows but Willie [Maugham] and myself' he said. 'There are little things that make me shudder. And that man has been my dearest friend for 20 years. And now I'm the laughing stock of London. And he

1. The poets William Butler Yeats (1865–1939) and Walter de la Mare (1873–1956). Virginia's impressions of de la Mare seem to be linked to his famous dreamlike poetry, as in *The Listener and Other Poems* (1912). Yeats had written about his spiritualist system in *A Vision* (1926).

writes to say he didn't mean it for me.' 'Oh but he undoubtedly did that' said Vita cheerfully. 'And he might have been jugged' said Hugh. 'You dont know the kind of life that Willie has led. I do. I could put him in a book. But then I call it a dastardly thing to do.' And so on, round and round, round and round, like a dog with a tin on its tail, till it was half past 12. Then he said it was all in the strictest confidence, and he had told no one else. But of course, Clive met Christabel [McLaren] next night, and Christabel had met Hugh that afternoon – and had been ever so much more tactful than Vita. [. . .]

B.

2277: To Ethel Smyth   *Monks House [Rodmell,*
                                         Sussex]

Friday [14 November 1930]

[. . .] I will now tell you about my parties (you say its a case of eating 6 meringues and being sick). Now thats unjust; thats the rasp of whooping cough; thats whats worse to me, *untrue*. Think of this: my 1st party was by command to Ottolines; and it was a shabby between the lights party, which is a compromise, for one can slip in without even putting on those black shoes which you carry about to propitiate the British aristocracy in a cardboard box mended with safety pins – no paper fasteners. In this twilight all the Italian furniture and pomegranates are faded to rose and amber, and now and then she flings a handful of cedar shavings upon the fire; dips her hand in a basket and brings up skeins like the entrails of flying fish, coloured wools, all tangled: these she drops again. And on one side of the fire sat the poet Yeats on the other the poet de la Mare – and what were they doing when I came in? Tossing between them higher and higher a dream of Napoleon with ruby eyes. All over my head it went – for what do I know of the inner meaning of dreams, I whose life is almost entirely founded on dreams (yes, I will come to the suicide dream one of these days) I mean I know nothing of the spiritual significance of ruby eyes, or a book with concentric rings of black, purple and orange. But Yeats said, as it might be a man identifying a rather rare grass, that is the third state of the soul in contemplation (or words to that effect – it will not surprise you if I got them wrong). And then? Did I like Milton? Yes. And then – De la Mare does not like Milton. And then – dreams and dreams. and then stories of Irish life in brogue; and then the soul's attitude to art; and then (here I was touched, you I daresay not –) then, as the talk got more and more rapt, refined and erratic, I saw Ottoline stoop her hand to what seemed a coal scuttle and apply it to her ear: An ordinary black ear trumpet it was, ungilt unfunnelled, and the apparition of this bare and ghastly object had somehow a sepulchral effect – and I cried out, in the midst of all the poetry. Heavens Ottoline, are you deaf? And she replied with a sort of noble negligence which struck me very much 'Yes, yes, quite deaf –' and then lifted the trumpet and listened. Does that touch you? Well it did me, and I saw in a flash all I admire her for; and think what people overlook, in the briarwood bramble of her obvious tortuousness and hypocrisy. [. . .]

V.

2330: To Clive Bell   *Monks House [Rodmell, Sussex]*

21st Feb. 1931

Dearest Clive,

[. . .] Aldous [Huxley] astounds me – his energy, his modernity. Is it that he can't see anything that he has to see so much? Not content with touring Europe with Sullivan[1] to ask all great men of all countries what they think of God, science, the soul, the future and so on, he spends his week in London visiting docks, where with [his wife] Maria's help he can just distinguish a tusk from a frozen bullock: and now is off on a tour of the Black Country, to visit works, to go down mines: and then to Moscow, and then America. I am very envious in my heart. I should like to die with a complete map of the world in my head. But shall I ever see a naked savage? I doubt it. Your son Julian, who dropped in yesterday, says the sight of Duncan is odder far than any savage. I think by the way from what I gathered at Cambridge that he has a very good chance of a fellowship – how odd that is too. I mean, how time passes, and how the young improve upon us, for none of us were ever made fellows, and remained charming and amorous and adventurous like Julian into the bargain.

Arnold Bennett lies, it is said, like the picture of a dying fox in Uncle Remus,[2] staring straight at the ceiling and beating the air with his front

1. J. W. N. Sullivan (1886–1937), who wrote on scientific and musical subjects.
2. The extremely popular American folk tales by Joel Chandler Harris (1848–1908). Bennett died on 27 March.

paws as he tries to say 'I met him in 1906'. After an hour's effort he comes out with this momentous fact; but will live they say to write another fifty novels.

I have finished my book [*The Waves*] – yes – but it is a failure. Too difficult: too jerky: too inchoate altogether. But what's the point of writing if one doesn't make a fool of oneself? Anyhow I am left high and dry and can turn my mind to other people's books. Will Rothenstein has brought out his memoirs,[1] in which Vanessa, Stella and Virginia Stephen figure, most inaccurately, all in black, like Watts paintings, having tea in the basement [of Hyde Park Gate], very beautiful, but shy, and only responding with freedom to Phil Burne-Jones[2] and Arthur Studd. Also there is my grandmother,[3] a violent old lady rapping the floor with a stick and descending to scold Will for his iniquitous portrait of her beautiful daughter, the stepmother [mother] of Mrs Bell and Mrs Woolf, who are now so well known. Do you think that all memoirs are as mendacious as this – Every fact I mean, all on one side? Lytton's little book of biographies is coming out,[4] and he wants to call it Lives in Aspic, but Carrington and Pippa [Strachey] forbid. And I am turning to Don Juan [Byron] and Aurora Leigh [Elizabeth Barrett Browning], together with all those vile memoirs, for which as you know, I have such a gluttonous appetite. [. . .]

V.

2335: To Ethel Smyth   *52 Tavistock Sqre.* [*W.C.1*]

11th March 1931

I feel, no doubt wrongly, simply from your voice and what you say mysteriously about 'discipline' that I have annoyed? – no, not annoyed, but perhaps hurt you? Well, I'm so blind and deaf psychologically, that I have to put these, to most people certainties, as questions, and now, because I'm blind and deaf, I'm going to lay before you the reason of the misunderstanding, if there is one. I expect you to ridicule me, but I dont mind being ridiculed, if you understand me, as there is always the chance that you will understand.

1. *Men and Memories*, by the painter Sir William Rothenstein (1872–1945), was published in two volumes in 1931–2.
2. Philip Burne-Jones (1861–1926), the son of Sir Edward Burne-Jones.
3. Maria Jackson, *née* Pattle (1818–92).
4. *Portraits in Miniature* (1931).

It was the party.[1] I dont know when I have suffered more; and yet why did I suffer? and what did I suffer? Humiliation: that I had been dragged to that awful Exhibition of insincerity and inanity against my will (I used to be dragged by my half-brothers against my will – hence perhaps some latent sense of outrage) Then, that you liked the party – you who are uncompromising, truthful, vehement. 'Ethel likes this sort of thing' I said, disillusion filled me: all belief fell off me. 'And she has planned this, and worse still, subjected me to it. Gulfs separate us.' And I felt betrayed – I who have spoken to you so freely of all my weaknesses – I to whom this chatter and clatter on top of any art, music, pictures, which I dont understand, – is an abomination. Oh then, the elderly butlers, peers, champagne and sugared cakes! It seemed to me that you wantonly inflicted this indignity upon me for no reason, and that I was pinioned there and betrayed and made to smile at our damnation – I who was reeling and shocked, as I see now, (to excuse myself,) by my own struggle with The Waves – who had vainly perhaps but honestly tried to understand you, H.B.[2] the Prison: there I was mocking and mowing, and you forced me to it and you didn't mind it. I went home therefore more jangled and dazed and out of touch with reality than I have been for years. I could not sleep. I took chloral. I spent the next day in a state of horror and disillusion. When you rang me up you seemed to guess at none of all this, and I felt that I could never approach you so as to touch you again. (And without exaggeration you dont know how I have honoured and respected you – come, oddly, to depend upon your sanity) So then I put off [Sibyl] Colefax and Ottoline and resolved to be quit of the posturing and insincerity and being hauled about and made to exhibit myself for ever.

This no doubt seems to you wantonly exaggerated to excuse a fit of temper. But it is not. I see of course that it is morbid, that it is through this even to me inexplicable susceptibility to some impressions suddenly that I approach madness and that end of a drainpipe with a gibbering old

1. The Woolfs had gone to hear the first London performance of Ethel Smyth's oratorio, *The Prison*, on 24 February. Afterwards they went to the party given for her by the Countess of Rosebery.
2. Henry Brewster (1850–1908), always referred to as H.B. by Ethel, was a wealthy man, half American, who lived most of his life in France and Italy. Ethel was in love with his sister-in-law, and when she met him at 25, she fell in love with him too. He was the only man who aroused her passionate affections. Brewster wrote several books of philosophy. One of them, *The Prison: a Dialogue* was the basis for her oratorio.

man. But this is me; and you cant know me and merely brush this aside and disregard it as a fit of temper. I dont attempt to rationalise; but I can now, after 2 weeks, see how selfish, cold, and indeed brutal I may have seemed to you, when in fact I felt more strongly about you and therefore about your betrayal of me to wolves and vultures than ever before. Excuse this; and continue whatever your scheme may be. I dont suppose I shall understand your explanation, if you give one, or you mine. But I venture it, trusting in your sanity as I do: and because of what I call my respect for you.

V.

2339a: To Ethel Smyth [*52 Tavistock Square,*] *London.* [*W.C.1*]
[23 March 1931]

[...] I've just read your letter hastily – about HB's [Brewster's] writing – As I say my remarks applied to his letters; I should never say that his books were badly written because they're not literary – in fact, for me, like most Americans, he is much too literary in one sense – too finished, suave, polished and controlled; uses his brains and not his body; and if I call him not a born writer, its because he writes too well – takes no risks – doesn't plunge and stumble and jump at boughs beyond his grasp, as I, to be modest, have done in my day; and you. It trickles off me – his beauty – instead of raising the nerves in my spine – But this is the way with all Americans – they cant throw things about as we do. cant take liberties: are so d–d refined for example Henry James. Enough: I'm rushed; and incoherent.

2342: To Ethel Smyth   *52 Tavistock Sqre.* [*W.C.1*]
1st April (fools day) [1931]

[...] Write me long letters. In the country – they unfurl like flowers in water. The worst of my suffering is that its half the scratching of an eczematic dog. Little things people say; nods and hints: these stick in my pelt; and not the arrows always of destiny. No: what you give me is protection, so far as I am capable of it. I look at you and (being blind to most things except violent impressions) think if Ethel can be so downright and plainspoken and on the spot, I need not fear instant dismemberment by wild horses. Its the child crying for the nurses hand in the dark. You do it by being so uninhibited: so magnificently unself-conscious. This is what people pay £20 a sitting to get from Psycho-analysts – liberation from their own egotism. Never mind now – here's Vita coming like a ship in full sail. I think you're right – we all cry for nurses hand.

V.

2343: To Ethel Smyth   *Monks House [Rodmell, Sussex]*

7th April]1931]

[. . .] I wrote you a long letter [. . .] which was all on the theme of the absurd and irrational happiness of our lives – yes, even poor Leonard, whose breast I pierce daily with hot steel, is divinely happy here; we giggle and joke, and go and poke at roots and plan beds of nasturtium; and altogether, life is a childish happy affair – no reason for happiness, dear me no: and therefore one never talks of it, I suppose: but only of the other state which can be made to sound reasonable. 'I'm the happiest woman in England' I said to Leonard yesterday, for no reason, except that we had hot rolls for breakfast and the cat had eaten the chicken. But also the most egotistical – no I think, with all due respect, Ethel's that. Lord, Ethel, did you think I was ever so blind as to say that you, of all people, had conquered egotism? It is only that you ride it so magnificently that one doesn't care if its egotism or altruism – its your uncautiousness I envy; not your selflessness. [. . .]

V.

2354: To Ethel Smyth   *Hotel de France et d'Angleterre, La Rochelle [France]*

Monday 20th April 1931

[. . .] I'm reading Lawrence, Sons and Lovers, for the first time; and so ponder your question about contemporaries. [J. M.] Murry, that bald necked blood dripping vulture, kept me off Lawrence with his obscene objurgations. Now I realise with regret that a man of genius wrote in my time and I never read him. Yes, but genius obscured and distorted I think: the fact about contemporaries (I write hand to mouth) is that they're doing the same thing on another railway line: one resents their distracting one, flashing past, the wrong way – something like that: from timidity, partly, one keeps ones eyes on one's own road. Stella Benson[1] I dont read because what I did read seemed to me all quivering – saccharine with sentimentality; brittle with the kind of wit that means sentiment freezing: But I'll try again: I'll think about jealousy. Its true that death makes judgment easier. [. . .]

V

2372: To Ethel Smyth   *52 T.[avistock] S.[quare, W.C.1]*

12th May [1931]

No Ethel, dear, no; I didn't make my meaning plain. I wasnt alluding to any particular instance, of misunderstanding, so much as to the general impossibility, which over comes me sometimes, of *any* understanding between two people. This instance – your behaviour about critics and your music –[2] doesnt seem to me of importance. That is, if I give my mind seriously to it for five minutes – a thing I seldom do – I can imagine, by imagining you as a whole, – with all your outriders and trembling thickets of personality, exactly why you do it; and sympathise; and admire; and feel the oddest mixture of admiration and pity and championship such as I used to feel for a white tailless cat of ours which we forgot to have castrated. This superb brute used to spend his nights fighting; and at last got so many wounds that they wouldnt heal; and he had to be put out of life by a vet. And I respected him; and I respect you.

1. The novelist (1892–1933), whose best-known work was *Tobit Transformed*, published in this year and awarded the *Femina Vie Heureuse* prize. She had met Virginia when Leonard, who had published some of her articles in the *Nation*, invited her to tea in the summer of 1925. She knew several of Virginia's friends, including Vita Sackville-West. Her social intercourse with Virginia was sporadic since Benson lived with her husband, J.C. O'G. Anderson, a customs official, in the remote outreaches of China. But the recent discovery of several letters, the best of which (2695a) is printed here, documents a previously little-known literary relationship.
2. Ethel had been set off by the music critic of the *New Statesman*, W. J. Turner, who had written of *The Prison* on 7 March: 'Both Ethel Smyth and Henry Brewster have made brave attempts at mediocrity, but both have failed without attaining that bottomness which is completely diverting.' Ethel replied in print throughout March, April and May, enlarging the terrain as she went. Her theme was that women composers and performers were rarely seen in the proper perspective. She had just published her latest riposte, 'Composers and Critics' (*New Statesman*, 9 May 1931). See also Letter 2393.

Only I think you dont altogether realise how, to the casual onlooker you seem exaggerated – how it strikes an outsider. I think sometimes you let the poison ferment. Never mind. I can't altogether lay hands on my meaning. The other thing anyhow interests me much more – the impossibility of one person understanding another. Oh, and when I write to you, I put it off till the end of the day when my careful typed letters to publishers and so on are done with and I write with a flick of the pen, leaving things to be understood. Hence my unintelligible remark about 'not believing in causes.' This, as I see, now, reverts to Murrys life of Lawrence [*Son of Woman*]; the whole doctrine of preaching, of causes; of converting; teaching etc which has been working vaguely in my mind and penetrating into my Waves; so that I let it fly, casually, in my letter, without a word to explain it. I think what I mean is that all teaching at the present moment seems to me a blasphemy; this hooked itself on to your cause; and so obliquely, to Laura Riding, whom I despise for writing perpetually to explain her own cause when reviewers say what is true – that she is a damned bad poet.[1] There! Not very well put I admit; but hurried. [. . .]

V.

2374: To Ethel Smyth   *52 Tavistock Sqre.* [*W.C.1*]

18th May 1931

[. . .] Now, about Causes. Of course, and of course, I'm not such a pacifist as to deny that practical evils must be put to the sword: I admit fighting to the death for votes, wages, peace, and so on: what I can't abide is the man who wishes to convert other men's minds; that tampering with beliefs seems to be impertinent, insolent, corrupt beyond measure. I never pass through Hyde Park without cursing separately every God inventor there. This is partly because; unbaptised as we were, our religious friends, some cousins in particular [Katherine and Dorothea Stephen], the daughters of Fitzjames, rasped and agonised us as children by perpetual attempts at conversion. As they were ugly women, who sweated, I conceived a greater hatred for them than

1. The American poet and critic Laura Riding (b. 1901), who was intensely influential within a small circle of poets and thinkers, was then the partner of the poet Robert Graves. Hogarth had published her work in 1926 and 1927. In a recent journal she had replied vehemently to a reviewer who had damned four of her books, a habit she continued all her life.

ever for anyone. And even now, when no one tries, I still draw in and shiver at the suspicion – he's got a finger in my mind. I will try to read [Stella Benson's] Tobit one of these days but the repulsion of the early book, whatever it was [*Goodbye, Stranger* (1926)], still poisons my mind. And I cant read when I'm writing; everything flies off at such an odd angle (This is another pen: no: no: I must revolutionise my life – a new pen: no smoking)

Now this is not in the least the letter I meant to write: but the illusion of the perfect letter still hovers. A Mrs Stack to see you 'Who is Mrs Stack?' 'A lady who wishes to talk about your book' 'To hell with Mrs Stack.' L. comes in. 'I've an estimate to show you'. This is life: and I adore it

V.

2375: To Vanessa Bell   *Monks House [Rodmell, Sussex]*

23rd May [1931]

Dearest Dolphin,

[. . .] I've had to retire to bed for 2 days with a headache, but am now practically recovered. This was not due to my Jolly, but to Ethel Smyth, whom I think, seriously, to be deranged in the head. We'd spent the morning trapesing round the Chelsea flower show, a very remarkable sight, banks and banks of flowers, all colours, under a livid awning, for it was perishing cold, and all the county families parading with their noses red against the lilies, – a fascinating but rather exhausting performance, and then Ethel appeared, stamping like a dragoon with a wallet full of documents. For 3 hours she nailed me to my chair while she rehearsed the story of her iniquitous treatment by Adrian Boult.[1] I cant (you'll be glad to hear) go into it all, but she seems to have gone into the green room, after he'd been conducting a Bach Mass for 6 hours, and insisted that he should do the Prison at the BBC; whereafter, according to her, he grossly insulted her, in the presence of the finest artists in Europe, and finally after a screaming and scratching which rung through The Queen's Hall, ordered her out of the room. She then went through, with the minuteness and ingenuity of a maniac, the whole history of her

---

1. Musical Director of the BBC (1930–42) and founding conductor of the BBC Symphony Orchestra (1930–49).

persecution for the past 50 years; brought out old letters and documents and read them aloud, beat on my chair with her fists; made me listen, and answer, and agree at every moment; and finally I had to shout that I had such a headache that unless she stopped talking I should burst into flames and be combusted. One is perfectly powerless. She raves and rants; yet has a demoniac shrewdness, so that there's no escape. 'You've got to listen to me – You've got to listen' she kept saying and indeed the whole of 52 rang with her vociferations. And its all fabricated, contorted, twisted with red hot egotism; and she's now launched on a campaign which means bullying every conductor and worrying every publisher, and rich man or woman, as well as unfortunate friends, until she gets that hopeless farrago of birds and last posts played and all HB's rubbish printed again. I dont feel I can even face her unless 2 keepers are present with red hot pokers – at the same, considering her age, I suppose she's a marvel – I see her merits as a writer – but undoubtedly sex and egotism have brewed some bitter insanity. [. . .]

Then we had Violet Hunt-Hueffer[1] (it appears she's a married woman in certain streets in Berlin, where she signed a document; but not otherwise) and had a lewd and lascivious talk about her statements as to Ruskins private parts and so on. It is all based upon things she heard gentlemen saying to her mother as she was going up to bed at the age of 8. These she has since reflected upon and drawn her own conclusions – erratic, slightly; and I ought to be going through the revised version at this moment, instead of scribbling to you. Its hot, ink black: now its pouring; now blue as a rooks egg: very odd weather; The only advantage over November is that its hot. Lytton and Raymond (to go on gossiping) dined with us – Lytton, as one always says, very charming: Raymond with every virtue except charm. Lytton's book [*Portraits in Miniature*] is out – I think its far better than Elizabeth [*and Essex*], indeed rather masterly in technique, and the essays read much better together than separate. Also, I think he's combed out his rhetoric somewhat in respect for us. He had seen Julian and Helen[2] he said, and deplores the Cambridge infection, as I do – but whats to be done? He's bound to get a Fellowship, and there Helen will sit forever, talking, Lytton said, minute provincialities about exams; and Cambridge parties.

1. Violet Hunt (1866–1942), the novelist, daughter of A. W. Hunt, the painter. She lived with the novelist Ford Madox Hueffer, who changed his surname to Ford. The Hogarth Press rejected Hunt's book on Elizabeth Siddal, called *The Wife of Rossetti, Her Life and Death*, as unreliable and sensationalist.
2. Helen Soutar, with whom Julian Bell was in love.

Percy[1] has got appendicitis, so we have a day gardener from Glynde and it is said our flowers wont be as good as usual. Nevertheless, our garage and our new rooms are very remarkable: the frigidaire is installed, but not working which matters the less as nature is seeing to it; and we have electric light everywhere. I dont see what further improvements can be made – Our way of life here – cooking messes, cutting fresh asparagus from the earth seems to me almost divine (quite if there were a Dolphin in the pond with the fish) and I dont (you'll be sorry to hear) really envy you Rome, as I want to write, which needs a table, and then – Lord – how violently our taste in friends opposes itself! Thus you can go to Rome and there meet Jimmy Sheehan – to me the dullest of good Americans – and Peter Morris,[2] who is explained by your brilliant analysis, as the cousin of a duke without a skin – I cannot imagine. Far rather would I stay in Surbiton and consort with [Sylvia's sister] Ida Milman and Emma Vaughan. Those are my sentiments – not, I suppose yours. I suppose Jimmy, Peter and Angus have some mystic charm as I see that Vita has none in your eyes. I suppose its something to do with the illusion of sex: the male sex illudes you; the female me: Thus I see the male in its reality; you the female. Or how do you account for it? About books and pictures our taste is respectable; about people, so crazy I wouldn't trust a dead leaf to cross a pond in it. [. . .]

B.

2376: To V. Sackville-West   *Monks House, Rodmell*
                                     [Sussex]

Sunday [24 May 1931]

Dearest Creature

[. . .] I've wasted 4 days when I wanted to write. And I've spent them partly reading Princess Daisy of Pless,[3] speculating upon her real character and life and longing for a full account from you – who appear

---

1. Percy Bartholomew had been the Woolfs' gardener at Monk's House since 1928.
2. James Vincent Sheean (1899–1975), an American correspondent who achieved great popularity in English society, and Peter Morris, a painter – both sometime lovers of Duncan Grant, as was Angus Davidson, mentioned later.
3. *From My Private Diary* (1931), by Princess Daisy of Pless, *née* Mary Theresa Olivia Cornwallis-West. She was the daughter of Colonel W. ('Poppets') Cornwallis-West, and distantly related to Vita through the De la Warrs.

in a footnote as a distinguished author. What a chance the British aristocracy had and lost – I mean if they'd only grafted brains on to those splendid bodies and wholesome minds – for I cant help liking her, in her wild idiocy, and her frankness '7 days late – can it be a child –' seems to me the highest human quality, if it werent combined with a housemaids sensibility and the sentimentality of a Surbiton cook. Could Bloomsbury be grafted on to Mayfair: but no: we're too ugly and they're too stupid. And so the world goes to rack and ruin. [. . .]

V.

2378: To V. Sackville-West   *Monks House [Rodmell, Sussex]*

Wednesday 27th May [1931]

[. . .] I'm quite recovered and have been sauntering over the downs alone – Lord – why go back to London? They look so lovely this evening, from my garden room, with the low barns that always make me think of Greek Temples. And we've been to a village wedding and seen the bridal party perched on kitchen chairs driven off in a great blue wagon, drawn by colossal farm horses with ribbons in their tails, and little pyramids of bells on their foreheads. What an odd mixture English country life is of squalor and magnificence! [. . .]

V.

Perhaps Ethel is sleeping with you tonight?[1]

2380: To Vanessa Bell   *52 Tavistock Square [W.C.1]*

June 1st [1931]

What an angel I am to write, seeing youve never written in answer to my long last – but good hearted as I am, I write to say we spent yesterday with Angelica;[2] who was in high spirits; in blue; in a new coat; we went off to a field to picnic; but owing to my sense of duty we took Judith [Bagenal] too. They were very amusing – both brought gloves.

---

1. Ethel Smyth was spending the night with Vita at Sissinghurst.
2. Angelica Bell, then aged 12, was at Langford Grove School, Essex, where her Headmistress was Mrs Elizabeth Curtis, and one of her best friends was Elizabeth Carr ('Beetle').

Angelica a pair of furred ones. Judith brought only one, because as she pointed out, one only brings gloves to show that one has gloves, so that one is enough; and then if one loses it one can bring the other. Angelica saw the sense of this, but of course left both of hers in the car. Then she refused to touch tongue, but devoured tomatoes raw; and lettuce and liqueur chocolates and a whole box of pineapple chunks. Then we went down to the sea, and she caught a furry bear caterpillar and put it in her hat. Then we stole up behind an old gentleman who was sketching. We also found a lamb being led by a boy on a string, and she stroked its ears. We then went to tea at the Blue Lion where you stay, because she said there is a dear old lady who knows all about her and gives one hot buttered toast. It was a broiling hot day. We had a good deal of conversation at tea. They were both extremely pathetic (to me) about their being so bad at arithmetic that they would never be able to to go to Cambridge as Mrs Curtis would say they could not pass the entrance. Angelica said that she had been able to do decimals, but they had put her so low in the class she was not now allowed to learn any sums. They spoke with great sadness about this. She said Quentin had never written to her, and she is so devoted to him that she cannot bear his being so long away. I said he had gone to Cassis. She said Thank goodness, then he will come back at last; but he may have grown very thin, or very fat. She said you were coming back in a week to Paris. We are all to come to what they call Parrots day. She sang us some drinking songs in a rollicking voice. Also some Mozart. She blacked all her face by accident and I had to wipe her, then she went to the looking glass and said how dreadful she looked. Of course she looked like a fantastic blue butterfly beside a tidy cob. Not but what Judith is not a sensible child with a very sad view of life and her responsibilities. She always knew the right road and Angelica never did. This rather depressed Angelica. Then we went back to school and A. asked me not to come and see Beetle, as it would make her shy. Beetle has fallen off a desk and torn her ligaments, so that she has to lie on a chair in the garden. A. tied up the few remaining cherries with gold string from the sweets and took them to Beetle. Then she implored me to come and see Mrs Curtis, which I did not want to do, but A. was so pressing that I yielded, and we went off to the drawing room but Mrs C. was at a service. So I went over the school with A. and saw all the bedrooms and photographs of army officers and a new dress which A. admired very much. As you see I have fallen in love with her, but think her mother very heartless, gallivanting in Rome and never casting a thought my way. Then we left them, they were going to be read aloud to and do hymn practise. It was on the whole very fine and a great success but how pathetic children are to be sure; full of the wildest feelings I could see, and adumbrations of the future and jealousies and torments, though I think very happy there. Judith said the worst of school is one is never alone, but A. seemed to like this. So no more. Though had you written I would have told you some very interesting pieces of news and one that bodes no good to us all this summer. So there.

B.

2393: To Ethel Smyth   [*52 Tavistock Square, W.C.1*]

Saturday [27 June 1931]

[...] What I should like would be, in another article, a purely objective statement of the exact disabilities (not being allowed to play in orchestras etc which women suffer in music.) Also, though you make out a good case, the critics, damn them, cant be so destructive or why are the classics the classics; and why is this so, even in the case of Wagner, so often during their life time? Somehow the big apples come to the top of the basket, and generally before the composer is under the sod. But of course I realise that the musician's apple lies longest at the bottom and has the hardest struggle to rise – thats clear. And then I detest people dwelling on their own injuries – its so infinitely sterile. And then I think the creative thing to do would be to furbish up some orchestra and run the things on your own. This I did – oh yes, in a modest way, when the publishers told me to write what they liked. I said No. I'll publish myself and write what I like. Which I did, and for many years, owing to lack of organisation travellers etc. lost much money thereby. Yes there I am blowing my own trumpet. But its a harsh raw noise – ones own trumpet. If I were you I'd train typists and street singers rather than go on whipping these gentrys hard and horny behinds. You will say however that I know nothing, feel nothing and understand less than nothing. So be it. I realise why I am so essential to you – precisely my quality of scratching post, what the granite pillar in the Cornish field gives the rough-haired, burr-tangled Cornish pig – thats you. An uncastrated pig into the bargain; a wild boar, a savage sow, and my fate in life is to stand there, a granite pillar, and be scraped by Ethel's hoary hide. Yes, because not another soul in Woking but lies under you like sweet lavender; there you roll and trample and bellow. I'm the only friend you have who is thoroughly and disgustingly upright and blind and deaf and dumb. Now isnt that a psychological discovery of the first water? But I cant be here till 5 or so on Wednesday owing to my infernal fate – to listen to a poetess singing her own songs to music written by a brother at some blasted hall. I've seen Barretts;[1] rather feeble I thought; and have written (to come out next week) an 'essay' on Mrs Browning.[2] But perhaps we may meet, if youll arrange it – one scrape more, one more grind of your infuriated hide and rasping tusks. What you call euphemistically 'putting cards on the table;' when its more like rending a rib open with a knife.

– hah hah. V,

2406: To Ethel Smyth   [*Monk's House, Rodmell, Sussex*]

Sunday [19 July 1931]

Well Ethel, Leonard has read it – The Waves – and likes it,[3] and I'm so relieved I'm like a girl with an engagement ring. Its true he thinks very few people will survive the first 100 pages. And I must now see if I cant simplify and clarify a little on his hints; but he doubts that I can. Anyhow thats over: and I'm, as I say, as light as a trout, with sheer irresponsible relief, and feel now I can spend a whole hour putting sweet peas in water and needn't hurry down to my commas and semi-colons in a state of torpor, distrust, and somnolent sordidity. Here's an eldritch screech of egotism if you like. But my word – think of getting that MS. out of the house on Tuesday perhaps, and no proofs for a fortnight. A very stormy week end: elm trees almost down, and flowers broken by rutting cats howling all night in the wind. They made their marriage bed in the sweet williams, and their progeny will be pied, I imagine. And I'm buying a boat and taking to the sea. Why should all physical delight rest with you – why shouldn't I stretch my muscles in a gale and haul down sheets and anchors and fly before the North East to the Pole?

---

1. The play, *The Barretts of Wimpole Street* (1930), by Rudolph Besier.
2. On 'Aurora Leigh' (*TLS*, 2 July 1931, *Essays*, V). Virginia was to write one of her most popular books, *Flush* (1933), about Mrs Browning's spaniel.
3. Leonard had in fact called *The Waves* (published in September of this year) a masterpiece and the best of her books.

2418: To V. Sackville-West   [*Monk's House, Rodmell, Sussex*]

Saturday [8 August 1931]

[. . .] As for Katherine [Mansfield], I think you've got it very nearly right. We did not ever coalesce; but I was fascinated, and she respectful, only I thought her cheap, and she thought me priggish; and yet we were both compelled to meet simply in order to talk about writing. This we did by the hour. Only then she came out with a swarm of little stories, and I was jealous, no doubt; because they were so praised; but gave up reading them not on that account, but because of their cheap sharp sentimentality, which was all the worse, I thought, because she had, as you say, the zest and the resonance – I mean she could permeate one with her quality; and if one felt this cheap scent in it, it reeked in ones nostrils. But I must read her some day. Also, she was for ever pursued by her dying; and had to press on through stages that should have taken years in ten minutes – so that our relationship became unreal also. And there was Murry squirming and oozing a sort of thick motor oil in the background – dinners with them were about the most unpleasant exhibitions, humanly speaking, I've ever been to. But the fact remains – I mean, that she had a quality I adored, and needed; I think her sharpness and reality – her having knocked about with prostitutes and so on, whereas I had always been respectable – was the thing I wanted then. I dream of her often – now thats an odd reflection – how one's relation with a person seems to be continued after death in dreams, and with some odd reality too. [. . .]

                                                 V.

2426: To Ethel Smyth   *Monks House* [*Rodmell, Sussex*]

Wednesday 2nd Sept [1931]

[. . .] Why did you tear up the Wreckers[1] letter? I've often told you, letters are a way of penetrating for those who are, like me, blind into the dark damp deeps of your soul. No, the headache isnt the period – how you love periods, w.c.'s, excrement of all sorts – it interests me – I'm going into that in my life of you – not the period but God. I was struck with a brilliant idea; wrote and wrote; he smashed his fist on my head.

1. Ethel Smyth's opera, composed in 1904–05, with a libretto by Henry Brewster.

Lord, I said, I will write. Then he altogether took from me the power of adding word to word. So I went to bed. A head like wood, instead of one like fire – thats your God. What he like is to take away, to destroy, to give pain for pleasure – L. says if I'll stay in bed till Monday God will let me alone for another 6 months. But no: bed, with Ivanhoe and Hugh Walpole [*Judith Paris*] for my companions, bed with God for my protector, is intolerable. I'm up, but dont dare go to the Lodge and write. That little inspiration therefore is doomed. I shall never catch it again. And it rains and what is life without writing?

I was highly amused, and maliciously pleased by your letter, saying how you had never seen me in such good condition – so social, sober, cheerful and healthy (I mean spiritually, not bodily). Lord Ethel – that day you came I was so bothered, so irritated in a rage about everything (unreasonably as it turned out) that I almost put you off; thought I could never sit an afternoon of talk out; had a mind, on top of the down to explain and excuse; almost write to ask pardon for having given you such a wretched time. And you saw nothing! Then you talk of your insight – then you wonder that I dont 'want' more than 2 people – Here we sit in dark tunnels, tapping on the wall – Thats friendship – thats communication. But do tell me why that visit was so momentous – I thought you must be bored, disillusioned, and caustic though restrained. But of course (forgive this leap) you have Style. Never a postcard without it. Its the flight and droop of the sentence; where the accent falls, the full stop. Ah, how beautifully you wing your way from phrase to phrase! When one feels something remote, separate, pure, thats style. And, I think, almost the only permanent quality, the one that survives, that satisfies. And now why was that visit momentous?

V.

2437: To John Lehmann[1]

Monks House, Rodmell
[*Sussex*]

Sept 17th [1931]

Dear John,

I'm most grateful to you for your letter. It made me happy all

1. The poet John Lehmann (1907–87), was brought into the Woolfs' lives by their nephew Julian Bell, whom Lehmann knew at Cambridge. And through Lehmann came more contact with the new generation of young poets, W. H. Auden (1907–73), Stephen Spender (b. 1909), and Cecil Day Lewis (1904–72, Poet Laureate, 1968). All three of them were published by The Hogarth Press, but only Spender became a friend. Lehmann was more. At the beginning of this year he had started to work with

yesterday. I had become firmly convinced that the Waves was a failure, in the sense that it wouldn't convey anything to anybody. And now you've been so perceptive, and gone so much further and deeper in understanding my drift than I thought possible that I'm immensely relieved.

Not that I expect many such readers. And I'm rather dismayed to hear we've printed 7,000: for I'm sure 3,000 will feed all appetites; and then the other 4 will sit round me like decaying corpses for ever in the Studio (I cleared up the table – for you, not the corpses). I agree that it's very difficult – bristling with horrors, though I've never worked so hard as I did here, to smooth them out. But it was, I think, a difficult attempt – I wanted to eliminate all detail; all fact; and analysis; and my self; and yet not be frigid and rhetorical; and not monotonous (which I am) and to keep the swiftness of prose and yet strike one or two sparks, and not write poetical, but purebred prose, and keep the elements of character; and yet that there should be many characters, and only one; and also an infinity, a background behind – well, I admit I was biting off too much.

But enough, as the poets say. If I live another 50 years I think I shall put this method to some use, but as in 50 years I shall be under the pond, with the gold fish swimming over me, I daresay these vast ambitions are a little foolish, and will ruin the press. That reminds me – I think your idea of a Letter most brilliant – To a Young Poet?[1] because I'm seething with immature and ill considered and wild and annoying ideas about prose and poetry. So lend me your name – (and let me sketch a character of you by way of frontispiece) – and then I'll pour forth all I can think of about you young, and we old, and novels – how damned they are – and poetry, how dead. But I must take a look into the subject, and you must reply, 'To an old novelist' – I must read Auden, whom I've not read, and Spender (his novel I swear I will tackle tonight).[2] The whole subject is crying out for letters – flocks, volleys, of them, from every side. Why not get Spender and Auden and Day Lewis to join in? [. . .]

Yr

Virginia Woolf

1. Virginia published *Letter to a Young Poet* in July 1932 as one of the Hogarth Letters Series.
2. Spender had submitted a novel to the press. Virginia thought it had some strong features, but she rejected it, advising the 22-year-old author to throw it out and write something completely different. He published it in 1988, with revisions, as *The Temple*.

the Press as a manager trainee. Although he left eighteen months later to live in Vienna, he returned in 1938 as a full partner, having bought out Virginia's share.

2451: To Vanessa Bell   [*52 Tavistock Square, W.C.1*]

Thursday [15 October 1931]

Dearest dearest Dolphin,

O what a mercy that you should like that book! I cant tell you, (this is literal truth) what it meant to me getting your letter this morning.

Nobody except Leonard matters to me as you matter, and nothing would ever make up for it if you didn't like what I did. So its an amazing relief – I always feel I'm writing more for you than for anybody: only I cant express this, as I'm rushing off, and have been interrupted by Peter [F. L. Lucas] coming. Never mind – I couldn't say if I'd the whole day how happy you make me.

And Lord – what I owe to you!

But I cant write more now, and only send this as an inarticulate thanksgiving and shall write again tomorrow –

You didnt think it sentimental, did you, about Thoby?[1] I had him so much in my mind, – I have a dumb rage still at his not being with us always.

Dearest Dolphin, how I adore you, whether you like what I write or not

B.

I'm frightfully interested about your picture.[2]

1. Vanessa wrote about *The Waves*: 'For its quite as real an experience as having a baby or anything else, being moved as you have succeeded in moving me – Of course there's the personal side – the feelings you describe on what I must take to be Thoby's [Perceval's] death. [. . .] Even then I know its only because of your art that I am so moved. I think you made one's human feelings into something less personal – if you wouldn't think me foolish I should say that you have found the "lullaby capable of singing him to rest" [*Hamlet*]' (October 1931, Berg Collection).

2. In the same letter Vanessa wrote: 'I've been working hard lately at an absurd great picture I've been painting off and on the last 2 years – and if I could only do what I want to – but I can't – it seems to me it would have some sort of analogous meaning to what you've done. How can one explain, but to me painting a floor covered with toys and keeping them all in relation to each other and the figures and the space of the floor and the light on it means something of the same sort that you seem to me to mean.' The painting (*The Nursery*) is reproduced in Frances Spalding, *Vanessa Bell*, 1983, opposite p. 272. Its present location is unknown.

2453: To Margaret Llewelyn Davies
52 Tavistock Square [*W.C.1*]

Sunday 18th Oct. [1931]

Dearest Margaret,

[...] Did you see a very good review of L's book by Laski in the Statesman?[1] I must say I feel rather triumphant that he has come through with that book in spite of all his other occupations: and now there are seven more volumes to be written. I cant conceive how you politicians can go on being political. All the summer we had nothing but political arguments with Maynard and others; and I finally felt it so completely silly, futile, petty, personal and unreal – all this about money – that I retired to my room and read poetry in a rage. Well, I know you dont agree; but if everyone read poetry then there'd be no politics; no crisis; none of this place hunting and party spite. All they do is to abuse each other. This shows you how little I grasp the true meaning of events. [...]

Yrs V

2454: To George Duckworth   *52 Tavistock Square, W.C.1*

18th October [1931]

My dear George,

I am delighted you find the Waves plain sailing and common sense. I shall quote your opinion I daresay in an advertisement. [...]

Many thanks from

Your affectionate
GOAT

2460: To G. L. Dickinson   *52 Tavistock Square, W.C.1*

Oct. 27th 1931

My dear Goldie,

How extraordinarily nice of you to write to me – I cant tell you what

1. A review by Harold Laski of *After the Deluge*. There were to be two more volumes of Leonard's book. The next appeared in 1939, and the third, under the title of *Principia Politica*, in 1953. They dealt with the ideas of liberty, equality and fraternity and their effect upon communal political motivation.

pleasure your letter gave me.[1] What you say you felt about the Waves is exactly what I wanted to convey. Many people say that it is hopelessly sad – but I didnt mean that. I did want somehow to make out if only for my own satisfaction a reason for things. That of course is putting it more definitely than I have a right to, for my reasons are only general conceptions, that strike me as I walk about London and then I try to fit my little figures in. But I did mean that in some vague way we are the same person, and not separate people. The six characters were supposed to be one. I'm getting old myself – I shall be fifty next year; and I come to feel more and more how difficult it is to collect oneself into one Virginia; even though the special Virginia in whose body I live for the moment is violently susceptible to all sorts of separate feelings. Therefore I wanted to give the sense of continuity, instead of which most people say, no you've given the sense of flowing and passing away and that nothing matters. Yet I feel things matter quite immensely. What the significance is, heaven knows I cant guess; but there is significance – that I feel overwhelmingly. Perhaps for me, with my limitations, – I mean lack of reasoning power and so on – all I can do is to make an artistic whole; and leave it at that. But then I'm annoyed to be told that I am nothing but a stringer together of words and words and words. I begin to doubt beautiful words. How one longs sometimes to have done something in the world – So you see how it comforts me to think that anyhow you had me in mind on the river bank. Then the world I live in – for I dont see how to live in any other – seems at any rate to have that justification. So thank you again – very very sincerely – for writing. [. . .]

Yours always
Virginia Woolf

2467: To Hugh Walpole   *Monks House [Rodmell, Sussex]*

Sunday [8 November 1931]

My dear Hugh,

[. . .] Well – I'm very much interested about unreality and the Waves – we must discuss it. I mean why do you think The Waves unreal, and

1. Dickinson wrote: 'Your book is a poem, and as I think a great poem. [. . .] there is throbbing under it the mystery which all the poets and philosophers worth mentioning have felt' (in Robin Majumdar and Allen McLaurin, *Virginia Woolf: The Critical Heritage*, 1975, p. 271).

why was that the very word I was using of Judith Paris [Walpole'e novel] – 'These people aren't *real* to me' – though I do think, and you wont believe it, it has all kinds of qualities I admire and envy. But unreality does take the colour out of a book of course; at the same time, I dont see that it's a final judgment on either of us. You're real to some – I to others. Who's to decide what reality is? Not dear old Harold, anyhow, whom I've not heard, but if as you say, he sweeps us all into separate schools one hostile to the other, then he's utterly and damnably wrong, and to teach the public that's the way to read us is a crime and a scandal, and accounts for the imbecility which makes all criticism worthless. Lord – how tired I am of being caged with Aldous, Joyce and Lawrence![1] Can't we exchange cages for a lark? How horrified all the professors would be! Yes, greatly to my surprise The Waves is selling better than any of my novels, which pleases me, and E. M. Forster says it moves him more than any of them, which pleases me still more.[2] Otherwise, opinions good and bad, seem to me increasingly futile and beside the mark.

I'm reading Middlemarch with even greater pleasure than I remembered: and Ford M. Ford's memoirs [*Thus to Revisit*] – fascinating, and even endearing; but I long to know the truth about him – the truth which I'm sure you know, as you know the truth about all these great figures. I wish, to please me, you'd write your own memoirs – why not? The truth and nothing but the truth.

Anyhow come and see us; for we must discuss Reality and Ford M. Ford at length. Why is he no longer the same name as he was 20 years ago when I met him[3] – and her – at the [George] Protheros?

Yours
V.W.

---

1. In a BBC talk on 29 September, Harold Nicolson labelled as modernist writers Virginia, T. S. Eliot, D. H. Lawrence, James Joyce and Evelyn Waugh. He excluded John Galsworthy, James Barrie, J. B. Priestley and Hugh Walpole on the grounds that they were old-fashioned.
2. Virginia quoted from Forster's letter in her diary for 16 November: 'I've the sort of excitement over it which comes from believing that one's encountered a classic' (*Diary*, IV, 52).
3. Ford Madox Hueffer changed his Germanic surname after the war, in 1919.

2481: To Lytton Strachey   *52 Tavistock Sqre. [W.C.1]*

10 Dec [1931]

'I arise from dreams of thee'[1] – that's why I write. I have just woken from a dream in which I was at a play, in the pit and suddenly you, who were sitting across a gangway in a row in front, turned and looked at me, and we both went into fits of laughter. What the play was, what we laughed at, I've no notion, but we were both very young (no, for you had your beard) and at the age when we used to write to each other. Why are these dreams more vivid than real life? – Anyhow while it hangs about me, I can't help writing to the bearded serpent, especially as Clive tells me you are off to Malaya for months[2] and the chances are we shan't meet till Gordon Sqre. is full of tulips and [Arthur] Waley is playing tennis with Alix [Strachey] in white flannels.

I'm recumbent, lazy, content, reading book after book. And what are you doing? Reading Shakespeare I hope and occasionally making a note very neatly in a very beautiful book. By the way I read As you like it the other day and was almost sending you a wire to ask what is the truth about Jacques – What is it? His last speech reads so very odd.[3]

This is all my news, as I see no one, not Ottoline, not Charlie Chaplin[4] – no one but Clive who runs in to see me between a lunch party that ends at 5 and a dinner party that begins at 8.30 and goes on till the sparrows are rising in flocks from the Embankment. Lord – how I'd like to lead his life.

Well this is only a dream letter and needs no answer, unless you can tell me what we laughed at; but when you're in London with the tulips and Waley's white flannels, please come and see your old and attached friend

Virginia

---

1. Shelley, 'The Indian Serenade'.
2. In fact, Lytton was desperately ill.
3. 'To see no pastime, I: what you would have
   I'll stay to know at your abandon'd cave.' (V, iv, 79–80)
4. Charlie Chaplin, who was then 42, was paying a prolonged visit to London, and was much lionised by Sibyl Colefax and Ottoline Morrell.

2484: To Dora Carrington   *52 Tavistock Sqre. [W.C.1]*

Tuesday [15 December 1931]

Dearest Carrington,

We're so unhappy to hear that Lytton is ill. We didnt know it. If you or Ralph [Partridge] could ever let us have a card to say how he is we should be more than grateful.

Our best love. If there was anything I could do you would let me know wouldn't you –

Yours Virginia

2486: To Ethel Smyth   *[52 Tavistock Square, W.C.1]*

[19 December 1931]

This is only again 'just a line' to catch the early post so that you may get it this evening. L. S. is about the same. The next days are the critical ones – fear of perforation.[1] But there's nothing to be done. Nessa comes back tomorrow, and I shall know on Monday if its any use our going for the night on Tuesday. I suspect Nessa has told them not to ask me, unless she sees they really are in need of an outsider. They – all the relations – sitting there waiting find it a relief to drive over to Hungerford – and anything one can do, as you will realise, is to me a relief. After all, I dont suppose I care for anyone more than for Lytton. (after my Jew) He's in all my past – my youth. But never mind. Its my form of tenderness, that – well, I wont go on. I feel your form, dearest E – oh yes – sitting by me so strong – so quiet. Yes. Its the being used up, after these attacks of headache – thats the nuisance now. Its always so – a general complete influenza drowse. But fresh air at Rodmell will cure that in no time

Will write tomorrow.

Yr

V.

2498: To Ethel Smyth   *Monks House [Rodmell, Sussex]*

Tuesday, 29th Dec [1931]

[. . .] I think you grossly underrate the strength of my feelings – so

1. The doctors' latest diagnosis of Lytton Strachey's condition was an ulcerated colon.

strong they are – such caverns of gloom and horror open round me I
daren't look in – and also their number. Do you know how I cared for
Katherine Mansfield, for Charlie Sanger[1] – to mention friends only? No,
you dont. But then, for months on first knowing you, I said to myself
here's one of these talkers. They dont know what feeling is, happily for
them. Because everyone I most honour is silent – Nessa, Lytton,
Leonard, Maynard: all silent; and so I have trained myself to silence;
induced to it also by the terror I have of my own unlimited capacity for
feeling – when Lytton seemed to be dying – well yes: I cant go into that,
even now. But to my surprise, as time went on, I found that you are
perhaps the only person I know who shows feeling and feels. Still I cant
imagine talking about my love for people, as you do. Is it training? Is it
the perpetual fear I have of the unknown force that lurks just under the
floor? I never cease to feel that I must step very lightly on top of that
volcano. No Ethel, there's a mint of things about me, I say egotistically,
you've no notion of; the strength of my feelings is only one. [. . .]

About Gwen Raverat [. . .] – well, Gwen is one of my oldest friends,
George Darwins daughter, all Cambridge, all Darwin solidity, integrity, force and sense – What must she do, but take to art. This she did
with a scientific thoroughness that used to make us jeer. But somehow
she persevered, went to France, met – no this was at Cambridge – a
French boy, Jacques R; fell violently in love; forced him, we used to
think, to give up his lighter and more lascivious loves, to marry her.
What a passion her love was! I came in for some flashes of jealousy – not
of me – of another woman [Ka Cox]: and was blinded – never saw such
crude what they call elemental passion unscrupulous, tyrannic, pure –
before or since. And then she married him: they both painted; she like a
Darwin, by science, force, sense; and he rather gifted but lyrical, and
exact and very French. And then he began to stumble; the doctors said
his spine was affected: Through 10 years I suppose he slowly stiffened,
till the paralysis reached his hands, which had to be tied to the paint
brushes; and Gwen lifted him, rubbed him, drove him in a pony cart over
the hills at Vence, to paint; and so he was finally tortured to death,
watching it come, with rage, with obscenity – he wrote me page after
page, and she at last wrote for him – of despair, of defiance – They were
incredibly brave; and yet it was unspeakably sordid, for he couldn't die,
and was jealous, and sexually tormented, and abused her, and loved her,

1. The barrister had died in February 1930.

and she suffered, as I imagine, more than seemed humanly possible, till at last she almost killed him, with one dose of morphia after another – the doctors saying she mustn't, and she defying them. After he died, 7 years ago, she came back to England, with the two children; and used to say to me, her unhappiness was such that she ought not to see me. She became set, frozen, like an old log dried out of all sensation, save for the children. And then she fell in love again:[1] and the man married somebody else. And somehow I got her a job on Time and Tide; and she stumps about, to me still frozen, formidable – I cant get over her past; but if you see her as a living and normal woman, probably its true. And I avoid seeing her, because I know of her past; and I feel that she wishes to avoid that, and so lunches with Lady Rhondda.[2]

Good bye
V.

1. During Jacques' last years, Gwen Raverat fell in love with a neighbour at Vence, the painter Jean Marchand (1883–1941), who was already married.
2. Margaret Haig Thomas, the Viscountess Rhondda (1883–1958) succeeded to her father's title in 1918. An ardent feminist, she founded *Time and Tide* in 1920, and from 1926 was its editor.

1932-1933

Virginia was deeply shaken by Lytton Strachey's death, which immediately preceded her 50th birthday, and saddened by Carrington's two months later. But she continued in the full stride of her age. She was offered – and refused – public honours, made new friends, among them Elizabeth Bowen, and twice travelled abroad during these years. She dashed off her lightest book, Flush, *and began what would be for her the most arduous,* The Years. *In the midst of all this, her health occasionally trembled.*

Her relations with Ethel Smyth were, as usual, confrontational, a mode about which Virginia continued to complain, but at which she was fairly adept herself. She gave Ethel cutting advice on her feminist essays, thinking they were too concerned with Ethel's own grievances and not the general good. Vita was still fascinating. She bought and was restoring Sissinghurst Castle, where she would create her famous garden. When Vita and her husband travelled in the United States, Virginia expressed envy (Virginia's own transatlantic travel plans never materialised) but also prejudice against Americans. Vita was still alluring too. So Virginia was pained about Vita's new intimates. Quentin Bell's pulmonary illnesses sent him to bed, where he was treated to the stimulus of his aunt's frequent letters.

2517: To Dora Carrington   *52 Tavistock Sqre. [W.C.1]*

Sunday [31 January 1932]

Carrington dearest, I hope you dont mind my writing to you sometimes – it is such a comfort because there is nobody to talk to about Lytton who knew him as you did[1] – and of course dont answer. One hates so the feeling that things begin again here in London without him. I find I cant write without suddenly thinking Oh but Lytton wont read this, and it takes all the point out of it. I always put away things in my mind to say to Lytton. And what it must be for you – I wish some time I could see you

1. Lytton Strachey had died ten days earlier, aged 52. Virginia's grief was great: 'It is like having the globe of the future perpetually smashed' (*Diary*, IV, 64).

and tell you about the time, after Thoby's death, before you knew him, when I used to see him. But I could never give him what you did. I used to laugh at him for having grown so mellow and good tempered (you know how I loved laughing at him) and he said, 'Oh but you know, it is rather wonderful – Ham Spray and all that – and its all Carrington's doing.' This is no help to you now, but it is for us. Before he knew you, he was so depressed and restless – and all that changed when you had Tidmarsh. [...]

Virginia

Leonard sends his love.

2542: To Dora Carrington   *52 T.[avistock] S.[quare, W.C.1]*

2nd March [1932]

I loved those little pictures, darling Carrington. How it seizes upon one, the longing for Lytton, when one sees them. But then how happy he looks – that is one comfort – and then again I thank you. We would always have come to Ham Spray: it was only the feeling we had that that belonged to another side of Lytton's life: I dont mean that you didn't want us, but that it was simpler for him to come here. But heavens – how I wish we had brushed aside all that, and come and stayed: or made him come here oftener. Of course one gets involved in things, and there is always the press, and Leonards different things – how worthless it seems now compared with one hour of being with Lytton. Yes, I think it does get harder – I cant describe to you the sense I have of wanting to tell Lytton something. I never read a book even with the same pleasure now. He was part of all I did – I have dream after dream about him and the oddest sense of seeing him coming in the street.

Oh but Carrington we have to live and be ourselves – and I feel it is more for you to live than for any one; because he loved you so, and loved your oddities and the way you have of being yourself. I cant explain it; but it seems to me that as long as you are there, something we loved in Lytton, something of the best part of his life still goes on. But goodness knows, blind as I am, I know all day long, whatever I'm doing, what you're suffering. And no one can help you. [...]

Goodbye, darling Carrington

your old attached friend
Virginia

2549: To Lady Ottoline Morrell
[*52 Tavistock Square, W.C.1*]

Friday [11 March 1932]

Dearest Ottoline,

This is just to tell you that Carrington died this morning. We were there yesterday and talked and she seemed quiet and very gentle. That is all I know now, but I wanted you to know.

My love
Virginia

2553: To Lady Ottoline Morrell
[*52 Tavistock Square, W.C.1*]

Tuesday [15 March 1932]

Dearest Ottoline,

I've been away till this evening or I would have written. Yes, of course it was suicide, but at first I didn't like to say so, as they were anxious to get the verdict that it was an accident. She had borrowed a gun from Brian Guinness,[1] and shot herself early on Friday morning. She died in 3 or 4 hours. Ralph arrived while she was still conscious. She told him it was an accident – that she had been shooting at a rabbit and had slipped. But she had already tried once before when Lytton was dying. That was why we went down – the only chance seemed to be to give her some interruption. But I felt, as we sat talking about Lytton in Lytton's room that afternoon, that she could not go on much longer. She said she had failed with everything except with Lytton – she was very gentle and affectionate. I could only tell her how much we all needed her – indeed, she kept so much of Lytton that her death makes his loss more complete. But she had suffered so terribly and could not believe that there was anything to come in life. I feel that he would have hated it – Pippa [Strachey] came back last night on hearing of it. Carrington made every preparation and rang up Ralph after we had gone to say that she felt more cheerful. But it was terrible leaving her alone that night, without anybody in the house.

yrs
Virginia

1. Bryan Guinness (b. 1905), later 2nd Lord Moyne and a writer. On 29 February, while visiting him in Andover, Carrington borrowed his gun, ostensibly to shoot rabbits at Ham Spray.

2570: To Vanessa Bell   [*52 Tavistock Square, W.C.1*]

Monday, April 11th 1932

Dearest,

[. . .] Barbara [Bagenal] takes the cake. Never never can there have been a woman so sealed from birth to all the subtleties sensibilities and harmonies of civilised life. To dump her mumpish brat [Judith] on you at the last moment seems the last straw. Couldnt this be tactfully conveyed her, by Duncan say, on a card? Of course its a form of morbid love for you – thus to inflict these scars. Any contact is some sort of ecstasy to her – But after this, dont despise me for Ethel Smyth and the rest. Nan [Hudson] has been humbly rhapsodising about your genius for art – a subject that leaves me cold. But she says you are one of the 3 people she loves. The third is a dog. Would you believe it, she has altered all her plans because her summer bull dog might have been left with an unsympathetic servant; was about to start for Cannes, and is going as it is to live at Dieppe alone with him for a fortnight. She told me a long story about a Swiss who copulates with cows. I take this to mean that she has relations with Peter [the bulldog]. I dont blame her, save that he's old, blind and smells. Then she said people take her for a Sapphist. By dint of praising incontinence as an aid to landscape painting I almost brought her to admit that she has, once or twice, on a pale May night, embraced Ethel [Sands] in a coppice. But she flitted off to a party – I like her though, and feel that there is brick beneath the – is it called rubble? – which I doubt with Ethel.

I've been seeing the usual sort of people – that, is the Keynes' at Rodmell, and Ethel [Smyth] and Vita and Harold. We went over to Sissinghurst[1] which is now a complete 15th Century Castle, with moat, drawbridge, seneschal, greyhound, ghost, bowling green and I daresay buried treasure. Its rather a lovely rose-red though. Then we had tea with Maurice Baring at Rottingdean – 2 dirty footmen to hand anchovy sandwiches, which I loathe and so had to put in my bag. When asked for a match by Baring I handed him my sandwich. Ethel Smyth was there, straddled like a major in front of the fire. Then I saw James and Alix [Strachey]; James rather dried up and stratified I thought: Alix flowing with a queer phosphorescent beauty. Old Mrs S. Florence has just

1. In 1930 Vita Sackville-West had purchased the centuries-old ruined buildings at Sissinghurst Castle, near Cranbrook, Kent, which she and Harold Nicolson skilfully rebuilt and there created what is still one of the loveliest gardens in England.

proved in 10 vols. that colour is the same as sound: the question is who will publish it?[1] James is Lyttons executor, and has found masses of poems and plays, mostly unfinished, also box upon box of letters. We advised him to have the letters typed and circulated among us. He says Lytton said very unpleasant things about us all. But as we all do that, I dont see that it matters. Ott [Morrell] and Roger Senhouse[2] neednt be included, if it hurts their feelings. Our letters aren't there – it was an earlier series. James says that Lytton meant to write one more book on George Washington; and then retire, probably abroad, and write violently, proclaiming his sodomy, and cutting adrift from society. I must say I doubt it. [. . .]

[. . .] Write, write write, good Dolphin; and I will remember you to your blue brothers in the Aegean.[3] Leonard sends love.

B.

2573: To Vanessa Bell
[On board the Lloyd Triestino s.s. Tevere]

19th April [19]32

Well here we are floating past the Greek islands. Not a ripple on the sea, so hot one can sit naked on deck – an occasional fowl settles on the masts – Roger comes running to say thats Corcyra [Corfu] which it isnt – a Greek gentleman corrects him – asked his name he says he is Christ son of Christ. There is also Mr Hutchinson,[4] the archaeologist, who plays chess. But we are in the first class, and all this seething life surrounds the Frys in the Second. I have withdrawn to our palatial writing room, where there are only bald headed merchants. The truth is it is impossible to do anything at sea. We were to reach Athens this evening, but rocks have fallen and blocked the Gulf of Corinth so we have to go round, and shant arrive till 6 tomorrow morning – rather a bore, as there is a limit to ones love of sea life. We have a cinema in the evening: tray upon tray of ham sandwiches; beef tea half hourly; and an

1. Alix Strachey's mother, Mary Sargant-Florence, did not publish her study, *Colour Coordination*, until 1940, when it appeared in a single volume.
2. The publisher and bibliophile Roger Senhouse (1900–70) had been the male focus of Lytton's affections during his last years.
3. The Woolfs planned to leave on the 15th to travel by train and boat *via* Venice to Greece. Their companions were Roger Fry and his sister Margery ('Ha') Fry.
4. Perhaps Richard Wyatt Hutchinson, best known for his excavations at Nineveh.

occasional melancholy waltz. So far, the Frys and the Wolves have been as sweet as nuts and soft as silk, and I daresay we haven't stopped talking, completely, for half an hour. There was dinner in Paris, at a little place where Roger took his wife 36 years ago: and then a night and a half day at Venice. Roger oozes knowledge, but kindly warmly like an aromatic – what? Shower bath, it'll have to be, as my wits are dazed. We only had time for 3 churches and part of the Academia [Galleria dell'Accademia] – and Florias [Florians café]. Ha – (I've once called her so, by mistake) dressed like an elderly yak in a white pelt constrained by a girdle, is admirable in bearing the brunt of aesthetic criticism. I've heard her even contradict Roger about Bellini, and she always has a feeling about a sky or a pillar or the use of bald heads in design which turns the blade off the poor ignorant Wolves. I did however, attack Titian and Leonard says he made a point about a diagonal – anyhow, it doesnt matter, as Roger is urbanity itself, and realised from the first that one must let pass Venice and concentrate upon Greece.

We drove round Brindisi yesterday, in search of a dome that Roger had seen from the boat, but we only found the railway station and one locked church. This was a diversion however, as Leonard had beaten Roger twice at chess, and I gather there was some feeling, – what Roger does is to take his Queen back, and then says – which is exasperating, – he cant play well when Leonard is so slow. But this is the only rub. We talk, talk, talk. Sometimes Ha and I (but I must call her Margery) pace the deck discussing Herbert Fisher, or Pamela,[1] I think she suspects me of being an intellectual and moral and social snob; so I do my best to climb off my perch and roll on the floor; and sometimes she likes me; and then she's fearfully humble. When I say 'but Ha – I mean Margery – you know all about politics' she says 'My dear Virginia, when will you get that silly illusion out of your head? I'm merely good at bluff. That's how I take people in.' – I think she was probably a good deal chastened by Rogers infatuation with Bloomsbury, and suspects me of being in conspiracy against her, But Lord lord – I know nothing about anyone; and merely advance my antennae and generally get snubbed – yesterday I lost my spectacles, (but had packed them): this morning I came down to breakfast holding my sponge bag, and have once wandered, in my night gown, into the barbers shop. This is what comes of dreaming of

1. Roger Fry's daughter, a painter, then aged 30, who was married to another painter, Micu Diamand.

Duncan all night. Why dream of Duncan? He never dreams of me, nor thinks of me either; nor writes to me into the bargain. Yet my lust for love remains undiminished by the Greek islands. We are just in time for Easter in Athens. Christ the son of Christ – how Roger picks up dusky jews at every turn, and Ha too. We shall have a following like a bitch on heat – says we must spend the 1st of May night in the churches and the streets: all lights but one go out. That is the Easter rite, and more beautiful he says than any other. Roger has a special box of canvases; Ha is also going to sketch. We think of going to Crete. Roger thinks of meeting Helen [Anrep] at Venice. What thoughts are in your head? Well this, though a terrible letter from a born writer – which you cant deny I am – not a good one but a born one – that's the sort of thing Roger and I argue about – is long, and adoring and full of the most tender if unexpressed – but aren't the tenderest feelings precisely those – emotions. This is whats called 'crossing' a letter. Please, please write, Poste Restante, Athens Greece.

I could have described the scenery but I know of old how you hate that.

B.

2575: To V. Sackville-West   [*Hotel Majestic*] *Athens*

April 24th [1932]

Well, you haven't written to me, not one word, not one post card, so perhaps Sissigt. is blotted out – the Tower fell, crushing the daughter of the Sackvilles to pink pulp – a very fitting end for a woman who forgets old but humble, humble but old, friends. Its Sunday at Athens; we've been lunching, not too well, and looking for 2 hours at Byzantine relics – because its a sultry wet day; and now we're off to Hymettus, and yesterday we went on a ship to Aegina, and saw the loveliest temple, and an island all carved in terraces with olives and wild flowers, and the sea running into the bays (it was pouring wet, I must admit, and we were herded with 50 American archaeologists) Still it is a beautiful island, and I padded to the hill top, picking wild irises and unknown yellow stars, and little purple, violet, blue, white, pearl flowers, all about as big as the stone on your ring no bigger. And we went to Daphnis, and wandered in olive woods, and to Sunium, the Temple on a cliff, which cliff is soft with flowers, all again no bigger than pearls or topazes. Margery Fry is a maniacal botanist, and squats – she's the size of a Russian bear – on the rocks digging with a penknife. And we saw the Greek shepherds huts in a wood near Marathon, and a lovely dark olive, red lipped, pink shawled girl wandering and spinning thread from a lump of wool from her own flock of sheep. There! Thats to make you feel envious. (I see you've got foot and mouth disease in Kent.)

Our drawbacks – these you'll want to know – are bitter winds, stormy grey skies, and vast helpings of soft sweet pudding. Also Roger has the piles – cant walk, also Margery suffers, like all spinsters aged 63 [60] from unrequited loves 20 years ago for Englishmen who were killed in the war. But this means that she is full of the most obsolete and erudite information about archaeology; has everything an invalid can want in a huge wooden box, and makes arrowroot for those who like arrowroot the last thing at night. Tomorrow, if the rain stops, we're off for 3 nights in the Peloponese. (cant spell) and then back here, and then, I think to Crete, and then, I suppose home. But I dont want Tavistock Sqre at the moment: I like the life here – you should see the donkeys, with paniers full of anemones; and the Square, all ablaze with flowers, and the Acropolis. Have I described our afternoon on The Acropolis – when a storm rushed up from the Aegean, black as arrows, and the blue was as blue as hard china, and the storm and the blue fell upon each other and 10 million German tourists rushed across the temple precisely like suppliants in their grey and purple mackintoshes – no I haven't described the Acropolis – You may thank your stars I know my place as a prose writer and leave all that to someone who, about this time 4 years since, won from Jack Squire, a silver beaker [symbolising the Hawthornden Prize] to drink her pop from. There! Thats my revenge for your not thinking of me. Ethel thinks of me. The first thing I got here from Giolmann the tourist agent was a sheet from Woking bidding him buy a man's saddle 2nd hand for her to ride on this autumn 'as I'm growing stiff and rather past middle life now'. I picture you and Ethel jogging up Hymettus together on a second hand man's saddle. [...] Please write. Roger is angelic, and exudes knowledge of the most sympathetic kind.

L sends his love – but is catching a flea –

V.

2579: To Ethel Smyth   [*Hotel Majestic, Athens*]

Wednesday May 4th 1932 A.D.

There, whats wrong with that date? Whats Einstein got to do with it? For your further information I will add 11.35 on a blazing hot morning.

I'm sitting on my bed with my ink pot on the po-cupboard, a large boil on my chin, result of wind and sun, a sore throat, result of cold and dust, but almost perfectly happy all the same. Why did you never tell me that Greece was beautiful? Why did you never mention the sea and the hills and the valleys and the flowers? Am I the only person who has eyes in my head? I solemnly inform you, Ethel, that Greece is the most beautiful country in the whole world; May is the most beautiful season in the whole year; Greece and May together – ! There were the nightingales for example singing in the cypresses where we sat beside the stream: and I filled my lap with scarlet anemones; Yes, but you want facts; Baedeker. Well then, we went from Athens to Corinth; town being rebuilt after earthquake; gulf [canal] stopped owing to heavy fall of rock; six donkeys engaged in carting fall away; will take 6 months or year: all traffic meanwhile held up: Delphi cut off; oranges unobtainable in hotel: from Corinth (all this in a great open car of Giolmann's perfectly driven over roads like coagulated craters by enchanting driver) to Mycenae: my word. magnificent. Bees booming in the Tomb of Agamemnon. (What is the line about 'his helmet made a hive for bees')[1] tea at Belle Helene [inn]; among the plains, with frogs barking: so to Nauplia in the evenings; oh and then next day up the most nerve racking pass, shooting like an arrow along a razor with caverns of rock in abysses a million feet deep under one's left eye, and donkeys emerging round the corners to Mitrovitza; so to Mistra; Byzantine church magnificent; peasants delightful; coffee in a peasants room; so to Athens again; all the time the heat increasing and the wind, and the flowering trees visibly opening and making tassels of violet and white and crimson (dont ask me to document these facts) against a sky of flawless blue. Then a day at Athens, which was good Friday according to their barbarian reckoning, but Lord, Ethel, how infinitely I prefer their barbarian reckonings to your protestant orthodoxy! At night, in the still heat, we stood on the balcony and saw the procession go by, singing in a minor key, some, to me, impressive and solemn dirge round a bier; and the clergy with beards and long hair and stiff catafalque like robes sang, and I can assure you all that is in me of stunted and deformed religion flowered under this hot sensuality, so thick, so yellow, so waxen; and I thought of the lights of the herring fleet at sea; everyone holding a yellow taper along the street and all the lights coming out in the windows. Why, we almost wept, we pagans. [. . .]

1. 'His helmet now shall make a hive for bees' (George Peele, 'Polyhymnia', 1590).

2592: To Ethel Smyth   *52 T.[avistock] S.[quare, W.C.1]*

Thursday [26 May 1932]

[. . .] I cant tell you how down in the mud and the brambles I've been
– nearer one of those climaxes of despair that I used to have than any
time these 6 years – Lord knows why. Oh how I suffer! and whats
worse, for nothing, no reason thats respectable. Only coming back from
Greece here to the incessant rubbing and rasping; and then one thing
going bad on my hands after another – here's one friend in a divorce
case, another fallen in love; and an odious quarrel fastened on me, and
the whole Press upset and in process of death or birth, heaven knows
which – these I suppose were reasons why I answered you so grumpily:
and was incapable of any vision of hope. This evening is the first
evening, nearly, I've had to myself; and slowly I'm renewing my soul.
I'm reading over the fire. Can it be possible I shall one day wish to write
again – Can there be peace and hope on t'other side of this blazing
cauldron? I repeat – how one suffers: and why? No doubt you have a
reason when you suffer. I wouldn't live last week again for £33.10/- and
6d. [. . .]

V.

2625: To Ethel Smyth   *Monks House [Rodmell, Sussex]*

Aug 18th [1932]

[. . .] Lord how hot it is here – the downs fizzling across the marsh:
the village sunk in portentous silence. I'm much better but dont do more
than creep from my bedroom to my [writing] lodge, holding a parasol to
placate L. who follows me like a dog – About the faint – I wish I could
gratify your morbid curiosity, but one packs about 10 lives into these
moments – I could write 3 volumes – how odd it is to break through the
usual suddenly and so violently. It wasn't in the afternoon; but after
dinner, sitting on the terrace, in the cool. I was looking at Caburn and
thinking how the night of a hot day differs from cool nights – thinking
about all that was cool and quiet – the white owl crossing the meadow
when suddenly my heart leapt; stopped; ran away, like a four in hand. I
cant stop it, I said. Lord, now its in my head. This pounding must must
must break something. So I said 'I'm going to faint' and slid down and
lay flat on the grass at L's feet. He dashed into the house and came back

with the ice tray of the frigidaire, which he put under my neck. And then I thought of everything under the sun: he says it lasted 30 minutes. Then the pounding lessened; and he helped me up; and I felt very faint – trees; flowers, stretching, fading: and I thought I could never get to the house – really that was painful, walking and fainting, but I did; and flopped on the bed; and said to L. with my usual sense, Would it be a good thing to use the Po? Certainly he said and I used it: and began shaking and he said can you take your temperature? But I couldnt hold the tube in my lips; however, I did later, and instead of being very high as the dr. expected, it was very low: and gradually I became sleepy and comfortable, only afraid to move, as if all my limbs were separate, and so fell asleep and woke, drowsy, sleepy, content – and that all. L. rang up the dr. who is seeing a specialist who knows about heat fainting and will inform us. But there's no need. There is nothing whatever wrong with me. I've always had what they call an intermittent pulse, and this – so a heart dr told me – tires the heart and makes it sensitive to strain, but the heart is perfectly sound, strong, and loving as you know. [. . .]

V.

2628: To Lady Ottoline Morrell   *Monks House* [*Rodmell, Sussex*]

6th Sept. [1932]

Dearest Ottoline,

I wish I could write you as nice a letter as you wrote me, but I have been out walking on the Downs, with a black spaniel who will chase sheep – hence my hand with which I tried to hold him in, shakes like an aspen. But you must try to decipher – only it wont be worth while.

Do you think people (I'm thinking of Lytton and Walpole[1]) do write letters to be published? I'm as vain as a cockatoo myself; but I dont think I do that. Because when one is writing a letter, the whole point is to rush ahead; and anything may come out of the spout of the tea pot. Now, if I thought, Ottoline will put this letter in a box, I should at once apply the tip of my finger to the end of the spout. When one was very young perhaps one did: perhaps one believed in immortality. I think Lytton's letters were freer as he got older and rid of this illusion: hence they're not printable; [. . .]

V.

1. Horace Walpole, 4th Earl of Oxford (1717–97), whose *Letters*, edited in nineteen volumes (1903–25), are his most famous literary legacy.

2645: To V. Sackville-West   *52 Tavistock Square* [*W.C.1*]

Tuesday 18th [October 1932]

Yes dearest Creature – that was very nice of you. Pinka and I sat erect, blushing, as our praises poured forth from the trumpet.[1] I think you gave me too much – I hope the three you suppressed weren't listening too. But anyhow, you soothed my vanity – there are people who say I'm vain – did you know it? – like cream poured onto the sore nose of a feverish – I shall say cat – having just had tea with two cats. (Nessa brought up the Charleston cat; as we drank tea it split into two – one of those miracles that do happen in peoples studios) Anyhow you said what I most wanted – not that I'm an enchanting gossip, but that my standard is high. I loathe being called enchanting. Did you see Priestly on Harold you and me? I thought if I were a cat I should not split so much into two as into one glutinous stream of unadulterated disgust.[2] You would have been still nicer if you had told me you were in London, and come here. I prefer you, bodily, to you vocally.

Oh I was in such a rage of jealousy the other night, thinking you had been in love with Hilda [Matheson] that summer [1929] you went to the Alps together! Because you said you werent. Now were you? Did you do the act under the Dolomites? Why I should mind this, when its all over – that tour – I dont know. But I do. D'yu remember coming to confession, or rather justification, in my lodge? And you weren't guilty then were you? You swore you werent. Anyhow my Elizabeth[3] comes to see me, alone, tomorrow. I rather think, as I told you, that her emotions sway in a certain way. (thats an elegiac) I'm reading her novel to find out. Whats so interesting is when one uncovers an emotion that the person themselves, I should say herself, doesn't suspect. And its a sort of duty dont you think – revealing peoples true selves to themselves? I dont like these sleeping princesses. Talking of the upper

1. On 17 October Vita reviewed *The Common Reader: Second Series* in her radio talk about new publications, throwing out three other books to make room for a full treatment of Virginia's.
2. Virginia translated her fury at Priestley into a lively essay called 'Middlebrow' (cast in the form of a letter to the editor of the *New Statesman*, but an essay nonetheless). It was published posthumously in *The Death of the Moth* (see *Essays*, V). The article to which Virginia refers has not been traced, but it is clear from her essay that Priestley had labelled her 'Bloomsbury' and 'highbrow', using both terms pejoratively, as Virginia thought.
3. Virginia had met the Irish novelist Elizabeth Bowen (1899–1973) through Ottoline Morrell. Since 1923 Bowen had been married to Alan Cameron.

classes, I went to the David–Rachel wedding.[1] To see Lady Salisbury with Desmond was entirely worth 5/6 white gloves. And Molly with Ld. Salisbury:

So when are you coming to see me!

V.

2660: To V. Sackville-West *52 T.[avistock] S.[quare, W.C.1]*

[8? November 1932]

Well, my faithless sheep dog, – yes, you'll be turned into a very old collie if you dont look out, blind of one eye, and afflicted with mange on the rump – why dont you come and see me? Poor Virginia can't come to you. She – that is, I suppose, I – had another, very slight though, fainting; and Elly Rendel[2] brought her misanthropic stethoscope, and says the systolic action of my heart – what used to be called my intermittent pulse – is too wild; and thats why I faint; and I must be quieter, and drink digitalis, and there's nothing whatever wrong with my heart! And I mustn't go into hot rooms, like Sibyls [Colefax]. So I doubt if I can come to Sst. [Sissinghurst] at the moment – not that its a very hot room – the bedroom might be though – For which reason I ask again (I'm in such a rush) when could you come and see me? I'm divinely happy, because I wrote all the morning – Oh how you'll hate my new novel, and how it amuses me![3] – and then I go for a walk, or drive, and then I come back to tea, carrying one muffin which I eat, with honey, and then I lie on the sofa, and – who d'you think came and talked to me t'other night? Three guesses. All wrong. It was Violet Trefusis – your Violet.[4] Lord what fun! I quite see now why you were so enamoured – then: she's a little too full, now, overblown rather; but what seduction! What a voice – lisping, faltering, what warmth, suppleness, and in her way – its not mine – I'm a good deal more refined – but

1. The wedding of Lord David Cecil, the son of the 4th Marquess of Salisbury, and Rachel MacCarthy, daughter of Desmond and Molly, took place on 13 October.
2. Virginia had been a patient of Elinor Rendel (1885–1942), Lytton Strachey's niece, since 1924.
3. Nearing the end of *Flush*, Virginia suddenly put it aside to begin an 'essay-novel', at first called *The Pargiters*, but published in 1937, after periods of great agony, as *The Years*.
4. Vita's former lover had come to talk to The Hogarth Press about her third novel, *Tandem*, 1933.

thats not altogether an advantage – how lovely, like a squirrel among buck hares – a red squirrel among brown nuts. We glanced and winked through the leaves; and called each other punctiliously Mrs Trefusis and Mrs Woolf – and she asked me to give her the Common R. which I did, and said smiling, 'By the way, are you an Honourable, too?' No, no, she smiled, taking my point, you, to wit. And she's written to ask me to go and stay with her in France, and says how much she enjoyed meeting me: and Leonard: and we positively must come for a whole week soon. Also Mrs Keppel [Violet's mother] loves me, and is giving a dinner partly [*sic*] solely for me in January. How I enjoyed myself! To be loved by Mrs Keppel, who loved, it is said – quite a different pair of shoes [Edward VII].

Well, what I was going to say, but have no time, is that I dont altogether agree with you (on the wireless) about Lawrence. No, I think you exaggerate. Genius, I admit: but not first rate genius. No. And such a cad to Ottoline. My word, what a cheap little bounder he was, taking her money, books, food, lodging and then writing that book.[1] And the other night they broadcast a poem, writer unknown; and L and I listened in; and we said who's that? some modern, quite 2nd rate, but trying to be first rate – pretentious – not genuine. Behold, Lawrence again, so they say. I admit the genius, in Sons and Lovers: but thats the sum and pinnacle of it all (I've not read anymore)[2] the rest is all a dilution, a flood, a mix up of inspiration, and prophecy – which I loathe – Oh yes, a genius, but not first rate. So there.

And come and see me

V.

2686: To Ethel Smyth   *Monks House [Rodmell, Sussex]*

Dec. 28th or thereabouts [1932]

[. . .] I am actually writing the very day I get your letter – a proof of the divine peace of Monks House. Nobody but the postman can possibly interrupt me between today and tomorrow. Therefore I am sunk deep in

1. *Women in Love* (1921), in which he cruelly portrayed Ottoline Morrell in the character of Hermione Roddice. *The Letters of D. H. Lawrence*, edited by Aldous Huxley, had been published in September, and Virginia had read at least some of them.
2. Not true. See Letter 2178, p. 266, note 1.

books. Oh yes, I write in the morning – just a little joke [*Flush*] to boil my years pot: but from 4.30 to 11.30 I read, Ethel. Isn't that gorgeous? And not only those damned flimsy MSS: no: books: printed, solid, entire: D'you know I get such a passion for reading sometimes its like the other passion – writing – only the wrong side of the carpet. Heaven knows what either amounts to. My own brain is to me the most unaccountable of machinery – always buzzing, humming, soaring roaring diving, and then buried in mud. And why? Whats this passion for? You, who love questions, answer me that. No – nobody can. And then this passion, which has been so well advised, lands me tonight in a book like the reek of stale cabbage and cheap face powder – a book called The Story of San Michele by [Axel] Munthe [1929]. Now dont say its your favourite work. A book more porous with humbug, reeking more suddenly with insincerity, I've never read. I'm at page 50. I rather suspect you of knowing him. My mother in law loves him – his d——d sentimental book, she being the mother of 9 children, and used to darn their socks on waking in the time of her calamity. And I'm reading Stella Benson [*Tobit Transplanted* (1931)]: with pleasure, and – oh so many books – doesn't it break your heart almost to think of me, with this passion, always consumed with the desire to read, chopped, chafed, bugged, battered by the voices, the hands, the faces, the bodily presence of those who are pleased to call themselves my friends? Its like knocking a bluebottle off its lump of sugar perpetually. I am in an exaggerative mood. I should qualify all this with a thin red line signifying 'exaggeration' – but God knows if Ethel Smyth – I think of calling you so in future – cant read Virginia by this time, let her eyes fall into a well and there drown. [. . .]

                                                                    V.

2687: To Hugh Walpole   *Monks House, Rodmell*
                                                               [*Sussex*]

28th Dec [1932]

My dear Hugh,

I can assure you that I liked your present better than any – better than the peach fed Virginian ham even, for literature, if you wont think me too high brow, is something – not I suppose if you are starving on a desert island – I was going to say that literature – but I become too self conscious to go on – is more than ham. Well, anyhow, this book of yours[1] is to me, anyhow, more than ham, first because I love finding myself quoted and called mysterious on the first page – considering I'm wallowing in ham and grilled turkey – and then because as you know, of all literature (yes, I think this is more or less true) I love autobiography most.

In fact I sometimes think only autobiography is literature – novels are what we peel off, and come at last to the core, which is only you or me. And I think this little book – why so small? – peels off all the things I dont like in fiction and leaves the thing I do like – you. [. . .]

Love from us both V.

2694: To V. Sackville-West   *Monks House, Rodmell*
[Sussex]

7th Jan 1933

[. . .] O Lord that I could see you, as you are – sitting on a tight plush seat in a car, I imagine, with views of the Middle West – an unattractive land, largely sprinkled with old tin kettles – racing across vast slabs of plate glass. For you are now travelling across America; the negroes are spitting in the carriage next door; and after 25 more hours, the train will stop at a town like Peacehaven, only 75 times larger, called Balmoral-ville, where you will get out, and after a brief snack off clams and iced pear drops with the Mayor, who is called, I should think Cyrus K. Hinks – but thats a detail I leave to you, you will go to a large baptist Hall, and deliver a lecture on Rimbaud. [. . .]

I was seized with gloom when you left – ask Ethel. Isn't it odd what tricks affection – to leave it at that – plays? I dont see you for six weeks sometimes; yet the moment I know you're not there to be seen, all the fishmongers shops in the world go dark.[2] I always think of you as a pink shop with a porpoise in a tank. Now there are no porpoises. No, Sissinghurst is grey; Sevenoaks a drab coloured puce. Here I sit at Rodmell, with a whole patch of my internal globe extinct. Yes – thats a compliment for you. [. . .]

1. Hugh Walpole's *The Apple Tree*, a volume of reminiscences, was published for Christmas 1932. The first words of the book are: 'There is a fearful passage in Virginia Woolf's beautiful and mysterious book *The Waves*, which when I read it, gave me an acute shock of unanticipated reminiscence.' He then quotes a long passage in which he found his title: 'The apple-tree leaves became fixed in the sky; the moon glared.'
2. Virginia often returned to her memory of Vita imperiously ordering fish at a Sevenoaks shop in December 1925 when the physical part of their relationship began.

By the way, are you lecturing on me at Albertvilleapolis Pa? If so, do send me your notes. Please do. And let them say something of love, and Horne the butler [at Long Barn]. Let them slip in one word to say Vita loves Virginia better than the whole world wrapped in a nutshell. Better than all those ardent but anaemic herring grillers with whom – Lord love her soul! – she consorts. Because Virginia is so clever, so good; and Virginia – this is a fact, not merely an idle boast – Virginia has been asked to write for the London Mercury by Jack Squire. What he says is, Will I send him a story and he'll see if it'll do. Oh my God – how I envy you, slipping off your skin and adventuring through fields where the flamingoes rise in flocks and the old black women stand at the doors, a baby at each breast! Thats what I adore and honour and cherish the Nicolsons for – sloughing their skins, every spring in a heap of drab scales and plunging naked into nothingness. Yes; you are a venturous woman, and make me envious. Please, for Gods sake, dont catch the flu, or the pneumonia – both I see rampant in New York. Dont do a thing that can diminish your splendour in my eyes, Come back soon, before I start, as I intend, for the East.

I'm told that Bunny Garnett's book on Pocahontas is very good.[1] Is it? Please tell me. I can read nothing but my own novel [*The Pargiters*], which is just as well, because nobody else will ever get through it.

Shall you now clear a space among the spittoons and write to me? Describe everything, down to the lace on womens nightgowns. Then add a terse but compendious statement why I love Virginia next best to my husband and sons.

And take great care of yourself.

V.

2695a: To Stella Benson   *Monks House, Rodmell,*
                                           [Sussex]

Jan 12th 1933

My dear Stella

I am ashamed indeed to see that your letter is dated the 1st of September; and here am I waiting till January to answer it. But I wanted to read Tobit in peace – you remember that I insisted upon your giving

---

1. *Pocahontas, or The Nonpareil of Virginia* (1933), by David Garnett, a fictionalised biography of the American Indian princess.

me a copy? And what I call peace is a mind not entirely saturated with novels that I have read in MS; and people running in and out of the room as they do at Tavistock Square. So I waited for Christmas and I have just finished Tobit and so can say – well, what am I to say? I like it immensely. You're quite right – you are getting at the bones of things, and I love the bareness, the whiteness the hardness of your bones. But I dont think that when you say that you are dealing with what is common (you say you live so much with very common people that you watch for common things) you mean what is cheap, nasty, commonplace, trivial, silly, affected. Not at all. I should say what you have done in Tobit is precisely the opposite – you've eaten away the soft mush and laid bare the bone. And I admit I envy you. I suspect that in some ways it is easier for you, living on an island in the China seas (my geography is vague in the extreme, but so I figure you) to shed the relics of the sort of mush that collects round one in London. I meet somebody who says 'youre this or that', and I dont want to be anything when I'm writing. Now in the China seas you only meet people like my sister in law,[1] who is kind and good, but as for seeing you, you might be a zebra or an elephant for all she sees of you. And so when you sit down to write Tobit you haven't a mist in front of your eyes, and that I think is a healthy state, though horribly painful in the obtaining. I should be driven desperate if I lived in a wilderness of Bellas – she sends home photographs of herself opening golf clubs from which I get my only idea of English life in China; but no doubt I should write much better if I did.

Anyhow I like and admire and envy the bareness of Tobit and feel it exists there as bright and hard and strange as a landscape of China. I think I liked the landscape, and the beginning with the men burying the dead, as well as anything. But in what sense are the characters 'common'? Tanya, for instance? The old man? Anna? I dont see that. No, I think they are subtle, rare, and hard – thats what I admire. You dont box them up together to brew personal emotions, and yet what more by way of character could one want?

I'm writing in some confusion, but if I stop to make my meaning plainer, I shall only plunge deeper into obscurity. But please tell me what you mean by 'common' one of these days.

Are the aeroplanes dropping bombs in your back garden? Are you chasing the smugglers across the bay? You remember how you told us

---

1. Bella Southorn (1877–1960), Leonard's sister, who was married to Sir Thomas Southorn, Colonial Secretary in Hong Kong.

they said they were taking presents to their Aunts? And what is your daily life like now? Are you riding? Does the General come to dinner with a servant to see that you dont put poison into the soup?

There is nothing of the kind happening in Sussex at the moment. It is a summer day – oddly enough. We have been walking over Mount Caburn, the down you saw – here is the picture of us sitting and looking at it – from the terrace that afternoon. (We aren't looking our best, either of us) On the top of Mount Caburn I saw a man running like mad. Leonard said he was a murderer; I said No, a poet. And sure enough when we came out on top there was a horrid little sentimental poem about the view, written on an envelope and weighted down with small pieces of chalk – snail shells to a seat. Such is Sussex.

On Sunday we go back to London, rather foolishly to the Hogarth Press and the telephone and the popping in and out of charming but too distracting people. I was going to ask Cornelia Sorabji[1] to come, but having fainted was rather feeble for a time and supposed she had gone back. Then I saw she was in London but was too shy by that time to do anything about it. Should you be writing to her, please ask her to let me know next time she is in London. I should like very much to see her.

I told them to send you a Common Reader. But honestly I dont want you to write to me about it – it was only the word 'common' that caught my eye.

Leonard, who is just about to wash his head, asks me to send you his regards and to say – what I say too – please come back soon and pay us another, and a longer visit.

Yours ever
Virginia Woolf

University Library, Cambridge

2698: To V. Sackville-West   *52 Tavistock Square [W.C.1]*

Jan 24th 1933

Yes, dearest Creature, I did write to you [letter 2694] but I called you Nicolson, and did not say forward; so you may not have got it. As it was the very most passionate letter I ever wrote, and the loveliest and wittiest what a pity. (This is trusting you never got it.)

1. Benson's friend Cornelia Sorabji (1866–1954), the daughter of an Indian teacher, was educated at Somerville College, Oxford. She became a barrister, did much for women's causes in India, and was a prolific author and lecturer.

You wrote to me from the high seas. How like you – to have waves 80 miles high, and to stand on the Bridge with the Captain [of the *Bremen*].

Now the point of you is that everything is like you – thats very profound. Here it is freezing, sneezing. You knew we had June last month – well, all the roses will be burnt by frost. Leonard is always talking about his buds. And the pipes are frozen here, and when I've had my bath Nelly [Boxall] and I have to bale it down the w.c. filling a pail with a tumbler. Heaven be praised, the w.c. is not yet frozen; but tomorrow the pipes will burst. I tell you all this to bring you in touch with England. I daresay you're eating clams on a skyscraper at this moment – 5:30 on Tuesday evening, the time you should be with me. And we wasted our last evening. I raging against Eddy [Sackville West], you very honourably upholding him. Did you ever discuss it with him? I've not seen him since; nor ever shall, I daresay, for I cant manoeuvre my friends tempers.

They're all dying, my friends – only Mrs Hunter, I mean, and George Moore and Alan Parsons[1] – none of them my friends, but the air is full of funerals, and old Ethel is in the highest glee.

She was here, pounding the arm of the chair the other night, and I said Wont you be late for Mrs Hunter? Dont care if I am said Ethel. At last I packed her off, and Mrs Hunter died 10 minutes after she got there. I'm rather pleased; she was such a time dying, and yet, if one has to die – as they say – I like her drinking champagne on yellow satin as well as anyway. I am writing all the morning: and I like writing; but you wont much care for it. Never mind. Oh and tonight theyre dancing Orlando on the ice,[2] and I shant be there. Its a remarkable fact – the whole British peerage says they descend from the Courtiers I invented, and still have the snow boots which they wore on the frost which I invented too. Its all true, every word of it.

They charge 30/- a ticket, and I would willingly have gone and hired skates if you'd have come. But now my porpoise no longer crowns the fishmongers shop – thats a quotation from the Scholar-Gypsy.[3]

1. The dead were Ethel Smyth's sister, Mary Hunter, the novelist George Moore, and Alan Parsons (1889–1933), drama critic of the *Daily Mail* and husband of Viola Tree.
2. 'A Gawdy on the Frozen Thames' (but actually on the Grosvenor House ice rink) was organised by Lord Riddell, Lady Newnes and Lady Burney in recollection of James I's ice carnival in 1604, described in *Orlando*. Lady Newnes appeared in a sleigh as Queen Anne of Denmark, and there were skating ballets performed by debutantes.
3. Matthew Arnold – but of course Virginia has recast his famous image with allusions to her relationship with Vita.

Dotty (excuse this leaping and jumping – I have to dine out) has given up the Poets Series[1] – I'm afraid she's grumpy, but oh dear, I cant smooth out all her grumps and glooms. She should be mated with a stallion and pour her humours down that sink, And the Press badly wants a filip of some sort. Shall you have your new novel ready for October? – its about America;[2] and it has a storm at Sea. We've had an American – head of Macmillans – here today.[3] Thats my boast. Oh I must boast, for I cant bear to think of all you're doing and seeing, and I not there, and I not there! Please, please, write down every scrap for me; you know how not a tassel on a table or a stain on a mat comes amiss. And how I miss you! You wouldn't believe it. I want coloured windows, red towers, moats and swans, and one old Bull walking up and down an empty stable: you, in short. But you dont want me. You are enchanting, chiefly with the glamour of your title and the glow of your pearls, all the Coons in Canada. Tell me that too: about the white soft women and their blazing eyes. I wish I couldn't see them so clearly couched on glittering frosty grass with the daughter of The Sackvilles.

Now I must dress. We are dining in Addison Road with the Laskis. Who is Mrs Laski?[4] What shall I say to her? And the pipes are frozen. Hail and Farewell[5] – that was the one book of G.M's I admired wholly. Write to me – write.

V.

2737: To Vanessa Bell   *Lucca [Italy]*

Wednesday May 17th [1933]

Dearest Dolphin

I have tried several times to write to you, but it is almost impossible, owing to every sort of noise, and then I'm so sleepy after a bottle of chianti; and as a matter of fact there is only description of natural objects and works of art to offer you. And you dont write. Post after post comes;

1. Dorothy Wellesley had chosen and subsidised the Hogarth Living Poets series.
2. Vita's next novel was *The Dark Island* (1934), which was not about America; but in 1942 she wrote *Grand Canyon*, which was.
3. The President of Macmillan's Publishing Company, New York, was then George Brett (1858–1936).
4. She was Frida Kerry, the daughter of a Suffolk landowner, whom Harold Laski had married when he was in his late teens.
5. George Moore's autobiography (1911–14).

none from Dolphin. So far we have had no accidents, but some moments of agony when the fluid wheel has stuck, or the gear gone wrong. And we have been all through France, and as far as Siena; indeed only 50 miles short of Rome. Undoubtedly Tuscany beyond Siena is the most beautiful of all lands anywhere – it is, at the moment, every inch of it laden with flowers: then there are nightingales: but it is the hills, – no, I will not describe for your annoyance. what is to me the loveliest, the most sympathetic, and I may say Virgilian of countries; for its years since we read Virgil together and you very properly told me not to write a word about landscape or art either.

And the peasants are infinitely the nicest of our kind – oh how much preferable to the Sands, the Smyths, the Logans! My Italian lands me in all kinds of wayside conversations, as we generally lunch under olives, beside streams with frogs barking. Why didn't you come? I should have thought the pictures very good at Siena – and then I like the old maids one meets: but the truth is this is only a discovery – we must come and settle at Fabbria [in Tuscany], a little farm we found, for ever and ever. There is no news. We called in at the Bussy's[1] as we passed, and found Janie and Dorothy, perfectly equipped, neat and bright as pins, sipping coffee; I dont care, I must admit for that view, or hill – but then the whole Riviera seems to me Raymonds [Mortimer] country – a pink pyjama country – however they seemed very friendly and want us to sleep the night going back; but I doubt it. Simon [Bussy] appeared, more of an organ monkey than ever, and theyre all about to start for Gordon Square. Why should I be snubbed for asking to be shown the Studio? Sure enough, I was – He said 'Not today. Perhaps next time.' Considering everything I cant see why I should be snubbed – simpleton as I am. We've seen a great many pictures – San Gimignano today, and yesterday we went to a place where I shall be buried, if bones can walk – that is, Monte Oliveto; oh oh oh – Cypresses, square tanks, oxen, and not big bony hills, little velvety hills – and the monastery: and as hot as August. But I wont deny that we've had some very cold days, and some violent tempests, one at Volterra for example – all because a peasant woman whose vines were perishing, came in and offered 2 candles to the

1. The Bussys lived in the hills above Monte Carlo. Simon (1870–1954) painted, and Dorothy (*née* Strachey, 1866–1960) wrote. Janie (1906–60), also a painter, was their only child.

Madonna for rain – which promptly came. Now its thundery again, and we've been walking all over Lucca, trying to find an antiquity shop, but the only one there was has gone. Its a most busy town. full of different markets; and the building – but as I said, I wont commit any faux pas on that head.

I suppose London is rocketing like a Catherine Wheel with various splendours – Rumours reach me from Ethel and so on – I hear she came to see you, but you could only talk of her dogs private parts – We now start home, rather slowly, and shall be back on the 27th I think – at Rodmell. The car is miraculous – not a bump comes through – and in France, of course it reaches unparallelled speed;

Shall you be glad to see me? Oh but you never realised I had gone – yet to me it seems years and years and as if I had seen all the countries of the earth spread before me. This is certainly the only way to see Italy. [. . .]

Yr
B.

2738: To Ethel Smyth   *Lerici* [*Italy*]

May 18th [1933]

Yes I have meant to write, again and again, but again and again I have fallen fast asleep. Moreover, whats the use of writing? Here am I sitting, by an open window, by a balcony, by the bay in which Shelley was drowned,[1] wasn't he, 113 years ago, on a hot day like this – which indeed I might describe, but how describe the hills, the tall pink yellow white houses, and the in fact, not fiction, purple brown sea, not rolling in waves, as I made my sea [in *The Waves*], but now and again giving a little shiver, like that which runs through a field of corn, or the back of a race horse! No, my good general's daughter, Italy beats me – Tuscany above all, which is incomparably the finest and purest of Italy, where I've been sitting, these 5 or 6 days, on hills like songs, like poems, thought of all in one flash and for ever, you would say by God, but then you're a general's daughter. I'm burnt like a grilled bone, and for the most part a little tipsy; and now we're starting home, over the Apennines

1. Shelley was drowned on 8 July 1822, together with his friend Edward Williams, when their small schooner capsized in a squall. Their bodies were washed ashore a few weeks later and were cremated on the beach.

tomorrow, to Parma, to Piacenza, so to Avignon, which leads to Dieppe, to Monks House, and so once more to the 52nd house in Tavistock Sqre.

Well, what are you doing? – inducing a large penis into a small hole? And I suppose rehearsing masses and comic operas, tippling, browbeating, and leading the forces of womanhood, massed, against ignorance and corruption? I dont like Fascist Italy at all – but hist! – there's the black shirt under the window – so no more.

Addio.
V.

Mrs Shelley and Mary Williams walked up and down the balcony of the house next door [Casa Magni] waiting while Shelleys body rolled round with pearls – it is the best death bed place I've ever seen –

2746: To Ethel Smyth [*52 Tavistock Square, W.C.1*]

Thursday June 8th 1933

No I dont think I put my point effectively; I did not mean that I dislike facts and dates; What I did mean was – oh dear how silly to try and explain – but my conscience is tender about writing – I meant, give all the facts and all the dates; the more the better; but let them be about other people, not E.S. My own longing in reading your article[1] is to escape the individual; and to be told simply, plainly, objectively in 1880 there was not a single woman in an orchestra; there was not a single teacher to teach women harmony; the expense of going to Berlin was 165 pound ten; eight women were educated partly by 1891; in 1902 Wood[2] took five violinists women into his orchestra; the number increased, and is now – (here a table) . . . and so on, all the way through. But to be told *My* opera was not played because – *My* mass was only played once, Elgars 17 times – to have to listen to anecdotes, hearsay, verbal anecdotes about how some unknown Austrian said that some unnamed conductor ought to be very proud of ES makes me feel, and will I think make any moderately intelligent moderately sensitive man or woman feel – Oh the womans got a grievance about herself; Shes

1. Virginia had long been providing blunt criticism of the articles that Ethel was collecting for her *Female Pipings in Eden*, published later this year. The particular article under consideration was 'Women's Training Hitherto'.
2. Sir Henry Wood (1869–1944), the conductor of the Queen's Hall Orchestra, who organised the Promenade concerts in London, where some of Ethel's music was performed.

unable to think of any one else. Now I know that this is deliberate on your part therefore I think you should try to see how very possible it is that your policy is wrong. Leonard to whom I recited passages said exactly the same. I dont believe anyone whose hands have lately been dipped in ink can judge this sort of thing – to give an instance; I was wound to a pitch of fury the other day by a reviewers attacks upon a friend of mine to do a thing I have never yet done – to write to the papers a long letter. 'Yes' said L. when I showed it to him; but itll do more harm than good; its all about yourself. When a fortnight later in cold blood I read it, there was 'I' as large, and ugly as could be; thanks to God, I didn't send it. You will say Oh but I must cite my case because there is no other. But my dear Ethel your case is that there are a thousand others. Leave your own case out of it; theirs will be far far stronger. Enough, I only say this because – well, I didnt write 'A room [*of One's Own*]' without considerable feeling even you will admit; I'm not cool on the subject. And I forced myself to keep my own figure fictitious; legendary. If I had said, Look here am I uneducated, because my brothers used all the family funds which is the fact – Well theyd have said; she has an axe to grind; and no one would have taken me seriously, though I agree I should have had many more of the wrong kind of reader; who will read you and go away and rejoice in the personalities, not because they are lively and easy reading; but because they prove once more how vain, how personal, so they will say, rubbing their hands with glee, women always are; I can hear them as I write. One thing more; and silence for ever; Nancy girls to me seems in bad taste.[1] Why? I dont know.

V

2767: To Quentin Bell   *52 T[avistock] S[quare, W.C.1]*

Wednesday [26 July 1933]

Dearest Quentin,

I'm very sorry to hear that youre in bed.[2] Please recover instantly, as I want you to come and meet Miss Elizabeth Read, a virgin, living with a large dog, rhapsodical, slim – about eighteen; now lodged in an Inn – but

1. 'Nancy girls' does not appear in the published text. But Ethel ignored Virginia's central message to omit her personal grievances, with which *Female Pipings* is replete.
2. With whooping cough and pleurisy.

for the past six months at Quentins, in the village.[1] I enclose a letter from our dear Cousin James.[2] Never did I see a more dumpish, foolish, chattering ugly man; his trousers stained; his pockets done up with string, bolt eyed, shock headed, with a lolling swollen tongue like a mad dogs. He is a confounded bore and I gave him your address.

Yesterday I went to see the Burne Joneses;[3] no I dont like them; save as remnants of Nessas and my youth – floating lilies; things that have gone down the stream of time; which image is more just than you would think; for every picture has one white face looking down, and another looking up out of water. The suavity, the sinuosity, the way the private parts are merely clouded – it's all a romantic dream, which makes me think of tea at Hyde Park Gate. Oh I'm dripping with heat. Last night we dined with Julia Tomlin, and met Peter Quennell; Dorothy Bussy and Wogan[4] (who asked a great deal after you,) who may spell his other name with two l's or one – I dont know. As youre notoriously indiscreet and Charleston, Nessa says, a warren of literary gents, I will not give you my candid opinion of anybody, but I prefer Wogan to Quennel; on the other hand, Q. has more knives in his brain. And I met a Mlle Chaunèse, and before I knew what was up, she had whipped out a note book and was taking my opinion of Joyce, Lawrence, life, death and the chances of an immortal soul. Then I lost my temper; and told her if she printed a word – shes an interviewer – I'd shoot her dead. This created an incident.

Talking of death and bullets, have you heard that Mrs Eliot is on the war path, said to have a carving knife with which first to skin Tom; then Ottoline; finally me? For she says Ott and I are Tom's mistresses; now as I never had a favour from that man its rather hard to give my life on the pavement.

I'm sending you a book of short stories; one – by [James] Joyce – seems to me very good. The others Ive not read. But please tell me what

1. Elizabeth Read was a social worker with literary ambitions. She was lodging at Quentins, a house in Rodmell, and had approached Virginia as an admirer of her writing. The 'virgin' had a live-in lover.
2. James Stephen, then aged 25, succeeded his father Harry as 4th baronet in 1945, the same year in which he was certified insane. He was not discharged from hospital until 1972.
3. An exhibition at the Tate Gallery in commemoration of the centenary of Edward Burne-Jones' birth.
4. Peter Quennell (b. 1905), the man of letters. Wogan Philipps (b. 1902, later 2nd Baron Milford). He was a painter and the husband of novelist Rosamond Lehmann.

you think, as I must thank for it. We dined with Jack and Mary [Hutchinson]; Mary is to me ravishing; in chalk white with a yellow turban, like an Arab horse, or a pierrot. And we met two Frogs – Masson[1] and another [Simon Bussy], and went to the Zoo. And now I'm dining with Vita. But I wish I were sitting by my own fish pond with my own nephew writing indecent and vulgar lives of the living. Shall we revive our stories?

I hope to see you soon.

Virginia

2783: To Ethel Smyth   *Monk's House [Rodmell, Sussex]*

22nd August [1933]

No, my dear Ethel, Your psychology is much at fault. If I hadn't a heart of gold under the skin of a shark I should never write to you again, after your comments upon my poor little note. Thats the trouble with the daughters of generals – either things are black, or they're white; either theyre sobs or they're 'shouts –' whereas, I always glide from semi-tone to semitone; and you never hear the difference between one and another. Thats why you dont understand a word I write, either in MS. or print; for its long been plain to me that you dont. Oh no: Dickens is your favourite author; after him Mr Priestly. Ah hah! (There is an element of very profound truth in this) But I've forgotten now the lecture I meant to write upon your letters. One incident I do however remember. When you came that afternoon, I jumped out of bed and stood outside the drawing room door. I was about to go in. Then I thought, not of you, but of Leonard.[2] Unravel this riddle, as you float above the [Hebridean] islands. [. . .]

I wish I knew the geography of the British Isles. I dont at once visualise Hebrides, Skye, and the rest. I only see a black blot in mid air which is you, astride an aeroplane; firmly grasping a rail, keenly envisaging the seascape; and completely master of your feet and

1. The artist and ballet designer André Masson.
2. There had been yet another scene. Ethel had been hurt by Virginia's refusal to see her when she came to Rodmell on 14 August. Virginia had a headache and was resting in bed. Ethel complained that Leonard would not understand that she wished to see Virginia for only two minutes. 'Does one want to talk to a landscape? to a fine sunset? No – only to bathe in it for half a second' (Ethel to Virginia, 15 August, Berg Collection).

faculties. I daresay you drop down upon a British fortress and drink rum with the officers. Do they think you a jolly good fellow? Are you always moving on? Do you ever think? – read? – or are you dazed, as I am in the car, when we drive, and drive and drive, and my mind is a long peaceful smudge? [. . .]

V.

2788: To Ethel Smyth

*Monk's House, Rodmell,
near Lewes, Sussex*

Wednesday [6 September 1933]

[. . .] For Gods sake tell me about the maiden-head removal – what a lark![1]

Shall we go and be done together? Side by side in Bond Street?

V.

2795: To Quentin Bell

*Monks House [Rodmell,
Sussex]*

Tuesday [19 September 1933]

Dearest Quentin,

[. . .] The reason why Ethel Smyth is so repulsive, tell Nessa, is her table manners. She oozes; she chortles; and she half blew her rather red nose on her table napkin. Then she poured the cream – oh the blackberries were divine – into her beer; and I had rather dine with a dog. But you can tell people they are murderers; you can not tell them that they eat like hogs. That is wisdom. She was however full – after dinner – of vigorous charm; she walked four miles; she sang Brahms; the sheep looked up and were not fed. And we packed her off before midnight.

Now the [F. L.] Lucases are coming; and then we go to London; and then – well, have you read the mornings paper on Lydia?[2] The D.T. is

1. Ethel wrote to Virginia on 26 August that she had met a young woman who 'tells me lots of girls have themselves operated on nowadays so as not to endure tortures on marriage nights. [. . .] Why not try it now? (Its never to late to rend)' (Berg).

2. In spite of her heavily accented English, Lydia Lopokova (Mrs Maynard Keynes) now began to turn her attention from the ballet to the theatre. She had just opened as Olivia in *Twelfth Night* at the Old Vic and had asked Virginia to write a review, which she did, publishing it in the *New Statesman & Nation* (there had been another journalistic merger) for 30 September (see *Essays*, VI).

scathing. My god; what shall I say? I think the only possible line to take is how very exciting it is to see Shakespr mauled; of course one might make play with the idea that the Elizabethans were just as unintelligible; and throw in a hint about opposites being the same thing as equalities – if you take my meaning. Either the worst, or the best – that sort of remark. Well. Pity me. [. . .]

V.

2801: To David Garnett   *52 Tavistock Sq. [W.C.1]*

Sunday [8 October 1933]

My dear Bunny,

You were more than generous and wholly delightful [in the *New Statesman* review] about Flush and Virginia last week; and I had meant to write and thank you before, but not being altogether a dog, as you justly observe, had no time to go to the London Library and prove that I'm not so inaccurate as you think. No. I am rather proud of my facts. About license, for instance; surely I made plain that I was referring to nature, not the post office? license natural to his age – well, I ask you, what has that license got to do with the Encyclopaedia? or the Post Office, or six and eightpence? Natures license, sometimes called lust. About the working mans cottage; I agree it looks a farm in the picture; but Mr Orion Horne calls it a working mans cottage; and he saw it; and was not a picturesque artist.[1] Painters at that date always enlarge houses out of consideration for their owners. Such is my view as a biographer (and oh lord how does any one pretend to be a biographer?) As for asphalt, I admit I have my doubts; but I suspect that the Prince Regent like asphalt – asphalt seems to me implied by the [Brighton] Pavilion. But how could you let slip the horrid anachronism which stares at you, bright red, on page I dont know what? There were no pillar boxes in the year 1846. They were invented by Anthony Trollope about 1852. Dont expose me. If you do, my sales will prick like a bubble. Old gentlemen will die in fury. I could go on, but will stop, having I hope partly vindicated my claim to truth speaking. Yes, the last paragraph as

1. The illustration captioned 'Flush's Birthplace' in *Flush* is a nineteenth-century engraving, unsigned. Richard Hengist Horne (1803–84), author of *Orion*, collaborated with Robert Browning and Elizabeth Barrett (who was the spaniel Flush's owner) on *New Spirit of the Age* (1844).

originally written was simply Queen Victoria dying all over again –
Flush remembered his entire past in Lyttons best manner; but I cut it
out, when he was not there to see the joke. But what a good critic you are
– lots of things you said I think of in the watches of the night; they stick
like burs; whereas the others, save Desmond's [MacCarthy in the
Sunday Times], run off my coat like water.

Yours affectionate old English springer spaniel Virginia

2806: To Quentin Bell   *52 Tavistock Sq. [W.C.1]*

Saturday [14 October 1933]

Dearest Quentin,

I saw Julian and hear that though dilapidated and tied up with string,
and skidding and skadding you reached home safe. No sooner had you
gone, than Hugh Walpole burst in; much elated and also discomposed.
He had been to the next door house by mistake; a lady with purple hair
and carmine lips answered him. No I am not Mrs Woolf she said –
indeed it was obvious what her trade was – not mine; and when Hugh
said he must go; Oh no she said, just come in all the same. This was very
upsetting Hugh said; his tastes being what they are. He looks down
nightly upon the heads of prostitutes in Piccadilly; and never knows
more of them than that. [. . .]

Last night we went to the Cherry Orchard – oh and Lydia came in to
see us; and says she is now happier; but they were both in the depths of
gloom; and they liked my article on her. So thats all right. We dont think
on the whole the Cherry Orchard can be acted by the English. Even the
dog is English. I think it ought to be rewritten in sea gulls language like
Synge.[1] But they acted very well, but I doubt if it is as great a play as I
thought it when I was young. Our Miss Walton [Hogarth Press] waited
an hour and a half to see it, and was delighted. Now Kingsley Martin has
just rung up to ask L. to go and talk about Hitler. He thinks there is
going to be a world revolution. L. thinks he is optimistic and emotional.
I dont like his table manners. [. . .]

Virginia

1. John Millington Synge (1871–1909) based his plays on the people, customs, and
language of the Aran Islands, off Galway.

2813: To V. Sackville-West 52 *T.[avistock]* S.*[quare, W.C.1]*

Wednesday 1st Nov. [1933]

'I saw Vita lunching at the Café Royal today' said Jack Hutchinson last night.

Oh such a pang of rage shot through me! All through dinner, and the supper, which ended with champagne and iced cake at 12.30, I was going back and foraging in my mind for the seed in my pillow: (you know what I mean: the pea under the mattress) and that was it. And I couldn't say 'who was with her?'[1] And it burnt a hole in my mind, that you should have been lunching at the Cafe Royal and not come to see me.

How pleased you'll be! You did it on purpose I daresay. But who were you with? You knew I should get wind of it – yes and it was a woman you were lunching with, and there was I, sitting alone and and and . . . . . I break off my writing, which is all dish water, to make this heated exclamation:

In fact we've been having the devil of [a] time, what with one thing and another. Quentin's going to Switzerland.[2] Nessa's flying with him to Geneva. We're motoring them to Croydon at 6 on Friday morning: then go to Brighton to see Francis,[3] who can only haul himself round a table, hanging on to Desmond and a male nurse. Then back on Monday.

And when shall I see you? Dearest Creature, do write and tell me who you were lunching with at the Cafe Royal – and I sitting alone over the fire!

I've had your book [*Collected Poems*] in my hands – and very stately it is, like a slab of ivory engraved with steel; but I didn't read it, because you are giving it me.

Oh the Cafe Royal! When Jack said that – not to me, but to the company, you could have seen my hand tremble; and then we all went on talking and the Rothschild's[4] came in, and a fat man called Shearman,

1. Vita had been lunching with Harold's sister, Gwen St Aubyn (b. 1896), who for the next few years was her most intimate friend.
2. Because of suspected tuberculosis.
3. Francis Birrell had been operated on for a brain tumour. He died at the beginning of 1935.
4. Victor (later 3rd Lord) Rothschild (b. 1910), who married St John and Mary Hutchinson's daughter Barbara (b. 1911) in the next month. This was their engagement party. One of the guests was Sir Montague Shearman (1885–1940), the barrister and collector of pictures.

and the candles were lit, and I chose mine, a green one, and it was the first to die, which means they say that out of the 8 or 9 people there, I shall be the first to wear a winding sheet. But you'll be lunching at the Cafe Royal!

Y

V.

2821: To Quentin Bell   *Monks House* [*Rodmell,*
                                         Sussex]

Saturday 18th Nov. [1933]

Dearest Quentin,

[. . .] I wonder if you've met Mrs Bottome [at the Swiss sanatorium], Nessa's friend, who is a friend of Vita's – a lady who, being married to a Forbes, sticks to Bottome heroically as her pen name.[1] Dear me – I should never have had the courage to be Virginia Bottome. Or have you preferred, as I should, to lie by yourself sublimely? I used to think it rather sublime, being shut up but then I was not as firm in the wits as you are. I had Ottoline to tea, and now she's sent me more memoirs.[2] Oh and she sent her love. Her memoirs are full of appalling revelations – of course she lies, but not entirely. And how she was torn by Bertie [Russell], Lytton, Henry Lamb, Lawrence. Since Helen of Troy I dont think any woman can have launched so many ships. [. . .]

Yrs Virginia

2826: To Quentin Bell   *52 Tavistock Sq.* [*W.C.1*]

Sunday 26th Nov [1933]

Dearest Quentin,

I read your letter with great pleasure in Time and Tide;[3] it seemed to me put with masterly brevity; most true. But I am no politician – how do

1. Phyllis Bottome (1882–1963), the novelist, who in 1917 married A. E. Forbes-Dennis.
2. In the early 1930s Ottoline Morrell began to write her memoirs based on her diaries, but they were not published until after her death, when they were edited in two volumes by Robert Gathorne-Hardy (1963 and 1974).
3. Attacking the argument that Germany was entitled to claim Austria as part of the German Reich.

you come by that queer instinct? I had such a party the other night at Mary's [Hutchinson] – she bet me I wouldn't go, to meet Michael Arlen,[1] who wrote The Green Hat. So I did go; and there he was, and a mort of other notables; including Elizabeth Princess Bibesco,[2] all in flamingo feathers which parted to give view to her own brown down, (how coarse this is; but true). M.A. is a rubber faced little sweaty Armenian monkey, full of protestations, as if I'd just whipped him on the behind for writing the Green Hat. He never stopped apologising, said he only did it to make money, and made fifty thousand pounds; and so married a Greek wife, who was there, silent as an image and stupid, they said, as a mummy; but rather in the style of the Venus of Milo all the same. 'She's very silent', he said to me, 'but a perfect lady'. He is *not* a perfect gentleman. But then he has made fifty thousand pounds, and is now going to write a book for highbrows. Barbara and Victor [Rothschild] were also there; – well, I wont be indiscreet, but between you and me, that's a marriage bound for the rocks.[3] Victor would make me shoot him in ten minutes. He's a Jew; that I rather like but – no, I wont be indiscreet. He had come in the other morning carrying a cardboard box big enough to hold a top hat; and said to B. 'Here's a little present'. She, thinking it was a muff or a pair of shoes, never cut the string till he'd gone; when out there fell box upon box of pure red rubies – crowns made of rubies, bracelets, rings, breastplates, festoons – all ruby; all red as the morning star and bright as dawn. Jack [Hutchinson] said the whole room was lit up. They are worth £300,000 pounds. So they can't insure them and they have to be taken to the Bank in a steel lined case and kept there. An old Rothschild bought them 100 years ago for his wife; but she kept them under her bed; I am making Barbara dine here in them next week; and am having the police staff in the Square enlarged. But no – not for all the rubies in the mines of Africa – no, Quentin; no. But I'm discreet.

Then I'm involved with your friend Sickert. I went to his show, and was so much impressed that Nessa made me write to him; and he said 'Do me the favour to write about my pictures and say you like them'. 'I

1. Michael Arlen (1895–1956), the novelist, was born in Bulgaria of Armenian parents, but was educated in England and became a British subject in 1922. He achieved sudden fame in 1924 with *The Green Hat*, described by one critic as 'a combination of sexual farce and melodrama'. In 1928 he married a Greek Countess, Atalanta Mercati.
2. The novelist Elizabeth Bibesco, *née* Asquith (1897–1945), who was married to Prince Antoine Bibesco.
3. It ended in 1946.

have always been a literary painter, thank goodness, like all the decent painters. Do be the first to say so' he says. I rather think of trying. Nessa is going to take me to tea with him.[1] Do you think one could treat his paintings like novels? I went to Agnews yesterday and Mr Colin [Agnew] had them all brought down, and lined a room; and he asked me to write a book on them. What do you think of Sickert's painting? I gather Roger is rather down on it; so is Clive. It seems to me all that painting ought to be. Am I wrong? if so, why? Are the Alps looking fine? Are there eagles?

So goodbye,
Virginia

2828: To Quentin Bell   *Monks House [Rodmell, Sussex]*

Sunday 3rd Dec [1933]

Dearest Quentin,

[...] I've seen a good deal of life, so called, since I wrote, I spent a night with the [H.A.L.] Fishers at the Wardens Lodgings [New College, Oxford] – rather an impressive 14th century house, part tithe barn, but then came the eighteenth century and cut up the barn into bedrooms with panels; and modern youth flourishes, discreetly, decorously, all over the house. I should think there were one hundred promising undergraduates in after dinner; and I shook hands with all; and tried to think what to say, but oh dear what a farce! One might as well go to a school treat and hand out penny buns. There was the great Isaiah Berlin,[2] a Portugese Jew by the look of him, Oxford's leading light; a communist, I think, a fire eater – but at Herbert's everyone minces and mouths and you wouldn't guess to talk to them that they had a spark or a spunk. Herbert is all that is refined and stately; he looks much like Adrian [Stephen]; but office has smoothed out all corrugosities. He told me story after story about the Cabinet of 1916. To him that was what a Christmas tree is to a child, and the poor old moth still haunts those extinct, but once radiant, candles. He adores Lloyd George; he sniffs at

---

1. This invitation led to Virginia's *Walter Sickert: a Conversation*, published by The Hogarth Press in October 1934.
2. Isaiah Berlin (b. 1909), the philosopher and historian of ideas, was a Fellow of All Souls.

Bloomsbury. 'No I cannot see much to be said for Mr Eliot; no music'. He thinks Winston Churchill a very good painter. He deplores the present state of everything. But he does his bit like a Bishop. And he was very kind to me, and we cracked a little about Madge and Will [Vaughan] and George [Duckworth] and Uncle Halford[1] – the dead, or practically dead. And there was one lovely girl, I think called [Maire] Lynd [b. 1911], daughter of Robert, who boards with the Fishers; having been, I gather – but may be wrong – turned out of Somerville for being caught fully dressed talking about the gold standard with a young man. Why are officials so noble but so chilly? As for Lettice [Mrs Fisher], she is an old henwife, cheese paring, wispy, all brawn and muscle; no flesh; no humour; but again as kind as they make them – which, if you leave out imagination, humour, music, humanity – doesn't go the whole length. And the beds were hard.

Then we had old Tom Eliot to tea, and sat over the fire and gossiped. He was primed with Clive's brandy, for he had been lunching till tea time on old brandy with Clive, Rebecca West and Lady Colefax. So he was bemused and mellow; and only wanted the W.C. For as he said, he had been drinking since one thirty. What a phantasma one's friends lives are! Tom is writing a pageant [*The Rock*] to be acted at Sadlers Wells in the spring on *London*; in order to collect one quarter of a million to build forty six churches in the suburbs. 'Why' asked Leonard. And Tom merely chuckled. I rather think his God is dwindling. But he likes clerical society, and was going to call on the Vicar of Clerkenwell. Dear me, I wish you would come back soon, and then we could go into all these matters together.

Roger and Helen also dined with us. Looked at in a half light Helen reminds me of a red rose just falling on a June night. Dont you think she has a kind of foull (should read 'full') blown beauty? And one or two rain drops might be added. But she was very kind and not too thorny that night. Roger never stops lecturing. So very tactfully we said What is the use of criticism? And he said I think – but its all in his Cambridge lecture[2] – criticism is useless, save as it – but here I lost count, being very sleepy that night. Have you seen his lecture? 'Well', he said to me, 'you wouldn't find any literature in my paintings – this referred to my essay

1. Henry Halford Vaughan (1811–85) was, like the others mentioned, a relative of both Herbert Fisher and Virginia. The object of Virginia's early romantic affection, Madge Vaughan, died in 1925.

2. Roger Fry's inaugural lecture as Slade Professor at Cambridge: 'Art History as an Academic Study'.

on Sickert. 'What should I find?' I asked. Happily he was stumping down the stairs. So you see old Bloomsbury still crackles under the pot. We have a memoir meeting [the Memoir Club] next week; and I have Ethel Smyth and Rebecca West to tea to discuss the life of Mrs Pankhurst. In strict confidence, Ethel used to love Emmeline – they shared a bed.[1]

Its a howling gale here.

Virginia

2836: To Lady Ottoline Morrell   *52 Tavistock Square,*
W.C.

19th Dec. [1933]

Dearest Ottoline,

Now we are off, and I haven't seen you, but what was the use of asking you on top of Ethel Smyth, Rebecca West, Vita Nicolson and so on? – which reminds me that Vita wants to see you, and also reminds me that Rebecca was fascinating – ungainly, awkward, powerful, arborial, like some sloth or mandrill; but oh what a joy to grapple with her hairy arms! I mean she was very upstanding and outspoken, and we discussed religion, sex, literature and other problems, violently, in a roar, to catch Ethel's ear, for 3 hours. This is to corroborate my view, and in opposition to yours – but who knows? The human soul is deaf, and next time she may bite my fingers to the bone. Did you know Stella Benson? I'm sorry for her death – I think one of these days she might have written something I liked – And I wanted to see her, apart from the dull little man [her husband, J. Anderson] who never left her alone a moment.

Now as I say we are going, why I cant think, to Rodmell, where life will be a flight from the cold to the fire; but perhaps we shall see the downs sometimes. And I cant go on with this scribble, because, owing entirely to you, Stephen Spender is dining here, and I must wash. Mark my words – the whole evening will be spent in talking of Stephen Spender, and when the stars are in the sky, I shall stumble to bed wondering by what alchemy you refine these rough youths to gold. So no more.

yrs V

1. Ethel Smyth was certainly an ardent supporter of both the Women's Suffrage Movement and its redoubtable leader, Emmeline Pankhurst (1858–1928). The bed bit is less certain, but Ethel herself wrote (in *Female Pipings in Eden*) about some intense emotional intimacy in a two-bedded room.

2837: To Quentin Bell   *52 Tavistock Sq.* [*W.C.1*]

21st Dec 1933

Dearest Quentin,

This is a black foggy Christmas week; and the human race is distracted and unlovable. That is, I spent yesterday in Oxford Street buying things like gloves and stockings. A drought is imminent; Rodmell has long ceased to wash; and it is said that Communion is no longer possible, owing to the congealed state of the holy blood. We go down today and I shall think of you when the owl comes out of the ivy bush and the bells toll. It was thus that we ushered out the old clergyman's soul, if you remember.[1] Stephen Spender and Miss [Maire] Lynd – I cant name her, for being Irish her parents have christened her some faery Celtic name – dined here last night. She is dusky, twilit, silent, secretive. He on the other hand talks incessantly and will pan out in years to come a prodigious bore. But he's a nice poetic youth; big nosed, bright eyed, like a giant thrush. The worst of being a poet is one must be a genius; and so he cant talk long without bringing in the abilities and disabilities of great poets; Yeats has praised him; I see being young is hellish. One wants to cut a figure. He is writing about Henry James and has tea alone with Ottoline and is married to a Sergeant in the Guards.[2] They have set up a new quarter in Maida Vale; I propose to call them the Lilies of the Valley. Theres William Plomer, with his policeman; then Stephen, then [Wystan] Auden and Joe Ackerly,[3] all lodged in Maida Vale, and wearing different coloured Lilies.

Their great sorrow at the moment is Siegfried Sassoon's defection,[4] he's gone and married a woman, and says – Rosamond[5] showed me his letter – that he has never till now known what love meant. It is the saving of life he says; and this greatly worries the Lilies of the Valley, among whom is Morgan [Forster] of course, who loves a crippled bootmaker; why this passion for the porter, the policeman and the bootmaker? Well, we must go into the matter when you come back.

1. The Rev. James Hawkesford, Rector of Rodmell, who died in January 1928.
2. Spender, then 24, lived with Jimmy Younger, who had joined the Army for three years at 18, but was now unemployed.
3. J. R. Ackerley (1896–1967), author, playwright and, from 1935–59, literary editor of *The Listener*.
4. The poet Siegfried Sassoon, now 47, married Hester Gatty.
5. The novelist Rosamond Lehmann (b. 1903) was known to the Woolfs through her brother John. They also knew her husband, Wogan Philipps.

Angelica [Bell] is once more in town; and the place is therefore humming. I suppose in two years there will be a series of bullets flying and knives gashing – for Gods sake dont let her marry a policeman. [. . .]

Virginia

2841: To Lady Ottoline Morrell   *Monks House, Rodmell [Sussex]*

31st Dec. [1933]

Dearest Ottoline,

[. . .] This morning I had a remarkable letter, for the first time, from Vivienne Haigh Eliot. Happily she doesn't ask me to do anything. She merely says that Tom refuses to come back to her, and that it is a great tragedy – so I suppose I can agree and say no more. She has made Leonard her executor, but writes sensibly – rather severely, and with some dignity poor woman, believing, she says, that I respect marriage.

And Vita came with her sons, one Eton, one Oxford,[1] which explains why she has to spin those sleepwalking servant girl novels. I told her you would like to see her. I remain always very fond of her – this I say because on the surface, she's rather red and black and gaudy, I know: and very slow; and very, compared to us, primitive: but she is incapable of insincerity or pose, and digs and digs, and waters, and walks her dogs, and reads her poets, and falls in love with every pretty woman, just like a man, and is to my mind genuinely aristocratic; but I cant swear that she wont bore you: certainly she'll fall in love with you. But do let her come down from her rose-red tower where she sits with thousands of pigeons cooing over her head. [. . .]

yrs Virginia

1. The Etonian was Nigel Nicolson (b. 1917), later a publisher, an MP, a writer and an editor – of his father's diaries and Virginia Woolf's letters. His brother Benedict (1914–78), who was to become an art historian, was at Balliol.

1934–1935

The political temperature of the Continent was rising. The Nazis were causing such trouble in Germany and Austria that even Virginia, as she put it, was alarmed. Notwithstanding the risks, she and her Jewish husband travelled through Germany and Holland to Italy. Another of their holiday journeys took them to Ireland.

There Virginia learned of the death of her half-brother, George Duckworth, whom she remembered with incongruous feelings of affection and horror. The death of Roger Fry moved her far more deeply, compounded by its devastating effect upon Vanessa. Helen Anrep and Margery Fry wanted Virginia to write his biography, and she reluctantly agreed. For a long time the Fry project – along with The Years, *which dragged on and on – was a great burden to her.*

Vita had moved away emotionally. Virginia wrote far more often now to Ethel, with whom she shared her unhappiness about Vita, their mutual friend. She also wrote frequently to her nephew Julian Bell, particularly after he took a university teaching position in China. Trying to address his interests, she sent letters about politics and the literary world. To Quentin Bell, she wrote witty letters that depended upon general, occasionally hostile gossip. Her niece, Angelica, now in her mid-teens, received letters filled with fantasy.

After eighteen exasperating years with the cook, Nelly Boxall, Virginia finally found the courage to give her notice (see Letter 2867), a drama every bit as real and important to Virginia as what was happening in the outside world.

2857: To Quentin Bell   *52 Tavistock Sq, W.C.1*

15th Feb [1934]

Dearest Quentin,

[. . .] I dined with Colefax and met Noel Coward;[1] and he called me Darling, and gave me his glass to drink out of. These are dramatic

---

1. The actor, playwright and composer (1899–1973), whose works Virginia claimed to despise. His 'opera' was *Conversation Piece*, which Coward called a play, although it had a libretto.

342

manners. I find them rather congenial. Anyhow theres no beating about the bush, as Nessa would say, rather coarsely. Then he played his new opera on Sybils grand piano and sang like a tipsy crow – quite without self consciousness. It is about Brighton in the time of the Regency – you can imagine. I am to go and see him in his retreat. He makes about twenty thousand a year, but has several decayed uncles and aunts to keep; and they will dine with him, he says, coming out of Surbiton, and harking back to his poverty stricken days. So he has to combine them with the half naked nymphs who sing his parts, which is difficult.

There is a terrible amount of politics about at the moment. You are nearer Vienna than I am – but everybody says here this is the beginning of the end.[1] We are to have Mosley[2] within five years. I suppose you and Julian will be in for it. What Angelica will live to see boggles me. But after all there are many advantages today over yesterday – one can write to a nephew in a manner that my Aunt Mary [Fisher] could not. Julian is caballing as usual. He darts in, like a very nimble elephant, and seizes books on Manchuria and then departs to his room in Taviton Street. Roger is gone. Clive in Paris. I missed the memoir club owing to my disease; but it sounded rather good.

I have just refused to sit for my portrait for the Nat. Portrait Gallery; dont you agree I am right? They send a wretched boy to draw one in one sitting; then they keep the drawing in a cellar, and when I've been dead ten years they have it out and say Does anyone want to know what Mrs Woolf looked like? No, say all the others. Then its torn up. So why should I defile a whole day by sitting? [. . .]

Virginia

2859: To Ethel Smyth   *52 T[avistock] S.[quare, W.C.1]*

Monday [26 February 1934]

No 'I'll tell this' to copy your style at its sweetest, when I get a letter from you, beating your breast, and going into all the usual attitudes, 'how have I wasted my affection – what a serpent Virginia is – what a

---

1. On 12–14 February there were widespread riots in Vienna when the Catholic Chancellor tried to suppress the Socialists. The Austrian Nazis took advantage of the turmoil to increase their own terrorist activities.
2. Sir Oswald Mosley (1896–1980), leader of the New Party and, since 1932, the British Union of Fascists.

genius, what an Undine[1] –' then I harden harder, and colden cooler, for I think Ethel Smyths the most attitudinising unreal woman I've ever known – living in a mid Victorian dentists waiting room of emotional falsity – likes beating up quarrels for the sake of dramatising herself, enjoys publicity and titles from universities and Kings, surrounded by flatterers, a swallower of falsehoods, why should I stand this manhandling, this brawling this bullying, this malusage? When I've friends that respect me and love me and treat me honestly generously and according to the fair light of day? Why pray why cowtow to the bragging of a Brigadier Generals daughter? Why?

V.

2863: To Quentin Bell   *52 Tavistock Sq [W.C.1]*

March 8th 1934

Dearest Quentin,

I am as usual delighted and shocked by your letter. How you carry on in the High Alps, to be sure – I thought the pure snows had their tempering effect on human passions – but what you tell me of the clergy on the Alp brings a flush even to the cheek of Mont Blanc. And I am not a mountain. No, but I'm hardly distinguishable from an old sack of onions at the moment. That damnable Duke of Bedford is making us entirely redecorate the whole house[2] – from top to bottom; bricks, walls, windows, cellars, cupboards – all have to be painted; rehung; with the result that here I am marooned in a space the size of a rather large tabby cat, books to right of me, pictures to left of me, and not a drop to drink.[3] It is hell – and hell lasting as long as Mr Ridge the builder chooses. We dine on scraps on our knees. Leonard has ardent politicians, five of them at this moment, encamped on the bottoms of cupboards while clouds of dust rise; and our food tastes of plaster; and our noses stink of oil paint. Oh for a whiff of your air, contaminated as it is by the clergy! [...]

Also there was Lydias Dolls house,[4] which was a triumphant

1. A mythological water sprite, mortal but soulless, and also the title of a romance (1811) by Baron de la Motte Fouque, in which such a sprite is caught by a fisherman.
2. The Woolfs leased 52 Tavistock Square from the Duke of Bedford's Estates.
3. A fancifully mixed allusion to Tennyson ('The Charge of the Light Brigade') and Coleridge (*The Rime of the Ancient Mariner*).
4. Lydia Lopokova appeared as Nora in Ibsen's *The Doll's House* on 4 March at the Arts Theatre Club, London.

success, much to our surprise. Dear Old Maynard was – this is exactly true – streaming tears; and I kissed him in the stalls between the acts; really, she was a marvel, not only a light leaf in the wind, but edged, profound, and her English was exactly what Ibsen meant – it gave the right aroma. So shes in the 7th Heaven and runs about kissing and crying. Whether it means business I dont know.

Then I was sitting brushing the dust off the bread and butter when Nelly said a very old man called Secker was at the door. I thought she meant a carpenter; but it was old Walter Sickert, come to thank me for my article on him. Up he stumped, in a green peaked cap; and said I had written the only criticism worth having in all his life. That means, it praises him to the skies. He is rather sunk, like a cracked canvas; but he sang a few bawdy songs over his cake, and smoked a cigar. He is bitter though against all Rogers and Clives I imagine; says they dont know a picture from a triangle; here he kissed my hand and said, 'Whereas you – youre an angel.' Thats what comes of laying it on with skill and thickness, my dear Quentin. However he's 74 and not long for this side of the grave I daresay, so his vanity and weariness must be excused.

Then we had a crazy party in a Lyons tea shop, where half the aristocracy in England sat on hard chairs, drank tea like vinegar and ate rancid butter. This was old Ethel Smyths celebration after the passion of her Mass. 'I hate religion' I roared into her deaf ears; and there was lovely Lady Lovat,[1] a Catholic, repining on the next chair. Ethel was in tearing spirits, fresh from the side of the Queen. What a sight they made in the Royal Box together! You are still her paragon. 'What a boy!' she keeps on saying. 'Were I only sixty years younger –'

Julian is rather bothered about his fellowship which will be out next week.[2] He thinks he may get a job at the BBC. He is writing poetry too, and editing Pope and asking about jobs in China. [. . .]

Virginia

1. Lady Lovat, *née* the Hon. Laura Lister (1892–1965), the daughter of Lord Ribblesdale. The performance of Ethel Smyth's Mass in D, part of the celebration of her 75th birthday, was conducted by Sir Thomas Beecham in the Albert Hall on 3 March. Queen Mary was in attendance.
2. Julian Bell failed in his second attempt to become a Fellow of King's, and was living mainly in London, writing poetry, but without paid employment until he went to China in 1935.

2867: To Ethel Smyth   *Monks House.* [*Rodmell,*
                                    Sussex]

Thursday 29th March (1934]

[...] Do you know – no you dont – I have gone through almost the
most disagreeable six weeks of my life, and I'm so happy, so free today.
Well this was what happened; only it sounds a little absurd after this
preamble. Nelly [Boxall], the cook, the cook we've had 18 years, has
been worrying me the past 12 months or so, and gradually I was coming
convinced we must part – d'you remember she had her kidneys out, and
the dr. appealed to me to take her back, which I did against my
judgment? Well, she's been lapsing again into her old tempers and
glooms, and I could not decide what to do. In the intervals she was
angelic and an admirable cook – and then 6 weeks ago today, when I was
ill, there was a row over an elecric oven, which we wanted to try; and she
wouldn't. And suddenly I felt this is the end; if I let her stay she will grow
on us and wither and decay. But I could not face a month with her under
notice, so I laid down a scheme to which I kept for 6 weeks, until I almost
died of it – that is I kept serenely but severely at a distance; and again and
again she tried to break me down; she cajoled and apologised, and half
suspected what was up, but not quite. And we had the whole house
decorated – floors up, books down, every room a muddle, and agony,
and she was determined not to let a word escape her; and so we went on
till this Tuesday when I sent for her to the drawing room and told her
plainly that I could stand the strain no longer and she must go. And all
Tuesday and yesterday we lived in a storm of abuse and apology, and
hysterics and appeals and maniacal threats, she entirely refusing to go,
and refusing my notice and the cheque – a handsome one – stuffing it
back in my pocket, following me about the house, till I was driven in the
cold wind to spend yesterday morning parading Oxford Street, as my
study is once more in the builders hands.

Well, we had arranged to drive off here at 2.30: and then came the
final battle, the final appeal and abuse and tears, and she refused to shake
hands with L. and so we left her, grasping a wet cloth at the sink and
glaring at us, and off we went, and she still says she will not go. 'No, no,
no, I will not leave you' I heard her vociferate, to which I said, Ah but
you must, and so we slammed the door.

Why does this scene, this long drawn out struggle with a poor
drudge demoralise one more than any love or anger scene with ones own
kind? I felt such a weight on me all those weeks thinking of how I must

dismiss her that sometimes I could hardly sit in my chair. Honestly, I have hardly sat down seriously to a book. Once the moment came, my horror vanished and I didn't mind the abuse and the tears; indeed I saw so deep into her poor muddled terrified but completely self seeking mind that I felt a thousand times reassured. And now its over, and that aching tooth removed for ever! I suppose this reads very absurd, but you dont know how she's clung all these years, or how difficult it was, considering her virtues and her complete determination to stay for ever, to make the effort. So this may excuse some of my stony-hearted silence. In the midst of our house horror – and that was intolerably sordid – every cup tasted of dust – I had to spend every afternoon for ten days dusting books and putting them back, with these awful ingratiating advances from Nelly every hour or so – 'Do let me make you a cup of tea – you look so tired' and so on – in the midst of this, Elizabeth [Williamson] came. I took her round to a room I borrowed at the Stracheys. I thought her a most stalwart and upstanding woman (please dont copy this and send it to her) full of character and interest. I shall try to see her again, – oh dear how nice the summer will be without Nelly! I shall only get a daily; I shall be free; I shall dine at the Zoo; I shall make no attachments ever again: oh how cool and quiet I feel this morning; we chuckle and chatter like a pair of pigeons.

I saw Vita who had seen you, and you saw the adored sister in law I hear [Gwen St Aubyn]. I broached the subject of C. St. J:[1] but V. would have none of it. I expect in her absorption with G. she was blind, – blinder than usual. No, I did not admire St J's article on the Mass: I thought it very skimming and surface interesting only, not criticism, only enthusiasm. But what is the worth of my opinion? On this, nothing. We plan – oh I feel so free, I repeat – a visit to Ireland at the end of the month; and one to Scotland in June, but only short tours. This is a scrabbled dull letter, but the emotions of the last 2 days have made scrambled eggs of my wits; I sit in my lodge and look, like a child of 3, at a bird; at a flower; at a butterfly. There was a butterfly, in spite of the raging wind.

V.

1. The drama critic and future biographer of Ethel Smyth, (Miss) Christopher St John (c. 1875–1960), lived with Edith Craig, Ellen Terry's daughter. St John was, however, in love with Vita, who did not return her affections.

2875: To V. Sackville-West

52 *T.*[avistock] *S.*[quare, W.C.1]

Friday 13th [April 1934]

Yes, I must really write to you, because I want to know what is happening. But that said, I've nothing to say. Thats because you're in love with another, damn you! Aren't I a nice nature, though, like a flight of green birds alighting now and then? I had meant, God knows, to apologise for being so d—d dull, so obtuse, drowsy and dreary that night at Kings Bench [Harold Nicolson's London flat]. I said to myself, no wonder Vita no longer loves you, because you bore her and if there's one thing love wont stand, its boredom. The truth was Ottoline and Nelly between them – oh what a scene I had – never will I let a servant stay 18 years again – had ground me to a kind of gray dust. That reminds me – your amethyst is on the mantelpiece beneath the stone that came from Persepolis – the 3 curls of the Emperor's head, I always think it is. [. . .]

The week after next we go to Ireland, driving all across by land, and then leaping the Channel, and staying with Eli Bowen, and so up to the wildest islands, where the seals bark and the old women croon over corpses of drowned men, dont they. And there I may be windswept in to the sea. But what would Vita care. 'No', she'd say, we had Petulaneum Ridentis in that bed last year: we'll try the Scrofulotum Penneum there this.' So she'd bury me under, wouldnt she, Vita? And yet how clever, how charming I am!

V.

2887: To Vanessa Bell   *Glenbeith, Kerry*

Thursday May 4th [3rd 1934]

We only got the Times yesterday and read about George.[1] Well, there's nothing much to be said at this distance, in the wilds of Kerry. Poor old creature – I wonder what happened and why he was at Freshwater. But I must wait till I see you, unless you've had the charity to write. Did you go to the funeral? I've just with great labour composed a letter to Margaret [his widow]. Now suppose this had happened 30

1. Sir George Duckworth, Virginia and Vanessa's half-brother, died on 27 April, aged 66, at Freshwater on the Isle of Wight, where he was staying with friends.

years ago, it would have seemed very odd to take it so calmly. As a matter of fact I feel more affection for him now than I did 10 years ago. In fact I think he had a sort of half insane quality – I cant quite make out what – about family and food and so on. But your memoir[1] so flooded me with horror that I cant be pure minded on the subject. I hope to goodness somebody went to the service – I wish I had been able to.

But here we are a great deal further and wilder than if in Italy or Greece. We only see Irish papers, now and then; there are no towns, only an occasional small fishing village and as we changed our plans, all our letters have gone wrong. It was mere chance we found a copy of the Times lying about.

We have had a most garrulous time. We never stop talking. The Irish are the most gifted of people in that line. After dinner the innkeeper comes in and sits down and talks till bedtime, perfect English, much more amusing than any London society, and if its not the innkeeper, as it was last night, then the other guests, if there are any. They all make bosom friends at once, and we're already committed practically, to buy a house at Glengariff. Its a mixture of Italy Greece and Cornwall: I suppose too romantic in parts; but extremely subtle, greys, browns, yellows, an occasional donkey, absolutely deserted, not a house ever to be seen, no gentry, everybody lamenting, because nobody comes any more, and the gentry have all fled. I daresay it would be too depressing to live in, but after Sussex I find it heavenly, and so far we have only had one bad day. We spent a night with the Bowens, where, to our horror we found the Connollys[2] – a less appetising pair I have never seen out of the Zoo, and the apes are considerably preferable to Cyril. She has the face of a golliwog and they brought the reek of Chelsea with them. However Elizabeth was very nice, and her husband [Alan Cameron], though stout and garrulous, was better than rumour reported. It is an 18th Century house, but the remarkable thing about Ireland is that (here Mrs Fitzgerald the landlady broke in for another outburst of conversation: she has given me a receipt for a perfect Onion soup) There is no architecture of any kind: all the villages are hideous; built entirely of slate in the year 1850: so Elizabeths home was merely a great stone box, but full of Italian mantelpieces and decayed 18th Century furniture, and carpets all in holes – however they insisted upon keeping up a ramshackle kind of state, dressing for dinner and so on. – Lord! this is all

1. This memoir is probably Vanessa's 'Life at Hyde Park Gate, 1897–1904, or Adventures in Society'. The manuscript is in family hands.
2. The writer and critic Cyril Connolly (1903–74) and his first wife Jean, *née* Bakewell.

very dull, but garrulity has seized upon me too. Now I must copy out the onion soup, and then we pack and go on to a place called Adare, and so to Dublin and we shall be back on Wednesday.

How is my dear Dolphin? I feel that I have been away a hundred years and dipped in the depths of the sea and anything may have happened.

Leonard says Laura[1] is the one we could have spared.

So goodbye and let me know when we can meet.

B.

2894: To Ethel Smyth   *Monk's House, Rodmell*
                                        near Lewes, Sussex

Monday [21 May 1934]

[. . .] So I came back lit the fire; and read Proust, which is of course so magnificent that I cant write myself within its arc; that's true; for years I've put off finishing it; but now, thinking I may, and indeed so they say must die one of these years, I've returned, and let my own scribble do what it likes. Lord what a hopeless bad book mine will be! [*The Years*] I tried to start it going; but its verbose, foolish, all about hollow reeds. At lunch I told L: who said anyhow one could burn it. And then I lit the fire and read Mrs Wharton; Memoirs[2] and she knew Mrs Hunter [Ethel's sister], and probably you. Please tell me sometime what you thought of her. Theres the shell of a distinguished mind; I like the way she places colour in her sentences, but I vaguely surmise that there's something you hated and loathed in her. Is there? [. . .]

Talk of my obstinacy and folly in not liking my letters to be quoted! I wrote one, casually, to an unknown but accredited American the other day, hinting at a mild literary scandal. She replies that she gave it to a friend of hers who is publishing it in The Atlantic Monthly![3] So thats why I write *Private* or should, in future. [. . .]

V.

1. Their disturbed half-sister, Laura Stephen, lived in institutions until her death in 1945.
2. The memoirs of the American novelist Edith Wharton (1862–1937) were entitled *A Backward Glance* (1934).
3. No such letter was published in the *Atlantic Monthly*.

2907: To Ethel Smyth   *52 T.[avistock] S.[quare, W.C.1.]*

Monday [2 July 1934]

[...] For the first time almost in my life I am honestly, without exaggeration, appalled by the Germans.[1] Cant get over it. How can you or anyone explain last week end! Their faces! Hitler! Think of that hung before us as the ideal of human life! Sometimes I feel that we are all pent up in the stalls at a bull fight – I go out into the Strand and read the placards, Buses passing. Nobody caring. Well as you would say, Basta. [...]

V.

2910: To Stephen Spender   *52 Tavistock Square [W.C.1]*

July 10th [1934]

Dear Stephen,

[...] I'm so happy that you read the Lighthouse with pleasure, when there are so many other books you might be reading. Some people say it is the best I wrote – others say the Waves: I never know: do you – I mean about your own books? It used to worry and puzzle me – this diversity of opinion: no I'm becoming resigned to the fact that one cant get any settled opinion, and its rather a relief, for then one can go ahead on one's own; and merely stop and enjoy the praise if one gets it.

Who was your tutors wife, I wonder?[2] I wish there were some means of circulating the people who are as beautiful and charming as that – As it is, they remain on one shelf, and we on another. I never thought Oxford bred mothers and children – only very distinguished elderly men: but I'm still under the influence as you see, of my party at the Fishers.

I'm very glad to hear that you are writing a long poem [*Vienna*]. Yes, of course I agree that poetry makes statements; and perhaps the most important; but aren't there some shades of being that it cant state? And

1. In the early morning of 30 June, Ernst Röhm, chief of the SA, the Nazi private army, was murdered by Hitler's order, and during the weekend several hundred other prominent Nazis, accused of plotting a *coup d'état* and other crimes, were ruthlessly executed.
2. Winifred Carritt, *née* Etty, wife of E. F. Carritt (1876–1964), University Lecturer in Philosophy at Oxford. Spender and his friends thought her like Mrs Ramsay in *To the Lighthouse*.

aren't these just as valuable, or whatever the term is, as any other? I am writing with prejudice, I admit, for I spent last week describing the state of reading poetry together, and I dont think you could say that in poetry.

So with an infinite number of feelings: or such is my feeling. Then I go on to say that prose, as written, is only half fledged; and has a future, and should grow – but thats my private prejudice, and no doubt rises, not from conviction, but because I am in some way stunted. Its all very complex and immensely interesting. I should like to write four lines at a time, describing the same feeling, as a musician does; because it always seems to me that things are going on at so many different levels simultaneously. I shall like anytime to read your poem; I want to read nothing but poetry.

The rock [by T. S. Eliot] disappointed me. I couldn't go and see it, having caught the influenza in Ireland; and in reading, without seeing, perhaps one got the horror of that cheap farce and Cockney dialogue and dogmatism too full in the face. Roger Fry, though, went and came out in a rage. But I thought even the choruses tainted; and rather like an old ship swaying in the same track as the Waste Land – a repetition, I mean. But I cant be sure that I wasn't unfairly influenced by my anti-religious bias. He seems to me to be petrifying into a priest – poor old Tom.

What about politics? Even I am shocked by the last week in Germany into taking part: but that only means reading the newspapers. Do write again, should you have time.

Greetings from Leonard
Yrs VW

2915: To Ethel Smyth
Monks House [Rodmell, Sussex]

Sunday [29 July 1934]

[. . .] We got here on Thursday, all Friday was spent at Worthing [with Leonard's mother]; today, like a butterfly whose wings have been crinkled up to a frazzle, (American) I begin to shake them out, and plane through the air. I've not read so many hours for how many months. Sometimes I think heaven must be one continuous unexhausted reading. Its a disembodied trance-like intense rapture that used to seize me as a girl, and comes back now and again down here, with a violence that lays me low. Did I say I was flying? How then can I be low? Because, my dear Ethel, the state of reading consists in the complete elimination of the *ego*;

and its the ego that erects itself like another part of the body I dont dare to name.

Yes I will, I suppose, I must I know, get Maurices [Baring] 'Dulwich Lady [*The Lonely Lady of Dulwich* (1934)];' but oh dear me, I dont want to. I never can submit myself to his silvery bald fingers (as a writer I mean) with any gusto. He's too white waistcoated, urbane, and in the old Etonian style for my rough palate. I cant get a thrill or a jar or any kind of acceleration out of him, any more than I can out of my dear infrequently met but always welcome Desmond MacCarthy – No, they're both what the fashion writers call 'immaculate'. But I'll try once more in deference to you. But then, since the heart has got into your brain, about Maurice, I dont think you a safe guide in those groves, those scented garden paths, down which he for ever leads some noble crinoline. I am scurrying and hurrying to write this letter, and cover this virgin page, before L: who is reading a vast history of all histories – the sort of book Mr Casaubon tried to write in Middlemarch – finally shuts the page, and says Bed, whereupon Pinka jumps down from her chair, and we go in procession through the garden to my room: where I lie, and look through the apple leaves, at the clouds that hide the stars. [. . .]

V.

2929: To Ethel Smyth   *Monks House [Rodmell,*
Sussex]

11th Sept. 1934

[. . .] we've had an awful blow – Roger Fry's death – You'll have seen – It is terrible for Nessa.[1] We took her up to London yesterday and shall probably go up on Thursday again for the service – music only I think. He was to me the most heavenly of men – so I know you'll understand my dumb mood. – so rich so infinitely gifted – and oh how we've talked and talked – for 20 years now.

V.

1. After their love affair ended in 1914, Vanessa Bell and Roger Fry had remained close friends.

2936: To George Rylands   *Monks House, Rodmell,*
Near Lewes, Sussex

Sept 27th [1934]

Dearest Dadie,

I don't know that I had anything very definite in mind about dialogue – only a few random generalisations. My feeling, as a novelist, is that when you make a character speak directly you're in a different state of mind from that in which you describe him indirectly: more 'possessed', less self conscious, more random, and rather excited by the sense of his character and your audience. I think the great Victorians, Scott (no – he wasn't a Vn.) but Dickens, Trollope, to some extent Hardy all had this sense of an audience and created their characters mainly through dialogue. Then I think the novelist became aware of something that can't be said by the character himself; and also lost the sense of an audience. (I've a vague feeling that the play persisted in the novelist's mind, long after it was dead – but this may be fantastic: only as you say novelists are fantastic.) Middlemarch I should say is the transition novel: Mr Brooke done directly by dialogue: Dorothea indirectly. Hence its great interest – the first modern novel. Henry James of course receded further and further from the spoken word, and finally I think only used dialogue when he wanted a very high light.

This is all rather incoherent, and also, as is the case with all theories, too definite. At the same time I do feel in the great Victorian characters, Gamp, Micawber, Becky Sharp, Edie Ochiltree [in Scott's *The Antiquary*], an abandonment, richness, surprise, as well as a redundancy, tediousness and superficiality which makes them different from the post Middlemarch characters. Perhaps we must now put our toes to the ground again and get back to the spoken word, only from a different angle; to gain richness, and surprise. [. . .]

2946: To Ethel Smyth   *52 Tavistock Square, W.C.1.*

Thursday [1 November 1934]

[. . .] I sat up so late last night talking to Aldous Huxley a most witty and cosmopolitan minded man that I'm in a state which cant be called either one or other – [. . .]

Aldous fired me to read Italian Latin Greek to travel, to see – its true he's blind of one eye, which accounts I think for his erudition – If I had only one eye I should cease to flaunt and flare (I've been walking up Kingsway merely to gaze my fill) and should (so I say) learn my letters. And you've done it all – thats what I like about you, looked and lusted, and tasted, and learnt, and lolled in a quarry – surely that quarry in the Aldershot region ought to have its tablet 'Here Ethel Smyth, dismounted from her bicycle, and lost her virginity.' I'll see to it. A chaste circle of blue china. Think of the tourists coming to peer. Do you give me leave? How are you getting on with the memoirs? I'll read or not read just as you like. Did I tell you I met Yeats, at Ottolines? And he said (this is my vanity) 'I'm writing about The Waves; which . . .' Now I took that for a compliment, on the lips of our greatest living poet.

V.

2949: To Ethel Smyth   *52 T.[avistock] S.[quare, W.C.1]*

Tuesday [6 November 1934]

[. . .] I long to hear your impressions of P^{ss}. Mary.[1] I'm told she is mutton-faced, mutton-minded, and sheep-natured: that she slightly repels; and has only one remark 'Good luck'. – to those who win races. So what did she say to you? And how did she endure the musical harmonies? It is said (I've been seeing a courtier[2]) that H.M. the Queen [Mary] is so constituted that Beethoven causes her acute indigestion. [. . .]

V.

2966: To Victoria Ocampo[3]   *Monk's House, Rodmell, Lewes [Sussex]*

Dec 22nd 34

Dear Victoria,
    [. . .] I like Aldous's mind immensely: not his imagination. I mean,

1. Only daughter of King George V and married to the Earl of Harewood. She had attended one of Ethel's concerts.
2. She may have meant the young Director of the National Gallery, Kenneth Clark, (1903–83), whom she had met dining with Clive Bell on 31 October.
3. Virginia had met Victoria Ocampo (1890–1979) with Aldous Huxley at a recent exhibition of Man Ray's photographs. She was an Argentinian of wealth and cultural influence through her magazine *Sur*. She and Virginia formed a quick friendship that continued through correspondence and meetings during Ocampo's frequent trips to London.

when he says 'I Aldous...' I'm with him: what I dont like is 'I Rampion –' or whatever the mans' name may be.[1] But you've said all this and much more to my liking. I hope you will go on to Dante, and then to Victoria Okampo. Very few women yet have written truthful autobiographies. It is my favourite form of reading (I mean when I'm incapable of Shakespeare, and one often is) [. . .]

V.W

2973: To Ethel Smyth   *Monks House [Rodmell, Sussex]*

Tuesday 9th [8] Jan. 1935

It is so cold I cant stretch out far enough from the fire to get a blameless sheet. I think this one has been sat on by the marmozet.[2] I admit I've been silent – oh but what a compliment to you that is! Every day I polish off a crop of nettles; never do I get any letter (except from Woking) of pure affection. All the rest implore, command, badger, worry. Here's Lady Rhondda, heres a man who wants a puff, a woman who wants a preface; and that d——d ass Elizabeth Bibesco – So we go round and round the prickly pear: only Ethel remains unredeemed, a very flagstaff of British oak. Its an age since I unloaded my breast. In the first place did I tell you about the death of that dear bright little – no rather heroic – Francis Birrell? He had cancer of the brain, and I had to go and sit with him 2 or 3 times after he knew he was dying; might linger paralysed, or die mad. And did he show it? No, in spite of being an atheist, there he lay cracking his little jokes, with his face paralysed. But what, my dear Ethel, do you think it all means? What would you have said to a friend – 25 years I've known him – dying at 45, full of love of life, – just beginning to live? And we both knew he was dying: and what was there to say about it? Nothing. I feel like a dead blue sea after all these deaths – cant feel any more.

So to the Sitwells. One night before coming here I met Osbert, who said Hows Ethel Smyth? Do ask her when you see her, – did my father propose to her? Because thats the family story. So I ask you. Did he?

---

1. Mark Rampion, a character in Huxley's *Point Counter Point* (1928), was modelled on D. H. Lawrence.
2. In July of the previous year Leonard had been given a marmoset, which accompanied him everywhere.

And was that why he married the woman who went to prison,[1] (hereby breeding O. and Edith and Sashy [Sacheverell] – not I think to the ultimate glory of the British tongue, fond as I am of parts of them.)

At the same time how happy we are here! Cooking dinner; and walking – oh what miles I've walked, right into remote valleys; with a thorn tree, and a shell. I always think the ice has only melted off the downs a year or two ago – the primeval ice – green ice, smooth ice

Its true, we had a childrens' party and I judged the clothes. All the mothers gazed, and I felt like – who's the man in the bible[2] – ? Which by the way, I have bought and am reading. And Renan.[3] And the New Testament; so dont call me heathen in future. I'm pained, rather, to use my grandmother's language, about Vita and Gwen. I had a moments talk with Harold, and he hinted, and I hinted: the upshot of it being he thinks V. has grown very slack. So I said, 'she sits in her red tower and – dreams'. Upon which he cocked his eyebrow and said 'Thats precisely it. She refuses to see anyone but' – Now this has taken me 7 mins. ¾ to write. And all the MSS. remain unread. And the log is blazing. And I shall sleep sound. And write in my new garden hut which looks over the marsh: – did I tell you? So raise your voice and thank me for this now 10 minute letter; and hook the ink to you and reply.

Yr V.

2978: To Ethel Smyth   52 T[avistock] S[quare, W.C.1]

Wednesday (23 January 1935]

[. . .] why do you always compound 'intelligence' with destructive criticism? Roger [Fry], who was the most intelligent of my friends was profusely, ridiculously, perpetually creative: couldnt see 2 matches without making them into a boat. That was the secret of his charm and genius. Its some grit thats got into your eye from meeting [F.L.] Peter Lucas here – a prig and a pedant if ever there was one: but a sweet prig: and anyhow he's the only one. And you're always protesting and self-conscious and with your hackles pricked about critics. But enough

---

1. This incident fascinated Virginia. See Letter 1414, p. 176, note 2.
2. Probably Solomon – I Kings 3, vv. 16–28.
3. Ernest Renan (1823–92), the French historian of religion, whose work included *St Paul* (1869), which Virginia was reading, and the more famous *Vie de Jésus* (1863).

as Lady Ponsonby[1] used to say. What a convenience it is to make your friends speak for me! Oh I've been in such a howling duststorm – to sit alone and read the Bible is like drawing into a sunny submarine hollow between deep waves.

Adieu
VW

2984: To Ethel Smyth   *Monks House, Rodmell*
                                            [Sussex]

9th Feb: [1935]

When a person's thick to the lips in finishing a book [*Beecham and Pharaoh*], (like you) its no use pretending that they have bodies and souls so far as the rest of the world is concerned. They turn the sickle side of the moon to [the] world: the globe to the other. This profound psychological truth I've so often proved, and now respect in you, so dont write. One of these days our moons shall shine broad in each others' faces – when I come to Woking. [. . .]

So I kiss the top of your head and farewell

V.

What a comfort to think that nothing I could say or do would make you think better or worse of me.

3015: To Vanessa Bell   *Hotel des Pays-Bas, Utrecht,*
                                            Holland

May 7th [1935]

Here we are in the middle of Holland.[2] So far it has been perfect – blazing sun, until today no accidents, except killing one hen, but it was the hen's fault. It is extremely difficult driving however, as the streets are very narrow, and there are millions of cyclists – like flocks of swallows, and innumerable racing cars. Even Cousin Thea [Dorothea Stephen,

---

1. The wife of Sir Henry Ponsonby (1825–95), who was for many years Private Secretary to Queen Victoria. After his death, Lady Ponsonby became a Lady-in-Waiting and was said to be the only person of whom the Queen was frightened. Ethel's stormy friendship with her lasted nearly thirty years until Lady Ponsonby's death in 1916. Ethel wrote about her at length in *As Time Went On* (1936).
2. This was a month's excursion by car to Holland, Germany, Italy (where the Woolfs met Vanessa, Quentin and Angelica), and back through France.

aged 64] would cycle if she were a dutchwoman. We have been to Amsterdam, Dordrecht, Zutphen and Haarlem. Its all next door – I mean towns are only across 6 fields. The great point about it is the beauty of the architecture; and the awnings, which are all colours, and the canals, and the tulips, and flowering trees, weeping their reflections into the water – can such a thing be said? [. . .]

Tomorrow we start for Germany: but I dont think we shall be interned,[1] owing to Mitzi [the marmoset]. We are received everywhere like film stars, generally there is a crowd of 20 round the car when we stop. All the children come running; old ladies are sent for: they always end by offering to show us the way or do anything for us – such is their love of Apes[2] (please consider this). [. . .]

Its very expensive here, and I think we have spent more in one week than in 3 elsewhere, and there is not much human beauty, but every virtue – cleanliness, honesty and so on: bad coffee; delicious biscuits: the cows wear brown holland coats; and its amazingly lovely – the streets and the water and the marshes and the barges and the . . . but I will stop this sentence, for the plain fact I cant form my letters only I must say you ought to paint the tulip fields and the hyacinth fields all laid out flat with about 20 miles of water in and out, 18 sheep, 6 windmills, sun setting, moon rising. So goodbye. I agree about Vitas transformation. Harold says its the Change of life – I say its love –

B

3025: To Ethel Smyth   [*52 Tavistock Square, W.C.1*]

[2 June 1935]

I'm sorry I've been incommunicative, but I can only write letters when my mind is full of bubble and foam; when I'm not aware of the niceties of the English language. You dont know the bother it is, using for one purpose what I'm perpetually using for another. Could you sit down and improvise a dance at the piano after tea to please your friends? And now, home here, I shall drink no more wine – now we're landed, and are strewn with bills, letters, manuscripts, dark men from the East who must see Leonard – etc etc. I cant count the number of flies settled on this dead horse.

1. Not entirely a joke. That Leonard was a Jew was a cause for realistic concern in Germany at this time.
2. A reversion to one of Virginia's childhood nicknames for herself.

And talking of death, the first thing that happened as we drew up at Monks House was meeting poor old Pinka's dead body. She had a fit and died the day before we came. and here was Percy [Bartholomew, the gardener] burying her in her basket and we were both very unhappy – This you'll call sentimental – perhaps – but then a dog somehow represents – no I cant think of the word – the private side of life – the play side.

Did I tell you in my drunken bout that I was offered a red ribbon, and to be one of the 18 or so ladies and gentlemen calling themselves Companions of Honour, and to walk into the room behind you, the Dames? I said No thanks; I dont believe in Honours, though Ethel Smyth, I said, does. Was I right? – Would you like to see me wearing a red ribbon and walking behind you? Oh what d——d nonsense it all is! [. . .]

V

3047: To Vanessa Bell   *52 Tavistock Sqre. [W.C.1]*

17th July [1935]

I was just sitting down to write to you last night when Julian came in to say that he has got the Chinese professorship.[1] You will have heard from him already. He seemed very excited, though also rather alarmed at the prospect. I wish it weren't for so long – though he says he can come back after a year. Still I suppose its a great chance, and means that he will easily get something in England afterwards. Leonard thinks it an extraordinarily interesting job as it will mean being in the thick of Chinese politics, and Julian also felt this – what it means Chinese politics, I dont know, nor I suppose do you. We had a long talk, and he was very charming and said that he felt it was time he made a complete break. [. . .]

This is the most exciting news naturally. Otherwise I was going to tell you about the horrors of going to Bristol to open Roger's show. Really the Frys – in the first place, it was broiling hot; then we lost our way and only got there just in time. Then there was a large audience, all of the most stodgy and respectable; then they kept an electric fan going

1. Julian Bell had applied more than a year before to the Cambridge Appointments Board for a teaching job in a foreign university, preferably in the Far East. He was now offered, and accepted, the Professorship of English at Wuhan University, 400 miles up the Yangtze River from Nanking.

so that I could hardly make myself heard – then I felt in my bones that neither Margery [Fry] nor Pamela [Diamand] much liked what I said. In short it was all rather an absurd waste of time and energy, I felt – though I thought Roger's pictures, as far as I could see them in the crowd, a good deal better than I expected. Margery never wrote and thanked me – and in fact I feel that the Frys view of Roger is completely different from ours, and I'm in rather a puzzle to know what to do about seeing Margery before I go. I'm sure she'll disapprove of anything I write.[1] Yet I feel she means to hold me to it. Julian agrees – thinks her almost crazed on the subject, and advises me to keep clear of her: but how am I to? Anyhow, I feel sure she didn't like my innocent and highly eulogistic speech for some reason. [. . .]

B.

I have been asked to be President of the P E. N Club in succession to Wells: this is about the greatest insult that could be offered a writer, or a human being.

3056: To Ethel Smyth   *Monks House [Rodmell, Sussex]*

Saturday [10 August 1935]

[. . .] Since coming here I have poured out tea for 15 self-invited guests: I have been to London; I have read a dozen MSS. of tepid trash and then you call me lazy! Then you say I forget old friends! – ranking yourself apparently with the fairy who bent over my cradle and whispered music in my ear. Well, aint it odd, how, a mere four year old like you – for it is now precisely four years since you caught me a cuff over the head for telling you – I forget what, but I remember falling flat on the drawing room floor – aint it odd how free and easy we are together: and what pains over your heart is like a breeze over corn in mine. Now any critic, anyone trained in the art of letters at Cambridge, like your friend Peter Lucas, could tell from that last sentence, with its recurring rhythm, and visual emblem – why dont they make me Prof. of English – I'd teach em – would know from that sentence that I've just come in from a long hot walk over the downs and sat by myself in a

---

1. Margery Fry had first thought to write her brother's life herself, but then, as his literary executor, she asked Virginia to undertake the project. In spite of her misgivings, Virginia agreed.

cornfield. If ever you come this way, I'll take you to Muggery Poke [a farm]. There we'll seal our love on a floor where the nettles push among the cow droppings. It was deserted 50 years ago, and I go there every Saturday to muse upon my youth – [. . .]

V.

3060: To ETHEL SMYTH   *Monks House [Rodmell, Sussex]*

Tuesday [3 September 1935]

[. . .] I went to Siss^t: and Vita was so seductive in her sailors trousers, and we had 15 minutes alone – the first this year – and I'm sorry you dismiss her. G. [Gwen] was there, like a drowning cat; wet, white, and Harold – Red, robust.

V.

3069: To JULIAN BELL   *52 Tavistock Square [W.C.1]*

14th Oct 1935

Dearest Julian,

Nessa says it is possible to write to you, which for some reason I had thought doubtful. Now the great thing is to make a beginning, and then to trust that you will answer. So I lead off – only I'm told one must be careful. Well, we had a great family meeting the other night and Nessa read your journey letter aloud and it was we all said a very good letter; only rather melancholy. You were on board ship, and it had been very hot in the Red Sea. Then she had a cable to say youd arrived. Now I suppose you are teaching the Chinks about Mrs Gaskell – which seems an odd thing to do. Oh dear how I wish television were now installed and I could switch on and see you, instead of tap tapping [i.e. typing], which curtails my ideas and castrates my style. But then, I take it, you cant read the only hand that gives me any currency.

As for news – well, after you left we had old Tom [Eliot] to stay the week end; he was urbanity itself, and we had a good deal of old crones talk about people like Middleton Murry, Wyndham Lewis and so on. He's determined to write plays about modern life in verse, and rather crusty when reviewers say he's an old fogy. In fact I think he feels that hes only just beginning to write what he wants. Whether hes on the turn, religiously speaking, I'm not sure. He had an early cup of tea on Sunday and went to Communion. It was a wet morning too, and when I came down to get breakfast there he was dew sprinkled, saying that he had met three old women in the churchyard and one of them said, as he passed, 'Yes, there she was lying in bed with a still born child by her side'. A nice way of beginning Sunday. We dined with the Keynses, and Maynard commissioned him to write a play for the new theatre.[1]

Then we went to the Brighton conference, which was better than any play.[2] To hear first old Lansbury a true Christian, but with an eye, I thought to the gallery – I mean the [Brighton] Dome, not Heaven; and then [Ernest] Bevin like a snake whos swallowed a toad, denouncing him, crushing him 'Some people like to go hawking their consciences about' he said – while poor Lansbury squirmed behind him; this was as good as any play – not that Ive seen one. But I wont write politics; They are now all in a stir about the election, said to come off in November.

I am beginning to work at Rogers letters [for her biography], and have by the way had a scrawl from Ha to say that the Mallarmé is all off, owing to the monstrous behaviour of the Mallarmé people in Paris.[3] I gather theyve refused to have any further dealings; but on what grounds I dont know. Doubtless she'll tell you. Rogers letters are fascinating; an awful mix; the family ones very stiff; the travel ones rather dull; but always some flash of interest; and some to Basil Williams[4] extremely amusing. But I cant think how to deal with it – or whether to deal with it. I wish you were here to discuss the whole thing. Did you write anything [about Fry]? I hope so. One might write a whole long book; I rather suspect its a case either of a long book or a short essay. But I must go on

1. The Cambridge Arts Theatre, which Keynes inspired and helped to finance. Eliot did not write for it.
2. At the Labour Party conference the Woolfs heard George Lansbury (1859–1940), the Labour leader and pacifist, who opposed the imposition of sanctions on Italy for invading Abyssinia. He had to resign his leadership in the face of opposition led by Ernest Bevin (1881–1951), General Secretary of the TGWU, 1921–40.
3. Nonetheless, in the next year there did appear Roger Fry's translations of some Stéphane Mallarmé poems, with a commentary by Charles Mauron. Julian Bell helped with the editing and translated some of the poems.
4. A friend from Fry's Cambridge days, Basil Williams was Professor of History at Edinburgh University, 1925–37.

reading. Your C.O. book has come for L. to review.[1] I thought Adrian very good – the only one Ive looked at.

Last night we dined with Clive; present, Nessa, Duncan and Sally [the Woolfs' spaniel]. We discussed criticism; and at what point the critical faculty dies. I think mine is just able to deal with poetry this year; but will be dead next year. So hurry up and write some.

We are all well in health, and spry in spirit; but rather miss you, and I wish Q. wasnt going up to the potteries,[2] however I rather suspect we shall make a push and come to China.

I must now go and see an importunate and unfortunate Gerwoman[3] who thinks I can help her with facts about Women under Democracy – little she knows – what you do about your poor old Virginia.

3082: TO ANGELICA BELL[4]

52 *Tavistock Square* [*W.C.1*]
(*but we're really at Monks
House for the moment.*)

Sunday Nov. 18th [17th, 1935]

Darling dearest Pix;

Here we are, in a down pour; frogs weather; but I was so delighted to get your deceitful letter that I try to dry my webbed claws, having become to all purposes a toad, and write. Again once again you took me in. 'Beale Cunningham as I live!' I howled, seeing your envelope on my plate.[5] How do you know precisely how to take me in with her writing? – And then it turns into you. And then the very next day comes her book; which is all about keeping goldfish in Paris; and falling in love with Jews; and it begins well; but swells into such a mish-mash of words, about love and Jews and how to train vines over pergolas and wear silk pyjamas – In fact I think she must be mad; and I ought to write and tell her so. If you should meet a dumpy but washy woman, who loved a Jew

1. *We Did Not Fight* (1935), a collection of eighteen autobiographical essays by British conscientious objectors in the First World War, edited with an introduction by Julian Bell. Among the contributors were Virginia's brother Adrian Stephen, David Garnett and Siegfried Sassoon.
2. To learn the craft of pottery at Stoke-on-Trent.
3. Ruth Grüber, who wrote, in English, *Virginia Woolf: a Study* (1935).
4. Angelica Bell, who would soon be 17, was in Paris to learn French. She was staying with friends of the Bussys, Zoum and François (b. 1903) Walter. He was an active Socialist and the editor of the French anti-Fascist journal *Vigilance*. Virginia had met him in October.
5. Beall Cunningham, whose new novel was *Wide White Page*.

in the Palais Royal, drop a pebble down her back and tell her to empty her ink pot into the Seine and never write another word, with my love.

We came down here on Thursday for the Election. Leonard had to drive voters to the Poll – not parrot – would that it had been – for three hours in a downpour. And after all our Mr [F. R.] Hancock [Labour] was ten thousand votes behind Mr [J. de V.] Loder [Conservative]. However I will not send politics to the Asses house, for thats what he lives on. I imagine you coming down to breakfast, lifting the cover off your plate and finding nothing but AntiFascist hay, chopped very fine; with a few old herring bones. However this is not strictly according to fact; for from what you say I think you have a good eye for a witch. [. . .]

I was oh so happy to read a little common sense in your letter about sunsets and witches. The woman who thought you such a good actress[1] was Elizabeth Bowen; whos a very good writer in her way; and moves about the world and sees all sorts of actors and actresses; and she said she could see you had the real gift. We went to see Tom Eliot's play [*Murder in the Cathedral*] the other night. I think what is wanted is for some actress to make plays in which people are like ourselves only heightened; what is so bad is the complete break between the acting, the words and the scenery. Thus you lose all feeling of harmony. Why dont you make a play all in one? Thus it is much better to read plays than to see them. I am almost dazed with writing my book; and think it would be better acted. I shall make the end into a play for you to act. Some of it is good; most of it is bad. It is too long. And I have to write about Roger. At least Nessa wants me to; and Margery Fry has given me masses of letters; and all his diaries; how he dined out or went to Paris. Do you think it is possible to write a life of anyone? I doubt it; because people are all over the place. Here are you, for instance, walking in the Tuileries; and buying necklaces; and seeing the sunset; and writing to me; now which is you? Eh? I will give Mummy all your messages; only some of them are scratched out on the envelope. I like dinner better than tea; but when one has to see people one doesnt know, tea is over quicker. [. . .]

I'm dining with your admirer Raymond [Mortimer] tomorrow; to meet Aldous Huxley; oh you dont like Raymond; – Tom is bringing an American[2] to tea; and I had a long visit from Ottoline. I was late; and found her curled in my chair like a viper reading a book. We had a vipers

1. Angelica now hoped for a stage career.
2. Emily Hale, formerly from Boston, who taught at Claremont College, California. She wrote an interesting letter to Ruth George describing Virginia's conversational manner. The letter is held by Scripps College, Claremont.

talk; fascinating; about her life when she was a Duke's sister and wore a great hat and sat on the box seat for his four in hand and went to Ascot. That was thirty years ago. She took the Duke of Portland, her brother, to tea with Sheppard[1] at Kings; and Maynard was there and Lydia. The Duke said, 'Who was that Don, who married the dancing girl?' He'd never heard of Maynard. So Ottoline said, 'Hes Maynard Keynes. Very well known.' And the Duke said, 'Maynard? Any relation of the Miss Maynard who married Lord Warwick?' So you see Bloomsbury is still very very obscure.

Sally has just run in to send her love to you; but the truth is shes so passionately in love with Leonard that she cant stay in my garden room, and has just galloped off in the pouring wet because she thinks Leonard is taking flowers out of the greenhouse. And heres Leonard; and he sends his love. We want to come to Fontainebleau after Christmas. What are your plans?

Ginny

I think I shall call my book 'The Years'. Do you think it a good name? Mummy is going to do a jacket full of Donkeys Ears.

3085: To Julian Bell   *52 Tavistock Square* [*W.C.1*]

1st Dec 1935

Dearest Julian,

[...] Oh Lord – how I hate these parsons! We went to Toms play, the Murder, last week; and I had almost to carry Leonard out, shrieking. What was odd was how much better it reads than acts; the tightness, chillness, deadness and general worship of the decay and skeleton made one near sickness. The truth is when he has live bodies on the stage his words thin out, and no rhetoric will save them. Then we met Stephen Spender, who also was green at the gills with dislike, and came on to dinner one night; and told us how he has quarrelled with your friend John [Lehmann]. He wrote a story and put John in; then he sent the proofs to John, who was furious; whereupon Stephen stopped the story from appearing and rewrote it; but Johns vanity – for such I suppose it to be – was outraged; and they are on tiger-cat terms; in fact, broken off entirely. Stephen is off to Portugal with Isherwood[2]

1. J. T. Sheppard (1881–1968), Provost of King's College, Cambridge.
2. The novelist Christopher Isherwood (1904–86), another of the group of leading young writers who met Virginia and Leonard in the 1930s.

and a friend; two friends I think; of the lower orders and the male sex [. . .]

3rd Dec. I see Id better make this a diary letter; as I never get time to write for more than a minute or two. I try to read Roger in the lapses of finishing my book; but it won't finish; its like some snake thats been half run over but always pops its head up. Ive just come on this in one of Rogers letters from Charleston 1926: – youd all been to dine with the Keyneses, and Lydia would talk, 'I felt hardly able to play up and relapsed into talk with Julian and Quentin who accompanied us. Julian's very beautiful, and very charming and extremely intelligent. Hes got much of Clive but is a more serious character with bigger ambitions and altogether more to him. I've been teaching him chess and hes got on with astonishing rapidity so that I have to reduce my handicap every day.' I like compliments myself; and so hand this on. There are others equally good; but be discreet; for he says very sharp things about Clive. In fact his irritation with Clive seems to become almost an obsession – about his bagging Rogers ideas; his lack of understanding of art; his reverting to the Bell type and so on. I must ask Nessa.

Friday 6th Dec. [. . .] We had such a meeting at Adrian's last night to form a group to encourage the French [anti-Fascists]; Nessa will tell you what for. I was dumb with helpless wonder at the competence of the political; and his loquacity. There was dear old Peter [Lucas] and Aldous and Auden; besides a mass of vociferous nonentities, chiefly journalists and scrubby men with rough hair – you know the sort. Anyhow L. is doomed to another Committee; much may it profit the world. Peter's in a fuss because no one reviews his two latest efforts; and then the N.S., that is Stonier,[1] comes out with what I thought the most immoral review I almost ever read; unfair; untrue; written with a squint and a bitter poison; to which Peter, like an ass, thought good to reply, and only to say 'What a great poet am I'. Better leave others to say it. He's parching and tanning; red as a herring; and one that has no roe. (See Romeo and Juliet [II, iv, 40]) – to which we went two nights ago; and how it curled up Tom's Cathedral, and dropped it down the W.C.! Do you appreciate Shakespeare? I think you used not to. To me he becomes so miraculous, I felt, sitting there – not that Romeos one of the best – like the crowd who watch a rope go up into the air with a heavy basket on top. A thing one cant account for. Still acting it they spoil the poetry. [. . .]

I hope you wont follow Dadies [Rylands] example; I see in the paper

1. G. W. Stonier, an assistant editor at the *New Statesman & Nation* 1928–45.

hes been made [Cambridge] University lecturer in English for three years. But why teach English? As you say, all one can do is to herd books into groups, and then these submissive young, who are far too frightened and callow to have a bone in their backs, swallow it down; and tie it up; and thus we get English literature into ABC; one, two, three; and lose all sense of what its about. Thats why Auden, Spender and Day Lewis are bound together in a holy trinity – nobody reads with open eyes. All are mere catalogue makers; and thats what comes of teaching in a Chinese university. I make no doubt though that they scoop up pailsfull of what is worth having from seeing you walk about the fields with your glasses in your hands, and no nonsense about being a learned man. In fact, as the ambassador of reason and love, I can quite see you wearing a halo, bright winged, with eyes – dear me, I had thought of such a nice phrase for you, as the Chinese, of both sexes see you – and now its lunch time; and I must rush up. [. . .]

So good bye for the moment dearest Julian but let us continue this spasmodic chirp, as it is a way of converse. Love from L.

V.

1936–1937

Throughout 1936 Virginia struggled with The Years. *It made her ill and more unstable than she had been, she said, since 1913. Consequently, Leonard had to lie to her about the quality of her book, which nonetheless sold very well when it was published in 1937.*

The activities of Hitler, Mussolini and Franco inevitably increased Leonard's political work. Virginia attempted to take part, but after a brief membership in a writers' committee to fight Fascism, she turned to the pen, producing an essay for the Daily Worker *and beginning* Three Guineas, *a strong feminist statement against war. Politics became most personal when Julian Bell decided to return from China in order to participate in the Spanish Civil War against Franco. His death in Spain at the age of 29 devastated his mother Vanessa, to whom Virginia wrote almost daily letters of consolation and diversion.*

3101: To Julian Bell   *52 Tavistock Square, W.C.*

30th Jan. 1936

Dearest Julian,

[. . .] We have been, as everyone will tell you, deluged in tears and muffled in crape for the past ten days.[1] The British public has had a fit of grief which surpasses all ever known. It was a curious survival of barbarism, emotionalism, heraldry, ecclesiasticism, sheer sentimentality, snobbery, and some feeling for the very commonplace man who was so like ourselves. But it's over today thank God; the sun is shining; prize fighting has begun again; there's a splendid murder – a mans body found in a field with five shots in it – and we are all cheering up. We had a completely aquatic Christmas at Rodmell; and I kept my head down so low upon my desk trying to finish my book, that I hardly saw or spoke; in fact laid it at last on a pillow and groaned. Leonard however went the usual round, and now here we are again, involved in the usual uproar of politics, society, Indians, niggers, poets, Ethyl Smyth, – from which

1. For the death and funeral of King George V. He was buried at Windsor on 28 January.

racket I except Ann,[1] who stumped in looking like a rugger blue the other night, and Christopher Strachey, whom you ought I think to elect to the Society [The Apostles]. At least he seemed to me a bubbling Strachey, with all their brains and the Costello guts; who might turn out much to the point, Ann too, – but L. says the Society is doomed, for he's had the sacred books [minutes] on his table since June and only yesterday did the Archangel [Secretary] – is that his name – write and ask if they were lost. [. . .]

I am told on the very best authority that the new King [Edward VIII] is a cheap second rate little bounder; whose only good points are that he keeps two mistresses and won't marry and make a home; and that he likes dropping into tea with the wives of miners. But this is from Iris Origo[2] who danced with him several times; those who are more remote say on the contrary he has every virtue though not every grace; and was daily so insulted by the King that when the King died the only thing Edward could do to show his feelings was to have all the clocks put back half an hour.[3]

Love
Virginia

3104: To Hugh Walpole   *Monks House [Rodmell, Sussex]*

8th Feb. [1936]

My dear Hugh,

[. . .] I'm reading David Copperfield for the 6th time with almost complete satisfaction. I'd forgotten how magnificent it is. Whats wrong, I can't help asking myself? Why wasn't he the greatest writer in the world? For alas – no, I won't try to go into my crabbings and diminishings. So enthusiastic am I that I've got a new life of him: which makes me dislike him as a human being. Did you know – you who know

1. Ann Stephen (b. 1916), daughter of Adrian and Karin, *née* Costelloe, was then an undergraduate at Cambridge, as was her cousin Christopher Strachey (1916–75), the son of Rachel (Karin's sister) and Oliver Strachey.
2. Marchesa Iris Origo (*née* Cutting, 1902–88), whose second book, *Allegra*, was published by The Hogarth Press in 1935. She lived in Siena with her husband, Marchese Antonio Origo.
3. The fact, but not the implied motive, was correct. King George had always kept the clocks at Sandringham half an hour fast. The first decision of the new King was to restore them to Greenwich time.

everything – the story of the actress?[1] He was an actor, I think; very hard; meretricious? Something had shrivelled? And then his velvet suit, and his stupendous genius? But you wont want to be discussing Dickens at the moment.

I too must fling my clothes into a bag and drive up through the villa residences to London.

You meanwhile are sitting with vast blue plains rolling round you: a virgin forest at your back; a marble city [Los Angeles] gleaming at your feet; and people so new, so brave, so beautiful and so utterly uncontaminated by civilization popping in out of booths and theatres with pistols in their hands and aeroplanes soaring over their heads – sometimes you find a bleeding corpse in the street but nobody thinks much of that – Well, I've no space to describe Hollywood to you, and so must leave you to your cocktail. When are you coming back?

yrs aff
V.W.

3111: To Julian Bell   *52 T[avistock] S[quare, W.C.1]*

11th March 1936

Dearest Julian,

[. . .] As you can imagine, we are all under the shadow of Hitler at the moment[2] – even Nessa and Duncan start a conversation by saying, What is your opinion, Leonard, of whats-his-name? They ask intelligent questions about colonies. As for Leonard he works all day, drafting measures for the Labour party; answering that gaby Kingsley Martin,[3] who cant make up his own mind without tapping every other mind within a radius of twenty miles. He always interrupts our one resource against politics which is music. That's why I curse him. [. . .]

We're all very well; and I think Nessa seems more than usually cheerful. She's taken her own line in London life; refuses to be a celebrated painter; buys no clothes; sees whom she likes as she likes; and altogether leads an indomitable, sensible and very sublime existence. I

1. In Thomas Wright's *Life of Charles Dickens* (1935), Virginia had read about the novelist's affair with the actress Frances Eleanor Ternan, which lasted many years and contributed to his estrangement from his wife.
2. On 7 March Hitler sent his troops into the Rhineland in defiance of the Treaty of Versailles and the Locarno Pact. Britain and France took no action to force him to withdraw.
3. Kingsley Martin, editor of the *New Statesman & Nation*, 1931–60.

won't go into the Duncan Queen Mary affair as I expect you have it first hand already.[1] And L. will put you wise one of these days when he gets a chink of time about politics. As for Clive, he's been to Paris; and then dines out, so that we seldom meet. And when we meet, theres a kind of straining to keep the two dogs from each others throats. Not that I mind a good row; but for all you say about the Apostles, your father is now such a flibbertigibbet one can't expect him to hit it off with L. who takes it all like doom and destruction. I think Clive got on Roger's nerves towards the end, and I expect he was hard on him. But it also seems to me pretty clear that Clive did pilfer a good deal without acknowledge-ment from Roger; and as Roger was half persecution mad – only he was far too sweet and sane to let the disease rip – he minded being pilfered far more than was reasonable. Then Helen [Anrep] was inclined to rub the spot.

As for your Apostles, much though I respect them singly, I begin to think that these Societies do more harm than good, merely by rousing jealousies and vanities. What d'you think? it seems to me the wrong way to live, drawing chalk marks round ones feet, and saying to the Clives etc you can't come in. However that maybe a private whim of my own; nothing would make me take a feather of any dye to stick in my hat. [. . .]

much love dearest Julian from us both.

Virginia

3136a: To Julian Bell   *Monk's House, Rodmell*
                                         [Lewes, Sussex]

May 21st 1936

Dearest Julian,

[. . .] I think you are much to be envied. I wish I had spent three years in China at your age – the difference was, though, that at your age, what with all the family deaths and extreme intensities – father, mother, Stella, Thoby, George Jack [Waller Hills] – I felt I had lived through all emotions and only wanted peace and loneliness. All the horrors of life had been pressed in to our eyes so very crude and raw. And then came the burst of splendour, those two years at Gordon Square before Thoby

---

1. The decorative panels which Duncan Grant had been commissioned to paint for the lounge of the new Cunard liner *Queen Mary* had been rejected by the Chairman of the Company as unlikely to please the type of passenger he hoped to attract. This action struck many of Duncan's friends as both unethical and philistine, and they demanded that he be compensated.

died, a kind of Elizabethan renaissance, much though I disliked the airs that young Cambridge gave itself. I found an old diary which was one violent shriek of rage at Saxon and Lytton sitting there saying nothing, and with no emotional experience, I said. But I mustn't begin writing my autobiography. How I wish I had known you in those days. Only I should have fallen in love with you, after my fashion, and you would have loved Nessa, because I always thought her so very much more lovable than I was. More autobiography! [...]

I don't much want to plunge into London at the moment; what I wish is that we could take a lonely farm on the moor above Zennor [Cornwall]. You can't think what a place that is. We stayed with the Arnold Forsters, who are a highly commendable, public spirited pair, without much of the charm or succulence of our group, despising the flesh, with very hard beds, very mangy meals, but always rung up by the local committees and always speaking, administering the law, helping the poor, lecturing in remote coves on Peace, giving large teas to unknown struggling down-at-heels intellectuals of a very minor sort – what a snob I am! The fact is I like Bloomsbury much best; but can't help seeing how valuable and necessary the other sort is, the world being what the world is. Will is rather acid, and paints like a typewriter, line after line, and then whips off to America and preaches. I don't feel at my ease with him; and Leonard thinks him probably a humbug. He's very vain that is, and his wife, who loved Rupert Brooke, praises him at every other moment as wives praise husbands they don't love, by way of excusing their own marriage. You know the sort, and how obvious their commendation sounds and how hollow. Also she loves the County; can't open her mouth without bringing in some titled Squire, and falls in with all their respectabilities. Still she, again, is a good hearted woman; and a model of all a magistrate should be. But what I liked was the country. We must go there together. There were ravens at Bosigran; I heard them barking, and then they flew round my head. Ka had seen a badger the night before we came. It's the most lovely and peculiar of all countries I think. We stayed at a very large country house now an hotel [Budock Vean] near Falmouth and dribbled in and out of all those little bays, incredibly lonely and unspoilt, with here an old castle, there a granite cross and the sea always at the end of the lane. Yes, I am going to buy a cottage there, because Sussex is getting far too pretty and suburban. Will you share it with me? We will live there for months at a time roaming the moors, sitting on the top of the cliffs, watching birds. [...]

I don't see why you should worry yourself to write a novel. It's such a long gradual cold handed business. What I wish is that you'd invent some medium that's half poetry half play half novel. (Three halves, I see; well, you must correct my arithmetic.) I think there ought to be a scrambling together of mediums now. The old are too rigid; but then one must have a terrific technique to explode the old forms and make a new one, to say nothing of a lump of fire in one's brain, or the new form is merely a pose. Still I don't see why, with your odd assortment of gifts – philosophy, poetry, politics, and some human interest, you shouldn't be the one to do it. These other young men always seem to be stuck in some hypnotic trance; partly fear of what other young men will say, partly dread of their own emotions. Now when you've been away in China you'll have much less sensitiveness to current opinion. [. . .]

Love V

3140: To Ethel Smyth *M.[onk's] H.[ouse, Rodmell, Sussex*

Saturday [6 June 1936]

[. . .] I'm afraid I wrote a wail to you – No – I'm not feeling 'at an end' at all. Rather the other way. Heres my brain teeming with books I want to write – Roger, Lytton, Room of ones Own[1] etc etc – and I can only just manage one wretched ¾ hour proof correcting [*The Years*]. Thats my plaint. If only I could be free from this recurring nuisance! But its much better. Never trust a letter of mine not to exaggerate thats written after a night lying awake looking at a bottle of chloral and saying no, no, no, you shall not take it. Its odd why sleeplessness, even of a modified kind has this power to frighten me. Its connected I think with those awful other times when I couldn't control myself.[2] But enough, as Lady P [Ponsonby] (was it?) would say. I'm ever so much better today, and making up unwritten books at a great rate. My folly was I would do all

1. *Roger Fry*, which was not finished until 1940; a biography of Lytton Strachey, requested by the Strachey family, but never undertaken; and a sequel to *A Room of One's Own*, which eventually emerged in 1938 as *Three Guineas*.
2. The strain of finishing her now dreaded novel *The Years* had caused Virginia to collapse at Monk's House in April. In her diary of 11 June, Virginia wrote: 'I can only, after 2 months, make this brief note, to say at last after 2 months dismal and worse, almost catastrophic illness – never been so near the precipice to my own feeling since 1913 – I'm again on top' (*Diary*, V, 24). She was wrong. The full burden was not lifted until she finished the novel at the end of November.

the Fry papers in between times up till Easter: made 3 stout volumes of extracts: which takes thought.

I rather think I shall try a few days in London. I'm longing to see you, to talk, to dine out, to go to operas, ballets, pictures, to walk in Bond Street – but no.

You understand that if I dont ask you to come it is simply that I dare not get another bout and see my poor L. look as if we were both standing on the gallows. He has been most perfectly angelic – but eno' as Lady P. wd. say

Let me hear about the puppy.

V.

3146: To Ethel Smyth   *[52 Tavistock Square, W.C.1]*

[25 June 1936]

[. . .] I'm almost floored by the extreme dexterity insight and beauty of Colette.[1] How does she do it? No one in all England could do a thing like that. If a copy is ever going I should like to have one – to read it again. and see how its done: or guess. And to think I scarcely know her books! Are they all novels? Is it the great French tradition that lifts her so serenely, and yet with such a flare down, down to what she's saying? I'm green with envy: (all the same I've just done my first batch of proofs: considering my head was mostly like a boiled pudding laced about with red hot nerves this is to my credit as a woman – bad though the book is as a book) [. . .]

V.

3146a: To Julian Bell   *Monk's House, Rodmell [Sussex]*

June 28th 1936

My dearest Julian,

[. . .] I read your thing on Roger[2] only very slowly. I think it's full of ideas; full of sharp insights; and there are a mass of things I would like to

1. Ethel had sent Virginia an article on Anna de Noailles by the French fiction writer Sidonie-Gabrielle Colette (1873–1954). Virginia read at least three of Colette's books, two of autobiography (*Mes Apprentissages*, 1934, *Sido*, 1929), and one of fiction (*Duo*, 1934), and the two writers sent each other messages through mutual friends.
2. Julian's critical essay, 'On Roger Fry', was offered to the Woolfs for the Hogarth Letters series. It was also intended to help Virginia with Fry's biography. Julian was terribly hurt by this response and did not write to his aunt for several months.

pilfer if I write, as I hope next autumn. My criticism is; first that you've not mastered the colloquial style, which is the hardest, so that it seemed to me (but my mind was weak) to be discursive, loose knit, and uneasy in its familiarities and conventions. However you could easily pull it together. Prose has to be so tight, if it's not to smear one with mist. L. has read it and agrees with me on the whole. As Nessa may have told you, we can't use it as a letter, because it's too long; also, the letter series has proved a failure, and we have stopped it. What L. suggests is that it should be sent to [R. A.] Scott James [editor] of the Mercury, who might print it in two parts. Even so, I expect he would ask you to shorten it. [. . .]

I am in trouble with the Writers Society – got up by Aldous [Huxley] and Morgan [Forster], which held a conference in London last week,[1] which I did not attend. There M. Malraux[2] developed violent symptoms of rabid communism; and Raymond [Mortimer], who was present, thinks I must resign on these grounds. As I've already said, Societies seem wrong for me, as I do nothing; and with Leonard meeting a dozen times a week and filling the drawing room with Bernal and Miss Gardiner[3] and Ha [Margery Fry] and Aldous we do our bit for liberty. What can I do but Write? Hadn't I better go on writing – even by the light of the last combustion? And it all ends in private squabbles. M. [François] Walter has quarrelled with M. somebody else; so it goes on. But I assure you, never a day passes but we don't get asked either to sign a protest, telegraph a message, or join a new group. [. . .]

[. . .] we had tea at Charleston, on Sunday, and found them all very well, and I think once more hopped out of the frying pan on to the cool green pastures of the painters art. How I envy them! There they sit, looking at pinks and yellows, and when Europe blazes all they do is to screw their eyes up and complain of a temporary glare in the foreground. Unfortunately, politics get between me and fiction. I feel I must write something when this book is over – something vaguely political; doubtless worthless, certainly useless. [. . .]

1. The second meeting (the first was held in Paris in 1935) of the International Congress of Writers, a left-wing society whose avowed objective was the 'Defence of Culture' against Fascism.
2. The political novelist (*Man's Fate*) André Malraux (1901–79) had organised the first meeting.
3. John Desmond Bernal (1901–71), always called 'Sage'. A crystallographer at Cambridge, he was afterwards (1937–63) Professor of Physics at the University of London and a well-known Marxist who received the Lenin Peace Prize in 1953. He shared his house with Margaret Gardiner.

You've heard of Clive's honour [the Legion of Honour] – now what induced him to tie that blob of red ribbon to his tail? Aren't human beings ridiculous? He made a speech at Oxford in French to air the fact – rather to the undergraduates amazement, according to David Cecil, who heard him. [. . .]

Vita has produced a life of Joan of Arc; a solid, wordy, worthy work, in every way the opposite of Lytton, of whom my opinion rises the more I read other peoples lives and essays. He had mastered the art of saying what he meant – and in prose how difficult that is! They remain stated finished controlled – even those little biographies of his.[1] Lord, how I wish he'd lived – I sometimes feel that old Bloomsbury though fast dying, is still our bulwark against the tawny flood. So come back and drive your stake in, before we are overwhelmed. [. . .]

V

3147: TO V. SACKVILLE-WEST   *Monks House [Rodmell, Sussex]*

Monday 29th June [1936]

[. . .] Whats interesting [about *Saint Joan of Arc*] is the whole, however, not the parts. I keep speculating – which is what I enjoy most in all books: not themselves: what they make me think. How I wish you'd write another chapter on superstition: what the French peasant at that time believed. I cant help thinking the general state of mind was so different from ours that voices, saints, came, not through God, but through a common psychology: why was everyone able to write poetry: to carve statues; paint pictures? – then, and not now. So that they believed where we cant. Or rather, our belief is hardly perceptible to us, but will be to those who write our lives in 600 years. Therefore . . . but I've no sense to follow this out. I agree, we *do* believe, not in God though: not one anyhow. And I cant lay hands satisfactorily on your 'unity'. Perhaps I mean, belief is almost unconscious. And the living belief now is in human beings. For example, to whisk off a little, how angelically you behave to the Hogarth Press! Generous, humane, honourable. In Jeanne's time none of those qualities existed. *Therefore*

---

1. Virginia is probably thinking mainly of *Portraits in Miniature* (1931), but other 'little biographies' are in *Books and Characters* (1922) and the posthumous *Characters and Commentaries* (1933).

they heard heavenly voices for no doubt the human vessel is so limited that it can only contain a few exalted detached and impersonal feelings at one time. As a psychologist Proust is far in advance of Ronsard. My perception or your perception is far finer that any 2 womens in 1456. On the other hand, the Rodmell church bells rouse in me nothing but antipathy to the Xtian religion – more especially as they set Miss Emery's dogs barking. [. . .]

Look at this: I did it myself.

[*stamped:*] Virginia
        Woolf
        Virginia
        Woolf

3152: To Leonard Woolf   *Monk's House* [*Rodmell, Sussex*]

Tuesday [14 July 1936]

A very good, though very dull day. No headache this morning, brain rather active in fact: but didn't write – did nothing but lie in bed and read Macaulay. Then there was a telephone, to which I flew, thinking it was you: but it was only a wire from Ethel 'dont forget Coachman's hat' – the photograph she means, which I must now send her. Then I lunched – Louie[1] very friendly and attentive – listened to a little dance music – took half an hour's stroll in the marsh – saw a grass snake – came back – lay in bed – slept over Blunt[2] had tea, and am now listening to the Mcnaghton 4 tet (daughters of Malcolm)[3] playing Haydn. But they play too slowly.

Percy [Bartholomew, gardener] is mowing the lawn in front, having mown the Croft this morning. So thats all my news. Its not a nice day, though fine; hot and windy with black clouds; and when I've posted this I shall take another little stroll. No letters; but my cigars.

The fact is its damned dull without you, dearest M[ongoose]: and if you didn't come back I should have to take to writing by way of fillip. I cant help thinking I can now – if I dandle my brain a bit and have frequent lie downs.

1. Louie Everest came to Monk's House in 1934 and worked for the Woolfs (and then for Leonard alone) for nearly forty years.
2. *My Diaries* (1919 and 1920) by Wilfrid Scawen Blunt (1840–1922), poet, traveller and politician.
3. Malcolm Macnaghten (1869–1955), a barrister, who married the daughter of Charles Booth, a friend of Leslie Stephen.

Could you bring some *cream?* Thats all I can think of to worry you with. But of course make Mabel [Haskins, maid] get it 1/- worth. Oh how we adore you! how angelic you are to us – I say its sentimental to say this, and that you know it already but the M's [marmots] insist, and say a Bird in the bush is worth 2 in the hand. Indeed you cant think how like a widow bird I am, all makes a frozen sound; and how I miss Sally [dog] and Mitz [marmoset] too. But you most, dearest of all Ms. Take care: dont sit up to all hours: dont let the Bore [Kingsley Martin] entirely exhaust you and come back safe tomorrow. Lord how nice to hear you!

M [andrill]

I hope you'll ask Elly [Dr Elinor Rendel] about your prophylactic.

3160: To Ethel Smyth   *Monks House* [*Rodmell, Sussex*]

Aug. 13th [1936]

[. . .] you'll be amused to hear, you made the blood come to my head the other day by some remarks of yours in a letter on 'Bloomsbury' Now here on the very second page I think you say 'important – to use the great Bloomsbury word' and again the blood rushes. To explain would take too long. But I daresay you'll twig from the following quotation. A young man the other day sent me a book in which he perpetually used 'Bloomsbury' as a convenient hold all for everything silly, cheap, indecent, conceited and so on. Upon which I wrote to him: All the people I most respect and admire have been what you call 'Bloomsbury'. Thus, though you have every right to despise and dislike them, you cant expect me to agree. Moreover, to use a general term like this, without giving instances and names, so that the people you sneer at can defend themselves, seems to me a cowardly subterfuge, of which you ought to be ashamed. Anyhow, never come and see me, who live in Bloomsbury, again. (Maurice [Baring] I see talks of Bloomsbury too)

And as you have once more trodden on that toe – I admit all the cheap journalists, ever since Roger and Lytton died, have been jumping on it, – I see red: which colour is not favourable to criticism: an art that should be impersonal; and so I wont tell you what I think of your article, for this second reason too. The first however, is the more important (to use a Bloomsbury word) I've read almost all Baring; and to sum up our differences would, as I say, use more time and brain power than are mine.

Lord! how I loathe Wokingism.[1]

Yr V.

3164: To Ethel Smyth   [*Monk's House, Rodmell, Sussex*]

Saturday [22 August 1936]

[...] Abuse By. [Bloomsbury] as much as you like, and I take this second sheet – a proof of health, for I've scarcely written a letter – all cards – mostly illegible – to say how you grow on me. Isnt that odd? Absence; thinking of some one – then the real feeling has room to expand. like the sights that one only sees afterwards: Is that peculiar to me, or common to all? Anyhow, lying in bed, or listlessly turning books I could hardly read, over and over again I've thought of you; and dwelt on your affection – Lord, how that pleased me, what you said to Dotty [Wellesley] – as if it were a red sun I could see and feel hot through the mist. And what a superb friend you are! telling all those people not to bother me! So many of my friends insist that I ought to do this and that – you, on the contrary accept me, and dont fritter and fuss me. And then how I adore your broad human bottom – how it kindles me to think of you, worried and bothered, yet lunching at a party of 12, and I'm convinced keeping the table in an uproar; and plunging like a blue Italian Dolphin into all the nets of the Sitwells; always battling and battering – and with it all keeping a mushroom sensibility intact. But enough: as – who was it? – would say. What I should like would be that you should come one of these days to Wotton [Sussex], and let us meet calmly and quietly – The packed visit is what gives my brain a screw. Still I'm so much better, I daresay it could stand a screw.

Now what else? Oh if you've time some day tell me about Dotty. I've always wondered how the Vita affair went with her. My relations were a good deal obscured by Vita – I mean, she left Dotty originally, I think, mostly on my account. [...]

V.

1. Ethel lived in Woking.

3173: To Ethel Smyth   *Monks House [Rodmell,*
                                        Sussex]

18th Sept. [1936]

[...] [Wordsworth's] The Prelude. Have you read it lately? Do you know, its so good, so succulent, so suggestive, that I have to hoard it, as a child keeps a crumb of cake? And then people say he's dull! Why have we no great poet? You know thats what would keep us straight: but for our sins we only have a few pipers on hedges like Yeats and Tom Eliot, de la Mare – exquisite frail twittering voices one has to hollow one's hand to hear, whereas old W^{th} fills the room. [...]

                                                                    V.

3189: To Julian Bell   *52 Tavistock Square [W.C.1]*

14th Nov. 1936

My dearest Julian,

[...] Let me see – since we came back we have been on the run and on the talk almost incessantly. I have seen the young poets – Spender and Plomer, and been induced to subscribe to the young poets paper, The Left review.[1] That shows you that politics are still raging faster and fiercer. I've even had to write an article for the Daily Worker on the Artist and politics.[2] Aldous [Huxley] is on the rampage with his peace propaganda; and Leonard is trying to convince the labour party that the policy of isolation is now the only one. Berties book[3] convinced him. But then when it comes to making a practical suggestion, which will convince Mr Gillies,[4] Berties book is not much use. However, I leave this out of my letters – that and Spain [the Civil War], which is now the most flaming of all the problems, since no doubt you'd rather hear gossip from me. [...]

That brings me to the present state of literature; which in my case is to the effect that I've cut down my book from close on 700 to 420 pages; its pretty bad; but I can't help it; and though doubtful (genuinely) if its

1. A monthly which ran from October 1934 to May 1938.
2. 'Why Art Today Follows Politics' (14 December).
3. Bertrand Russell's *Which Way to Peace?* (1936).
4. William Gillies, the Secretary of the International Department of the Labour Party.

worth publishing, shall publish, on Leonard's advice.[1] I'm so sick of it I can't judge. Now I'm free, almost, to tackle Roger, and shall try to get the papers in order. [...]

This morning I got a packet of photographs from Spain all of dead children, killed by bombs – a cheerful present. Privately we keep up our spirits. I take tea with Nessa – my great resource; and old Duncan stumbles over his words and Angelica takes the winds of March with beauty [*The Winter's Tale*, IV, iii, 118]. But lord, what a career – acting. [...]

Virginia

3197: To Violet Dickinson   *52 Tavistock Square, W.C.1*

Dec. 6th [1936]

My Violet,

It was extremely good of you to keep and bind up so much better than they deserved all those scattered fragments of my very disjected and egotistic youth.[2] Do you like that girl? I'm not sure that I do, though I think she had some spirit in her, and certainly was rather ground down harshly by fate. I'm glad Angelica hasn't to go through all her Aunt did by her age. At points I became filled with such a gust from her tragic past, I couldn't read on. Letters seem more than anything to keep the past – out it comes, when one opens the box. And so much I'd forgotten.

All I beg of you is dont let anybody else read those letters. Should I ever write my own memoirs there are some scenes and a few sentences I should like to quote: but I don't suppose a memoir-writing fit will fall on me. As John Bailey[3] must have said, letters aren't written nowadays: compare these with the 18th Century: what jerks and spasms they come in.

---

1. On 5 November Virginia had written in her diary: 'L. put down the last sheet about 12 last night, and could not speak. He was in tears. He says it is "a most remarkable book – he *likes* it better than The Waves." and has not a spark of doubt that it must be published' (*Diary*, V, 30). But in *Downhill All the Way* (1967), Leonard confessed: 'To Virginia I praised the book more than I should have done if she had been well' (p. 155).
2. Virginia's old friend Violet Dickinson, long since abandoned, had sent her typescript copies of some 350 of Virginia's letters to her, bound in two volumes.
3. John Cann Bailey (1864–1931), the critic and essayist.

But one thing emerges whole and lucid – how very good you were to me, and how very trying I was – all agog, all aquiver: and so full of storms and rhapsodies. [. . .]

Sp[arroy].

3206: To V. Sackville-West   *Monk's House, Rodmell,*
                                      near Lewes, Sussex

27th Dec [1936]

[. . .] Ethel's new dog is dead. The truth is, no dog can stand the strain of living with Ethel. I went down one day and found it on the verge of nervous collapse, simply from listening to her conversation. Never shall I forget a walk all round Worplesdon [Surrey] Golf Club in the rain – she lame, also taken short, not to put a fine point on it, in the pavilion. Well, well – if we all weather as red and roaring, we shant do so badly. [. . .]

V.W.

3206a: To Julian Bell   *Monk's House, Rodmell,*
                                Lewes, Sussex

Dec 30th 36

Dearest Julian,

Your letter came this morning – the one in which you say that you didn't write because you were hurt that I didn't like your Roger better. I just send a line, though I doubt if you'll get it, to say how sorry I am – indeed angry with myself. The truth was I read your paper and wrote my letter when I was in a complete state of daze what with London, proofs, and having headaches; I ought to have kept both for a clearer time; probably I expressed myself very badly and read very imperfectly. But all I want to say is that though I can't remember what I wrote, I certainly didn't mean to say anything that could possibly hurt you. Probably my impressions were mixed and incoherent; probably too you broached questions that I dont understand. But it is absurd to go over it at this distance of time – all I write to say is I'm very sorry.

We're dining at Charleston tomorrow – no more news as I wrote so lately; a hot June day, and we shall be very glad when you're back.[1] Don't for Gods sake let us quarrel about writing – [...]

Love from us both.

Virginia

3224: To Ethel Smyth   *52 T[avistock] S.[quare, W.C.1]*

Sunday [7 March 1937]

[...] I'm much interested by your theory that I like you but in absence: also that I dislike your presence because it drags me to the surface. No – there are 2 ways of doing it: the reviewers way I hate; yours I feel on the contrary bracing and invigorating. But then to explain the difference I should have to write several rather involved pages of psychological analysis. I think Proust explains it, but I cant remember where. Something I mean about the soul, how its elements are united differently by different stimulants; shaken together like those scraps of colour in a funnel [kaleidoscope] that we played with as children. [...]

V.

3230: To Stephen Spender   *52 Tavistock Sqre., [W.C.1.]*

7th April [1937]

Dear Stephen,

[...] I said I'd write about it [*The Years*], but I've been so plagued by the usual spate of reviews, even more contradictory than usual – oh why haven't we got a single decent critic among us? – that I've almost forgotten the book. But what I meant I think was to give a picture of society as a whole; give characters from every side; turn them towards society, not private life; exhibit the effect of ceremonies; Keep one toe on the ground by means of dates, facts: envelop the whole in a changing temporal atmosphere; Compose into one vast many-sided group at the end; and then shift the stress from present to future; and show the old fabric insensibly changing without death or violence into the future – suggesting that there is no break, but a continuous development,

1. Against the strong protests of his family, especially his mother Vanessa, who was miserable about it, Julian had decided to return from China in order to join the fight against Fascism in Spain as a member of the International Brigade.

possibly a recurrence of some pattern; of which of course we actors are ignorant. And the future was gradually to dawn.

Of course I completely failed, partly through illness – I've had to leave out one whole section which I could not revise in time for the press – partly through sheer incompetence. The theme was too ambitious. However I enjoyed the writing immensely, though not the revision; and am longing to go on to something else. I expect I muted down the characters too much, in order to shorten and keep their faces towards society; and altogether muffed the proportions: which should have given a round, not a thin line.

Julian is thinking of going to drive a lorry. I wish you could talk to him before he goes; but I daresay you're busy, and he is all over the place, interviewing Labour party, communists and so on. Your letter came in the nick of time to set him against the CP.[1] – we of course kept your name and confidence intact: it was most interesting. [. . .]

Your affate
V.W.

3240: TO STEPHEN SPENDER   *52 Tavistock Sq., [W.C.1.]*

April 30th [1937]

Dear Stephen,

[. . .] I dont think I agree with you though that *all* the characters felt the unreality, the invalidity of their experience. Eleanor's experience though limited partly by sex and the cramp of the Victorian upbringing was meant to be all right; sound and rooted; the others were crippled in one way or another – though I meant Maggie and Sara to be outside that particular prison. I couldnt bring in the Front as you say partly because fighting isnt within my experience, as a woman; partly because I think action generally unreal. Its the thing we do in the dark that is more real; the thing we do because peoples eyes are on us seems to me histrionic, small boyish; However I havent got this expressed, and I daresay difference of sex makes a different view. Which is right? God knows.

But I'm very glad you saw that the tend of the book, its slope to one quarter of the compass and not another, was different from the tend in

---

1. The letter contained accounts of the Communist-led International Brigade written by Spender's friend Jimmy Younger, who had joined it in Spain and become terribly disillusioned. Partly because of his mother's distress, Julian decided not to go to Spain as a soldier, but as an ambulance driver. He left on 7 June.

my other books. Yes, I am very anxious to develop it further; and almost tried a poetry section in this book; wanted to get some chorus; some quite different level. But once the narrative gets going the impetus is very heavy and difficult to interrupt, thats the horror to me of the novel. And in the Years I wanted to catch the general readers attention: perhaps I did this too much. But ever so many thanks for reading it so carefully. I've just been abused by the Dean of Durham[1] for irreligion and for saying that wrist watches were invented in 1880. [...]

yr aff
V.W.

3265: To Lady Ottoline Morrell   *Monk's House, Rodmell*
                                    [Sussex]

June 27th [1937]

Dearest Ottoline,

That is very bad news – that you've been so ill.[2] I hadn't heard. When you last wrote you said you were going to Tunbridge Wells, only for a rest I hoped. Please dont wave your adieu just yet. I can assure you the world requires the presence of your golden wing, not its vanishing. But now all thats over, I hope; and we can owl for a moment – its as dark as midnight at the moment, with a storm coming up over Caburn.

It was very stormy in France[3] – otherwise perhaps it would have been too perfect. We roamed about in the Dordogne valley – Souillac, Sarlat, Treysac – do you know these little towns, on the river, near Cahors and Perigueux, but almost lost; no tourists; the loveliest farms, old houses that Montaigne's friends lived in and are now lived in by shoemakers – but I wont describe – England seems like a chocolate box bursting with trippers afterward. As for London, from which we've escaped this week end, I cant describe its horror – fascination too, since

1. Cyril Alington, former Head Master of Eton, had been Dean of Durham since 1933. In his 'Book Talk' broadcast on 15 April, he had said in connection with *The Years*: 'The one thing from which I pray heaven to defend me [...] is from the dreary adventures of men and women who are confronted with problems for which they can find no answer, because neither they nor their creators have any sure standard to which they can refer.'
2. Ottoline had suffered a stroke and was now recovering at Dr Cameron's Tunbridge Wells Clinic, where she was also found to have heart disease. She died there in April of the next year, aged 64.
3. Where the Woolfs had driven 7–25 May.

people are so odd – but how they swarm, and what a din they keep up. If I had any sense I should only see the ones I like, but I lose my head, and in consequence see the ones I dont like.

Anyhow you are spared that. And illness is a very sublime state, if one can read; I'm so glad you liked my little Gibbon; I'm doing Congreve now.[1] If you want sheer joy read him; if you dont want anything so ecstatic, but broad and mellow and satisfactory, try the Memoires of George Sand. 10 little volumes; I'm in the 5th, and find it absorbing: We went to Nohant and saw her Chateau,[2] her pens and desk and bed, all as she left them – the very wallpapers, and the table set for Flaubert and Chopins spinet and the little theatre where they acted, with Maurices [her son] dolls in a cupboard.

I must now pick a dish of raspberries for dinner, and cease to try your eyes. But if Philip [Morrell] some day would send a card to say how you are – no, I daresay he's too busy. Our love to you. L. is clipping his hedge.

V.W.

3275: To V. Sackville-West   [*52 Tavistock Square, W.C.1*]

Wednesday [21 July 1937]

Dearest Creature

I wired to you because Julian was killed yesterday in Spain.[3] Nessa likes to have me and so I'm round there most of the time. It is very terrible. You will understand.

V.

1. Virginia was reading the Restoration dramatist for an essay that she called 'Congreve's Comedies: Speed, Stillness and Meaning' (*Essays*, VI).
2. The French novelist George Sand lived in the Château de Nohant most of her life and died there in 1876. It was a favourite resort of a remarkable group of intellectuals and artists, including Chopin, Liszt, Flaubert and Balzac.
3. Julian Bell had been attached to a British medical unit based on the Palace of the Escorial for the big Republican offensive to cut the supply route of the Nationalist forces encircling Madrid. Having survived great dangers, Julian was wounded by a shell on 18 July and died a few hours later. He was 29 years old.

3285: To V. Sackville-West   *52 Tavistock Square, W.C.1.*

[26? July 1937]

Dearest Creature,

I was very glad of your letter. I couldnt write, as I've been round with Vanessa all day. It has been an incredible nightmare. We had both been certain he would be killed, and the strain on her is now, perhaps mercifully, making her so exhausted she can only stay in bed. But I think we shall drive her down to Charleston on Thursday.

Lord, why do these things happen? I'm not clear enough in the head to feel anything but varieties of dull anger and despair. He had every sort of gift – above everything vitality and enjoyment. Why must he get set on going to Spain? – But it was useless to argue. And his feelings were so mixed. I mean, interest in war, and conviction, and a longing to be in the thick of things. He was the first of Nessa babies, and I cant describe how close and real and always alive our relation was. As for Nessa – but as I say I'm so stupid what with ordering the char to buy mutton, and generally doing odd jobs I cant think, or as you see write – so forgive this egotism. *Shall* you come over to M.H. one day? I should like to see you. And dear old Clive, – he is such a pathetic, and always honest, man, cracking his jokes, to try and make us all laugh – wh. I admire

Yr V.

3286: To Vanessa Bell   *[Monk's House, Rodmell, Sussex]*

Tuesday [3 August 1937]

This is only to say that I'm coming over to tea tomorrow, which is Wednesday, unless you stop me – unless that is, you've had enough of your singe, who adores you, and cant stay away from you. I find there are all sorts of trains and omnibuses and possible combinations, so that I can trot on my own toes.

Its a hazy hot day here; Leonard has been clipping his yews; I have been maundering over the downs, and trying to write Congreve, and theres not much village news, save that Louie [Everest] went in a boat yesterday for the first time in her life. How, being a mother at 14, she preserves this innocence of all other adventures I dont know. Then her friend, the Welshwoman, Mrs Polock, came to help in the house, and looks like the most sophisticated Bloomsbury Bunny,[1] only more competent. There's no doubt civilisation is beginning at the bottom, so that we shall all be overtaken, before long. No letters yet, but then thats Bank holiday; and Leonard is glad, because he can write his book [*After the Deluge*, Volume II), but I like opening a letter, and thinking myself loved. I've written to Margery [Fry] to tell her to find more articles, and we'll bring them when we go up on Tuesday. I wonder if you've dipped into Helen's [Anrep] box. Monks House is like a green cave, no light to eat by in the dining room, so we dine in the kitchen: this comes of the romantic profusion of our Vine, which blocks all the windows. You'd say it was natural to Wolves – this dim leafage; and now I must stop chattering to my darling dolphin and go to the post, and hope for a letter and then play bowls, and then put the kettle on; but all the time adoring my lovely dolphin, and longing to see her.

B.

3294: To Vanessa Bell   *Monks House [Rodnell, Sussex]*

Tuesday [17 August 1937]

[. . .] There have been no great adventures to speak of, save that the Bridge was open last night as we came through, in a storm of rain, a sailing ship passing, and all very romantic, and as usual I thought of you. Do you think we have the same pair of eyes, only different spectacles? I rather think I'm more nearly attached to you than sisters should be. Why is it I never stop thinking of you, even when walking in the marsh this afternoon and seeing a great snake like a sea serpent gliding among the grass? You were right about the American magazine: they now say they will, take my story if I wire a suitable synopsis – which is a sketch of the plot; so I've made up a story about a jeweller and a duchess, and cabled the plot – how he buys her pearls, for £10,000, knowing them to be false – thats not all of it by any means. Do you think, knowing the Americans as you do, that this will fetch them? It means £200 if it does.[2] I'm

---

1. A phrase invented by Molly MacCarthy in 1917 for Carrington, Dorothy Brett and Barbara Hiles, who attended the Slade School of Art and wore their hair cropped short.
2. 'The Duchess and the Jeweller' was published in *Harper's Bazaar* (London, April 1938; New York, May 1938).

completely stuck on my war pamphlet [*Three Guineas*], so I may as well write about Duchesses. I'm always wanting to argue it with Julian – in fact I wrote it as an argument with him. Somehow he stirred me up to argue – I wish I'd got his essays to read – they might give me some ideas. I suppose Charles will discuss them with you,[1] and I shant see you alone for ever so long. unless I creep over tomorrow, but I hardly think you'll want to see me so soon again. A letter from Tom [Eliot], who wants to come late in September: a letter from a lady who has described me in a French newspaper – 'a noble lady with a great shock of white hair' – Lord, are we as old as all that? I feel only about six and a half. And now I must play bowls, be beaten once more, and then have out the scope and see if I can pry into your bedroom. If you notice a dancing light on the water, that's me. The light kisses your nose, then your eyes, and you cant rub it off; my darling honey how I adore you, and Lord knows I cant say what it means to me to come into the room and find you sitting there. Roger felt just the same. Have you noted any extracts in his letters? I think you must begin at the beginning with old Lady Fry [his mother]. So no more.

B.

3299: To Vanessa Bell   *Monks House* [*Rodmell,*
                                          Sussex]

Monday [23 August 1937]

[. . .] Oh I'm so furious! Just as we'd cleared off our weekend visits, the telephone rings, and there comes to lunch, late, hungry yet eating with the deliberation and mastication of a Toad, Mr [William] Gillies of the Labour Party. It's 5.30. He's still there, masticating. Half a plum cake has gone down crumb by crumb. Mercifully he was ceased [*sic*] with such a choking fit that I made off to my Lodge to write this. You cant conceive what the mind of a Labour party leader is like – George [Duckworth] is advanced, Saxon [Sydney-Turner] rash, and Barbara [Bagenal] wildly imaginative in comparison. And they scrape their knives on their plates. Never let Angelica marry a Labour leader: on the other hand dont tell Leonard this, for he lives in the delusion that they are good men. [. . .]

B

G[illies]. is going!!!

1. Vanessa and Virginia – with the help of Roger Fry's and Julian's friend, Charles Mauron – were planning to publish a collection of Julian's essays, poems and letters. It appeared in 1938, edited by Quentin Bell.

3309: To Ethel Smyth   *Monks House, Rodmell*
                                              [Sussex]

19th Sept 37

Well, are you still tramping the Roman wall? or have you come back
South, and if you have come South what are you doing South? I shant be
told unless I ask, so, merciful heaven having provided a wet day, so that
our visitors have put us off, I'm writing, though I've nothing to say.
How was it that in such circumstances our ancestors at once wrote such
letters as could be printed verbatim? Was it nice to get Horace Walpoles
letters? Was it better than reading Hugh Walpoles novels? At Sissinghurst two days ago – we took Quentin and Angelica over – Harold was
saying he more or less agrees with you about MB's [Maurice Baring]
novels. But when pressed to explain rather wobbled, so I thought. Gwen
wasn't there – and oh the difference to me, as the poem says.[1] And the
whole place was a magnificent proof of our old English aristocratic
tradition. When I got back here I was positively ashamed of my middle
class origin. It was a wet night and the kitchen was damp and my room
all strewn with old clothes. But I recouped my spirits by saying L. and I
wouldn't like to live at Siss'. Vita was perfect in her way and Harold in
his. How I adore nice people. What else makes life worth living? Are
you a nice woman? What do you think you live for? Of course, if one
believed in God, as you do, it would make a very great difference. Tom
Eliot is coming here next week end. I shall ask him, if I dare – but to ask
him a question is like putting a penny in the slot of the Albert Hall –
what he thinks about God. Audens Iceland[2] seemed to me mainly
attitudinising, as if he were uneasy at heart, and must talk about himself
in order to rid himself of some scabby itch: a kind of public scratching. I
dont send this off as a specimen of a very good letter, but as a request for
news. If I can I'm going to make a shot at seeing Paris before we settle in.
Only its so difficult

                                                              V.

---

1. She lived unknown, and few could know
   When Lucy ceased to be;
   But she is in her grave, and, oh,
   The difference to me!
      Wordsworth, 'She Dwelt Among the Untrodden Ways'
2. W. H. Auden's *Letters from Iceland* (1937), written with Louis MacNeice.

3313: To Elaine Robson[1]   *Monk's House, Rodmell,*
                                      Lewes, Sussex

SUNDAY. SEPTEMBER TWENTY SIXTH [1937]

MY DEAR ELAINE,

I LIKED YOUR POEM AND YOUR STORY VERY MUCH INDEED. I HAVE NOT SEEN A RABBIT WASHING HIS CEILING BUT YESTERDAY I SAW A HARE WHO WAS MAKING A WARM BED FOR HIS WINTER LODGING IN THE MARSH. HE HAD JUST LAID DOWN A NICE BLANKET MADE OF THISTLE-DOWN WHEN HE SAW ME AND RAN AWAY. HIS BED WAS QUITE HOT, AND I PUT A MUSHROOM THERE FOR HIM TO EAT. THE MARSH IS FULL OF MUSHROOMS. I WISH YOU AND DADDY AND MUMMIE WERE ALL HERE TO PICK THEM AND THEN WE WOULD COOK THEM AND HAVE THEM FOR SUPPER. I ALSO SAW A KINGFISHER. HIS BED IS IN THE BANK OF THE RIVER BUT I HAVE NEVER FOUND IT. SALLY HAS HAD A THORN IN HER PAW AND WE HAVE HAD TO POULT-ICE IT. AT LAST THE THORN CAME OUT AND HER PAW IS ONLY AS BIG AS A PENNY BUN. IT WAS AS BIG AS A SOUP PLATE. MITZI HAD A MACAROON FOR BREAKFAST THIS MORNING. WHEN YOU ARE IN LONDON WILL YOU COME TO TEA WITH US AND MAKE A BINDING FOR YOUR LOVELY POEM AND STORY. DO YOU LIKE WRITING PROSE OR POETRY BEST. THIS TYPEWRITER CANNOT SPELL AND SOMETIMES USES WRONG TYPE. XXXXXX UNCLE LEONARD SENDS HIS LOVE: SALLY HAS JUST BARKED HER LOVE ALSO AND MITZ BIT ME IN THE EAR WHICH MEANS SHE SENDS YOU HER LOVE TOO.

                    YOUR AFFECTIONATE AUNT VIRGINIA

1. The daughter (then aged 6) of Juliette Alvin (d. 1982), the cellist and music therapist, and W. A. Robson (1895–1980) of the London School of Economics, who, with Leonard Woolf, was co-founder of the *Political Quarterly* in 1930 and co-editor until 1959. Elaine Robson later studied biology at Cambridge and became Lecturer in Zoology at Reading University in 1969.

3315: To V. Sackville-West   *Monks House [Rodmell, Sussex]*

Oct 1st [1937]

We have been so ridden with visitors that I never had a moment to write. In fact I was so touched by your letter that I couldnt. Isnt it odd? Nessa's saying that to you, I mean, meant something I cant speak of.[1] And I cant tell anyone – but I think you guess – how terrible it is to me, watching her: if I could do anything – sometimes I feel hopeless. But that message gives me something to hold to. [. . .]

V.

3325: To Ethel Smyth   *52 T.[avistock] S.[quare, W.C.1]*

Tuesday Oct 26th [1937]

[. . .] As for Pepita,[2] the other question, is it good? Well, whats your standard? Boswell? Rousseau? or merely the current pitter patter? One never knows. I think it's of its kind whatever that means, admirable: as easy to read as velvet glove to slip into; and very skilful; and compact; and not a schoolboys essay like Joan [*Saint Joan of Arc*]; great fun; and should certainly sweep the market, break the Bank. The odd thing is, I detest Lady Sackville at the end of it: an insipid, selfish, rather stupid housemaid of amorous propensities jumped up into the Peerage. But Vita says she is adorable. So I'm no doubt wrong. And this hasty estimate is only for your own ears – Did you ever meet her? Oh I get so bored with her extravagances after the first fun! and the vanity and the illiteracy, and the magpie's claws.

We were on the front at Seaford during the gale. That's as near as I got to Paris. The waves broke over the car. Vast spouts of white water all along the coast. Why does a smash of water satisfy all one's religious aspirations? And its all I can do not to throw myself in – a queer animal rhapsody, restrained by L. [. . .]

V.

---

1. Vanessa had written to Vita telling her that Virginia had helped her after Julian's death more than she could say, and asking Vita to make Virginia believe this.
2. Vita's *Pepita*, a biography of her grandmother, the Spanish dancer, and of her mother, Lady Sackville, was published in this month by The Hogarth Press.

3327: To V. Sackville-West

52 T.[avistock] S.[quare, W.C.1]

15 Nov. [1937]

Why 'once' Virginia?[1] Why mayn't I answer your letter? That of course is the way to make me sit down at once and answer it. Why are you a dustbin? And why shouldn't we go for a jaunt? Why, why, why?

Just because you choose to sit in the mud in Kent and I on the flags of London, thats no reason why love should fade is it? Why the pearls and the porpoise should vanish?[2]

No. I cant see your argument. In January I will take you to the place where we once had a glass of wine in a bow window overlooking the river. Also I'll take you to The Tower – I've just been there, this dripping Sunday; because almost every day I take my walk through the City. I like it better than Kent – Bread Street, Camomile Street, Seething Lane, All Hallows, St Olaves – Then out one comes at The Tower, and there I walk on the terrace by the guns, with the ships coming up or down – which is it? Last week [5 November] we went to Guy Fawkes at Lewes. Lordloveme, why didn't you come? Tossing torches all up and down the streets: people rigged up as courtiers, gondoliers, old farmers in black Spanish hats. Then we all trooped onto the downs, and burnt the Pope. It was the very image of an Italian picture of Calvary; crowds gazing up: the figure falling

As you say though, Spains burning and Hitler booming.[3] A french politician is dining here: I have to cook the dinner, and cant, as you know, talk what you would call, French. (d'you remember the rough sea on the channel boat? and how skilfully I christened it?)[4]

So no more – But if your pen should again take to twisting, let it.

Because, my dear Vita, whats the use of saying '*once* Virginia' when I'm alive here and now? So's Potto if it comes to that

yr faithful old servants
and adorers
P and V

1. On 13 November Vita had begun her letter 'My (once) Virginia'.
2. See p. 319, n. 2.
3. 1937 was the 'year of no surprises' from the dictators, but Hitler was stepping up his claim for the return of the German colonies surrendered to the Allies after World War I, and he and Mussolini continued to intervene actively in the Spanish War.
4. While crossing the Channel for their holiday in France in September 1928, Vita overheard Virginia asking a French sailor, 'Est-ce que la mer est brusque?'

3342: TO VANESSA BELL   *Monks House [Rodmell, Sussex]*

Tuesday, 28th Dec. [1937]

[. . .] [Sibyl Colefax] gave us a verbatim, hot from the Kings mouth, account of the Abdication:[1] swore that he and Wally had never been to bed; says Wally is a simple good devoted soul, who implored the King to keep her as his mistress or let her go. 'If you do' he said 'I shall dog you to the ends of the earth in an aeroplane.' Whenever S. goes abroad they ring her up and she stays with them. Unfortunately they refuse to take her advice – which is to go to South America – and are going to live in Paris, where no one will visit them, because of propriety. I gathered that Sibyl is going to act as liaison officer between them and the implacable Queen Mary, and I'm not at all sure that I'm not going to help David to have recourse to the classics – which, as Sibyl says, might do him a world of good. As for Wally, Leonard wd. feel perfectly at home with her. And so on, all in odds and ends, for 1 hour and 30 minutes. [. . .]

Now good Dolphin, be careful; and warm; and eat and love

poor worm eaten
Singe

1. Edward VIII ('David') abdicated on 10 December 1936 and married his mistress, Wallis Simpson, on 4 June 1937.

1938–1939

There were fewer splendid letters of the old sort in this period, almost as if Virginia were disengaging herself a bit from people. Her other writing was not deeply satisfying to her either. After the difficulty of The Years, *there followed two non-fictional works –* Three Guineas *and 'the compromise of biography',* Roger Fry. *She longed to write fiction again, and began to plan her last novel,* Between the Acts. *At least she was freed from some of the burden of The Hogarth Press when John Lehmann bought out her half of that successful enterprise.*

The Woolfs had two holidays, one in Scotland, the other in France. Friends died. But the overriding news was always Hitler. The Munich Crisis in the autumn of 1938 spurred Virginia to write some absorbing letters of 'inner history' to Vanessa, who was abroad. After war was declared in September 1939, Virginia again described London, 'this doomed and devastated but at the same time morbidly fascinating town'. She and Leonard were forced to move. They chose another Bloomsbury square house, but, for safety's sake, made the country their base.

3358: To Ethel Smyth   *52 Tavistock Square, W.C.1.*

Thursday 27 Jan. [1938]

[...] Our bitch [Sally], mated for the 2nd time 5 weeks ago, again shows no signs of childbirth, like Princess Juliana [of the Netherlands], and its laid to L's charge. Love for him they say, has turned her barren. [...]

V.

3361: To Vanessa Bell   *52, Tavistock Square,*
                                          [London,] W.C.1.

[3 February 1938]

I was so furious today not to see you properly dearest creature: I was thinking tomorrow is Julian's birthday and how I saw him in his cradle. You know I'd do anything I could to help you, and its so awful not to be able to: except to adore you as I do.

This doesnt want an answer: its only Singe's kiss my own darling.

3362: To Philip Morrell   *52 Tavistock Square, W.C.1.*

Feb 3rd [1938]

My dear Philip,

Of course I am much touched, as well as flattered, that you should write to me[1] – and I would have written before, except that, like you and all the rest of the world, I'm in the grip of influenza. So excuse both handwriting and mind weakness. I cant conceive why you should be afraid of writing when you have such extremely nice things to say. However, I admit I often tear up letters myself: one cant, even at my age, believe that other people want affection or admiration; yet one knows that there's nothing in the whole world so important. Why is it? Why are we all so tongue tied and spellbound? Why, as you say, do we live three streets off and yet never meet? I think human beings are fundamentally crushed by a sense of their insignificance. You and Ottoline seem to me to have everything: why should you care a bent farthing what I think or feel? Thats the line it takes with me: and to my surprise, apparently with you.

But merely as an author, that curious extension or excrescence on the original V.W – I'm delighted with – first: your liking Jacobs Room [1922]: my own favourite, the only one I can sometimes read a page of without disgust: second, that you should actually have read, still more marvellously have liked, Night and Day [1919]: a book written in half hour laps in bed, and so tedious to remember, and, I have always been told, a complete failure to read. Nothing will make me read it: but owing to your letter, a faint sunset glow surrounds it on the shelf.

I'm so glad Ottoline is better. I always hope you both realise what a part – and an unthanked part – you both played in the old civilisation. But why dont we renew it? Perhaps when I'm up and about you'll come to tea. Anyhow thank you for your letter, and excuse this feeble answer.

Yrs V.W.

1. In 1927 Philip Morrell had fallen quite seriously in love with Virginia. She regarded his position as touching but pathetic. Now he had written again in the same vein.

3364: To T. S. Eliot   *52 Tavistock Square, W.C.1*

Wednesday [9 February 1938]

The Wolves hope that The O'Possum,[1] who is hereby created King of all Possums, and an Irish Monarch, will come to tea, 4.30, on Tuesday 15th: one Wolf has now recovered, it is hoped, from kidney disease, the other from influenza: recurring; and both would relish a little cheerful talk about ptomaine poisoning and laryngitis, – the Wolf who is holding the pen cant spell tonight or form her letters, but thats nothing to the discredit of her heart, which is true and tender as the poet says the North is:[2] and oh god what a good poem [Shakespeare's] Venus and Adonis is compared with Mr – I forget his name but must now read his MS.

V

3377: To Ling Su-Hua[3]   *52 Tavistock Square, W.C.1*

5th April 1938

Dear Sue Ling,

I hope you have had the letter I wrote in answer to your first letter. I wrote only a few days after I had yours. Now Vanessa has just sent on

1. In November 1937 Eliot had sent the following verse to Virginia:

> Among the various Middle Classes
> (who live on treacle and molasses)
> A custom has (for want of better)
> Been called the Bread and Butter letter
> But Mrs Woolf would not rejoice
> At anything that's so bourgeoise,
> So what can poor Old Possum do,
> Who's upper-middle through and through?
> . . .
>
> (copy at Sussex University)

Eliot's most famous use of this persona is in his book of poetry for children, *Old Possum's Book of Practical Cats* (1939).

2. Oh tell her Swallow, thou that knowest each,
   That bright and fierce and fickle is the South,
   And dark and true and tender is the North.
           Tennyson, *The Princess*, IV, 73–5

3. The wife of Professor Chen of Wuhan University and an intimate friend of Julian Bell while he worked there. She had written to Virginia that she was helplessly depressed by Japan's invasion of China and her refugee life in the western province of Szechuan. In 1947 she came with her husband to England, where he worked first with the

your letter of March 3rd. I wish I could help you. I know that you have much more reason to be unhappy than we have even; and therefore how foolish any advice must be. But my only advice – and I have tried to take it myself – is to work. So let us think how you could fix your mind upon something worth doing in itself. I have not read any of your writing, but Julian often wrote to me about it, and meant to show me some of it. He said too that you had lived a most interesting life; indeed, we had discussed – I think in letters – the chance that you would try to write an account of your life in English. That is what I would suggest now. Your English is quite good enough to give the impression you wish to make; and I could change anything difficult to understand.

Will you make a beginning, and put down exactly anything you remember? As no one in England knows you, the book could be more free than usual. Then I would see if it could not be printed. But please think of this: not merely as a distraction, but as a work that would be of great value to other people too. I find autobiographies much better than novels. You ask what books I would advise you to read: I think the English in the 18th Century wrote in the best way for a foreigner to learn from. Do you like letters? There are Cowpers, Walpoles; very clear and easy; Scotts novels; (Rob Roy); Jane Austen: then Mrs Gaskells life of Charlotte Brontë: then among modern writers, George Moore's novels – they are simply written too. I could send you English books, but I do not know if you have them already. But from your letters I see that you write very well; you need not copy others, only find new words by reading quickly. I say nothing about politics. You know from what I said before how strongly the English are on your side but cannot do anything to help. We hear about China from friends here. But perhaps now there will be a change. The worst may be over.

At any rate please remember that I am always glad if you will write and tell me anything about yourself: or politics: and it would be a great pleasure to me to read some of your writing, and criticise it: so think of writing your life, and if you only write a few pages at a time, I could read them and we could discuss it. I wish I could do more. We send you our best sympathy.

Yours
Virginia Woolf

Sino-British Culture Association and later with UNESCO. The autobiography which Virginia urged her to write was eventually published by The Hogarth Press in 1953 under the title *Ancient Melodies*, with a foreword by Vita Sackville-West.

3383: To V. Sackville-West   *52 Tavistock Square* [*W.C.1*]

May 3rd [1938]

[. . .] We think of driving up to The Hebrides, the furthest seas –
where the cuckoo calls – whats the quotation Im thinking of? – breaking
the silence of the seas[1] – anyhow, thats what we mean to do in June. Oh
I'm so sick of this blasted London; its perpetual drab, its drip today, its
grey everyday, and all these people. The Press however is now chained
to John Lehmann,[2] or will be in October; and I hope (not with great
sanguinity though) to be quit of those eternal MSS. Six lie before me at
this moment. And we've had such a good year and made so much
money, and I cant help some pride when I think of the type in the carpet
at Hogarth House [in 1917]; and now they say its worth, The Press,
£10,000. Much thanks to the noble daughter of all the Sackvilles.

My God, how does one write a Biography? Tell me. I'm fairly
distracted with Fry papers. How can one deal with facts – so many and
so many and so many? Or ought one, as I incline, to be purely fictitious.
And what is a life? And what was Roger? And if one cant say, whats the
good of trying? Yet its my favourite reading – short of shall we say
Shakespeare and Sackville West: biography. I am reading for the first
time a book which I think a very good book – Mandeville's Fable of the
Bees [1714]. Only I must turn to Libby Benedicts Fable on Libby
Benedict.[3] As I began by saying this is merely a fish without any bait for
news. of you. I was at Ottolines funeral services.[4] I miss her; I mean
Gower Street looks to me dumb and dismal. I used to go round between
tea and dinner, and now – so dont put the light out which as you
remember lit up the porpoise at Sevenoaks. And excuse so very mild a
dribble – Its Potto's fault

V.

1. A voice so thrilling ne'er was heard
   In spring-time from the cuckoo-bird,
   Breaking the silence of the seas
   Among the farthest Hebrides.
      Wordsworth, 'The Solitary Reaper'
2. John Lehmann had purchased Virginia's half-share in The Hogarth Press.
3. The author of *The Refugees*, published by the Press in March 1938. Virginia met her for
   the first time on this day.
4. On 26 April at St Martin-in-the-Fields, Trafalgar Square.

3389: To T. S. Eliot   *52 Tavistock Square* [*W.C.1*]
26th May [1938]

Dear Tom,

Whichever Woolf it was, it wasnt this Woolf; but now it is this Woolf – which sounds like a passage from the works of the inspired Miss [Gertrude] Stein.

This is only to say in soberer language, that we go away for Whitsun on Wednesday; would therefore suggest tea on Sunday next at 4.30; failing that, tea on Tuesday next at the same hour; the snag then being an Italian woman at five thirty who might cut into our great pleasure in unadulterated conversation. But from your engagements, and their lieu, it looks as if neither day would do; in which case, we must leave it to you. Perceive how I rhyme – how instinctively and in the manner of George Herbert!

I'm longing I needn't say to hear how the visit to the water closet at Netherhampton went off;[1] if you met Miss Edith Olivier; if she's as nice as she says she is; if Mr Stephen Tennant (to me an incredible bore) is as she says Oscar Wilde incarnate; and so on and so on.[2] Yes, I murmured 'I'm Mrs Woolf,' at Ottolines funeral; then in a bold loud voice BUT I REPRESENT T. S. ELIOT – the proudest moment of my life; passing, alas, like spring flowers.

Affectionately V. W.

3392: To Ethel Smyth   *52 Tavistock Square* [*W.C.1*]
1st June. 38

Ethel you're a trump. A heart of gold under a somewhat charming exterior. They will be overjoyed. And I've told them you might add a book or two. If you know which you want to shed, write the titles on a card and send to Miss Douie, Librarian, 29 Marsham St. SW1.[3] Theyre

1. An old joke between them about the 'imperfect drainage' at Netherhampton, Salisbury, the home of Sir Bruce Richmond, formerly editor of *The Times Literary Supplement*. Eliot had been staying with the Richmonds while he lectured in Salisbury on the poetry of George Herbert.
2. Edith Olivier (d. 1948) was the author of several books. In 1938–9 she was Mayor of Wilton, Wiltshire. Stephen Tennant (1906–88) was the fourth son of Lord Glenconner. He was a painter, but he was known chiefly for his glamorous parties and pretty appearance.
3. Virginia was a great supporter of the library founded by the London Society for Women's Service, of which Philippa Strachey was secretary. Vera Douie was its librarian, 1926–67.

so cramped they have to choose which to house. I think its almost the only satisfactory deposit for stray guineas, because half the readers are bookless at home, working all day, eager to know anything and everything, and a very nice room, with a fire even, and a chair or two, is provided. So you were as usual, under your exterior, as wise as Goethe, and as good as gold. I'm rather distressed, all the same, at taking your money.

I will send you 3 guineas (the book only I mean) tomorrow. I hadn't meant to, as it only repeats The Years, with facts to prove it, not fiction; and is a hurried piece of work – though it was hard work collecting the facts – and you wont like it or agree with it.[1] So lets say no more about it.

I am also to thank you for the letter about Scotland. It comes in the nick of time, as there are difficulties about Skye, and we think of confining ourselves to [mainland] Scotland. Your nephew is a very kind good man to have troubled. Will you thank him? or shall I? Another friend [Ka Arnold-Forster, aged 51] has died suddenly on a Cornish moor. Oh dear me, I cant keep pace with all these deaths. And so count on you to keep on the sunny side of the grave a little longer. We are going to M. H. today, because L. has to inspect the village school. There are too many things to do, on the sunny side, but such is the ... I cant finish what I meant to say, because L. says I must pack. And I've all Roger's letters to tie up and take. But I will get a quiet evening at Rodmell and write a long long letter, a love letter, one of the very sweet, the very rare the very few and to you.

V.

3395: To Ethel Smyth   *M[onks] H.[ouse, Rodmell, Sussex]*

June 7th [1938]

[. . .] 2) I cant generalise about young men and war. I only know that my own nephew had a passion for the art; and a longing – instinctive and irrational – to fight himself. Yet why? And if you can, as in this village, beat up recruits from the farm, on the strength of red coats and pay, surely the instinct must be there, if mitigated in the more sophisticated quarter. But I do suggest that there's a strong turn against it – witness pacifism growing; only routed by the 'virile' conception. And suggest indifference.

1. But Ethel replied: 'Your book is so splendid that it makes me hot' (3 June 1938, Berg Collection).

3) Patriotism. My dear E . . . of course I'm 'patriotic': that is English, the language, farms, dogs, people: only we must enlarge the imaginative, and take stock of the emotion. And I'm sure I can; because I'm an outsider partly; and can get outside the vested interest better than Leonard even – tho' a Jew.

4) Notes. Yes that was a question; bottom of the page or end. I decided for end, thinking people might read them, the most meaty part of the book, separately. Gibbon wished to do this, but gave way to friends. Pippa Strachey writes that she's glad they are at the end. I had a mass more and still have. Yes – very hard work that was

5) Alas, there wont be a 2nd edition in my lifetime. L. printed 15 thousand! – against my judgment.

6. The Times photograph[1] – damn them. They rang up and asked for me. Were given the stock reply. 'Mrs W. doesn't want her photograph published' – whereupon they go to a shop and buy the Lady in the Lit Sup. who gave me a shock. No I dont think she's a beauty: but her nose looks sharp eno' to cut hay with. Why shd. I reflect 'what a beautiful woman' I am? I'm not, and never think so. (This is true) [. . .]

V.

3405: To V. Sackville-West   *George Inn, Chollerford*
                                    Northumberland

19th June [1938]

[. . .] Of course I knew you wouldn't like 3 gs – thats why I wouldn't, unless you had sent a postcard with a question, have given it you. All the same, I dont quite understand. You say you don't agree with 50% of it – no, of course you dont. But when you say that you are exasperated by my 'misleading arguments' – then I ask, what do you mean? If I said, I dont agree with your conception of Joan of Arc's character, thats one thing. But if I said, your arguments about her are 'misleading' shouldn't I mean, Vita has cooked the facts in a dishonest way in order to produce an effect which she knows to be untrue? If *thats* what you mean by 'misleading' then we shall have to have the matter out, whether with swords or fisticuffs. And I dont think *whichever we use*, you will, as you say, knock me down. It may be a silly book, and I dont agree that its a well-written book; but its certainly an honest book: and I took more

1. The *TLS* on 4 June published one of the photographs taken of Virginia by Lenare in January 1929.

pains to get up the facts and state them plainly than I ever took with any thing in my life. However, I daresay I'm reading more into 'misleading' than's there. But oh Lord how sick I get of all this talk about 'lovely prose' and charm when all I wanted was to state a very intricate case as plainly and readable as I could. [. . .]

V.

3406: To Vanessa Bell   *Flodigarry Hotel, Portree, Isle of Skye*

25th June [1938]

Well, here we are in Skye, and it feels like the South Seas – completely remote, surrounded by sea, people speaking Gaelic, no railways, no London papers, hardly any inhabitants. Believe it or not, it is (in its way, as people say) so far as I can judge on a level with Italy, Greece or Florence. No one in Fitzroy Street will believe this, and descriptions are your abhorrence – further the room is pullulating and popping with Edinburgh tourists, one of whom owns spaniels, like Sally, but 'all mine are gun trained, the only thing they wont carry being hares' – so I cant run on, did you wish it. Only – well, in Duncan's highlands,[1] the colours in a perfectly still deep blue lake of green and purple trees reflected in the middle of the water which was enclosed with green reeds, and yellow flags, and the whole sky and a purple hill – well, enough. One should be a painter. As a writer, I feel the beauty, which is almost entirely colour, very subtle, very changeable, running over my pen, as if you poured a large jug of champagne over a hairpin. I must here tender my congratulations to Duncan upon being a Grant. We've driven round the island today, seen Dunvegan, encountered the children of the 27th Chieftain, nice red headed brats:[2] the Castle door being open I walked in; they very politely told me the Castle was shut to visitors, but I could see the gardens. Here I found a gamekeepers larder with the tails of two wild cats. Eagles are said to abound and often carry off sheep: sheep and Skye Terriers are the only industries; the old women live in round huts exactly the shape of skye terriers; and you can count all the natives on 20 feet: but they are very rapacious in the towns, and

1. The Grants were from Rothiemurchus, Inverness-shire.
2. Dunvegan Castle in the north of Skye was the hereditary seat of the McLeods of McLeod. The 27th Chief of Clan McLeod had died in 1935 and was succeeded by his daughter Flora, whose grandsons Virginia saw.

its no use trying to buy anything, as the price, even of Sally's meat, is at least 6 times higher than in our honest land. All the same, the Scotch are great charmers, and sing through their noses like musical tea kettles. The only local gossip I've collected for you is about your Mr Hambro's wife – [1]the one who was drowned in Loch Ness. We met a charming Irish couple in an Inn, who were in touch, through friends, with The Monster. They had seen him. He is like several broken telegraph posts and swims at immense speed. He has no head. He is constantly seen. Well, after Mrs Hambro was drowned, the Insurance Company sent divers after her, as she was wearing 30,000 pounds of pearls on her head. They dived and came to the mouth of a vast cavern, from which hot water poured; and the current was so strong, and the horror they felt so great, they refused to go further, being convinced The Monster lived there, in a hollow under the hill. In short, Mrs Hambro was swallowed. No drowned body is ever recovered and now the natives refuse to boat or to bathe. That is all the local gossip. And I will *not* describe the colour. [...]

B –

3435: To Ethel Smyth   *Monk's House, Rodmell,*
                                        near Lewes, Sussex

29th Aug [1938]

I dont know, or indeed care, whose turn it is to break this long silence – last time you wrote from Harrogate: and did I answer, or didn't I? I cant remember what we were talking about. Operas? Workmen? Thats the curse of letter writing – Why should you be agog to hear how the new room's going on – how L. suddenly invented a balcony and a verandah – how there are sheets everywhere: dust falling – hammer and nails – workmen peeping in at me breakfasting in bed. You will skip all that. As for politics, I feel as if we were all sitting downstairs while someone slowly dies. So why write letters? Nevertheless, here we've been to Seaford today to mate Sally, in spite of the politics. She wouldn't mate. Leonard has gone to fetch her after 2 hours further solicitation. And I've been walking; found a dead tortoise on the top of the downs; also several clouded yellows [butterflies]. All the morning I work my

1. Winifred Hambro (wife of Ronald Olaf Hambro, Chairman of Hambro's Bank) was drowned in Loch Ness in August 1932 when her speedboat exploded.

brain into a screw over Roger – what did he do in 1904 – when did his wife go mad, and how on earth does one explain madness and love in sober prose, with dates attached? I saw Vita and I saw Gwen. Vita has written a long poem [*Solitude*], L. says very good: I've not read it. That I think I told you. And you now – now drop your trumpet, which by the way is upside down, and tell me: about the opera; about the orchestra: about Mary [Ethel's maid] and Woking and the Balfours.[1] Why is the aristocratic mind invariably middle class when the body is divine? Just finished Lady Fred Cavendish's diaries:[2] no vigour, no insight, no originality. All as drab and dowdy as Mabels Sunday best (Mabel is our maid of all work.) Explain this to me. And such damned condescension to artists. Yet all else is fine and flowing and thoroughbred – only the mind cluttered with curtains and ferns. I want to settle in and read some entire pure classic to rid me of the infection. But instead I play bowls with fanatic fury like yours for golf. So we approach, you and I, from different points of the compass. Here I cook dinner, so must stop, just, it happens, as a flock of fine feathered ideas perches on my wire. No I dont like Harolds BBC manner,[3] oh and every day I get a packet of abuse or ecstasy. Letters, I mean from that hysterical and illiterate ass the Public.

As I said before I must cook dinner, and wait the return of the Bride [Sally]. I had tea today at Seaford with the bastard son [Philip Hugh-Jones] of Philip Morrell. Did you know that ante-chamber to Ottolines drawing room? Now Ethel, answer.

V.

3441: To Ethel Smyth   *Monks House [Rodmell, Sussex]*

Sunday [11 September 1938]

[...] Oh I've had such a drubbing and a scourging from the Cambridge ladies – the professors of Eng. lit: at Cambridge for 3gs.[4] I'm

1. Lady Elizabeth Balfour, a daughter of the Earl of Lytton who married the 2nd Earl of Balfour in 1887, was Ethel's friend and neighbour at Woking.
2. *The Diary of Lady Frederick Cavendish*, edited by John Bailey in 1927. She was Lucy (d. 1925), daughter of the 4th Lord Lyttelton, and wife of the Chief Secretary for Ireland, who was murdered in Phoenix Park, Dublin.
3. Harold Nicolson was broadcasting regular talks on current political affairs.
4. The Cambridge teacher Q. D. Leavis (1906–81), who with her husband F. R. Leavis was the force behind the influential critical journal *Scrutiny*, wrote in the September

a disgrace to my sex: and a caterpillar on the community. I thought I should raise their hackles – poor old strumpets.

3443: To Ethel Smyth   *M.[onks] H.[ouse, Rodmell, Sussex]*

Sat. 17th Sept. [1938]

[. . .] Lets leave the letters till we're both dead. Thats my plan. I dont keep or destroy but collect miscellaneous bundles of odds and ends, and let posterity, if there is one, burn or not. Lets forget all about death and all about Posterity. [. . .]

Yr
V.

3447: To Vanessa Bell   *Monks House [Rodmell, Lewes, Sussex]*

1st October. [1938]

[. . .] In London it was hectic and gloomy and at the same time despairing and yet cynical and calm.[1] The streets were crowded. People were everywhere talking loudly about war. There were heaps of sandbags in the streets, also men digging trenches, lorries delivering planks, loud speakers slowly driving and solemnly exhorting the citizens of Westminster Go and fit your gas masks. There was a long queue of people waiting outside the Mary Ward settlement[2] to be fitted. L. went off at once to see K.M. [Kingsley Martin]. I discussed matters

1. With Duncan, Quentin and Angelica, Vanessa had left England on 16 September to drive across France to Cassis. Meanwhile, Hitler maintained his threat to invade Czechoslovakia. On 15 September the Prime Minister, Neville Chamberlain, had flown to Germany, and agreed in principle to the secession to Hitler of certain areas. On 22 September Hitler increased the pressure, and five days later the French Army and the British fleet were partially mobilised. At the last moment, while Chamberlain was addressing the House of Commons on the 28th, he was handed a message from Hitler, who wrote at Mussolini's suggestion, proposing a conference at Munich the next day to settle the crisis.
2. An education centre at 36–37 Tavistock Place.

issue a vitriolic review of *Three Guineas*. Her case was mainly against what she perceived to be Virginia's class and therefore her false assumptions about women's position: 'It seems to me the art of living as conceived by a social parasite.'

with Mabel [their maid]. We agreed that she had better go to Bristol – whether she has or not I dont yet know. Then L came back and said Kingsley was in despair; they had talked for two hours; everybody came into the N. S [*New Statesman*] office and talked; telephones rang incessantly. They all said war was certain; also that there would be no war. Kingsley came to dinner. He had smudges of black charcoal round his eyes and was more melodramatic and histrionic than ever. Hitler was going to make his speech at 8. We had no wireless, but he said he would ring up the BBC after it was over and find out the truth. Then we sat and discussed the inevitable end of civilisation. He strode up and down the room, hinting that he meant to kill himself. He said the war would last our life time; also we should very likely be beaten. Anyhow Hitler meant to bombard London, probably with no warning; the plan was to drop bombs on London with twenty minutes intervals for forty eight hours. Also he meant to destroy all roads and railways; therefore Rodmell would be about as dangerous as Bloomsbury. Then he broke off; rang up Clark, the news man at The BBC;[1] 'Ah – so its hopeless . . .' Then to us, 'Hitler is bawling; the crowds howling like wild beasts.' More conversation of a lugubrious kind. Now I think I'll ring up Clark again . . . Ah so it couldnt be worse . . . To us. No Hitler is more mad than ever . . . Have some Whiskey Kingsley, said L. Well, it dont much matter either way, said K. At last he went. What are you going to do? I asked. Walk the streets. Its no good – I cant sleep. So we clasped hands, as I understood for the last time.

Next morning Tuesday every one was certain it was war. Everyone, except one poor little boy in a shop who had lost his head and was half crying when I asked for a packet of envelopes (and he may have been in some sort of row) was perfectly calm; and also without hope. It was quite different from 1914. Every one said Probably we shall win but it'll be just as bad if we do. I went to the London Library to look up some papers about Roger. I sat in the basement with the Times open of the year 1910. An old man was dusting. He went away; then came back and said very kindly, 'Theyre telling us to put on our gas masks, Madam' I thought the raid had begun. However, he explained that it was the loudspeaker once more addressing the citizens of Westminster. Then he asked if he could dust under my chair; and said they had laid in a supply of sand bags, but if a bomb dropped there wouldnt be many books left

1. John Beresford Clark (1902–68), Director of the BBC Empire Service, 1935, and Assistant Controller of the Overseas and European Service, 1939.

over. After that I walked to the National Gallery, and a voice again urged me to fit my gas mask at once. The Nat Gallery was fuller than usual; a nice old man was lecturing to an attentive crowd on Watteau. I suppose they were all having a last look.

I went home, and found that L. had arranged that the Press was to go on; but the clerks to go away into the country if they liked. Then Miss Hepworth the traveller said the shops were mostly refusing to buy at all, and were mostly going to close. So it seemed we should have to shut down. The clerks wanted to go on, as they had no place in the country; and of course no money. We arranged to pay wages as long as we could – but plans were vague. Mrs [Norah] Nicholls [manager] said she should prefer to lie in the trench that was being dug in the square; Miss Perkins [clerk] preferred to sit in the stock room, which she had partly prepared with mattresses etc. Then, after lunch, an American editor[1] arrived to ask me to write an article upon Culture in the United States. We agreed however that culture was in danger In fact she said most English authors were either in Suffolk, or starting for America. In Suffolk they were already billeting children from the East end in cottages. Then Rosinsky[2] came; he thought he had a visa for America and was going to try to go at once. Then Mrs Woolf rang up to say she was going to Maidenhead if she could get rooms. Then an express arrived from Victoria Ocampo who had just landed from South America, wished to see me at once, was trying to fly to America and what could she do with a sister who was ill – could we advise a safe retreat? Also Phil Baker[3] and others rang up Leonard. With it all we were rather harassed; what should we need if we were marooned in Rodmell, without petrol, or bicycles? L. took his mackintosh and a thick coat; I Rogers letters to you, and a packet of stamped envelopes. Then we had to say good bye to the press, and I felt rather a coward, as clearly they were nervous although very sensible; and they had no garden. But the Govt; asked all who could to leave London; and there was John [Lehmann] in command. So off we went.

It was pouring terrific torrents; the roads packed; men nailing up shutters in shop windows; sandbags being piled; and a general feeling of flight and hurry. Also it was very dark; and we took about three hours to

1. Phyllis Moir of the *Forum*, New York, for which Virginia had written before.
2. Herbert Rosinski, a refugee from Nazi Germany, was the author of *The German Army*, published by The Hogarth Press in 1939.
3. Philip Noel-Baker (1889–1982), the Labour MP whose work for disarmament and world peace was rewarded with the Nobel Peace Prize in 1959. Virginia had known his wife Irene Noel since before her marriage in 1915.

get back. At ten oclock Mr Perkins[1] knocked and entered with a box of gas bags which he fitted on us. No sooner had he gone. than Mr [Guy] Janson [South Farm] came with another box. He said that children were arriving from the East End next morning. Sure enough, next day, – but I wrote to you and told you how we had the news of the Prime Ministers sensational statement [the Munich announcement] – we thought it meant anyhow a pause – well, after that, Mr Perkins came and said the children were coming – 9,000 had to be billeted in Sussex; fifty in Rodmell; how many could we put up? We arranged to take two. By that time, the nightmare feeling was becoming more nightmarish; more and more absurd; for no one knew what was happening; and yet everyone was behaving as if the war had begun. Mr Hartman [of Southease] had turned his barn into a hospital and so on. Of course we thought it was ridiculous; yet still they went on broadcasting messages about leaving London; about post cards with stamps being given to refugees who would be deposited safely, but they must not ask where. At any moment the fifty children might arrive. Also the Archbishop would offer up prayers; and at one moment the Pope's voice was heard . . . But I will shorten; and skip to Sissinghurst; where we went on Thursday; and heard that the Italian King had saved the situation by threatening to abdicate. Harold had seen the PM grow visibly ten years younger as he read the message which was handed him. It was all over. And I must play bowls. Leonard sends a message to Q[uentin]; in his opinion we have peace without honour for six months.

I'll write again. Maynard comes tomorrow. Plans vague; but we write here, where we shall probably stay at present. No time to read this through.

Post going,
B.

3449: To Vanessa Bell   *Monks House, [Rodmell,
Lewes, Sussex]*

Monday, October 3rd [1938]

[. . .] You say you would like gossip about the inner history, so I'll use my fragment of time before lunch – I've been trying to describe the first PIP show[2] without success – to go on with my scrambled and

---

1. A. F. Perkins, clerk to Chailey Rural District Council, which was responsible for civil defence in Rodmell.
2. For her biography of Roger Fry, Virginia was writing about the First Post-Impressionist Exhibition in November 1910.

inarticulate story. Everything is still incoherent; but you'll excuse . . .

Well, I think I broke off at Sissinghurst last Thursday. We found that Harold had been kept in London, to arrange a counterblast to Chamb[erlain]. with Eden, Churchill etc. He had just rung up Vita and said she was to show us his diary. This was very interesting. They had all been convinced that war was inevitable. The cabinet had tried to control Chamb – the younger members that is. They were certain he was going to sell us. However off he flew [to Godesberg]. When the House met that Wednesday [28 September] they all believed it was to announce war. He spoke very wearily yet precisely, like a business man making a statement. Then they saw the note [from Hitler] handed him. He lit up, looked ten years younger, made his announcement; whereupon they all went mad, threw hats in the air, rushed about the lobbies shouting. That was all he knew when he wrote. Then Vita showed us the great barn with windows covered with frames that didnt fit and doors half sealed. Thirty people were to sleep there. I forget how many children were to be put up in hop oasts. The farmer [Ozzy Beale] arrived to ask what was now to be done.

Then Gwen St Aubyn arrived from Lewes; she had been taking her daughters school [Frances Holland] from London to Stanmer Park [near Brighton], which Lady Chichester had given over; and sixty girls were already lying in the picture gallery on mattresses, and blackboards were ready for next days lessons. Miracles of organisation had been performed by everyone. The roads, she said were crowded with lorries full of escaping schools. Vita said it was known for certain that London was to be attacked at twenty minutes intervals for twenty four hours with gas and bombs. Also that Mussolini had been stiffened at the last moment by The King of Italy who had said he would abdicate. Hence his pressure upon Hitler; which had turned the tide at the last moment. We came back, half expecting to find our refugees waiting us at Monks House. Mercifully there was no one.

Then next day we all turned rather cynical, and were sure of peace with dishonour. Then the BBC kept on saying that nothing was safe; we were all to go on expecting war; until finally Chamberlain arrived; and we heard him read the terms from Heston;[1] frantic cheers; hysterical

---

1. The London airport where Chamberlain arrived on 30 September, bringing with him a declaration signed by himself and Hitler early that morning in Munich, by which Britain and Germany pledged themselves 'never to go to war with one another again'. From the windows of Downing Street he assured the cheering crowds that he brought back 'peace with honour'.

cries from old ladies; then the Archbishop praying; then bells pealing; while here at Rodmell a service was hastily got up; our bells made a perfectly infernal din; Mrs Ebbs [wife of the rector] in vain tried to whip up the villagers to some excitement; but one and all they remained perfectly sure that it was a dirty business; and meant only another war when we should be unable to resist. Of course the country was much calmer than London. Leonard was amazed by the sagacity of the old gaffers. The Postman stayed and talked good sense for about half an hour. The BBC however still announced that all reptiles would be shot at the Zoo; and any tiger that escaped killed at sight. I think they were so proud of their organisation that they wanted to air it, though it began to leak out that the air defence had been found full of holes; and that the carnage would have been immense in London.

Yesterday the Keynes came to tea. Maynard had already summed up the situation in a very good article which he read us; I'll send you the N.S on Friday in which it appears. His view is that the whole thing was staged by Chamb.; that there was never any fear of war; that he never even consulted Russia; that it was a put up job between him and Hitler; that he would now call a general election; that our business is to fight Chamberlain; that we are sure of peace during our life time; that Hitler wants the Ukraine; that he'll get it; that Italy will be wiped out; that we shall do a deal with the colonies; that Chamberlain is a mere Birmingham politician; and so on. We all analysed our complexities of shame, and fear; Lydia said Maynard had really been a great deal alarmed; and excited. Of course the truth was that one felt all along that Chamb. had something up his sleeve; only one couldnt say how much. Also the feeling of despair and coming death was very genuine in London, however irrational. I am proud to say that my last words on leaving the Press were 'There wont be war' but I was hooted down. I suppose everyone, except Kingsley Martin, chopped and changed. For instance some of the Gordon Square pundits – friends of Maynards – refused to agree to trenches being dug in the square and held out that war was impossible. On the other hand, the whole Royal Society has fled to the country; and Cambridge was so disorganised – all the colleges fitted up as hospitals – that it has had to put off term for some days. If it was all a piece of stage management on Chambs part, he took in a great many authorities. But you'll have had enough of this; and I expect I am sending, as you would say, coals to Birmingham. Duff Cooper,[1] much

1. Duff Cooper (1890–1954), First Lord of the Admiralty, objected profoundly to Chamberlain's sacrifice of Czechoslovakia and resigned his office in protest.

to Maynards surprise and admiration, has resigned. There is now going
to be a great reaction against the terms; and I'm afraid L. will be drawn
in. Already John [Lehmann] wants us to go to London to discuss plans
for the Press tomorrow. But we mean to stay here at all costs this week.
The hubbub is incessant in London; and one simply repeats the same
thing, and is exposed to all the bray of all the donkeys. [. . .]

B

3454: To Vanessa Bell   *Monks House [Rodmell,*
Lewes, Sussex]

Saturday Oct 8th [1938]

[. . .] You say you want details. England has now settled down to the
usual cat and dog; I mean, I told you so, its your fault no its not; Kettle
yourself; pot yourself; or whatever the phrase is. Trenches were dug
because if you lie at the bottom of a sloping hole, a shell will burst at
either side and miss you. Two workmen were buried alive making them.
As for gas masks, many have died through testing them on the exhaust
pipes of cars. Govt; has now issued an edict that theyre not to be tried on
gas pipes as they dont work. Black boxes are being issued to keep them
in against the next war. Some grateful owners have paid the Treasury
one guinea apiece. Ours lie on the drawing room table. I did not say the
press was fortifying my studio; I said the stock room [Tavistock Square].
This is a firmly built stone lined compartment behind the front room;
most suitable, therefore as Miss Perkins said. Lined with books and
mattresses practically impregnable. [. . .]

What am I to say about you?[1] Its rather as if you had to paint a
portrait using dozens of snapshots in the paint. Either one ought to dash
it off freehand, red, green, purple out of ones inner eye; or toil like a fly
over a loaf of bread, As it is I'm compromising; and its a muddle; and
unreadable; and will have to be used, like the letter, to wipe a gooses
rump. But Roger himself is so magnificent, I'm so in love with him; and
see dimly such a masterpiece that cant be painted, that on I go. Also,
reading his books one after another I realise that he's the only great critic
that ever lived. For instance Cezanne [1927] – a miracle. [Characteristics
of] French Art [1932] – another. Why did one only read his little articles?

1. About Vanessa's affair with Roger Fry. In the biography Virginia simply referred to
  'their friendship'.

So, as you see, on I go; and grumble; and sweat; and sometimes get so hot in the head I roll in the cabbage bed. Do give me some views; how to deal with love so that we're not all blushing. [. . .]

We get snatches of divine loneliness here; a day or two; and sanguine as I am I said to L. as we strolled through the mushroom fields, Thank the Lord, we shall be alone; we'll play bowls; then I shall read Sévigné; then have grilled ham and mushrooms for dinner; then Mozart – and why not stay here for ever and ever, enjoying this immortal rhythm, in which both eye and soul are at rest? So I said, and for once L. said; Youre not such a fool as you seem. We were so sane; so happy; and then, I went in; put the kettle on; ran up stairs looked at the room; almost done; fireplace lovely; wood wrong stained; but still felt floating on the wings of peace. Made tea; got out a new loaf; and honey and was about to call in L from the ladder on the high tree – where he looked so beautiful my heart stood still with pride that he ever married me; and then . . . A face at the window. A voice. May we come in, Virginia? A jersey; trousers; bright red cheeks; glassy blue eyes. Barbara [Bagenal]. An interval of sheer horror; of unmitigated despair; my life crashed; my soul broke; my tongue faltered; and there was Nick [her husband].

So we had them both for four hours by the clock. Lodging with Mrs Curtis they had tried to find you; were told by the pistmas (I mean postman) Charleston was empty; so came without the decency of a card or a telephone; planted their dismality on me. Such crude brutality, such denial of all human decency seems to me so unthinkably bestial that after they'd gone – and we had to drive them to Firle – I let fly; and for hours L. and I argued; he thought me too harsh; I thought him deplorably sentimental. But we both agreed that the poor Bags are in the lowest rung of life; water blooded; blowsy; grumpy; servile; their eyes all flies; one drip drip drip of complaint from Barbara, Judith [their daughter], such a trial; no friends; boys so stupid; cant pass exams; no money; no servants; no friends; and of course none of it said rhymically [*sic*] like this, with some arch to the back; but all verified and stated in words like hard boiled eggs; so that there I sat staring. L. took Nick round the garden. Nick too giggles. Not a drop of hope or health in them; and so we settled like creeping flies on Saxon [Sydney-Turner], who at least excites B's bitterness; she has found him a flat at Greenwich; why wont he face the fact that he must live there? Wont have money to go to the Opera. Has the eczema on his hands. Over eating. Yes, moaned Nick – hes terribly greedy. Eats grouse alone. Not a grouse had come their way these ten years. And why should it? And theyd no milk, nor eggs; had picked twenty dead mushrooms by way of gift; and I had to explore Itford Farm in the twilight, with Nick, to furbish up their miserable larder. But enough. Poor things – its a death to your door; the refrain was always Nessa and Duncan – Angelica and Quentin, as if you had obsessed them and dispossessed them. Tell Angelica, Judith considers her the only friend she has; 'But of course Angelica never invites her now . . .' [. . .]

Maynard is a great man, I rather think. They had caught three mice in one trap; this excited him to the verge of hysteria. Now thats true greatness; combined as it is with buying a whole flock of sheep; ditto of cows; he had been also dictating a letter to the Times; is overcoming the innumerable actors and actresses [at his Cambridge Arts Theatre] who wont act Phedre; they will act Phedre; had also a complete knowledge of Tuberculosis in cows; meanwhile gave permission for Auntie to drive with Edgar [chauffeur] to Lewes to buy stockings; all details are referred to him; yet he remains dominant, calm; intent as a terrier to every word of L's play; spotted at sight things Id never seen from sheer vacancy; and left me crushed but soaring with hope for a race that breeds men like Maynard. And I kissed him and praised to the skys his Memoir Club paper;[1] by which, most oddly to my thinking, he was really pleased. D'you ever feel such a worm as I almost always feel? Or are you always as beautiful as I thought you the last night at Charleston, when I could hardly breathe for fear of unsettling the magnificent human Camberwell beauty [butterfly, i.e. Vanessa] who was, I suppose, mending socks? [. . .]

B

3460: To Vanessa Bell   *52 Tavistock Sq[uare, W.C.1.]*

24th Oct [1938]

Your letter I may tell you very nearly had fatal consequences. I very nearly rushed off to Cassis, so intoxicating were your words; and the sense of heat; and vines; and beauty; and freedom; and silence; and no telephones. You very nearly had me on you; and then what a curse you would have found it! Only the timely revelation of the complete failure of our marriage prevented it. Only just in time to stop me taking my ticket. Its an awful confession – if I werent so hurried I would conceal it;

1. On Cambridge and George Moore, published in 1949 as *My Early Beliefs*.

but the fact is we are so unhappy apart that I cant come. Thats the worst failure imaginable – that marriage, as I suddenly for the first time realised walking in the Square, reduces one to damnable servility. Cant be helped. Im going to write a comedy about it. But if I had come your perfect globe would have been smashed; you know how careful I have to be, too, to bait my hook with little minows [*sic*] and other tit bits to disguise my rapacity for your society with whats acceptable to you. Had I come the hook would have been bare; all this winter you'd have had nothing but the rusty steel to grate your teeth upon. Also, its a good thing that Wolves and Bells should be separated sometimes in order that each may inspissate their identity. [. . .]

London is appalling, but also I admit fascinating – in its meretricious way. Also Exmouth Street Market, with a black corpse of a horse among flowers and cheap glass has its appeal; also Hampton Court where we went yesterday in the balm of a perfect summers day was worth all your black visaged spectacular south. We roamed the park, smelt the flowers, and mooned along the galleries where, thanks [to] Roger, I'm now seeing in chairs pictures tapestries a remote world of inexplicable significance.[1] I think the art of painting is the art for ones old age. I respect it more and more. I adore its severity; its bareness from impurity. All books are now rank with the slimy seaweed of politics; mouldy and mildewed. I wish I could settle to pure fiction; indeed had to rush headlong into a novel;[2] as a relief; but am now back at Roger and the compromise of biography again. That reminds me; please will you and Duncan write something quick about the Borough Polytechnic.[3] Any facts. Who were the artists? What were the subjects? Does the dining room still exist? Can one see it? Do answer this. I'm toiling in a maze; and no one so far has thrown me a single bone of help.

Now to gossip. Jack Hutch, youll be glad to hear was let blood copiously, and has recovered. Mary [Hutchinson] says it was a slight attack. He is at work again. This was imparted to me as I sat talking to [Sibyl] Colefax. You see I get from people what you get from vines.

1. Roger Fry had worked intermittently for several years, beginning in 1912, on the restoration of the Mantegna paintings, *The Triumphs of Caesar*, in the Royal Collection at Hampton Court.
2. *Between the Acts*, called at this stage *Pointz Hall*.
3. In 1911 Roger Fry was commissioned to decorate the students' dining room at the Borough Polytechnic, London. Roger, with the help of young artists (Duncan Grant, Frederick Etchells, Bernard Adeney, Macdonald Gill and Albert Rothenstein) did scenes of the amusements of London. Fry had painted a scene at the Zoo.

These distorted human characters are to me what the olive tree against the furrowed hill is to you. Colefax is an essential part of the composition; wrinkled I admit. I was led, by a spirit in my feet, (that is Shelley)[1] to denounce her life to her; her snobbery; her falsity; her damned dressed up dinner party society. I will only dine with you, I bellowed, (without you V. B. I become so vehement,) if I may walk out of my own house, as I am, to your door. 'Done!' she cried. Today I'm invited to meet Max Beerbohm and Lord Ivor[2] without washing; and will I bring [Christopher] Isherwood on the same terms? What am I to say? Why do I seek to change society, when it means that one has to act on ones words? L. says I can rat. [. . .]

B.

3464: TO VANESSA BELL *52 Tavistock Sq[uare, London, W.C.1.]*

Nov. 2nd [1938]

[. . .] My Colefax party was perhaps worth going to, as I didnt dress, and sat next Max [Beerbohm], and we talked writers shop. He's a charmer; rubicund; gay; apparently innocent; but in fact very astute and full of airy fantasies. He invented obituaries, and has an extraordinary gift for telling little stories that he makes up on the spur of the moment. When we went to Hastings the other day an old man stopped me in the street and said. 'Have I the honour of addressing Miss Edith Sitwell?' 'I'm Mrs Woolf,' I said. He then swept off his hat and said 'Not my old friend Leslie Stephen's daughter?' 'Who have I the honour of addressing' I said. 'Somebody whose name youve never heard,' he said . . . 'Coulson Kernahan!'[3] I told Max this; and he instantly told me the whole history of C.K.'s life; how he'd written a book called God and the Ant;

1. And a spirit in my feet
   Hath led me – who knows how?
   To thy chamber window, sweet!
      Shelley, 'The Indian Serenade'
2. Max Beerbohm (1872–1956), author (*Zuleika Dobson*, 1911) and caricaturist; Lord Ivor Spencer Churchill (1898–1956), youngest son of the 9th Duke of Marlborough, and an art collector.
3. Coulson Kernahan (1858–1943), the writer and soldier. Max Beerbohm's summary of his career is accurate, except that Kernahan wrote no book entitled *Celebrities I Did Not Know*. One of his books was *An Author in the Territorials*, with a foreword by Field-Marshal Lord Roberts of Kandahar (1832–1914), the hero of the Afghan and South African wars.

sold one million copies; also one called Celebrities I knew – how he visited Lord Roberts 'who rose from his chair and looked at me with eyes – were they blue? were they hazel? were they brown? No they were just soldiers eyes' He also wrote a book called Celebrities I did not know. Max Beerholm . . . for one . . . How much was true and how much invented I dont know. But it was very amusing as he told it; but I cant record it. Then there was Somerset Maugham.[1] a grim figure; rat eyed; dead man cheeked, unshaven; a criminal I should have said had I met him in a bus. Very suspicious and tortured. But youve met him. And Lord Ivor [Churchill]; and Lord de la Warr;[2] and Christopher I[sherwood] who seemed all agog with amusement; but is a shifty quicksilver little slip of a creature – very nimble and rather inscrutable and on his guard. I had no talk with him; but he said he had heard of you and would come and dine. Will you come and meet him? [. . .]

3467: To Duncan Grant   *52 Tavistock Square, W.C.1*

14th Nov. 38

Dearest Duncan,

I was greatly pleased to get a letter from you, and only wish you would take to the pen oftener. Like all painters, your sense of words is plastic, not linear, and I am on the side of the plastic myself. But this is not the time to broach that – only to welcome you back to civilisation; its a bear garden, and I'm entirely of your advice that we should rusticate. [. . .]

London is extremely beautiful at the moment, blue as June, soft as down. Think of my idiocy – I walked from Marble Arch to Horse Guards admiring two divine young men. So beautiful were they I circled round and round to hear what they said. In vain. Like young gods, with small chins, blue eyes, perfect hips and shoulders. Ouida[3] would have adored them. The sky like a Canaletto. [. . .]

I've lots to say but this paper cuts it short. Not however my affection,

1. This was the only time that Virginia met the playwright and novelist, who was then 64.
2. 'Buck', the 9th Earl de la Warr (1900–76), President of the Board of Education in Chamberlain's Government, and Vita Sackville-West's cousin.
3. Louise de la Ramée (1839–1908), the popular novelist who wrote under the name Ouida. Splendidly elegant guardsmen were frequent characters in her flamboyant novels.

or the desire I have to see you. 'You' in this context stands for the two divine women [Vanessa and Angelica] also.

V.

3481: To Ethel Smyth   *52 Tavistock Square, W.C.1.*

Tuesday 24th Jan. [1939]

[. . .] Oh dear Ethel, why did our parents conceive us so that we saw this particular stretch of time? I have such an immense capacity for sheer pleasure up my sleeve; and shant use it this side of the grave. So I burrow into Roger. And what are you doing? The same, I expect: Anyhow we artists have that anciliary – whats the word? – other world outside the real world I mean. If this is real. I am reading Sévigné; that leads to Michelet; that to Saint Simon; and I see Rabelais at the turn of the corner.[1] We're going to see the great Freud on Saturday.[2] [. . .]

V.

3485: To May Sarton[3]   *52 Tavistock Square [W.C.1]*

2nd Feb 39

Dear May Sarton,

I was glad to get your letter, in spite of the request you make in it; and in spite of the fact that I have no time to answer it. (I am rushing

1. Virginia was contemplating a book of criticism which she did not live to write. She called it a 'grand tour of literature' and planned to move as she pleased through time, space and genres. Beginning with the letters of Madame de Sévigné, she might continue with the nineteenth-century French historian Jules Michelet, then – going back a step through time – with the political philosopher Henri, Comte de Saint-Simon, and back further, to the fiction of François Rabelais. When she considered this project in her diary, Somerset Maugham was hooked on to the end of the list (*Diary*, V, 205).
2. The Hogarth Press had been publishing the works of Sigmund Freud since 1924, but Virginia had never met him. He was now a refugee from Vienna and had taken a house in Maresfield Gardens, Hampstead, where the Woolfs had tea with him. Freud was very courteous (he ceremoniously presented Virginia with a narcissus), but was suffering from the cancer which killed him eight months later at the age of 83.
3. The American poet and novelist May Sarton (b. 1912) had met Virginia in 1937 through Elizabeth Bowen, with whom Sarton was in love.

down to the country; and snatch ten minutes off what ought to be my work). About the MS. for the Refugees society. I am sure it is a good society; but my repulsion from societies is great; still greater my hatred of encouraging writers in their idiotic vanity about their own little doings. I tear up my manuscripts when I have any; but in fact I make such wild sketches in hand writing alter so completely on the type writer that a manuscript of mine is mostly nonsense. And I dont like to sell nonsense; nor do I think it would sell; for no sane person could make head or tail of it. Still, I promise that I will rout among my papers and see if there's some page not too incoherent. If so I'll do violence to my horror of this groping and send it to the address you give.[1]

I'm glad that youre writing poetry; also that youre teaching it. I have no recollection of hearing from Mrs Swift or that I ever had a book from her.[2] Please apologise for me, if she accuses me of not thanking her, as I fear she well may. But I think you know, among other objectionable characteristics, my hatred of thanking writers for their books. One cant say what one thinks; But its rude – uncivilised; a futile protest against the immense reciprocity required by civilisation. This will help to explain my dumbness about your own poetry; which I will read, and say nothing about. In fact, since we had a partner in the Press, two months ago, I gave myself a license to read no modern writing of any kind for one full year. I have been so steeped in modern manuscripts that I was losing all sense that one differed from another. I am reading Chaucer and hope in a year to have recovered my palate. At the moment Auden reads like Spender; Spender like Auden; and neither mean anything. So if I did read you I should only get another confused note in the general clamour; but I hope this will have sorted itself out by next January. As you can imagine, there are so many other things dinning in one's mind here – war, politics, and an infinite number of different people. I shall be seeing Elizabeth [Bowen] and a young man called Sean O'Faolain[3] next week; which I shall enjoy; and hope to see you when youre over. I'm ashamed to let this scribble cross the Atlantic; but if I dont, then you will give up your last relic of belief in me, which I have some vague wish to preserve.

There are half a dozen snowdrops out in our garden; and we are now

1. Virginia sent Sarton the manuscript of *Three Guineas*.
2. Elizabeth Townsend (Mrs Rodman) Swift had written a book on the psychology of women, which May Sarton had sent to Virginia in the hope that The Hogarth Press might publish it.
3. The Irish writer (b. 1900), known chiefly for his short stories.

driving through the bitter east wind to see them. Best wishes and thanks and apologies.

yrs
Virginia Woolf

3548: To V. Sackville-West   *Monk's House, Rodmell,*
                                  near Lewes, Sussex

Tuesday 29th Aug. [1939]

Well, there's another day of peace[1] – I mean we've just listened in to the P.M. I suppose Harold came back [from the House of Commons], so you didn't come [to Rodmell].

I cant help letting hope break in, – the other prospect is too mad.

But I dont think I'm philosophic – rather, numbed. Its so hot and sunny on our little island – L. gardening, playing bowls, cooking our dinner: and outside such a waste of gloom. Of course I'm not in the least patriotic, which may be a help, and not afraid, I mean for my own body. But thats an old body. And all the same I should like another ten years: and I like my friends: and I like the young. That'll all go forever if – Meanwhile, not a van will come to unpack furniture or remove books at 37:[2] all's held up: publishing and moving blocked. We go up on Thursday to see whats to be done.

Otherwise come at any time, and indeed, my dearest creature, whatever rung I'm on,[3] the ladder is a great comfort in this kind of intolerable suspension of all reality – something real.

But isn't it odd? – one cant fold it in any words.

V.

1. There were to be only four more. On 3 September England declared war on Germany.
2. The Woolfs had moved to 37 Mecklenburgh Square, Bloomsbury, but because of the war they lived in Sussex and made only occasional trips to London.
3. Virginia had asked about her standing with Vita, and Vita had replied (25 August 1939): 'Virginia darling, you are very high up on the rungs – always.'

3553: To ETHEL SMYTH   *Monk's House, Rodmell,*
                                        near Lewes, Sussex

Tuesday 26th [September 1939]

Yes it was angelic of you to write. And I would have answered – but since Sept 1st this house has been a refugee haunt – always a clerk from the Press, or some fugitive, and God knows, though I've no cause to complain, since we escaped 3 East end children, visitors fritter one's day to shreds. The last went this morning. So until raids begin we shall be alone – save for raids from neighbours. We're exposed to neighbours. Thank God though I've made my head work in the mornings, and so am more or less calm. But no reading. All talk. Some of the clerks turned out magnificent. One a publicans daughter, another a greengrocers, a third a photographers, a fourth a sheer adventuress with a fatherless, I mean Bastard child, for whom all her concern was. Then we dashed to London, decided to go on publishing, brought out all our books yesterday – L's 2nd volume: a masterly work [*After the Deluge*]. Pray God some one will buy it. But the confusion in the trade is confounded – no one buys in shops, no bagmen. And so ruin stares us in the face; and I begin to be stingy. I'm seeing Vita tomorrow. Both the boys [Ben and Nigel] are in the army, and Harold in London. I'm sorry – oh dear how sorry, for I know what waiting about means. [. . .]

Why you old wretch – how I laughed at the love over the garden wall, and yet was jealous.[1] So you see there's green fire in me if not red. [. . .]

                                                                        V.

3559: To ANGELICA BELL   [*37 Mecklenburgh Square, W.C.1*]

Monday [16 October 1939]

Dearest Pixie,

You cant think how difficult it is to write a letter in this doomed and devastated but at the same time morbidly fascinating town. Also there's a dearth of pens and a prevalence, indeed a pullulation of chamber pots. Oh and the books: all over the floor: oh and the pictures: all on their heads. Oh oh oh . . . [. . .]

1. The indefatigable Ethel was still falling in love. In a recent letter she had described two new loves, one a 35-year-old American woman she met in Ireland, and the other a next-door-neighbour of 81.

[. . .] we lunched with Mrs Drake[1] to meet Mrs Webb: and she was like a dead leaf spotted with fire – so crinkled so curled but invincible in spite of bladder trouble and cancer by the sheer might of disinterested intelligence. Another vol. required. Her nephew at the War Office says there'll be a raid tonight: (so this is no doubt my dying word) and the War will be over by Xmas, because its a fact that the German army is already in disruption. Hitler's last fling will be at our heads tonight and tomorrow. [. . .]

[. . .] you dont know what a queer place London is – Here we are running in and out of each other's houses with torches and gas masks. Black night descends. Rain pours. Vast caterpillars are now excavating trenches in the Square. Shops shut at 5 or so. Many windows remain black all day. The streets are a hurry scurry of people walking. Ambulances abound. Very stout women wear blue trousers. No one ever sits down. The buses are quick but rare. And in short – I've just pulled down the black blinds – rats in caves live as we do. [. . .]

V.

3565a: To Katharine Furse[2]   *Monks House, Rodmell,*
                                      tLewes Sussex.

9th Nov. 39

Dear Katharine,

I'm sorry I left your letter unanswered – but our flat is still very rickety, and no ink, or if ink, no pen. We stayed there a week or so, but now I'm glad to say are back again.

I'll consider pornographic when I re-read; and thank you for not insisting on anything; thats so rare.[3] In London, oddly enough, I heard a

1. Barbara, eldest daughter of Daniel Meinertzhagen, and a niece of Beatrice Webb. Her husband was Bernard Drake, a solicitor.

2. Madge Vaughan's youngest sister Katharine, widow of the painter Charles Furse, was created a Dame in 1917 for her work with the Red Cross Voluntary Aid Detachment. She was subsequently Director of the Women's Royal Naval Service and later of the World Association of the Girl Guides and Girl Scouts. This letter is one of several Woolf-Furse letters held by Bristol University Library.

3. Virginia had sent Katharine a passage from a letter by Roger Fry in which he describes her father, the poet and critic John Addington Symonds (1840–93), as 'the most pornographic person I ever saw'. After initial reluctance, which Virginia would not accept, Katharine agreed to the use of the phrase. But when *Roger Fry* was published, she wrote again to say that she was pained by Virginia's decision.

good deal about your father – that is I met someone who told me he had heard they'd had a meeting of the London Library Comm; to decide if you should be allowed to read the autobiography.[1] And chiefly because Desmond MacCarthy, Harold Nicolson and E. M. Forster were all shocked at its being withheld, agreed. Is there any truth in this? What then becomes of the story that it was burnt? If you ever have a moment, I'd so much like to know the facts. Also the same man asked me if you knew the account given by your father (anonymously) of his own sexual experience in Havelock Ellis's book. He said it was extremely interesting; and obviously by your father, though unsigned. Again, I met another man, who was on the point of writing a life of your father when he heard you were doing it. This shows – both of them were of the same persuasion – how much interest there is among them about him; not of course for that reason only. But I think they all wish the question openly discussed; and a woman could do it more openly. I don't think for a moment it would damage your character – rather the other way; not that you care. Ive seen so much of the nasty silly petty side of the homosexuals; which is obviously largely the result of secrecy.

I return Mr Cottam [unidentified]; of whom I've never heard. A very interesting letter. No I dont know Gosses son; he writes about pirates I think; and so sounds as if might be shockable.[2] I may be misjudging him.

Pornography I'm told derives [etymologically] from brothels not pigs. But it has an unpleasant smell to it I agree.

Yours affly,
Virginia Woolf

Bristol University

1. Dame Katharine was hoping to write a biography of her father and had applied to do research at the London Library, which held his candidly homosexual memoirs under a fifty-year embargo against publication. She did not read the autobiography until 1949, when the Symonds box was opened for the first time. In her own memoirs, *Hearts and Pomegranates* (1940), she includes a fairly straightforward discussion of her father's interest in homosexual research 'from personal experience'. The almost clinical account by Symonds of his homosexual awakening appeared in *Sexual Inversion* (1897) by the early sexologist Havelock Ellis (1859–1939).
2. Edmund Gosse's son was Philip (1879–1959), a physician and writer, whose books included *The Pirates' Who's Who* (1924).

3570: To Judith Stephen[1]   *Monk's House, Rodmell,*
                                  Lewes [Sussex]

2nd Dec 39

Dear Judith,

[...] What sort of creed are you coming to? As far as I remember, 21 was a devillish age; so intense; and so violently crabwise – this way, that way, and as you say back as much as forward. But it was amazingly exciting too. Never shall I forget arguing with Thoby, Lytton, even old Saxon, hour after hour about good and truth, and one's personal emotions as we called them.

I was asked to lecture the Cambridge English Soc. too, but really I've so often said lectures are damned things; also that no woman should give tongue to Camb. until Camb. has done its duty and made them members of the University – but what's the use of protesting? With this war on. However I'm more and more convinced that it is our duty to catch Hitler in his home haunts and prod him if even with only the end of an old inky pen. [...]

                                                          VW

---

1. Virginia's niece, the younger daughter (1918–72) of Adrian and Karin Stephen. Judith was at Newnham, where she was an excellent student.

1940

Virginia had ten years' worth of ideas left in her, she said, provided Hitler did not stop her. But as she worked on Between the Acts *and planned another book of criticism, her spirit was dampened because the war forced her to write in a vacuum: 'The audience has gone'. She finished* Roger Fry *with the help of some of his old friends, including George Bernard Shaw, from whom she received a flirtatious letter. She was dissatisfied with the book, but resoundingly defended its subject to Vita's son, Ben Nicolson, who had accused Fry of elitism.*

The sight of London bombed and blasted broke her heart. Her own house was hit and thereafter uninhabitable. But her aesthetic sense prevailed when the River Ouse in Sussex was bombed, making a temporary sea of the fields. Whatever the external stress, she could always read herself 'into a state of immunity'.

3580: To Shena, Lady Simon[1]   *Monk's House, Rodmell*
                                            Lewes, Sussex

Jan 22nd [1940]

My dear Shena,

I've had too many distractions to write – people staying here, London and so on. But not too many to read your paper. I find it useful, suggestive, and sound. I agree with most of your arguments. I wish we could meet and discuss them. What the Americans want of me is views on peace. Well, these spring from views on war. So I shall work on from your paper when the time comes.[2] Meanwhile, do cast your mind further that way: about sharing life after the war: about pooling men's and women's work: about the possibility, if disarmament comes, of removing men's disabilities. Can one change sex characteristics? How far is the

1. Shena Simon (1883–1972), an ardent social reformer like her husband, the Liberal MP Sir Ernest Simon, had met Virginia in 1933 and had since corresponded with her from time to time about feminist issues.
2. Virginia had been asked by the American magazine *Forum* to write an article for them (see *Essays*, VI). She had turned to Lady Simon, whose experience was so much broader, asking her to write down her views on women and war.

women's movement a remarkable experiment in that transformation? Mustn't our next task be the emancipation of man? How can we alter the crest and the spur of the fighting cock? Thats the one hope in this war: his soberer hues, and the unreality, (so I feel and I think he feels) of glory. No talk of white feathers anyhow; and the dulness comes through the gilt much more than last time. So it looks as if sexes can adapt themselves: and here (thats our work) we can, or the young women can, bring immense influence to bear. So many of the young men, could they get prestige and admiration, would give up glory and develop whats now so stunted – I mean the life of natural happiness. [. . .]

Yr V. W.

3582: To Ethel Smyth   *Monk's House, Rodmell,*
                                          near Lewes, Sussex

1st Feb 40

Yes, I'd like to look at South Riding,[1] if its no trouble to you to send it on. I think I meant that W.H. was a barrel organ writer. Vera is a scrambling and enthusing chatterbox, but of course very competent. I'm judging WH. only on her journalism – and she insisted to me that that was all she ever wanted to do – and the book on me, which I felt to be a painstaking effort rather to clear up her own muddles than to get the hang of mine. But I didnt want to be written about (not personally) and so never did more than whip through it with one eye shut. I dont like pulling out all the organ stops and 'humanising': I dont like regional novels: those are my prejudices; and I much prefer people who let all that settle down (like Hardy, like Tolstoy) and only write when the sediment is firm and the water clear. Therefore I'm not likely to be fair on W.H. And oh Lord how I loathe that scribbling business: 35 novels to be reviewed for Harpers Bazaar in one morning in a bungalow. So I'm not unprejudiced, but will try to be.

Here we are snow bound. All engagements in a muddle. We tried to go, but the car frozen, the roads impossible. I should be listening to

1. The most successful novel of Winifred Holtby, who in 1932 had published one of the early studies of Virginia. Holtby died in 1935, aged 37, and in 1940 her close friend, novelist and feminist Vera Brittain (1896–1970), published a tribute to her, *Testament of Friendship.*

Desire under the Elms[1] this moment. Never was there such a mediavel winter. The electricity broke down. We cooked over the fire, remained unwashed, slept in stockings and mufflers. And what about you?

I'm using this frozen pause to confront a long last grind at R.F. Then it'll be done. but goodness knows when. The [Fry] family has to pass it. Endless objections I foresee. And its not a book, only a piece of cabinet making, and only of interest to R's friends, for whom I've tried to stick together an amalgamation of all his letters. And what a job to do! And its of no interest that I can see, except to his half dozen devotees. Never mind – I've learnt a carpenter's trick or two.

Reading Burke. Reading Gide. and I have to lecture on the moderns to the working classes at Brighton.[2]

V.

3608a: To George Bernard Shaw   *Monk's House, Rodmell,*
near Lewes, Sussex

15th May 1940

Dear Mr Shaw,

Your letter reduced me to two days silence from sheer pleasure.[3] You wont be surprised to hear that I promptly lifted some paragraphs and inserted them in my proofs. You may take what action you like.

As for the falling in love, it was not, let me confess, one-sided. When I first met you at the Webbs [in 1916, see Letter 771] I was set against all great men, having been liberally fed on them in my father's house. I wanted only to meet business men – and (say) racing experts. But in a jiffy you made me re-consider all that and had me at your feet. Indeed you have acted a lover's part in my life for the past thirty years; and though I daresay its not much to boast of, I should have been a worser woman without Bernard Shaw. That is the reason – I mean the multiplicity of your lovers and what you must suffer from them – why Leonard and Virginia have never liked to impose themselves on you. But we have an intermittent perch – 37 Mecklenburgh Square – in

1. Eugene O'Neill's play, 1925.
2. Her lecture to the Workers' Educational Association (later published as 'The Leaning Tower') was about Auden, Spender, MacNeice and Day Lewis (see *Essays*, VI).
3. Shaw had written for Virginia a vivid description, complete with dialogue, of a 1917 luncheon with Roger Fry and the composer Edward Elgar. Parts of it appear in *Roger Fry*, p. 208.

London; and if ever Mr Shaw dropped his handkerchief – to recur to the love theme – we should ask nothing better than to come and see you.

As for the Roger Fry picture, I should accept it gratefully. For that offer, and for your letter, and for everything else that you have given me, I am always yours humbly and gratefully,

                                                        Virginia Woolf
Heartbreak House, by the way, is my favourite of all your works.[1]

The British Library

3609: TO ETHEL SMYTH   *Monk's House, Rodmell,*
                                        near Lewes, Sussex

17th May 40.

[. . .] Its a good thing to have books to believe in – and any number of little drudgeries: food to order: a village play to rehearse; and old Mrs West and her idiot boy – they took an hour this afternoon. We shant I suppose be killed; but I think of Montaigne, let death find me planting cabbages.[2] A disease has struck our gooseberries. Percy [Bartholomew] is mowing the lawn, and I have just forced myself to answer a lady who wants to know – what, dont matter. Still, in this numb and prosaic state, I should like a letter. [. . .] D'you know what I find? – reading a whole poet is consoling: Coleridge I bought in an old type copy tarnished cover, yellow and soft: and I began, and went on, and skipped the high peaks, and gradually climbed to the top of his pinnacle, by a winding unknown way. So then I bought a Shelley: tea stained, water marked; but also no edited anthology cabinet piece. Him too I'm going to explore in the same sauntering under the bramble way. I find the poets and Ethel Smyth very effective when I wake between the worlds – 3 and 4. [. . .]

                                                                    V.

1. 'There is a play of mine called Heartbreak House which I always connect with you because I conceived it in that house somewhere in Sussex where I first met you and, of course, fell in love with you. I suppose every man did' (Dan H. Laurence, ed., *Bernard Shaw, Collected Letters, 1926–1950,* 1988, 557).
2. 'Let death seize about me whilst I am setting my cabbages, careless of her dart, but more of my imperfect garden' ('To Study Philosophy is to Learn to Die', Book I, Chapter 19, Montaigne's *Essays*).

3612: To Ethel Smyth   *Monk's House, Rodmell,*
                                         near Lewes, Sussex

9th June 40

[. . .] I expect its right to bring out your book [*What Happened Next*];
and we incline to do the same. Only Longman has a big staff, and ours is
very small. I hope anyhow, for yours. I read myself into a state of
immunity. And, as you know, I find your drug very potent. I dont think I
was alone for 3 days for one moment [in London]; and each brought a
little jab of the war – each time the door opened or the telephone rang it
was war and war – and 'still we danced forward.' D'you remember that
quotation?[1]

My brain hums with scraps of poetry. Some of them were desperate;
others hopeful; and some 'plucking the flower while they may'[2] – thats
my niece Judith boating on the Lake in Regents Park, having just done
her tripos. 'We never talk about war at Cambridge' she said. 'We leave
that to the dons'. Then in came Kingsley Martin and Rose Macaulay, and
there we sat in the hot evening, till the stars came out, never lighting a
lamp, and gradually Kingsley Martin sucked every drop of lifeblood to
feed his great purple vampire body. The searchlights are very lovely
over the marsh, and the aeroplanes go over – one, a German, was shot
over Caburn, and my windows rattled when they dropped bombs at
Forest Row. But its like a Shakespeare song today – so merry, innocent,
and very English.

On Holmes[3] and my father. No, I dont know of any pamphlet: only
that they climbed [mountains] together, and Holmes was a great
charmer, and lunched with us. There were éclairs – and he pointed to
one, and said 'Why éclairs?' A question I've never answered: a beautifully urbane, witty, over cultivated American. [. . .]

                                                              V.

---

1. 'When one news straight came huddling on another
   Of death! and death! and death! still I danced forward.'

   From John Ford's *The Broken Heart* (1633), V, iii, and quoted by Virginia in the first
   Common Reader.
2. Virginia's adaptation of Robert Herrick's famous line, 'Gather ye rosebuds while ye
   may' from 'To Virgins, to Make Much of Time'.
3. Oliver Wendell Holmes (1809–94), the American poet and essayist, best remembered for *The Autocrat of the Breakfast Table* (1858).

3627: To Benedict Nicolson   *Monk's House, Rodmell,*
                                     Lewes [Sussex]

13 Aug. 1940

Dear Ben,

Just as I began to read your letter, an air raid warning sounded. I'll put down the reflections that occurred to me, as honestly, if I can, as you put down your reflections on reading my life of Roger Fry while giving air raid alarms at Chatham.[1]

There goes that damned siren, I said to myself, and dipped into your letter. You were making extracts from Roger's letters as you listened. 'Returning slowly through France he stopped in many of the towns and villages . . .' I began making extracts from your biography. 'Returning slowly from Italy with Jeremy Hutchinson,[2] Ben Nicolson reached Venice in May 1935 . . .'.

Here the raiders came over head. I went and looked at them. Then I returned to your letter. 'I am so struck by the fools paradise in which he and his friends lived. He shut himself out from all disagreeable actualities and allowed the spirit of Nazism to grow without taking any steps to check it . . .' Lord, I thought to myself, Roger shut himself out from disagreeable actualities did he? Roger who faced insanity [his wife's], death and every sort of disagreeable – what can Ben mean? Are Ben and I facing actualities because we're listening to bombs dropping on other people? And I went on with Ben Nicolson's biography. After returning from a delightful tour in Italy, for which his expensive education at Eton and Oxford had well fitted him, he got a job as keeper of the King's pictures. Well, I thought, Ben was a good deal luckier than Roger. Roger's people were the very devil; when he was Ben's age he was earning his living by extension lecturing and odd jobs of reviewing. He had to wait till he was over sixty before he got a Slade professorship. And I went on to think of that very delightful party that you gave in Guildford Street two months before the war. I remembered Isaiah Berlin discussing philosophy – not Spinozas – [G. E.] Moores – with Leonard; Stephen Spender flirting with a young Freud; Cressida Ridley[3] and all

1. Vita's older son was then serving as a lance-bombardier in an anti-aircraft battery at Chatham, Kent.
2. Jeremy (b. 1915), later Lord Hutchinson, Q.C., the son of Virginia's friends St John and Mary Hutchinson, had known Ben Nicolson at Oxford.
3. The daughter of Sir Maurice and Lady Violet Bonham Carter, who married Jasper Ridley, another Oxford friend of Ben Nicolson, in 1939.

the rest of the young talking exactly as we used to talk at Bernard Street [Fry's Bloomsbury house]. Then I looked at your letter. 'This intensely private world which Roger Fry cultivated could only be communicated to a few people as sensitive and intelligent as himself . . .' Why then did Ben Nicolson give these parties? Why did he take a job under Kenneth Clark at Windsor? Why didn't he chuck it all away and go into politics? After all, war was a great deal closer in 1939 than in 1900.

Here the raiders began emitting long trails of smoke. I wondered if a bomb was going to fall on top of me; I wondered if I was facing disagreeable actualities; I wondered what I could have done to stop bombs and disagreeable actualities . . . Then I dipped into your letter again. 'This all sounds as though I wish to say that the artist, the intellectual, has no place in modern society. On the contrary, his mission is now more vital than it has ever been. He will still be shocked by stupidity and untruth but instead of ignoring it he will set out to fight it; instead of retreating into his tower to uphold certain ethical standards his job will be to persuade as many other people as possible to think and behave in the same way – and on his success and failure depends the future of the world.'

Who on earth, I thought, did that job more incessantly and success-fully than Roger Fry? Didn't he spend half his life, not in a tower, but travelling about England addressing masses of people, who'd never looked at a picture and making them see what he saw? And wasn't that the best way of checking Nazism? Then I opened another letter; as it happened from Sebastian Sprott,[1] a lecturer at Nottingham; and I read how he'd once been mooning around the S. Kensington Museum '. . . then I saw Roger. All was changed. In ten minutes he caused me to enjoy what I was looking at. The objects became vivid and intelligible . . . There must be many people like me, people with scales on their eyes and wax in their ears . . . if only someone would come along and remove the scales and dig out the wax. Roger Fry did it . . .'

Then the raiders passed over. And I thought I cant have given Ben the least notion of what Roger was like. I suppose it was my fault. Or is it partly, and naturally, that he must have a scapegoat? I admit I want one. I loathe sitting here waiting for a bomb to fall; when I want to be writing. If it doesn't kill me its killing someone else. Where can I lay the

---

1. W. J. H. ('Sebastian') Sprott (1897–1971), a friend of Maynard Keynes and Lytton Strachey, was Lecturer in Psychology at Nottingham University.

blame? On the Sackvilles. On the Dufferins?[1] On Eton and Oxford? They did precious little it seems to me to check Nazism. People like Roger and Goldie Dickinson did an immense deal it seems to me. Well, we differ in our choice of scapegoats.

But what I'd like to know is, suppose we both survive this war, what ought we to do to prevent another? I shall be too old to do anything but write. But will you throw up your job as an art critic and take to politics? And if you stick to art criticism, how will you make it more public and less private than Roger did? About the particular points you raise; I think if you'll read some of last articles in Transformations [1926] you'll find that Roger got beyond the very classical and intellectual painters; and did include Rembrandt, Titian and so on. I've no doubt you're right in saying that his attempts at the sort of Berenson[2] connoiseurship were lamentable. I've never read BB, so I cant say. I did read Roger's last Slade lectures however; and was much impressed by the historical knowledge shown there. But of course I'm not an art critic; and have no right to express an opinion.

Well, the hostile aeroplanes have passed over my head now; I suppose they're dropping bombs over Newhaven and Seaford.

I hope this letter doesn't sound unkind. Its only because I liked your being honest so much that I've tried to be. And of course I know you're having a much worse time of it at the moment than I am ... Another siren has just sounded.

Yours ever
Virginia Woolf

3641: To Mrs R. C. Trevelyan[3]   *Monk's House, Rodmell*
Lewes, Sussex

4th Sept 40

Dear Bessie,

It was delightful of you to write to me about my life of Roger. You have found out exactly what I was trying to do when you compare it to a piece of music. Its odd, for I'm not regularly musical, but I always think

1. Ben's mother was, of course, a Sackville; his father's aunt Hariot married the Marquess of Dufferin and Ava, Viceroy of India.
2. Bernard Berenson (1865–1959), the art historian who specialised in attributions of Italian paintings.
3. Bob Trevelyan's Dutch wife, Elizabeth (1874–1957).

of my books as music before I write them. And especially with the life of Roger, -- there was such a mass of detail that the only way I could hold it together was by abstracting it into themes. I did try to state them in the first chapter, and then to bring in developments and variations, and then to make them all heard together and end by bringing back the first theme in the last chapter. Just as you say, I am extraordinarily pleased that you felt this. No one else has I think. And I dont wonder, for I was often crushed under the myriad details. It wasn't only the difficulty of making quotations fit – so many things had to be muted, or only hinted. And there is always a certain constraint, which one doesn't feel in fiction, a sense of other people looking over one's shoulder. I cant say how glad I am that you and Bob who both knew Roger so well think it a true portrait of him. Bob went all through his life even though, as so often happens, they met less often towards the end. I understand your being shy with him. I wasn't exactly shy, but I sometimes felt overpowered, and so uneasy. But nobody – none of my friends – made such a difference to my life as he did. And yet, writing about him, one had to keep that under. [. . .]

With love from us both.

Yr affectionate
Virginia Woolf

3644: To Ethel Smyth   *Monk's House, Rodmell,*
                                             near Lewes, Sussex

11th Sept. [1940]

[. . .] Yesterday we were up in London, and there was a crowd at Meck Sqre: a policeman stopped us: we got out – saw that the house just opposite ours across the road had been entirely crushed that night. A direct hit on top. It was nothing but a heap of bricks, smoking still. And we weren't allowed to go to 37, as a bomb was still in the square unexploded. Our house wasnt touched, but the windows are broken. So there was nothing for it but to come away. Everyone apparently in that house – one of those lovely houses at the side – had sheltered in the basement. All killed I suppose. We go up on Friday to arrange about moving the Press [to Letchworth, Hertfordshire]. and to bring back some of our valuables. that is if we're allowed. But everyone has been evacuated; the press cant work – And then we went and saw Holborn –

my word – its like a nightmare. All heaps of glass, water running, a great gap at top of Chancery Lane; my typists office demolished.

I've just seen a plane shot down on the hill beside Lewes. We heard firing, ran out, and saw the plane swerve and fall, and then a burst of black smoke. Then the English plane circled and made off. There's the all clear.

Thats why its so difficult to write a coherent letter. I try to write of a morning. Its odd to feel one's writing in a vacuum – no-one will read it. I feel the audience has gone. Still, so oddly is one made, I find I must spin my brain even in a vacuum.

But I want to know about you. Vita was coming but at the last moment she rang up. Bombs were dropping round Sissinghurst, and she had to stay, as she drives an ambulance. Rose Macaulay is doing the same in London. I admire that very much. Here we lead a disjointed jumping life. I had a niece staying here; another in a cottage. They collected friends in the airforce and so on. We had a fête: also a village play. The sirens sounded in the middle. All the mothers sat stolid. I also admired that very much. [. . .] Are you – doing what? Dear me: its true I should like to see you. You cohere like an orange globe, while the rest of the world scuds and streams.

V.

Post Script. Thursday [12 September]

[. . .] I've been up on the hill picking blackberries for dinner, and lost a glove that was to have lasted a winter, and suddenly conceived the idea of a new book,[1] and really I think I can weather – I mean weather cock – I mean brain spin – another ten years if Hitler doesn't drop a splinter into my machine. Churchill cheered me up.[2] Also this great gale thats blowing as it must have blown the other Armada. What touched and indeed raked what I call my heart in London was the grimy old woman

1. 'Oh, blackberrying, I conceived, or remoulded, an idea for a Common History Book – to read from one end of lit. including biog: and range at will, consecutively' (*Diary* V, p. 318, 12 September 1940). For some time Virginia had been toying with the idea of a book on social history and its effect on literature, both British and possibly foreign. The book took different shapes in her mind as she progressed. She worked at it intermittently until the end of her life, but left it unfinished. At first she called it *Reading at Random* or *Turning the Page*. See also Letter 3481, note 1.
2. Churchill's broadcast at 6 pm on 11 September cheered Virginia by its tone, but its substance was to warn England that the intensified bombing of London might be a preliminary to a German invasion. He said: 'It ranks with the days when the Spanish Armada was approaching the Channel and Drake was finishing his game of bowls.'

at the lodging house at the back, all dirty after the raid, and preparing to sit out another. We, after all, have at least been to Italy and read Shakespeare. They havent: dear me, I'm turning democrat. And then, the passion of my life, that is the City of London – to see London all blasted, that too raked my heart. Have you that feeling for certain alleys and little courts, between Chancery Lane and the City? I walked to the Tower the other day by way of caressing my love of all that. We might be in the Strand, here at night the raiders make such a noise of traffic – like buses and drays – in the sky. Now and then a bomb drops – but far away – Eastbourne I think. What about Woking? What does Mary [Ethel's maid] think? And Pan [sheepdog]? So you see, my thoughts curl round to you again, and indicate a letter. Werent we lucky to bring out our books when we did? [. . .]

V.

3658: To Ethel Smyth   *Monk's House, Rodmell,*
                                         near Lewes, Sussex

14th Nov 1940

[. . .] Another bomb in Meck Sqre: did I tell you? All the books down again. Did I tell you we half think of moving the furniture here? We brought down a car load last week. Then, to my infinite delight, they bombed our river. Cascades of water roared over the marsh – All the gulls came and rode the waves at the end of the field. It was, and still is, an inland sea, of such indescribable beauty, almost always changing, day and night, sun and rain, that I cant take my eyes off it. Yesterday, thinking to explore, I fell headlong into a six foot hole, and came home dripping like a spaniel, or water rugg (thats Shakespeare).[1] How odd to be swimming in a field! Mercifully I was wearing Leonards old brown trousers. Tomorrow I buy a pair of cords for myself. Its raining – raining . . . and I've been walking, walking. The road to the Bridge was 3 foot in water, and this meant a 2 mile round; but oh dear, how I love this savage medieval water moved, all floating tree trunks and flocks of birds and a man in an old punt, and myself so eliminated of human feature you might take me for a stake walking.

1. Ay, in the catalogue ye go for men;
   As hounds and greyhounds, mongrels, spaniels, curs,
   Shoughs, water-rugs, and demi-wolves are clept
   All by the name of dogs.
                                         Macbeth, III, i, 92–95

436

And tell me your opinion of Margot Oxford [formerly Asquith]. For some reason she writes to me passionately daily. She sent for me in London, and told me the story of her sexual organs. Cold, as you can imagine. [. . .]

Now I must put on our dinner – To do this I must crash through a meeting of farm labourers which Leonard is holding in the hall. They are going to grow co-operative potatoes; each man his strip. Why am I so much shyer of the labourer than of the gentry? I am almost – what d'you call a voracious cheese mite which has gnawed its way into a vast Stilton and is intoxicated with eating – as I am with reading history, and writing fiction[1] and planning – oh such an amusing book on English literature. Only room for exhortation: Write.

V

---

1. Virginia was writing her last novel, *Pointz Hall*, which was published posthumously as *Between the Acts*.

1941

In January Virginia was 59. By then Leonard was anxious about his wife's depression. Still, she continued to write perfectly normal letters during the next two months. She worked on her books, tried to keep up with her friends, and occupied herself with daily domestic life. However, her increasing instability so troubled Leonard that on 21 March he consulted a new friend, Octavia Wilberforce, who was also a physician, and on the 27th Virginia saw her in her professional capacity.

By that time, Virginia may have already tried to kill herself (see Letters, *Vol. VI, Appendix A, 'The Dating of Virginia Woolf's Last Letters'). She had begun to hear voices again and was convinced that this time she would not recover. She couldn't write. She couldn't read. She couldn't bear to burden Leonard. And the death of her choice had long seemed an option, even a reasonable one. She left three suicide notes, one for Vanessa and two, with overlapping content, for Leonard.*

3678: To Ethel Smyth   *Monks House, Rodmell*
                                                         [*Sussex*]

12th Jan 41

[. . .] I'm interested that you cant write about masturbation. That I understand. What puzzles me is how this reticence co-habits with your ability to talk openly magnificently, freely about – say H.B. [Henry Brewster]. I couldn't do one or the other. But as so much of life is sexual – or so they say – it rather limits autobiography if this is blacked out. It must be, I suspect, for many generations, for women; for its like breaking the hymen – if thats the membrane's name – a painful operation, and I suppose connected with all sorts of subterranean instincts. I still shiver with shame at the memory of my half brother,[1]

1. Not George Duckworth who later pushed his affection too far, but his brother
   Gerald (1870–1937). See Virginia's description of this encounter in 'A Sketch of the
   Past' (*Moments of Being*, 1976, p. 69), which she had written between April 1939 and
   November 1940.

standing me on a ledge, aged about 6, and so exploring my private parts. Why should I have felt shame then?

But why should I be writing these sexual speculations now? Every other second I take my eyes off the page to look at the elms outside – burning orange against a deep blue. Then theres the little cross of the Church against the snow. Only the snow is going. Yesterday it was a livid purple. Lord! How quickly the sun sets! Only one red slope now is left on Caburn. But I must add the smoke convoluting out of Asheham Cement Works is a ruffled pink that absolutely defies description – you'll be glad to hear.

How odd it is being a countrywoman after all these years of being Cockney! For almost the first time in my life I've not a bed in London. D'you know what I'm doing tomorrow? Going up to London Bridge. Then I shall walk, all along the Thames, in and out where I used to haunt, so through the Temple, up the Strand and out into Oxford Street, where I shall buy maccaroni and lunch. No. You never shared my passion for that great city. Yet its what, in some odd corner of my dreaming mind, represents Chaucer, Shakespeare, Dickens. Its my only patriotism: save one vision, in Warwickshire one spring [May 1934] when we were driving back from Ireland and I saw a stallion being led, under the may and the beeches, along a grass ride; and I thought that is England. [. . .]

By the way, youre coming to stay in the Spring: you will address the Womens Institute (as Vita is doing) then youll sleep here. Never mind Leonard. He is a good man: in his heart he respects my friends. But as for *my* staying with *you*, for some occult reason, he cries No no No. I think its a bad thing that we're so inseparable. But how, in this world of separation, dare one break it? I'm working really rather hard (for me) but whats the good of what I write, I havent the glimpse of an idea. You'll say, its good for you. So it is, I've no doubt. [. . .]

V.

3685: To Ethel Smyth   *Monks House, Rodmell*
                                        [Sussex]

Feb 1st 41

I've written you ever so many beautiful letters – cigarette letters – you know the kind, when one's devotion to Ethel rises like a silver smoke, too fine for words. These are the letters I write you, about 3 on a wet windy morning. Unlike Margot [Oxford], I dont keep a pencil at my head and I forget where we left off – you were going into the snow in snow boots. You had seduced the wife of the woodcutter – and then? I have a far away lover, to match your translator – a doctor, a cousin, a Wilberforce,[1] who lives at Brighton and has – by a miracle – heard of you. If I were in London, I'd ask you to meet. She has a herd of Jersey cows and sends me a pot of cream weekly. Oh theres Margot – I cant fathom her – I get now almost daily a letter written in bed at 3 am in the Savoy. Why at this last lap of time should she fabricate an entirely imaginary passion for me, who am utterly incongruous 'You and Frances Horner'[2] she says this morning 'are the only women I've ever loved'. The rest of womenkind, as I can well imagine, seeing her clothes, she hates. Yet she assures me she never bedded with a lover. And why assure me of anything? Is it that at the end of life she must somehow still collect some mirror? and I, being unused, still reflect whats no longer there? I suppose her lovers, male, are now grizzly old Peers, with whom its no use flirting. Extend your lighthouse Beam over this dark spot and tell me what you see. [. . .]

Did I tell you I'm reading the whole of English literature through? By the time I've reached Shakespeare the bombs will be falling. So I've arranged a very nice last scene: reading Shakespeare, having forgotten my gas mask, I shall fade far away, and quite forget . . . They brought down a raider the other side of Lewes yesterday. I was cycling in to get our butter, but only heard a drone in the clouds. Thank God, as you would say, one's fathers left one a taste for reading! Instead of thinking, by May we shall be – whatever it may be: I think, only 3 months to read Ben Jonson, Milton, Donne, and all the rest! Today however, to make me quicken my pace, I saw a yellow woodpecker bright green against ruby red willows. Lord! how I started, and then saw coming across the marsh, Leonard, looking like a Saxon Earl, because his old coat was torn and the lining flapped round his gum boots. [. . .]

Now, Ethel dear, you will perhaps very kindly write to me. You see what a long letter this is: also dated. Not a very coherent letter; but Leonards sawing logs under the window; and the marsh is all emerald

1. Virginia met Octavia Wilberforce (1888–1963) in 1937. Their families had been closely linked in the nineteenth century through the Clapham Sect, whose prime achievement was the abolition of slavery in the British Empire. Leslie Stephen's step-grandmother was a Wilberforce.
2. Lady Horner's daughter married Margot Oxford's stepson, Raymond, eldest son of the Prime Minister, Herbert Asquith.

green again, and the elms barred with rosy clouds, and pale pure blue behind that funny little extinguisher – the Church. For the past 3 weeks I've lived like a moth in a towel. Did I tell you I can now make lovely, rich, savoury vegetable soup? Tonight we shall have maccaroni au gratin and my lovers [Wilberforce] cream. [. . .]

I would like to ask, quite simply, do you still love me? Remember how I waved that day in Meck Sqre. Do love me.

V.

3700: To Elizabeth Robins[1]   *Monk's House, Rodmell Lewes, [Sussex]*

March 13th [1941]

Dear Miss Robins,

I was very sorry to hear from Octavia that you had had an accident. Selfishly, I'm afraid it may interfere with the book that I'm looking forward to. But I remember a saying of Henry James – all experiences are of use to a writer. I think he was talking about a nervous breakdown. So may it be worth a broken bone.

I now go on to say that I've been cycling into Lewes – not a very interesting remark, save that it connects with Octavia. Has she told you, I wonder – no, I dont suppose she has – of her amazing bi-weekly bounty – cream, milk, sometimes a cheese? Thats what I've been fetching. You cant think how it brightens our weekly bill of fare. Also, to fetch her empty basket, she sometimes comes over, and this has been, is, and will be, I hope, a great treat. Is it our drop of blood in common? Anyhow we sit over the fire, as if we'd known each other in the woods at Lavington.[2] Its odd how our lives have run just not meeting but through the same country. Thats the sort of woman I most admire – the reticence, the quiet, the power – Here I can imagine her look of enquiry – why? Well its difficult to say why. Its the variety and the calm partly. As you can imagine, she's healing the sick by day, and controlling the fires by night. [. . .]

1. Elizabeth Robins (1862–1952), actress, author (The Hogarth Press had published her essay *Ibsen and the Actress*, 1928, and, for private circulation, *Portrait of a Lady or The English Spirit Old and New*, 1941), and feminist. Born in America, she had long lived in England, had known Virginia's parents, and until 1940, when she returned to the States, shared a house in Brighton with Octavia Wilberforce.
2. Lavington House, near Chichester, Sussex, the family seat of the Wilberforces, where Octavia was born.

Its amazingly peaceful here, you can almost hear the grass grow; and the rooks are building; you wouldn't think that at 7.30 the planes will be over. Two nights ago they dropped incendiaries, in a row, like street lamps, all along the downs. Two hay stacks caught and made a lovely illumination – but no flesh was hurt. Indeed, every bomb they drop only casts up a crater so far. Its difficult, I find, to write. No audience. No private stimulus, only this outer roar. And in these circumstances, Octavia is very refreshing. [...]

Yrs
V.W.

3708: To Vanessa Bell   [*Monk's House, Rodmell,*
                                                                  Sussex]

Sunday [23? March 1941]

Dearest,

You cant think how I loved your letter.[1] But I feel that I have gone too far this time to come back again. I am certain now that I am going mad again. It is just as it was the first time, I am always hearing voices, and I know I shant get over it now.

All I want to say is that Leonard has been so astonishingly good, every day, always; I cant imagine that anyone could have done more for me than he has. We have been perfectly happy until the last few weeks, when this horror began. Will you assure him of this? I feel he has so much to do that he will go on, better without me, and you will help him.

I can hardly think clearly any more. If I could I would tell you what you and the children have meant to me. I think you know.

I have fought against it, but I cant any longer.

Virginia

1. On 20 March Vanessa wrote to Virginia: 'You *must* be sensible. Which means you must accept the fact that Leonard and I can judge better than you can. Its true I havent seen very much of you lately, but I have often thought you looked very tired and I'm sure that if you let yourself collapse and do nothing you would feel tired, and be only too glad to rest a little. You're in the state when one never admits whats the matter – but you must not go and get ill just now. What shall we do when we're invaded if you are a helpless invalid – what should I have done all these last 3 years if you hadnt been able to keep me alive and cheerful. You dont know how much I depend on you. [...] Both Leonard and I have always had a reputation for sense and honesty so you must believe us. [...] I shall ring you up sometime and find out what is happening' (University of Sussex, papers of Leonard Woolf).

3710: To Leonard Woolf   [*Monk's House, Rodmell, Sussex*]

[28 March 1941]

Dearest,

I want to tell you that you have given me complete happiness. No one could have done more than you have done. Please believe that.

But I know that I shall never get over this: and I am wasting your life. It is this madness. Nothing anyone says can persuade me. You can work, and you will be much better without me. You see I cant write this even, which shows I am right. All I want to say is that until this disease came on we were perfectly happy. It was all due to you. No one could have been so good as you have been, from the very first day till now. Everyone knows that.

V.

You will find Roger's letters to the Maurons in the writing table drawer in the Lodge. Will you destroy all my papers.

443

Epilogue

Virginia left her last letter on the writing block in her garden lodge. About 11.30 am she walked the half mile to the River Ouse, filled her pockets with stones, and threw herself into the water. Her body was not found until 18 April, when some children discovered it a short way downstream. She was cremated at Brighton on 21 April, with only Leonard present, and her ashes were buried under a great elm tree at Monk's House, with the penultimate words of The Waves as her epitaph: 'Against you I will fling myself, unvanquished and unyielding, O Death!'

Appendix

Appendix

1973	*Mrs Dalloway's Party*
1975–80	*Letters Volumes 1–6*
1976	*Moments of Being*
1976	*Freshwater*
1977–84	*Diary Volumes 1–5*
1977	*Books and Portraits*
1977	*The Pargiters*
1982	*The London Scene*
1985	*The Complete Shorter Fiction*
1986–94	*Essays Volumes 1–6*
1989	*Early Journals*

(Dates refer to first British edition)

FAMILY TREE
Showing the antecedents and relations of
VIRGINIA WOOLF

FAMILY

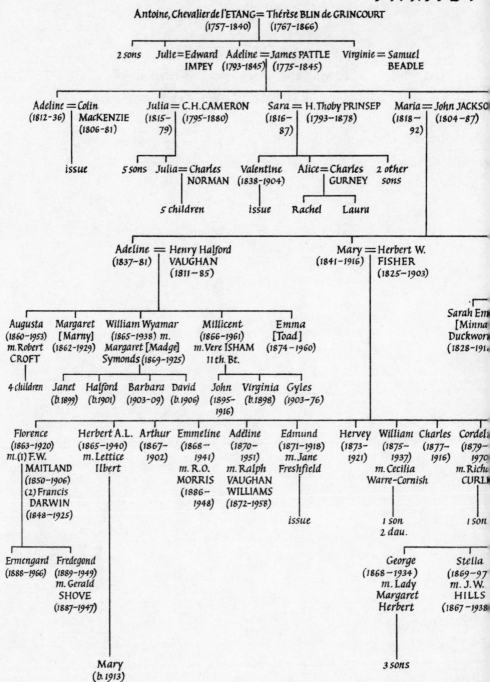

Antoine, Chevalier de l'ETANG = Thérèse BLIN de GRINCOURT
(1757–1840)   (1767–1866)

2 sons   Julie = Edward IMPEY   Adeline = James PATTLE   Virginie = Samuel BEADLE
     (1793–1845) (1775–1845)

Adeline = Colin MacKENZIE (1812–36) (1806–81)   Julia = C.H. CAMERON (1815–79) (1795–1880)   Sara = H. Thoby PRINSEP (1816–87) (1793–1878)   Maria = John JACKSON (1818–92) (1804–87)

issue   5 sons   Julia = Charles NORMAN   Valentine (1838–1904)   Alice = Charles GURNEY   2 other sons

5 children   issue   Rachel   Laura

Adeline = Henry Halford VAUGHAN (1837–81) (1811–85)   Mary = Herbert W. FISHER (1841–1916) (1825–1903)

Augusta (1860–1953) m. Robert CROFT   Margaret [Marny] (1862–1929)   William Wyamar (1865–1938) m. Margaret [Madge] Symonds (1869–1925)   Millicent (1866–1961) m. Vere ISHAM 11th. Bt.   Emma [Toad] (1874–1960)   Sarah Em[Minna Duckwor (1828–191

4 children   Janet (b.1899)   Halford (b.1901)   Barbara (1903–09)   David (b.1906)   John (1895–1916)   Virginia (b.1898)   Gyles (1903–76)

Florence (1863–1920) m.(1) F.W. MAITLAND (1850–1906) (2) Francis DARWIN (1848–1925)   Herbert A.L. (1865–1940) m. Lettice Ilbert   Arthur (1867–1902)   Emmeline (1868–1941) m. R.O. MORRIS (1886–1948)   Adeline (1870–1951) m. Ralph VAUGHAN WILLIAMS (1872–1958)   Edmund (1871–1918) m. Jane Freshfield   Hervey (1873–1921)   William (1875–1937) m. Cecilia Warre-Cornish   Charles (1877–1916)   Cordeli (1879– 1970 m. Richu CURL[

issue   1 son 2 dau.   1 son

Ermengard (1888–1966)   Fredegond (1889–1949) m. Gerald SHOVE (1887–1947)   George (1868–1934) m. Lady Margaret Herbert   Stella (1869–97) m. J.W. HILLS (1867–1938

Mary (b.1913)   3 sons

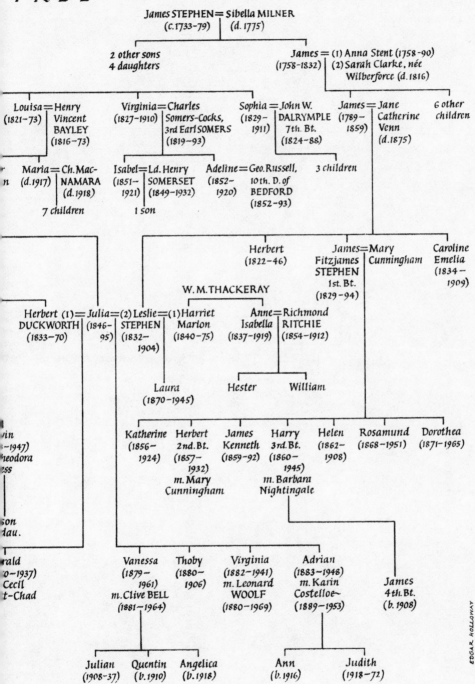

James STEPHEN = Sibella MILNER
(c.1733-79)   (d. 1775)

2 other sons
4 daughters

James = (1) Anna Stent (1758-90)
(1758-1832) (2) Sarah Clarke, née
                    Wilberforce (d. 1816)

Louisa = Henry
(1821-73) Vincent
           BAYLEY
           (1816-73)

Virginia = Charles
(1827-1910) Somers-Cocks,
             3rd Earl SOMERS
             (1819-93)

Sophia = John W.
(1829-   DALRYMPLE
1911)   7th. Bt.
         (1824-88)

James = Jane
(1789- Catherine
1859)   Venn
        (d. 1875)

6 other
children

Maria = Ch. Mac-
(d.1917) NAMARA
          (d. 1918)

7 children

Isabel = Ld. Henry
(1851-   SOMERSET
1921)   (1849-1932)

1 son

Adeline = Geo. Russell,
(1852-   10th. D. of
1920)   BEDFORD
         (1852-93)

3 children

Herbert
(1822-46)

James = Mary
Fitzjames Cunningham
STEPHEN
1st. Bt.
(1829-94)

Caroline
Emelia
(1834-
1909)

W. M. THACKERAY

Herbert (1) = Julia = (2) Leslie = (1) Harriet
DUCKWORTH (1846- STEPHEN Marion
(1833-70)   95)   (1832- (1840-75)
                   1904)

Anne = Richmond
Isabella RITCHIE
(1837-1919) (1854-1912)

Laura
(1870-1945)

Hester   William

Katherine   Herbert   James   Harry   Helen   Rosamund   Dorothea
(1856-   2nd. Bt.   Kenneth   3rd. Bt.   (1862-   (1868-1951) (1871-1965)
1924)   (1857-   (1859-92) (1860-   1908)
             1932)   1945)
             m. Mary   m. Barbara
             Cunningham   Nightingale

Vanessa   Thoby   Virginia   Adrian
(1879-   (1880-   (1882-1941) (1883-1948)
1961)   1906)   m. Leonard   m. Karin
m. Clive Bell   WOOLF   Costelloe
(1881-1964)   (1880-1969) (1889-1953)

James
4th. Bt.
(b. 1908)

Julian   Quentin   Angelica
(1908-37)   (b. 1910) (b. 1918)

Ann   Judith
(b. 1916)   (1918-72)

EDGAR HOLLOWAY

Index

This is an index of proper nouns. The names of people, animals and groups constitute the majority of the entries. The index also includes certain places, titles, events and institutions that are important in the life of Virginia Woolf. Normally, the page reference immediately following a person's name is the location of his or her biographical summary. For further convenience, many of the recurring figures are identified in parenthetical epithets. Virginia Woolf is everywhere abbreviated to V.

Aberconway, Christabel. *See* McLaren

Ackerley, J. R., 340&*n*

Alington, Cyril, 163&*n*, 386&*n*

Alington, Hester (Mrs Cyril), 163&*n*

Americans: overly refined, 147, 167, 177, 282, 430; yet salty, 185; uncivilised, 304, 319–20, 371; vivid and unEnglish language of, 245&*n*, 246

Anderson, J. C. O'G., 284*n*, 339

Anderson, Sherwood, 245&*n*

Anrep, Helen (Roger Fry's lover), 209&*n*; as mother, 222; her beauty, 338; and Roger Fry, 310, 342, 372, 389; visits V., 210–11, 248&*n*, 261

Apostles, The, 24*n*, 47*n*, 370, 372

Archilocus, 123

Aristotle, 123

Arlen, Michael, 336&*n*

Arnold, Matthew, 323&*n*

Arnold, Thomas, 100*n*

Arnold-Forster, Katharine ('Ka'), *née* Cox (Cambridge friend), 63&*n*; begins friendship with V., 58; nurses V., 80*n*, 179; surrounded by gallant youths, 145; pursued by Jacques Raverat, 144*n*, 302; marries, 102*n*; lives in Cornwall, 133&*n*; her bad taste, 105, 175; praises her husband, 102, 146, 179, 373; opinion of Vanessa, 105; a serious woman, 178; dull, 178–9, 373; public-spirited, 146, 373; dies, 402 Letters to: Nos. *645, 660, 709, 1016, 1073, 1084*

Arnold-Forster, Will (painter married to Ka Cox): marries, 63*n*, 102*n*; in hospital, ix, 101–2; his character, 105, 133, 146, 179, 373; his painting, 102, 105, 133, 179, 373

Asheham (Rodmell, Sussex), 70*n*

Asquith, Anthony ('Puffin'), 168&*n*

Asquith, H. H. (Lord Oxford), 148&*n*, 208, 210

Asquith, Margot (Lady Oxford), 148&*n*, 160, 162, 210, 440

Auden, W. H., 294*n*, 340, 367–8, 391, 420

Austen, Jane, 51*n*, 123, 154, 399

B. (for 'Billy', one of the 'Apes' or 'Synges', a persona V. took on in childhood and used throughout her life as her normal signature to Vanessa Bell), 48 & *passim*

Bacon, Francis, 244

Bagenal, Barbara, *née* Hiles (at Hogarth Press, friend of Saxon Sydney-Turner and Vanessa Bell), 95&*n*; and Saxon, 86, 95&*n*, 96, 102, 230; marries, 95–6; visit to Monk's House, 118; in hospital, x, 170; unimaginative, 260, 390; morbid love for Vanessa, 307; dreadful, 414–15 Letter to: No. *1405*

Bagenal, Judith (Barbara's daughter), 105&*n*, 230, 250, 289–91, 307, 414–15

Bagenal, Nicholas (Barbara's husband), 95&*n*, 118, 414–15

Bagnold, Enid, 96&*n*

Bailey, John Cann, 382&*n*

Balfour, Lady (Elizabeth), 406&*n*

Balzac, Honoré de, 243

Barclay, Florence, 124&*n*

Baring, Maurice, 263&*n*, 307, 353, 379–80, 391

Bartholomew, Percy (gardener), 288&*n*, 360, 378, 429

Bayreuth: V. attends opera in, 52&*n*, 53–4